# 2006
# Children's Writer's & Illustrator's Market.®

Alice Pope, Editor
Lauren Mosko & Mary Cox,
   Assistant Editors

**WRITER'S DIGEST BOOKS**
CINCINNATI, OH

Senior Editor, Writer's Digest Market Books: Kathryn S. Brogan
Supervisory Editor, Writer's Digest Market Books: Donna Poehner
Writer's Market website: www.writersmarket.com
Writer's Digest Books website: www.writersdigest.com

International Standard Serial Number 0897-9790
International Standard Book Number 1-58297-402-0

Cover design by Kelly Kofron
Interior design by Clare Finney
Production coordinated by Robin Richie

**Attention Booksellers:** This is an annual directory of F + W Publications. Return deadline for this edition is December 31, 2006.

# Get Instant Access
## to thousands of editors and agents @
# WRITERSMARKET.COM

## Register now and save $10!

Sure, you already know **Children's Writer's & Illustrator's Market** is the essential tool for selling your work for children. And now, to complement your trusty "children's writer's bible," subscribe to WritersMarket.com (see back for more information) for **$10 off the regular price!**

As a purchaser of **2006 Children's Writer's & Illustrator's Market**, get a $10 discount off the regular $29.99 subscription price for WritersMarket.com. Simply enter coupon code **WM6MB** on the subscription page at www.WritersMarket.com.

# www.WritersMarket.com
## The Ultimate Research Tool for Writers

## Tear out your handy bookmark
### for fast reference to symbols and abbreviations used in this book

CWIM06

---

## 2006 CHILDREN'S WRITER'S & ILLUSTRATOR'S MARKET KEY TO SYMBOLS

 market new to this edition

 Canadian market

 listing outside of the U.S. and Canada

 publisher producing educational material

 online opportunity

 book packager/producer

 publisher accepts agented submissions only

 award-winning publisher

**ms, mss** manuscript(s)

**SCBWI** Society of Children's Book Writers and Illustrators

**SAE** self-addressed envelope

**SASE** self-addressed, stamped envelope

**IRC** International Reply Coupon

**b&w** black & white

(For definitions of unfamiliar words and expressions relating to writing, illustration and publishing, see the Glossary.)

TEAR ALONG PERFORATION

## 2006 CHILDREN'S WRITER'S & ILLUSTRATOR'S MARKET KEY TO SYMBOLS

 market new to this edition

 Canadian market

 listing outside of the U.S. and Canada

 publisher producing educational material

 online opportunity

 book packager/producer

 publisher accepts agented submissions only

 award-winning publisher

**ms, mss** manuscript(s)

**SCBWI** Society of Children's Book Writers and Illustrators

**SAE** self-addressed envelope

**SASE** self-addressed, stamped envelope

**IRC** International Reply Coupon

**b&w** black & white

(For definitions of unfamiliar words and expressions relating to writing, illustration and publishing, see the Glossary.)

*TEAR ALONG PERFORATION*

# WRITERSMARKET.COM

## Here's what you'll find at WritersMarket.com:

**More than 5,700 listings** — At WritersMarket.com, you'll find thousands of listings that couldn't fit in the *2006 Writer's Market*! It's the most comprehensive database of verified markets available.

**Easy-to-use searchable database** — Looking for a specific magazine or book publisher? Just type in the title or keyword for broad category results.

**Listings updated daily** — It doesn't look good to address your query letter to the wrong editor or agent...and with WritersMarket.com, that will never happen. You'll be on top of all the industry developments...as soon as they happen!

**Personalized for you** — Stay on top of your publishing contacts with **Submission Tracker**; store your best-bet markets in **Favorites Folders**; and get **updates** to your publishing areas of interest, every time you log in.

**And so much more!**

## Subscribe today and save $10!
(enter coupon code WM6MB)

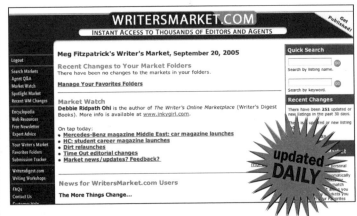

## Tear out your handy bookmark
for fast reference to symbols and abbreviations used in this book

CWIM06

# Contents

© 2003 Glin Dibley

Frank Morrison

© 2004 Amy Young

## MARKETS

# RESOURCES

© Maria de Lourdes Morales O'Meara

## INDEXES

© Jarrett J. Krosoczka

# From the Editor

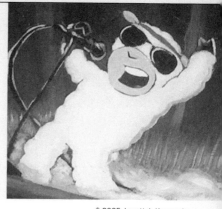

Often in articles and interviews with authors, they say *I wanted to be a writer from the time I was a kid.*

Here's a confession: When I was kid, I wanted to be a rock star. I spent countless hours jumping around on my bed singing into my hairbrush along with my favorite Journey album. There was even a short period in the '80s when I had big hair.

The only problem with my dream of being a rock star was that I can't play any instruments and I'm a terrible singer. (Run if you ever see me in a Karaoke bar). I became an editor instead.

Last year, about the same time the 2005 edition of *Children's Writer's & Illustrator's Market* sprung forth into the world, I had (another real) baby, Murray. These days when I walk into the room, Murray reacts like I'm a rock star: He squeals and smiles and wiggles around like a teenager at a Beatles concert. It's pretty cool.

When Murray was three months old, I took him to his very first book signing. We went to see Holly Hobbie at our local bookstore. For me, Holly Hobbie is a rock star. She created Toot & Puddle! I yelled and jumped up and down when I heard she was coming to town. I stood in line to get books signed and was nervous about what I would say (despite practicing in the car). Murray slept through the whole thing.

In her article Getting Back in the Saddle for a Tough Revision (page 25) author Christine Kole MacLean likens herself to a cowboy. Candice Ransom is a boxer in her piece Surviving in the Ever-Changing Publishing Biz (page 37). In First Books (page 85), Mona Michael talks about writers as superheroes with their own special powers.

So right now stop thinking of yourself as merely a writer or illustrator. *You're a cowboy—* bustin' the range to revise from sun up till sundown until your work is just right. *You're a boxer—*ducking blows, lasting 13 rounds, landing a one-two punch, and scoring contract after contract. *You're a superhero—*leaping tall deadlines in a single bound, juggling a day job, a family, and a writing life.

One day, if I do my job, authors and illustrators will be Murray's rock stars. And if you do your job (and follow the advice and use the information in this book) you could be that rock star. And maybe he'll stand in line, waiting for your autograph, not quite knowing what to say.

Alice Pope
cwim@fwpubs.com

*Editor's note: The illustration above is from Jarrett J. Krosoczka's rockin' picture book* Punk Farm. *See the Insider Report with Jarrett on page 164 and visit www.punkfarm.com.*

# Just Starting?

*Some Quick Tips for*
*Writers & Illustrators*

I f you're new to the world of children's publishing, buying *Children's Writer's & Illustrator's Market* may have been one of the first steps in your journey to publication. What follows is a list of suggestions and resources that can help make that journey a smooth and swift one:

**1. Make the most of *Children's Writer's & Illustrator's Market.*** Be sure to read How to Use This Book on page 5 for tips on reading the listings and using the indexes. Also be sure to take advantage of the articles and interviews in the book. The insights of the authors, illustrators, editors, and agents we've interviewed will inform and inspire you.

**2. Join the Society of Children's Books Writers and Illustrators.** SCBWI, more than 19,000 members strong, is an organization for both beginners and professionals interested in writing and illustrating for children. They offer members a slew of information and support through publications, a website, and a host of Regional Advisors overseeing chapters in almost every state in the U.S. and in a growing number of locations around the globe (including France, Canada, Japan, and Australia). SCBWI puts on a number of conferences, workshops, and events on the regional and national levels (many listed in the Conferences & Workshops section of this book). For more information, contact SCBWI, 8271 Beverly Blvd., Los Angeles CA 90048, (323)782-1010, or visit their website: www.scbwi.org.

**3. Read newsletters.** Newsletters, such as *Children's Book Insider*, *Children's Writer*, and the SCBWI *Bulletin*, offer updates and new information about publishers on a timely basis and are relatively inexpensive. Many local chapters of SCBWI offer regional newsletters as well. (See Helpful Books & Publications on page 368 for contact information on the newsletters listed above and others. For information on regional SCBWI newsletters, visit www.scbwi .org and click on "Publications.")

**4. Read trade and review publications.** Magazines like *Publishers Weekly* (which offers two special issues each year devoted to children's publishing and is available on newsstands), *The Horn Book*, and *Booklinks* offer news, articles, reviews of newly-published titles, and ads featuring upcoming and current releases. Referring to them will help you get a feel for what's happening in children's publishing.

**5. Read guidelines.** Most publishers and magazines offer writer's and artist's guidelines that provide detailed information on needs and submission requirements, and some magazines offer theme lists for upcoming issues. Many publishers and magazines state the availability of guidelines within their listings. Send a self-addressed, stamped envelope (SASE) to publishers who offer guidelines. You'll often find submission information on publishers' and magazines' websites.

**6. Look at publishers' catalogs.** Perusing publishers' catalogs can give you a feel for their line of books and help you decide where your work might fit in. If catalogs are available (often stated within listings), send for them with a SASE. Visit publishers' websites, which often contain their full catalogs. You can also ask librarians to look at catalogs they have on hand. You can even search Amazon.com (www.amazon.com) by publisher and year. (Click on "book search" then "publisher, date" and plug in, for example, "Lee & Low" under "publisher" and "2005" under year. You'll get a list of Lee & Low titles published in 2004, which you can peruse.)

**7. Visit bookstores.** It's not only informative to spend time in bookstores—it's fun, too! Frequently visit the children's section of your local bookstore (whether a chain or an independent) to see the latest from a variety of publishers and the most current issues of children's magazines. Look for books in the genre you're writing or with illustrations similar in style to yours, and spend some time studying them. It's also wise to get to know your local booksellers; they can tell you what's new in the store and provide insight into what kids and adults are buying.

**8. Read, read, read!** While you're at that bookstore, pick up a few things, or keep a list of the books that interest you and check them out of your library. Read and study the latest releases, the award winners, and the classics. You'll learn from other writers, get ideas, and get a feel for what's being published. Think about what works and doesn't work in a story. Pay attention to how plots are constructed and how characters are developed or the rhythm and pacing of picture book text. It's certainly enjoyable research!

**9. Take advantage of Internet resources.** There are innumerable sources of information available on the Internet about writing for children (and anything else you could possibly think of). It's also a great resource for getting (and staying) in touch with other writers and illustrators through listservs and e-mail, and it can serve as a vehicle for self-promotion. (Visit some authors' and illustators' sites for ideas. See Useful Online Resources on page 371 for a list of websites.)

**10. Consider attending a conference.** If time and finances allow, attending a conference is a great way to meet peers and network with professionals in the field of children's publishing. As mentioned above, SCBWI offers conferences in various locations year round. (See www.scbwi.org and click on "Events" for a full conference calendar.) General writers' conferences often offer specialized sessions just for those interested in children's writing. Many conferences offer optional manuscript and portfolio critiques as well, giving you a chance for feedback from seasoned professionals.

**11. Network, network, network!** Don't work in a vacuum. You can meet other writers and illustrators through a number of the things listed above—SCBWI, conferences, online. Attend local meetings for writers and illustrators whenever you can. Befriend other writers in your area (SCBWI offers members a roster broken down by state)—share guidelines, share subscriptions, be conference buddies and roommates, join a critique group or writing group, exchange information, and offer support. Get online—sign on to listservs, post on message boards, visit chatrooms. (The Institute of Children's Literature offers regularly scheduled live chats and open forums. Visit www.institutechildrenslit.com and click on Scheduled Events. Also, visit author Verla Kay's website, www.verlakay.com, for information on workshops. See Useful Online Resources on page 371 for more information.) Exchange addresses, phone numbers, and e-mail addresses with writers or illustrators you meet at events. And at conferences, don't be afraid to talk to people, ask strangers to join you for lunch, approach speakers and introduce yourself, or chat in elevators and hallways.

**12. Perfect your craft and don't submit until your work is its best.** It's often been said that a writer should try to write every day. Great manuscripts don't happen overnight; there's time, research, and revision involved. As you visit bookstores and study what others have written and illustrated, really step back and look at your own work and ask yourself—

honestly—*How does my work measure up? Is it ready for editors or art directors to see?* If it's not, keep working. Join a critique group or get a professional manuscript or portfolio critique.

**13. Be patient, learn from rejection, and don't give up!** Thousands of manuscripts land on editors' desks; thousands of illustration samples line art directors' file drawers. There are so many factors that come into play when evaluating submissions. Keep in mind that you might not hear back from publishers promptly. Persistence and patience are important qualities in writers and illustrators working toward publication. Keep at it—it will come. It can take a while, but when you get that first book contract or first assignment, you'll know it was worth the wait. (For proof, read First Books on page 85.)

# How to Use This Book

A s a writer, illustrator, or photographer first picking up *Children's Writer's & Illustrator's Market*, you may not know quite how to start using the book. Your impulse may be to flip through the book and quickly make a mailing list, then submit to everyone in hopes that someone will take interest in your work. Well, there's more to it. Finding the right market takes time and research. The more you know about a company that interests you, the better chance you have of getting work accepted.

We've made your job a little easier by putting a wealth of information at your fingertips. Besides providing listings, this directory includes a number of tools to help you determine which markets are the best ones for your work. By using these tools, as well as researching on your own, you raise your odds of being published.

## USING THE INDEXES

This book lists hundreds of potential buyers of freelance material. To learn which companies want the type of material you're interested in submitting, start with the indexes.

### The Age-Level Index

Age groups are broken down into these categories in the Age-Level Index:

- **Picture books or picture-oriented material** are written and illustrated for preschoolers to 8-year-olds.
- **Young readers** are for 5- to 8-year-olds.
- **Middle readers** are for 9- to 11-year-olds.
- **Young adults** are for ages 12 and up.

Age breakdowns may vary slightly from publisher to publisher, but using them as general guidelines will help you target appropriate markets. For example, if you've written an article about trends in teen fashion, check the Magazines Age-Level Index under the Young Adult subheading. Using this list, you'll quickly find the listings for young adult magazines.

### The Subject Index

But let's narrow the search further. Take your list of young adult magazines, turn to the Subject Index, and find the Fashion subheading. Then highlight the names that appear on both lists (Young Adult and Fashion). Now you have a smaller list of all the magazines that would be interested in your teen fashion article. Read through those listings and decide which ones sound best for your work.

Illustrators and photographers can use the Subject Index as well. If you specialize in painting

### 2006 CHILDREN'S WRITER'S & ILLUSTRATOR'S MARKET KEY TO SYMBOLS

**N**  market new to this edition

**•**  Canadian agency

**•**  listing outside U.S. and Canada

**•**  publisher producing educational material

**•**  electronic publisher or producer

**•**  book package/producer

**A**  publisher accepts agented submissions only

**•**  award-winning publisher

**ms, mss** manuscript(s)

**SCBWI** Society of Children's Book Writers and Illustrators

**SASE** self-addressed, stamped envelope

**SAE** self-addressed envelope

**IRC** International Reply Coupon, for use in countries other than your own

**b&w** black & white

(For definitions of unfamilliar words and expressions relating to writing, illustration and publishing, see the Glossary.)

**Find a handy pull-out bookmark, a quick reference to the icons used in this book, right inside the front cover.**

animals, for instance, consider sending samples to book and magazine publishers listed under Animals and, perhaps, Nature/Environment. Since illustrators can simply send general examples of their style to art directors to keep on file, the indexes may be more helpful to artists sending manuscripts/illustration packages who need to search for a specific subject. Always read the listings for the potential markets to see the type of work art directors prefer and what type of samples they'll keep on file, and send for art or photo guidelines if they're available.

### The Poetry Index
This index lists book publishers and magazines interested in submissions from poets. Always send for writer's guidelines from publishers and magazines that interest you.

### The Photography Index
In this index you'll find lists of book and magazine publishers, as well as greeting card, puzzle, and game manufacturers, that buy photos from freelancers. Refer to the list and read the listings for companies' specific photography needs. Send for photo guidelines if they're offered.

## USING THE LISTINGS
Many listings begin with one or more symbols. Refer to the inside back cover of the book for quick reference and find a handy pull-out bookmark (shown at left) right inside the front cover.

Many listings indicate whether submission guidelines are available. If a publisher you're interested in offers guidelines, send for them and read them. The same is true with catalogs. Sending for catalogs and reading about the books a publisher produces gives you a better idea of whether your work would fit in. (You should also look at a few of the books in the catalog at a library or bookstore to get a feel for the publisher's material.) Note that a number of publishers offer guidelines and catalogs on their websites.

### Especially for artists & photographers
Along with information for writers, listings provide information for photographers and illustrators. Illustrators will find numerous markets that maintain files of samples for possible future assignments. If you're both a writer and an illustrator, look for markets that accept manuscript/illustration packages.

If you're a photographer, after consulting the Photography Index, read the information under the **Photography** subhead within listings to see what format buyers prefer. For example, some want 35mm color transparencies, others want black and white prints. Note the type of photos a buyer wants to purchase and the procedures for submitting. It's not uncommon for a market to want a résumé and promotional literature, as well as tearsheets from previous work. Listings also note whether model releases and/or captions are required.

**EASY-TO-USE REFERENCE ICONS**

**WEBSITES**

**TIPS ON APPROACHING EACH PUBLISHER**

**SPECIFIC CONTACT NAMES**

**DETAILED SUBMISSION GUIDELINES**

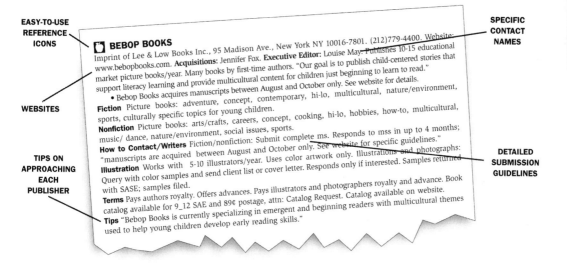

**BEBOP BOOKS**
Imprint of Lee & Low Books Inc., 95 Madison Ave., New York NY 10016-7801. (212)779-4400. Website: www.bebopbooks.com. **Acquisitions:** Jennifer Fox. **Executive Editor:** Louise May. Publishes 10-15 educational market picture books/year. Many books by first-time authors. "Our goal is to publish child-centered stories that support literacy learning and provide multicultural content for children just beginning to learn to read."
• Bebop Books acquires manuscripts between August and October only. See website for details.
**Fiction** Picture books: adventure, concept, contemporary, hi-lo, multicultural, nature/environment, sports, culturally specific topics for young children.
**Nonfiction** Picture books: arts/crafts, careers, concept, cooking, hi-lo, hobbies, how-to, multicultural, music/ dance, nature/environment, social issues, sports.
**How to Contact/Writers** Fiction/nonfiction: Submit complete ms. Responds to mss in up to 4 months; "manuscripts are acquired between August and October only. See website for specific guidelines."
**Illustration** Works with 5-10 illustrators/year. Uses color artwork only. Illustrations and photographs: Query with color samples and send client list or cover letter. Responds only if interested. Samples returned with SASE; samples filed.
**Terms** Pays authors royalty. Offers advances. Pays illustrators and photographers royalty and advance. Book catalog available for 9_12 SAE and 89¢ postage, attn: Catalog Request. Catalog available on website.
**Tips** "Bebop Books is currently specializing in emergent and beginning readers with multicultural themes used to help young children develop early reading skills."

## Especially for young writers

If you're a parent, teacher, or student, you may be interested in Young Writer's & Illustrator's Markets. The listings in this section encourage submissions from young writers and artists. Some may require a written statement from a teacher or parent noting the work is original. Also watch for age limits.

Young people should also check Contests & Awards for contests that accept work by young writers and artists. Some of the contests listed are especially for students; others accept both student and adult work. These listings contain the phrase **open to students** in bold. Some listings in Clubs & Organizations and Conferences & Workshops may also be of interest to students. Organizations and conferences which are open to or are especially for students also include **open to students**.

# Before Your First Sale

If you're just beginning to pursue your career as a children's book writer or illustrator, it's important to learn the proper procedures, formats, and protocol for the publishing industry. This article outlines the basics you need to know before you head to the post office with your submissions.

## FINDING THE BEST MARKETS FOR YOUR WORK

Researching publishers thoroughly is a basic element of submitting your work successfully. Editors and art directors hate to receive inappropriate submissions; handling them wastes a lot of their time, not to mention your time and money, and they are the main reason some publishers have chosen not to accept material over the transom. By randomly sending out material without knowing a company's needs, you're sure to meet with rejection.

If you're interested in submitting to a particular magazine, write to request a sample copy or see if it's available in your local library or bookstore. For a book publisher, obtain a book catalog and check a library or bookstore for titles produced by that publisher. Most publishers and magazines have websites that include catalogs or sample articles (websites are given within the listings). Studying such materials carefully will better acquaint you with a publisher's or magazine's writing, illustration, and photography styles and formats.

Most of the book publishers and magazines listed in this book (as well as some greeting card and paper product producers) offer some sort of writer's, artist's, or photographer's guidelines for a self-addressed, stamped envelope (SASE). Guidelines are also often found on publishers' websites. It's important to read and study guidelines before submitting work. You'll get a better understanding of what a particular publisher wants. You may even decide, after reading the submission guidelines, that your work isn't right for a company you considered.

## SUBMITTING YOUR WORK

Throughout the listings, you'll read requests for particular elements to include when contacting markets. Here are explanations of some of these important submission components.

### Queries, cover letters, & proposals

A query letter is a no-more-than-one-page, well-written piece meant to arouse an editor's interest in your work. Many query letters start with leads similar to those of actual manuscripts. In the rest of the letter, briefly outline the work you're proposing and include facts, anecdotes, interviews, or other pertinent information that give the editor a feel for the manuscript's premise—entice her to want to know more. End your letter with a straightforward request to write or submit the work, and include information on its approximate length, date it could be completed, and whether accompanying photos or artwork are available.

In a query letter, think about presenting your book as a publisher's catalog would present it. Read through a good catalog and examine how the publishers give enticing summaries of their books in a spare amount of words. It's also important that query letters give editors a taste of your writing style. For good advice and samples of queries, cover letters, and other correspondence, consult *Formatting & Submitting Your Manuscript*, Second Edition, by Cynthia Laufenberg and the editors of *Writer's Market* and *How to Write Attention-Grabbing Query & Cover Letters*, by John Wood (both Writer's Digest Books).

For More Info

- **Query letters for nonfiction.** Queries are usually required when submitting nonfiction material to a publisher. The goal of a nonfiction query is to convince the editor your idea is perfect for her readership and that you're qualified to do the job. Note any previous writing experience and include published samples to prove your credentials, especially samples related to the subject matter you're querying about.
- **Query letters for fiction.** More and more, queries are being requested for fiction manuscripts. For a fiction query, explain the story's plot, main characters, conflict, and resolution. Just as in nonfiction queries, make the editor eager to see more.
- **Cover letters for writers.** Some editors prefer to review complete manuscripts, especially for fiction. In such cases, the cover letter (which should be no longer than one page) serves as your introduction, establishes your credentials as a writer, and gives the editor an overview of the manuscript. If the editor asked for the manuscript because of a query, note this in your cover letter.
- **Cover letters for illustrators and photographers.** For an illustrator or photographer, the cover letter serves as an introduction to the art director and establishes professional credentials when submitting samples. Explain what services you can provide as well as what type of follow-up contact you plan to make, if any.
- **Résumés.** Often writers, illustrators, and photographers are asked to submit résumés with cover letters and samples. They can be created in a variety of formats, from a single page listing information to color brochures featuring your work. Keep your résumé brief, and focus on your achievements, including your clients and the work you've done for them, as well as your educational background and any awards you've received. Do not use the same résumé you'd use for a typical job application.
- **Book proposals.** Throughout the listings in the Book Publishers section, publishers refer to submitting a synopsis, outline, and sample chapters. Depending on an editor's preference, some or all of these components, along with a cover letter, make up a book proposal.

A *synopsis* summarizes the book, covering the basic plot (including the ending). It should be easy to read and flow well.

An *outline* covers your book chapter by chapter and provides highlights of each. If you're developing an outline for fiction, include major characters, plots and subplots, and book length.

*Sample chapters* give a more comprehensive idea of your writing skill. Some editors may request the first two or three chapters to determine if she's interested in seeing the whole book.

## Manuscript formats

When submitting a complete manuscript, follow some basic guidelines. In the upper-left corner of your title page, type your legal name (not pseudonym), address, and phone number. In the upper-right corner, type the approximate word count. All material in the upper corners should be single-spaced. Then type the title (centered) almost halfway down that page, the word "by" two spaces under that, and your name or pseudonym two spaces under "by."

The first page should also include the title (centered) one-third of the way down. Two spaces under that type "by" and your name or pseudonym. To begin the body of your manuscript, drop down two double spaces and indent five spaces for each new paragraph. There should be one-inch margins around all sides of a full typewritten page. (Manuscripts with wide margins are more readable and easier to edit.)

Set your computer on double-space for the manuscript body. From page two to the end of the manuscript, include your last name followed by a comma and the title (or key words of the title) in the upper-left corner. The page number should go in the top right corner. Drop down two double spaces to begin the body of each page. If you're submitting a novel, type each chapter title one-third of the way down the page. For more information on manuscript formats, read *Formatting & Submitting Your Manuscript*, by Cynthia Laufenberg and the editors of *Writer's Market* (Writer's Digest Books). SCBWI members and nonmembers can refer to their publication *From Keyboard to Printed Page: Facts You Need to Know*. Visit their website www.scbwi.org and click on "Publications."

For More Info

## Picture book formats

The majority of editors prefer to see complete manuscripts for picture books. When typing the text of a picture book, don't indicate page breaks and don't type each page of text on a new sheet of paper. And unless you are an illustrator, don't worry about supplying art. Editors will find their own illustrators for picture books. Most of the time, a writer and an illustrator who work on the same book never meet. The editor acts as a go-between and works with the writer and illustrator throughout the publishing process. *How to Write and Sell Children's Picture Books*, by Jean E. Karl (Writer's Digest Books), offers advice on preparing text and marketing your work.

If you're an illustrator who has written your own book, consider creating a dummy or storyboard containing both art and text, and then submit it along with your complete manuscript and sample pieces of final art (color photocopies or computer printouts—never originals). Publishers interested in picture books specify in their listings what should be submitted. For tips on creating a dummy, refer to *How to Write and Illustrate Children's Books and Get Them Published*, edited by Treld Pelkey Bicknell and Felicity Trotman (North Light Books), or Frieda Gates' book, *How to Write, Illustrate, and Design Children's Books* (Lloyd-Simone Publishing Company).

For More Info

Writers may also want to learn the art of dummy making to help them through their writing process with things like pacing, rhythm, and length. For a great explanation and helpful hints, see *You Can Write Children's Books*, by Tracey E. Dils (Writer's Digest Books).

## Mailing submissions

Your main concern when packaging material is to be sure it arrives undamaged. If your manuscript is less than six pages, simply fold it in thirds and send it in a #10 (business-size) envelope. For a SASE, either fold another #10 envelope in thirds or insert a #9 (reply) envelope which fits in a #10 neatly without folding.

Another option is folding your manuscript in half in a 6×9 envelope, with a #9 or #10 SASE enclosed. For larger manuscripts, use a 9×12 envelope both for mailing the submission and as a SASE (which can be folded in half). Book manuscripts require sturdy packaging for mailing. Include a self-addressed mailing label and return postage.

If asked to send artwork and photographs, remember they require a bit more care in packaging to guarantee they arrive in good condition. Sandwich illustrations and photos between heavy cardboard that is slightly larger than the work. The cardboard can be secured by rubber bands or with tape. If you tape the cardboard together, check that the artwork doesn't stick to the tape. Be sure your name and address appear on the back of each piece of art or each photo in case the material becomes separated. For the packaging, use either a manila envelope, a foam-padded envelope, brown paper, or a mailer lined with plastic air bubbles. Bind nonjoined edges with reinforced mailing tape and affix a typed mailing label or clearly write your address.

Mailing material first class ensures quick delivery. Also, first-class mail is forwarded for one year if the addressee has moved, and it can be returned if undeliverable. If you're concerned about your original material safely reaching its destination, consider other mailing options, such as UPS or certified mail. If material needs to reach your editor or art director quickly, use overnight delivery services.

Remember, companies outside your own country can't use your country's postage when returning a manuscript to you. When mailing a submission to another country, include a self-addressed envelope and International Reply Coupons, or IRCs. (You'll see this term in many listings in the Canadian & International Book Publishers section.) Your postmaster can tell you, based on a package's weight, the correct number of IRCs to include to ensure its return.

If it's not necessary for an editor to return your work (such as with photocopies), don't include return postage. You may want to track the status of your submission by enclosing a postage-paid reply postcard with options for the editor to check, such as "Yes, I am interested," "I'll keep the material on file," or "No, the material is not appropriate for my needs at this time."

Some writers elect to include a deadline date. If you don't hear from the editor by the specified date, your manuscript is automatically withdrawn from consideration. Because many publishing houses and companies are overstocked with material, a minimum deadline should be at least three months.

Unless requested, it's never a good idea to use a company's fax number or e-mail address to send manuscript submissions. This can disrupt a company's internal business. Some publishers, however, may be open to e-mail submissions. Study the Book Publishers listings for specifics and visit publishers' websites for more information.

## Keeping submission records

It's important to keep track of the material you submit. When recording each submission, include the date it was sent, the business and contact name, and any enclosures (such as samples of writing, artwork, or photography). You can create a record-keeping system of your own or look for record-keeping software in your area computer store.

Keep copies of articles or manuscripts you send together with related correspondence to make follow-up easier. When you sell rights to a manuscript, artwork, or photos, you can "close" your file on a particular submission by noting the date the material was accepted, what rights were purchased, the publication date, and payment.

Often writers, illustrators, and photographers fail to follow up on overdue responses. If you don't hear from a publisher within their stated response time, wait another month or so and follow up with a note asking about the status of your submission. Include the title or description, date sent, and a SASE for response. Ask the contact person when she anticipates making a decision. You may refresh the memory of a buyer who temporarily forgot about your submission. At the very least, you'll receive a definite "no" and free yourself to send the material to another publisher.

## Simultaneous submissions

If you opt for simultaneous (also called "multiple") submissions—sending the same material to several publishers at the same time—be sure to inform each editor to whom you submit that your work is being considered elsewhere. Many editors are reluctant to receive simultaneous submissions but understand that for hopeful writers and illustrators, waiting several months for a response can be frustrating. In some cases, an editor may actually be more inclined to read your manuscript sooner if she knows it's being considered by another publisher. The Society of Children's Book Writers and Illustrators cautions writers against simultaneous submissions. They recommend simultaneously submitting to publishers who state in their submission guidelines that they accept multiple submissions. In such cases, always specify in your cover letter that you've submitted to more than one editor.

It's especially important to keep track of simultaneous submissions, so if you get an offer on a manuscript sent to more than one publisher, you can instruct other publishers to withdraw your work from consideration.

## AGENTS & ART REPS

Most children's writers, illustrators, and photographers, especially those just beginning, are confused about whether to enlist the services of an agent or representative. The decision is strictly one that each writer, illustrator, or photographer must make for herself. Some are confident with their own negotiation skills and believe acquiring an agent or rep is not in their best interest. Others feel uncomfortable in the business arena or are not willing to sacrifice valuable creative time for marketing.

About half of children's publishers accept unagented work, so it's possible to break into children's publishing without an agent. Some agents avoid working with children's books because traditionally low advances and trickling royalty payments over long periods of time make children's books less lucrative. Writers targeting magazine markets don't need the services of an agent. In fact, it's practically impossible to find an agent interested in marketing articles and short stories—there simply isn't enough financial incentive.

One benefit of having an agent, though, is it may speed up the process of getting your work reviewed, especially by publishers who don't accept unagented submissions. If an agent has a good reputation and submits your manuscript to an editor, that manuscript will likely bypass the first-read stage (which is generally done by editorial assistants and junior editors) and end up on the editor's desk sooner.

When agreeing to have a reputable agent represent you, remember that she should be familiar with the needs of the current market and evaluate your manuscript/artwork/photos accordingly. She should also determine the quality of your piece and whether it is saleable. When your manuscript sells, your agent should negotiate a favorable contract and clear up any questions you have about payments.

Keep in mind that however reputable the agent or rep is, she has limitations. Representation does not guarantee sale of your work. It just means an agent or rep sees potential in your writing, art, or photos. Though an agent or rep may offer criticism or advice on how to improve your work, she cannot make you a better writer, artist, or photographer.

Literary agents typically charge a 15 percent commission from the sale of writing; art and photo representatives usually charge a 25 to 30 percent commission. Such fees are taken from advances and royalty earnings. If your agent sells foreign rights to your work, she will deduct a higher percentage because she will most likely be dealing with an overseas agent with whom she must split the fee.

Be advised that not every agent is open to representing a writer, artist, or photographer who lacks an established track record. Just as when approaching a publisher, the manuscript, artwork, or photos and query or cover letter you submit to a potential agent must be attractive and professional looking. Your first impression must be as an organized, articulate person.

For listings of agents and reps, turn to the Agents & Art Reps section. For additional listings of art reps, consult *Artist's & Graphic Designer's Market*; for photo reps, see *Photographer's Market* (both Writer's Digest Books).

# Running Your Business

*The Basics for Writers & Illustrators*

A career in children's publishing involves more than just writing skills or artistic talent. Successful authors and illustrators must be able to hold their own in negotiations, keep records, understand contract language, grasp copyright law, pay taxes, and take care of a number of other business concerns. Although agents and reps, accountants and lawyers, and writers' organizations offer help in sorting out such business issues, it's wise to have a basic understanding of them going in. This article offers just that—basic information. For a more in-depth look at the subjects covered here, check your library or bookstore for books and magazines to help you. We also tell you how to get information on issues like taxes and copyright from the federal government.

## CONTRACTS & NEGOTIATION

Before you see your work in print or begin working with an editor or art director on a project, there is negotiation. And whether negotiating a book contract, a magazine article assignment, or an illustration or photo assignment, there are a few things to keep in mind. First, if you find any clauses vague or confusing in a contract, get legal advice. The time and money invested in counseling up front could protect you from problems later. If you have an agent or rep, she will review any contract.

## Sources for Contract Help

Writers organizations offer a wealth of information to members, including contract advice:

**Society of Children's Book Writers and Illustrators** members can find information in the SCBWI publication Answers to Some Questions About Contracts. Contact SCBWI at 8271 Beverly Blvd., Los Angeles CA 90048, (323)782-1010, or visit their website: www.scbwi.org.

**The Authors Guild** also offers contract tips. Visit their website, www.authorsguild. org. (Members of the guild can receive a 75-point contract review from the guild's legal staff.) See the website for membership information and application form, or contact The Authors Guild at 31 E. 28th St., 10th Floor, New York NY 10016, (212)563-5904. Fax: (212)564-5363. E-mail: staff@authorsguild.org. Website: www. authorsguild.org.

A contract is an agreement between two or more parties that specifies the fees to be paid, services rendered, deadlines, rights purchased, and for artists and photographers, whether original work is returned. Most companies have standard contracts for writers, illustrators, and photographers. The specifics (such as royalty rates, advances, delivery dates, etc.) are typed in after negotiations.

Though it's okay to conduct negotiations over the phone, get a written contract once both parties have agreed on terms. Never depend on oral stipulations; written contracts protect both parties from misunderstandings. Watch for clauses that may not be in your best interest, such as "work-for-hire." When you do work-for-hire, you give up all rights to your creations.

When negotiating a book deal, find out whether your contract contains an option clause. This clause requires the author to give the publisher a first look at her next work before offering it to other publishers. Though it's editorial etiquette to give the publisher the first chance at publishing your next work, be wary of statements in the contract that could trap you. Don't allow the publisher to consider the next project for more than 30 days and be specific about what type of work should actually be considered "next work." (For example, if the book under contract is a young adult novel, specify that the publisher will receive an exclusive look at only your next young adult novel.)

For More Info

(For more information about SCBWI, The Authors Guild, and other organizations, turn to the Clubs & Organizations section and read the listings for the organizations that interest you.)

## Book publishers' payment methods

Book publishers pay authors and artists in royalties, a percentage of either the wholesale or retail price of each book sold. From large publishing houses, the author usually receives an advance issued against future royalties before the book is published. Half of the advance amount is issued upon signing the book contract; the other half is issued when the book is finished. For illustrations, one-third of the advance should be collected upon signing the contract; one-third upon delivery of sketches; and one-third upon delivery of finished art.

After your book has sold enough copies to earn back your advance, you'll start to get royalty checks. Some publishers hold a reserve against returns, which means a percentage of royalties is held back in case books are returned from bookstores. If you have a reserve clause in your contract, find out the exact percentage of total sales that will be withheld and the time period the publisher will hold this money. You should be reimbursed this amount after a reasonable time period, such as a year. Royalty percentages vary with each publisher, but there are standard ranges.

## Book publishers' rates

According to figures from the Society of Children's Book Writers and Illustrators, first-time picture book authors can expect advances of $2,000-3,000; first-time picture book illustrators' advances range from $5,000-7,000; text and illustration packages for first-timers can score $6,000-8,000. Rates go up for subsequent books: $3,500-5,000 for picture book text; $7,000-10,000 for picture book illustration; $8,000-10,000 for text and illustration. Experienced authors can expect higher advances. Royalties for picture books are generally about five percent (split between the author and illustrator) but can go as high as ten percent. Those who both write and illustrate a book, of course, receive the full royalty.

Advances for hardcover novels and nonfiction can fetch authors advances of $4,000-6,000 and 10 percent royalties; paperbacks bring in slightly lower advances of $3,000-5,000 and royalties of 6-8 percent.

As you might expect, advance and royalty figures vary from house to house and are affected by the time of year, the state of the economy, and other factors. Some smaller houses may not even pay royalties, just flat fees. Educational houses may not offer advances or offer smaller amounts. Religious publishers tend to offer smaller advances than trade publishers. First-time writers and illustrators generally start on the low end of the scale, while established and high-profile writers are paid more. For more information SCBWI members can request or download SCBWI publication "Answer to Some Questions About Contracts." (Visit www.scbwi.org.)

## Pay rates for magazines

For writers, fee structures for magazines are based on a per-word rate or range for a specific article length. Artists and photographers have a few more variables to contend with before contracting their services.

Payment for illustrations and photos can be set by such factors as whether the piece(s) will be black and white or four-color, how many are to be purchased, where the work appears (cover or inside), circulation, and the artist's or photographer's prior experience.

## Remaindering

When a book goes out of print, a publisher will sell any existing copies to a wholesaler who, in turn, sells the copies to stores at a discount. When the books are "remaindered" to a wholesaler, they are usually sold at a price just above the cost of printing. When negotiating a contract with a publisher, you may want to discuss the possibility of purchasing the remaindered copies before they are sold to a wholesaler, then you can market the copies you purchased and still make a profit.

## KNOW YOUR RIGHTS

A copyright is a form of protection provided to creators of original works, published or unpublished. In general, copyright protection ensures the writer, illustrator, or photographer the power to decide how her work is used and allows her to receive payment for each use.

Essentially, copyright also encourages the creation of new works by guaranteeing the creator power to sell rights to the work in the marketplace. The copyright holder can print, reprint, or copy her work; sell or distribute copies of her work; or prepare derivative works such as plays, collages, or recordings. The Copyright Law is designed to protect work (created on or after January 1, 1978) for her lifetime plus 70 years.

If you collaborate with someone else on a written or artistic project, the copyright will last for the lifetime of the last survivor plus 70 years. The creators' heirs may hold a copyright for an additional 70 years. After that, the work becomes public domain. Works created anonymously or under a pseudonym are protected for 120 years, or 95 years after publication. Under work-for-hire agreements, you relinquish your copyright to your "employer."

## Copyright notice & registration

Some feel a copyright notice should be included on all work, registered or not. Others feel it is not necessary and a copyright notice will only confuse publishers about whether the material is registered (acquiring rights to previously registered material is a more complicated process).

Although it's not necessary to include a copyright notice on unregistered work, if you don't feel your work is safe without the notice, it is your right to include one. Including a copyright notice—© (year of work, your name)—should help safeguard against plagiarism.

Registration is a legal formality intended to make copyright public record, and it can help you win more money in a court case. By registering work within three months of publication or before an infringement occurs, you are eligible to collect statutory damages and attorney's fees. If you register later than three months after publication, you will qualify only for actual damages and profits.

Ideas and concepts are not copyrightable, only expressions of those ideas and concepts. A character type or basic plot outline, for example, is not subject to a copyright infringement lawsuit. Also, titles, names, short phrases or slogans, and lists of contents are not subject to copyright protection, though titles and names may be protected through the Trademark Office.

You can register a group of articles, illustrations, or photos if it meets these criteria:

- the group is assembled in order, such as in a notebook
- the works bear a single title, such as "Works by (your name)"
- it is the work of one writer, artist, or photographer
- the material is the subject of a single claim to copyright

It's a publisher's responsibility to register your book for copyright. If you've previously registered the same material, you must inform your editor and supply the previous copyright information, otherwise, the publisher can't register the book in its published form.

For more information about the proper way to register works and to order the correct forms, contact the U.S. Copyright Office, (202)707-3000. The forms available are TX for writing (books, articles, etc.); VA for pictures (photographs, illustrations); and PA for plays and music. For information about how to use the copyright forms, request a copy of Circular I on Copyright Basics. All of the forms and circulars are free. Send the completed registration form along with the stated fee and a copy of the work to the Copyright Office.

**For More Info**

For specific answers to questions about copyright (but not legal advice), call the Copyright Public Information Office at (202)707-3000 weekdays between 8:30 a.m. and 5 p.m. EST. Forms can also be downloaded from the Library of Congress website: www.loc.gov/copyright. The site also includes a list of frequently asked questions, tips on filling out forms, general copyright information, and links to other sites related to copyright issues. For members of SCBWI, information about copyrights and the law is available in their publication: Copyright Facts for Writers.

## The rights publishers buy

The copyright law specifies that a writer, illustrator, or photographer generally sells one-time rights to her work unless she and the buyer agree otherwise in writing. Many publications will want more exclusive rights to your work than just one-time usage; some will even require you to sell all rights. Be sure you are monetarily compensated for the additional rights you relinquish. If you must give up all rights to a work, carefully consider the price you're being offered to determine whether you'll be compensated for the loss of other potential sales.

Writers who only give up limited rights to their work can then sell reprint rights to other publications, foreign rights to international publications, or even movie rights, should the opportunity arise. Artists and photographers can sell their work to other markets such as paper product companies who may use an image on a calendar, greeting card, or mug. Illustrators and photographers may even sell original work after it has been published. And there are a number of galleries throughout the U.S. that display and sell the original work of children's illustrators.

Rights acquired through the sale of a book manuscript are explained in each publisher's contract. Take time to read relevant clauses to be sure you understand what rights each contract is specifying before signing. Be sure your contract contains a clause allowing all rights to revert back to you in the event the publisher goes out of business. (You may even want to have the contract reviewed by an agent or an attorney specializing in publishing law.)

The following are the rights you'll most often sell to publishers, periodicals, and producers in the marketplace:

**First rights.** The buyer purchases the rights to use the work for the first time in any medium. All other rights remain with the creator. When material is excerpted from a soon-to-be-published book for use in a newspaper or periodical, first serial rights are also purchased.

**One-time rights.** The buyer has no guarantee that she is the first to use a piece. One-time permission to run written work, illustrations, or photos is acquired, then the rights revert back to the creator.

**First North American serial rights.** This is similar to first rights, except that companies who distribute both in the U.S. and Canada will stipulate these rights to ensure that another North American company won't come out with simultaneous usage of the same work.

**Second serial (reprint) rights.** In this case, newspapers and magazines are granted the right to reproduce a work that has already appeared in another publication. These rights are also purchased by a newspaper or magazine editor who wants to publish part of a book after the book has been published. The proceeds from reprint rights for a book are often split evenly between the author and his publishing company.

**Simultaneous rights.** More than one publication buys one-time rights to the same work at the same time. Use of such rights occurs among magazines with circulations that don't overlap, such as many religious publications.

**All rights.** Just as it sounds, the writer, illustrator, or photographer relinquishes all rights to a piece—she no longer has any say in who acquires rights to use it. All rights are purchased by publishers who pay premium usage fees, have an exclusive format, or have other book or magazine interests from which the purchased work can generate more mileage. If a company insists on acquiring all rights to your work, see if you can negotiate for the rights to revert back to you after a reasonable period of time. If they agree to such a proposal, get it in writing.

Note: Writers, illustrators, and photographers should be wary of "work-for-hire" arrangements. If you sign an agreement stipulating that your work will be done as work-for-hire, you will not control the copyrights of the completed work—the company that hired you will be the copyright owner.

**Foreign serial rights.** Be sure before you market to foreign publications that you have sold only North American—not worldwide—serial rights to previous markets. If so, you are free to market to publications that may be interested in material that's appeared in a North American-based periodical.

**Syndication rights.** This is a division of serial rights. For example, if a syndicate prints portions of a book in installments in its newspapers, it would be syndicating second serial rights. The syndicate would receive a commission and leave the remainder to be split between the author and publisher.

**Subsidiary rights.** These include serial rights, dramatic rights, book club rights, or translation rights. The contract should specify what percentage of profits from sales of these rights go to the author and publisher.

**Dramatic, television, and motion picture rights.** During a specified time, the interested party tries to sell a story to a producer or director. Many times options are renewed because the selling process can be lengthy.

**Display rights or electronic publishing rights.** They're also known as "Data, Storage, and Retrieval." Usually listed under subsidiary rights, the marketing of electronic rights in this era of rapidly expanding capabilities and markets for electronic material can be tricky. Display rights can cover text or images to be used in a CD-ROM or online, or they may cover use of material in formats not even fully developed yet. If a display rights clause is listed in your contract, try to negotiate its elimination. Otherwise, be sure to pin down which electronic rights are being purchased. Demand the clause be restricted to things designed to be read only. By doing this, you maintain your rights to use your work for things such as games and interactive software.

## STRICTLY BUSINESS

An essential part of being a freelance writer, illustrator, or photographer is running your freelance business. It's imperative to maintain accurate business records to determine if you're making a profit as a freelancer. Keeping correct, organized records will also make your life easier as you approach tax time.

When setting up your system, begin by keeping a bank account and ledger for your business finances apart from your personal finances. Also, if writing, illustration, or photography is secondary to another freelance career, keep separate business records for each.

You will likely accumulate some business expenses before showing any profit when you start out as a freelancer. To substantiate your income and expenses to the IRS, keep all invoices, cash receipts, sales slips, bank statements, canceled checks, and receipts related to travel expenses and entertaining clients. For entertainment expenditures, record the date, place, and purpose of the business meeting, as well as gas mileage. Keep records for all purchases, big and small. Don't take the small purchases for granted; they can add up to a substantial amount. File all receipts in chronological order. Maintaining a separate file for each month simplifies retrieving records at the end of the year.

## Record keeping

When setting up a single-entry bookkeeping system, record income and expenses separately. Use some of the subheads that appear on Schedule C (the form used for recording income from a business) of the 1040 tax form so you can easily transfer information onto the tax form when filing your return. In your ledger include a description of each transaction—the date, source of income (or debts from business purchases), description of what was purchased or sold, the amount of the transaction, and whether payment was by cash, check, or credit card.

Don't wait until January 1 to start keeping records. The moment you first make a business-related purchase or sell an article, book manuscript, illustration, or photo, begin tracking your profits and losses. If you keep records from January 1 to December 31, you're using a calendar-year accounting period. Any other accounting period is called a fiscal year.

There are two types of accounting methods you can choose from—the cash method and the accrual method. The cash method is used more often: You record income when it is received and expenses when they're disbursed.

Using the accrual method, you report income at the time you earn it rather than when it's actually received. Similarly, expenses are recorded at the time they're incurred rather than when you actually pay them. If you choose this method, keep separate records for "accounts receivable" and "accounts payable."

## Satisfying the IRS

To successfully—and legally—work as a freelancer, you must know what income you should report and what deductions you can claim. But before you can do that, you must prove to the IRS you're in business to make a profit, that your writing, illustration, or photography is not merely a hobby.

The Tax Reform Act of 1986 says you should show a profit for three years out of a five-year period to attain professional status. The IRS considers these factors as proof of your professionalism:

- accurate financial records
- a business bank account separate from your personal account
- proven time devoted to your profession
- whether it's your main or secondary source of income
- your history of profits and losses
- the amount of training you have invested in your field
- your expertise

If your business is unincorporated, you'll fill out tax information on Schedule C of Form 1040.

If you're unsure of what deductions you can take, request the IRS publication containing this information. Under the Tax Reform Act, only 30 percent of business meals, entertainment and related tips, and parking charges are deductible. Other deductible expenses allowed on Schedule C include: car expenses for business-related trips; professional courses and seminars; depreciation of office equipment, such as a computer; dues and publication subscriptions; and miscellaneous expenses, such as postage used for business needs.

If you're working out of a home office, a portion of your mortgage interest (or rent), related utilities, property taxes, repair costs, and depreciation may be deducted as business expenses—under special circumstances. To learn more about the possibility of home office deductions, consult IRS Publication 587, Business Use of Your Home

The method of paying taxes on income not subject to withholding is called "estimated tax" for individuals. If you expect to owe more than $500 at year's end and if the total amount of income tax that will be withheld during the year will be less than 90 percent of the tax shown on the current year's return, you'll generally make estimated tax payments. Estimated tax payments are made in four equal installments due on April 15, June 15, September 15, and January 15 (assuming you're a calendar-year taxpayer). For more information, request Publication 533, Self-Employment Tax.

The Internal Revenue Service's website (www.irs.gov) offers tips and instant access to IRS forms and publications.

**For More Info**

## Social Security tax

Depending on your net income as a freelancer, you may be liable for a Social Security tax. This is a tax designed for those who don't have Social Security withheld from their paychecks. You're liable if your net income is $400 or more per year. Net income is the difference between your income and allowable business deductions. Request Schedule SE, Computation of Social Security Self-Employment Tax, if you qualify.

If completing your income tax return proves to be too complex, consider hiring an accountant (the fee is a deductible business expense) or contact the IRS for assistance. (Look in the White Pages under U.S. Government—Internal Revenue Service or check their website, www.irs.gov.) In addition to offering numerous publications to instruct you in various facets of preparing a tax return, the IRS also has walk-in centers in some cities.

## Insurance

As a self-employed professional, be aware of what health and business insurance coverage is available to you. Unless you're a Canadian who is covered by national health insurance or a full-time freelancer covered by your spouse's policy, health insurance will no doubt be one of your biggest expenses. Under the terms of a 1985 government act (COBRA), if you leave a job with health benefits, you're entitled to continue that coverage for up to 18 months—you pay 100 percent of the premium and sometimes a small administration fee. Eventually, you must search for your own health plan. You may also choose to purchase disability and life insurance. Disability insurance is offered through many private insurance companies and state governments. This insurance pays a monthly fee that covers living and business expenses during periods of long-term recuperation from a health problem. The amount of money paid is based on the recipient's annual earnings.

Before contacting any insurance representative, talk to other writers, illustrators, or photographers to learn which insurance companies they recommend. If you belong to a writers' or artists' organization, ask the organization if it offers insurance coverage for professionals. (SCBWI has a plan available to members in certain states. Look through the Clubs & Organizations section for other groups that may offer coverage.) Group coverage may be more affordable and provide more comprehensive coverage than an individual policy.

# Research for Fiction Writers

*Hitting the Books (& the Web)*

by Lauren Mosko

With so many works of creative nonfiction receiving critical attention and brisk sales in the last few years, writers are beginning to spend time discussing their *pre-writing* process, specifically the months and even years they invest in research for their books. Of course writers of nonfiction are expected to conduct thorough research, but fiction writers can also gain a great deal by hitting the books before they ever put pen to paper (or fingers to keyboard).

It might seem strange to spend time doing research for a story that's not grounded in fact, but fiction writers need their readers to believe in the characters, settings, and circumstances of their stories just as much as nonfiction writers do. Research helps writers create a convincing and colorful world—the kind that draws in readers and keeps them turning pages. No matter what you're writing about, what you discover while investigating your subject can help you do two things:

- Include details that make your scenes more realistic and reinforce your authority
- Inform the tone, mood, and style of your writing so that your reader not only believes the story is authentic but also connects with it mentally and emotionally

For example, let's say I've got an idea for a young adult novel about a lifeguard who is devastated after a child drowns on her shift. I imagine the vague circumstances of the main event like this: My protagonist is sharing the shift with another lifeguard. She starts to get overheated and asks the other guard to watch the pool while she goes for a glass of water. The other lifeguard becomes distracted by a struggling swimmer near his stand and doesn't see a toddler slip under the water in the shallow end. My protagonist returns, sees the little boy at the bottom of the pool, drags him out, and tries to resuscitate him to no avail.

This could be a very powerful scene or it could be a disaster. Here are some things I need to know in order to make it work:

- How big and what shape is the pool if there are only two guards on duty?
- Where is the pool? Is it a public neighborhood pool or a private apartment complex pool? At which place is a toddler more likely to be left unattended by a parent or guardian?
- How do lifeguards act while on duty? Do they converse casually or are their exchanges strictly business? Is there usually music playing in the background?

**LAUREN MOSKO** is editor of *Novel & Short Story Writer's Market* and former assistant editor of *Children's Writer's & Illustrator's Market*.

- What's the official procedure for pulling a child from the bottom of a pool? (And in what year is my story set? How would the procedure be different if my story were set in the 1980s instead of in present day?) Would my lifeguard have any special equipment?
- Would my protagonist perform Rescue Breathing or CPR? Both? How are they performed?
- What would the other lifeguard be doing in the meantime?

If I don't take the time to learn the answers to these questions, I might be able to fool a reader who has never worked at a pool or doesn't know how to perform CPR. But since my protagonist has a job that many other teens also hold (and studied very hard to earn), I can't risk revealing to them that I haven't done my homework. If I blow this scene, they'll stop reading. Instead of getting emotionally invested in the crisis of a girl who did her best to save a little boy, they'll be furious with her (and me) because, for example, she *clearly could have* saved the little boy if she knew children need one breath for every five chest compressions—not two breaths after 15 compressions like adults. That might seem like a small detail, but in this case it was a matter of life and death (for my poor toddler and my scene).

## CONDUCTING YOUR RESEARCH

It's easy to become paralyzed when you're faced with the prospect of research. Mounds of material are available from innumerable sources. Where should you even begin? Can all your research be done from home? Take some time before you start to set up a research strategy. Make a list of the sites (physical and cyber) you could visit and what you hope or expect to find there. Here's a basic plan to help get you started.

### The Internet

Probably the easiest place to begin your research is at your own desk. The Internet is the perfect tool if you're looking for fast facts or general overviews. To return to my example story, if I wanted to know the basic steps for CPR, all I'd have to do is choose a search engine like Google or Yahoo and input ''CPR'' (or more specifically ''CPR for children''), and dozens of sites with simple instructions are returned.

Be careful, though. A search engine is only as good as its conductor, and if I didn't already know that professional rescuers of all kinds, from EMTs to lifeguards, are required to use a mask to perform CPR now instead of just doing the old mouth-to-mouth technique, I'd still be getting wrong information. A quick Internet search can confirm the 5-compressions-to-2-breaths part of the procedure, but I'll probably need to get my hands on a lifeguard manual if I really want my protagonist to do the job correctly.

In addition to the search engines, also visit the websites of organizations or publications that are related to your topic. A fairly obvious site I could visit for my story is that of the American Red Cross (www.redcross.org), the most well-known organization that certifies lifeguards. If I wanted to know what pop music might be playing on the radio while the guards were working (since I have no idea what teenagers listen to now), I'd visit the website of Billboard (www.billboard.com), the trade magazine for the music industry, and check out their famous Billboard Pop Charts.

### The library

After you've collected as much cursory information as possible from the Internet, it's time to head to the library to further explore your topic. The first item on your agenda should be to read other people's books—as many and as great a variety as you can carry. Nonfiction, narrative nonfiction, and fiction all offer valuable insights, so don't overlook anything that might be pertinent. On my trip, I'd seek out the American Red Cross manuals *Lifeguarding*

*Today* and *CPR for the Professional Rescuer* (nonfiction), as well as R.L. Stine's *The Dead Lifeguard* from the Fear Street Super Chiller Series and something from the *Baywatch Junior Lifeguard* book series (fiction). If I was considering setting this scene in the past, perhaps I'd also pick up Robert C. Baxley's *The Lifeguards* (narrative nonfiction). Remember that you're not just looking for facts; you're seeking to absorb as much information as possible about the context for your story and how it's been treated in others' works. You want to understand as much as you can about the history, culture, economics, and politics of your subject so that the world you create is as complete as possible.

Next, hit the newspaper and periodical archives. These will be great sources for factual first- or second-hand accounts of events or circumstances that can give you ideas about how real people might act in a situation like the one you're about to create. Don't limit yourself to your local newspaper or local magazines; think about any source that relates to your subject.

If you still can't find what you need, try the library's online research databases. These resources catalog articles from popular magazines and even more obscure journals and often backdate farther than what's physically present in your library. To make searching easier, they are usually organized by subject.

Before you leave the library, don't forget to stop by the multimedia desk. Movies, documentaries, and audiotapes are invaluable supplements to your printed research. In some cases, they might even be the best research material. (For example, a video about child CPR will instruct me much more clearly than any book's diagram.) In addition to giving you more information about people and cultures, the pictures, faces, music, and voices that multimedia materials offer can help you when it's time to invent your own pictures and voices.

## The adventure

While your home computer and the local library are wonderful resources, don't let yourself be limited by them. If it's possible to travel, consider visiting a museum or archive devoted to your subject. The volume of material devoted specifically to your area of interest is well worth the tank of gas or plane ticket, but make sure that you've already done preliminary Internet and library research before going. Materials in a museum or archive cannot be checked out so you'll want to make the most of your time there. Go with a detailed list of the information for which you're looking so you don't waste time wandering aimlessly and also prepare a few very specific questions, in the event that you have the opportunity to talk to a curator or special collections librarian.

Next, go "on location." If your story is set in another country, state, or even another neighborhood, visit it. You can re-create this world fairly well with the information you've gathered in your other research, but nothing is better than being there. Keep in mind that this adventure doesn't have to be extravagant. If your story is about two children who grew up in the plains of Africa but your budget does not afford you a safari, a trip to the nearest city zoo to watch how the elephants move and interact and how giraffes feed is better than any pictures you might find in *National Geographic*. Similarly, I have no intention of going to a local pool and staging a drowning in order to research my hypothetical story, but going and absorbing the atmosphere at a few different pools—the patron demographics, the life-guard demographics, their interactions, etc.—will help me so much when I sit down to write my dramatic scene.

## The interview

Once you've exhausted *places* for research, think about the *people* you could talk to. Interviews are wonderful primary sources of information, and the proliferation of e-mail has made them easier than ever to conduct. Sit down and brainstorm all the types of people who might be able to shed light upon your subject. Are there scholars or specialists in your subject area at a local high school or college? What about practitioners in the field? Can you think of anyone who has participated in or witnessed a similar event?

If so, first do a little more research. Head back to the computer or the library and search for anything your potential interviewees have written, any public appearances, or any previous interviews they've granted. You'll eventually use this information to help you formulate questions tailored to your interviewees' area of expertise, but for now, just make sure that they have the knowledge that will actually further your research. (For example, I wouldn't want to waste my time [and his] interviewing an Aquatics Director at a facility that's used strictly for physical therapy. He wouldn't be able to tell me much about lifeguards or patrons if they don't exist at his site.) Once you've got a list of solid interview candidates, use the Internet or the trusty phone book to track them down.

Once you've found them, write, e-mail, or call to ask if they have time for a brief interview. Explain who you are and what you're working on. Promise them no more than five questions. (Even if you only ask five questions, once you get people started talking about themselves, they'll usually go on until you've gotten everything you came for and more.) If they agree to the interview, set up a time to meet, phone, or send them your questions via e-mail. Give yourself at least a week to review your reserach and formulate your questions. After you've set a "date," write and revise your questions. Make them as specific and open-ended as possible. Nothing is more frustrating than a shy or aloof interviewee who answers you mono-syllabically, so don't even give them the opportunity.

If you're interviewing in person, take along a tape recorder if you have one. (Don't forget to ask your interviewees if they mind being taped.) It's much easier to hold a conversation if you're not trying to write as fast as you can and listen at the same time. Also bring along a typed copy of your questions and some paper and pens in case you want to jot down a few notes. If you're conducting the interview by e-mail, send the questions on the agreed-upon date, along with a deadline for return of responses. (A week is good.) If you're doing a phone interview, you can either invest in a tape recorder that hooks up to your phone (about $80 at Radio Shack) or you can just scribble furiously while they talk. No matter what method you use, when the interview is over, always remember to send a thank-you card.

## ORGANIZING YOUR NOTES

Now that you're up to your elbows in notebooks and index cards, it's time to organize them and decide what you're going to use in your actual text. The most important thing to keep in mind is that every bit of information you collected does not need to be included in your story. Resist the urge to load your manuscript with names and dates that don't further the plot or develop your characters. The idea is to use your research to learn the background information and then do what you do best—make the rest up.

To illustrate, in her 2004 SCBWI Annual Conference address "Once Upon a Time: The Power of Story," author Karen Cushman (*Catherine Called Birdy, The Midwife's Apprentice, Rodzina*) said that she probably only uses 10 percent of the information she gathers for her books; the other 90 percent gives her the security to write with authority. In other words, use your research to create a few sentences that authenticate each scene, and then let the rest serve as your own mental proof. In her 2004 SCBWI Annual Conference address entitled "Truth Versus Fact: Research as the Skeleton for Your Story," author Donna Jo Napoli (*Sirena, Breath, North*) offered that a good rule of thumb is that the amount of detail you use in any given scene should be proportional to the weight of that scene in the grand scheme of the book. If you're still not sure if you've included too much or too little information, have someone else read your story and ask her if the amount of research overwhelms the story.

## WRITING YOUR STORY

This sample research plan is a good place to start, but you should feel free to modify it any way that best fits your project. No matter what you read or where you travel, you're still the author and the integrity of *your* story is still the most important thing. If in your research you discover two sources that seem to contradict or oppose each other, Napoli encourages writers to just pick and choose the parts that make the best story. With art, as in life, you can't please everyone. If you are looking for the answer to a specific question but can't find it anywhere, she urged writers not to be afraid to just give themselves creative license. (If no one can tell me whether or not it's proper for lifeguards to don footwear while perched on their stands, I can write that my protagonist always wears sandals because she is self-conscious of her pointy toes. Problem solved!) After all, it's that creative license that set your story—and your research—in motion in the first place.

# Getting Back in the Saddle for a Tough Revision

by Christine Kole MacLean

was in the middle of New York City when I fell off my horse—my writing horse, that is. I had just come from a meeting with my editor, who had given me yet another two-page, single-spaced editorial letter about my work in progress. I spent the next few months doing precious little writing. I was too busy baying at the moon, feeling sorry for myself.

As far as I was concerned, the time off was justified. By then, I had been on the dusty trail of revision for almost a year. When I had first submitted the manuscript for what would become *Mary Margaret and the Perfect Pet Plan* to Stephanie Owens Lurie at Dutton at the end of 2001, it had been as a 1,000-word picture book. She had liked the idea, but couldn't use it as a picture book. Would I like to try it as something longer—maybe an early chapter book?

I hadn't ever written a story that long before, but my main character was fun and the idea of spending a little more time with her appealed to me. I did the work and resubmitted the 7,000-word manuscript in February of 2002. While my editor thought it was coming along nicely, she expressed some concerns in her editorial letter. Most of them seemed easy enough to address—until the one that recommended I add a major subplot. "But then it will be too long," I said in an e-mail, hoping to deter her. "Don't worry about the length," she replied cheerfully. "I think it wants to be a novel."

I thought not. Having never written a novel before, the idea of building the story into one terrified me. Mary Margaret still amused me, but could I *quintuple* the number of words I'd already written about her?

It occurred to me that I could quit. The book was not under contract; I felt I could politely decline ("Dear Ms. Lurie, I'm sorry but I think you have me confused with another writer, since I don't actually *write* novels") and remain on friendly terms. But I've learned that if something scares me, it's a sign I should at least try it. So I groped and stumbled and cursed my way through that particular revision and resubmitted the story, now 30,000 words, in May of 2002. Pleased with the result, my editor rewarded me with a compliment about my willingness to revise (a foreshadowing of what was to come, no doubt) and a contract. For one brief moment, I thought that perhaps I could write novels after all.

Then she sent a second editorial letter. Any confidence I had gained was replaced with

---

**CHRISTINE KOLE MACLEAN** (www.christinekolemaclean.com) has written about everything from celebrities and work/life balance to institutional investing and corporate culture. Nothing has been as difficult or as personally satisfying as finishing *Mary Margaret and the Perfect Pet Plan*. She recently finished a sequel, *Mary Margaret, Center Stage* (Dutton/Penguin), which is forthcoming.

Through revision after revision, *Mary Margaret and the Perfect Pet Plan* evolved from a 1,000-word picture book to a 10,000-word novel. Christine Kole MacLean worked under the guidance of Dutton editor Stephanie Owens Lurie to expand the story spending well over a year on the process. MacLean's hard work was rewarded with the 2004 publication of *Mary Margaret*. The author has just completed a follow-up featuring the same character.

raw fear. But the book was under contract, and no matter how badly I was shaking in my boots, turning back was no longer an option. I saddled up for another revision and set out to make my main character more convincing, give her brother a bigger role in the story, and temper some of the adult humor.

That fall, weary and saddle sore but satisfied that the story was better as a result of my editor's suggestions and my work, I sent the manuscript to her again. She said she needed some time to think but her gut reaction was that it was "just a matter of pacing." Still being a greenhorn at writing novels, this sounded a lot like "tweaking" to me. I took off my chaps and relaxed in the belief that I was almost finished with the book.

## HOLD UP THERE, LITTLE MISSY

In December, I joined my husband on a business trip to New York so I could meet my editor for the first time and discuss final revisions. I knew there was still some work to be done on the manuscript, but I pictured the two of us jawing about how far the story had come. Instead, as we went over the editorial letter she had written (her third—but who's counting?), she gently told me how far it still had to go. The pacing was off. The ending was pat. Worst of all, I needed to give my character a best friend, which definitely does not fall into the category of "tweaking." I left her office facing the most daunting revision of all, and I was dog-tired from all the previous revisions.

I took the holiday season off, thinking that I'd have a renewed sense of energy after the New Year. But January came and went, and I still couldn't drag my sorry be-hind out of the bunkhouse. Then in February, I had several upheavals in my personal life—the kind of things that don't get resolved in a week or a month or even six months. My old lack of energy coupled with this new lack of focus meant that I was in a heap of hurt.

## RIDING HERD

I wish I could say that this is the part of the story where I took the bull by the horns, but it's not. Instead, it was my editor who inadvertently spurred me into action. In an e-mail exchange with her I mentioned what was going on in my personal life. Although she hadn't ever set a firm deadline for the revision (thinking that I'd be sending her a new draft in a few months, as I had with previous revisions), she replied that she could extend the deadline for the revision, if that would help.

*Deadline.* The word triggered something in me. In addition to writing fiction, I write for corporate clients—nice people who don't put much stock in writer's block and don't care about self-doubt or any other writer's neuroses I might have. Their expectation is that I'll deliver quality work on time, and somehow I deliver quality work on time. Having my editor mention the word *deadline* in that e-mail was an "a-ha" moment for me in which I realized it was possible to bring the same discipline to my creative writing that I had been bringing to my freelance writing for 20 years. Instead of taking my editor up on her kind offer to be flexible about the deadline, I asked her to set a firm one. I steeled myself for the journey ahead and hit the trail for what I hoped would be the last time.

Once I had figured out that regardless of whether I was writing fiction or corporate bro-chures, I still saddled up the same way, I was able to get back to the chore at hand. Unfortu-nately, getting back to it is not the same thing as *doing* it. As with the previous revisions, I stumbled my way through. But because by now it was clear to me that I was going to be spending a lot of time riding the wide open range of revision, this time I paid attention to how I got my footing after I stumbled. Here are a few things I learned.

**To go the distance, concentrate on the miles.** The deadline my editor had set for me was approximately eight weeks out, and my book was about 16 chapters long. So I put myself on a strict schedule of revising two chapters each week. That's all. Just two chapters. This

EDITORS ON REVISION...

# Caitlyn Dlouhy

*Caitlyn Dlouhy is Executive Editor for Atheneum Books for Young Readers*

**What qualities does a writer need to be good at revision?**

W hat qualities does a writer need to be good at revision? A great revisionist is one who is truly open to editorial suggestions; one who will trust his or her editor, knowing that any suggestion is aimed toward making the text as strong as it can possibly be; and one who will follow changes throughout his/her entire manuscript. For instance, rather than slicing open the one section that needs the fix, he or she will look carefully at how that change might resonate throughout the rest of the work.

**What are the most common revision mistakes new writers make?**

One is rushing! I think especially with new or not-yet-contracted writers, they have a misperception that if they don't get their revision in quickly enough, the editor might lose her enthusiasm for a project, and they'll have lost their "moment," so they'll do a fast, perfunctory, but not necessarily well-thought-through revision that is almost always disappointing.

Another common mistake is, ahem, disregarding most of the editor's suggestions. If your editor is telling you that a character is unrealistic or a scene isn't working, while you don't necessarily have to take the editor's suggestions on how to fix these problems, you do have to fix these problems in some way.

**What don't writers understand about the revision process that you wish they did?**

What I most wish writers understood is that we aren't trying to torture writers, nor are we trying to impose our own creative desires into their work. Most often we get a strong sense of how good a writer can be, and we want to help bring out their very best. We're terrifically busy, and it would be so much easier to just slip the manuscript into copyediting; writing a six or eight page editorial letter can take *days*. But we do it because we want your manuscript to shine.

**Who is a writer you've worked with you feel is outstanding at revision and why?**

Frances O'Roark Dowell. While working on her upcoming novel, *Chicken Boy*, she rewrote her entire first draft because we realized that the story wasn't being told from the strongest point of view—the narrator's best pal, Tobin, actually had the more unique voice, and could tell a more compelling story. There was no moaning and groaning. Frances went into Tobin's head, coaxed out his story, and sent me a second draft that was nearly an entirely new manuscript, and one that knocked my socks off.

**Working with a writer who is really great at revision is like . . .**

. . . working with a master chef—you just have to supply a few key ingredients, and he creates a multi-layered, carefully nuanced, full-bodied feast.

**Working with a writer who doesn't understand or isn't good at the revision process is like . . .**

. . . throwing leaves into the wind—they rarely end up where you're hoping they will.

**Is there a part of the revision process that you particularly enjoy or dread?**

I dread having to bring up the same issues in a second or third revision letter. I love love *love* seeing where a good revisionist will take his or her manuscript—when I read the rewrite and think wow wow wow, he/she really did it!

seemed manageable to me. I knew, however, that if I didn't complete those two chapters, time would quickly get away from me and I'd be scrambling at the end to make the deadline. So I did what all good fiction writers do: I raised the stakes. I told my editor that she could expect to see 25 percent of the book every two weeks. And when I got down to work, I kept my anxiety at bay by thinking only about the work I had to complete for the next mini-deadline.

**Let amigos give you a hand.** Afraid that I'll lose the compulsion to write a story if I talk about it too much, I don't usually talk about my work in progress. Furthermore, for a long time, I felt like it would be cheating somehow if I didn't figure out every element of the revision myself. But I was so stymied during that last revision by the problem of what kind of person my main character would choose as a best friend that when a writer friend asked why I had such a hangdog look on my face, I blurted out everything. By the end of our conversation, I had a good idea of who the best friend was and why my main character would choose him. Since then, I've opened up and talked about my works in progress more often. There's a difference between talking a problem through and talking the story out, and you never know when something someone else says will spark that perfect solution you've been hoping for.

An editor can be the best friend of all during a revision. At a critical point during that last revision, my editor—who must have a sixth sense that tells her when a writer is flagging—sent words of encouragement. "Take your time and enjoy the ride," she said in an e-mail. "Relax with the knowledge that you have my full confidence." Those words, which I reread

EDITORS ON REVISION...
# Melanie Kroupa

*Melanie Kroupa is Publisher of Melanie Kroupa Books, an imprint of Farrar, Straus & Giroux.*

**What qualities does a writer need to be good at revision?**
A willingness to step back and look at what she's written with a fresh eye. If a writer has a good grasp on what it is she's set out to do—and can express that—and can keep an open mind as she (and others) look at it to consider if she's accomplished what she set out to do, a writer's taken a good first step in the revision process.

It's useful if a writer can listen to (and hear) an editor's point of view, considering questions, specific suggestions or ideas for change that an editor might suggest—and then decide if those ideas make sense and are in line with what she set out to write. The suggestions should ring true to the author. If they don't, and they don't work to strengthen the book, the author should consider whether she wants to make the changes. If they do ring true, then it's important that the author internalize the suggestions, let them lead her to their own solutions that fit the author's particular style and seem integral to the whole of the manuscript being revised.

**What are some common revision mistakes?**
Listening to too many different critics—other writers, friends, family, even editors—and trying to revise according to the suggestions of everyone. The danger is in losing your own vision and voice, losing your grasp on the story you want to tell. If you try to please everyone the result is likely to be a mishmash.

countless times, always took the edge off my anxiety enough so that I could keep going.

**It is possible to rope and hogtie the Muse.** I know. I did it every day for eight weeks because I couldn't risk her leaving. I suppose this is just a variation on the old saw that writing is one percent inspiration and 99 percent perspiration. What I discovered was that I needed to do my 99 percent first, *then* the Muse would—sometimes grudgingly—pitch in her measly one percent. Every day I lit the same scented candle (sandalwood) and played the same classical CD (Bach: The Goldberg Variations) not as a way of summoning the Muse to do her part but as a way of signaling to myself that it was time to do mine. This daily routine helped me get into the writing groove quickly.

**The right analogy is as valuable as a good cow pony.** Two analogies helped steady me during the final revision of my book. The first comes from *Star Wars*. The hardships in my personal life were making it difficult to concentrate on the revision even when I was finally ready to tackle it. I began to think of myself as Luke Skywalker in the scene at the end of the first movie where he is flying through an alley in the Death Star, at the end of which is the target that he must hit if he is to destroy the Death Star and accomplish his mission. Meanwhile, Imperial forces—and Darth Vader himself—are firing missiles at him from all sides. I thought of all the distractions in my life as those missiles that Luke had to ignore if he was to have any chance of hitting his target. When I was at my desk, I couldn't worry about all the other things going on in my life. Like Luke, I had to block them out and focus on the mission.

The second analogy came from *Indiana Jones and the Last Crusade*, when Indiana's father is dying and the only way Indiana can save him is by getting water from the cup of life. To get to it, he must leap over a giant crevasse. Intellectually, he knows it's impossible—no man can jump that far. But he takes the step of faith required of him and the bridge appears beneath his feet. He realizes it was an optical illusion; the bridge was there all along. Whenever I began to doubt myself, I would think of that scene and remember how Indiana had to take the first step before he could know that the bridge was there. The only difference was that Indiana only had to take that first step once for him to see the whole bridge, while I had to take the step of faith over and over again because I could only see my own "bridge" materialize one step at a time.

**Don't hang onto the saddle horn.** Throughout the revision process I was plagued by the fear that in fixing what was *wrong* I might get rid of something that was *right*. During the last revision, I finally let go of that. I realized that all editorial letters, no matter how long or how daunting, can be boiled down to three words: Make it better. After more than a year of working on *Mary Margaret and the Perfect Pet Plan*, I was bored with it. I needed to find a way to reconnect with it, but I wasn't sure how. One night, because I had been doing my 99 percent the Muse finally kicked in her one percent, and I came up with a new opening. My editor hadn't told me I needed a new opening, and she may in fact have liked the old opening better. I don't know. All I know is that the new beginning sparked my interest in the story again and if I had still been afraid to mess with something that apparently was working for my editor, I might never have found a way to reconnect with my story. And if I hadn't found a way to reconnect with it, I wouldn't have been able to keep going.

## THE END OF THE TRAIL

Back in June of 2002, the day after I got my very first editorial letter, I attended a conference where Kate DiCamillo (author of Newbery Award-winner *Tale of Despereaux*) and Kara LaReau, her editor at Candlewick, spoke about the revision process. They were honest and witty and entertaining. DiCamillo said that for her, getting an editorial letter "feels like you've baked a cake for your editor and frosted it, and then she looks at it and says, 'It's a lovely cake. Now can you go back and add an egg?'" After the session, I approached her and asked her what I now realize is an impossible question: "But *how*? How do you add the egg?" She gave me an empathetic look and said, "You just do."

While some of what worked for me might work for others who are on that long, lonely, revision trail, in truth I can't offer a satisfying answer to the question of "how," either. What I can offer is hope and encouragement. You may think that you've got nothing left to it, but you do. Maybe all you've got left is that you're too stubborn to be licked by it. If so, I tip my ten-gallon hat to you, because that's really all you need. I can also offer a glimpse of what lies at the end of the trail: a book, yes, but something that's even better—a bit more confidence than you had before.

EDITORS ON REVISION...

# Stephanie Owens Lurie

*Stephanie Owens Lurie is President and Publisher of Dutton Children's Books (and Christine Kole MacLean's editor).*

**What qualities does a writer need to be good at revision?**
The ability to revise in the true sense of the word, i.e., envision something again; to listen to constructive feedback without getting upset; and to incorporate suggestions—sometimes vague ones—in a way that remains true to your vision, story, and characters. I think the latter is the most important quality.

**What are the most common revision mistakes that new writers make?**
They refuse to let go of something that isn't working. They take input too literally and can't go beyond the editor's suggestions, which essentially means that the editor is doing the rewriting.

**What are some revision mistakes that even experienced writers make?**
Problems occur less frequently with the veterans, of course, but sometimes it can take several drafts before the author can come up with the perfect solution. Experienced writers may suffer from the belief that they don't need to do so many drafts.

**Who is a writer you've worked with you feel is outstanding at revision and why?**
I recently worked on a novel called *Wishing Moon* with Michael O. Tunnell. We went through at least three major revisions, and each draft was a huge improvement over the last. He welcomed my input, telling me he prefers revision to writing from scratch, and it shows!

**Working with a writer who is really great at revision is like . . .**
. . . standing in an artist's studio and watching her carve a perfect sculpture from a chunk of marble.

**Working with a writer who doesn't understand or isn't good at the revision process is like . . .**
. . . trying to tutor a diligent, well-intentioned student who has an undiagnosed learning disability.

**Is there a part of the revision process that you particularly enjoy or dread?**
I enjoy seeing how the author responds to my suggestions. It's magical when the author can address a problem I identified, but in a way I never would have thought of!

Articles & Interviews

# Repeat Performances

*Reprints and Reslants*

by Sue Bradford Edwards

For many writers, completing a project is a heady experience. We seal the envelope or zap the piece off through cyberspace, congratulating ourselves on a goal well met. Then we look around for something new to research. Finding reliable sources, double checking facts, and tracking down knowledgeable sources for interviews all take time. Doesn't it make more sense to use our research again and again to generate as many sales as possible? You can do this by recycling your work as either a reprint or a reslant of the original topic.

## Play it again, Sam

Perhaps the easiest way to recycle your work is to sell it again. If you've sold first North American serial rights or first rights, wait until the piece is in print and then find another market that needs this particular story, article or poem. With nonexclusive world rights or one-time rights, you may not have to wait until the piece is in print.

Finding another market is especially easy to do if a piece is religious with broad appeal, because weekly publications use a lot of work and many writers find them an excellent market. "Religious markets, particularly the Sunday School take-home papers have been the best for exact reprint selling," says author Kathryn Lay. "As long as the markets don't cross over, it's not a problem. I've sold the same Christmas essay nearly every year since 1989 to Baptist, Catholic, Methodist, Assembly of God, Mennonite, Non-Denominational and so on." In this way, the piece brings her income again and again with no additional research or writing involved. Lay simply submits the piece as she would any other manuscript, informing the editor in the cover letter that she is offering "reprint" or "one-time" rights and that is has appeared elsewhere.

If you are going to submit something as a reprint, but aren't sure your target publication wants previously published material, just be up front about what rights you are offering and that the piece has already been published. "As editors, we always appreciate knowing whether a piece is being offered as a reprint or otherwise. We trust writers, and we trust that writers trust editors!" says Randy Fishell, *Guide* editor. "At *Guide*, we encourage reprint submission. We'd rather have the opportunity to review a story than have it kept in the

**SUE BRADFORD EDWARDS** is a full-time freelance writer based in Missouri specializing in nonfiction. Her work appears regularly in the *St. Louis Post-Dispatch*, *Children's Writer* newsletter, and through a variety of educational publishers. She supplements her writing habit by teaching a course on children's nonfiction. To find out more about this and her other work, visit her website, www.SueBradfordEdwards.8m.com.

writer's hands due to uncertainty about rights.'' After all, a piece that has met a market need once may be able to do so again.

Writers seeking to sell reprints should keep careful records. ''When I sell a piece, I make a list on the back of the page in my notebook of the possible places for reprint. Once it's published and my rights are mine again,'' explains Lay, ''I begin sending it out to the places on that list and search for new ones that I may have discovered since I sold it originally. If I only sell one-time rights, such as some religious publications purchase, I immediately start looking for noncompetitive markets to submit it to.'' Once Lay has sold a piece to a Catholic publication, other Catholic publications probably won't want to buy it, so it's best to submit first to markets that don't take reprints or the ones that pay the best.

### We were wondering if you could help us . . .

Writers don't always have to market their work to publishers to make reprint sales. If you have a lot of published work in magazines, in books and online, you have a visible presence and those wanting to use your work may come looking for you.

This is especially true in the field of educational publishing. ''Textbook companies like Harcourt have often asked for reprints,'' says author Jane Yolen. These companies contact authors when putting together literature anthologies. They also contact authors like Yolen and Sneed Collard III when they are assembling packets of testing materials—comprehension tests often used in school districts or at the state level. ''By far the most successful markets for me have been to companies needing passages for school tests,'' Collard says. ''I would say I've sold some of my articles five or six times in this way.'' The companies will ask to use an article, story or poem.

Editors of anthologies and collected works may also come looking for authors. Kathryn Lay sold a piece on holding a Marketing Day to *Inklings*, a now out-of-print e-zine. ''*The Writer* magazine group contacted me to print it in their 2002 *Writer's Handbook* and it became the very first article in the book,'' she says. Such contacts may also lead to sales of new material or previously published pieces the editor hasn't seen. ''An editor from a *Guideposts* anthology saw my piece in *Chicken Soup for the Mother's Soul*,'' says Lay, ''found me online and asked to reprint it. I later sold her three other pieces.''

And it isn't just traditional publishers that approach authors. ''My poem 'Alone on a Broom' was in a collection of my halloween poems,'' says Yolen. ''Someone creating gourd witches asked for permission to attach the poem to her product. Often I hear from storytellers, musicians, etc. who want to use my stories and poems in new ways.''

But don't sit and wait for publishers, storytellers, and gourd artists to come find you. You need to seek them out, too. ''I get requests from young adult, sci-fi and fantasy anthologies in both England and the U.S., as well as anthologies on specific subjects,'' says Yolen. ''I am also not loathe to query a specific editor on reprints when I hear about someone doing a new book whose subject matter matches something I have already written about. I hear of these books at conferences, online, and reading trade magazines.'' Network and you will find places to resell your work even if they don't approach you first.

### You have the right . . . or do you?

In order to sell a piece as is or with only minor changes, you have to have retained some of your rights. This can be difficult in the current magazine market. ''One big problem is that most magazine publishers now buy only all rights, which is a terrible deal for a writer,'' says Collard. ''Because of this, I have all but stopped writing magazine articles. The time and effort just aren't worth it. To give you an idea, I might originally make $500 for a magazine piece. With reprint rights, the income from that piece might eventually reach $3,000 or more.''

Sell only first rights, first North American serial rights, nonexclusive world rights, or one-time rights, and you have room to seek additional sales and make added income from your work. If, on the other hand, you've sold all rights to a particular piece or done a work for hire project, you cannot sell it again.

Does this mean you might as well start researching something new? Not at all. You can still make another sale, but first you will have to reslant your work.

### Finding a new angle—reslanting

Coming up with a new slant on a topic is one way you can reuse the research you've done for an all rights or work-for-hire project. "If it's a topic you are enthusiastic about, writing another article, using all fresh phrasing, is one way to overcome the limits of all-rights sales. They have purchased the words in that order," says author Sue Uhlig. You just have to come up with a way to reuse the material in another similar piece.

Just be sure that you are really writing a new piece. "It doesn't mean you can mess around, changing the order of what you've written. Instead start over as if you hadn't written anything about the topic," says Uhlig. "Think about a different slant or focus or a different audience as you write."

This means that if you sold *Highlights* a piece on grizzly bears that focuses on one cub, you shouldn't try simply focusing on another cub or the sow. Instead you might concentrate on how modernization has altered the bears' habitat, how one human family co-exists with

## Reprints: The Editor's Perspective

It's all well and good to decide to remarket your work, but what types of pieces will editors accept as reprints? Randy Fishell, *Guide* editor, shares his perspective.

"As a writer myself, it always made sense to me that more than one market could be served by at least some of the pieces I'd penned," Fishell says. "I've brought that same viewpoint to the editorship of *Guide*. We'll take a look at virtually any reprint piece that fits the criteria outlined in our writer's guidelines and hasn't appeared in a market that conflicts with our own."

A conflicting market doesn't mean one that holds differing religious views but one that competes for sales. "We do not encourage the submission of stories that have appeared in one of our denomination's 'sister' publications," says Fishell. "Regarding 'competing' markets, in our view we don't have many of them. More important to us is whether a story meets our editorial requirements, the foremost of which is that the story must be true." So if your piece has appeared in another Seventh-Day Adventist publication, Fishell isn't the editor to send it to next. But if it's appeared in a Baptist, Presbyterian, or Methodist publication, you might consider *Guide*.

Particularly good markets for reprints, as for any manuscripts, are those that publish a large volume of work. "Because of our weekly frequency and story volume need, *Guide* may be more open to a wide range of reprint options than many other publications," Fishell explains. "This does not mean we publish lower-quality work. We simply require more manuscripts from which to choose. Specifically, true stories that reflect a strong grasp of our denomination's standards and viewpoints would gain the editors' attention."

Create a piece that is good enough to be published once and, if you've retained the rights, you may find you have a frequent seller.

its ursine neighbors, or even how the grizzly is adapted to its environment versus that of the black or polar bear.

Don't limit yourself to reslanting only those topics you researched for a work-for-hire or all-rights sale. Collard also reslants book topics to make additional sales. "I've reslanted topics in several ways," he says. "One is to write magazine articles based on one, more narrowly defined, topic from one of my books. When I write a YA or older nonfiction book, I have often also gone on to write an introductory picture book that covers some aspects of the original book."

One of the easiest ways to reslant a subject is to rework it for a different age level. "For the topic of my YA book *Monteverde—Science and Scientists in a Cloud Forest*, I wrote an elementary-age book called *The Forest in the Clouds*," says Collard. "The main challenge is choosing the new topic. I always try to just pick a slice of the original work. For instance in my cloud forest pieces, I didn't try to just rearrange the information from my original books. I looked for smaller topics within the main umbrella that would interest kids, e.g. strangler figs or nocturnal animals. I ask myself what I can write without doing a huge amount of additional research."

Reslanting can also give you the opportunity to use tangential information that didn't find its way into the original project. "When I'm working on research for a nonfiction piece, I don't always use all the information and can salvage some of it for other uses," says Lay. "A few years ago I wrote a feature article for *Woman's Day* on "Safety In Your World." It dealt with safety issues with appliances, home security, automotive, weather, etc. Later I used some of the weather stuff they weren't interested in and redid it as a weather safety piece for a childcare magazine. I also used some of the information I'd seen during my research on children's playground and bicycle and swimming safety and queried Kiwanis about an article for parents to teach their children to be safe when they were on their own, titled 'Playing It Safe.' " In this way, one research stint gives rise to multiple articles and greater opportunity for repeat income through reprints.

Have a religious piece you can't sell as a straight reprint due to denominational differences? Sometimes a slightly different slant is necessary. "I make the appropriate changes that are particular for a specific religion. For example, Seventh Day Adventists don't have Sunday School but Sabbath School. I also discovered through editorial changes that they don't drink coffee," Uhlig says. "Sometimes what needs to be reslanted is the age or sex of main character and all that would follow with either or both. I've done this so a story would fit more closely the audience age or for boys- or girls-only markets." As denominational changes reverberate throughout the story or a character's gender changes, change after change mounts and soon a new story is born.

Can't immediately come up with a new focus or market for your topic? Sometimes it takes time. "The first book I wrote was YA nonfiction, *Pirates in Petticoats*, about women pirates," says Yolen. "About thirty years later, I did a picture book ballad called *The Ballad of the Pirate Queens* about two of those same women pirates. Now I am trying to sell a 48-page nonfiction picture book/group bios about women pirates."

Changing the format of the topic can also provide additional sales. "I recently completed a sign language learning guide for Barnes & Noble," says author Carol Parenzan Smalley. "Quick on its heels is a set of ASL flashcards for the same publisher. And, I am working on a series of children's picture books that incorporates sign language too. And teachers' guides." Multiple formats often open multiple markets.

Yolen's work shows that you shouldn't limit your reslants to nonfiction. Your information can also find its way into fiction. "I did a nonfiction book about the Shakers, called *Simple Gifts*," says Yolen. "I found them so fascinating that a couple of years later, I wrote a YA novel about them called *The Gift of Sarah Barker*. Then right after that, I wrote an sci-fi novel,

*Dragon's Blood* in which the dragon farm looks suspiciously like the Shaker community I had visited, complete with a round barn."

Whether it's multiple sales of a single piece or multiple takes on a single topic, using your work multiple times pays off. As Yolen says, " I think that good research is like a salmon, swimming upstream to spawn again."

Don't limit yourself and the possibilities may prove endless.

## Money in the Bank

Is it worth the time spent marketing to sell reprints and reslants? "About a third of my income is from resales," says Jane Yolen, "including foreign rights, magazine, anthology resales, repackaging my own stories and poems into different volumes, movies, audio and even gourds! I even have had a poem reprinted on a coffee can."

The long and short of it is that more sales equal more income and reusing your work can add to your sales. On the topic of safety, Kathryn Lay has sold six different pieces and sold reprints for some of these. Add to this the ideas she has for still more work on this topic, you can see the lines of text—and entries in her checkbook—adding up.

For Sneed Collard III, the Costa Rican cloud forest had yielded the greatest amount of material. "Besides *Monteverde—Science and Scientists in a Cloud Forest* and *The Forest in the Clouds*, I have a forthcoming book on one of the scientists who works in the forest canopy. I have also written at least four related articles on the topics of nocturnal animals, epiphytic plants, a scientist's research, and strangling fig trees for which I won the Society of Children's Book Writers and Illustrators Magazine Merit Award."

What if someone contacts you asking for a reprint and asks what you wish to be paid? "Depending on the size of the publication," says Lay, "I usually asked for one-half or one-third of the original payment." Often the publisher soliciting the sale will also make a specific offer for payment. Advises Collard, "There are no hard-and-fast rules for pricing except never accept a first offer. It is almost always too low."

Just remember when ideas multiply and your work works for you, your income grows!

Articles & Interviews

# Surviving in the Ever-Changing Publishing Biz

by Candice Ransom

When I sold my first children's book in 1982, I believed my feet were set on a golden path that would carry me ever higher to the pinnacle of success. Little did I know that my career would actually resemble ten rounds with a world heavyweight boxing champion. And I was just a flyweight.

## In this corner

Spring, 1967. I sat on the floor in my living room, studying *The Washington Post* children's book announcements as intently as an algebra problem. *I'm going to sell a book*, I told myself. That may have been an odd goal for most fifteen-year-olds, but I longed to be a children's writer. Hapless publishers were already receiving my dreadful submissions. After graduation from high school, I pursued my dream. Without a college degree, though, I felt like a ninety-eight pound weakling matched against strong, bright writers.

When my first book—a paperback original—was accepted, I became a contender. Nothing would hold me back. Or so I thought.

## On the ropes

My career developed muscle. I sold my second book, then a third; acquired a second publisher, then a third; moved from fiction into nonfiction, paperback to hardcover. Often I balanced five or six contracts on my calendar, juggling weekend projects, weekday projects, revisions, galleys, and school visits. I handled my own contract negotiations, publicity, and speaking engagements, month after month, year after year.

At first fancy footwork helped me dodge major problems. My professional day was sacrosanct: if it didn't require a tourniquet, it didn't interfere with my work. Then the real world jabbed one-two punches. My parents died. My cat died. I suffered with depression. Not one but *three* major illnesses battered me. My husband retired. We moved three times in a year.

Life, I discovered, does not wait until your writing day or current project is over before intruding.

**CANDICE RANSOM** is the author of 95 books for children, with more than 45 titles translated into 12 languages. Her books have been named IRA Teachers Choice, *The New York Times* Ten Best Illustrated Book, ALA Recommended Book for Reluctant Readers, and many other honors. She holds an M.F.A. in Writing for Children from Vermont College and is currently earning he M.A. in Children's Literature at Hollins University. She lives in Fredericksburg, Virginia, with her husband and four cats.

Candice Ransom • Illustrations by Eric Velasquez

With a writing career spanning several decade, author Candice Ransom has been a master of reinvention, publishing picture books, early readers, chapter books, midgrades, biographies, and nonfiction. One of her recent offerings, *Libery Street*, is one of a several titles with Civil War themes by the Virginia-based author.

## David vs. Goliath

When my first book came out in 1982, children's publishing was on the cusp of enormous changes. "Children's Books Mean Business" touted the theme of one trade show. Bottom-liners realized children's books made money. Conglomerates swallowed up smaller publishing houses. Editors and imprints vanished overnight. I paid little attention to all this activity until one memorable year when seven of my books were canceled. Not seven contracts—*books*, well into production. Suddenly the rules had changed and it was no longer a fair fight.

## Knock-out punch

While I lost editors who had published one or two books, I still retained my original editor. She bought my first book and launched my career. But around the time of the mass book cancellation, she retired. I was devastated. We had worked on 30 books together. She had been my trainer, my mentor, my friend.

A new generation of editors were coaching fresh, young writers. When I submitted manuscripts to these editors, they asked for my credentials. How could I condense a six-page book list or summarize a career that began when most of them were in middle school? When some editors remarked, *What a lot of B. Dalton bestsellers*, it seemed they were implying, *What have you done lately?*

## Down for the count

Not all of these catastrophes pummeled me at once. Yet I felt I was forever fending off blows. Then the biggest wallop of all flattened me—loss of faith. I became disillusioned with the accumulation of changes. Who needed another book by Candice Ransom? I didn't hang up my gloves for good, but shadow-boxed, writing work-for-hire projects and formula books. I avoided the children's section of the library and bookstores, unable to face other people's success . . . and my own failure.

Healing a broken spirit was harder than overcoming the worst case of writer's block, I found. I limped through *The Artist's Way* program, scribbling my pain in Morning Pages. On one Artist Date I toured a garden where forget-me-nots bloomed in blue profusion. I was so struck by their beauty, I stitched a picture of forget-me-nots and hung it in my bedroom. When I opened my eyes every morning, the needlepoint bouquet reminded me of my life's work. *Forget-me-not.*

But it would be five long years before I climbed back into the ring.

## The comeback kid

Journaling, reading inspirational books, soul-searching, taking long walks, and talking to my husband all helped me understand no one had done anything to me *personally*. By turning my back on the field of children's books, I had only been hurting myself.

On New Year's Eve, 1999, I sat on my study floor, surrounded by children's books. I missed reading kids' books, looking at them, touching them. I missed *writing* them, working on projects that engaged my soul. Time to come out swinging.

Self-imposed exile taught me to get help. And there's plenty of it out there now. Doors that I had slammed shut opened wide when I subscribed to newsletters, attended conferences, reviewed trade journals, and read five years of children's books. A resource that hadn't existed early in my career—the Internet—opened even more doors with its wealth of message boards and chat rooms.

Five years away brought even more changes in the field. Series books and picture books—the mainstay of my work—were on the downswing. Editors and imprints were still shifting. I obtained an agent to whip me back into fighting shape. I also formed an online critique group. With fellow writers rooting in my corner, I didn't feel so isolated.

## Going the distance

My agent scrolled through my book list, commenting I had reinvented myself several times. That was deliberate. The key to my longevity, I believe, is flexibility.

When I began selling in the early '80s, hardcover books were suffering due to library budget cuts. Paperback originals were blossoming. It was no accident that my first book was a paperback. Rather than duke it out in the hardcover market, I sought out markets where writers were *wanted*.

Over the years I've followed my own desires, as well as moving with the marketplace. While no one advocates following trends, it is futile to write the same old books if no one is buying them. Other writers agree.

Author/illustrator Rosalyn Schanzer is keenly aware of the dynamics of publishing. "No matter how long authors and illustrators have been in this business," she says, "we might have to impress a different editor or a new audience at any moment."

Schanzer views change as a challenge. Her latest book proves her point. *George vs. George: The American Revolution as Seen from Both Sides* takes an innovative look at the Revolutionary War. She adds, "Shifting sands dare me to improve my work, encourage me to think up unique cutting-edge ideas, ensure that I'm never bored, kick me out of ruts, keep me current, and actually help make my job a lot more fun."

## Learning curve

Curiosity and a tendency toward boredom led me to sample new genres. Once I had the midgrade novel down, I branched out into picture books, then nonfiction. Next I tackled historical fiction and biographies. I enjoy the versatility and never feel trapped by any one genre, in case it falls out of favor.

Jane Yolen, whose amazing career has spanned 40 years, knows a thing or two about survival. She attributes her longevity to mastering picture books, baby books, middle grade chapter books, nonfiction, YA—everything. The author of *The Perfect Wizard: Hans Christian Anderson, Pay the Piper,* and scores of other titles, states, "I can do fantasy, realistic, historical. Rhymed, unrhymed. So if one kind of book is no longer in vogue, I still am."

Another veteran, Marion Dane Bauer, uses the same approach. It isn't easy to keep passion intense for thirty years, but Bauer believes you should "try genres you've never thought of before, explore new topics." The author of *A Bear Named Trouble* also suggests "getting energy from reading what the young writers, just coming into the field, are doing."

Author Kathleen Karr also works in a variety of genres. Though she wishes publishers took more risks with books that don't always fit within sales projections, she continues to explore new directions. With her latest entries, a picture book called *Mama Went to Jail for the Vote,* and a YA historical, *Worlds Apart,* she has moved to opposite ends of the field.

Articles & Interviews

## New editors for old

When my editors were fired, or left the company, or their jobs simply disappeared, new editors with their own contenders took their places. The new editors had no obligation to keep me on, but they asked about my work. This time around I introduced myself with jazzy promotional material, grabbing their attention with the number of books I'd written and emphasizing *recent* projects to avoid appearing stuck in the past.

At the same time, I maintained my relationships with my previous editors. If they choose not to stay in the business, they may resurface one day, if not as an editor, then as an agent, publisher, or packager.

Susan L. Roth, author/illustrator of 24 books, holds the same opinion. "If you lose the editor, keep the publisher. And vice versa. There's safety in numbers. Always have at least two of each."

Even writers who have been lucky enough to work with the same editor throughout their career admit the business has changed. Mary Downing Hahn, author of such award-winning books as *The Dead Man in Indian Creek* and *Stepping on the Cracks*, lost her paperback editors due to mergers. Though her new books garner excellent reviews, no one has offered to pick up reprint rights. "After 24 years in the business," she says, "it seems I have no paperback publisher. Since schools and many other children's literature venues prefer to sell paperbacks, I face an uncertain financial future."

What's a writer to do? Karr, who has worked with several publishers and editors, counters the editor/publisher problem by "seeking out smaller houses, with editors who are still willing to take a modest chance on the theory that eventually the quality of good writing will out."

## Training camp

What about those life-altering events? In my case, journaling was an integral part of my recovery process. Pouring out my thoughts allowed me to step back and gain perspective.

Try to incorporate these events into your work. Not immediately, of course, but make time to record your emotions. There is no substitute for personal experience. What exactly *does* depression feel like? Are the bathroom tiles refreshingly cool or brutally hard when you are too sick to get off the floor?

During my career I attended countless writing conferences and seminars in children's literature. Sometimes I spoke at these events, but if I was a participant, I listened to the presenters with the attitude I could *always* learn something new.

When I entered the MFA in Writing for Children program at Vermont College, people asked, "Why are *you* going?" I replied that everyone was on their own journey in this life. After 20 years of writing, I believed a degree would boost my career, deepen my critical thinking, and help me produce better work from my inner core.

Two intense years later, I had ventured into preschool and board books, started doing my own illustrations, and wrote the kind of novel I never thought I could, the kind of book I'd dreamed about writing when I was 15.

A taste of learning made me crave more. I'm currently earning my Masters in Children's Literature at Hollins University.

## Keeping the faith

If someone had counseled me during my five-year crisis, maybe I wouldn't have hit the canvas like a pole-axed ox. Susan Roth, whose books include *My Love for You* and *Hard Hat Area*, credits good friends and professional groups such as the Children's Book Guild of Washington D.C., for support. When she moved from D.C. to New York City, a Guild member gave her an introduction to *her* old writing group. "We all speak the language," says a grateful Roth.

A writer's success doesn't rely on talent alone. Kathi Appelt, author of *Miss Lady Bird's Wildflowers: How a First Lady Changed America*, acknowledges the love of her editors, agents, teachers, students, her family, and finally "the children who call to me in my dreams and on the pages. Yes, in the end, it is a matter of love. That's what gets me through."

My own love of children's books—their sheer wonderfulness—called me back into the field.

Katherine Paterson, whose books have earned two Newbery Medals and two National Book Awards, modestly credits her success to her long-time editor and a Higher Power. "Honestly," she admits, "I believe I have survived by the grace of God and the help of Virginia Buckley, my wonderful editor since 1970."

## Staying on your feet

Much of my own success was due to my desire to make my childhood dream come true. That, and the fact I can't do anything else. Along the way in becoming a children's book writer I failed to learn to cook, iron shirts, balance a checkbook, decipher a phone bill, and a host of other tasks most people perform with ease.

Keeping my eyes on the prize, I followed writer, mentor, and teacher Jane Resh Thomas's sage advice: *Do your work*. The author of *The Counterfeit Princess* says, "You can't control the market or editors or even the quality of your writing. All you can do is keep your butt in the chair and work."

On a recent school visit, the district librarian thanked me for coming and, she added quietly, for what I do. It is rare an outsider understands that behind the joy of writing for children, the work is often dicey, the pay minimal, the hours of butt-in-the-chair long. The librarian supervisor thanked me for those who couldn't—the children who read our books, need our books.

We can all be champions in this field. Prepare to go the distance. Stay in shape. Get plenty of rest. And when the bell rings, come out *writing*.

# Tips for Staying Alive

You may run into walls, lose heart, or need motivation during your long-term career. These books offer solace and solutions:

- *Art and Fear: Observations on the Perils (and Rewards) of Artmaking*, by David Bayles and Ted Orland (Image Continuum, 1993).

- *Writing Past Dark: Envy, Fear, Distraction, and Other Dilemmas in the Writer's Life*, by Bonnie Friedman (HarperCollins, 1993).

- *The Artist's Way: A Spiritual Path to Higher Creativity*, by Julia Cameron (Tarcher, 1992).

- *The Vein of Gold: A Journey to Your Creative Heart*, by Julia Cameron (Putnam, 1997).

Don't box yourself into a corner. In addition to your professional organizations, join or start a critique/schmooze group, in-person or online.

Assume *nothing* will remain status quo. Keep on your toes!

# Tackling Tough Topics in YA Lit

by Lauren Mosko

In the opening chapter of her young adult novel *The First Part Last*, Angela Johnson's protagonist Bobby—a 16-year-old African-American single father—observes his infant daughter asleep on his chest and muses, "if the world were really right, humans would live life backward and do the first part last. They'd be all knowing in the beginning and innocent in the end."

Bobby continues, reasoning that "then everybody could end their life on their momma or daddy's stomach in a warm room, waiting for the soft morning light." Johnson has another explanation. "Ultimately it would save us the pain of adolescence," she says. "I think I'm mired in my 14th year. Life would be so much easier if I'd had all the answers in the beginning, then I wouldn't have had to worry about anything. It's so much easier to deal with things when you're young and strong."

In fact, many writers of young adult literature share Johnson's sentiments and view their work as an opportunity not only to offer a compelling story to an audience that is often made up of reluctant readers but also to equip those readers with information—through the telling of stories and the sharing of experiences—the readers would otherwise have to stumble upon the hard way or never learn at all. Of course, writers of YA lit can't provide kids with all the answers or spare them all the heartache of their preteen and teen years, but the stories can and do alleviate some angst by showing readers that they're not alone in their struggles and by opening their minds and hearts to the struggles of others.

Young people should know the comfort of camaraderie and develop feelings of understanding and empathy for others. These lessons are common undercurrents in YA lit, yet some outside the YA lit community gasp at the thought of finding their son curled up on the couch with a book about a single teenage father. Or a 16-year-old Palestinian suicide bomber. Or a high school where the quarterback is a drag queen. Or a boy whose circle of friends has been touched by AIDS.

Writers who wish to venture into the world of YA lit may feel anxious—or downright afraid—when they see the work of well-loved authors like Chris Crutcher, Katherine Paterson, Louis Lowry, Maurice Sendak, and Judy Blume turn up regularly on lists of "challenged" or "banned" books. It seems to be a paradox: write books that deal frankly with real young adult issues in an effort to reach that audience and risk getting your books pulled from library shelves; steer clear of the most difficult and controversial issues and risk not connecting with

**LAUREN MOSKO** is editor of *Novel & Short Story Writer's Market* and former assistant editor of *Children's Writer's & Illustrator's Market*.

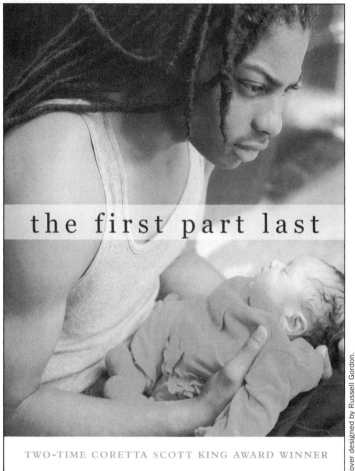

"Brief, poetic, and absolutely riveting, this gem of a novel tells the story of a young father struggling to raise an infant," says *School Library Journal* about Angela Johnson's *First Part Last*. It's likely, however, that Johnson hasn't read this praise of her novel; she says she doesn't concern herself with reviews: "It's lovely if some reviewer likes the book, but I'm interested in catching that eighth-grade boy who's a reluctant reader."

the first part last

TWO-TIME CORETTA SCOTT KING AWARD WINNER

ANGELA JOHNSON

Cover photo © 2003 John Healy. Cover designed by Russell Gordon. Reprinted with permission of Simon & Schuster.

your readers' generational experiences. So what do you do if you are compelled to tell a story that addresses topics that venture off the well-worn, "safe" path?

Here authors **Angela Johnson**, **David Levithan**, **Billy Merrell**, and **Pnina Moed Kass**—who all have created books that address sensitive subject matter—discuss the current climate and the need for YA literature and how they feel about their work, in addition to offering tips for creating and submitting your own story.

## THE TRUTH, THE WHOLE TRUTH

Blazing the thorny trail less traveled is never easy, but Johnson insists that our modern cultural and historical contexts demand a more forthright kind of reading material for young

As editor of Scholastic's PUSH imprint, David Levithan publishes writers who tell it like it is, offering readers: "No preaching. No false endings. No stereotypes or contrivance. Just an honest dose of reality." Levithan himself is author of the critically acclaimed *Boy Meets Boy*. Says *Booklist* of the novel: "In its blithe acceptance and celebration of human differences, this is arguably the most important gay novel since Nancy Garden's *Annie on My Mind*; it certainly seems to represent a revolution in the publishing of gay-themed books for adolescents."

adults than what she was exposed to in high school in the late 1970s. "From the time I was in sixth grade, I read adult books. I mean, 'YA literature'? If you could find it in the library it was Nancy Drew," she says. But she recalls that in the early 1980s, as the generation of Baby Boomer children began to come of age, those types of books weren't sufficient enough to address young adult needs. "You were faced with drugs, teen pregnancy, AIDS, broken homes and blended families; it was just a reality. You couldn't keep hitting kids with Nancy Drew mystery books. Someone had to belly up and start telling the truth," she says.

Johnson strives to present true snapshots of life in all of her YA novels, which include popular titles like *Heaven* (winner of the Coretta Scott King Award) and *Looking for Red*, in addition to *The First Part Last*, which earned both the Coretta Scott King and Michael Printz Awards. She admits that her books sometimes frustrate kids who are looking for happy endings or "pat answers" to tough situations but her point is to expand the way they look at the world by offering other viewpoints—other kids' realities. "Anyone who would think *The First Part Last* is a valentine to teenage pregnancy hasn't read it. It's ugly. There's a kid who hasn't gotten sleep—a kid who's lost his childhood. There's a young girl in a coma. The parents can't deal or won't deal or they deal the way they want to deal. I'm not touting teenage pregnancy," she laughs. "By *no* means," she adds. "Bobby handles more than I think I could ever handle. But again, that's the point. Somewhere on the planet there is a Bobby."

Among those writers working along with Johnson to open kids' minds to experiences outside their own is David Levithan. Levithan is the editor of Scholastic's PUSH imprint but is perhaps best known for his critically acclaimed novel *Boy Meets Boy*. This self-proclaimed "gaytopia" focuses on a down-to-earth protagonist named Paul and his quest to maintain a relationship with artistic, introverted Noah and also features a cast of vivid characters that includes Infinite Darlene, the high school's quarterback and a diva drag queen undaunted. Levithan explains, "I just wanted a world where Paul's sexuality wasn't an issue, where he'd been out since kindergarten and hadn't really suffered for it. And from that one desire came this whole world and all of its ideals."

Another author who opens up his world for YA readers is Billy Merrell, a 24-year-old poet whose memoir *Talking in the Dark* is a modern coming-of-age tale, tender and painfully honest. In addition to the joy and sorrow experienced in the changing of the narrator's family unit and during his homosexual awakening, he also copes with the fear and grief that accompany a friend's AIDS diagnosis. "The book's narrator is gay but the circumstances of his life are complicated," Merrell explains. "I like to think that the poems get at what it is like to find and lose love in general, not only for an upper-middle-class gay white boy from Florida."

Together, Levithan and Merrell are also in the process of editing *Queerthology* (Knopf), an anthology of personal nonfiction stories centered on the changing LGBTQ (lesbian/gay/bisexual/transgender/questioning) youth experience. "We're looking to make a cultural document that exhibits complicated, diverse points of view about these issues young people face," explains Merrell. Unfortunately, many of the stories submitted have not been tales as peacefully introspective as his own or as colorful and carefree as the world that Levithan has created. "Helping edit and compile *Queerthology* has shown me just how naive I was about the real world," says Merrell. " I honestly felt we were farther along politically than we are. It haunts me to read some young people's accounts of family violence, school antagonisms, and irresponsible adult influences. I'm hopeful that the collection, while acknowledging there is work to be done in our communities, will make us all appreciate how far we've come."

Billy Merrell offers YA readers an honest coming-of-age memoir in poems with *Talking in the Dark*. "The book's narrator is gay but the circumstances of his life are complicated," Merrell explains. "I like to think that the poems get at what it is like to find and lose love in general, not only for an upper-middle-class gay white boy from Florida."

Cover photo by Brad Wilson/Photonica. Cover design by Steve Scott. Reprinted with permission of PUSH, an imprint of Scholastic, Inc.

Despite the dystopian stories, Merrell is hopeful about the culture in which he writes because he feels that we are reaching a time when young people (especially LGBTQ teens) can be less defined by their sexuality. "I came of age in a culture that is not only conscious of various sexualities and lifestyles but in a culture that cherishes diversity—which is not to say that being a LGBTQ youth isn't difficult. It is. Though children and teens are able to deal with it in a way that adults even a generation older than me weren't able to. There are so many more modes of communication and connection than ever before," he says.

Levithan adds another ray of light by offering that the world of publishing is becoming more open to these modes of communication and connection. "The market is very accepting of queer lit right now, especially if it's good. It's like *Will & Grace* or *Queer Eye for the Straight Guy* in popular culture—although certainly some people in this country won't go for it, most people will," he says.

Of course, dealing with burgeoning sexuality isn't the only difficult task young adults in the 21st century face. Worries about terrorism and war were thrust to the forefront of American consciousness after the attacks on the World Trade Center in 2001. In her novel *Real Time* (winner of the Sydney Taylor Prize in 2004 and honored as one of the CBC/NCSS 2005 Notable Social Studies Trade Books for Young People), Pnina Moed Kass, an American-born writer living in Israel, strives to educate young readers about these horrors and the way they are manifested in the Israeli-Palestinian conflict—a subject barely explained (if at all) in most social studies textbooks.

*Real Time* begins by following several characters through one fateful day when the actions of a young suicide bomber affect each character's life. Kass does not shy away from the grittiness of fear, hatred, religious zealotry, or the physical aftermath of a car bomb because they are very much a part of modern reality in the Middle East. ''The subjects of genocide, suicide, and terrorism are horrendous. They are large in scope, weighty in their moral implications, and difficult emotionally for teens or adults,'' Kass says. ''I think it is crucially important that everyone—regardless of age or reading level, whether they are young adults or adults—gains an insight into the human aspects of the causes of terrorism and in particular the tragic impetus for young people to kill themselves and others. I would hope the readers of *Real Time* would gain an understanding of the complexity of the Israeli-Palestinian conflict. I think readers are ready to accept the ambivalence implicit in this long-running struggle for nationhood. I am also sure that readers are ready to empathize with characters who initially they thought repulsive. As a writer I want to present as many facets and faces as I can.''

Told from varying points of view, Pnina Moed Kass' *Real Time* takes place in contemporary Israel and centers around a suicide bombing. ''I think it is crucially important that everyone—regardless of age or reading level, whether they are young adults or adults—gains an insight into the human aspects of the causes of terrorism and in particular the tragic impetus for young people to kill themselves and others,'' says Kass. Her book received the 2004 Sydney Taylor Prize from the Association of Jewish Libraries.

Jacket photo © Stockbyte./PictureQuest

Kass's goal—to present as many facets and faces as she can—is one achieved not only in her work and in the work of Johnson, Levithan, and Merrell but also in the work of all writers of YA lit. Presenting these rich and differing points of view helps to ease the readers' transition from the simplistic black-and-white truths of their childhood to the complicated Technicolor world of adulthood by showing kids that nothing they experience—be it scary, dramatic, or awkward—isolates them.

## TELLING YOUR TRUTH

Those of you who are parents of teenagers, are close to a teenager or just remember your teenage years know there's *always* a struggle. Chances are, you have a cache of material from which to draw, but you may be reluctant to embark on such an emotional journey. How should you approach it?

**Don't be afraid to tell your truth.** "Looking at the wide range of subjects that the contemporary novel deals with, I don't think any topic needs to be avoided," says Kass. "Ironically, fiction is the most honest of genres."

Johnson agrees, "There's nothing in the world that you can write that hasn't happened or isn't true. I've never shied away from that. To me, these are just stories of life."

Merrell offers, "I have never been reluctant to reveal myself—not in my writing or in my life. Sometime growing up I found that I respond to intimacy in a certain way. Knowing difficult truths about a person, no matter who it is, made me feel closer to them. Whether it is naive or not, I guess I started believing that truly opening up, even to strangers, initiates a relationship and trust that is different from other exchanges. In many ways I feel blessed to have been able to share so much of myself with people in my life. I believe everyone has important insights and realities to express, and that the world would be a better place if more people were expressing them."

**Be honest in your writing.** Speaking about the submissions he received for *Queerthology*, Merrell says, "So far, the weakest pieces seem false, fed by clichés and generalities instead of by the revelation of honest experience. The best pieces should get at what they attempt to express by giving details from life instead of editorialization or by telling the reader what to think. The most touching and convincing writing lets readers make their own decisions, revealing a situation through specific information showing that no moment in a life is like any other."

**Remember that the story and the characters always come first.** "Just tell the story you want to tell," says Levithan. "Don't try to be sensational or exploitive. Story and character have to come first. If you write an 'issue novel' where it's all about the problem and not about anything else, then it's not going to work and probably won't be published."

As an editor, he has another pet peeve. "Sometimes the melodrama gets to be a bit much, as does the body count or misery count. And if I get a sense that anything is gratuitous, I'll back away."

Kass adds, "A story, even one of the most horrifying nature, gains veracity when the characters are true. Fake emotions, easy solutions, premeditated plotting will all stifle the heartbeat of a story. First and foremost comes the person, then the problem."

**Don't worry about criticism—from your family or anyone else.** "When dealing with personal material, you have to forget all consequences," says Merrell. In the writing of *Talking in the Dark*, I approached each poem singularly, trying not to be conscious of the fact that strangers or family might read it eventually. Once you get at something that may be difficult to say to yourself, it is far more difficult to ignore it. Also, know whom you're writing for. A piece will be better if it's written for your own understanding, your own complicated relationships with hope and survival, than it will written for revenge, spite, or denial."

Johnson says that she doesn't even read reviews for her books because that's not the real audience with which she concerns herself. "It's lovely if some reviewer likes the book, but I'm interested in catching that eighth grade boy who's a reluctant reader," she explains.

**Have confidence in your story.** "No apologies," says Johnson. "Once you present your work and there is difficult subject matter or there is going to be controversial subject matter, it is all about the way you feel about the work. If the work is true, there should be no apologies. An editor will know that your strength behind the work is enough for him to be strong about the work. You're completely lost if you don't believe in the work and you have no confidence."

## SHARING YOUR TRUTH

Once the exciting, grueling, wonderful process of creation is complete, it's time to share your story. Sending any piece of your writing out into the world is nerve-racking, but when you're dealing with an issue that's close to your heart or writing about your own life it's natural that you might feel even more vulnerable. Still, as in the process of creation, our writers urge you to be brave and stay true. Despite the sensitive subject matter of their books, none of them have submission horror stories to share, but several of them agreed upon this one piece of advice: Resist the urge to focus on the "issue" in your query letter.

Levithan says you shouldn't even call attention to something you feel may be sticky. "Let the editor decide whether something is controversial or not."

Johnson agrees. "Let the editor discover. I always think the best cover letter in the world is 'Hello, my name is . . . , I'm presenting this YA novel to you. Please let me know. I hope that you do enjoy it.' And let them discover it. Because it's almost like a present—something to be unwrapped. We never do the work justice if we try to explain it," she says.

Kass' agent pitched her book so she didn't have to write an actual query, but she suggests you focus on the elements of the book instead of on the issue. "When asked what *Real Time* is about, I have described it as a mosaic of characters, from many backgrounds and personal histories, affected by one catastrophic act. I have pointed out that the structure of the book is a framework of time, moments that tick away, and not a plot divided into chapters," she says.

## THE TRUTH WILL OUT

If you have an idea for a young adult book that presents some potentially controversial subjects or situations, don't censor yourself. Don't worry about those few people who would rather open their mouths than open their minds. Angela Johnson could only recall a couple of instances when a parent or an administrator objected to something she'd written and even then she wasn't upset. "To me, it just means someone is reading it. Let them make some noise; that can't hurt," she says. "There are basic truths and I don't understand some people's need to keep truth out of children's hands. We're not saying it's *their children's* truth; we're just saying it's a truth. And there's nothing wrong with truth."

# Authors Rise to the Challenge of Censorship

by Kelly Milner Halls

Congress shall make no law respecting an establishment of religion, or prohibiting the free exercise thereof; or abridging the freedom of speech, or of the press; or the right of the people peaceably to assemble, and to petition the Government for a redress of grievances.

—The First Amendment to the U.S. Constitution

D id James Madison have children's books in mind when he drafted those powerful words? Probably not; books and libraries were elitist commodities during our nation's infancy, even after the Bill of Rights (including the First Amendment) was made law on December 15, 1791.

Books for young readers were rare until Andrew Carnegie funded libraries for the common man. According to Carnegie Life Trustee Glenn A. Walsh, the first children's library "was created with the opening of the Main Branch of The Carnegie Library of Pittsburgh on November 5, 1895." The Newbery Award was established 26 years later in 1921.

Today, books for young readers are common in all walks of American life. But where there is access, there will be challenges—formal motions that question the value and decency of material written for and accessed by kids. And frequently, those book challenges strike terror in the hearts of their authors.

Do children's writers have a defense against the dogs of censorship nipping at their heels? Absolutely. As is so often true, when it comes to censorship, knowledge is power, and the squeaky wheel gets oil to spin with ease.

## KNOW YOUR RIGHTS

According to the American Library Association's Intellectual Freedom experts, these four targets are most likely to draw fire—sexual content, "bad" language, racism, and religion.

---

**KELLY MILNER HALLS** has been a full-time freelance writer for almost 15 years, with 1,600 articles and reviews to her credit and 14 children's books, including *Dinosaur Mummies* (Darby Creek, 2003), a Booklist Top Ten Science Book for Young Readers, and *Albino Animals* (Darby Creek, 2004), an ALA Quick Pick for Reluctant Readers. *Wild Dogs* (Darby Creek) and the *JPI Dinosaur Travel Book* (Random House) will be released in late 2005 and early 2006 and five other children's books are under contract. Halls makes her home in Spokane, Washington, the single mother of two great daughters, seven assorted cats and three rat-like dogs. She works as YA novelist Chris Crutcher's assistant in Spokane when she's not writing books and articles of her own.

The ALA would defend any individual's right to register a complaint. But when it comes to the removal of books from library shelves, the United States Supreme Court has been crystal clear. In a 1957 court decision synopsized by the First Amendment Center in Washington, D.C., material defined as "obscene" (largely by community standards) is not protected under the First Amendment rules of free speech. But in 1966, Medal of Freedom recipient, the late Justice William J. Brennan ruled that even a work declared obscene cannot be banned, "unless it is found to be utterly without redeeming social value." That ruling—Memoirs vs. Massachusetts—still stands today.

Can a work be banned simply because it includes bawdy language? Not according to the highest court in the land. In Cohen vs. California, a 1971 case where an antiwar demonstrator defended his right to wear a jacket imprinted with the words, "F— the Draft," the U.S. Supreme Court ruled that, "offensive and profane speech are protected by the First Amendment."

With regards to religion, can a community with a population committed to one religious value ban books from library shelves? Thanks to the determination of a 17-year-old named Steven Pico, the answer is No. In the Board of Education vs. Pico, the U.S. Supreme Court ruled in favor of the teen, and said school officials could not remove books from school libraries merely because they disagreed with the ideas contained within the books.

School officials can discontinue the use of "offensive" books as school curriculum. But those same books cannot be removed from library shelves based on personal opinion.

Will being aware of these and other Supreme Court rulings on free speech guarantee your books are shielded from censors? No. Many books pulled are done so without fanfare or due process, regardless of law. But knowing what your rights are can empower you as an author when it comes to battling official book challenges.

## BE EVER WATCHFUL

Which brings us to the next censorship hurdle. How will an author know if and when his or her book has been challenged?

"Often, as author, you don't find out about a censorship attempt," says Bruce Coville, whose short story "Am I Blue?" was unsuccessfully challenged in Solon, Iowa in 2004. "That's partly because most censors, and schools for that matter, want to keep what they're doing quiet. They know that frequently a lot of the community will not be supportive of what they're doing."

Lois Duncan agrees. "I am almost never informed when a book of mine has been challenged," she said in a January 2002 interview. "I learn about it only if a reporter contacts me for a comment and then, since I don't know the specifics of the problem, I don't know how to respond."

Being watchful and willing to help can be an author's best defenses. "My assistant scans the Internet search engines for news of potential book challenges," says author Chris Crutcher, whose work—including *Whale Talk* and *Athletic Shorts*—is often challenged. "And because I have a reputation for standing up against censors, I frequently hear directly from the teachers and librarians, even from students who know my books are being challenged."

"I subscribe to the ALA's Newsletter on Intellectual Freedom, which is the best single-source gathering spot for information on what's been censored," says Coville. "I also am a big fan of the NCAC (National Coalition Against Censorship). Judy Blume does a lot of work with them, and they're a terrific organization."

When an author is made aware, book challengers face something unexpected—knowledgeable and even passionate opposition. But it's up to us to develop an information network to keep us in the know.

## MAKE CONTACT—THE CHALLENGED

If your books are challenged, you have several choices.

You can ignore the challenge and keep writing your next book. According to Lois Duncan, being banned hasn't hurt her book sales. In fact, one anonymous industry insider said, "We don't think it's good when any book gets banned, but sometimes banned books get more attention and sell more copies, which is the opposite of what their banners want."

You can make contact with the school or library in question, and offer to lend a virtual hand. "Chris Crutcher contacted me and offered to help," said Iowa teacher Sue Protheroe, who was using Crutcher's and Coville's work to support her gay-tolerance unit in 2004. "He provided encouragement and affirmation and he wrote a powerful statement that I used in my presentation to the Materials Reconsideration Committee. The final part of that statement brought the audience of kids, parents and community members to their feet."

"When we turn away from tough material in stories that kids face every day in real life," Crutcher wrote, "we take ourselves off the short list of people to turn to. Kids would much rather we found ways to discuss those tough issues with them than to pretend they don't exist. They will always come up in real life, and it seems to me we want to be there when they do. Kids say over and over, 'You as adults don't understand us.' Why don't we see if we can prove them wrong once in a while."

## MAKE CONTACT—HEAD-TO-HEAD

Nikki Grimes met her censor head on, after a librarian hosting her school visit said students would not be exposed to *Jazmin's Notebook* because it touched upon drugs and sexual truths.

"I was shocked," Grimes admitted. "The material was handled responsibly and was quite explicitly treated as cautionary tales. I asked the librarian to reconsider, but to no avail. When I did the school visit, I took a copy of *Jazmin's Notebook* with me and read some of the 'offensive material' during my talk. No one commented on this, not in my presence, at any rate! I don't know whether the complaining parties had, in fact, read the entire book before deciding on their policy."

Grimes insists the true test is a question of context. "People who ban books rarely consider the context. In the case of my own work, I encourage self-esteem, critical thinking, moral choices. When I write about drugs, I am saying 'This is a bad thing. Don't do it.' When I write about sex, I am saying 'This is serious stuff. Think carefully. Be responsible. Consider waiting.' Why would any school want to ban that?"

Even so, she's opposed to banning books, even those she might consider objectionable. "If every book containing objectionable material were to be banned," Grimes says, "the Holy Bible would be the first book on the pyre! Within its pages, you will find sex, adultery, murder, molestation, prostitution, incest, witches, mediums, suicide, beheadings, and wars without end. So, do we ban it? I don't think so. I continue to write what I think is important without being overly concerned with censorship. I want my readers to make their own choices about what they do, or don't read."

## MEET THE PRESS

Coville also provided statements to back Protheroe's classroom use of his short story, "Am I Blue?" Parents had suggested his work and the teacher's desire to encourage tolerance was an endorsement of homosexual behavior. Coville's response went out through the voice of the local press.

"There is no overt sexuality," Coville said in the *Iowa City Press Citizen* on October 28, 2004. "It's a story about ideas. But I do find it disturbing that the idea of tolerance is something people find dangerous. The parents' concerns are coming from the heart, but they don't stand up to reasoned approach. Why would anybody choose to be part of a subgroup that is mocked, made fun of, that has one of the highest suicide rates in the country? Why would you choose a lifestyle that would make you the butt of jokes, susceptible to bashing because of who you are?'' he asked.

Author Julius Lester also uses the press to help defend the First Amendment. When his book, *When Dad Killed Mom* was challenged in Wyoming in 2002, Lester didn't wait for the reporter's call. He wrote a letter to the editor.

"Given how serious domestic abuse is in this country," Lester says, "given how many children have been killed along with their mothers by their fathers, given how many children have been orphaned by their fathers killing their mothers, I find people's focusing on language or references to sex to be somewhat misguided, to put it mildly. The novel attempts to deal with a serious issue but from the point of view of children who carry lifelong scars of domestic abuse. To focus on language and sexuality in the book is sticking one's head in the sand.''

Lester didn't apologize for his fiction's gritty realism. He stood firmly for the readers who might one day need it to survive challenges of their own. He did so with eloquence via the free press.

## MAKE POWERFUL FRIENDS

Being challenged may feel like an exercise in isolation, but when you take a stand, you're not alone—not if you reach out for help generously offered.

The American Library Association welcomes and encourages the report of banned and challenged books. You can print the challenge form out via the ALA's robust and user-friendly website (www.ala.org/ala/oif/challengesupport/), fill it in, and mail it with the appropriate postage. You can fill out a similar form online. Or you can fax the printed from to Beverley Becker, the Associate director of the Office for Intellectual Freedom at (312)280-4227.

The National Council of Teachers of English also has an online report option to document book challenges at www.ncte.org/forms/censorship/. Once those reports are filed, the NCTE often has materials available to help defend free speech. You can also write for more information: 1111 W. Kenyon Road, Urbana, Illinois 61801-1096; or call (217)328-3870 and ask to speak with someone about anticensorship support.

Another powerful resource is the National Coalition Against Censorship. Stewarded by the very able Joan Bertin, the NCAC offers tips and support to anyone as passionate about protecting the First Amendment as they are. Judy Blume is vocally in support of the NCAC, which offers a hearty censorship defense primer on their website at www.ncac.org/action/suggestions.html.

Last but not least, the American Civil Liberties Union was founded in 1920 to help protect the Bill of Rights, including our First Amendment right to free speech. One trip to their website at www.aclu.org/ can help you locate your local ACLU branch and advice or assistance to meet your anticensorship needs.

## WORK THE WEB

Once you take a stand on the challenge of your work, document your efforts online. Make most of the information you've seen outlined in this article readily available on your personal website, along with personal accounts of how you've fought against censorship, firsthand. Share your passion, your experience and your resources with every other writer or educator at risk. To keep our First Amendment rights safe, we must all enjoy the same, guaranteed liberties.

## BE A TRUE PATRIOT—DARE TO DEBATE

Some people suggest standing up against the loss of freedom is subversive—that going against the will of some Americans is more important than defending the rights of all. But not everyone agrees.

". . . debate on public issues should be uninhibited, robust, and wide-open and it may well include vehement, caustic, and sometimes unpleasantly sharp attacks on government and public officials," according to Supreme Court Justice Brennan.

Brennan also said, "The progress of the law depends on a dialogue between heart and head." Call out boldly to both, and you'll stand true to your work and the readers who believe in it, whether you win every challenge, or lose.

## Frequently Banned Children's Books

Here are some (but certainly not all) of the children's books that appear in the American Library Association's list of the 100 Most Frequently Challenged Books of 1990–2000. You'll recognize many of these titles—and may be surprised by some that made the list.

*Daddy's Roommate*, by Michael Willhoite
*The Chocolate War*, by Robert Cormier
*The Adventures of Huckleberry Finn*, by Mark Twain
Harry Potter series, by J.K. Rowling
*Forever*, by Judy Blume
*Bridge to Terabithia*, by Katherine Paterson
Alice series, by Phyllis Reynolds Naylor
*The Giver*, by Lois Lowry
*It's Perfectly Normal*, by Robie Harris
Goosebumps series, by R.L. Stine
*The Great Gilly Hopkins*, by Katherine Paterson
*A Wrinkle in Time*, by Madeleine L'Engle
*Fallen Angels*, by Walter Dean Myers
*In the Night Kitchen*, by Maurice Sendak
Anastasia Krupnik series, by Lois Lowry
*The Goats*, by Brock Cole
*Blubber*, by Judy Blume
*Killing Mr. Griffin*, by Lois Duncan
*Halloween ABC*, by Eve Merriam
*Julie of the Wolves*, by Jean Craighead George
*The Outsiders*, by S.E. Hinton
*The Pigman*, by Paul Zindel
*Deenie*, by Judy Blume
*Annie on My Mind*, by Nancy Garden
*A Light in the Attic*, by Shel Silverstein
*Asking About Sex and Growing Up*, by Joanna Cole
*James and the Giant Peach*, by Roald Dahl
*Boys and Sex*, by Wardell Pomeroy
*Are You There, God? It's Me, Margaret*, by Judy Blume
*Athletic Shorts*, by Chris Crutcher

Articles & Interviews

# Writing for the School & Library Market

by JoAnn Early Macken

E very year, scores of publishers produce thousands of books that never appear on bookstore shelves. Where do they all go? To schools and libraries, both huge buyers of children's books. Educational publishers cater to this monstrous market by publishing books that are linked to the school curriculum. Writing for educational publishers is one way to break into the children's book market, satisfy your desire to write for children, and earn a reliable income. I've written dozens of these books and edited hundreds more, and I'm still tickled to be working on them. You might find your own joy in the field.

## WHAT IS AN EDUCATIONAL PUBLISHER?

Educational publishers produce books specifically aimed at the school and library market. The audience for these books ranges from prekindergarten to 12th grade. The books are often published in series. They are not textbooks, but many expand on subjects studied in schools. Younger children use them in classrooms to learn how to read. Older children use them to research and write reports. Subjects include science, social studies, history, math, and almost anything else you can imagine.

Some of the better known educational book publishers include Capstone Press, Enslow Publishers, Heinemann-Raintree Publishers, Lerner Publishing Group, Marshall Cavendish, Rosen Publishing Group, and Scholastic Library Publishing. Many less familiar book publishers offer equally rewarding opportunities to writers who are willing to do their homework. Other publishers produce supplemental classroom materials such as teachers' guides, activity books, workbooks, reference books, tests and test preparation materials, flashcards, and software components. Writers with teaching experience might be especially suited for writing supplemental materials.

A book sale in the educational market can be different from one in the trade market in several important ways. Payment is one of them. Copyright is another. In a typical sale to a trade publisher, an author receives an advance against royalties and keeps the copyright. An educational publisher might pay an advance against royalties, royalties alone, or a flat fee. Fees vary widely according to the publisher and the project. Many educational publishers only offer work-for-hire contracts. Under such an agreement, the copyright belongs to the

**JOANN EARLY MACKEN** (www.joannmacken.com) is the author of *Sing-Along Song* (Viking, 2004) and more than 50 nonfiction books for beginning readers. A graduate of the M.F.A. in Writing for Children and Young Adults Program at Vermont College, she lives in Wisconsin with her husband and their two sons. Between books, she takes photographs, paddles a canoe, and speaks to children and adults about writing.

publisher, not the author. The publisher can revise the material to fit its perception of the market and publish it in any form. The author's name may or may not appear on the book. As in trade publishing, contracts come with a wide variety of clauses.

The format of an educational book can also be different from that of a trade book. It might include extra features at the end known as back matter. Glossaries, indexes, timelines, and lists of related books and websites all fit into this category.

## FINDING EDUCATIONAL PUBLISHERS

Have you already written something you think is appropriate for an educational publisher? Look for one that accepts unsolicited manuscripts. Do you have an idea for a book or series? Search for a publisher that accepts queries. Are you an established writer looking for a new assignment? Send a résumé and writing samples to a company that accepts them. Whatever your situation, you can start

© 2005 Weekly Reader Early Learning Library

Author JoAnn Early Macken wrote *Art Classes* for a Weekly Reader series called After-School Fun. "This series is different from the previous ones I had worked on because the photographs feature one main character throughout each book instead of different children on every page," says Macken. The photographer for the series had to match the text exactly, she says, to get the close correlation between text and illustrations that is so important for beginning readers.

by looking at publishers. Research each company thoroughly before you submit.

A wealth of information is available about educational publishers if you know where to look. Start with this book. Educational publishers in *Children's Writer's & Illustrator's Market* are marked with an apple symbol.

Check the listings to locate an educational publisher and find out what the company accepts. Visit the company's website to see what kinds of work it publishes. See if the catalog is posted, and study it to find out if the work you want to do fits into a category and age level the publisher already provides. You may even be able to contribute titles to an existing series.

Book producers, also known as packagers or book developers, work with publishers to prepare books for publication. Book producers sometimes suggest topics to publishers and sometimes respond to requests from publishers for books on specific topics. They often hire freelance writers. They rarely accept unsolicited submissions or queries. In *Children's Writer's & Illustrator's Market*, book producers are marked with the symbol of an open book.

If you are a member of the Society of Children's Book Writers and Illustrators (SCBWI), you can order a copy of the "Directory Guide to Educational Markets" or download it from the website (www.scbwi.org). The 2003 directory lists about 40 educational publishers, their locations and contact information, the kinds of publications they publish, details about submissions, and company websites.

SCBWI also offers a list of book producers. Members can order a copy or download it from the website. The American Book Producers Association website includes a member directory at www.abpaonline.org/directory.html. The directory includes links to more detailed information about member companies. Many member companies have websites, too.

You can also find educational publishers through the books they publish. Spend some time browsing in a school or public library. Check the nonfiction section for books on topics that appeal to you and find the publishers' names inside. After you study enough books, you'll get a feel for the kinds you like and the companies that publish them.

Searching online will reveal more companies. I entered "educational publisher" into a search engine and found thousands of results. The first few pages alone included many names I recognized. One site, at www.ourcreativespace.com/educate.html, includes a list of educational publishers.

Attend trade shows and pick up publishers' catalogs. Study the catalogs for examples of series and titles the company produces.

Network! Other writers can be the best sources of information and might even know which companies are actively seeking authors. Go to conferences, join listservs, and check writers' websites.

Some educational publishers avoid controversial subjects. Others specialize in problem-solving books, biographies, nature, or crafts. Some focus on specific age levels. One company might have several imprints with different requirements. Look for publishers that accept what you have to offer.

## IDEAS YOU CAN SINK YOUR TEETH INTO

You've probably heard the old advice to write what you care about. What do you care about? What have you always wanted to learn more about? Do you have expert knowledge of a subject you can put into language young readers can understand? Pick a topic you can live with for the time it takes to investigate it and share what you discover. Explore websites intended for kids to see what interests them. Keep a file of topics that capture your attention. These subjects can be the basis for query letters.

Because many educational books are tied to the school curriculum, it helps to know what children study in each grade. If you know in what grade students study a certain topic, you can target your writing to that age level. The Education World website lists national education standards for Fine Arts, Language Arts, Mathematics, PE and Health, Science, Social Sciences, and Technology at www.education-world.com/standards/national/index.shtml. The site also provides links to state standards. If you want to know what second graders study in science in Texas, you can find out there. State standards are helpful because many national standards stretch across several grades. In reality, publishers can't keep up with all the standards of individual states any more than writers can. It's probably enough to check the standards of several large states such as Texas, California, and New York.

## SEARCHING & RESEARCHING

Meticulous research is critical. SCBWI members can download or order a copy of "From Idea to Completed Project: Resources You Can Use." It includes lists of reference books and journals, books about writing and illustrating, and research tips.

Some publishers require authors to use only research materials written for adults. In theory, a book intended for children might already be simplified; if you simplify what you read in a children's book, you risk accidentally altering the meaning. As you research, keep track of important terms, dates, and events to include in the back matter.

You might need to provide several sources for the facts you include. Try to find at least two or three reliable sources for each fact. Be sure to keep good records! Find out what documentation is required by the publisher. It's always a good idea to photocopy the title page, copyright page, and every book page where you find information. Highlight the facts so the editor doesn't have to search for them.

For websites, include the site name, URL, and date accessed along with the printed pages. Reliable websites usually end in .gov, .edu, or .org. Be wary of sites that end in .com because they might be biased, and be especially leery of personal websites. You might not be able to tell whether the contents represent expert knowledge or personal opinion.

If printing or photocopying isn't practical, take careful notes. A good researcher once told me that if you always write exactly what you read, you'll never be confused about whether you are paraphrasing or plagiarizing.

## GETTING THE WORDS DOWN

I realized that I really wanted to write for children when our kids were young. I had worked as a technical writer for many years, and I was ready for a change. I enrolled in the M.F.A. in Writing for Children and Young Adults program at Vermont College. There, I concentrated on writing picture books and poetry. I also absorbed tons of general information about writing for children. After graduation, I worked as a freelance writer, editor, and proofreader. As a freelancer, I learned some valuable lessons.

"I suggested a series about forest animals to Weekly Reader after I wrote two other series called Animals I See at the Zoo and Animals That Live on the Farm," says author JoAnn Early Macken. *Owls* is one of the books resulting from her query, part of the Animals That Live in the Forest series. "The fact that I had some input into the process made it extra fun to write," says Macken.

**Keep your options open.** I started as an editor and later took on writing and proofreading work. Occasionally, I helped with photo selection. Eventually, I started contributing my own photographs. The department also hired fact checkers, translators, indexers, and other freelancers. If you have another related skill, offer it. If you have an opportunity, be willing to learn.

**Be flexible.** Educational publishers sometimes have unusual requirements. My first writing assignment was a series of four books, each about a different habitat and eight animals that lived there. The company had purchased the rights to use the illustrations from an existing series but not the text. I had to write new text to match the illustrations—the opposite of the typical process.

**Be sure you understand the specifications for a project before you begin.** For one series I wrote, I was given a word count for each book that included the glossary, the index, and a list of related books and websites. I made the mistake of thinking that the word count only applied to the main text. The books were intended for beginning readers, so a small change in the number of words made a big difference. All six books were too long, and I had to revise them quickly to meet the deadline.

**Ask for samples and guidelines.** If you write for an existing series, you might have to follow established standards for consistency. I wrote six books in a series that had six previously published titles because the original author was too busy. To understand the format, I studied the previous books. If you contribute to an existing series, be sure you know which features are consistent throughout a series and which are subject to change.

**Keep a lookout for new ideas.** The first series I wrote were assigned to me. After I became comfortable with the process, I suggested some topics of my own and was thrilled to be able to write those series myself.

When you write for children, remember the books you read in school. Some were deadly boring, and others made you want to learn more about the subject. Model your writing after the intriguing ones.

- Use lively, figurative language and active verbs. Let your enthusiasm for the subject show.
- Relate the facts to a child's world by using examples that a child would recognize.
- Make your descriptions clear and concise.
- Use transitions to make the reading flow smoothly.
- Vary the sentence structure to keep it interesting.
- Avoid stereotypes. Strive for diversity and balance in the characters you portray.

All the books I've written for the school and library market are intended for first and second grade beginning readers. I love writing for this age because keeping the writing at an appropriate reading level is like a solving a puzzle. If you write for younger readers, keep the sentences simple and pay special attention to the vocabulary. *Children's Writer's Word Book*, by Alijandra Mogilner (Writer's Digest Books), contains lists of words that children should be able to understand at age levels from kindergarten through sixth grade. It also includes a Thesaurus that lists the grade level for each word and its synonyms—a very helpful tool for finding age-appropriate substitutes.

Your word-processing software might have a feature for checking the reading level of a document. In Microsoft® Office Word, for example, you can determine the Flesch-Kincaid Grade Level for a sentence, a paragraph, or an entire document. Although the number might not correspond exactly to other leveling systems, it can give you a clue to the readability of your work.

## SUBMITTING

As in trade publishing, you'll find a range of submission policies. Some educational publishers accept unsolicited submissions. Some only accept agented material. Others prefer to receive queries or résumés with writing samples so they can assign work based on their needs. Some publishers focus on a narrow age range or a specific topic or geographical area. Know your market before you submit.

If you haven't been published before, you might have better luck submitting a query for a topic you know well. Rely on your expert knowledge to sell your idea.

## AN EDITOR'S POINT OF VIEW

After several years of freelancing, I took a job as a managing editor for an educational publishing company. The company published about two hundred books every six months. From the other side of the desk, I gained a whole new perspective.

In a little more than two years, I was responsible for editing or supervising the editing of nearly three hundred books. Every editor in the department worked on dozens of books in many different series each year. Very few were written by authors we contracted directly. Most were either developed by book producers or copublished with other companies in foreign countries.

Most of the books I worked on were short and simple, but producing them was still a complicated process. I worked with authors, designers, photo researchers, book producers, reading specialists, translators, and production people. Changes in the schedule were constant and inevitable. Manuscripts came in late, problems cropped up with photo permissions, authors got sick, translators took unexpected vacations, and no matter what happened, the books had to be finished on time. Sometimes a book or series had to be switched from one editor to another. Close to deadline time, many projects were shuffled around or shared by several editors.

So if you have a book or a series in progress and you don't hear from an editor for a while, it may be that she's struggling to keep her head above water. Don't contact her without a good reason.

Do ask questions if you're not sure what's expected of you. Keep your editor informed if anything changes in your schedule, especially if it affects your deadline. Each step in the publishing process depends on previous ones. If you are late and don't notify the editor, you can create havoc with the rest of the schedule.

When I started editing those beginning reader books, I asked authors to submit the first book in each series for approval before writing the rest of the series. I recommend a similar process for any series project. Having the initial approval can alleviate your concerns while you write the remaining books. Making a correction in one book is much easier than fixing six with the same problem. Depending on the length of the books you write, you might need to submit an outline first. Consider it a road map that keeps you on the right track.

My experience is certainly not typical, but I'm not sure there is such a thing. People find their way into this type of writing from many different angles. As I write this, I've just returned to freelance writing. I have a stack of ideas I'm itching to explore, and I'm about to venture back into the realm of market research and query letters. I can't wait to see which of those ideas become books. If you are bursting with enthusiasm for a subject you'd like to investigate, try sharing it with children through school and library books. The best reward will be knowing that somewhere a child will open a book you wrote and be wowed by the fascinating facts you've provided.

# Holiday Books

## *A Hungry, Hearty Children's Niche*

by Kelly Milner Halls

**B**reaking into the realm of writing for young readers can be tough without finding a niche. But step into the world of seasonal or holiday books, and your relationship with acquiring editors could have the shelf life of a battery bunny. It could keep going, and going, and going. . . .

Consider, for example, the quirky zeal of author/illustrator David Carter's pop-up holiday books. Carter has dedicated 11 of his 28 books to holiday themes, 10 of those to fun-natured holiday bugs.

Why bugs? ''I was asked to describe a day in the life of 8-year-old David Carter,'' he says on fellow author/illustrator Robert Sabuda's website (www.robertsabuda.com). ''I would spend hours on end searching the foothills and fields around my home in Bountiful, Utah, for rocks and boards.''

When bugs popped up from outdoor hiding places, Carter explained, so did ideas. And as an adult, holiday bugs took on a lucrative appeal. *Jingle Bugs*, (Simon & Schuster, 1992), Carter's first holiday venture (his third children's book) was released with an initial print run of 225,000 copies according to Simon & Schuster, and a hefty advertising budget to go with it.

Holiday-themed bug books soon joined the Carter parade as a result of some editorial brainstorming. ''After the success of *How Many Bugs in a Box?* (Simon & Schuster, 1988),'' Carter says, ''we created a list of ideas that included a Christmas book. With a little nudge from my editor, *Jingle Bugs* became the third book in the Bugs series, which led to *Love Bugs* (Simon & Schuster, 1995)—and the rest is history.''

Which holidays offer the most bookselling potential? Carter has mined almost every field. In addition to the two bug books that started his seasonal trend, he created *The Twelve Bugs of Christmas* in 1999, *Easter Bugs* in 2001, *Chanukah Bugs* in 2002, *Halloween Bugs* in 2003 and *Birthday Bugs* in 2004—along with two other Christmas pop-up books not populated by insects at all. But is Christmas oversold?

''Though we often hear that the market is glutted with Christmas books, this holiday still drives the most sales,'' says Stephanie Owens Lurie, President and Publisher of Dutton

**KELLY MILNER HALLS** has been a full-time freelance writer for almost 15 years, with 1,600 articles and reviews to her credit and 14 children's books, including *Dinosaur Mummies* (Darby Creek, 2003), a Booklist Top Ten Science Book for Young Readers, and *Albino Animals* (Darby Creek, 2004), an ALA Quick Pick for Reluctant Readers. *Wild Dogs* (Darby Creek) and the *JPI Dinosaur Travel Book* (Random House) will be released in late 2005 and early 2006 and five other children's books are under contract. Halls makes her home in Spokane, Washington, the single mother of two great daughters, seven assorted cats and three rat-like dogs. She works as YA novelist Chris Crutcher's assistant in Spokane when she's not writing books and articles of her own.

Children's Books. "But some holidays, such as Halloween, are good for lower-priced, mass market books, but not hardcovers. Mother's Day has been over-published, but not Father's Day, which is ironic, since Father's Day books tend to sell better (because mothers buy more books than fathers do)."

Lurie agrees that Carter-like quirk can help capture a children's book editor's imagination. "Because the market is so crowded (approximately 9,000 new children's books are published each year), the more clever or fresh a story is, the more attention it may receive. On the other hand, if it is *too* quirky, it may have too limited an audience."

To walk the fine line between traditional and unique, think craftsmanship. "We look for stories with distinct but sympathetic characters and a new twist on universal themes," Lurie says. "The best ones offer a memorable character who changes in the course of the story, a little bit of dramatic tension to keep readers turning the pages, and an element of magic or mystery to set the mood."

Dennis R. Shealy, Director of Novelty Publishing and Licensed Publishing at Random House Books for Young Readers has a slightly different, mass-market perspective. "The majority of my titles are licensed, so I have almost no opportunity to take original titles," he says. "For the few seasonal titles I publish that are not licensed, I usually mine the Golden Books backlist for old titles that are sweet and nostalgic. Or we might publish a mass (less

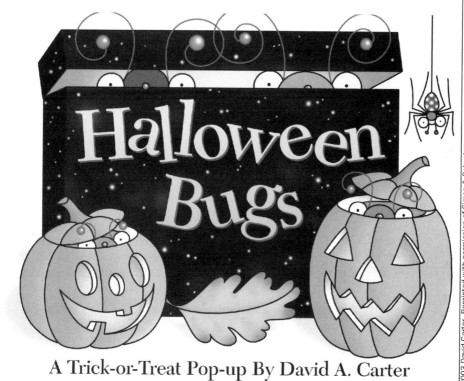

# Halloween Bugs

## A Trick-or-Treat Pop-up By David A. Carter

David Carter's *Halloween Bugs: A Trick-or-Treat Pop-Up* is just one of almost a dozen holiday-themed bug pop-up books from the author/illustrator, who has also created Easter-, Christmas-, and Chanukah-themed titles. Editor Stepahnie Owens Lurie feels that Carter-like quirk can help capture a children's book editor's imagination. "Because the market is so crowded, the more clever or fresh a story is, the more attention it may receive," she says.

# Holiday Stories for Magazines

With more than 15 years of experience in the children's writing business I can say with some authority that editors are always in need of fresh holiday-themed articles. Through the years I've earned a quirky reputation when it comes to holiday fare, because when an editor says "holiday," I think beyond Christmas trees, pumpkin patches, and cutout hearts. And that's the key to catching an editor's eye.

Brainstorming is the most effective train on the alternative track. List as many standard holiday keywords or themes as you can across the top of a sheet of paper. Then, under each word, list new words or short phrases about each of those individual themes. For example, if one of your themes is "Christmas tree," you might list *ornaments, pine, tinsel, colored lights, paper chains,* or *popcorn strings* underneath it.

Thanks to Internet search engines, researching is easier than ever. Ask yourself related questions and prospective answers. Who invented the popcorn string as a holiday decoration? Why? You may find a 10-year-old prince or princess started the tradition, and that's a great article topic. But even if you don't find authentic, verifiable answers, you can still mine sheer inspiration. No clue on why popcorn strings were added in Christmases past? Then consider how they could be used in the future. Write "Christmas Is for the Birds," an article on nature-friendly decorating to bring the holidays outdoors.

### Ho, ho, oh no!

When the *Chicago Tribune KidNews* asked me to explore the season, my weird wheels were already turning. I made my list. I checked it twice. Rudolf was one of my keywords, so I started researching reindeer and discovered they were the focus of a new agricultural trend.

In just over 600 words, I offered reindeer ranching—from milk to meat to mittens—for readers under 16. Who knew the country of Finland considered reindeer ranching a vital source of commerce? And who knew ranchers in Colorado and Minnesota were trotting along the same frosty tracks? The *Tribune*'s youngest readers did—as soon as my article hit the section's front page.

To my benefit, one of the ranchers had children's author and illustrator Jan Brett as a frequent visitor, so I had a perfect sidebar. How does an illustrator ranch (or get) her reindeer ideas? For young readers, it was the perfect short companion piece.

### Talking turkey

When *Guidepost for Kids* asked for a hearty serving of Thanksgiving sass, I made a list of Turkey Day details—the big birds, pilgrims, Native Americans, parades. I researched turkey breeds and breeders, and came up with a few variations on the theme, including the New Preston, Connecticut, Turkey Olympics. For more than a decade, the Inn at Lake Waramaug had sponsored a series of costume contests for gobblers and their human partners. I interviewed participants and the hotel owners that hosted the event about the nature of the competition. Then I wrote a sidebar about animal rights activists opposed to the scene.

"I *Love* my Turkey" was my submission for the *Chicago Tribune KidNews*. It profiled people who had raised turkeys as pets rather than entrees. From 4-H members to people who came across turkey chicks on a whim, these poultry people admitted it was hard to eat the drumsticks if the rest of the body came running at the sound of your voice.

## Holy Halloween horrors

Spooks rule the October skies, but how do you put a new face on an old monster? My research told me to do it with make-up and prosthetics, via an interview with Hollywood special-effects artist Rick Baker. Talking with the man who breathed life into Michael Jackson's dead dancers (*Thriller*, 1980) and 2004's alternative movie hero, *Hellboy*, took Halloween to a new level for the piece I wrote for online publication KidsReads.com.

*Freezone/Curiocity for Kids*, a syndicated children's newspaper supplement, published my feature on phantom photos—how real-life ghostbusters take pictures of their flesh-challenged friends. "Dead End Jobs" won the *Chicago Tribune Kidnews* cover slot for Halloween, profiling six professions—from grave digging to forensic toxicology—in which dead bodies were required to get the job done.

The next time you want to break into a children's magazine market, put your Santa hat on inside-out and crack an ostrich egg at Easter. Turn things upside down and see what jumbled holiday thoughts come to mind.

—*Kelly Milner Halls*

expensive) version of a trade title or spruce up a mass title (better paper, larger size, etc.) that sold well the year before."

When Shealy does take interest in a fresh author, he admits, a new twist on an old theme has potential, but not so much in terms of content. "My corner of the mass market is usually more of a place for quirky formats (some interesting new bell or whistle, pop-ups, things that light up and make sounds). In terms of content, the 'quirk' needs to tie in with a quirky new format. We are trying to reach a mass audience—so again, it has to be appealing to all types of people."

Are there elements holiday editors do not want to see in their slush piles? Absolutely. "When I get submissions they are often based very specifically on the writer's family or some specific incident. For the kinds of mass market books that I publish, you need to be much more general, i.e., it will appeal to all children of all types," says Shealy.

Rhyming texts lead the list of tired submissions for Lurie along with, "stories that borrow too much from familiar holiday stories, e.g. *A Christmas Carol* or *Rudolph the Red-Nosed Reindeer*; stories written to teach a moral; overly long texts (more than 2,000 words)."

Both industry experts agree market research can help prospective authors better their odds. "I think the biggest mistake writers make is just sending out manuscripts blindly," Shealy says. "I was always impressed by writers who had sent it to me or the company for a specific reason—I loved Book X and if you published that book, here are three reasons why I think you will want to publish my manuscript; or I think my book would fit into this series for reasons x, y, and z. Don't just say it, but do some research and know who you are sending your manuscript to and why."

Lurie agrees. "Read what is being published now. Look at various publishers' lists, either in catalogs at your local library, or in the Spring and Fall announcement issues of *Publishers Weekly*. Try to identify the best home for your work. Write from the heart and take time to hone your craft. Stay true to your own vision, but realize that creating a picture book is a very collaborative process. You'll need patience and perseverance in order to succeed in this business."

But don't forget the fun and the dazzle, Carter says. "It's what this business is all about; that certain something that brings a smile to a child's face. I do it by imagining what would make a 5-year-old David Carter chuckle. So rely on your memories and create to please yourself."

## A Sprinkling of Seasonal Classics

### Christmas
*The Night Before Christmas Pop-Up*, illustrated by Robert Sabuda
*The Polar Express*, by Chris Van Allsburg
*How the Grinch Stole Christmas*, by Dr. Seuss
*Merry Christmas Maisy* (Chistmas and Hanukkah), by Lucy Cousins

### Hanukkah
*Festival of Lights: The Story of Hanukkah*, by Maida Silverman
*My First Hanukkah Board Book*, by Clare Lister

### Valentine's Day
*Roses are Pink, Your Feet Really Stink*, by Diane deGroat
*Junie B. Jones and the Mushy Gushy Valentine*, by Barbara Park
*Max's Valentine*, by Rosemary Wells

### Easter
*The Dumb Bunnies' Easter*, by Sue Denim, illustrated by Dav Pilkey
*It's the Easter Beagle, Charlie Brown*, by Charles M. Schulz
*Easter Bugs: A Springtime Pop-Up*, by David Carter

### Halloween
*Clifford's Halloween*, by Norman Bridwell
*Dragon's Halloween*, by Dav Pilkey
*Franklin's Halloween*, by Paulette Bourgeois

# The Page Is the Thing

*An Adult Author Tackles Picture Books*

by Heather Sellers

There's a famous quote in which the writer says, "This letter is long because I didn't have time to make it shorter."

Moving from writing for adults—stories, a memoir, articles, and a guide to the writing life—to writing a picture book for 4- to 8-year olds was to be—for me—a nice break, a fun diversion. I expected, like most writers new to the field, that the story would come easily, the writing would be fun, and because the book is *short*, that much less time would be involved.

No.

Almost always, new picture book manuscripts are sent by their authors directly to the publisher, where, if accepted, an artist is chosen, by the publisher. When my dear friend Amy Young and I decided to join forces on a picture book, we knew we were taking a risk in breaking the rules. She is a well-established professional illustrator; I have been writing for twenty years; we thought, Why Not?

I'm a writer. Should be easy.

The first manuscript I shared with Amy was five pages, single-spaced. I opened with a beautiful description of the village where our characters, Cubby and Spike, went about their daily routines. Beautifully written passages of dialogue developed their characters; quirks and little gestures differentiated the characters; and two subplots subtly appeared, developed, and resolved. I spent weeks on the draft, writing late into the night, thrilled to be inside the world I had developed. Visions of a wildly successful children's book career danced in my head.

"You know it has to be shorter," Amy said. We were sitting on her couch, midsummer. My five pages were spread on the coffee table. "A lot shorter."

"This is the shortest thing I have ever written."

"Don't you write poetry? Think poem-short."

"But a lot of this is important. And, I want there to be stuff for the parents—they buy the books."

"By a lot shorter, I mean, four-fifths of this has to go."

I was surprised, because I have worked as a writer for twenty years, but I felt really hurt

**HEATHER SELLERS** is the author of *Page After Page: how to start writing and keep writing no matter what!* (Writer's Digest Books), short story collection *Georgia Under Water* (Sarabande Books), and picture book *Spike & Cubby's Ice Cream Island Adventure!* (Henry Holt). She teaches writing workshops at Hope College and around the country. She is currently completing a novel.

when Amy said that. "What about Patricia Polacco?" I said softly. "She has a lot of words."

"She's Patricia Polacco!" Amy held up a pile of books, and started opening to random pages. One sentence. Two short sentences. Lots of the pages she pointed to had *no words*.

My mistake was that I thought moving from writing for adults to writing for children meant simplify. Just that. Do what I do, but simpler.

Again: No.

## A TOUGH TRIP BACK TO THE DRAWING BOARD

I left Amy's house that afternoon with my five pages. Amy crossed out paragraphs, chunks of text, all of page four!, but there was, she said, still much cutting to do. I would have to figure it out she said. I was frustrated. I had looked at hundreds of picture books, I had read the bible, Nancy Lamb's *Writer's Guide to Crafting Stories for Children*. I *knew* the size of my canvas—why was I painting murals when I was supposed to be doing a miniature? Why was this so hard?

How could I take what I already knew about writing (I have a PhD in creative writing, two volumes of poetry, an award-winning story collection) and use it? Was all my training and practice in writing for adults going to help? Or hinder?

In writing for adults, the paragraph is the thing. You learn structure by building scenes, and you build scenes to make a narrative sequence. You layer action, always including a secondary track to amplify and complicate the central narrative line. As I worked, hard— and it was hard, hard as crafting a poem—to cut my tome-version of Spike and Cubby's story into something short and rich and tight and wonderful, something that was concise, but read large and deep and wide—I realized that in a picture book, the page is the thing.

Each page is a step. Like a stanza in a poem.

And on each page you deliver a beat—something that shifts the direction of the story.

A lot happens in the child's mind when the page is turned, and paying attention to that gap, that space, was a large part of my breakthrough as a children's book writer.

The page is the thing.

Not true for adult audiences—page breaks just aren't a significant part of the reading experience.

The next thing I learned was that each sentence has to have tension in it. You can't do what you must do for adult writers, build sentences into paragraphs, like waves that accrue energy. Each sentence has to have a "story" in it. It has to do what a paragraph does for an adult. I think of picture book sentences like this: there's a pole at the beginning, and a pole at the end, and the writer's job is to push those two poles as far apart as possible.

It turns out, my training as a poet is what I draw on in writing for children. Every word counts, every line counts. Sounds obvious. But the narrative writer, the prose person, thinks in terms of explaining, building, developing—that's *writing* to us. When I was thinking "children's story" I was thinking plot points, development, arc. Yes, that's all got to be there, but I would have saved a lot of time had I written short and tight at the outset.

And, like poems, a picture book is best built from the middle out. A picture book is, again, just One Thing. It's not a series of micro-stories. When I had my five-page story (soon to be a lean mean two-and-a-half page piece), I didn't really have A Story. I had great characters facing myriad fabulous obstacles. That's not a picture book, and that was my mistake. I had a series of events. A picture book—and this is why they, and great poems are so hard to write—has at its core a turning, a change, a transformation. A problem is solved and a person realizes and changes in *that same moment*. This turn is at the center of the story, and I would have saved a lot of time as a writer if I had started with that turn, that character-action moment upon which the book would be built. Instead, I wrote from beginning to end, and kept adding, adding, adding. Writing for adults is like surfing. You paddle out, gather all this energy and surf to shore. Writing for children is like a perfect dive off the high platform—lean, neat, an arrow piercing the water.

An adult story is an experience—you become someone else and see through their eyes. A story for a child, age 4-8 is more like a puzzle, and the child knows it when he's in it. He is still learning to see the world through *his own* eyes—completely different. Story is the apparatus that sucks him up—the mystery, the desire, the promise of a satisfying outcome. It's not a place where you play out the complexities of human emotion. A picture book is less narrative and more experience.

But, nor is a picture book a snack while a novel for adults is a full seven course meal. I wanted to write picture books that were nourishing and delightful, quality tales that enlightened, charmed, and uplifted the child and parent. I didn't want an easy lesson, or a simplistic outcome. I wanted to write a great picture book, like *Where the Wild Things Are* or *Goodnight, Moon*. I wanted it to be rich and beautiful and smart and pure.

So, I brought back to Amy, a month later, a highly revised, brutally cut two-page manu-

Author Heather Sellers' first foray into writing for children is *Spike & Cubby's Ice Cream Island Adventure*, her picture book collaboration with author/illustrator pal Amy Young. Through the process of revising and cutting her manuscript Sellers learned there are many differences in writing for adults and writing for children.

script. Single spaced. Eleven point font. Just over one thousand words. We sat on the sofa, our dogs (the real Cubby and the real Spike) snuggled in with rawhide.

"It's still too long." She showed me two giant pieces of paper, on which she had drafted out sketches for 24 pages. "You have to think in terms of the page. We don't even need words on each page."

My face flushed. I was the writer. I knew writing. Why didn't she stick to art? "You get one sentence—one beat per page, Heather. I don't mean to sound harsh. But this is too long. What's the story?"

"Can't you draw it, and then I can write it?" I said desperately.

"It's the middle," she said. "The middles are always the hard part." And she took a bite of her sandwich, and stared at me, hard. The story ball was in my court, no getting around it.

So I started over.

## WORKING STORY BACKWARDS, FROM THE INSIDE OUT

Beats.

Steps. Back to the drawing board.

Literally. I went home, and put 28 pieces of typing paper on my study floor. I knew the story would end with a picture of the two dogs, friends forever, so I sketched that in.

That sentence could write itself, later on.

And that is when I got the idea. The sentence writing itself. Somehow, the dogs would get into an adventure that would unblock Cubby. At the end of the book, he would be able to write again—he would thus have to be blocked at the outset.

The story is a nut, the puzzle in the middle, the question that the book would answer. It came to me like that—in a flash—when I had the visual layout of the pages where my words would be. I shuffled pages with just a word or two to anchor the image, until I saw how the "answer" to the question came sooner than the ending, and the last three pages, the ending, were really a playing out of Life Post Answer.

I kept shuffling—not writing, but *seeing* the story in the kid's mind. The art is the main story vehicle. The words are cues for what happens in between the pages. And—hardest lesson of all for the writer—if the story is good, not every page in the picture book *needs to have words on it.*

Once I had the middle, I got the end. There's no doubt what the beginning has to be, when you work from the inside out. You just have to go in order: middle, end, beginning. I stood up from my spread of construction paper and Post-its. I went to my computer, and wrote the first sentence (one of the few that remained unchanged during the production phase of the book): "Cubby was stuck on his book, Dogs of the Sea. He couldn't think of anything to put for the second half of his first sentence."

What I had learned through doing all these drafts of words, words, words was that the words are the sound score, almost like the orchestra under the stage at the *Nutcracker*. The words should not really show up; the words support the art and give the story its structure, its frame. The actors, the dancers, on stage come to life through your words, but the movie-in-the-mind thing is happening via the illustrations. Your mission as picture-book-writer is not to be writerly, but to keep those pages turning, and invite the child to fall head first into the world on the next page.

For adults, you try to make an image play out in their brain. For kids, your words are a guide, scaffolding, arrows pointing at what is necessary, what is essential, what will *turn* in the narrative. Follow this path, your words say. But look out—danger is on the horizon— pay attention to this kind of clue.

# DOS AND DON'TS FOR WRITING PICTURE BOOKS

The main lesson I learned when I moved from writing for adults to writing for children was how and where to begin. The role of the language is almost the opposite of its purpose in a novel or a memoir for older readers. At first, I chafed against the differences. When working visually, I had my breakthrough. Writing picture books uses such different parts of the brain. The entire conception of the purpose of the written word, the nature of a story, and where to begin work on a picture story is almost at odds with writing for adults. But, I did use some of my training as a writer (that old PhD in creative writing, not quite paying for itself, but coming in handy!) when I turned to writing for children. Those carry-over lessons include:

**DO work from your own experience.** Cubby, in my series, is a writer; his best friend, Spike, a.k.a. Amy, is an artist, who illustrates Cubby's works.

**DO have a clear conflict, but not a simple one.** Cubby believes in work work work, but he is often stuck. Sound familiar? Spike represents creative flow—he takes breaks, lots, trusts the process. Thanks, Amy! Obviously, their personalities are parts of a whole—we all have both attributes. Splitting the human personality into pieces is a clear way to create a stage for interesting cohesive conflicts kids will track.

**DON'T try to re-create the world with pattern, texture, and symbol.** That's what the illustrator is for. Much of writing for adults is manipulating your words so that the reader has an experience of a world you are drawing—you want a movie to play out in her mind. The 4- to 8-year-old enters the world of the book through the illustrations. The words are a counterpoint, a voice-over, a separate but complementary apparatus designed to tease the page-turning and provide the story's framework.

**DO ask yourself this question:** What can the pictures *not* say? What is Cubby's greatest fear? What does Spike think he is getting away with? What are they worried will happen next? What would they see as a good outcome? What are they expecting to have happen? What do the characters have to say to each other, in dialogue? (Remember, that dialogue always has to have the tension poles in it, every line.)

In sum, your words are rails that keep the story on its track. They're like dotted lines. The pictures will fill in the lines, beautifully.

Finally, at the end of the summer, literally dozens of drafts later, I brought to Amy a crisp tight draft of 700 perfect words. She took the pages from me, and said thanks, and disappeared for *one year* in order to make the paintings.

My words were revised many, many times before being published.

I always tell my students, borrowing from William Stafford, revise your writing life. If you are practiced at writing for adults, you already know the secrets to good writing: do it every day, stay with it, read aloud to hear the rhythms and catch clunky phrasing. My love for strong verbs, alliteration, a catchy turn of phrase, humor and whimsy all fed my picture book writing; again, mostly things I practiced in poetry classes, more than in fiction work-shop. But the important aspects of writing for children required learning new skills: I had to draw heavily on lessons from the visual arts and to conceive of the story from the child's perspective.

Articles & Interviews

# Adult Authors Cross Over to YA Lit

by Kelly Milner Halls

We like to think our young adult writers emerge from a rare place in humanity. We imagine they are storytellers who respect youth more than the average adult possibly could. They are authors who fondly or painfully reflect upon coming-of-age with more clarity than the average woman or man. To us, they are historians who tell a tale with the wisdom of an adult but the voice of a believable kid.

When the brave few dare cross that invisible divide—when they leap from adult book circles, into the world of young reader lit, we worry and wonder, "Will Carl Hiaasen do kids justice the way Bruce Coville has?" "Can Dave Barry capture teen humor as well as Chris Crutcher does?" "If Catherine Ryan Hyde has written grown-up bestsellers, will her work relate to the Judy Blume crowd?"

According to prominent book review sources, the answers depend on who's making the jump.

"Esteemed adult author [Francine] Prose wants to make a political statement about the gradual process by which we lose personal freedom," says *Booklist* editor Bill Ott of her first young adult novel, *After* (HarperCollins, 2003), "but she runs into trouble. Caught somewhere between allegory, dystopian fantasy, and YA problem novel, her book never finds a home for itself."

But Joyce Carol Oates mastered the young adult task in *Big Mouth & Ugly Girl* (HarperCollins, 2002) a year earlier.

"Oates has a good ear for the speech, the family relations, the e-mail messaging, the rumor mills, and the easy cruelties waiting just beneath the veneer of civility," according to the *School Library Journal* reviewer Mariam Lang Budin. "Matt's character and especially the heroic Ursula's are depicted with a raw honesty. Readers will be propelled through these pages by an intense curiosity to learn how events will play out. Oates has written a fast-moving, timely, compelling story."

Like any other gene pool, skill shines where skill has been endowed. Like any other gene pool, the strong will survive long after the weak sink back into the mire.

---

**KELLY MILNER HALLS** has been a full-time freelance writer for almost 15 years, with 1,600 articles and reviews to her credit and 14 children's books, including *Dinosaur Mummies* (Darby Creek, 2003), a Booklist Top Ten Science Book for Young Readers, and *Albino Animals* (Darby Creek, 2004), an ALA Quick Pick for Reluctant Readers. *Wild Dogs* (Darby Creek) and the *JPI Dinosaur Travel Book* (Random House) will be released in late 2005 and early 2006 and five other children's books are under contract. Halls makes her home in Spokane, Washington, the single mother of two great daughters, seven assorted cats and three rat-like dogs. She works as YA novelist Chris Crutcher's assistant in Spokane when she's not writing books and articles of her own.

We asked four prominent adults-only authors who have made the transition to PG-13 and back why they crossed over and what it felt like on the other side.

**Carl Hiaasen,** author of such adult fare as *Skinny Dip* (Knopf 2004), saw success in the YA market with Newbery Honor-winning *Hoot* (Knopf 2002). His latest for young readers, *Flush*, is a September 2005 release from Knopf.

**Catherine Ryan Hyde** wrote *Pay It Forward* (Simon & Schuster 2000) the popular novel-turned-movie and turned to YA with *Becoming Chloe* (Knopf 2007).

**Dave Barry,** prolific humor writer whose adult titles include *Big Trouble* (Putnam 1999), delved into YA penning *Peter and the Starcatchers* (Disney 2004).

**Ridley Pearson,** Barry's co-author for *Peter*, is the best-selling author of *The Body of David Hayes* (Hyperion 2004) among other novels for the adult market.

These authors were remarkably candid in their responses to our questions. So sit back and make the discovery. Story is story, and we are all kids on the inside (at least a little).

## What made you want to write for kids?

**Carl Hiaasen:** First, it was something I'd never done before, and it's important for writers to take chances. Secondly, I really wanted to write something that I could give to my nephew, nieces and stepson without worrying about the salty language of adult situations. They've all been asking to read my other novels and I've been trying to stall them, at least until they hit the teenage years.

Carl Hiaasen

**Catherine Ryan Hyde:** It just all came together like a map I had been failing to see in perspective. Even the criticism I'd been receiving for my adult work—that it was too "positive," maybe too thematic and not as subtle as some of the stuff on *The New York Times* list. It just hit me that my style of writing would be better suited to a younger reader. And I was relieved by the change of direction, because I believed (and still do, fingers crossed) that the YA market is still more about the work and less about the marketing hook. One more factor I have to throw in: A lot of the fan mail I received regarding *Pay It Forward* was from young readers. A big handful said, "I used to think I didn't like reading until I read your book." Enough said?

**Dave Barry:** I have kids, and wanted to write something they could read without concluding that their father was insane.

**Ridley Pearson:** So much changes when kids enter your life. I basically have to keep my thrillers locked up in the house, so the kids don't open them and read them. The idea of writing something for them was a major inspiration for this project.

## What were some of the challenges you faced in writing for this new audience?

**Hiaasen:** The biggest challenge was trying not to subconsciously "write down" for younger readers. As J.K. Rowling and others have proven, kids are sophisticated readers with terrific vocabularies. They're also quite aware when adults are underestimating them.

**Hyde:** My themes and situations tend to be dark and fairly adult. I had a lot of questions about what you could and could not "do" in YA fiction. When I purposely tried to write for that audience, I found myself pulling my punches in ways I didn't even see. Then I found out you can do dark stuff in today's YA fiction. What you can't do is pull any punches. So I had to find that middle ground.

**Barry:** The challenges were basically the same ones you face with any novel—coming up with a good story, and telling it in an interesting, fast-paced way. Although it's obviously a story that appeals to younger readers, we didn't make any special effort to simplify it or limit the vocabulary; we just tried to tell the story the best possible way.

**Pearson:** Dave and I are both storytellers. We wanted to write something compelling and exciting that hopefully would last for years. We were working with a classic—J.M. Barrie's original *Peter Pan*—and we were mindful these were big shoes to step into.

### Would you say writing for kids is harder or easier than writing for adults?

**Hiaasen:** All writing is hard work, or at least it ought to be. When you pick a different audience for your work, the task becomes finding the right voice and the right tone in which to tell your story.

**Hyde:** For me I'd say it's easier. I think it comes down to your own sensibility—how your mind works and what you yourself like to write and read. For me, if I just act natural, it's more likely to fit the YA audience.

**Barry:** It's not easier, but it's definitely more fun.

**Pearson:** Writing with a partner—when he's Dave Barry—makes it *way* easier, than writing alone.

### Did you approach this book differently than you would an adult novel?

**Hiaasen:** It didn't take me as long to write *Hoot* as it did to write the other novels, partly because it was slightly shorter and partly because the plot wasn't quite as multilayered. Another reason it went along so quickly, frankly, is that I was having so much fun writing it.

**Hyde:** Interesting story: I recently sold two YA titles to Knopf. One, *Broken People*, had been written expressly for the YA market. The other, *Becoming Chloe*, was my favorite unpublished adult novel. I had revised it for the YA market, but in doing so, all I really did was shorten it by dropping a very adult subplot. I didn't change the prose at all. I was waiting for my new editor to tell me what I would have to do to make it suitable for YA. Instead she is publishing that novel nearly verbatim. She had me go into *Broken People* and go deeper into the characters, into the feelings. Not hold anything back. In other words, I had to rewrite the one that had initially been intended for YA to make it more like the one that hadn't. Go figure.

Catherine Ryan Hyde

**Barry:** The main change was that we were writing the book together, so we needed a system for collaborating. We ended up with what we came to call "ping pong"—sending each chapter back and forth by e-mail until we were both happy with it.

**Pearson:** We made a point, in our discussions of being careful not to write "down" to kids or get preachy. We wanted to write something that we'd enjoy reading as much we'd enjoy reading it to our kids.

### Did you ever have to consciously avoid slipping into an adult sensibility to maintain a youthful point of view?

**Hiaasen:** Once I got rolling, I was pretty comfortable inside the heads of the young characters in *Hoot*. Once in a while, a piece of dialogue would start sounding too much like grownups yapping, so I'd throw it out and start over.

**Hyde:** If anything, I've had to try to keep the voices out of my head that tell me to write "younger." It seems that when I write a books about teens that I think my adult readers would like, things go better.

**Barry:** Not really. It's an action-adventure-magic story that lends itself well to an innocent, childlike point of view. And fortunately Ridley and I are both immature.

**Pearson:** Dave and I never passed age 14. It's been a hindrance for both us most of our lives, but now it's finally paying off.

Dave Barry

**Did you look back at your own childhood or at your own children to keep your characterizations authentic?**

**Hiaasen:** When I was creating the characters in *Hoot*, I'm sure I stole liberally from my own preadolescence. It also helped to have a stepson in the fifth grade. Between Little League games and school functions, I'm constantly around kids who are roughly Roy's age, so there was no shortage of inspiration.

**Hyde:** I have no children of my own to analyze. But I have a secret weapon: My own arrested development. People used to ask me about Trevor, "Do you have a 12-year-old? Do you know a 12-year-old?" I'd say, "No. I *am* a 12-year-old."

**Barry:** I suppose we did some of both.

**Pearson:** I think we just turned inward. You thought we were kidding about still being 14 at heart?

**Were you a writer at an early age? Did you have any idea this career was in the cards?**

**Hiaasen:** I knew from a young age that I wanted to be a writer. I got a typewriter when I was six and I was hooked. I wrote a neighborhood sports paper and handed out the carbons to my friends. Kickball scores, stuff like that.

## Who's Crossing Over (and Back)?

Here's a list of just a few adult authors who have entered the world of YA fiction.

Isabel Allende, *City of the Beasts* (HarperCollins)
Julia Alvarez, *Finding Miracles* (Knopf)
Clive Barker, *Abarat: Days of Magic, Nights of War* (Joanna Cotler)
Dave Barry and Ridley Pearson, *Peter and the Starcatchers* (Disney)
Michael Chabon, *Summerland* (Miramax)
Charles de Lint, *The Blue Girl* (Viking)
Louise Erdrich, *The Birchbark House* (Hyperion)
Neil Gaiman, *Coraline* (HarperCollins)
Carl Hiassen, *Hoot* and *Flush* (both Knopf)
Alice Hoffman, *Aquamarine* and *Green Angel* (both Scholastic)
Stephen King, *The Girl Who Loved Tom Gordon* (Simon & Schuster)
Elmore Leonard, *A Coyote's in the House* (HarperCollins)
Joyce Carol Oates, *Big Mouth & Ugly Girl* and *Freaky Green Eyes* (both HarperCollins)
Francine Prose, *After* (Joanna Cotler)

**Hyde:** Yes. My mother was a writer, and I was quite enchanted by the whole idea. When I was a sophomore in high school my English teacher, Lenny Horowitz, told me I could write. I made up my mind to be a writer then and there, but it took decades to achieve any real follow-through.

**Barry:** I always loved to write, but I never imagined it would be my career.

**Pearson:** Ditto. Taught myself how to type (on a manual typewriter, of course) at age 10. Never dreamed I'd be a published writer.

### Did any kid advance readers go over your books before the "world" did?

**Hiaasen:** My stepson Ryan offered some gentle pointers on dialogue while I was writing the book. Later, he read an early draft and gave me a thumbs-up, which from a fifth grader, is practically a rave review.

**Hyde:** No, I've been trusting my agent and editor, both of whom are quite experienced in YA, to be my judges.

**Barry:** We had several—some older, some younger—and we were gratified by the response from both age groups.

**Pearson:** A boy named Tanner Walters was the first child (along with my daughter Paige) to read the early published version of the novel (and advanced readers copy). But no one saw the book ahead of publication.

**Ridley Pearson**

### What, if any criticism, did you experience as an adult writer crossing over into the world of children's literature?

**Hiaasen:** I was lucky because I didn't get any criticism, or at least I didn't see any of it. I'm sure there was a good deal of curiosity about what kind of book *Hoot* would turn out to be, considering the tone and content of my adult novels. My main goal was to make it just as funny in a way that kids would appreciate.

**Hyde:** I wouldn't say criticism. A bit of wonderment, as though I've given myself some sort of demotion. Which seems odd to me, because, if anything, I think literature for young readers is a higher calling.

**Barry:** I think some of the fans of J.M. Barrie's original Peter Pan works—especially the novel—felt we strayed too far from Barrie's tone, which is more surreal and sometimes sort of mystical. We think Barrie was a wonderful writer, and of course we're indebted to him, but our goal was to create a story for today's younger readers, most of whom are less familiar with Barrie's original work than the way it has been interpreted in the Disney cartoon and various movies.

**Pearson:** Thankfully, the novel has been extremely well received. Readers see this for what it is, I think: a sometimes amusing, but engaging *story*. It may not be great or classic literature, but if we've told a fun story, then we met our goals. We want kids to have fun books to read.

### Do you think children's writers should have the same chance to cross-market to adults?

**Hiaasen:** Young readers are going to cross over to adult books no matter what—lots of them are showing up at book signings for my adult novels, so I know that's true. When you learn to love reading as a kid, it's natural to reach out for different works by authors you like, or by other authors you've heard about from your friends.

These days, there's not much happening in adult fiction that could shock or traumatize a young reader. What they see regularly on television—whether it's MTV or the news from Iraq—is far more likely to strip away their innocence than a book is.

**Hyde:** Absolutely. If you can tell a good story, you can probably entertain people of all ages. Most good YA novels are already suitable adult fare. My dream for the entire industry is that we stop putting writers in "boxes." Let each work be judged independently from what came before and what will come after. Then there would be less fanfare about changes in career direction, and writers would be free to follow their hearts.

**Barry:** Sure. Writers change genres all the time, sometimes with great success.

**Pearson:** No other writers should be allowed to write children's books. Only Dave and me.

## Why Change to YA?

### Catherine Ryan Hyde's story

A couple of years ago, I went through a kind of "dark night of the soul" (not to be overly dramatic) regarding my career. After years of being "too literary" to impress a New York publisher, *Pay It Forward* put me into a new box—"too corny/inspiration-y" for sophisticated adult readers. Though I feel this is not true of my body of work as a whole (nor is it true of *Pay It Forward* in many minds), some reviewers carried that theme of criticism over into my other, more literary titles (such as *Electric God*)—seeing, I firmly believe, what they expected to see.

I felt like my agents and editors were telling me whatever I handed them was not quite "it." What exactly is "it" in adult publishing? No one really knows, but they are quick to tell you that something isn't. "It" seems to have more to do with the marketing department than editorial. I remember I was on a trip to New York, with some time to kill, walking in Central Park, and I was ready to throw the whole thing over and go into a different line of work. Not because I thought I couldn't publish again (I wasn't positive I could, but that had never held me back) but because I wasn't happy.

The answer came through: no matter what choices I made about my career, I would always write—I couldn't *not* write. So, what was I going to do? A happy accident that influenced my direction.

Much to my surprise, *Pay It Forward* crossed over into the YA audience with a bang by appearing on the ALA's "Best Books for Young Adults" list. A lot of the fan mail I received regarding *Pay It Forward* was from young readers. A big handful said, "I used to think I didn't like reading until I read your book."

That was the beginning of the pull. But there was more, a weird convergence of people pointing out things I might well have seen for myself: When asked about my favorite books, I tend to go all the way back to the YA lit I read in my formative years; the fact that my strongest characters were teens (the youthful Hayden in *Electric God*, Ella in the "Then" chapters of *Funerals for Horses*, etc.); the fact that I'd been getting more and more discouraged trying to find adult fiction I loved. I couldn't name one book I'd read from the last couple of years with genuine enthusiasm until someone gave me a copy of Jerry Spinelli's *Stargirl*.

It all came together like a map I had been failing to see in perspective. Even the criticism I'd been receiving for my adult work—that it was too "positive," maybe too thematic and not as subtle as some of the stuff on *The New York Times* bestseller list. It just hit me that my style of writing would be better suited to younger readers. And I was relieved by the change of direction, because I believed (and still do, fingers crossed) that the YA market is still more about the work and less about the marketing hook.

—*Catherine Ryan Hyde*

# Skateboard Mom's Guide to Self-Promotion

by Barb Odanaka

Editor's Note: How does a first-time, noncelebrity children's author land on *Good Morning America*, CNN, *The Early Show*, National Public Radio and the cover of *USA Today* all in the same month? If you're Barb Odanaka, it's simply a matter of being on a roll—quite literally, that is.

Odanaka used her skateboarding skills to promote not only her first children's book (*Skateboard Mom*, Putnam, 2004) and website (www.skateboardmom.com), but also her club, the International Society of Skateboarding Moms, a 200-member organization of "women who dare to have fun."

A former reporter at the *Los Angeles Times*, Odanaka knew a thing or two about the machinations of the media and figured she had a decent chance of getting some exposure for her book—if only the media would bite. Devour is more like it. At last count, Odanaka and her band of skater moms have been featured in more than 100 newspapers, magazines and television outlets worldwide, gracing the pages of the *Los Angeles Times*, *Miami Herald*, *New York Daily News*, *Connecticut Post*, *Philadelphia Inquirer*, *Chicago Tribune* and *Women's Day*.

Odanaka, whose *Smash! Mash! Crash! There Goes the Trash* is on the Summer 2006 list with Simon & Schuster/Margaret K. McElderry Books, has been interviewing children's book insiders for several years. Her "Getting to Know . . ." column runs every other month on the SCBWI website (www.scbwi.org) and her own website features many Q&As with leading industry professionals.

With that in mind, we thought it best for Skateboard Mom to interview . . . herself. She did so in the comfort of her own home in Laguna Beach, California.

### Let's just get right down to it: how did you get so much publicity?
The short answer? I have a gimmick—a club of moms who ride skateboards—that ties directly into my book, *Skateboard Mom*. As a reporter, I asked myself early on what would kind of news articles might tie into my book. I had already started the skateboard mom club and thought it might attract a bit of media attention.

### A bit.
Yeah. I never expected it to catch on quite to the extent that it did.

---

**BARB ODANAKA** left a journalism career at the *Los Angeles Times* to backpack around the world, write children's books, and ride her skateboard (though not necessarily in that order). Today, the author of *Skateboard Mom* (Putnam) and *Smash! Mash! Crash! There Goes the Trash* (Margaret K. McElderry Books) lives with her family in Laguna Beach, California. For more about her, please glide over to her website, www.skateboardmom.com.

## When did you say to yourself, "Wow, this is big"?

Probably when I saw myself on the front page of *USA Today*—a ridiculously large photo of me skateboarding, with an article about our club and a mention of my book. That's when my phone started ringing. It got to the point where I had to turn things down—like a producer of ABC's reality TV show, *Wife Swap*. He said I'd be perfect for the show—and offered me $5,000 to do it. I told him $5,000 wouldn't even cover the first month of psychotherapy my family would likely have to go through to recover from the experience. Thanks but no thanks.

## Let's get down to the nuts and bolts of your self-promotion strategy. How exactly did you plot all this?

I guess I started thinking about it right after I sold *Skateboard Mom* to Putnam in 2001. Nothing in detail, but you know, every author has those dreams of landing on *Oprah* and so forth. I certainly never dreamed of *Oprah*—okay, maybe just a little—but I figured I could come up with something to attract attention for the book. I guess it swirled in my head for about a year before I came up with the idea of the skateboard mom society. At the time, it seemed kind of like a long shot. But it was the best idea I could come up with. Besides, I'd been hankering to find more women to skate with; I was hoping to start the club one way or the other.

## Did you do this on your own, or did your publisher get behind it?

I realized early on that it was probably going to be up to me, and only me, if I wanted my book to get any attention. Let's face it, the major publishers have so many authors and so many books to promote. I reviewed children's books for several years, so I knew, just by the heaps of inch-thick catalogs that arrived on my doorstep, what my book was up against. There are just so many books out there and publishers can only dedicate so much in terms of marketing dollars. So from the very beginning, I thought of it as my own enterprise, my own little business. It sounds funny now, but I actually registered the domain for my website (www.skateboardmom.com) before I'd even written the *Skateboard Mom* manuscript! I guess I was pretty confident that I'd write a manuscript that would sell. Point is, I was marketing this particular book, subconsciously perhaps, from the very beginning. I know a lot of writing purists will cringe at this, but that's the truth of it.

## How about your publisher? Were they supportive?

Putnam was quite generous. They offered me a nice little publicity bonus after things started rolling, which helped pay for a promotional video I'd made. It wasn't huge, but I never expected it so it was greatly appreciated.

## A video?

I figured if I was going to get attention from TV stations, I needed some video—"B roll" as they call it—that would show me talking about my book and doing my skateboard tricks. I now have it on DVD along with the TV segments from CNN, *The Early Show* and *Good Morning America* so it makes for nice background material for schools and media outlets. I knew going in it was a risk to make, that I might never recoup the investment. But it's turned out OK.

## You sound like a publicist.

That would have been a big insult back in my *LA Times* years, but now I can honestly say I've enjoyed the publicity process. And, as odd as it sounds, I think my antipublicist stance as a reporter helped me with my book promotion. As a reporter, I was trained to be highly skeptical—unwelcoming, really—when it came to publicists. Despite what some publicists tell you, most reporters are not waiting by the phone for their call. I know as a reporter, the

Using her knowledge as a former reporter, *Skateboard Mom* author Barb Odanaka orchestrated a media blitz that landed her on *Good Morning America*, CNN, NPR, and the front page of *USA Today*, among other venues. As founder of the International Society of Skateboarding Moms, Odanaka had the perfect hook to get the media interested.

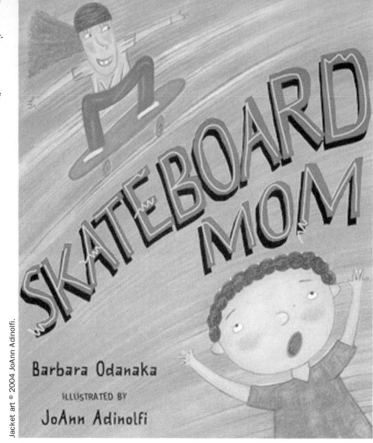

Jacket art © 2004 JoAnn Adinolfi.

glossier the press packet, the faster I would toss it into the recycling bin. It was a pride issue. Reporters worth their press pass go out and find stories; they don't let publicity people feed stories to them. Knowing this, I approached most of the media contacts differently. I've never written a press release or put together a press kit yet.

### Publicists are just going to love that.

The funny thing is, I actually did hire a publicist early on. My first idea was to launch my book with an event—the Mighty Mama Skate-O-Rama, on Mother's Day, 2004. My hope was to get a bunch of moms on skateboards, all in one place, in a festive way. Although I was pretty sure I could draw print media to the event, I hadn't a clue how the radio and TV people work. I figured I'd better consider making the investment in a freelance publicist. I knew it was a risk financially—after all, I'm a picture book author and that 5 percent royalty is only going to go so far. But, as with my promotional video, I justified it as a long-term investment in my career.

### How'd it go?

Well, the publicist I hired made a lot of phone calls, put out a lot of feelers, and scored a couple of interviews for me—a radio interview and TV coverage of the Mother's Day event by Fox Sports Net. She brought in a former producer at ABC to put me through some "media training" (pretty hilarious, since I was a former reporter and conditioned to hate this kind of thing) and she also was a lot of fun to work with, which is always a plus.

But would I do it again? Not likely. While her rate—$1,800 for a two-month period—was considerably lower than others I interviewed (the going rate seems to be $5,000 per month!) it didn't seem worth it in the end. I knew I could contact the media as well as she, and I would do it through a reporter's point of view.

### But you didn't use a press kit. What did you do, send out Morse Code?

It depended on the situation. Sometimes I'd e-mail a TV station or newspaper with a brief, to-the-point paragraph about the International Society of Skateboarding Moms, and just leave it at that. Of course, I left my e-mail, phone number, and my website. A very soft sell. Other times, I might write to a reporter directly, particularly if I'd seen that they'd written about skateboarding or other extreme sports. Granted, the fact that I had been a reporter myself didn't hurt. I expect it helped my credibility somewhat.

### Sounds like you had a huge advantage.

Not huge. If I had published a counting book about farm animals, I wouldn't have attempted what I attempted. But having been a features writer, I knew what types of newspaper stories I liked to write about, and I know I personally would have jumped at a story about skateboarding moms. Everyone likes a paradox, and the image of a mom on a skateboard speaks to that I think.

### Speaking of skateboarding, what's up with that?

I've loved it ever since Santa brought me my first board when I was 10 years old. I stopped skating as a teenager, then started again at 35 when I became a mom. At that point, it became something like a full-blown obsession. I own 22 skateboards, including three I use as bookshelves. I skateboard around the house. I literally dream about it. Some women play tennis. Others go to scrapbooking parties. I skateboard. The fact that I could use it to promote my book was, to me, way cool.

### Were there any disappointments in this publicity whirl?

Well, it was great fun skateboarding on *Good Morning America* but it didn't exactly turn out as planned. They had planned a whole segment on us, with an in-studio chat to follow, but the morning of the show, President Bush decided to grant Iraq its independence three days earlier than planned, so that big news trumped everything. They ended up showing us skateboarding in Times Square about five times throughout the program and Charlie Gibson and Diane Sawyer came out and interviewed us at the end. But my book was never mentioned. Pretty crushing from a publicity standpoint, but otherwise it was a blast. How many people can say they gave Charlie Gibson a skateboard lesson?

### Sounds surreal.

There have been many surreal moments. *People* magazine sent a team of four to my house for a photo shoot—photographer, assistant photographer, hair/makeup stylist, and wardrobe stylist. The first thing the wardrobe person did was open my closet, inspect my meager collection of clothes and shake her head pitifully. The shoot was going to be at a skateboard park. I didn't really think I needed to load up on the designer clothes. They even had us pose in the middle of the skatepark drinking milk and eating apples, apparently to boost that "wholesome mom" image. We all had to roll our eyes at that. No one drinks milk while skateboarding.

### How has all the exposure helped the book?

Like anyone, I'd hoped for sky-high sales. The initial numbers were good—the book went into a second printing within five or six months—but it wasn't like I snagged a spot on the bestseller list. Where it has helped is in school visits and such. Also, it was an incredible crash course in so many aspects of the business—marketing, publicity, even aspects of the media that I didn't quite get. I worked really hard to get *Skateboard Mom* out there—at least eight hours a day for six or seven months. It was satisfying just knowing I gave it just about everything I could.

### That brings up an obvious question: your next book, *Smash! Mash! Crash! There Goes the Trash*, comes out this year. What are you going to do, start a society of moms who drive trash trucks?

I'll admit I've thought about it! Truth is, I have confidence that this book will sell itself without a lot of theatrics. Kids love trash trucks. I feel good about the writing. And Will Hillenbrand is the illustrator. I wore a skateboard helmet while promoting my first book. It'll be nice to wear my author hat for the next!

# Six Lessons I Learned from Paula Danziger

by Greg R. Fishbone

n July of 2004, the children's book community lost one of its most unique and colorful members, Paula Danziger—the irreplaceable author of *The Cat Ate My Gymsuit*; *Barfburger Baby, I was Here First*; and the beloved Amber Brown series, among many others. Paula would have been amused by that word, *lost*, used as if she'd merely wandered from the group while shopping for another pair of purple-sequined Doc Martens. I imagine Paula reading this article up in Children's Writer Heaven and listening for an announcement: *Attention shoppers! Would the party who lost Paula Danziger please report to the service desk?*

In her books and in her life, Paula always maintained a healthy sense of fun. Her humor ranged from the puns in the Amber Brown books to seasonal gifts of plastic reindeer that "pooped" jellybeans. Her snot jokes were infamous: "Why is snot better than broccoli? Because little kids won't eat broccoli!"

But as silly as she could be, she was always serious about writing.

Paula was my friend and mentor, and one of the people I admired most. She was a teacher whose lessons beg to be spread. Here are as many of them as I can cram into an article plus a couple more.

## Lesson #1: Share your passion

I met Paula Danziger in an Internet chat room. That sounds like a joke, but it's not.

It was Verla Kay's chat room for children's writers (www.verlakay.com), and Paula spoke to us as she often spoke to groups of writers, educators, librarians, and children. She spoke to us by keyboard even as she recovered from a life-threatening physical assault that occurred in her hotel during a reading association conference. Not even such a traumatic incident could dampen her enthusiasm for reaching out to people.

Conference planners loved Paula. I once saw someone ask Paula if she would be the keynote speaker at an event for writers and illustrators. Not only did she agree to speak, she pulled out her cell phone and within ten minutes got a picture book illustrator, a children's book editor, and a literary agent to join her.

Paula's primary life lesson was about sharing. All writers are driven to share words and stories, but Paula shared her enthusiasm, her knowledge, and her passion as well.

**GREG R. FISHBONE** is Assistant Regional Advisor and Webmaster for New England SCBWI and head of the Writing City online university (www.writingcity.com). He maintains a weblog at http://gfishbone.com and is currently applying Paula Danziger's advice to a number of not-yet-published novels.

# What I Learned from Paula Danziger . . .

Well, for one thing, I've learned what it's like to miss someone every day, and how hard it is to write without our daily phone calls and jokes about "now we really must write. . . ."

But the lesson that I most want to keep close is Paula's hatred of bullies and meanness. She was so funny that jokes came rolling out of her, but she had a deep passion for kindness. When I would read her something I wrote, she would be quick to tell me if she thought someone was being too mean. I hope to keep her voice in my head, steering me away from the joke that has cruelty in it.

And then, of course, I can always use a snot joke. Snot jokes aren't cruel, they're just disgusting, and Paula loved funny snot jokes.

—*Elizabeth Levy*

## Lesson #2: Join a community

During the first week I knew her, Paula pointed me toward the Society of Children's Book Writers and Illustrators. She did the same with every aspiring writer or illustrator she met. At the time I worried whether it would be worth the cost, but I've come to believe, as Paula did, in the importance of community.

Writing a book is a solitary process, and publishing that book can be a difficult journey. Many people only get so far before giving up, unless they have a network of like-minded friends to provide support, encouragement, and commiseration.

In addition to SCBWI, there are other organizations dedicated to romance (Romance Writers of America), speculative fiction (The Science Fiction and Fantasy Writers Association), horror (Horror Writers Association), and other genres. Joining is no guarantee of publication, but the conferences, workshops, newsletters, and critique groups of SCBWI have been as helpful to me as Paula promised they would be.

## Lesson #3: Keep current

Another thing Paula taught me was how important it is for children's writers to know and understand the children of today. Paula was so in tune with children that she could guess the age and grade of just about any child she came across, but she never stopped researching what kids were playing with, eating, or wearing. Paula even "adopted" a second grade class in Texas when she was researching her young Amber Brown books.

At one point, I told Paula that I preferred to draw upon personal experiences for my writing. After all, I wasn't so long out of school that I couldn't remember how it felt.

"That's important," she said, "but keep in mind how quickly the culture changes. Four years is a high school generation. By the time you're twelve years out of high school, your own experiences are three generations removed."

That made me feel old, but it put the problem into a proper context. Even if you know exactly how today's children and teens act, speak, and think, you still need to keep up with the trends because a new generation is only four years away.

This is also why Paula didn't write much about computers, with the notable exception of *Snail Mail No More*, co-authored with Ann M. Martin. Even though Paula was plugged into the world of e-mail, chat rooms, and instant messaging, the technology was changing too fast for her to comfortably include it in her books.

## Lesson #4: Build characters

I used to struggle with characterization. Fortunately, Paula taught me an exercise for developing characters. She used webbing—putting a character's name in the center of a page and extending a web of facts around the name. Then she would add more facts around those first facts and connect them into a web.

If a character loved horses, that fact would be added to the web, but it also raised a question. Why did she love horses so much? If it was from summer visits to her aunt's farm in the country, that fact was also added. And if her love of horses led her to read books about horses, that fact was added as well. Each new insight made the character more dimensional, more interesting, and more realistic.

For expressing the inner lives of her characters, Paula drew inspiration from acting. One of the books she recommended to me was *Respect for Acting*, by Uta Hagen, a proponent of the Stanislavsky Method. I was skeptical about whether acting lessons could apply to characters on a written page, but once again Paula was right. By thinking about my characters as if I were portraying them in a play, I could focus better on their motivations and mannerisms.

I will never have Paula's instincts for well-drawn characters, but with my webs of facts and modified Stanislavsky Method, I've improved quite a bit.

Paula once even created a character web based on my sister and used it to help me choose a perfect birthday gift. There really was no limit to her skills!

## Lesson #5: Connect with readers

I went with Paula on classroom visits and book signings, hoping to get an idea of how a successful author worked. Paula's method was to make a big impression, which was easy enough with her outrageous clothes, big glasses, and chunky amber jewelry. Yet somehow, she still managed to connect with her audience and remain accessible.

# What I Learned from Paula Danziger . . .

Like many in our field, I can't say enough good things about Paula, and what she meant to me personally and professionally.

I first met Paula when I was in college. At that time, I was known primarily as a Canadian author; I was just breaking into the U.S. kids' book field. Paula took me under her wing, and—I later learned—"talked me up" at every single school visit she did. She never took credit for this. Paula wasn't looking to be patted on the back. The truth only sunk in over years of appearances, when I realized how many recommendations had come from her.

The most important literary lesson I took and continue to take from Paula was when *not* to be funny—don't try to blow the doors off with every paragraph. "Be yourself and be honest," she told me, "and the humor will come." It was natural for her, but I started writing as a kid, when overkill is a virtue. I still remind myself of that almost daily.

—*Gordon Korman*

## What I Learned from Paula Danziger . . .

Be generous with your time, and always remember to be considerate of people who help you in any way.

Paula was so great about writing thank you notes, and just plain *caring* about the people she worked with that did things to help her in her career. Her example will always shine brightly in my mind.

—*Verla Kay*

The secret, she told me, was to always, always, always make eye-contact. She also drew out shy people with her easy smile and interested conversation. As a result, nobody who had a book signed by Paula ever forgot the experience.

Also it didn't hurt that she could also sign her name backward or upside down as easily as forward and right side up.

### Lesson #6: Hopefully ever after

Another of Paula's favorite lessons used John Frederick Nims's "Love Poem." Paula would underline each funny line in red, including the entire first stanza. Then she would underline each sad line in blue, including the entire second stanza. By the end of the poem, the blocks of blue and red came together in a blend of purple, sad and funny at the same time.

Many of Paula's books also come together in a blend of sad and funny. Paula didn't believe in happy endings. She believed in hopeful endings. From what I understand, life in a hopeful ending is a little better than yesterday but not quite as good as tomorrow. I like that, and a legion of Paula's readers seem to agree.

Paula also didn't believe in writing a "series" of books, although she had respect for authors who did. She always insisted that her Amber Brown books were not a series, nor were they sequels. Paula used the term "sequelizer" because each was written without relying on previous or upcoming books.

### Lessons Paula couldn't teach me

There were lots of other things I learned from Paula, but one thing Paula couldn't teach me was how to follow rules. For her, most rules did not seem to apply.

For example, I met her for lunch once and we each brought manuscripts. I was very proud of my manuscript because it looked like all my writing manuals said it should: double-spaced with a proportional font and one-inch margins on bright 24-pound white paper.

Paula's manuscript was printed in a sans-serif font on screaming neon red paper.

When Paula looked at my pages she seemed surprised to see that my name was on every page. "What a great idea," she said. "Does everyone do that?"

From this I learned that rules are merely guidelines to be followed with common sense. They can be safely disregarded once you've earned enough knowledge, or enough of a reputation.

Another thing Paula couldn't teach me was how to deal with rejection. When I got my first rejection letter I called Paula for advice. She was very interested in what the letter said, what I was going to do, and what it felt like to get such a note.

Paula had never received a single rejection letter in her entire career, so she had to learn what that was like from me.

# First Books

by Mona Michael

"Can I really do this?" "Is my writing any good?" "Maybe I'm just not good enough for children's picture books?" Every writer or illustrator knows the self-doubt gremlin's voice. It creeps in despite your best efforts to keep it away. This year's first books' authors dispel the nasty creature, both in their stories and in their books.

A boy unwittingly incites the greatest gathering of jazz icons ever, only to begin his own journey to greatness with his first ever clarinet; a misfit, downtrodden by bullies discovers his own powers of resilience; a geeky teenager overcomes misunderstandings and misnomers to get the girl; and a boy obsessed with a superhero learns the real hero is himself. They are all triumphant, telling the stories of young people discovering and reaching for their own dreams—defeating bullies, obsessions, and most of all, self-doubt.

The characters, like their creators come from different backgrounds, overcome different obstacles and travel different roads. But they all discover that they are worthy and possessed of powers all their own. Read on to learn about their super powers. Then, make sure you're taking advantage of your own.

## Janice Repka, *The Stupendous Dodgeball Fiasco* (Dutton)

"I declare the *Stupendous Dodgeball Fiasco* a must-read for all young dodgeballers. It has everything you could want in a story: drama, suspense, great characters, humor, and, of course, dodgeball," says Ed Prentiss, President of The National Dodgeball League. What other book can boast such praise? But Janice Repka's first book is a fun ride no matter what your age or position on dodgeball. Her journey, while not always fun, bears no fewer twists and turns.

**Janice Repka**

She began as a U.S. Army newspaper journalist and became interested in law during a magazine internship. She set out on a successful career as a civil litigation lawyer. But the fiction bug never left her. Then came a wake up call. At 35 and eight months pregnant, Repka was diagnosed with breast

**MONA MICHAEL** is associate editor for North Light/IMPACT Books where she works with fantasy, comic, and fine artists to make super-spectacular art instruction books. When she's not looking at pictures, she working as a writing consultant for a local business and tutoring ESL students ages 7 to 14.

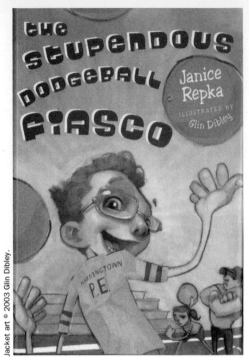

Jacket art © 2003 Glin Dibley.

Janice Repka's debut mid-grade novel *The Stupendous Dodgeball Fiasco* features a circus family, a bully/dodgeball champ, and a blind lawyer as main character Phillip Stanislaw battles in court against his town's beloved pastime after relocating to the unofficial Dodgeball Capital of the World. "Its subject matter couldn't be more appealing to kids, and the humorous situations will keep the pages turning," says *School Library Journal*.

cancer. It took years for her to recover from her illness enough to consider returning to work. By then her outlook had changed, though. It was time to pursue her dream.

Repka knew that she wanted to write a book for middle-graders about an 11-year-old boy representing himself in court. "The struggle was finding a conflict that was not too complex or boring," she says. Then, out of the blue, the idea hit her—dodgeball! "I loved the potential of a sports neophyte moving to the dodgeball capital of the world, getting his glasses broken in a game and taking the school bully to court," she says.

She made her neophyte a misfit 11-year-old boy whose father was a clown and whose mother was the fat lady. The stage set, Repka began a deliberate research and writing schedule. She wrote 500 words a day, pouring out phrases like, "You can't stuff more than six clowns in a phone booth." Repka delighted in her discoveries. "There's this wonderful world of circus jargon and folklore," she says. "Readers are often surprised to find out that they really do wash elephant hide with furniture soap and that once you teach a dog to ride a bicycle it really is difficult to get him to stop." Slowly and methodically, Repka wrote and revised.

She knew it was time to start submissions once she found herself replacing commas that she'd earlier removed. "It's the law of diminishing returns," she says. "You can only rewrite so many times." She opted to look for agents only so her agent could handle submissions and she could get to work on another book. She compiled a wish list and thrilled at a series of "nibbles." Then Scott Treimel asked for a 90-day exclusive. That meant she would have to stop submitting her manuscript and withdraw it from consideration for anyone she'd previously sent it to. "I was hesitant," says Repka. "But his credentials and client list won out." Treimel requested revisions, but in the meantime sent it to Dutton. "One rewrite and a few months later, Scott was drafting the contract," says Repka. "I felt like Cinderella."

Amidst all the fun, *Dodgeball Fiasco* shares important lessons for its readers, old and young. Repka says she wasn't trying to write a lesson book, but her own values and beliefs came through. And while she's happy that the book's gaining popularity with teachers as an anti-bullying book, she says the real compliment is that "kids are telling me it's a funny book that they enjoyed reading."

Repka's just finished a young adult novel with another intriguing title, *The Sweet Art of Chewing Glass*. "It's an edgy coming-of-age story, quite different from *The Stupendous Dodgeball Fiasco*," she says. "As I change and grow as a writer, I expect my stories will too."

## Debbie A. Taylor, *Sweet Music in Harlem* (Lee & Low)

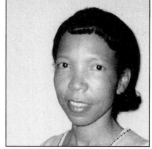

**Debbie Taylor**

How does University of Michigan's Director of Women in Engineering become a children's book writer? Debbie Taylor, author of the critically acclaimed picture book *Sweet Music in Harlem* answers, "You might wonder how a writer became director of Women in Engineering! I was a writer long before I aspired to increase the numbers of women in science and engineering fields." Taylor wrote stories all through her school years and majored in English in college. She only began working on women in science issues when she moved to Ann Arbor in 1992. But all the time she's been a writer.

Her first book, *Sweet Music in Harlem* was prompted by a T-shirt, a question and two words. The T-shirt belonged to Taylor's husband and featured the famous Art Kane photograph of 57 jazz legends. Along with the visages of Dizzy Gillespie, Count Basie, and Thelonius Monk, the photograph preserves the fresh faces of several Harlem children. While Taylor says her husband knew the name and instrument of every musician in the photo, he had no idea who the children were. "I wonder what those kids thought when those stars showed up on their street?" Taylor said out loud. Taylor wrote the words "jazz story" to remember for later.

Jacket art © 2004 Frank Morrison.

The idea for Debbie Taylor's debut picture book came from a T-shirt of her husband's featuring a famous Art Kane photograph of 57 jazz legends. Taylor submitted the manuscript for *Sweet Music in Harlem* to Lee & Low's New Voices Contest, and while it didn't win, it garnered interest from a Lee & Low editor. Says *School Library Journal*: "This dazzling tale is filled with energy, rhythm, and style."

"During the next few months I visited Kansas City," she says. "There I noticed signs with jazz-related names. In the hotel coffee shop, a boy named CJ ran past my glass of orange juice looking for something his uncle lost. The story emerged between bites of eggs and toast." It was a story about CJ, the nephew of a famous Harlem musician (Uncle Click). Uncle Click is to have his photo taken by famed photographer Max Kane, but he's lost his hat and sends CJ off to find it. CJ's search for the hat brings the rest of the greats to the photo spot and turns CJ's wonder at the world of music into his very own clarinet.

Taylor worked on the story for months, relying on her writing groups and family members for advice. After she got the story down, she settled in to do some research. There was much to investigate in the wide world of Harlem's jazz scene in the 1950s. "I didn't even look up the names of the musicians in the photograph until months later," she says. She turned to her husband's vinyl collection, and then sought out books, magazines and live recordings. She also had to investigate basic facts such as subway schedules for Harlem during the period.

Two years after she wrote the words, "jazz story," the story was finished. She sent it to publishers, and then entered the Lee & Low New Voices Contest. It was her second entry and she didn't win for either. But editor Jennifer Hunt asked if Taylor was interested in working with them to develop one or both of the stories for "possible publication." Taylor agreed immediately.

She knew from published friends and her involvement in the active Michigan SCBWI chapter that it would be a long time before her book made it to print. Her only surprise was just how quickly that time passed. "With revising the manuscript, producing other work, a full time job and family obligations, I was too busy to fret constantly," she says.

When the book finally came out, she aided Lee & Low's promotions with those of her own. She worked with local libraries and bookstores, created a website (www.sweetmusicinh arlem.com), connected with a local jazz station and even signed books during a blues and jazz festival. When asked about the attention and great reviews that the book's received, Taylor remains humble, saying only, "I have indeed been blessed."

## D.L. Garfinkle, *Storky: How I Lost My Nickname and Won the Girl* (G.P. Putnam's Sons)

Debra Garfinkle, the self-described "happily married soccer mom/writer in the suburbs" came up with the idea for *Storky* in 1984 as a one-page writing assignment. "In love" with the character, in 1990 she expanded that story into a longer one. A busy part-time attorney and mother, she didn't touch the story again for a long time. Then, in 1997, she had a cancer scare that caused her to re-evaluate her life. "I decided what I was most proud of was my two children and the one short story I had published. I decided to quit my job, have another child, and start writing a novel." In 1999 Storky came back as the main character for that novel.

**D.L. Garfinkle**

Michael "Storky" Pomerantz, is a teen misfit just entering high school. He wants to fit in and find a girlfriend. His parents are an embarrassment, the only friend he has is an old man at a nursing home, and he's stuck with a decidedly uncool nickname. His journey is one of self-discovery and acceptance. But the lessons involved never encroach on the novel's easy humor.

It took Garfinkle 14 months to finish the novel. "By that time, I had a six-year-old, a three-year-old, and a brand new baby," she says. The secret to writing with such a full house?

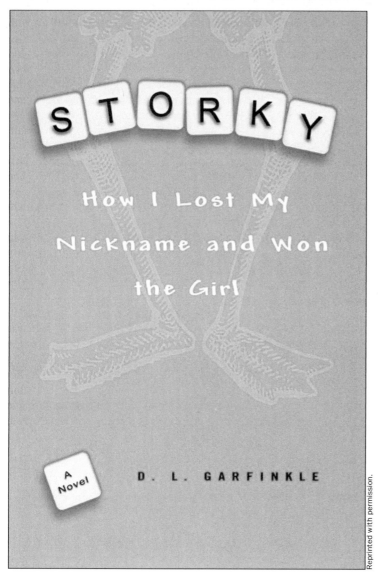

After numerous rejections and rewrites, Debra Garfinkle's debut novel *Storky* was finally published by Putman in 2005. Her book features Michael ''Storky'' Pomerantz, a teen misfit just entering high school who wants to fit in and find a girlfriend. His journey is one of self-discovery and acceptance told with an easy humor.

Reprinted with permission.

''Marry a wonderful guy,'' she says. ''My husband often takes over all childcare responsibilities when he's home so I can write.'' In addition, Garfinkle says her critique group helped immensely. As she writes she can still hear their voices: ''You can rephrase this without the adverb.'' ''Go deeper into your character.'' ''That doesn't ring true.''

Garfinkle brought the manuscript to a writers' retreat in Santa Fe, then decided it was time to send *Storky* out into the world. She opted to send the manuscript to agents only, a decision she credits partly to her own inexperience. ''I didn't know how difficult it was for an unpublished writer to get a good agent,'' she says. She also worried that a long list of rejections from editors would hurt her chances for getting an agent later. Rejections from agents, however, might provide her with feedback that would leave her options for publishers wide open.

Her strategy worked. ''I got a request for a rewrite from a great agent, a kind rejection letter from another, lots of form rejections, and an offer from Laura Rennert of the Andrea Brown Literary Agency that I accepted enthusiastically,'' says Garfinkle. Sure that her quest for publication was ending, she happily incorporated Rennert's suggestions into another rewrite. That finished, she relaxed and waited for a bidding war, leaving herself unprepared for what happened next. ''I got rejected. And rejected. And rejected,'' she says. Each time the manuscript was rejected, or ''declined'' as Rennert put it, Garfinkle used the advice and comments the editor made for rewrites. After long months of this cycle, and even the award for Best Unpublished Novel from the San Diego Book Awards, Garfinkle got some hopeful news. An editor from a major publisher said she ''hadn't been so excited about a manuscript in years.''

''I hadn't been so excited in years either!'' says Garfinkle. She did the revisions. The editor was happy. Garfinkle was happy. Rennert was happy. The committee, however, said no. Crushed, Garfinkle had no choice but to wait again. Months later, ''August 22, 2003, but who's counting,'' she says. The phone rang again. At first, Garfinkle remained skeptical. She didn't want to ride the same wave of excitement, rewriting her way to disappointment, again. But this call wasn't a request for a rewrite. John Rudolph of G.P. Putnam's Sons was making an offer.

After ''the happiest scream of her life'' Garfinkle has no plans to stop writing. Hard at work on her second and third novel, though, she says the process remains difficult. ''I hope to keep on writing until the day I die,'' she says. ''I just hope my next novel doesn't take 21 years from concept to publication.''

## Troy Wilson, *Perfect Man* (Orca)

**Troy Wilson**

Troy Wilson appears at readings wearing Lycra, electric blue shoes and red cape. It may sound silly, but when comics giant Stan Lee says about your book, ''Both the story and the art are sensational. I hope it sells a gazillion copies!'' you know you're doing something right. ''The costume has opened a lot of doors. It's already landed me five television appearances. I'm still waiting for *Oprah* though.''

Longed-for *Oprah* appearance aside, Wilson's first book is a hit. The premise is simple. ''We're all superheroes,'' he says. ''We all have our own super powers.'' Writing is definitely Wilson's super power. His first book's gathering praise in both Canada and the U.S., but like so many other authors, he says he just wrote the story he had to write. ''The idea kept tapping me on the shoulder and wouldn't let up.'' That tapping became a boy named Michael Maxwell McAllum who is obsessed with a real live superhero named Perfect Man. Michael is so preoccupied with Perfect Man that he doesn't leave much time for anything else, a problem that the author identifies with.

''As a kid, I was obsessed with comics,'' says Wilson. ''Because of my obsession, real life passed me by sometimes.'' Not anymore though. Wilson's first book story is atypical in many ways. While the idea rattled around in his head for a long period, once it came out, it came out quickly. ''It took about a week of steady work to get it 90 percent right. After that, it was all fine-tuning.''

''I was in a hurry,'' he says. ''I didn't show the story to anyone before I sent it away.'' And he never received a rejection for Perfect Man. He simultaneously submitted the manuscript to two publishers: Orca and a small, newer publisher. Orca had previously rejected another of Wilson's picture book manuscripts, but editor Maggie DeVries ''scribbled a note on the form letter complimenting the manuscript but saying that they published more straightforward stories.'' Wilson thought, ''Hey, she likes my stuff enough to write a comment. I just didn't send her the right kind of story.'' So he sent her *Perfect Man*.

After waiting six months, he phoned to ask about his manuscript. ''I expected to hear that they'd lost it, or that they were really backed up,'' says Wilson. ''When Maggie said they wanted to publish it, I was stunned.'' He hadn't heard from the other publisher, so he withdrew it. No rejections. Figures for a superhero right?

It took two and a half years for the book's release, giving Wilson plenty of time to think about promotion. He noticed that most of Orca's picture books contained no author photo. ''I wanted my author photo, darn it,'' he says. ''So I suggested they include photos of Dean [the illustrator] and me on the jacket— superhero pictures.'' Orca said okay. Wilson created a logo and taped it to his chest for the photo. That was all there was to the costume at that point. But then he thought about it some more.

''Why not assemble a full superhero outfit and wear it to all appearances,'' he thought. He bought the shiny shorts and bright blue shoes. He bought a Little Red Riding Hood cape and cut off the hood. He found cotton-lycra tights at a local dancewear company that even put a ''T'' on the chest for him.

These days, Wilson frequents classrooms, bookstores and libraries, donning the costume for every visit. Follow-

Jacket art © 2004 Dean Griffiths.

The premise of Troy Wilson's debut *Perfect Man* is simple. ''We're all superheroes,'' he says. ''We all have our own super powers.'' Wilson drew on his childhood obsession with comic books as he penned the picture book, and shows up to book signings and school visits in a makeshift superhero costume, asking young readers to identify their own special powers.

ing the theme of his book, he asks the children about their own super powers. But what's next for superhero Troy Wilson? ''*Oprah*. I figure if she's barraged by enough messages from *Children's Writer's & Illustrator's Market* readers, she'll have no choice but to invite me on her show (hint, hint).'' Did I mention one of Wilson's super powers is ''shameless self-promotion''?

# Book Publishers

There's no magic formula for getting published. It's a matter of getting the right manuscript on the right editor's desk at the right time. Before you submit it's important to learn publishers' needs, see what kind of books they're producing and decide which publishers your work is best suited for. *Children's Writer's & Illustrator's Market* is but one tool in this process. (Those just starting out, turn to Just Starting? Some Quick Tips for Writers & Illustrators on page 2.)

To help you narrow down the list of possible publishers for your work, we've included several indexes at the back of this book. The **Subject Index** lists book and magazine publishers according to their fiction and nonfiction needs or interests. The **Age-Level Index** indicates which age groups publishers cater to. The **Photography Index** indicates which markets buy photography for children's publications. The **Poetry Index** lists publishers accepting poetry.

If you write contemporary fiction for young adults, for example, and you're trying to place a book manuscript, go first to the Subject Index. Locate the fiction categories under Book Publishers and copy the list under Contemporary. Then go to the Age-Level Index and highlight the publishers on the Contemporary list that are included under the Young Adults heading. Read the listings for the highlighted publishers to see if your work matches their needs.

Remember, *Children's Writer's & Illustrator's Market* should not be your only source for researching publishers. Here are a few other sources of information:

- The Society of Children's Book Writers and Illustrators (SCBWI) offers members an annual market survey of children's book publishers for the cost of postage or free online at www.scbwi.org. (SCBWI membership information can also be found at www.scbwi.org.)
- The Children's Book Council website (www.cbcbooks.org) gives information on member publishers.
- If a publisher interests you, send a SASE for submission guidelines *before* submitting. To quickly find guidelines on the Internet, visit The Colossal Directory of Children's Publishers at www.signaleader.com/childrens-writers/.
- Check publishers' websites. Many include their complete catalogs that you can browse. Web addresses are included in many publishers' listings.
- Spend time at your local bookstore to see who's publishing what. While you're there, browse through *Publishers Weekly* and *The Horn Book*.

## SUBSIDY & SELF-PUBLISHING

Some determined writers who receive rejections from royalty publishers may look to subsidy and co-op publishers as an option for getting their work into print. These publishers ask writers to pay all or part of the costs of producing a book. We strongly advise writers and illustrators to work only with publishers who pay them. For this reason, we've adopted a policy not to include any subsidy or co-op publishers in *Children's Writer's & Illustrator's Market* (or any other Writer's Digest Books market books).

If you're interested in publishing your book just to share it with friends and relatives, self-publishing is a viable option, but it involves time, energy, and money. You oversee all book production details. Check with a local printer for advice and information on cost or check online for print-on-demand publishing options (which are often more affordable).

Whatever path you choose, keep in mind that the market is flooded with submissions, so it's important for you to hone your craft and submit the best work possible. Competition from thousands of other writers and illustrators makes it more important than ever to research publishers before submitting—read their guidelines, look at their catalogs, check out a few of their titles and visit their websites.

## ADVICE FROM INSIDERS
For insight and advice on getting published from a variety of perspectives, be sure to read the Insider Reports in this section. Subjects include authors and illustrators **Yuyi Morales** (page 112), **Amy Timberlake** (page 124), **Bruce Hale** (page 132), **Linda Zinnen** (page 144), **Peter McCarty** (page 154), and **Jarrett J. Krosoczka** (page 164); librarian **John Peters** (page 174); and editor **Deborah Brodie** (page 182).

**Information on book publishers listed in the previous edition but not included in this edition of *Children's Writer's & Illustrator's Market* may be found in the General Index.**

### A/V CONCEPTS CORP.
30 Montauk Blvd., Oakdale NY 11769. (631)567-7227. Fax: (631)567-8745. E-mail: info@edcompublishing.com. Specializes in nonfiction, fiction, educational material. **Writers contact:** Laura Solimene, editorial director. **Illustrators contact:** Dale Solimene, president. Produces 6 young readers/year; 6 middle readers/year; 6 young adult books/year. 20% of books by first-time authors. "Primary theme of books and multimedia is classic literature, math, science, language arts, self-esteem. We also hire writers to adapt classic literature."
**Fiction** Middle readers: hi-lo. Young adults/teens: hi-lo, multicultural, special needs. Recently published *The Taming of the Shrew*, adaptation by Lewann Sotnak, illustrated by Don Lannon and Ken Landgraf; *The Twelfth Night*, adaptation by Julianne Davidow; *The Merchant of Venice*, adaptation by Rachel Armington; *The Pioneers*, adaptation by Annie Laura Smith, illustrated by Matthew Archambault and Ken Landgraf.
**Nonfiction** Picture books, young readers, middle readers: activity books. Young adults/teens: activity books, hi-lo, multicultural, science, self help, textbooks. Average word length: middle readers—300-400; young adult books—500-950.
**How to Contact/Writers** Nonfiction: Submit outline/synopsis and 1 sample chapter. Responds to queries in 1 month.
**Illustration** Works with 4-6 illustrators/year. Reviews ms/illustration packages from artists. Submit ms with 3-4 pieces of final art. Illustrations only: Query with samples. Responds in 1 month. Samples returned with SASE. Samples filed.
**Photography** Submit samples.
**Terms** Work purchased outright for $50-1,000. Illustrators paid by the project $50-1,000. Photographers paid per photo $25-250. Offers writer's, artist's guidelines for SASE.

### ABINGDON PRESS
The United Methodist Publishing House, 201 Eighth Ave. S., Nashville TN 37203. (615)749-6384. Fax: (615)749-6512. E-mail: paugustine@umpublishing.org. Estab. 1789. **Acquisitions:** Peg Augustine, children's book editor. "Abingdon Press, America's oldest theological publisher, provides an ecumenical publishing program dedicated to serving the Christian community."
**Nonfiction** All levels: religion.
**How to Contact/Writers** Query or submit outline/synopsis and 1 sample chapter. Prefers submissions by e-mail. Responds to queries in 3 months; mss in 6 months.

**Illustration** Uses color artwork only. Reviews ms/illustration packages from artists. Query with photocopies only. Samples returned with SASE; samples not filed.
**Photography** Buys stock images. Wants scenic, landscape, still life and multiracial photos. Model/property release required. Uses color prints. Submit stock photo list.
**Terms** Pays authors royalty of 5-10% based on retail price. Work purchased outright from authors ($100-1,000).

## HARRY N. ABRAMS BOOKS FOR YOUNG READERS
115 W. 18th St., New York NY 10011. (212)519-1200. **Director, Children's Books:** Howard W. Reeves.
• Abrams Books for Young Readers no longer accepts unsolicited works of fiction. Nonfiction manuscripts may be sent via mail.
**Nonfiction** Picture books, young readers, middle readers, young adult.
**How to Contact/Writers** Nonfiction: Submit complete ms or proposal with SASE. Responds in 6 months only with SASE. Will consider multiple submissions.
**Illustration** Illustrations only: Do not submit original material; copies only. Contact: Becky Terhune.

## ABSEY & CO.
23011 Northcrest Dr., Spring TX 77389. (281)257-2340. Fax: (281)251-4676. E-mail: abseyandco@aol.com. Website: www.absey.com. **Publisher:** Edward Wilson. "We are looking primarily for education books, especially those with teaching strategies based upon research." Publishes hardcover, trade paperback and mass market paperback originals. Publishes 5-10 titles/year. 50% of books from first-time authors; 50% from unagented writers.
**Fiction** "Since we are a small, new press, we are looking for good manuscripts with a firm intended audience." Recently published *Saving the Scrolls*, by Mary Kerry.
**How to Contact/Writers** Fiction: Query with SASE. Nonfiction: Query with outline and 1-2 sample chapters. Does not consider simultaneous submissions. Responds to queries in 3 months.
**Illustration** Reviews ms/illustration packages. Send photocopies, transparencies, etc.
**Photography** Reviews ms/photo packages. Send photocopies, transparencies, etc.
**Terms** Pays 8-15% royalty on wholesale price. Publishes book 1 year after acceptance of ms. Manuscript guidelines for #10 SASE.
**Tips** "Absey publishes a few titles every year. We like the author and the illustrator working together to create something magical. Authors and illustrators have input into every phase of production."

## ACTION PUBLISHING
P.O. Box 391, Glendale CA 91209-0391. (323)478-1667. Fax: (323)478-1767. Website: www.actionpublishing.com. **Art Acquisitions:** Art Director. Publishes 2 middle readers/year.
**Fiction** Picture book: fantasy. Middle readers: adventure. Recently published The Family of Ree series, by Scott E. Sutton.
**How to Contact/Writers Only interested in agented material.**
**Illustration** Works with 2-4 illustrators/year. Reviews illustration packages from artists. Query. Contact: Publisher. Send promotional literature. Contact: Art Director. Responds only if interested. Samples returned with SASE or kept on file if interested and OK with illustrator.
**Photography** Buys stock and assigns work. Contact: Art Director. "We use photos on an as-needed basis. Mainly publicity, advertising and copy work." Uses 35mm or 4×5 transparencies. Submit cover letter and promo piece.
**Terms** Pays authors royalty based on wholesale price. Offers advances against royalties. Pays illustrators by the project or royalty. Pays photographers by the project or per photo. Sends galleys to authors. Original art returned as negotiated depending on project.

## ADVOCACY PRESS
P.O. Box 236, Santa Barbara CA 93102. (805)962-2728. Fax: (805)963-3580. E-mail: advocasypress@girlsincsb.org. Website: www.advocacypress.com. **Publisher:** Joan Bowman. Publishes 1-2 children's books/year. Specializes in life skills development books for youth, and children's titles with a gender equity focus.
• Advocacy Press title *My Way Sally* won the Benjamin Franklin Award for Best Children's Picture Book from the Publishing Marketing Associaion.
**Fiction** Picture books, young readers, middle readers: adventure, animal, concepts in self-esteem, contemporary, fantasy, folktales, gender equity, multicultural, nature/environment, poetry. "Illustrated children's stories incorporate self-esteem, gender equity, self-awareness concepts." Published *Father Gander Nursery Rhymes*, by Doug Larche, illustrated by Carolyn Blattel; *Minou*, by Mindy Bingham, illustrated by Itoko Maeno; *My Way Sally*, by Penelope Paine, illustrated by Itoko Maeno; *Shawdow in the Ready Time*, by Patty Sheehan, illustrated

by Itoko Maeno. "Most publications are 32-48 page picture stories for readers 4-11 years. Most feature adventures of animals in interesting/educational locales."

**Nonfiction** Middle readers, young adults: careers, multicultural, self-help, social issues, textbooks.

**How to Contact/Writers** "Because of the required focus of our publications, most have been written in-house. We are not currently publishing new titles, but would like samples to keep on file."

**Illustration** "Require intimate integration of art with story. Therefore, almost always use local illustrators." Average about 30 illustrations per story. Reviews ms/illustration packages from artists. Submit ms with dummy. Contact: Ruth Vitale. Responds in 2 months. Samples returned with SASE.

**Terms** Authors paid by royalty or outright purchase. Pays illustrators by project or royalty. Book catalog and ms guidelines for SASE.

**Tips** "We are not presently looking for new titles."

## ALADDIN PAPERBACKS/SIMON PULSE PAPERBACK BOOKS

1230 Avenue of the Americas, 4th Floor, New York NY 10020. (212)698-2707. Fax: (212)698-7337. Website: www.simonsays.com. Associate Vice President/Editorial Director: Ellen Krieger, associate publisher for Aladdin; Bethany Buck, associate publisher for Simon Pulse; Julia Richardson, executive editor; Jennifer Klonsky (all areas); Michelle Nagler, editor for Simon Pulse.

**Manuscript Acquisitions** Attn: Submissions Editor. **Art Acquisitions:** Debra Sfetsios, Aladdin; Russel Gordon, Simon Pulse. Paperback imprints of Simon & Schuster Children's Publishing Children's Division. Publishes 130 titles/year.

- Aladdin publishes primarily reprints of successful hardcovers from other Simon & Schuster imprints. They accept query letters with proposals for middle-grade series and single-title fiction, beginning readers, middle grade and commercial nonfiction. Simon Pulse primarily publishes Young Adult series and fiction, as well as reprints of successful hardcovers from other Simon & Schuster imprints. They accept query letters for young adult series and single-title fiction.

**Fiction** Recently published The Unicorn series chapter book series by Kathleen Duey (ages 7-10, edited by Ellen Krieger; fantasy chapter books, Aladdin Paperbacks); *Pendragon*, by D.J. MacHale (middle grade, fiction, edited by Julia Richardson); *The Keeper's Trilogy* (mid-grade); *Star Power* (edited by Jennifer Klonsky); *The Robin Hill School Series* (edited by Julia Richardson); *The Freaky Joe Club* (edited by Ellen Krieger).

## ALASKA NORTHWEST BOOKS

Imprint of Graphic Arts Center Publishing Co., P.O. Box 10306, Portland OR 97296-0306. (503)226-2402. Fax: (503)223-1410. E-mail: tricia@gacpc.com. Website: www.gacpc.com. **Aquisitions Editor:** Tricia Brown. Imprints: Alaska Northwest Books. Publishes 3 picture books/year; 1 young reader/year. 20% of books by first-time authors. "We publish books that teach and entertain as well as inform the reader about Alaska or the western U.S. We're interested in wildlife, adventure, unusual sports, inspirational nature stories, traditions, but we also like plain old silly stories that make kids giggle. We are particular about protecting Native American story-telling traditions, and ask that writers ensure that it's clear whether they are writing from within the culture or about the culture. We encourage Native American writers to share their stories."

**Fiction** Picture books, young readers: adventure, animal, contemporary, fantasy, history, humor, multicultural, nature/environment, poetry. Middle readers, young adult/teens: adventure, animal, anthology, contemporary, history, humor, multicultural, nature/environment, suspense/mystery. Average word length: picture books—500-1,000; young readers—500-1,500; middle readers—1,500-2,000; young adults—35,000. Recently published *Seldovia Sam and the Wildfire Rescue*, by Susan Woodward Springer, illustrated by Amy Meissner (ages 6-10, early chapter book); *Ten Rowdy Ravens*, by Susan Ewing, illustrated by Evon Zerbetz (age 5 and up, humor); *Berry Magic*, by Teri Sloat and Betty Huffmon, illustrated by Teri Sloat (age 6 and up , legend).

**Nonfiction** Picture books: animal. Young readers: animal, multicultural, sports. Middle readers, young adults/teens: animal, history, multicultural, nature/environment, sports, Alaska- or Western-themed adventure. Average word length: picture books—500-1,000; young readers—500-1,500; middle readers—1,500-2,000; young adults—35,000. Recently published *Big-Enough Anna: The Little Sled Dog Who Braved the Arctic*, by Pam Flowers and Ann Dixon, illustrated by Bill Farnsworth (5 and up); *Recess at 20 Below*, by Cindy Lou Aillaud (ages 6-10).

**How to Contact/Writers** Fiction: Submit complete ms for picture books or submit outline/synopsis and 2 sample chapters for YA novels. Nonfiction: Submit complete ms for picture books or submit 2 sample chapters for YA nonfiction chapter books. Responds to queries/mss in 3-5 months. Publishes book 2 years after acceptance. Will consider simultaneous submissions.

**Illustration** Works with 4-5 illustrators/year. Uses color artwork only. Reviews ms/illustration packages from artists. Submit ms with dummy or scans of final art on CD. Contact: Tricia Brown. Illustrations only: Query with résumé, scans on CD. Responds only if interested. Samples not returned; samples filed.

**Photography** Buys stock and assigns work. "We rarely illustrate with photos—only if the book is more educational in content.'' Photo captions required. Uses color and 35mm or 4×5 transparencies. Submit cover letter, résumé, slides, portfolio on CD, color promo piece.

**Terms** Pays authors royalty of 5-7% based on net revenues. Offers advances (average amount: $2,000). Pays illustrators royalty of 5-7% based on net revenues. Pays photographers royalty of 5-7% based on net revenues. Sends galleys to authors; dummies to illustrators. Originals returned to artist at job's completion. Book catalog available for 9×12 SASE and $3.85 postage; ms, art, and photo guidelines available for SASE. All imprints included in a single catalog. Catalog available on website.

**Tips** ''As a regional publisher, we seek books about Alaska and the West. We rarely publish YA novels, but are more interested in the pre-school to early reader segment. A proposal that shows that the author has researched the market, in addition to submitting a unique story, will get our attention.''

### ALL ABOUT KIDS PUBLISHING

117 Bernal Rd. #70, PMB 405, San Jose CA 95119. (408)846-1833. Fax: (408)846-1835. E-mail: lguevara@aakp.c om. Website: www.aakp.com. **Acquisitions:** Linda Guevara. Publishes 5-10 picture books/year. 80% of books by first-time authors.

**Fiction** Picture books, young readers: adventure, animal, concept, fantasy, folktales, history, humor, multicultural, nature/environment, poetry, religion, suspense/mystery. Average word length: picture books—450 words. Recently published *A, My Name is Andrew*, by Mary McManus-Burke (picture book).

**Nonfiction** Picture books, young readers: activity books, animal, biography, concept, history, multicultural, nature/environment, religion. Average word length: picture books—450 words. Recently published *Shadowbox Hunt: A Search & Find Odyssey*, by Laura L. Seeley (picture book).

**How to Contact/Writers** Fiction: Submit complete ms. Nonfiction: Submit complete ms for picture books; outline synopsis and 2 sample chapters for young readers. Responds to mss in 3 months. Publishes a book 2-3 years after acceptance. Manuscript returned with SASE.

**Illustration** Works with 5-10 illustrators/year. Reviews ms/illustration packages from artists. Submit ms with dummy or ms with 2-3 pieces of final art. Contact: Linda Guevara, editor. Illustrations only: Arrange personal portfolio review or send résumé, portfolio and client list. Responds in 3 months. Samples returned with SASE; samples filed.

**Photography** Works on assignment only. Contact: Linda Guevara, editor. Model/property releases required. Uses 35mm transparencies. Submit portfolio, résumé, client list.

**Terms** Pays author royalty. Offers advances (average amount: $1,000). Pays illustrators by the project (range: $3,000 minimum) or royalty of 3-5% based on retail price. Pays photographers by the project (range: $500 minimum) or royalty of 5% based on wholesale price. Sends galleys to authors; dummies to illustrators. All imprints included in a single catalog. Writer's, artist's and photographer's guidelines available for SASE.

**Tips** ''Write from the heart and for the love of children. Submit only one manuscript per envelope.''

### ALYSON PUBLICATIONS, INC.

P.O. Box 4371, Los Angeles CA 90078. (323)860-6065. Fax: (323)467-0152. **Acquisitions:** Editorial Department. Publishes 1-3 picture books/year; 1-3 young adult titles/year.

**Fiction** Will only consider submissions that deal with gay or lesbian topics. Picture books subjects, children with gay or lesbian parents.

**Nonfiction** Teens: concept, social issues. ''We like books that incorporate all racial, religious and body types. Books should deal with issues faced by kids growing up gay or lesbian.'' Published *The Daddy Machine*, by Johnny Valentine.

**How to Contact/Writers** Submit outline/synopsis and sample chapters (young adults). Responds to queries/ mss within 3 months. Include SASE. Picture books only considered with text accompanied by art.

**Terms** Pays authors royalty of 8-12% based on wholesale price. ''We *do* offer advances.'' Book catalog and/or ms guidelines free for SASE.

### AMERICAN GIRL PUBLICATIONS

(formerly Pleasant Company Publications), 8400 Fairway Place, Middleton WI 53562-2554. (608)836-4768. Fax: (608)836-1999. Website: www.americangirl.com. **Manuscript Acquisitions:** Submissions Editor. Jodi Evert, editorial director fiction; Michelle Watkins, editorial director, American Girl Library. **Art Acquisitions:** Jane Varda, art director. Imprints: The American Girls Collection, American Girl Library, History Mysteries, AG Fiction, Girls of Many Lands. Publishes 30 middle readers/year. 10% of books by first-time authors. Publishes fiction and nonfiction for girls 7 and up. ''Pleasant Company's mission is to educate and entertain girls with high-quality products and experiences that build self-esteem and reinforce positive social and moral values.''

● American Girl Publications does not accept ideas or manuscripts for The American Girls Collection, but does accept manuscripts for stand-alone historical fiction, and is seeking manuscripts for AG Fiction, its contemporary middle-grade fiction imprint for girls 10 and up. Request writers' guidelines for more information. Also publishes *American Girl* magazine. See the listing for *American Girl* in the Magazines section.

**Nonfiction** Middle readers: activity books, arts/crafts, cooking, history, hobbies, how-to, self help, sports. Recently published *A Smart Girl's Guide to Friendship Troubles*, by Patti Kelley Crisswell, (ages 8 and up; self-help); *Paper Punch Art*, by Laura Torres (ages 8 and up; craft); *Quiz Book 2*, by Sarah Jane Brian, illustrated by Debbie Tilley (ages 8 and up; activity).

**How to Contact/Writers** Nonfiction: Submit well-focused concepts for activity, craft or advice books. "Proposals should include a detailed descripton of your concept, sample chapters or spreads and lists of previous publications. Complete manuscripts also accepted." Responds in 3 months. Will consider simultaneous submissions.

**Illustration** Works with 10 illustrators/year. Reviews ms/illustration packages from artists. Illustrations only: Query with samples. Contact: Jane Varda, senior art director. Responds only if interested. Samples returned with SASE; copies of samples filed.

**Photography** Buys stock and assigns work. Submit cover letter, published samples, promo piece.

**Terms** Pays authors royalty or work purchased outright. Pays illustrators by the project. Pays photographers by the project. Sends galleys to authors; dummies to illustrators. Originals returned to artist at job's completion. Book catalog available for 8½×11 SAE and 4 first-class stamps. All imprints included in a single catalog.

**Tips** "We want nonfiction specifically targeted to girls. If the approach would appeal to boys as well as girls, it is not right for American Girl Library."

## □ AMIRAH PUBLISHING

P.O. Box 541146, Flushing NY 11354. E-mail: amirahpbco@aol.com. Website: www.ifna.net. **Acquisitions:** Yahiya Emerick, president. Publishes 2 young readers/year; 5 middle readers/year; 3 young adult titles/year. 25% of books by first-time authors. "Our goal is to produce quality books for children and young adults with a spiritually uplifting application."

• Amirah accepts submissions only through e-mail.

**Fiction** Picture books, young readers, middle readers, young adults: adventure, animal, history, multicultural, religion, Islamic. Average word length: picture books—200; young readers—1,000; middle readers—5,000; young adults—5,000. Recently published *Ahmad Deen and the Curse of the Aztec Warrior*, by Yahiya Emerick (ages 8-11); *Burhaan Khan*, by Qasim Najar (ages 6-8); *The Memory of Hands*, by Reshma Baig (ages 15 to adult).

**Nonfiction** Picture books, young readers, middle readers, young adults: history, religion, Islamic. Average word length: picture books—200; young readers—1,000; middle readers—5,000; young adults—5,000. Recently published *Color and Learn Salah*, by Yahiya Emerick (ages 5-7, religious); *Learning About Islam*, by Yahiya Emerick (ages 9-11, religious); *What Islam Is All About*, by Yahiya Emerick (ages 14 and up, religious).

**How to Contact/Writers** Fiction/nonfiction: Query via e-mail only. Responds to queries in 2 weeks; mss in 3 months. Publishes a book 6-12 months after acceptance. Will consider electronic submissions via disk or modem.

**Illustration** Works with 2-4 illustrators/year. Reviews ms/illustration packages from artists. Query. Contact: Qasim Najar, vice president. Illustrations only: Query with samples. Contact: Yahiya Emerick, president. Responds in 1 month. Samples returned with SASE.

**Photography** Works on assignment only. Contact: Yahiya Emerick, president. Uses images of the Middle East, children, nature. Model/property releases required. Uses 4×6, matte, color prints. Submit cover letter.

**Terms** Work purchased outright from authors for $1,000-3,000. Pays illustrators by the project (range: $20-40). Pays photographers by the project (range: $20-40). Sends galleys to authors; dummies to illustrators. Originals returned to artist at job's completion. Book catalog available for SASE and 2 first-class stamps. All imprints included in a single catalog. Catalog available on website.

**Tips** "We specialize in materials relating to the Middle East and Muslim-oriented culture such as stories, learning materials and such. These are the only types of items we currently are publishing."

## Ⓝ AMULET BOOKS

Abrams Books for Young Readers, 115 W. 18th St., New York NY 10001. (212)229-8000. Website: www.abramsbooks.com. Estab. 2004. Specializes in trade books, fiction. **Manuscript Acquisitions:** Susan Van Metre, senior editor. **Art Acquisitions:** Becky Terhune, art director. Produces 4 middle readers/year, 4 young adult titles/year. 10% of books by first-time authors.

**Fiction** Middle readers: adventure, contemporary, fantasy, history, science fiction, sports. Young adults/teens: adventure, contemporary, fantasy, history, science fiction, sports, suspense. Recently published *The Boy Who Couldn't Die*, by William Sleator (YA novel); *ttyl*, by Lauren Miracle (YA novel); *The Golden Hour*, by Maiya Williams (middle grade novel).

**How to Contact/Writers** Fiction: Query. Responds to queries in 2-3 months. Publishes book 18-24 months after acceptance. Considers simultaneous submissions.

**Illustration** Works with 6-8 illustrators/year. Uses both color and b&w. Query with samples. Contact: Becky Terhune, art director. Samples filed.

**Photography** Buys stock images and assigns work.

**Terms** Offers advance against royalties. Illustrators paid by the project . Author sees galleys for review. Illustrators see dummies for review. Originals returned to artist at job's completion. Catalog available for $9 \times 12$ SASE and 4 first-class stamps.

## ☒ ATHENEUM BOOKS FOR YOUNG READERS

1230 Avenue of the Americas, New York NY 10020. (212)698-2715. Website: www.simonsayskids.com. Book publisher. Vice President and Editorial Director: Emma Dryden. Estab. 1960. **Manuscript Acquisitions:** Send queries with SASE to: Ginee Seo, editorial director, Ginee Seo Books; Hilary Goddman, assistant to Richard Jackson, editorial director of Richard Jackson Books; Caitlyn Dlouhy, executive editor. "All editors consider all types of projects." **Art Acquisitions:** Ann Bobco. Imprint of Simon & Schuster Children's Publishing Division. Publishes 20-30 picture books/year; 4-5 young readers/year; 20-25 middle readers/year; 10-15 young adults/year. 10% of books by first-time authors; 50% from agented writers. "Atheneum publishes original hardcover trade books for children from pre-school age through young adult. Our list includes picture books, chapter books, mysteries, biography, science fiction, fantasy, graphic novels, middle grade and young adult fiction and nonfiction. The style and subject matter of the books we publish is almost unlimited. We do not, however, publish textbooks, coloring or activity books, greeting cards, magazines or pamphlets or religious publications. The lists of Charles Scribner's Sons Books for Young Readers have been folded into the Atheneum program."

- Atheneum does not accept unsolicited manuscripts. Send query letter only. Atheneum title *Kira-Kira*, by Cynthia Kadohata, won the 2005 Newbery Medal.

**How to Contact/Writers** Send query letter and 3 sample chapters. Responds to queries in 1 month; requested mss in 3 months. Publishes a book 18-24 months after acceptance. Will consider simultaneous queries from previously unpublished authors and those submitted to other publishers, "though we request that the author let us know it is a simultaneous query." Please do not call to query or follow up.

**Illustration** Works with 40-50 illustrators/year. Send art samples résumé, tearsheets to Ann Bobco, Design Dept. 4th Floor, 1230 Avenue of the Americas, New York NY 10020. Samples filed. Responds to art samples only if interested.

**Terms** Pays authors in royalties of 8-10% based on retail price. Pays illustrators royalty of 5-6% or by the project. Pays photographers by the project. Sends galleys and proofs to authors; proofs to illustrators. Original artwork returned at job's completion. Manuscript guidelines for #10 SAE and 1 first-class stamp.

**Tips** "Atheneum has a 40+ year tradition of publishing distinguished books for children. Study our titles."

## AVISSON PRESS, INC.

3007 Taliaferro Rd., Greensboro NC 27408. (336)288-6989. Fax: (336)288-6989. **Manuscript Acquisitions:** Martin Hester, publisher. Publishes 5-7 young adult titles/year. 70% of books by first-time authors.

**Nonfiction** Young adults: biography. Average word length: young adults—25,000. Recently published *I Can Do Anything: The Sammy Davis, Jr. Story*, by William Schoell (ages 12-18, young adult biography); *The Girl He Left Behind: The Life and Times of Libbie Custer*, by Suzanne Middendorf Arruda (ages 12-18, young adult biography); *Randolph Caldecott: An Illustrated Life*, by Claudette Hagel.

**How to Contact/Writers** Accepts material from residents of U.S. only. Nonfiction: Submit outline/synopsis and 2 sample chapters. Responds to queries/mss in 3 weeks. Publishes a book 9-12 months after acceptance. Will consider simultaneous submissions.

**Terms** Pays author royalty of 8-10% based on wholesale price. Offers advances (average amount: $400). Sends galleys to authors. Book catalog available for #10 SAE and 1 first-class stamp; ms guidelines available for SASE.

**Tips** "We publish *only* YA biographies. All artwork is done in-house."

## Ⓐ AVON BOOKS/BOOKS FOR YOUNG READERS

1350 Avenue of the Americas, New York NY 10019. (212)261-6500. Fax: (212)261-6668. E-mail: books@harperchildrens.com. Website: www.harperchildrens.com.

- Avon is not accepting unagented submissions. See listing for HarperCollins Children's Books.

## ☒ AZRO PRESS

PMB 342, 1704 Llano St. B, Santa Fe NM 87505. (505)989-3272. Fax: (505)989-3832. E-mail: azropress@qwest.com. Website: www.azropress.com. Estab. 1997. Specializes in trade books, fiction. **Writers contact:** Gae Zisenhardt. Produces 3-4 picture books/year; 1 young reader/year. 75% of books by first-time authors. "We like to publish illustrated children's books by Southwestern authors and illustrators. We are always looking for books with a Southwestern look or theme."

**Fiction** Picture books: animal, history, humor, nature/environment. Young readers: adventure, animal, hi-lo, history, humor. Average word length: picture books—1,200; young readers—2,000-2,500. Recently published *Lucy's Journey to the Wild West*, by Charlotte Piepmeier, illustrated by Sally Blakemore (ages 5-9, geography); *Grow Grow Grow*, by Barbara Riley, illustrated by Janet Guggenheim (ages 2-4, fiction); *Who Will Save Mr. Squeaky?*, written and illustrated by Terry Avery (ages 3-6, animals).

**Nonfiction** Picture books: animal, geography, history. Young readers: geography, hi-lo, history.

**How to Contact/Writers** Accepts international submissions. Fiction/nonfiction: Query or submit complete ms. Responds to queries/mss in 3-4 months. Publishes book 1½-2 years after acceptance. Considers simultaneous submissions.

**Illustration** Accepts material from international illustrators. Works with 3 illustrators/year. Uses color artwork only. Reviews ms/illustration packages. Reviews work for future assignments. Query with samples. Submit samples to illustrations editor. Responds in 3-4 months. Samples not returned. Samples not filed.

**Terms** Pays authors royalty of 10% based on wholesale price. Pays illustrators by the project ($2,000) or royalty of 5%. Author sees galleys for review. Illustrators see dummies for review. Originals returned to artist at job's completion. Catalog available for #10 SASE and 3 first-class stamps. Offers writer's guidelines for SASE. See website for artist's, photographer's guidelines.

**Tips** "We are not currently accepting new manuscripts. Please see our website for acceptance date."

## ☐ BALLYHOO BOOKWORKS INC.

P.O. Box 534, Shoreham NY 11792. E-mail: ballyhoo@optonline.net. **Acquisitions:** Liam Gerrity, editorial director. Publishes 2 picture books/year; 1 young reader/year. 30% of books by first-time authors. "We are a small press, but highly selective and want texts that flow from the tongue with clarity and are infused with the author's passion for the piece."

• Ballyhoo is not accepting new manuscripts until Spring 2006 due to a full schedule and an overwhelming increase in unsolicited submissions.

**Fiction** Young readers: animal, nature/environment. Average word length: picture books—up to 500; young readers—up to 1,000. Recently published *The Alley Cat* and *The Barnyard Cat*, by Brian J. Heinz, illustrated by June H. Blair (ages 5-9, picture books).

**Nonfiction** Picture books: arts/crafts, how-to. Young readers, middle readers: activity books, arts/crafts, hobbies, how-to. Average word length: picture books—up to 500; young readers—up to 1,000; middle readers—up to 10,000. Recently published *Metal Detecting for Treasure*, by Dorothy B. Francis (ages 10 and up, how-to).

**How to Contact/Writers** Accepts material from residents of U.S. only. Fiction/nonfiction: Query or submit outline/synopsis or outline/synopsis and 2 sample chapters. Responds to queries in 1 month; mss in 2 months. Publishes book 12-18 months after acceptance. Will consider simultaneous submissions.

**Illustration** Accepts material from residents of U.S. only. Works with 2-3 illustrators/year. Reviews ms/illustration packages from artists. Query or send ms with dummy. Contact: Editorial Director. Illustrations only: Send résumé, promo sheet and tearsheets. "We file all samples for future reference."

**Terms** Pays authors royalty of 5% based on retail price. Offers advances (average amount: $1,000-2,500). Pays illustrators 5% based on retail price. Sends galleys to authors. Originals returned to artist at job's completion. Manuscript guidelines available for SASE.

**Tips** "We don't see any value in trends, only in good writing."

## ☐ BANCROFT PRESS

P.O. Box 65360, Baltimore MD 21209. (410)358-0658. Fax: (410)637-7377. E-mail: bruceb@bancroftpress.com. Website: www.bancroftpress.com. **Manuscript Acquisitions:** Bruce Bortz, publisher. **Art Acquisitions:** Bruce Bortz, publisher. Publishes 1 middle reader/year; 2-4 young adult titles/year.

**Fiction** Middle readers, young adults: adventure, animal, contemporary, fantasy, humor, multicultural, problem novels, religion, science fiction, special needs, sports, suspense/mystery. Average word length: middle readers—40,000; young adults—50,000. Recently published *Finding the Forger: A Bianca Balducci Mystery*, by Libby Sternberg (ages 10 and up); *The Reappearance of Sam Webber*, by Jonathon Scott Fuqua (ages 10 and up) ; *Jake: The Second Novel in the Gunpowder Trilogy*, by Arch Montgomery (ages 13 and up); *Like We Care*, by Tom Matthews (ages 15 and up).

**Nonfiction** Middle readers, young adults: animal, biography, concept, health, history, multicultural, music/dance, nature/environment, reference, religion, science, self help, social issues, special needs, sports, textbooks.

**How to Contact/Writers** Fiction/nonfiction: Submit complete ms or submit outline/synopsis and 3 sample chapters. Responds to queries/mss in at least 6 months. Publishes book 18 months after acceptance. Will consider e-mail submissions, simultaneous submissions or previously published work.

**Terms** Pays authors royalty of 8% based on retail price. Offers advances (average amount: $1,000-3,000). Sends galleys to authors. Catalog and ms guidelines available on website.

**Tips** "We advise writers to visit our website and to be familiar with our previous work. Patience is the number one attribute contributors must have. It takes us a very long time to get through submitted material, because we are such a small company. Also, we only publish 4-6 books per year, so it may take a long time for your optioned book to be published. We like to be able to market our books to be used in schools and in libraries. We prefer fiction that bucks trends and moves in a new direction.We are especially interested in mysteries and humor (especially humorous mysteries)."

## Ⓐ BANTAM BOOKS FOR YOUNG READERS
Imprint of Random House Children's Book, Division of Random House, Inc., 1745 Broadway, New York NY 10019. (212)782-9000. Website: www.randomhouse.com/kids. Book publisher.
• See listings for Random House/Golden Books for Young Readers Group, Delacorte and Doubleday Books for Young Readers, Alfred A. Knopf and Crown Books for Young Readers, and Wendy Lamb Books.
**How to Contact/Writers** Not seeking mss at this time.
**Illustration** Contact: Isabel Warren-Lynch, executive director, art & design. Responds only if interested. Samples returned with SASE; samples filed.
**Terms** Pays illustrators and photographers by the project or royalties. Original artwork returned at job's completion.

## BAREFOOT BOOKS
2067 Massachusetts Ave., 5th Floor, Cambridge MA 02140. (617)576-0660. Website: www.barefootbooks.com. **Manuscript/Art Acquisitions:** U.S. editor. Publishes 35 picture books/year; 10 anthologies/year. 35% of books by first-time authors. "The Barefoot child represents the person who is in harmony with the natural world and moves freely across boundaries of many kinds. Barefoot Books explores this image with a range of high-quality picture books for children of all ages. We work with artists, writers and storytellers from many cultures, focusing on themes that encourage independence of spirit, promote understanding and acceptance of different traditions, and foster a life-long love of learning."
**Fiction** Picture books, young readers: animal, anthology, concept, fantasy, folktales, multicultural, nature/environment, poetry, spirituality. Middle readers, young adults: anthology, folktales. Average word length: picture books—500-1,000; young readers—2,000-3,000; anthologies—10,000-20,000. Recently published *We All Went on Safari*, by Laurie Krebs, illustrated by Julia Cairns (ages 3-7, picture book); *Thesaurus Rex*, by Laya Steinberg, illustrated by Debbie Harter (ages 2-6, concept book); *Goddesses: A World of Myth and Magic*, by Burleigh Muten, illustrated by Rebecca Guay (ages 7 to adult, anthology).
**How to Contact/Writers** Fiction: Submit complete ms for picture books; outline/synopsis and 1 sample story for collections. Responds in 4 months if SASE is included. Will consider simultaneous submissions and previously published work.
**Illustration** Works with 20 illustrators/year. Uses color artwork only. Reviews ms/illustration packages from artists. Send query and art samples or dummy for picture books. Illustrations only: Query with samples or send promo sheet and tearsheets. Responds only if interested. Samples returned with SASE.
**Terms** Pays authors royalty of 5% based on retail price. Offers advances. Sends galleys to authors. Originals returned to artist at job's completion. Book catalog available for 9×12 SAE and 5 first-class stamps; ms guidelines available for SASE. Catalog available on website.
**Tips** "We are looking for books that inspire and are filled with a sense of magic and wonder. We also look for strong stories from all different cultures, reflecting the ways of the individual culture while also touching deeper human truths that suggest we are all one. We welcome playful submissions for the very youngest children and also anthologies of stories for older readers, all focused around a universal theme. We encourage writers and artists to visit our website and read some of our books to get a sense of our editorial philosophy and what we publish before they submit to us. Always, we encourage them to stay true to their inner voice and artistic vision that reaches out for timeless stories, beyond the momentary trends that may exist in the market today."

## Ⓒ BARRONS EDUCATIONAL SERIES
250 Wireless Blvd., Hauppauge NY 11788. (800)645-3476, ext. 259. Fax: (631)434-3723. E-mail: waynebarr@bar ronseduc.com. Website: www.barronseduc.com. **Manuscript Acquisitions:** Wayne R. Barr, acquisitions manager. **Art Acquisitions:** Mary Ellen Owens. Publishes 20 picture books/year; 20 young readers/year; 20 middle readers/year; 10 young adult titles/year. 25% of books by first-time authors; 25% of books from agented writers.
**Fiction** Picture books: animal, concept, multicultural, nature/environment. Young readers: adventure, multicultural, nature/environment, fantasy, suspense/mystery. Middle readers: adventure, fantasy, multicultural, nature/environment, problem novels, suspense/mystery. Young adults: problem novels. Recently published *Everyday Witch*, by Sandra Forrester; *Word Wizardry* by Margaret and William Kenda.
**Nonfiction** Picture books: concept, reference. Young readers: how-to, reference, self help, social issues. Middle

readers: hi-lo, how-to, reference, self help, social issues. Young adults: biography, how-to, reference, self help, social issues, sports.

**How to Contact/Writers** Fiction: Query via e-mail. Nonfiction: Submit outline/synopsis and sample chapters. "Submissions must be accompanied by SASE for response." Responds to queries in 2 months; mss in 4 months. Publishes a book 1 year after acceptance. Will consider simultaneous submissions.

**Illustration** Works with 20 illustrators/year. Reviews ms/illustration packages from artists. Query first; 3 chapters of ms with 1 piece of final art, remainder roughs. Illustrations only: Submit tearsheets or slides plus résumé. Responds in 2 months.

**Terms** Pays authors royalty of 10-14% based on net price or buys ms outright for $2,000 minimum. Pays illustrators by the project based on retail price. Sends galleys to authors; dummies to illustrators. Book catalog, ms/artist's guidelines for 9 × 12 SAE.

**Tips** Writers: "We publish preschool storybooks, concept books and middle grade and YA chapter books. No romance novels." Illustrators: "We are happy to receive a sample illustration to keep on file for future consideration. Periodic notes reminding us of your work are acceptable." Children's book themes "are becoming much more contemporary and relevant to a child's day-to-day activities, fewer talking animals. We have a great interest in children's fiction (ages 7-11 and ages 12-16) with New Age topics."

## ⬤ BEBOP BOOKS

Imprint of Lee & Low Books Inc., 95 Madison Ave., New York NY 10016-7801. (212)779-4400. Website: www.bebopbooks.com. **Acquisitions:** Jennifer Fox. **Executive Editor:** Louise May. Publishes 10-15 educational market picture books/year. Many books by first-time authors. "Our goal is to publish child-centered stories that support literacy learning and provide multicultural content for children just beginning to learn to read. We make a special effort to work with writers and illustrators of diverse backgrounds. Current needs are posted on website."

● Bebop Books acquires manuscripts between August and October only. See website for details.

**Fiction** Picture books: adventure, concept, contemporary, hi-lo, multicultural, nature/environment, sports, culturally specific topics for young children.

**Nonfiction** Picture books: arts/crafts, careers, concept, cooking, hi-lo, hobbies, how-to, multicultural, music/dance, nature/environment, social issues, sports.

**How to Contact/Writers** Fiction/nonfiction: Submit complete ms. Responds to mss in up to 4 months; submit between August and October only. "See website for specific guidelines during this period. We will not respond to manuscripts received when our call for manuscripts is not open."

**Illustration** Works with 5-10 illustrators/year. Uses color artwork only. Illustrations and photographs: Query with color samples and send client list or cover letter. Responds only if interested. Samples returned with SASE; samples filed. "We are especially interested in submissions from artists of color, and we encourage artists new to the field of children's books to send us samples of their work."

**Terms** Pays authors royalty. Offers advances. Pays illustrators and photographers royalty and advance. Book catalog available for 9 × 12 SAE and 89¢ postage, attn: Catalog Request. Catalog available on website.

**Tips** "Bebop Books is currently specializing in emergent and beginning readers with multicultural themes. Often called 'little books,' they are used to help young children develop early reading skills and strategies. Each book is a small paperback, with full color illustrations and a story specifically written and illustrated to support beginning readers."

## BEHRMAN HOUSE INC.

11 Edison Place, Springfield NJ 07081. (973)379-7200. Fax: (973)379-7280. Website: www.behrmanhouse.com. **Managing Editor:** Editorial Department. Publishes 3 young readers/year; 3 middle readers/year; 3 young adult titles/year. 12% of books by first-time authors; 2% of books from agented writers. Publishes books on all aspects of Judaism: history, cultural, textbooks, holidays. "Behrman House publishes quality books of Jewish content—history, Bible, philosophy, holidays, ethics—for children and adults."

**Fiction** All levels: Judaism.

**Nonfiction** All levels: Judaism, Jewish educational textbooks. Average word length: young reader—1,200; middle reader—2,000; young adult—4,000. Recently published *I Kid's Mensch Handbook*, by Scott E. Blumenthal; *Shalom Ivrit 3*, by Nili Ziv.

**How to Contact/Writers** Fiction/nonfiction: Submit outline/synopsis and sample chapters. Responds to queries in 1 month; mss in 2 months. Publishes a book 2½ years after acceptance. Will consider simultaneous submissions.

**Illustration** Works with 6 children's illustrators/year. Reviews ms/illustration packages from artists. "Query first." Illustrations only: Query with samples; send unsolicited art samples by mail. Responds to queries in 1 month; mss in 2 months.

**Photography** Purchases photos from freelancers. Buys stock and assigns work. Uses photos of families involved in Jewish activities. Uses color and b&w prints. Photographers should query with samples. Send unsolicited photos by mail. Submit portfolio for review.

**Terms** Pays authors royalty of 3-10% based on retail price or buys ms outright for $1,000-5,000. Offers advance. Pays illustrators by the project (range: $500-5,000). Sends galleys to authors; dummies to illustrators. Book catalog free on request.

**Tips** Looking for "religious school texts" with Judaic themes or general trade Judaica.

## BENCHMARK BOOKS

Imprint of Marshall Cavendish, 99 White Plains Rd., Tarrytown NY 10591. (914)332-8888. Fax: (914)332-1888. E-mail: mbisson@marshallcavendish.com. Website: www.marshallcavendish.com. **Manuscript Acquisitions:** Michelle Bisson and Joyce Stanton. Publishes more than 100 young reader, middle reader and young adult books/year. "We look for interesting treatments of primarily nonfiction subjects related to elementary, middle school and high school curriculum."

**Nonfiction** Most nonfiction topics should be curriculum related. Average word length: 4,000-20,000. All books published as part of a series. Recently published *Life in the Middle Ages* (series), *The City, The Countryside, The Church, The Castle,* by Kathryn Hinds; *Lifeways: The Abache, The Cheyenne, The Haida, The Huron,* by Raymond Bial.

**How to Contact/Writers** Nonfiction: Submit complete ms or submit outline/synopsis and 1 or more sample chapters. Responds to queries/mss in 3 months. Publishes a book 2 years after acceptance. Will consider simultaneous submissions.

**Photography** Buys stock and assigns work.

**Terms** Pays authors royalty based on retail price or buys work outright. Offers advances. Sends galleys to authors. Book catalog available. All imprints included in a single catalog.

## THE BENEFACTORY

P.O. Box 128, Cohasset MA 02025. (781)383-8027. Fax: (781)383-8026. Website: www.readplay.com. **Manuscript/Art Acquisitions:** Cindy Germain, director, creative services. Publishes 6-12 picture books/year with the Humane Society of the United States; 6-12 picture books/year with Doris Day Animal Foundation. 50% of books by first-time authors. The Benefactory publishes "classic" true stories about real animals, through licenses with the Humane Society of the United States and Doris Day Animal Foundation. Each title is accompanied by a read-along audiocassette and a plush animal. A percentage of revenues benefits the licensor. Target age for DDAF titles: 4-7; for HSUS titles: 5-10.

**Nonfiction** Picture books: nature/environment; young readers: animal, nature/environment. Average word length: HSUS titles—1,200-1,500; DDAF titles—700-800. Recently published *Chessie, the Travelin' Man,* written by Randy Houk, illustrated by Paula Bartlett (ages 5-10, picture book); *Condor Magic,* written by Lyn Littlefield Hoopes, illustrated by Peter C. Stone (ages 5-10, picture book); *Caesar: On Deaf Ears,* written by Loren Spiotta-DiMare, illustrated by Kara Lee (ages 5-10, picture book).

**How to Contact/Writers** Query only—does not accept unsolicited mss. Responds to queries in 6 weeks. Publishes a book 1 year after acceptance. Will consider simultaneous submissions. Send SASE for writer's guidelines.

**Illustration** Works with 6-8 illustrators/year. Uses color artwork only. Reviews ms/illustration packages from artists. Query or send ms with dummy. Illustrations only: Send résumé, promo sheet and tearsheets to be kept on file. Responds in 6 months. Samples returned with SASE; samples filed. Send SASE for artist guidelines.

**Terms** Pays authors royalty of 3-5% based on wholesale price. Offers advances (average amount: $5,000). Pays illustrators royalty of 3-5% based on wholesale price. Sends galleys to authors; dummies to illustrators. Originals returned to artist at job's completion. Book catalog available for 8½×11 SASE; ms and art guidelines available for SASE.

## BESS PRESS

3565 Harding Ave., Honolulu HI 96816. (808)734-7159. Fax: (808)732-3627. E-mail: editor@besspress.com. Website: www.besspress.com. **Acquisitions Editor:** Reve Shapard. Publishes 3 picture books/year; 3 young readers/year; 1 middle reader/year. 5% of books by first-time authors. "We publish trade and educational books about Hawaii and Micronesia only. The perspective should be that of a resident, not a visitor."

**Fiction** Picture books: Hawaii. Average word length: picture books—600. Recently published *Hina and the Sea of Stars,* by Michael Nordenstrom (ages 5-8, picture book); *The Story of Hula,* by Carla Golembe (ages 5-8, picture book); *Waltah Melon: Local Kine Hero,* by Carmen Geshell and Jeff Pagay (ages 5-8, picture book).

**Nonfiction** Picture books, young readers, middle readers: Hawaii. Average word length: coloring books—1,200. Recently published *Dangerous Sea Creatures of Hawaii A to Z Coloring Book,* by Terry Pierce and Kristen Kofsky (ages 6-10, coloring book).

**How to Contact/Writers** Fiction/nonfiction: Submit complete ms. Responds to queries in 2-3 weeks; mss in 4-

6 weeks. Publishes book 1 year after acceptance. Will consider e-mail submissions, simultaneous submissions, and previously published work.

**Illustration** Works with 2-3 illustrators/year. Reviews ms/illustration packages from artists. "We prefer to use illustrators and photographers living in the region. We do not encourage samples from freelancers outside the region." Query. Contact: Reve Shapard, editor. Illustrations only: Query. Responds only if interested. Samples returned with SASE; samples filed.

**Photography** Works on assignment only. Uses Hawaii-Pacific photos only. Model/property releases required. Uses color and various size prints and transparencies. Submit cover letter.

**Terms** Pays authors royalty of 4-10% based on wholesale price or work purchased outright from authors for $250. Offers advances (average amount: $1,000). Pays illustrators by the project ($1,000) or royalty of 4-6% based on wholesale price. Pays photographers by the project ($500). Sends galleys to authors; dummies to illustrators. Originals returned to artist at job's completion. Book catalog available for SASE; ms guidelines available for SAE. All imprints included in a single catalog. Catalog available on website.

**Tips** "As a regional publisher, we are looking for material specific to the region (Hawaii and Micronesia), preferably from writers and illustrators living within (or very familiar with) the region."

## BETHANY HOUSE PUBLISHERS

11400 Hampshire Ave. S., Minneapolis MN 55438-2852. (952)829-2500. Fax: (952)829-2768. Website: www.bethanyhouse.com. **Manuscript Acquisitions:** Youth Department. **Art Acquisitions:** Paul Higdon. Publishes 10 middle-grade readers/year; 8 young adult titles/year. "Bethany House Publishers is an evangelical Christian publisher seeking to publish imaginative, excellent books that reflect an evangelical worldview without being preachy." Publishes picture books under Bethany Backyard imprint.

**Fiction** Children's and young adult fiction list is full.

**Nonfiction** Young readers, middle readers, young adults: religion/devotional, self-help, social issues. Recently published *God Called a Girl*, by Shannon Kubiak (young teen); *Total Devotion: A Growing-Up Guide*, by Sandra Byrd (middle readers).

**How to Contact/Writers** Considers unsolicited 1-page queries sent by fax only. "Bethany House no longer accepts unsolicited manuscripts or book proposals." Responds in 4 months. Publishes a book 12-18 months after acceptance.

**Illustration** Works with 5 illustrators/year. Reviews illustration samples from artists. Illustrations only: Query with samples. Responds in 2 months. Samples returned with SASE.

**Terms** Pays authors royalty based on net sales. Pays illustrators by the project. Pays photographers by the project. Sends galleys to authors. Book catalog available for 11 × 14 SAE and 5 first-class stamps. Write "Catalog Request" on outside of envelope.

**Tips** "Research the market, know what is already out there. Study our catalog before submitting material. We look for an evangelical message woven delicately into a strong plot and topics that seek to broaden the reader's experience and perspective."

## BEYOND WORDS PUBLISHING, INC.

20827 N.W. Cornell Rd., Hillsboro OR 97124-1808. (503)531-8700. Fax: (503)531-8773. E-mail: info@beyondword.com. Website: www.beyondword.com. **Acquisitions:** Summer Steele, managing editor children's division. Publishes 2-3 picture books/year; 1-2 nonfiction teen books/year. 50% of books by first-time authors. "Our company mission statement is 'Inspire to Integrity,' so it's crucial that your story inspires children in some way. Our books are high quality, gorgeously illustrated, meant to be enjoyed as a child and throughout life."

**Fiction** Picture books: contemporary, feminist, folktales, history, multicultural, nature/environment. "We are looking for authors/illustrators; stories that will appeal and inspire." Average length: picture books—32 pages. Recently published *Our Community Gardner*, written and illustrated by Barbara Pollack.

**Nonfiction** Picture books, young readers: advice, biography, history, multicultural, nature/environment. Recently published *Girls Know Best* (compilation of 38 teen girls' writing—ages 7-15); *So, You Wanna Be a Writer?* (ages 9-16, advice/career).

**How to Contact/Writers** Submit complete ms. Responds to queries/mss in 6 months. Will consider simultaneous submissions and previously published work.

**Illustration** Works with 4-6 illustrators/year. Reviews ms/illustration packages from artists. Submit ms with 2-3 pieces of final art. Illustrations only: Send résumé, promo sheet, "samples—no originals!" Responds in 6 months only if interested. Samples returned with SASE; samples filed.

**Photography** Works on assignment only.

**Terms** Sends galleys to authors; dummies to illustrators. Manuscript and artist's guidelines for SASE or available on website.

**Tips** "Please research the books we have previously published. This will give you a good idea if your proposal fits with our company."

Book Publishers

## BICK PUBLISHING HOUSE

307 Neck Rd., Madison CT 06443. (203)245-0073. Fax: (203)245-5990. E-mail: bickpubhse@aol.com. Website: www.bickpubhouse.com. **Aquisitions Editor:** Dale Carlson. "We publish psychological, philosophical, scientific information on health and recovery, wildlife rehabiliation, living with disabilities, teen psychology and science for adults and young adults."

**Nonfiction** Young adults: nature/environment, religion, science, self help, social issues, special needs. Average word length: young adults—60,000. Recently published *In and Out of Your Mind* (teen science); *Who Said What?* (philosophy quotes for teens), *What are You Doing with Your Life?*, by Krish Namurti (philosophy for teens).

**How to Contact/Writers** Fiction: Submit outline/synopsis and 3 sample chapters. Nonfiction: Submit outline/synopsis or outline/synopsis and 3 sample chapters. Responds to queries/mss in 2 weeks. Publishes book 1 year after acceptance. Will consider simultaneous submissions and previously published work.

**Illustration** Works with 1 illustrator/year. Uses b&w artwork only. Reviews ms/illustration packages from artists. Submit sketches of teens or science drawings. Contact: Dale Carlson, president. Illustrations only: Query with photocopies, résumé, SASE. Responds in 2 weeks. Samples returned with SASE.

**Terms** Pays authors royalty of 5-10%. Pays illustrators by the project (range: up to $1,000). Sends galleys to authors; dummies to illustrators. Book catalog available for SASE with 1 first-class stamp; writer's guidelines available for SAE. Catalog available on website.

**Tips** "Read our books!"

## BIRDSONG BOOKS

1322 Bayview Rd., Middletown DE 19709. (302)378-7274. E-mail: BirdsongBooks@Delaware.net. Website: www.BirdsongBooks.com. **Manuscript & Art Acquisitions:** Nancy Carol Willis, president. Publishes 1 picture book/year. "Birdsong Books seeks to spark the delight of discovering our wild neighbors and natural habitats. We believe knowledge and understanding of nature fosters caring and a desire to protect the Earth and all living things."

**Nonfiction** Picture books, young readers: activity books, animal, nature/environment. Average word length: picture books—800-1,000. Recently published *Raccoon Moon*, by Nancy Carol Willis (ages 5-8, natural science picture book); *The Robins In Your Backyard*, by Nancy Carol Willis (ages 4-7, nonfiction picture book).

**How to Contact/Writers** Nonfiction: Submit complete ms. Responds to mss in 3 months. Publishes book 3 years after acceptance. Will consider simultaneous submissions (if stated).

**Illustration** Accepts material from residents of U.S. Works with 1 illustrator/year. Reviews ms/illustration packages from artists. Send ms with dummy (plus samples/tearsheets for style). Illustrations only: Query with brochure, résumé, samples, SASE, or tearsheets. Responds only if interested. Samples returned with SASE.

**Photography** Uses North American animals and habitats (currently shorebirds and horseshoe crabs). Submit cover letter, résumé, promo piece, stock photo list.

**Tips** "We are a small independent press that is only interested in nonfiction, natural science picture books or educational activity books about North American animals and habitats. Our books include back matter suitable for early elementary classrooms. Mailed submissions with SASE only. No e-mail submissions or phone calls, please. Cover letters should sell author/illustrator and book idea."

## BLOOMSBURY CHILDRENS BOOKS

Imprint of Bloomsbury PLC, 175 Fifth Avenue, Suite 315, New York NY 10010. (646)307-5858. Fax: (212)982-2837. E-mail: bloomsburykids@bloomsburyusa.co. Website: www.bloomsbury.com/usa. Specializes in fiction, picture books. Publishes 20 picture books/year; 5 young readers/year; 10 middle readers/year; 15 young adult titles/year. 25% of books by first-time authors.

**Fiction** Picture books: adventure, animal, contemporary, fantasy, folktales, history, humor, multicultural, poetry, suspense/mystery. Young readers: adventure, animal, anthology, concept, contemporary, fantasy, folktales, history, humor, multicultural, suspense/mystery. Middle readers: adventure, animal, contemporary, fantasy, folktales, history, humor, multicultural, poetry, problem novels. Young adults: adventure, animal, anthology, contemporary, fantasy, folktales, history, humor, multicultural, problem novels, science fiction, sports, suspense/mystery. Recently published *Where is Coco Going?*, by Sloone Tanen (picture books); *Once Upon a Curse*, by E.D. Baker (middle reader); *Enna Burning*, by Shannon Hale (young adult fantasy).

**How to Contact/Writers** Submit synopsis and first 3 chapters with SASE. Responds to queries/mss in 6 months.

**Illustration** Works with 15 illustrators/year. Reviews ms/illustration packages from artists. Query or submit ms with dummy. Illustrations only: Query with samples. Responds only if interested. Samples returned with SASE; samples filed.

**Photography** Buys stock and assigns work. Uses color or b&w prints. Submit SASE.

**Terms** Pays authors royalty or work purchased outright for jackets. Offers advances. Pays illustrators by the project or royalty. Pays photographers by the project or per photo. Sends galleys to authors; dummies to illustrators. Originals returned to artist at job's completion. Writer's and art guidelines available for SASE. Catalog available on website.

**Tips** "Spend a lot of time in the bookstore and library to keep up on trends in market. Always send appropriate SASE to ensure response. Never send originals."

## BLUE SKY PRESS

557 Broadway, New York NY 10012-3999. (212)343-6100. Fax: (212)343-4713. Website: www.scholastic.com. **Acquisitions:** Bonnie Verburg. Publishes 15-20 titles/year. 1% of books by first-time authors. Publishes hardcover children's fiction and nonfiction including high-quality novels and picture books by new and established authors.

 • Blue Sky is currently not accepting unsolicited submissions due to a large backlog of books.

**Fiction** Picture books: adventure, animal, concept, contemporary, fantasy, folktales, history, humor, multicultural, nature/environment, poetry. Young readers: adventure, contemporary, fantasy, folktales, history, humor, multicultural, nature/environment, poetry. Young adults: adventure, anthology, contemporary, fantasy, history, humor, multicultural, poetry. Multicultural needs include "strong fictional or themes featuring non-white characters and cultures." Does not want to see mainstream religious, bibliotherapeutic, adult. Average length: picture books—varies; young adults—150 pages. Recently published *To Every Thing There Is a Season*, illustrated by Leo and Diane Dillon (all ages, picture book); *Bluish*, by Virginia Hamilton; *No, David!*, by David Shannon; *The Adventures of Captain Underpants*, by Dav Pilkey; *How Do Dinosaurs Say Good Night?*, by Jane Yolen, illustrated by Mark Teague.

**How to Contact/Writers** "Due to large numbers of submissions, we are discouraging unsolicited submissions—send query with SASE only if you feel certain we publish the type of book you have written." Fiction: Query (novels, picture books). Responds to queries in 6 months. Publishes a book 1-3 years after acceptance; depending on chosen illustrator's schedule. Will not consider simultaneous submissions. No electronic submissions or faxes.

**Illustration** Works with 10 illustrators/year. Reviews illustration packages "only if illustrator is the author." Submit ms with dummy. Illustrations only: Query with samples, tearsheets. Responds only if interested. Samples only returned with SASE. Original artwork returned at job's completion.

**Terms** Pays 10% royalty based on wholesale price split between author and illustrators. Advance varies.

**Tips** "Read currently published children's books. Revise—never send a first draft. Find your own voice, style, and subject. With material from new people we look for a theme or style strong enough to overcome the fact that the author/illustrator is unknown in the market."

## BOYDS MILLS PRESS

815 Church St., Honesdale PA 18431. (877)512-8366 or (570)253-1164. Fax: (570)253-0179. Website: www.boyd smillspress.com. Estab. 1990. **Manuscript Acquisitions:** J. DeLuca. Manuscript Coordinator. **Art Acquisitions:** Tim Gillner. 5% of books from agented writers. "We publish a wide range of quality children's books of literary merit, from preschool to young adult."

**Fiction** All levels: adventure, contemporary, history, humor, multicultural, poetry. Picture books: animal. Young readers, middle readers, young adult: problem novels, sports. Multicultural themes include any story showing a child as an integral part of a culture and which provides children with insight into a culture they otherwise might be unfamiliar with. "Please query us on the appropriateness of suggested topics for middle grade and young adult. For all other submissions send entire manuscript." Does not want to see talking animals, coming-of-age novels, romance and fantasy/science fiction.

**Nonfiction** All levels: nature/environment, science. Picture books, young readers, middle readers: animal, multicultural. Does not want to see reference/curricular text.

**How to Contact/Writers** Fiction/nonfiction: Submit complete ms or submit through agent. Query on middle reader, young adult and nonfiction. Responds to queries/mss in 1 month.

**Illustration** Works with 25 illustrators/year. Reviews ms/illustration packages from artists. Submit complete ms with 1 or 2 pieces of art. Illustrations only: Query with samples; send résumé and slides. Responds only if interested. Samples returned with SASE. Samples filed. Originals returned at job's completion.

**Photography** Assigns work.

**Terms** Authors paid royalty or work purchased outright. Offers advances. Illustrators paid by the project or royalties; varies. Photographers paid by the project, per photo, or royalties; varies. Manuscripts/artist's guidelines available for #10 SASE.

**Tips** "Picture books with fresh approaches, not worn themes, are our strongest need at this time. Check to see what's already on the market before submitting your story."

## ◘ BRIGHT RING PUBLISHING, INC.

P.O. Box 31338, Bellingham WA 98228. (360)398-9801. Fax: (360)383-0001. E-mail: maryann@brightring.com.

Website: www.brightring.com. **Acquisitions Editor:** MaryAnn Kohl. Publishes 1 young reader/year. Mission statement or editorial philosophy: ''to create fun, easy art ideas for kids and their parents.''

**Nonfiction** Young readers: arts/crafts, how-to (art). Average word length: young readers, middle readers—144 pages. Recently published *Storybook Art, Discovering Great Artists, Mudworks Bilingual*.

**How to Contact/Writers** Nonfiction: Query by e-mail. Responds to queries in 2 weeks; mss in 3 months. Publishes book 1 year after acceptance. Will consider e-mail submissions (query only). **No longer accepting unsolicited mss**.

**Illustration** Works with 1 illustrator/year. Uses b&w artwork only. Reviews ms/illustration packages from artists. Query by e-mail. Illustrations only: Query by e-mail or send postcard sample with brochure, photocopies, photographs, samples, SASE, tearsheets, URL. Responds in 1 week. Samples returned with SASE; samples filed.

**Terms** Work purchased outright from authors (range: $1,000-$3,000). Pays illustrators by the project (range: $1,000-$2,000). Sends galleys to authors; dummies to illustrators. Book catalog available for 8½×11 SASE with 60¢ postage; ms and art guidelines available for SASE. All imprints included in a single catalog. Catalog available on website. Manuscript guidelines also on website.

**Tips** ''We no longer pay by royalty—only authors who wish to collaborate with MaryAnn Kohl. Only art ideas for kids pre-K—age 12. No crafts or 'follow the steps'.'' Editorial staff attended or plans to attend the following conferences: NAEYC and BEA.

## BROADMAN & HOLMAN PUBLISHERS

LifeWay Christian Resources, 127 Ninth Ave. N., Nashville TN 37234-0115. Fax: (615)251-3752. Website: www. broadmanholman.com. **Contact:** Attn: Children's Area. Publishes 4-6 titles/year for ages 0-10. ''All books have Christian values/themes.''

**Nonfiction** Picture books: religion. Recently published *Word & Song Bible*, by Stephen Elkins, illustrated by Tim O'Conner; *LullaBible Series for Little Ones*, by Stephen Elkins, illustrated by Ellie Colton; *A Parable About the King*, by Beth Moore, illustrated by Beverly Wamen; *When the Creepy Things Come Out*, by Melody Carlson, illustrated by Susan Reagan.

**How to Contact/Writers Only interested in agented material.** Responds to queries/mss in 6-9 months. Publishes a book 1 year after acceptance.

**Illustration** Works with 3-4 illustrators/year. Samples returned with SASE; samples filed.

**Terms** Pays authors royalty of 10-18% based on wholesale price. Offers variable advance. Original artwork returned at job's completion. Book catalog available for 9×12 SAE and 2 first-class stamps. Manuscript guidelines available for SASE.

**Tips** ''We're looking for picture books with good family values; Bible story retellings; modern-day stories for children based on Bible themes and principles. Write us to ask for guidelines before submitting.''

## CALKINS CREEK BOOKS

Boyds Mills Press, 815 Church St., Honesdale PA 18431. (570)253-1164. Fax: (570)253-0179. E-mail: contact@bo ydsmillspress.com. Website: www.boydsmillspress.com. Estab. 2004. **Manuscripts Acquisitions:** Carolyn Yoder, editor. **Art Acquisitions:** Tim Gillner, art director. ''We aim to publish books that are a well-written blend of creative writing and extensive research which emphasize important events, people, and places in U.S. history.''

**Fiction** All levels: history. Recently published *Young Patriots*, by Marcella Fisher Anderson and Elizabeth Weiss Vollstadt (ages 10 and up, historical fiction); *Hour of Freedom*, by Milton Meltzer (ages 12 and up, American history in poetry).

**Nonfiction** All levels: history. Recently published *The President Is Shot*, by Harold Holzer (ages 8 and up, American history); *George Washington, the Writer*, edited by Carolyn P. Yoder (ages 8 and up, American history); *Dog of Discovery*, by Laurence Pringle (ages 8 and up, American history).

**How to Contact/Writers** Accepts international submissions. Fiction: Submit outline/synopsis and 3 sample chapters. Nonfiction: Submit outline/synopsis and 3 sample chapters. Considers simultaneous submissions.

**Illustration** Accepts material from international illustrators. Works with 25 (for all Boyds Mills Press imprints) illustrators/year. Uses both color and b&w. Reviews ms/illustration packages. For ms/illustration packages: Submit ms with 2 pieces of final art. Submit ms/illustration packages to Tim Gillner, art director. Reviews work for future assignments. If interested in illustrating future titles, query with samples. Submit samples to Tim Gillner, art director.

**Photography** Buys stock images and assigns work. Submit photos to: Tim Gillner, art director. Uses color or b&w 8×10 prints. For first contact, send promo piece (color or b&w).

**Terms** Authors paid royalty. Offers advance against royalties. Author sees galleys for review. Illustrators see dummies for review. Catalog available for 9×12 SASE with 6 first-class stamps. Offers writer's, artist's guidelines for SASE.

**Tips** ''Read through our recently-published titles and review our catalog. When selecting titles to publish, our emphasis will be on important events, people, and places in U.S. history. Writers are encouraged to submit a detailed bibliography, including secondary and primary sources, and expert reviews with their submissions."

## CANDLEWICK PRESS

2067 Massachusetts Ave., Cambridge MA 02140. (617)661-3330. Fax: (617)661-0565. E-mail: bigbear@candlewick.com. Website: www.candlewick.com. **Manuscript Acquisitions:** Karen Lotz , publisher; Liz Bicknell, editorial director; Mary Lee Donovan, executive editor; Kara LaReau, senior editor; Sarah Ketchersid, editor; Deborah Wayshak, editor. **Art Acquisitions:** Anne Moore. Publishes 160 picture books/year; 15 middle readers/year; 15 young adult titles/year. 5% of books by first-time authors. "Our books are truly for children, and we strive for the very highest standards in the writing, illustrating, designing and production of all of our books. And we are not averse to risk."
- Candlewick Press is not accepting queries and unsolicited manuscripts at this time. A movie was made of *Because of Winn-Dixie*, by Kate DiCamillo—The Newbery Honor book is now available in a movie tie-in edition.

**Fiction** Picture books: animal, concept, contemporary, fantasy, history, humor, multicultural, nature/environment, poetry. Middle readers, young adults: contemporary, fantasy, history, humor, multicultural, poetry, science fiction, sports, suspense/mystery. Recently published *The Earth, My Butt, and Other Big Round Things*, by Carolyn Mackler (young adult fiction); *Seeing the Blue Between*, edited by Paul B. Janeczko (young adult poetry collection); *Dragonlady*, by Ernest Drrake.

**Nonfiction** Picture books: concept, biography, geography, nature/environment. Young readers: biography, geography, nature/environment. Recently published *Top Secret : A Handbook of Codes, Ciphers, and Secret Writing*, by Paul B. Janeczko, illustrated by Jenna LaReau.

**Illustration** Works with approx. 40 illustrators/year. "We prefer to see a range of styles from artists along with samples showing strong characters (human or animals) in various settings with various emotions." Receives unsolicited illustration packages/dummies from artists. Color or b&w copies only, please; no originals. Illustrations only: Submit color samples to Art Resource Coordinator. Samples returned with SASE; samples filed.

**Terms** Pays authors royalty of 2½-10% based on retail price. Offers advances. Pays illustrators 2½-10% royalty based on retail price. Sends galleys to authors; dummies to illustrators. Pays photographers 2½-10% royalty. Original artwork returned at job's completion.

## CAPSTONE PRESS INC.

151 Good Counsel Dr., P.O. Box 669, Mankato MN 55438. Fax: (888)262-0705. Website: www.capstone-press.com. Book publisher. **Contact:** Helen Moore. Imprints: A+ Books, Bridgestone Books, Pebble Books, Blue Earth Books, Edge Books, Capstone High-Interest Books, Fact Finders, First Facts, Pebble Plus, Yellow Umbrella Books, Let Freedom Ring Books. "Capstone Press books provide new and struggling readers with a strong foundation on which to build reading success. Our nonfiction books are effective tools for reaching readers, with precisely-leveled text tailored to their individual needs."
- Capstone Press does not accept unsolicited manuscripts.

**Nonfiction** Publishes only nonfiction books. All levels: animals, arts/crafts, biography, geography, health, history, hobbies, science, and social studies.

**How to Contact/Writers** Does not accept submissions. Do not send mss. Instead, request author brochure with SASE, then send query letter, résumé, samples of nonfiction writing to be considered for assignment, and references

**Terms** Authors paid flat fee. Buys all rights. Book catalog available for large format SAE.

**Tips** "See website prior to sending query letter."

## CAROLRHODA BOOKS, INC.

Division of the Lerner Publishing Group, 241 First Ave. N., Minneapolis MN 55401. (612)332-3344 or (800)328-4929. Fax: (612)332-7615. E-mail: tdeslaurier@lernerbooks.com. Website: www.lernerbooks.com. **Manuscript Acquisitions:** Jennifer Zimian (nonfiction) and Zelda Wagner (fiction). Publishes 50-60 titles/year. 10% of books by first-time authors. "Carolrhoda Books is a children's publisher focused on producing high-quality, socially conscious nonfiction and fiction books for young readers K through grade 12, that help them learn about and explore the world around them." List includes picture books, biographies, nature and science titles, multicultural and introductory geography books and fiction for beginning readers.

**Fiction** Picture books, middle readers, young readers, young adult: "We like to see unique, honest stories that stay away from unoriginal plots, moralizing, and religious themes. We're also interested in seeing science fiction/fantasy for young readers."
- Carolrhoda only accepts submissions during the month of November. Also see listing for Lerner Publishing Group and Kar-Ben Publishing.

**Nonfiction** Picture books, young readers, middle readers: arts/crafts, biography, geography, history, nature/

environment, social issues, sports. Recently published *The War*, by Anais Vaugelade; *Little Wolf's Haunted Hall for Small Horrors*, by Ian Whybrow.

**How to Contact/Writers** Fiction: Submit complete ms for picture books, brief outline/synopsis and sample chapters not more than 50 pages for longer fiction. Nonfiction: Submit complete ms. Submissions are accepted in the months of November only. Submissions received in any other month will be returned unopened to the sender. A SASE is required for all submissions. Responds in 6-8 months.

**Terms** Pays authors royalty or purchases work outright.

**Tips** Carolrhoda does not publish alphabet books, puzzle books, songbooks, textbooks, workbooks, religious subject matter or plays. Address requests for guidelines to: GUIDELINE REQUEST with #10 SASE. Address requests for catalogs to CATALOG REQUEST and include 9×12 SAE with $3.85 postage.

## CARTWHEEL BOOKS, for the Very Young

Imprint of Scholastic Inc., 557 Broadway, New York NY 10012. (212)343-4425. Website: www.scholastic.com. Estab. 1991. Book publisher. Vice President/Editorial Director: Ken Geist. **Manuscript Acquisitions:** Grace Maccarone, executive editor; J. Elizabeth Mills, associate editor. **Art Acquisitions:** Stephen Hughs, art director; Keirsten Geise, associate art director. Publishes 25-30 picture books/year; 30-35 easy readers/year; 15-20 novelty/concept books/year. "With each Cartwheel list, we strive for a pleasing balance among board books and novelty books, hardcover picture books and gift books, nonfiction, paperback storybooks and easy readers. Cartwheel seeks to acquire novelties that are books first; play objects second. Even without its gimmick, a Cartwheel book should stand alone as a valid piece of children's literature. We want all our books to be inviting and appealing, and to have inherent educational and social value. We believe that small children who develop personal relationships with books and grow up with a love of reading, become book consumers, and ultimately better human beings."

**Fiction** Picture books, young readers: humor, suspense/mystery. Average work length: picture books—1-3,000; easy readers—100-3,000.

**Nonfiction** Picture books, young readers: animal, history, nature/environment, science, sports. "Most of our nonfiction is either written on assignment or is within a series. We do not want to see any arts/crafts or cooking." Average word length: picture books—100-3,000; young readers—100-3,000.

**How to Contact/Writers** Cartwheel Books is no longer accepting unsolicited mss. Query. All unsolicited materials will be returned unread. Fiction/nonfiction: For previously published or agented authors, submit complete ms. Responds to mss in 6 months. Publishes a book within 2 years after acceptance. SASE required with all submissions.

**Illustration** Works with 100 illustrators/year. Reviews ms/illustration packages from artists. Send ms with dummy. Illustrations only: Query with samples; arrange personal portfolio review; send promo sheet, tearsheets to be kept on file. Contact: Art Director. Responds in 2 months. Samples returned with SASE; samples filed. Please do not send original artwork.

**Photography** Buys stock and assigns work. Uses photos of kids, families, vehicles, toys, animals. Submit published samples, color promo piece.

**Terms** Pays advance against royalty or flat fee. Sends galley to authors; dummy to illustrators. Originals returned to artist at job's completion. Book catalog available for 9×12 SAE and 2 first-class stamps; ms guidelines for SASE.

**Tips** "Know what types of books we do. Check out bookstores or catalogs to see where your work would fit best."

## CAVENDISH CHILDREN'S BOOKS

Imprint of Marshal Cavendish, 99 White Plains Rd., Tarrytown NY 10591-9001. (914)332-8888. **Editorial Director:** Margery Cuyler. **Art Acquisitions:** Anahid Hamparian, art director. Publishes 20-25 books/year.

**Fiction/Nonfiction** All levels.

**How to Contact/Writers** Query nonfiction. Submit 3 chapters or more for fiction. No picture book submissions. Enclose SASE.

**Illustration** Contact: Art Director.

**Terms** Pays authors/illustrators advance and royalties.

## ☐ CHARLESBRIDGE

85 Main St., Watertown MA 02472. (617)926-0329. Fax: (617)926-5720. E-mail: tradeeditorial@charlesbridge.com. Website: www.charlesbridge.com. Estab. 1980. Book publisher. **Contact:** Trade Editorial Department, submissions editor or School Editorial Department. Publishes 60% nonfiction, 40% fiction picture books and early chapter books. Publishes nature, science, multicultural, social studies and fiction picture books. Charlesbridge also has an educational division.

**Fiction** Picture books and chapter books: "Strong, realistic stories with enduring themes." Considers the following categories: adventure, concept, contemporary, health, history, humor, multicultural, nature/environment, special needs, sports, suspense/mystery. Recently published *Picasso and Minou*, by P.I. Maltbie; *Fluffy: Scourge of the Sea*, by Teresa Bateman.

**Nonfiction** Picture books: animal, biography, careers, concept, geography, health, history, multicultural, music/dance, nature/environment, religion, science, social issues, special needs, hobbies, sports. Average word length: picture books—1,000. Recently published *The Bumblebee Queen*, by April Pulley Sayre; *Yum! Yuck!*, by Linda Sue Park and Julia Durango, illustrated by Sue Rama.

**How to Contact/Writers** Send ms and SASE. Accepts exclusive submissions only. Responds to mss in 3 months. Full mss only; no queries.

**Illustration** Works with 5-10 illustrators/year. Uses color artwork only. Illustrations only: Query with samples; provide résumé, tearsheets to be kept on file. "Send no original artwork, please." Responds only if interested. Samples returned with SASE; samples filed. Originals returned at job's completion.

**Terms** Pays authors and illustrators in royalties or work purchased outright. Manuscript/art guidelines available for SASE. Exclusive submissions only.

**Tips** "We want books that have humor and are factually correct. See our website for more tips."

## Ⓝ CHELSEA HOUSE PUBLISHERS

Haights Cross Communications, 2080 Cabot Blvd., Suite 201, Langhorne PA 19047. (215)487-9266. Fax: (215)757-8419. E-mail: ssharpless@chelseahouse.com. Website: www.chelseahouse.com. Specializes in nonfiction, educational material. **Manuscript Acquisitions:** Sarah Sharpless, editorial assistant. **Art Acquisitions:** Kim Shinners, director of production. Imprints: Chelsea Clubhouse; Chelsea House. Produces 150 middle readers/year, 150 young adult books/year. 10% of books by first-time authors.

## Ⓒ CHICAGO REVIEW PRESS

814 N. Franklin St., Chicago IL 60610. (312)337-0747. Fax: (312)337-5110. E-mail: csherry@chicagoreviewpress. Website: www.chicagoreviewpress.com. **Manuscript Acquisitions:** Cynthia Sherry, associate publisher. **Art Acquisitions:** Gerilee Hundt, art director. Publishes 3-4 middle readers/year; 4 young adult titles/year. 33% of books by first-time authors; 30% of books from agented authors. "Chicago Review Press publishes high-quality, nonfiction, educational activity books that extend the learning process through hands-on projects and accurate and interesting text. We look for activity books that are as much fun as they are constructive and informative."

**Nonfiction** Picture books, young readers, middle readers and young adults: activity books, arts/crafts, multicultural, history, nature/environment, science. "We're interested in hands-on, educational books; anything else probably will be rejected." Average length: young readers and young adults—144-160 pages. Recently published *Deserts*, by Nancy Castaldo (ages 6-9); *The Underground Railroad for Kids*, by Mary Kay Carson (ages 9 and up); *American Folk Art for Kids*, by Richard Panchyk (ages 9 and up).

**How to Contact/Writers** Enclose cover letter and no more than table of contents and 1-2 sample chapters; prefers not to receive e-mail queries. Send for guidelines. Responds to queries/mss in 2 months. Publishes a book 1-2 years after acceptance. Will consider simultaneous submissions and previously published work.

**Illustration** Works with 6 illustrators/year. Uses primarily b&w artwork. Reviews ms/illustration packages from artists. Submit 1-2 chapters of ms with corresponding pieces of final art. Illustrations only: Query with samples, résumé. Responds only if interested. Samples returned with SASE.

**Photography** Buys photos from freelancers ("but not often". Buys stock and assigns work. Wants "instructive photos. We consult our files when we know what we're looking for on a book-by-book basis." Uses b&w prints.

**Terms** Pays authors royalty of $7^{1}/_{2}$-$12^{1}/_{2}$% based on retail price. Offers advances of $3,000-6,000. Pays illustrators by the project (range varies considerably). Pays photographers by the project (range varies considerably). Original artwork "usually" returned at job's completion. Book catalog/ms guidelines available for $3.

**Tips** "We're looking for original activity books for small children and the adults caring for them—new themes and enticing projects to occupy kids' imaginations and promote their sense of personal creativity. We like activity books that are as much fun as they are constructive. Please write for guidelines so you'll know what we're looking for."

## CHILDREN'S BOOK PRESS

2211 Mission St., San Francisco CA 94110. (415)821-3080. Fax: (415)821-3081. E-mail: info@cbookpress.org. Website: www.cbookpress.org. **Acquisitions:** Submissions Editor. "Children's Book Press is a nonprofit publisher of multicultural and bilingual children's literature. We publish contemporary stories reflecting the traditions and culture of minorities and new immigrants in the United States. Our goal is to help broaden the base of children's literature in this country to include stories from the African-American, Asian-American, Latino/Chicano and Native American communities. Stories should encourage critical thinking about social and/or personal issues. These ideas must be an integral part of the story."

**Fiction** Picture books: contemporary, history, multicultural, poetry. Average word length: picture books—750-1,500.

**Nonfiction** Picture books, young readers: multicultural.

**How to Contact/Writers** Submit complete ms to Submissions Editor. Responds to mss in roughly 4 months. "Please do not inquire about your manuscript. We can only return/respond to manuscripts with a SASE." Publishes a book 1-2 years after acceptance. Will consider simultaneous submissions.

**Illustration** Works with 4-5 illustrators/year. Uses color artwork only. Reviews ms/illustration packages from artists. Send ms with 3 or 4 color photocopies. Illustrations only: color copies only, no original artwork. Responds in 8-10 weeks. Samples returned with SASE.

**Terms** Original artwork returned at job's completion. Book catalog available; ms guidelines available via website or with SASE.

**Tips** "Vocabulary level should be approximately third grade (eight years old) or below. Keep in mind, however, that many of the young people who read our books may be nine, ten, or eleven years old or older. Their life experiences are often more advanced than their reading level, so try to write a story that will appeal to a fairly wide age range. We are especially interested in humorous stories and original stories about contemporary life from the multicultural communities mentioned above by writers *from* those communities."

## CHRISTIAN ED. PUBLISHERS

P.O. Box 26639, San Diego CA 92196. (858)578-4700. E-mail: jackelson@cehouse.com. Website: www.Christian EdWarehouse.com. Book publisher. **Acquisitions:** Janet Ackelson, assistant editor; Carol Rogers, managing editor; Clint Kruger, design coordinator. Publishes 80 Bible curriculum titles/year. "We publish curriculum for children and youth, including program and student books and take-home papers—all handled by our assigned freelance writers only."

**Fiction** Young readers: contemporary. Middle readers: adventure, contemporary, suspense/mystery. "We publish fiction for Bible club take-home papers. All fiction is on assignment only."

**Nonfiction** Publishes Bible curriculum and take-home papers for all ages. Recently published *All-Stars for Jesus*, by Treena Herrington and Letitia Zook, illustrated by Aline Heiser (Bible club curriculum for grades 4-6); *Honeybees Classroom Activity Sheets*, by Janet Miller and Wanda Pelfrey, illustrated by Brenda Warren and Terry Walderhaug (Bible club curriculum for ages 2-3).

**How to Contact/Writers** Fiction/nonfiction: Query. Responds to queries in 5 weeks. Publishes a book 1 year after acceptance. Send SASE for guidelines or contact Christian Ed. at cgast@cehouse.com.

**Illustration** Works with 6-7 illustrators/year. Query by e-mail. Contact: Clint Kruger, design coordinator (ckruger @cehouse.com). Responds in 1 month. Samples returned with SASE.

**Terms** Work purchased outright from authors for 3¢/word. Pays illustrators by the project (range: $300-400/book). Book catalog available for 9×12 SAE and 4 first-class stamps; ms and art guidelines available for SASE or via e-mail.

**Tips** "Read our guidelines carefully before sending us a manuscript or illustrations. All writing and illustrating is done on assignment only and must be age-appropriate (preschool-6th grade)."

## CHRONICLE BOOKS

85 Second St., 6th Floor, San Francisco CA 94105. (415)537-4422. Fax: (415)537-4415. Website: www.chroniclek ids.com. Book publisher. **Acquisitions:** Victoria Rock, associate publisher, children's books. Publishes 35-60 (both fiction and nonfiction) books/year; 5-10% middle readers/year; young adult nonfiction titles/year. 10-25% of books by first-time authors; 20-40% of books from agented writers.

**Fiction** Picture books: animal, folktales, history, multicultural, nature/environment. Young readers: animal, folktales, history, multicultural, nature/environment, poetry. Middle readers: animal, history, multicultural, nature/environment, poetry, problem novels. Young adults: multicultural needs include "projects that feature diverse children in everyday situations." Recently published *Papa Do You Love Me?*, by Barbara Joosse, illustrated by Barbara Lavallee (ages 0-6, picture books); *I Love the Rain*, by Margaret Park Bridges, illustrated by Christine Davenier (ages 6 and up, picture book).

**Nonfiction** Picture books: animal, history, multicultural, nature/environment, science. Young readers: animal, arts/crafts, cooking, geography, history, multicultural and science. Middle readers: animal, arts/crafts, biography, cooking, geography, history, multicultural and nature/environment. Young adults: biography and multicultural. Recently published *Middle School: How to Deal*, by Sara Borden, Sarah Miller, Alex Strikeleather, Maria Valladares, and Miriam Yelton; *Postmark Paris*, by Leslie Jonath.

**How to Contact/Writers** Fiction/nonfiction: Submit complete ms (picture books); submit outline/synopsis and 3 sample chapters (for older readers). Responds to queries in 1 month; mss in 6-7 months. Publishes a book 1-3 years after acceptance. Will consider simultaneous submissions, as long as they are marked "multiple submissions." Will not consider submissions by fax or e-mail. Must include SASE or projects will not be returned.

**Illustration** Works with 15-20 illustrators/year. Wants "unusual art, graphically strong, something that will stand out on the shelves. Either bright and modern or very traditional. Fine art, not mass market." Reviews ms/illustration packages from artists. "Indicate if project *must* be considered jointly, or if editor may consider text and art separately." Illustrations only: Submit samples of artist's work (not necessarily from book, but in the envisioned style). Slides, tearsheets and color photocopies OK. (No original art.) Dummies helpful. Résumé helpful. "If samples sent for files, generally no response—unless samples are not suited to list, in which case samples are returned. Queries and project proposals responded to in same time frame as author query/proposals."

**Photography** Purchases photos from freelancers. Works on assignment only. Wants nature/natural history photos.

**Terms** Generally pays authors in royalties based on retail price, "though we do occasionally work on a flat fee basis." Advance varies. Illustrators paid royalty based on retail price or flat fee. Sends proofs to authors and illustrators. Book catalog for 9×12 SAE and 8 first-class stamps; ms guidelines for #10 SASE.

**Tips** "Chronicle Books publishes an eclectic mixture of traditional and innovative children's books. We are interested in taking on projects that have a unique bend to them—be it subject matter, writing style, or illustrative technique. As a small list, we are looking for books that will lend us a distinctive flavor. Primarily we are interested in fiction and nonfiction picture books for children ages infant-8 years, and nonfiction books for children ages 8-12 years. We are also interested in developing a middle grade/YA fiction program, and are looking for literary fiction that deals with relevant issues. Our sales reps are witnessing a resistance to alphabet books. And the market has become increasingly competitive. The '80s boom in children's publishing has passed, and the market is demanding high-quality books that work on many different levels."

## CLARION BOOKS
215 Park Ave. S., New York NY 10003. (212)420-5800. Website: www.clarionbooks.com. **Manuscript Acquisitions:** Dinah Stevenson, associate publisher; Virginia Buckley, contributing editor; Jennifer Greene, senior editor. **Art Acquisitions:** Joann Hill, art director.
- Clarion title *The Voice That Challenged a Nation: Marian Anderson and the Struggle for Equal Rights,* by Russell Freedman, won a 2005 Newbery Honor Award and the 2005 Robert F. Sibert Award. Their title *Lizzie Bright and the Buckminster Boy,* by Gary Schmidt, won a Newbery Honor and a Printz Honor Award. Their title *Real Time,* by Pnina Moed Kass, won the 2005 Sydney Taylor Book Award. See Tackling Tough Topics in YA Lit to read more about Kass and her book.

**How to Contact/Writers** Fiction and picture books: Send complete mss. Nonfiction: Send query with up to 3 sample chapters. Must include SASE. Will accept simultaneous submissions if informed.

**Illustration** Send samples (no originals).

**Terms** Pays illustrators royalty; flat fee for jacket illustration. Pays royalties and advance to writers; both vary. Guidelines available on website.

## CLEAR LIGHT PUBLISHERS
823 Don Diego, Santa Fe NM 87505. (505)989-9590. Fax: (505)989-9519. Website: www.clearlightbooks.com. **Acquisitions:** Harmon Houghton, publisher. Publishes 4 middle readers/year; 4 young adult titles/year.

**Nonfiction** Middle readers and young adults: multicultural, American Indian and Hispanic only.

**How to Contact/Writers** Fiction/nonfiction: Submit complete ms with SASE. "No e-mail submissions. Authors supply art. Manuscripts not considered without art or artist's renderings." Will consider simultaneous submissions. Responds in 3 months. Only send *copies.*

**Illustration** Reviews ms/illustration packages from artists. "No originals please." Submit ms with dummy and SASE.

**Terms** Pays authors royalty of 10% based on wholesale price. Offers advances (average amount: up to 50% of expected net sales within the first year). Sends galleys to authors.

**Tips** "We're looking for authentic American Indian art and folklore."

## CONCORDIA PUBLISHING HOUSE
3558 S. Jefferson Ave., St. Louis MO 63118. (314)268-1187. Fax: (314)268-1329. Website: cph.org. **Contact:** Peggy Kuethe. "Concordia Publishing House produces quality resources which communicate and nurture the Christian faith and ministry of people of all ages, lay and professional. These resources include curriculum, worship aids, books, and religious supplies. We publish approximately 30 quality children's books each year. We boldly provide Gospel resources that are Christ-centered, Bible-based and faithful to our Lutheran heritage."

**Nonfiction** Picture books, young readers, middle readers, young adults: activity books, arts/crafts, concept, contemporary, religion. Picture books: poetry. "All books must contain explicit Christian content." Recently published *A Tree for Christmas,* by Dandi Daley Mackall (picture book for ages 6-10); *Lies and Deceptions,* by Christina Hergenrader (ages over 12, youth fiction).

# Yuyi Morales

*Critique groups, culture
& the creative process*

**W**hen Yuyi Morales stood to accept her Golden Kite award for picture book illustration at the Society of Children's Book Writers and Illustrators award luncheon, she told the room full of writers, illustrators, and editors that had it not been for her critique group, her award-winning book might not have been written.

"The Revisionaries," as her group called themselves, consisted simply of Morales and several friends she met at a class on writing children's books. "After the course was over we stayed together as a critique group and our bond grew very strong," Morales says. "We not only criticized each other's work, but gave each other support and found ways to keep learning together." Because all three writers were also interested in illustrating, they decided to enroll in an evening class taught by illustrator Ashley Wolf.

Here, Morales tells how that class led to a book, *Just a Minute: A Trickster Tale and Counting Book*, the story of a grandmother with twinkling eyes who outsmarts Death. She also discusses cultural differences, her experience with publishers, and her passion for writing and illustrating children's books. To read more about Morales, visit her website, www.yuyimorales.com.

### So, the idea for *Just a Minute* came because of an evening class?

Yes. Our first assignment was to come up with either an alphabet or counting book to use as a framework for our illustrations. Our teacher gave us one week to hand in the story and sketches. I decided on a counting book. But what to count? I always loved the folktales from my country—especially those where ordinary folks defeat great enemies. Taking inspiration from the Mexican tradition, I sat down to write.

Sometimes stories seem to come out of nowhere. In reality our stories come from very deep inside us. Grandma Beetle came alive as the embodiment of the women who took care of me when I was a child—hard-working woman like my grandma, my mother, my aunts, and my sisters. Always tending their chores, these women love their children more than anything in the world. In my mind Grandma was also the personification of a beetle from my homeland—round and brown, always flaying and moving.

### Did everybody tell you not to write about death in such a humorous way?

*Many* people told me my story would never find a place in the children's book world. Death was a delicate subject, they said, and my story was scary. Growing up in Mexico, I was surrounded by the image of death as an inevitable companion. Our sayings, our traditions—even our candies and toys—have a playful affair with the image of death. I understood the cultural differences and how they affected my chances of having my book published. But I also felt my story was valid, and I pushed it forward.

## How did you get your book deal with Chronicle?

I didn't have an agent at that time, so I mailed a cover letter, manuscript, dummy, and two color samples to a handful of houses that accepted multiple submissions. Soon rejection letters started coming in saying things like "we like your artwork, but your skeleton is scary. We would never be able to sell this book. Do you have any other work?"

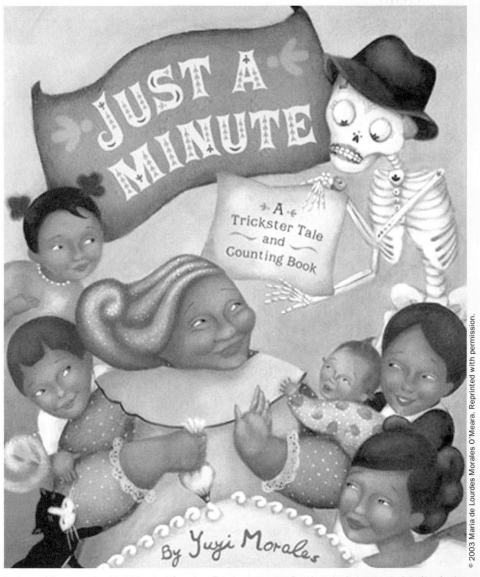

In *Just a Minute*, author Yuyi Morales' Grandma Beetle outsmarts Death—who has come to her door in the form of Senior Calavera ("Mr. Skull")—and teaches readers to count from one to ten in both English and Spanish. "Even if children don't grasp the implications of the skeleton's visit, they'll enjoy seeing him join the fun," says a starred *Booklist* review. "And when he extends Grandma's lease on life, the relieved, loving embrace she gives her grandchildren will satisfy young ones at a gut level."

More than a year passed. I had already gotten a contract to illustrate a school market book, and was accepting an offer to illustrate a book about César Chávez. Then one day I got a call from an editor at Tricycle Press. She found my manuscript, lost in the limbo of their offices for more than a year. She wanted to know if it was still available, for she loved the book! I was still catching my breath from the excitement when, a few days later, I got a call from Chronicle asking me to resubmit that "death story"! I had just started meeting with my agent Charlotte Sheedy, so she took charge of talking with the publishers. Although both houses were excellent matches for my book, in the end we signed with Chronicle.

### Once you started getting book deals, what was it like working with editors and art directors?

The process was slightly different with each house. For *Harvesting Hope: The Story of César Chávez* (Harcourt) I worked with editor Jeannette Larson who was my link to the art department. The cover was the most strenuous part. It took me a long time to come up with the right design. I originally took inspiration from my favorite muralist, Jorge Gonzales Camarena, trying to recreate the regal feeling he portrayed in his subjects. But my attempts were very stiff. I sketched many versions, none of them right. But like the great editor she is, Jeannette helped me without interfering in my creative process. She kept me going by sending me images of fruit crate labels for inspiration. She gave suggestions, told me what worked and what needed revision. Throughout the long process, she stirred my imagination, helping me come up with the right piece of artwork all by myself.

With *Just a Minute* for Chronicle, I worked on the text with editor Samantha McFerrin, and illustrations with art director Sarah Gulliham. Both kept me focused and happy while I was hard at work.

### Did you do any research for *Harvesting Hope*?

I immediately loved the manuscript by Kathleen Krull, but I had no knowledge of the life and work of César Chávez. So I embarked on a journey of learning about this man of gentle ways but strong resolutions. I read books, old newspapers, searched the Internet and traveled with my brother, my son, and husband to places where Chávez worked and lived.

I am not a realistic-style painter, but my illustrations still have to tell the truth. The landscape, the people, the feelings I experienced, found a way into my work that was more in accordance with my feelings and emotions than with what my eyes saw.

### How important is it for illustrators and authors to do school visits?

I did school visits before I had a book contract. After the publication of my first two books, I found myself traveling all over the country. It is exhausting, but once I shake the librarian's hand, or walk into a room full with children, every effort is worth it. Writing your book is only the beginning. It isn't until you see your readers face to face, that the

Jacket Illustration © 2003 Yuyi Morales.

Yuyi Morales credits Harcourt editor Jeannette Larson with helping her hone her vision for the illustrations for Kathleen Krull's *Harvesting Hope: The Story of César Chávez* (here shown in the Spanish-language edition). "I sketched many versions, none of them right," says Morales. She gave suggestions and stirred my imagination, helping me come up with the right piece of artwork all by myself."

real connection begins. It is then that reader and author become linked forever. I usually come back home all hugged and kissed, and with my hands still feeling warm from holding so many tiny beautiful hands.

## What motivates you? How do you stay inspired?

Before I start any new project, I clean and reorganize my workspace. It might be just one more way of procrastinating, but it is useful. To prepare to start working, I decided I must, one, put on music; and, two, be inspired.

Being inspired mostly means that I have gone and looked at a bunch of books I like from other authors and illustrators. It means I searched for reference pictures on the Internet, and, most important, that I *believe* I am about to create—even though I probably don't have the slightest idea what I am going to do.

The beautiful thing is that we don't need to know what we will create, because inside every one of us there are files and files brimming with the knowledge. These files are full with memories, fears, passion, dreams, and many, many more. It is never ending.

Because of this interior knowledge, all I need to do is sit with a pencil in my hand, and I let my body work. As my hand moves and writes the first word—any word—or draws a line—any line—I have to push myself to do it again and again. And it is chaos at first! Words make no sense; my drawings are horrible and pointless. But exploration is like that. How can I know what I want to write or paint if I don't look for it first?

## Tell us about your workspace. Do you have a studio?

When we moved to our new house my husband encouraged me to take the biggest, sunniest room as my studio. It was such a shock! I came from having created my books inside a working space the size of a small closet, with only a drawing table and a chair. In that tiny space my world revolved. Now I have all the space I need. Tim built me a drawing table and a long desk full of shelves and drawers. I painted the walls *Rosa Mexicano*, hot pink. My desk is yellow, my chair is red, and my organizing boxes are orange. It wasn't my intention, but I realized that my new studio is beginning to look like a page for my book *Just a Minute*. What a great place to be.

## So, life as an author and illustrator sounds good? What are you working on now?

I am currently working on a book written by Puerto Rican author Marisa Montes. Her story is a very playful interaction of English and Spanish, combined in a Halloween book. And I love it! I am painting all kinds of sketetons, monsters, ghosts, witches, you name it. But the most thrilling part for me is that they are coming out looking like people I know! As for writing, I am currently working on a longer piece, perhaps a novel. I won't know 'til I get it all out of me.

## What advice would you give those hoping to write and illustrate children's books?

Create from your inside out—from your dreams, from the things you are passionate about, and from the themes that trigger your wonderment. Writing and illustrating, like all art, is an exploration of oneself. If we keep writing or painting consistently, we begin to recognize ourselves, and what makes us powerful. And when one is feeling powerful, everything can happen!

—*Mary Cox*

Book Publishers

**How to Contact/Writers** Submit complete ms (picture books); submit outline/synopsis and sample chapters for longer mss. May also query. Responds to queries in 1 month; mss in 3 months. Publishes a book 2 years after acceptance. Will consider simultaneous submissions. "No phone queries."

**Illustration** Works with 20 illustrators/year. Illustrations only: Query with samples. Contact: Ed Luhmann, art director. Responds only if interested. Samples returned with SASE; samples filed.

**Terms** Pays authors royalties based on retail price or work purchased outright ($750-2,000). Sends galleys to author. Manuscript guidelines for 1 first-class stamp and a #10 envelope. Pays illustrators by the project.

**Tips** "Do not send finished artwork with the manuscript. If sketches will help in the presentation of the manuscript, they may be sent. If stories are taken from the Bible, they should follow the Biblical account closely. Liberties should not be taken in fantasizing Biblical stories."

## CREATIVE EDUCATION

Imprint of The Creative Company, 123 South Broad St., Mankato MN 56001. (800)445-6209. Fax: (507)388-2746. E-mail: The_Creative_Company@hotmail.com. **Manuscript Acquisitions:** Aaron Frisch. **Art Acquisitions:** Rita Marshall, art director. Publishes 5 picture books/year; 10 young readers/year; 30 middle readers/year; 10 young adult titles/year. 5% of books by first-time authors.

**Fiction** Picture books, young readers, middle readers, young adult/teens: adventure, animal, anthology, contemporary, fantasy, folktales, history, nature/environment, poetry, sports. Average word length: picture books—1,000; young readers—1,500; middle readers—3,000; young adults—6,000. Recently published *Erika's Story*, by Ruth Vander Zee, illustrated by Roberto Innocanti (ages 6-adult); *Swan Song*, by J. Patrick Lewis, illustrated by Christopher Wormell (ages 10-adult, poetry); *T Is for Toscana*, by Gary Kelley (ages 8-adult).

**Nonfiction** Picture books, young readers, middle readers, young adults: animal, arts/crafts, biography, careers, geography, health, history, hobbies, multicultural, music/dance, nature/environment, religion, science, social issues, special needs, sports. Average word length: young readers—500; middle readers—3,000; young adults—6,000. Recently published *Dairy Products*, by Jill Kalz (age 7, young reader); *Ships & Boats*, by John Hudson Tiner (age 11, middle reader); *William Shakespeare*, by Jennifer Fandel (age 14, young adult/teen).

**How to Contact/Writers** Fiction: Submit complete ms. Nonfiction: Submit outline/synopsis and 2 sample chapters. Responds to queries in 6 weeks; mss in 2 months. Publishes book 2 years after acceptance.

**Illustration** Works with 3 illustrators/year. Reviews ms/illustration packages from artists. Query. Contact: Aaron Frisch, editor. Illustrations only: Query with samples. Contact: Rita Marshall, art director. Responds only if interested. Samples not returned; samples filed.

**Photography** Buys stock. Contact: Bobby Nuytten, photo editor. Model/property releases not required; captions required. Uses b&w prints. Submit cover letter, promo piece.

**Terms** Sends dummies to illustrators. Book catalog available for 9×12 SASE and $1.60 postage; ms and photographer guidelines available for SAE. All imprints included in a single catalog.

**Tips** "We are very selective about fiction picture books, publishing five or fewer annually. Nonfiction submissions should be in series (of 4, 6, or 8), rather than single, as we are a nonfiction series publisher."

## CRICKET BOOKS

Carus Publishing Company, P.O. Box 300, Peru IL 61354. (815)224-5803, ext. 656. E-mail: cricketbooks@caruspub.com. Website: www.cricketbooks.net. **Art Acquisitions:** Ron McCutchan. Publishes 6 titles/year. "For 25 years we've published the best children's literary magazines in America, and choose only the same high-quality material for our book imprint."

● Cricket books has a moratorium on unsolicited manuscripts. Submissions from agents and authors already working with Cricket Books or magazines are still welcome. Watch website for updates.

**Fiction** Young readers, middle readers, young adult/teen: adventure, animal, contemporary, fantasy, history, multicultural, humor, sports, suspense/mystery, science fiction, problem novels. Recently published *Breakout*, by Paul Fleischman; *Robert and the Weird & Wacky Facts*, by Barbara Seuling, illustrated by Paul Brewer.

**How to Contact Not accepting unsolicited mss.** See website for details and updates on submissions policy.

**Illustration** Works with 4 illustrators/year. Use color and b&w. Illustration only: Submit samples, tearsheets. Contact: Ron McCutchan, 315 Fifth St., Peru IL 61354. Responds only if interested. Samples returned with SASE; sample filed.

**Terms** Pays authors royalty of 7-10% based on retail price. Offers advances. Pays illustrators royalty of 3% based on retail price. Sends galleys to authors; dummies to illustrators. Originals returned to artist at job's completion. Writer's guidelines available for SASE. Catalog available at website.

**Tips** "Primarily interested in chapter books, middle-grade fiction, but will also consider picture books."

## CSS PUBLISHING

517 S. Main St., Lima OH 45802-4503. (419)227-1818. Fax: (419)222-4647. E-mail: acquisitions@csspub.com. Website: www.csspub.com. **Manuscript Acquisitions:** Stan Purdum. Publishes books with religious themes. "We are seeking material for use by clergy, Christian education directors and Sunday school teachers for mainline Protestant churches. Our market is mainline Protestant clergy."

**Fiction** Young readers, middle readers, young adults: religion, religious poetry and humor. Needs children's sermons (object lesson) for Sunday morning worship services; dramas for Advent, Christmas or Epiphany involving children for church services; activity and craft ideas for Sunday school or mid-week services for children (particularly pre-school and first and second grade). Published *That Seeing, They May Believe*, by Kenneth Mortonson (lessons for adults to present during worship services to pre-schoolers-third graders); *What Shall We Do With This Baby?*, by Jan Spence (Christmas Eve worship service involving youngsters from newborn babies-high school youth); *Miracle in the Bethlehem Inn*, by Mary Lou Warstler (Advent drama involving pre-schoolers-high school youth and adult.)

**Nonfiction** Young readers, middle readers, young adults: religion. Young adults only: social issues and self help. Needs children's sermons (object lesson) for Sunday morning worship services; dramas for Advent, Christmas or Epiphany involving children for church services; activity and craft ideas for Sunday school or mid-week services for children (particularly pre-school and first and second grade). Published *Mustard Seeds*, by Ellen Humbert (activity bulletins for pre-schoolers-first graders to use during church); *This Is The King*, by Cynthia Cowen.

**How to Contact/Writers** Responds to queries in 2 weeks; mss in 3 months. Publishes a book 9 months after acceptance. Will consider simultaneous submissions.

**Terms** Work purchased outright from authors. Manuscript guidelines and book catalog available for SASE and on website.

## DARBY CREEK PUBLISHING

7858 Industrial Pkwy., Plain City OH 43064. (614)873-7955. Fax: (614)873-7135. E-mail: info@darbycreekpublishing .com. **Manuscript/Art Acquisitions:** Tanya Dean, editorial director. Publishes 10-15 children's books/year.

**Fiction** Middle readers, young adult. Recently published *The Warriors*, by Joseph Bruchac (ages 10 and up); *Dog Days*, by David Lubar (ages 10 and up).

**Nonfiction** Middle readers: biography, history, science, sports. Recently published *Dinosaur Mummies*, by Kelly Milner Halls, illustrated by Rick Spears; *Miracle: The True Story of the Wreck of the Sea Venture*, by Gail Karwoski.

**How to Contact/Writers** Accepts international material only with U.S. postage on SASE for return; no IRCs. Fiction/nonfiction: Submit publishing history and/or résumé and complete ms for short works or outline/synopsis and 2-3 sample chapters for longer works, such as novels. Responds in 6 weeks. Does not consider previously published work.

**Illustration** Illustrations only: Send photocopies and résumé with publishing history. "Indicate which samples we may keep on file and include SASE and appropriate packing materials for any samples you wish to have returned."

**Terms** Offers advance-against-royalty contracts.

**Tips** "We like to see nonfiction with a unique slant that is kid friendly, well researched and endorsed by experts. We're interested in fiction or nonfiction with sports themes for future lists. No series, please."

## ⊞ MAY DAVENPORT, PUBLISHERS

26313 Purissima Rd., Los Altos Hills CA 94022-4539. (650)947-1275. Fax: (650)947-1373. E-mail: mdbooks@eart hlink.net. Website: www.maydavenportpublishers.com. **Acquisitions:** May Davenport, editor/publisher. Publishes 1-2 picture books/year; 2-3 young adult titles/year. 99% of books by first-time authors. Seeks books with literary merit. "We like to think that we are selecting talented writers who have something humorous to write about today's unglued generation in 30,000-50,000 words for teens and young adults in junior/senior high school before they become tomorrow's 'functional illiterates.' We are interested in publishing literature that teachers in middle and high schools can use in their Language Arts, English and Creative Writing courses. There's more to literary fare than the chit-chat Internet dialog and fantasy trips on television with cartoons or humanoids." This publisher is overstocked with picture book/elementary reading material.

**Fiction** Young adults (ages 15-18): contemporary, humorous fictional literature for use in English courses in junior-senior high schools in U.S. Average word length: 40,000-60,000. Recently published *The Lesson Plan*, by Irvin Gay (about an illiterate black boy who grows up to become a teacher, ages 15-18); *A Life on the Line*, by Michael Horton (about a juvenile delinquent boy who becomes a teacher, ages 15-18); *Making My Escape*, by David Lee Finkle (about a young boy who daydreams movie-making in outer space to escape unhappy family life, ages 12-18).

**Nonfiction** Teens: humorous. Recently published *The Runaway Game*, by Kevin Casey (a literary board game of street life in Hollywood, ages 15-18).

**How to Contact/Writers** Fiction: Query. Responds to queries/mss in 3 weeks. "We do not answer queries or manuscripts which do not have SASE attached." Publishes a book 6-12 months after acceptance.

**Illustration** Works with 1-2 illustrators/year. "Have enough on file for future reference." Responds only if interested. Samples returned with SASE; samples filed. Originals returned at job's completion.

**Terms** Pays authors royalty of 15% based on retail price; negotiable. Pays "by mutual agreement, no advances." Pays illustrators by the project (range: $75-350). Book catalog, ms guidelines free on request with SASE.

**Tips** "Create stories to enrich the non-reading high school readers. They might not appreciate your similies and metaphors and may find fault with your alliterations, but show them how you do it with memorable characters in today's society. Just project your humorous talent and entertain with more than two sentences in a paragraph."

## DAWN PUBLICATIONS

12402 Bitney Springs Rd., Nevada City CA 95959. (530)274-7775. Fax: (530)275-7778. E-mail: glenn@dawnpub.com. Website: www.dawnpub.com. Book publisher. Co-Publishers: Muffy Weaver and Glenn J. Hovemann. **Acquisitions:** Glenn J. Hovemann. Publishes works with holistic themes dealing with nature. "Dawn Publications is dedicated to inspiring in children a deeper appreciation and understanding of nature."

**Nonfiction** Picture books: animal, nature/environment. Biographies of naturalists recently published *John Muir: My Life With Nature*, by Joseph Cornell (80-page biography); *Do Animals Have Feelings Too?*, by David L. Rice (32-page picture book).

**How to Contact/Writers** Nonfiction: Query or submit complete ms. Responds to queries/mss in 3 months maximum. Publishes a book 1 year after acceptance. Will consider simultaneous submissions.

**Illustration** Works with 5 illustrators/year. Will review ms/illustration packages from artists. Query; send ms with dummy. Illustrations only: Query with samples, résumé.

**Terms** Pays authors royalty based on net sales. Offers advance. Book catalog and ms guidelines available online.

**Tips** Looking for "picture books expressing nature awareness with inspirational quality leading to enhanced self-awareness. Usually no animal dialogue."

## DELACORTE AND DOUBLEDAY BOOKS FOR YOUNG READERS

Random House Children's Books/Random House, Inc., 1745 Broadway, New York NY 10019. (212)782-9000. Website: www.randomhouse.com/kids. Imprints of Random House Children's Books. 90% of books published through agents.

- See listings for Random House Golden Books for Young Readers and Alfred A. Knopf and Crown Books for Young Readers.

**Fiction** Unsolicited mss are only being accepted as submissions to either the Delacorte Dell Yearling Contest for a First Mid-Grade Novel or Delacorte Press Contest for a First Young Adult Novel. See website for submission guidelines.

**Illustration** Illustration only: Contact: Isabel Warren-Lynch, executive art and design director. Responds only if interested. Samples returned with SASE; samples filed.

**Terms** Pays illustrators and photographers by the project or royalties. Original artwork returned at job's completion.

## DIAL BOOKS FOR YOUNG READERS

Penguin Young Readers Group, 345 Hudson St., New York NY 10014. Website: www.penguin.com. Associate Publishers and Editorial Director:Lauri Hornik. **Acquisitions:** Nancy Mercado, editor; Cecile Goyette, senior editor; Rebecca Waugh, editor. **Art Director:** Lily Malcom. Publishes 35 picture books/year; 3 young readers/year; 6 middle readers/year; 9 young adult titles/year.

**Fiction** Picture books, young readers: adventure, animal, fantasy, folktales, history, humor, multicultural, poetry, sports. Middle readers, young adults: adventure, fantasy, folktales, history, humor, multicultural, poetry, problem novels, science fiction, sports, mystery/adventure. Published *A Year Down Yonder*, by Richard Peck (ages 10 and up); *The Sea Chest*, by Toni Buzzeo, illustrated by Mary Grand Pre (all ages, picture book); *A Penguin Pup for Pinkerton*, by Steven Kellogg (ages 3-7, picture book).

**Nonfiction** Will consider query letters for submissions of outstanding literary merit. Picture books, young readers, middle readers: biography, history, sports. Young adults: biography, history, sports. Recently published *A Strong Right Arm*, by Michelle Y. Green (ages 10 and up) ; *Dirt on their Skirts*, by Doreen Rappaport and Lyndall Callan (ages 4-8, picture book).

**How to Contact/Writers** Accepts picture book mss and queries for longer works. Do not send more than 10 pages. Responds to queries/mss in 4 months. "We do not supply specific guidelines, but we will send you a recent catalog if you send us a 9×12 SAE with 4 first-class stamps attached. Questions and queries should only be made in writing. We will not reply to anything without a SASE.'' No e-mail queries.

**Illustration** Works with 35 illustrators/year. Art samples should be sent to Dial Design and will not be returned without a SASE. ''No phone calls please. Only artists with portfolios that suit the house's needs will be interviewed.''

**Terms** Pays authors and illustrators in royalties based on retail price. Average advance payment ''varies.''

**Tips** ''We can only read longer manuscripts specifically requested through the query system. In addition, we can only keep track of these requested manuscripts; we do not track unsoliciteds. *Never* call or fax to inquire about the status of an unsolicited submission. Write a letter only if the reply time has exceeded four months. We will not reply to anything that is sent without a self-addressed stamped envelope. If you do not live in the United States, you must send an international reply coupon. We recycle all letters and manuscripts sent without sufficient postage. We will send you a recent catalogue if you send us a 9×12 envelope with four 37¢ stamps attached. This is one way to become informed as to the style, subject matter, and format of our books, as is a trip to your local library or bookshop. Reading a variety of current children's books is also very helpful.''

## Ⓐ DK PUBLISHING, INC.

DK Ink, 375 Hudson St., New York NY 10014. Website: www.dk.com. **Acquisitions:** submissions editor.
• DK Publishing does not accept unagented manuscripts.

## Ⓐ DOG-EARED PUBLICATIONS

P.O. Box 620863, Middletown WI 53562-0863. (608)831-1410 or (608)831-1410. Fax: (608)831-1410. E-mail: field@dog-eared.com. Website: www.dog-eared.com. **Art Acquisitions:** Nancy Field , publisher. Publishes 2-3 middle readers/year. 1% of books by first-time authors. ''Dog-Eared Publications creates action-packed nature books for children. We aim to turn young readers into environmentally aware citizens and to foster a love for science and nature in the new generation.''

**Nonfiction** Middle readers: activity books, animal, nature/environment, science. Average word length: varies. Recently published *Discovering Sharks and Rays*, by Nancy Field, illustrated by Michael Maydak (middle readers, activity book); *Leapfrogging Through Wetlands*, by Margaret Anderson, Nancy Field and Karen Stephenson, illustrated by Michael Maydak (middle readers, activity book); *Ancient Forests*, by Margaret Anderson, Nancy Field and Karen Stephenson, illustrated by Sharon Torvik (middle readers, activity book).

**How to Contact/Writers** Nonfiction: **Currently not accepting unsolicited mss**.

**Illustration** Works with 2-3 illustrators/year. Reviews ms/illustration packages from artists. Submit query and a few art samples. Illustrations only: Query with samples. Responds only if interested. Samples not returned; samples filed. ''Interested in realistic, nature art!''

**Terms** Pays authors royalty based on wholesale price. Offers advances (amount varies). Pays illustrators royalty based on wholesale price. Sends galleys to authors. Originals returned to artist at job's completion. Brochure available for SASE and 1 first-class stamp or on website.

## DOWN EAST BOOKS

P.O. Box 679, Camden, ME 04843-0679. (207)594-9544. Fax: (207)594-7215. E-mail: msteere@downeast.com. **Acquisitions:** Michael Steere , managing editor. Publishes 3-4 young readers and middle readers/year. 70% of books by first-time authors. ''As a small regional publisher Down East Books specializes in nonfiction books with a Maine or New England theme. Down East Books' mission is to publish superbly crafted books which capture and illuminate the astonishing beauty and unique character of New England's people, culture and wild places; the very aspects that distinguish New England from the rest of the United States.''

**Fiction** Picture books, middle readers, young readers, young adults: animal, adventure, history, nature/environment. Young adults: suspense/mystery. Recently published *Miss Renee's Mice*, by Elizabeth Hoffman, illustrated by Dawn Pete.

**Nonfiction** Picture books, middle readers, young readers, young adults: animal, history, nature/environment. Recently published *A Loon Alone*, by Pamela Love, illustrated by Shannon Sycks.

**How to Contact/Writers** Fiction/nonfiction: Query. Responds to queries/mss in 2 months. Publishes a book 6-18 months after acceptance. Will consider simultaneous and previously published submissions.

**Illustration** Works with 2-3 illustrators/year. Reviews ms/illustration packages from artists. Query. Illustrations only: Query with samples. Responds in 2 months. Samples returned with SASE; samples filed sometimes. Originals returned at job's completion.

**Terms** Pays authors royalty of 7-12% based on net receipts. Pays illustrators by the project or by royalty of 7-10% based on net receipts. Sends galleys to authors; dummies to illustrators. Original artwork returned at job's completion. Book catalog available. Manuscript guidelines available for SASE.

## 🌑 DUTTON CHILDREN'S BOOKS

Penguin Group (USA), 345 Hudson St., New York NY 10014-4502. (212)414-3700. Website: www.penguin.com. **Acquisitions:** Lucia Monfried. (easy-to-read, middle-grade fiction); Meredith Mundy Wasinger (middle-grade fiction, picture books); Michele Coppola (picture books, middle-grade fiction, upper young adult fiction), Julie Strauss-Gabel (picture books, middle-grade fiction, young adult). **Art Acquisitions:** Sara Reynolds, art director. Publishes approximately 50% fiction—fewer picture books, mostly YA and mid-grade novels. 10% of books by first-time authors.

● Dutton is open to query letters only.

**Fiction** Picture books: adventure, animal, history, humor, multicultural, nature/environment, poetry, contemporary. Young readers: adventure, animal, contemporary, fantasy. Middle readers: adventure, animal, contemporary, fantasy, history, multicultural, nature/environment. Young adults: adventure, animal, contemporary, fantasy, history, multicultural, nature/environment, poetry. Recently published *The Boy Who Spoke Dog*, by Clay Morgan (middle-grade); *Skippyjon Jones*, by Judy Schachner (picture book); *PREP*, by Jake Coburn (young adult).

**Nonfiction** Picture books. Recently published *Jack*, by Ilene Cooper; *Portraits of African American Heroes*, by Tonya Bolder.

**How to Contact/Writers** Query only. Does not accept unsolicited mss. Responds to queries in 3 months. Publishes a book 12-18 months after acceptance. Will consider simultaneous submissions.

**Illustration** Works with 40-60 illustrators/year. Reviews ms/illustration packages from artists. Query first. Illustrations only: Query with samples; send résumé, portfolio, slides—no original art please. Responds to art samples only if interested. Samples returned with SASE; samples filed. Original artwork returned at job's completion.

**Terms** Pays authors royalty of 4-10% based on retail price or outright purchase. Book catalog, ms guidelines for SAE with 8 first-class stamps. Pays illustrators royalty of 2-5% based on retail price unless jacket illustration—then pays by flat fee. Pays photographers by the project or royalty based on retail price.

**Tips** "Avoid topics that appear frequently. Illustrators: "We would like to see samples and portfolios from potential illustrators of picture books (full color), young novels (b&w) and jacket artists (full color)." Dutton is actively building its fiction lists, particularly upper YA titles. Humor welcome across all genres.

## 📕 EDUCATORS PUBLISHING SERVICE

Imprint of Delta Education, LLC, P.O. Box 9031, Cambridge MA 02139-9031. (617)547-6706. Fax: (617)547-3805. E-mail: epsbooks@epsbooks.com. Website: www.epsbooks.com. **Manuscript Acquisitions:** Charlie Heinle. **Art Acquisitions:** Sheila Neylon, senior editorial manager. Publishes 30-40 educational books/year. 50% of books by first-time authors.

**How to Contact/Writers** Responds to queries/mss in 5 weeks. Publishes book 6-12 months after acceptance. Will consider e-mail submissions, simultaneous submissions, previously published work. See website for submission guidelines.

**Illustration** Works with 12-18 illustrators/year. Reviews ms/illustration packages from artists. Query. Illustrations only: Query with samples; send promo sheet. Responds only if interested. Samples not returned; samples filed.

**Photography** Buys stock and assigns work. Submit cover letter, samples.

**Terms** Pays authors royalty of 5-12% based on retail price or work purchased outright from authors. Offers advances. Pays illustrators and photographers by the project. Sends galleys to authors. Book catalog free. All imprints included in a single catalog. Catalog available on website.

**Tips** "We accept queries from educators writing for the school market, primarily in the reading and language arts areas, grades K-8. We are interested in materials that follow certain pedagogical constraints (such as decodable texts and leveled readers) and we would consider queries and samples from authors who might be interested in working with us on ongoing or future projects."

## 📕 EDUPRESS, INC.

W5527 State Road 106, Ft. Atkinson WI 53538. (920)563-9571. Fax: (920)563-7395. E-mail: edupress@highsmith.com. Website: www.edupressinc.com. **Manuscript Acquisitions:** Nancy Crane. "Our mission is to create products that make kids want to go to school!"

**How to Contact/Writers** Nonfiction: Submit complete ms. Responds to queries/mss in 3 months. Publishes book 2 years after acceptance.

**Illustration** Uses b&w artwork only. Illustrations only: Query with samples. Contact: Kathy Rogers, production manager. Responds only if interested. Samples returned with SASE.

**Photography** Buys stock.

**Terms** Work purchased outright from authors. Pays illustrators by the project. Book catalog available at no cost. Catalog available on website.

**Tips** "Our materials are intended for classroom and home schooling use."

## EERDMAN'S BOOKS FOR YOUNG READERS

An imprint of Wm. B. Eerdmans Publishing Co., 255 Jefferson Ave. SE, Grand Rapids MI 49503. (616)459-4591. Fax: (616)776-7683. E-mail: youngreaders@eerdmans.com. Website: www.eerdmans.com/youngreaders. We are an independent book packager/producer. **Writers contact:** Judy Zylstra, editor-in-chief. **Illustrators contact:** Gayle Brown, art director. Produces 14 picture books/year; 3 middle readers/year; 3 young adult books/year. 10% of books by first-time authors. ''We seek high-quality manuscripts that celebrate the wonder of this world. At one time we only published religious material but we have broadened our interest and now publish books for the school, library, and general trade markets.''

**Fiction** Picture books: animal, concept, contemporary, folktales, history, humor, multicultural, nature/environment, poetry, religion, special needs, sports, suspense. Young readers: animal, concept, contemporary, folktales, history, humor, multicultural, poetry, religion, special needs, sports, suspense. Middle readers: adventure, contemporary, fantasy, folktales, history, humor, multicultural, nature/environment, problem novels, religion, sports, suspense. Young adults/teens: adventure, contemporary, fantasy, folktales, history, humor, multicultural, nature/environment, problem novels, religion, sports, suspense. Average word length: picture books—1,000; middle readers—15,000; young adult—45,000. Recently published *Circles of Hope*, by Karen Lynn Williams, illustrated by Linda Saport (picture book, ages 4 and up); *Going for the Record*, by Julie Swanson (novel, ages 12 and up); *Mississippi Morning*, by Ruth Vander Zee, illustrated by Floyd Cooper (picture book, ages 9 and up).

**Nonfiction** Middle readers: biography, history, multicultural, nature/environment, religion, science, social issues. Young adults/teens: biography, history, multicultural, nature/environment, religion, science, social issues. Average word length: middle readers—35,000; young adult books—35,000. Recently published *Maria Mitchell*, by Beatrice Gormley (ages 10 and up, biography); *Dororthy Day*, by Deborah Kent (ages 10 and up, biography).

**How to Contact/Writers** Accepts international submissions. Fiction/nonfiction: Query. Responds to queries/mss in 3-5 months. Considers simultaneous submissions.

**Illustration** Accepts material from international illustrators. Works with 10-12 illustrators/year. Uses color artwork only. Reviews work for future assignments. If interested in illustrating future titles, send promo sheet. Submit samples to Gayle Brown, art director. Samples not returned. Samples filed.

**Terms** Offers advance against royalties. Author sees galleys for review. Illustrators see dummies for review. Originals returned to artist at job's completion. Catalog available for 8 × 10 SASE and 4 first-class stamps. Offers writer's guidelines for SASE. See website for writer's guidelines.

**Tips** ''Find out who Eerdmans is before submitting a manuscript. Look at our website and check out our books.''

## ENSLOW PUBLISHERS INC.

Box 398, 40 Industrial Rd., Berkeley Heights NJ 07922-0398. Fax: (908)771-0925. E-mail: info@enslow.com. Website: www.enslow.com or www.myreportlinks.com. **Acquisitions:** Brian D. Enslow, vice president. Imprint: MyReportLinks.com Books. Publishes 30 young readers/year; 70 middle readers/year; 100 young adult titles/year. 30% of books by first-time authors.

- Enslow Imprint MyReportLinks.com Books produces books on animals, states, presidents, continents, countries, and a variety of other topics for middle readers and young adults, and offers links to online sources of information on topics covered in books.

**Nonfiction** Young readers, middle readers, young adults: animal, arts/crafts, biography, careers, geography, health, history, multicultural, nature/environment, science, social issues, sports. Middle readers, young adults: hi-lo. ''Enslow is moving into the elementary (grades 3-4) level and is looking for authors who can write biography and suggest other nonfiction themes at this level.'' Average word length: young readers—2,000; middle readers—5,000; young adult—18,000. Published *It's About Time! Science Projects*, by Robert Gardner (grades 3-6, science); *Georgia O'Keeffe: Legendary American Painter*, by Jodie A. Shull (grades 6-12, biography); *California: A MyReportLinks.com Book*, by Jeff Savaga (grades 5-8, social studies/history).

**How to Contact/Writers** Nonfiction: Send for guidelines. Query. Responds to queries/mss in 2 weeks. Publishes a book 18 months after acceptance. Will not consider simultaneous submissions.

**Illustration** Submit résumé, business card or tearsheets to be kept on file. Responds only if interested. Samples returned with SASE only.

**Terms** Pays authors royalties or work purchased outright. Pays illustrators by the project. Pays photographers by the project or per photo. Sends galleys to authors. Book catalog/ms guidelines available for $3, along with an 8½ × 11 SAE and $2 postage or via website.

## ☐ EVAN-MOOR EDUCATIONAL PUBLISHERS

18 Lower Ragsdale Dr., Monterey CA 93940-5746. (831)649-5901. Fax: (831)649-6256. E-mail: editorial@evan-moor.com. Website: www.evan-moor.com. **Manuscript Acquisitions:** Acquisitions Editor. **Art Acquisitions:** Cheryl Pucket, art director. Publishes 30-50 books/year. Less than 10% of books by first-time authors. '' 'Helping

Children Learn' is our motto. Evan-Moor is known for high-quality educational materials written by teachers for use in the classroom and at home. We publish teacher resource and reproducible materials in most all curriculum areas and activity books (language arts, math, science, social studies). No fiction or nonfiction literature books.''

**Nonfiction** Recently published *Daily Paragraph Editing* (5 book series, grades 2-5); *Nonfiction Reading Practice* (6 book series, grades 1-6); *Take It to Your Seat Learning Centers* (Math Centers K-1, Literacy Centers K-1, Literacy Centers 3-4).

**How to Contact/Writers** Query or submit outline, table of contents, and sample pages. Responds to queries in 2 months; mss in 4 months. Publishes a book 12-18 months after acceptance. Will consider simultaneous submissions if so noted. Submission guidelines available on our website. E-mail queries are responded to quickly. View our materials on our website to determine if your project fits in our product line.

**Illustration** Works with 8-12 illustrators/year. Uses b&w artwork primarily. Illustrations only: Query with samples; send résumé, tearsheets. Contact: Art Director. Responds only if interested. Samples returned with SASE; samples filed.

**Terms** Work purchased outright from authors, ''dependent solely on size of project and 'track record' of author.'' Pays illustrators by the project (range varies). Sends galleys to authors. Artwork is not returned. Book catalog available for 9×12 SAE; ms guidelines available for SASE.

**Tips** ''Writers—know the supplemental education or parent market. (These materials are *not* children's literature.) Tell us how your project is unique and what consumer needs it meets. Illustrators—you need to be able to produce quickly and be able to render realistic and charming children and animals.''

## EXCELSIOR CEE PUBLISHING

P.O. Box 5861, Norman OK 73070-5861. (405)329-3909. Fax: (405)329-6886. E-mail: ecp@oecadvantage.net. Website: www.excelsiorcee.com. **Manuscript Acquisitions:** J. Marshall.

**How to Contact/Writers** Nonfiction: Query or submit outline/synopsis. Responds to queries in 1 month. Publishes a book 1 year after acceptance. Will consider simultaneous submissions.

**Nonfiction** Recently published *Coming Full Circle*, by Loretta Hamilton-Geary; *About Face. Forward March*, by Robert Seikel.

**Tips** ''Excelsior Cee Publishing produces and markets books which speak through words of feeling. Whether it is a memoir, biography, humor, self-help, how-to or educational, the reader comes away with a sense of truth, feeling, and inspiration.''

## FACTS ON FILE

132 W. 31st St., New York NY 10001. (212)967-8800. Fax: (212)967-9196. Website: www.factsonfile.com. Estab. 1941. Book publisher. Editorial Director: Laurie Likoff. **Acquisitions:** Frank Darmstadt, science and technology/nature; Nicole Bowen, American history and studies; Jeff Soloway, language and literature; Owen Lancer, world studies; Jim Chambers, arts and entertainment. ''We produce high-quality reference materials for the school library market and the general nonfiction trade.'' Publishes 25-30 young adult titles/year. 5% of books by first-time authors; 25% of books from agented writers; additional titles through book packagers, co-publishers and unagented writers.

**Nonfiction** Middle readers, young adults: animal, biography, careers, geography, health, history, multicultural, nature/environment, reference, religion, science, social issues and sports.

**How to Contact/Writers** Nonfiction: Submit outline/synopsis and sample chapters. Responds to queries in 10 weeks. Publishes a book 10-12 months after acceptance. Will consider simultaneous submissions. Sends galleys to authors. Book catalog free on request. Send SASE for submission guidelines.

**Terms** Submission guidelines available via website or with SASE.

**Tips** ''Most projects have high reference value and fit into a series format.''

## ⚓ FARRAR, STRAUS & GIROUX INC.

19 Union Square W., New York NY 10003. (212)741-6900. Fax: (212)633-2427. Website: www.fsgkidsbooks.com. Estab. 1946. Book publisher. Imprints: Frances Foster Books, Melanie Kroupa Books. Children's Books Editorial Director: Margaret Ferguson. **Manuscript Acquisitions:** Margaret Ferguson, editorial director; Frances Foster, Frances Foster Books; Melanie Kroupa, Melanie Kroupa Books; Beverly Reingold, executive editor; Wesley Adams, executive editor; Robbie Mayes, editor. **Art Acquisitions:** Robbin Gourley, art director, books for young readers. Publishes 40 picture books/year; 15 middle readers/year; 15 young adult titles/year. 5% of books by first-time authors; 20% of books from agented writers.

• Farrar title *Jazzy Miz Mozetta*, by Frank Morrison, won a 2005 Coretta Scott King/John Steptoe New Talent Award for Illustration.

**Fiction** All levels: all categories. ''Original and well-written material for all ages.'' Recently published *The Search for Bell Prater*, by Ruth White; *That New Animal*, by Emily Jenkins.

**Nonfiction** All levels: all categories. "We publish only literary nonfiction."

**How to Contact/Writers** Fiction/nonfiction: Query with outline/synopsis and sample chapters. Do not fax submissions or queries. Responds to queries/mss in 3 months. Publishes a book 18 months after acceptance. Will consider simultaneous submissions.

**Illustration** Works with 30-60 illustrators/year. Reviews ms/illustration packages from artists. Submit ms with 1 example of final art, remainder roughs. Do not send originals. Illustrations only: Query with tearsheets. Responds if interested in 2 months. Samples returned with SASE; samples sometimes filed.

**Terms** "We offer an advance against royalties for both authors and illustrators." Sends galleys to authors; dummies to illustrators. Original artwork returned at job's completion. Book catalog available for 9×12 SAE and $1.95 postage; ms guidelines for 1 first-class stamp, or can be viewed at www.fsgkidsbooks.com.

**Tips** "Study our catalog before submitting. We will see illustrator's portfolios by appointment. Don't ask for criticism and/or advice—it's just not possible. Never send originals. Always enclose SASE."

## ☐ ☐ FIVE STAR PUBLICATIONS, INC.

P.O. Box 6698, Chandler AZ 85246-6698. (480)940-8182. Fax: (480)940-8787. E-mail: info@fivestarpublications. com. Website: www.fivestarpublications.com. **Art Acquisitions:** Sue DeFabis. Publishes 7 middle readers/year.

**Nonfiction** Recently published *Shakespeare for Children: The Story of Romeo & Juliet*, by Cass Foster; *The Sixty-Minute Shakespeare: Hamlet*, by Cass Foster; *The Sixty-Minute Shakespeare: Twelfth Night*, by Cass Foster.

**How to Contact/Writers** Nonfiction: Query.

**Illustration** Works with 3 illustrators/year. Reviews ms/illustration packages from artists. Query. Illustrations only: Query with samples. Responds only if interested. Samples filed.

**Photography** Buys stock and assigns work. Works on assignment only. Submit letter.

**Terms** Pays illustrators by the project. Pays photographers by the project. Sends galleys to authors; dummies to illustrators.

## FORWARD MOVEMENT PUBLICATIONS

300 West 4th St., 2nd Floor, Cincinnati OH 45202. (513)721-6659 or (800)543-1813. Fax: (513)721-0729. E-mail: orders@forwarddaybyday.com. Website: www.forwardmovement.org. **Acquisitions:** Edward S. Gleason, editor.

**Fiction** Middle readers and young adults: religion and religious problem novels, fantasy and science fiction.

**Nonfiction** Religion.

**How to Contact/Writers** Fiction/nonfiction: Query. Responds in 1 month. Does not accept mss via e-mail.

**Illustration** Query with samples. Samples returned with SASE.

**Terms** Pays authors honorarium. Pays illustrators by the project.

**Tips** "Forward Movement is now exploring publishing books for children and does not know its niche. We are an agency of the Episcopal Church and most of our market is to mainstream Protestants."

## FREE SPIRIT PUBLISHING

217 Fifth Ave. N., Suite 200, Minneapolis MN 55401-1299. (612)338-2068. Fax: (612)337-5050. E-mail: acquisitions@freespirit.com. Website: www.freespirit.com. **Acquisitions:** Editor. Publishes 16-22 titles/year for children and teens, teachers and parents. "Free Spirit Publishing is the home of SELF-HELP FOR KIDS® and SELF-HELP FOR TEENS® nonfiction, issue-driven, solution-focused books and materials for children and teens, and the parents and teachers who care for them."

• Free Spirit no longer accepts fiction or storybook submissions.

**Nonfiction** Areas of interest include emotional health, bullying and conflict resolution, tolerance and character development, social and study skills, creative learning and teaching, special needs learning, teaching, and parenting (gifted & talented and LD), family issues, healthy youth development, challenges specific to boys (including the parenting and teaching of boys), classroom activities, and innovative teaching techniques. We do not publish fiction or picture storybooks, books with animal or mythical characters, books with religious or New Age content, or single biographies, autobiographies, or memoirs. We prefer books written in a natural, friendly style, with little education/psychology jargon. We need books in our areas of emphasis and prefer titles written by specialists such as teachers, counselors, and other professionals who work with youth." Recently published *Talk and Work It Out and Know* and *Follow Rules*, by Cheri Meiners;*100 Things Guys Need to Know*, by Bill Zimmerman.

# Amy Timberlake

*Author breaks in with a (dirty) tale from her family lore*

**M**eet a children's book writer, and you'll likely be in the company of a person who remembers learning to love language and storytelling while perched on the knee of a family member. Amy Timberlake is no different.

The author of the 2004 SCBWI Golden Kite winner for best picture book text decided to commit to paper her family's fondest oral tradition, and the product is her debut *The Dirty Cowboy*. Her cowboy's tale is one supposedly reported in *The Silver City Enterprise* by her great-grandfather, Don Lusk, a newspaperman in Silver City, NM. Every summer, his son-in-law (Amy's grandfather "Papa") loved to recount the true story of a cowboy who decided to take his annual river bath, commanded his trusty canine companion to guard his wranglin' gear, and, as a result, was forced to run home naked through the desert when the dog refused to relinquish the clothes to the now-clean-smelling—and therefore suspect—cowboy.

"I hear my grandfather's version in my head more than I hear my own," reflects Timberlake. "I can see how he sat, slightly leaned forward, as he told the story. I remember how my brother and I had to promise to be quiet and not interrupt with too many questions. I remember how he'd pause, gather a few images in his head, and then continue the story. That memory of 'The Dirty Cowboy' is still the strongest."

Though Timberlake had been writing adult fiction as a graduate student at the University of Illinois at Chicago, she drew from her work as a seller and reviewer of children's books when she began her first writing project. "Even though I was exhausted from the effort of writing my Master's thesis, a novella, I wanted to continue to write regularly. As I wondered what to write, I remembered 'The Dirty Cowboy,' " she recalls. The familiarity and affinity she felt for picture books allowed her beloved childhood tale to take shape as one—the form that seemed most natural to her memory.

"What I remember is focusing on telling the story. I wanted my story to compete with Papa's story (which was a tall order)," she says. "In addition, I wanted to capture his language and make it funny. I truly wasn't thinking about the market while I wrote."

Timberlake finished her first version of *The Dirty Cowboy* in 1997—the same year that her grandfather passed away. Before he died, however, he was lucky enough to read an early manuscript. He sent Timberlake a letter, asserting the story was "for adults and not for children," but she remained firm. "I grew up knowing that my family exaggerated stories to make them more entertaining. Everyone told stories in their own way. I figured I had a right to my own version as much as Papa or my Dad or my brother have a right to their version," she says.

A few months later, Timberlake began submitting the manuscript to publishers, one at a time, hoping to ensure that even though her grandfather was no longer around to tell *his* version of the story, the dirty cowboy would live to bathe another day.

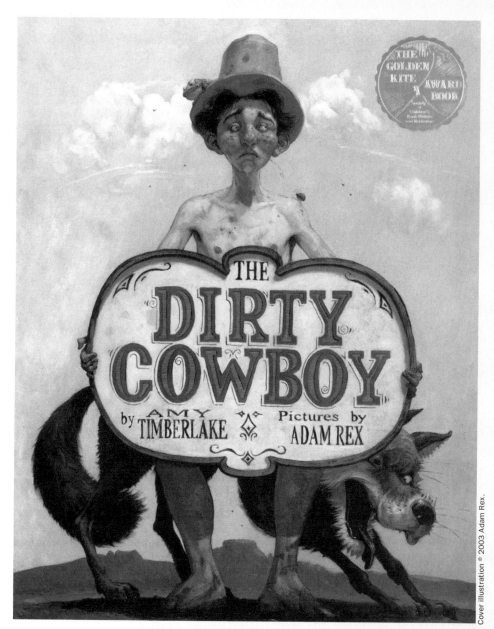

In what one Amazon.com reader-reviewer calls a "masterpiece of mesquite, mud, mayhem and scrub jays," author Amy Timberlake's first picture book *The Dirty Cowboy* (Farrar, Straus & Giroux) was a hit with readers and critics alike. In addition to SCBWI's 2003 Golden Kite Award for Excellence in Picture Book Text, Timberlake's tale earned, among others, a First Prize in the 2004 Marion Vannett Ridgway Awards, an International Reading Association 2004 Notable Book, a Parents Choice Gold Medal, and starred Reviews in *Kirkus*, *Publishers Weekly* and *The Bulletin for the Center of Children's Books*.

In 1999, she received an encouraging rejection letter from a well-respected editor who called *The Dirty Cowboy* a "tall tale." The comment sparked a new creative direction, and Timberlake and her cowboy went back to the computer.

"I thought, 'Okay, if you want a tall tale, I'll write you a tall tale,'" she remembers. "I did a major re-write, added all sorts of tall-tale elements like the dust devil scenes and crazed wrestling [between the cowboy and his dog] and then sent it out again."

A year passed before another house showed interest. At the request of its editor, Timberlake did another re-write and then waited patiently for a response. In the meantime, she decided to attend an SCBWI Illinois Writer's Retreat. During the retreat, Timberlake read a five-minute version of her story at an open mic event. Robbie Mayes of Farrar, Straus & Giroux was in the audience.

Timberlake spent the rest of the weekend working up the courage to approach Mayes. On the last day, she did, and she wasn't disappointed. "There was a particularly dreamy moment where he put his hand on my arm and said, 'If you wouldn't have come up and spoken to me, I would have talked to you. I'd really like it if you'd submit *The Dirty Cowboy* to me,'" she recalls. "I was stunned and very excited . . . except the manuscript was with the other editor at another house!"

When Timberlake returned home, she discovered that the editor she'd been corresponding with had left the house, and with that editor went the possibility of publishing her manuscript with them. She immediately submitted the manuscript to Mayes. A few months later he called with an offer, and Timberlake began her rewrites for FSG in November of 2000. Earlier that year, she had become the client of agent Steven Malk, who handled the contract with FSG for her. In June of 2001, the manuscript was finished; *The Dirty Cowboy* had finally found his way home.

The triumph of *The Dirty Cowboy* is not Timberlake's alone. After her first rewrite for FSG, Mayes sent Timberlake a sketch of the cowboy created by another emerging talent, illustrator Adam Rex.

"It was genius on Robbie's part. Adam Rex was the perfect partner for this story, and it was his first kid's book, too!" says Timberlake. "A week later, Robbie e-mailed me a full oil-painting of the cowboy trying to convince the dog to give up the clothes. I literally laughed out loud; it was perfect!"

Timberlake feels that Rex's art added "another beautiful layer" to the story that her family had treasured for generations, even though his interpretations of the characters were not exactly as her childhood imagination had conceived them.

"I think I'd always imagined the cowboy as someone about my grandfather's age. The dog I imagined as being more pathetic, and Adam's dog is clearly part wolf. But I never had a problem with any of this. Part of the joy of this picture book was the collaboration," she says.

In addition to learning the rewards of collaboration, Timberlake says the greatest thing she gained during the process of writing and publishing this book was confidence in her ability to work with a book editor. "For some reason, I was nervous about this," she recalls. "I wondered how it would feel to work with the edits. But I ended up loving the process. I knew if Robbie suggested a change, the sentence must—at the very least—be unclear. Eventually it felt like a game between the two of us: how many ways can I say the same thing, keep it in my language, and use just as strong an image."

Years of work, input from different editors, several rewrites, and the influence of an artist have done nothing to diminish or alter Timberlake's affection for her family's original story. "I still love it in the same way I did before sitting down to write the book. And being a picture book, the story now has a chance to reach many more children," she says.

Timberlake is currently working on a middle-grade novel called *Lucy Moon* for Hyperion due out in Spring 2006.

—*Lauren Mosko*

**How to Contact/Writers** "Submissions are accepted from prospective authors, including youth ages 16 and up, or through agents. Please review our catalog and author guidelines (both available online) before submitting proposal." Responds to queries/mss in 4-6 months. "If you'd like materials returned, enclose a SASE with sufficient postage." Write or call for catalog and submission guidelines before sending submission. Accepts queries only by e-mail. Submission guidelines available online.

**Illustration** Works with 5 illustrators/year. Submit samples to creative director for consideration. If appropriate, samples will be kept on file and artist will be contacted if a suitable project comes up. Enclose SASE if you'd like materials returned.

**Photography** Submit samples to creative director for consideration. If appropriate, samples will be kept on file and photographer will be contacted if a suitable project comes up. Enclose SASE if you'd like materials returned.

**Terms** Pays authors royalty based on net receipts. Offers advance. Pays illustrators by the project. Pays photographers by the project or per photo.

**Tips** "Free Spirit is a niche publisher known for high-quality books featuring a positive and practical focus and jargon free approach. Study our catalog, read our author guidelines, and be sure your proposal is the right 'fit' before submitting. Our preference is for books that help parents and teachers help kids [and that help kids themselves] gain personal strengths, succeed in school, stand up for themselves and others, and otherwise make a positive difference in today's world."

## FREESTONE/PEACHTREE, JR.

Peachtree Publishers, 1700 Chattahooche Ave., Atlanta GA 30318-2112. (404)876-8761. Fax: (404)875-2578. E-mail: hello@peachtree-online.com. Website: www.peachtree-online.com. **Acquisitions:** Helen Harriss. Publishes 4-8 young adult titles/year.

• Freestone and Peachtree, Jr. are imprints of Peachtree Publishers. See the listing for Peachtree for submission information. No e-mail or fax queries or submissions, please.

**Fiction** Picture books, young readers, middle readers, young adults: history, humor, multicultural, sports. Picture books: animal, folktales, nature/environment, special needs. Picture books, young readers: health. Middle readers, young adults/teens: adventure, contemporary, problem novels, suspense/mystery. Recently published *Saturdays & Teacakes*, by Lester L. Laminack, illustrated by Chris Soenpiet (ages 4-8, picture book); *The Amazing Mr. Franklin*, by Ruth Ashby, illustrated by Michael Montgomery (ages 7-10, early reader); *Quake*, by Gail Langer Karwoski, illustrated by Robert Papp (ages 8-12, middle reader/historical fiction).

**Nonfiction** Picture books, young readers, middle readers, young adults: history, sports. Picture books: animal, health, multicultural, nature/environment, science, social issues, special needs.

**How to Contact** Responds to queries/mss in 6 months.

**Illustration** Works with 10-20 illustrators/year. Responds only if interested. Samples not returned; samples filed. Originals returned at job's completion.

**Terms** Pays authors royalty. Pays illustrators by the project or royalty. Pays photographers by the project or per photo.

## ⚅ FRONT STREET BOOKS

862 Haywood Rd., Asheville NC 28806. (828)236-3097. Fax: (828)236-3098. E-mail: contactus@frontstreetbooks.com. Website: www.frontstreetbooks.com. **Acquisitions:** Joy Neaves, editor. Publishes 10-15 titles/year. "We are a small independent publisher of books for children and young adults. We do not publish pablum: we try to publish books that will attract, if not addict, children to literature, and books that are a pleasure to look at and a pleasure to hold, books that will be revelations to young minds."

• See Front Street's website for submission guidelines and complete catalog. Front Street focuses on fiction, but will publish poetry, anthologies, nonfiction and high-end picture books. They do not accept unsolicited picture book manuscripts. Front Street title *Fortune's Bones: The Manumission Requiem*, by Marilyn Nelson won a 2005 Coretta Scott King Author Honor Award.

**Fiction** Recently published *The Big House*, by Carolyn Coman; *Heck*, by Martine Leavitt; *MVP\**, by Doug Evans; *Fortunes Bones*, by Marilyn Nelson.

**How to Contact/Writers** Fiction: Submit cover letter and complete ms if under 30 pages; submit cover letter, 1 or 2 sample chapters and plot summary if over 30 pages. Nonfiction: Submit detailed proposal and sample chapters. Poetry: Submit no more than 25 poems. Include SASE with submissions if you want them returned. "Please allow four months for a response. If no response in four months, send a status query by mail."

**Illustration** "Send sample illustrations."

**Terms** Pays royalties.

## ⬜ FULCRUM KIDS

Imprint of Fulcrum Publishing, 16100 Table Mountain Parkway, #300, Golden CO 80403. (303)277-1623. Fax: (303)279-7111. Website: www.fulcrum-books.com. **Manuscript Acquisitions:** T. Baker , acquisitions editor.

**Nonfiction** Middle and early readers: activity books, multicultural, nature/environment.

**How to Contact/Writers** Submit complete ms or submit outline/synopsis and 2 sample chapters. Responds to queries in 3 weeks; mss in 2 months. Publishes a book 12-18 months after acceptance.

**Illustration** Works with 10 illustrators/year. Reviews ms/illustration packages from artists. Send ms with dummy or submit ms with 3 pieces of final art. Send résumé, promotional literature and tearsheets. Contact: Ann Douden. Responds only if interested. Samples not returned; samples filed.

**Photography** Works on assignment only.

**Terms** Pays authors royalty based on wholesale price. Offers advances. Pays illustrators by the project or royalty based on wholesale price. Sends galleys to authors; dummies to illustrators. Originals returned to artist at job's completion. Book catalog available for 9×12 SAE and 77¢ postage; ms guidelines available for SASE. Catalog available on website.

**Tips** "Research our line first. We are emphasizing science and nature nonfiction. We look for books that appeal to the school market and trade. Be sure to include SASE."

## LAURA GERINGER BOOKS

Imprint of HarperCollins Publishers, 1350 Avenue of the Americas, New York NY 10019. Website: www.haperch ildrens.com. **Manuscript and Art Acquisitions:** Laura Geringer. Publishes 6 picture books/year; 2 young readers/year; 4 middle readers/year; 1 young adult title/year. 15% of books by first-time authors.

**Fiction** Picture books, young readers: adventure, folktales, humor, multicultural, poetry. Middle readers: adventure, anthology, fantasy, history, humor, poetry, suspense/mystery. Young adults/teens: adventure, fantasy, history, humor, suspense/mystery. Average word length: picture books—500; young readers—1,000; middle readers—25,000; young adults—40,000. Recently published *If You Take a Mouse to School*, by Laura Numeroff, illustrated by Felicia Bond (ages 3-7); *The Dulcimer Boy*, by Tor Seidler, illustrated by Brian Selznick (ages 8 and up).

**How to Contact/Writers Only interested in agented material.**

**Illustration** Works with 8 illustrators/year. Reviews ms/illustration packages from artists. Send ms with dummy and 3 pieces of final art. Illustrations only: Query with color photocopies. Contact: Laura Geringer, publisher. Responds only if interested. Samples returned with SASE.

**Terms** Book catalog available for 11×9 SASE and $2 postage; all imprints included in a single catalog.

## GIBBS SMITH, PUBLISHER

P.O. Box 667, Layton UT 84041. (801)544-9800. Fax: (801)544-5582. E-mail: mbarlow@gibbs-smith.com. Website: www.gibbs-smith.com. **Manuscript Acquisitions:** Jennifer Grillone (picture books); Suzanne Taylor, vice president and editorial director (children's activity books). **Art Acquisitions:** Kurt Wahlner, art director. Book publisher; co-publisher of Sierra Club Books for Children. Imprint: Gibbs Smith. Publishes 2-3 books/year. 50% of books by first-time authors. 50% of books from agented authors. "We accept submissions for picture books with particular interest in those with a Western (cowboy or ranch life style) theme or backdrop."

- Gibbs Smith is not accepting fiction at this time.

**Nonfiction** Middle readers: activity, arts/crafts, cooking, how-to, nature/environment, science. Average word length: picture books—under 1,000 words; activity books—under 15,000 words. Recently published *Hiding in a Fort*, by G. Lawson Drinkard, illustrated by Fran Lee (ages 7-12); *Sleeping in a Sack: Camping Activities for Kids*, by Linda White, illustrated by Fran Lee (ages 7-12).

**How to Contact/Writers** Nonfiction: Submit an outline and writing samples for activity books; query for other types of books. Responds to queries/mss in 2 months. Publishes a book 1-2 years after acceptance. Will consider simultaneous submissions. Manuscript returned with SASE.

**Illustration** Works with 2 illustrators/year. Reviews ms/illustration packages from artists. Query. Submit ms with 3-5 pieces of final art. Illustrations only: Query with samples; provide résumé, promo sheet, slides (duplicate slides, not originals). Responds only if interested. Samples returned with SASE; samples filed.

**Terms** Pays authors royalty of 2% based on retail price or work purchased outright ($500 minimum). Offers advances (average amount: $2,000). Pays illustrators by the project or royalty of 2% based on retail price. Sends galleys to authors; color proofs to illustrators. Original artwork returned at job's completion. Book catalog available for 9×12 SAE and $2.30 postage. Manuscript guidelines availablee—mail duribe@gibbs-smith.com.

**Tips** "We target ages 5-11. We do not publish young adult novels or chapter books."

## ⓐ GOLDEN BOOKS

1745 Broadway, New York NY 10019. (212)782-9000. **Editorial Directors:** Courtney Silk , color and activity; Chris Angelilli, storybooks; Dennis Shealy, novelty. **Art Acquisitions:** Tracey Tyler, executive art director.

- See listing for Random House-Golden Books for Young Readers Group.

**How to Contact/Writers** Does not accept unsolicited submissions.

**Fiction** Publishes board books, novelty books, picture books, workbooks, series (mass market and trade).

## GRAPHIA

Houghton Mifflin Company, 222 Berkeley St., Boston MA 02116. (617)351-5000. Website: www.graphiabooks.com. **Manuscript Acquisitions:** Eden Edwards. "Graphia publishes quality paperbacks for today's teen readers. From fiction to nonfiction, poetry to graphic novels, Graphia runs the gamut, all unified by the quality writing that is the hallmark of this new imprint."

**Fiction** Young adults: adventure, contemporary, fantasy, history, humor, multicultural, poetry, problem novels, science fiction. Recently published: *I Can't Tell You*, by Hillary Frank; *Owl in Love*, by Patrice Kindl; *Zazoo*, by Richard Mosher (all novels for ages 14 and up).

**Nonfiction** Young adults: biography, history, multicultural, nature/environment, science, social issues.

**How to Contact/Writers** Query. Responds to queries/mss in 3 months. Will consider simultaneous submissions and previously published work.

**Illustration** Do not send original artwork or slides. Send color photocopies, tearsheets or photos to Art Dept. Include SASE fi you would like your samples mailed back to you.

**Terms** Pays author royalties. Offers advances. Sends galleys to authors. Catalog available on website (www.houghtonmifflin.com).

## GREENE BARK PRESS

P.O. Box 1108, Bridgeport CT 06601-1108. (203)372-4861. Fax: (203)371-5856. E-mail: greenebark@aol.com. Website: www.greenebarkpress.com. **Acquisitions:** Thomas J. Greene, publisher. Publishes 1-6 picture books/year; m ajority of books by first-time or repeat authors. "We publish quality hardcover picture books for children. Our stories are selected for originality, imagery and color. Our intention is to fire-up a child's imagination, encourage a desire to read in order to explore the world through books."

**Fiction** Picture books, young readers: adventure, fantasy, humor. Average word length: picture books—650; young readers—1,400. Recently published *Edith Ellen Eddy*, by Julee Ann Granger; *Hey, There's a Gobblin Under My Throne*, by Rhett Ranson Pennell.

**How to Contact/Writers** Responds to queries in 2 months; mss in 6 months; must include SASE. No response without SASE. Publishes a book 18 months after acceptance. Will consider simultaneous submissions. Prefer to review complete mss with illustrations.

**Illustration** Works with 1-2 illustrators/year. Uses color artwork only. Reviews ms/illustration packages from artists. Submit ms with 3 pieces of final art (copies only). Illustrations only: Query with samples. Responds in 2 months only if interested. Samples returned with SASE; samples filed. Originals returned at job's completion.

**Terms** Pays authors royalty of 10-12% based on wholesale price. Pays illustrators by the project (range: $1,500-3,000) or 5-7% royalty based on wholesale price. No advances. Sends galleys to authors; dummies to illustrators. Book catalog available for $2, which includes mailing. All imprints included in a single catalog. Manuscript; guidelines available for SASE or per e-mail request.

**Tips** "As a guide for future publications look to our latest publications, do not look to our older backlist. Please, no telephone, e-mail or fax queries."

## GREENHAVEN PRESS

Imprint of the Gale Group, 15822 Bermuda Center Drive, Suite C, San Diego CA 92127. Website: www.gale.com/greenhaven. **Acquisitions:** Chandra Howard., senior acquisitions editor. Publishes 300 young adult academic reference titles/year. 35% of books by first-time authors. Greenhaven continues to print quality nonfiction for libraries and classrooms. Our well known Opposing Viewpoints series is highly respected by students and librarians in need of material on controversial social issues.

● Greenhaven accepts no unsolicited manuscripts. All writing is done on a work-for-hire basis. See also listing for Lucent Books.

**Nonfiction** Young adults (high school): controversial topics, history, issues.

**How to Contact/Writers** Send query, résumé, and list of published works.

**Terms** Buys ms outright for $1,500-3,000. Sends galleys to authors. No phone calls. Short writing samples are appropriate; long unsolicited mss will not be read or returned.

## Ⓐ Ⓥ GREENWILLOW BOOKS

Imprint of HarperCollins, 1350 Avenue of the Americas, New York NY 10019. (212)261-6500. Website: www.harperchildrens.com. Book publisher. Vice President/Publisher: Virginia Duncan. **Art Acquisitions:** Paul Zakris, art director. Publishes 40 picture books/year; 5 middle readers/year; 5 young adult books/year. "Greenwillow Books publishes picture books, fiction for young readers of all ages, and nonfiction primarily for children under seven years of age."

● Greenwillow Books is currently accepting neither unsolicited manuscripts nor queries. Unsolicited mail will not be opened and will not be returned. Call (212)261-6627 for an update. Greenwillow title *Kitten's First Full Moon*, by Kevin Henkes, won the 2005 Caldecott Medal.

**Book Publishers**

**Illustration** Art samples (postcards only) should be sent in duplicate to Paul Zakris and Virginia Duncan.
**Terms** Pays authors royalty. Offers advances. Pays illustrators royalty or by the project. Sends galleys to authors.

## GROSSET & DUNLAP PUBLISHERS

Penguin Group (USA), 345 Hudson St., New York NY 10014. Estab. 1898. **Acquisitions:** Debra Dorfman, president/publisher. Publishes 175 titles/year. "Grosset & Dunlap publishes children's books that show children reading is fun with books that speak to their interests and are affordable so children can build a home library of their own. Focus on licensed properties, series, and readers."
**Fiction** Recently published Katie Kazoo (series); Zenda (series); Strawberry Shortcake (license); Dick & Jane (brand); The Wiggles (license).
**Nonfiction** Young readers: nature/environment, science.
**How to Contact/Writers Only interested in agented material.**

## GRYPHON HOUSE

P.O. Box 207, Beltsville MD 20704-0207. (301)595-9500. Fax: (301)595-0051. E-mail: kathyc@ghbooks.com. Website: www.gryphonhouse.com. **Acquisitions:** Kathy Charner, editor-in-chief.
**Nonfiction** Parent and teacher resource books—activity books, textbooks. Recently published *First Art: Art Experiences for Toddlers and Twos*, by MaryAnn F. Kohl; *Games to Play with Babies Third Edition*, by Jackie Silberg; *Creating Readers*, by Pam Schiller. " At Gryphon House, our goal is to publish books that help teachers and parents enrich the lives of children from birth through age eight. We strive to make our books useful for teachers at all levels of experience, as well as for parents, caregivers, and anyone interested in working with children."
**How to Contact/Writers** Query. Submit outline/synopsis and 2 sample chapters. Responds to queries/mss in 6 months. Publishes a book 18 months after acceptance. Will consider simultaneous submissions, e-mail submissions.
**Illustration** Works with 4-5 illustrators/year. Uses b&w artwork only. Illustrations only: Query with samples, promo sheet. Responds in 2 months. Samples returned with SASE; samples filed.
**Photography** Buys photos from freelancers. Buys stock and assigns work. Submit cover letter, published samples, stock photo list.
**Terms** Pays authors royalty based on wholesale price. Offers advances. Pays illustrators by the project. Pays photographers by the project or per photo. Sends edited ms copy to authors. Original artwork returned at job's completion. Book catalog and ms guidelines available via website or with SASE.
**Tips** "Send a SASE for our catalog and manuscript guidelines. Look at our books, then submit proposals that complement the books we already publish or supplement our existing books. We are looking for books of creative, participatory learning experiences that have a common conceptual theme to tie them together. The books should be on subjects that parents or teachers want to do on a daily basis."

## GULLIVER BOOKS

15 E. 26th St., New York NY 10010. (212)592-1000. Fax: (212)592-1030. E-mail: lvandoren@harcourt.com. Website: www.harcourtbooks.com. **Acquisitions:** Liz Van Doren, editorial director; Tamson Weston, editor; Kate Harrison, associate editor; Scott Piehl, art director. Publishes 25 titles/year.
● Gulliver only accepts manuscripts submitted by agents, previously published authors, or SCBWI members.
**Fiction** Emphasis on picture books: animal, contemporary, humor, history, multicultural, poetry. Also publishes middle grade and select young adult. Recently published *Won't You Be My Kissaroo*, by Joanne Ryder, illustrated by Melissa Sweet (ages 2-5, picture book); *Each Little Bird That Sings*, by Deborah Wiles (ages 8-12, middle grade).
**Nonfiction** Picture books: animal, biography, history, multicultural. Also publishes some middle grade and young adult.
**How to Contact/Writers Only interested in agented material.** Also accepts material from SCBWI members and previously published authors. Picture b ooks: Send m s. Middle grade/y oung a dult f iction/n onfiction: Query. Responds to queries/mss in 2 months.
**Illustrations** Responds in 2 months only if interested. Samples returned with SASE only; samples filed. Originals returned at job's completion.
**Terms** Authors and illustrators paid royalty.

## HACHAI PUBLISHING

156 Chester Ave., Brooklyn NY 11218-3020. (718)633-0100. Fax: (718)633-0103. E-mail: info@hachai.com. Website: www.hachai.com. **Manuscript Acquisitions:** Devorah Leah Rosenfeld, submissions editor. Publishes 4 picture books/year; 1 young reader/year; 1 middle reader/year. 75% of books published by first-time authors. "All books have spiritual/religious themes, specifically traditional Jewish content. We're seeking books about morals and

values; the Jewish experience in current and Biblical times; and Jewish observance, Sabbath and holidays.''

**Fiction** Picture books and young readers: contemporary, historical fiction, religion. Middle readers: adventure, contemporary, problem novels, religion. Does not want to see fantasy, animal stories, romance, problem novels depicting drug use or violence. Recently published *Let's Go to Shul*, written and illustrated by Rikki Benenfeld (ages 2-5, picture book); *Get Well Soon*, by Dina Rosenfeld, illustrated by Rina Lyampe (ages 2-5, picture book); *When the World Was Quiet*, by Phyllis Nutkis, illustrated by Patti Argoff (ages 2-5, picture book); *Once Upon a Time*, by Draizy Zelcer, illustrated by Vitaliy Romanenko (ages 3-6, picture book); *More Precious Than Gold*, by Evelyn Blatt (ages 7-10, short chapter book).

**Nonfiction** Published *My Jewish ABC's*, by Draizy Zelcer, illustrated by Patti Nemeroff (ages 3-6, picture book); *Nine Spoons* by Marci Stillerman, illustrated by Pesach Gerber (ages 5-8).

**How to Contact/Wrtiers** Fiction/nonfiction: Submit complete ms. Responds to queries/mss in 6 weeks.

**Illustration** Works with 4 illustrators/year. Uses primary color artwork, some b&w illustration. Reviews ms/ illustration packages from authors. Submit ms with 1 piece of final art. Illustrations only: Query with samples; arrange personal portfolio review. Responds in 6 weeks. Samples returned with SASE; samples filed.

**Terms** Work purchased outright from authors for $800-1,000. Pays illustrators by the project (range: $2,000-3,500). Book catalog, ms/artist's guidelines available for SASE.

**Tips** ''Write a story that incorporates a moral, not a preachy morality tale. Originality is the key. We feel Hachai publications will appeal to a wider readership as parents become more interested in positive values for their children.''

## HANDPRINT BOOKS

413 Sixth Ave., Brooklyn NY 11215. E-mail: submissions@handprintbooks.com. Website: www.handprintbook s.com. Submissions should be sent to e-mail address. Sample art (1 or 2 pieces) should be sent as a pdf or jpeg file.

**Tips** ''Please visit our website before submitting material to learn about the kinds of books we publish.''

## Ⓐ HARCOURT, INC.

15 East 26th Street, New York NY 10010. (212)592-1034. Fax: (212)592-1030. Children's Books Division includes: Harcourt Children's Books (Ms. Allyn Johnston, editorial director), Gulliver Books (Liz Van Doren, editorial director), Voyager Paperbacks, Odyssey Paperbacks, and Red Wagon Books. Book publisher. **Art Director:** Scott Piehl. Publishes 50-75 picture books/year; 10-20 middle readers/year; 25-50 young adult titles/ year. 20% of books by first-time authors; 50% of books from agented writers. ''Harcourt, Inc. owns some of the world's most prestigious publishing imprints—which distinguish quality products for children's educational and trade markets worldwide.''

• Harcourt Children's Books no longer accepts unsolicited manuscripts, queries or illustrations. Harcourt titles *How I Became a Pirate*, by Melinda Long, illustrated by David Shannon and *Tails*, by Matthew Van Fleet are both New York Times best sellers.

**Fiction** All levels: Considers all categories. Average word length: picture books—''varies greatly''; middle readers—20,000-50,000; young adults—35,000-65,000. Recently published *Pinduli*, by Janell Cannon; *The End of the Beginning*, by Avi; *Gifts*, by Ursula K. LeGuin; *The Librarian of Basra*, by Jeanette Winter.

**Nonfiction** All levels: animal, biography, concept, history, multicultural, music/dance, nature/environment, science, sports. Average word length: picture books—''varies greatly''; middle readers—20,000-50,000; young adults—35,000-65,000.

**How to Contact/Writers Only interested in agented material.**

Illustration Only interested in agented material.

**Photography** Works on assignment only.

**Terms** Pays authors and illustrators royalty based on retail price. Pays photographers by the project. Sends galleys to authors; dummies to illustrators. Original artwork returned at job's completion. Book catalog available for 8×10 SAE and 4 first-class stamps; ms/artist's guidelines available for business-size SASE. All imprints included in a single catalog.

## Ⓐ 🄥 HARPERCOLLINS CHILDREN'S BOOKS

1350 Avenue of the Americas, New York NY 10019. (212)261-6500. Website: www.harperchildrens.com. Book publisher. Editor-in-Chief: Kate Morgan Jackson. Editorial Director: Maria Modugno. **Art Acquisitions:** Martha Rago or Stephanie Berth-Horvath, director. Imprints: HarperTrophy, HarperTempest, Avon, HarperFestival, Greenwillow Books, Joanna Cotler Books, Laura Geringer Books, Katherine Tegen Books.

• HarperCollins Children's Books is not accepting unsolicited and/or unagented manuscripts or queries. Unfortunately, the volume of these submissions is so large that we cannot give them the attention they deserve. Such submissions will not be reviewed or returned. HarperCollins title *God Bless the Children*,

# Bruce Hale

*Cartoonist turned series author gets
kids connected with books*

I n Bruce Hale's popular Chet Gecko series, a pre-teen gecko takes on pro-bono detective work, solving crimes while hilariously misusing private eye lingo. Chet is part detective, part comedian, and he's also a student—something he'd like to forget. Like Chet Gecko himself, Hale's books resist categorization. It just may be that geckoes are a bit too slippery to pin down—and that's part of the draw.

Hale got the germ of the idea for his Chet Gecko series when he attended a Society of Children's Book Writers and Illustrators (SCBWI) conference back in 1997. After listening to several speakers from different publishing houses, he had a plan. "I was thinking, 'OK, what do publishers want?' So I listened to different editors talk, and they said, 'Oh, we love humor.' Another one said, 'We love animal stories.' And a couple of different houses said, 'We really love mysteries.' It came to my mind, why not do a combination of all three, a sort of humorous-mystery-animal story?" recalls Hale.

And that, as they say, was that. His idea may have seemed like a crazy mix, but it certainly worked for Hale's first nationally published book, *The Chameleon Wore Chartreuse*. Hale stuck with his winning recipe and kept going. Since 2000, he has published ten books in the Chet Gecko series and is currently working on the eleventh. In addition, he has published five Moki series picture books for children. (The tireless go-getter self-published his first Moki book in 1989.) But Hale won't rest on his laurels. He's spent his down time thinking up ideas for another series. "I'd like to keep a couple of series going concurrently, and just go back and forth between them," he says.

Although Hale began his creative life as a cartoonist, he has adapted very well to the demanding life of a writer—and a storyteller and workshop leader and speaker and illustrator and Fulbright scholar and actor and singer and screenwriter . . . So when does he sleep? "I get plenty of sleep," he claims. "Sleeping is very important to me. But I like to fill my working hours pretty well." Indeed.

Here Hale talks about the many hats he wears as a writer, illustrator and cartoonist, and about how he arrived at this point in his career. He also gives some sage, sometimes tongue-in-cheek advice to help other authors along their way.

### How did you get your first book published? Was the first Chet Gecko mystery the first book you published?

Actually, there are two answers to that question. The Chet Gecko series are the first books that I had published with a national publisher. However, before that I self-published five picture books, the first in 1989. I look at that as my learning curve. The early books were good and got better, and the whole time I was self-publishing, I was continuing to seek a national publisher. And then in 1998, I signed a contract with Harcourt for the first three Chet Gecko books.

## And how did that first self-published book go?

It worked out very well. I had started a business with a friend making little stuffed toy gift animals in Hawaii, Aloha-print critters, and I thought gosh, it would be kind of fun to do a book to go along with our gecko character. So I did a book called *Legend of the Laughing Gecko*, which explains why geckos are good luck in Hawaii. Initially we didn't know anything about publishing, and we sort of plunged into it. By sheer dumb luck, the book did very well, and now I think it's sold over 60,000 copies, which is pretty good for a self-published book.

## Would you recommend other people go the self-publishing route?

Only if you have deep pockets and are a little bit masochistic. It's really challenging. I had no idea how challenging it would be. You have to be not only the author—but also the book designer, in my case the illustrator, the publicist and the marketing team. I mean, you have to do everything yourself. It was very much learning on the job.

Private Eye Chet Gecko himself explains the setup for *The Malted Falcon*: "It was tall, dark, and chocolatey—the stuff dreams are made of. It was a treat so titanic that nobody had been able to finish one single-handedly (or even single-mouthedly). It was the Malted Falcon. How far would you go for the ultimate dessert? Somebody went too far, and that's where I came in." Visit www.brucehale.com for the rest of the story and the lowdown on Bruce Hale's Check Gecko series.

## At least you knew all sides of the business going into it.

Exactly. By the time I signed with Harcourt, they knew I understood the process of publishing a book and I would work hard on publicity and marketing and getting the books out there, getting my name out there, which is something I would imagine most publishers would want from any author.

## How did your first Chet Gecko book get published after you came up with the initial idea for it?

After I finished the initial manuscript, I submitted it to twelve different publishers, all of whom said no. Then I was at the SCBWI conference the following year, and I happened to hear an agent speak named Steven Malk, and I really liked what he had to say, and I thought we were sort of compatible. I sent him several stories, including *Chet Gecko*, which he really liked. Within three months of us meeting each other, he had a contract for me with Harcourt.

### So you would recommend getting an agent?

I don't think there's any one way to do it. It's certainly very helpful to have an agent, and there are some publishing houses that won't look at an unsolicited manuscript, and to get to them you need an agent. But I know some well-established authors who are really successful without one. For me, it proved to be a key to finally breaking through. My agent shared my viewpoint and was able to find an editor who also shared my twisted sense of humor and had a similar kind of viewpoint, and that was just a good match all the way around.

### What keeps you going as you write new books using the same characters?

Number one, it's great to be an employed writer. If the publisher says we want more of these, and I'm still having fun with the series, then why not? I really enjoy the characters, and I have fun playing in that world. As you can tell, I have a real fondness for the old-style detective mysteries, and I've read a ton of them. It's fun to write in that style and spoof it, but not entirely spoof it. It's a mystery on its own that I'm creating, not just a spoof. It's fun, kind of riffing on certain things, bringing a background character more into the foreground, and exploring relationships. That's one fun thing about series, once you've created the world, it's great to see how many variations you can make on it. I like to bring in something new every time. In my newest book, *Murder My Tweet*, Natalie, Chet's partner, is framed for a crime she didn't commit, and she's suspended from school. Chet's whole task is to find the guilty party, the blackmailer. And in the course of doing this, he finds this other plot going on which involves killer robots taking over the school. Killer robots! Oh yeah, how fun! One of the other books, *Hamster of the Baskervilles*, has a werehamster. Each time I think, what other fun things can I do within this environment?

### What's so attractive to you about having animals as protagonists?

I started out doing it because I liked drawing animals better than I liked drawing humans. And there are all kinds of cool animals around to draw in Hawaii. When I was starting to write *Chet Gecko*, I didn't want to do another gecko story. I wanted to do another animal protagonist, but something different. I was just writing the first introductory page of it, just kind of getting his voice in my head, and I could hear him so clearly. He said, "Who am I? I'm Chet Gecko, private eye." The name came out like that, and it sounded so great, I couldn't argue with it. So I had another gecko series on my hands. I've stuck with the animal characters because it offers sort of a universality. It's really easy for kids of any ethnicity or gender to relate to animals because animals are not human-specific to one ethnicity or gender themselves. It's also kind of a fun way to spoof human society. However, I am working on a longer fantasy book right now that has human protagonists. So, yes, I can write non-animals. I like to use all living things. Who knows, maybe we'll get a rock as the star of one of my books one of these days. It would be kind of limited in its motion, though.

### Maybe it has a really rich inner life?

Exactly.

### We touched on how you use humor, and when I was reading *The Mystery of Mr. Nice*, I was laughing a ton at the adult humor. Did you choose to make it work on two levels? Why do you think that works so well?

It was a deliberate choice. Initially, when I first wrote the book, it wasn't quite as conscious, because I was just writing what I enjoy. I had been writing some things that were heavy on the moral content, and nobody wanted to publish them, and now I see why. They were—if not didactic—just not as me. So I wrote something that would entertain me. Then part way into it I realized that I had taken as my model the old Warner Bros. cartoons which always had some jokes for the adults, like some bad puns and literary references, and some broad stuff for the kids. I maintained that for my model because I like connecting with both audiences. A lot of times in schools, teachers read to the kids, and then the teachers will laugh at something that the kids don't get, and it's an opportunity to explain things, to say, "This is a reference to this book." It makes it a teachable moment. It's fun for adults and it's fun for kids—that's the bottom line.

## Do you have a purpose for your writing?

With the Chet Gecko books, actually, my main purpose is to get kids excited about reading. I just want to write stories that are fun and hard to put down. I've gotten a lot of feedback from teachers and librarians that the series is really good for encouraging reluctant readers. And so I have sort of taken that as my mission, because I'm really passionate about getting kids connected with books. That more than anything is the reason I'm doing it. You know, in the books, sometimes a "teaching" scene will emerge, like in *Trouble is My Beeswax*. In that book, I deliberately chose cheating in the schools as my subject. There had been a cheating ring in the school, but it's not like teaching the kids a lesson, you know, "cheating is bad," but some things are revealed during the course of dealing with that theme over the course of the book, and some truth does emerge. It's just part of the scene. But I don't sit down and think, "What can I teach the kids this time?"

## What have you been working on lately?

Well, I'm not going to say much about it, because it's still in the rough draft stage, but I am working on a fantasy story. It involves time travel. It's fun to write something different, where there's not as much pressure to come up with rapid-fire jokes. And I've also written some short stories during this time off for some collections.

Actually, they're for two different collections. One of them is the Guys Read collection. Author John Scieszka started a group called Guys Read to encourage young guys to read. They're putting together a book to help fund the project. I contributed a story for that.

I've also been doing some screenwriting. I did a version of the Chet Gecko animated movie. It's under option right now, and it's actually been under option for a couple of years. It's slowly moving forward—this is the third version of the script I'm working on right now. Development in Hollywood is never a sure thing until the movie is actually being produced.

## What advice would you give other children's authors?

Persistence is even more important than talent in getting published. You can have all the talent in the world, but if you don't hang in there through the rejection, you'll never reach that stage of getting published. It's really important for beginning writers to realize that up front, that just because you can tell a good story it doesn't mean that the world will beat a path to your door and publish your book the first time out. You really have to want it enough to put up with that disappointment of rejection. It's no fun at all, but if you're willing to do what it takes you can become published, that's certainly what I've found myself. From the time I first started self-publishing, in 1989, to the time that *Chet Gecko* first came out, which was 2000—that's a good stretch of years. I was collecting a lot of rejection letters. It's important to not give up. That's my message to beginning writers.

*—Jessica Gordon*

illustrated by Jerry Pinkney, written by Billie Holiday and Arthur Herzog, Jr., won a 2005 Coretta Scott King Illustrator Honor Award. Harper title *Airborn*, by Kenneth Oppel, won a 2005 Printz Honor Award.
**Fiction** Publishes picture, chapter, novelty, board and TV/movie books.
**How to Contact/Writers Only interested in agented material.**
**Illustration** Art samples may be sent to Martha Rago or Stephanie Berth-Horvath. **Please do not send original art.** Works with over 100 illustrators/year. Responds only if interested. Samples returned with SASE; samples filed only if interested.
**Terms** Art guidelines available for SASE.

## ⬚ HAYES SCHOOL PUBLISHING CO. INC.
321 Pennwood Ave., Wilkinsburg PA 15221-3398. (412)371-2373. Fax: (800)543-8771. E-mail: chayes@hayespub.com. Website: www.hayespub.com. Estab. 1940. **Acquisitions:** Mr. Clair N. Hayes. Produces folders, workbooks, stickers, certificates. Wants to see supplementary teaching aids for grades K-12. Interested in all subject areas. Will consider simultaneous and electronic submissions.
**How to Contact/Writers** Query with description or complete ms. Responds in 6 weeks. SASE for return of submissions.
**Illustration** Works with 3-4 illustrators/year. Responds in 6 weeks. Samples returned with SASE; samples filed. Originals not returned at job's completion.
**Terms** Work purchased outright. Purchases all rights.

## HEALTH PRESS
 NA Inc., P.O. Box 37470, Albuquerque NM 87176-7479. (505)888-1394 or (877)411-0707. Fax: (505)888-1521. E-mail: goodbooks@healthpress.com. Website: www.healthpress.com. **Acquisitions:** Editor. Publishes 4 young readers/year. 100% of books by first-time authors.
**Fiction** Picture books, young readers: health, special needs. Average word length: young readers—1,000-1,500; middle readers—1,000-1,500. Recently published *The Girl With No Hair*, by Elizabeth Murphy-Melas, illustrated by Alex Hernandez (ages 8-12, picture book); *The Peanut Butter Jam*, by Elizabeth Sussman-Nassau, illustrated by Margot Ott (ages 6-12, picture book).
**Nonfiction** Picture books, young readers: health, special needs, social issues, self help.
**How to Contact/Writers** Submit complete ms. Responds in 3 month. Publishes a book 9 months after acceptance. Will consider simultaneous submissions.
**Terms** Pays authors royalty. Sends galleys to authors. Book catalog available.

## HENDRICK-LONG PUBLISHING COMPANY
10635 Tower Oaks, Suite D, Houston TX 77070. (832)912-READ. Fax: (832)912-7353. E-mail: hendrick-long@worldnet.att.net. **Acquisitions:** Vilma Long, vice president. Publishes 4 young readers/year; 4 middle readers/year. 20% of books by first-time authors. Publishes fiction/nonfiction about Texas of interest to young readers through young adults/teens.
**Fiction** Middle readers: history books on Texas and the Southwest. No fantasy or poetry.
**Nonfiction** Middle, young adults: history books on Texas and the Southwest, biography, multicultural. "Would like to see more workbook-type manuscripts."
**How to Contact/Writers** Fiction/nonfiction: Query with outline/synopsis and sample chapter. Responds to queries in 3 months; mss in 2 months. Publishes a book 18 months after acceptance. No simultaneous submissions. Include SASE.
**Illustration** Works with 2-3 illustrators/year. Uses primarily b&w interior artwork; color covers only. Illustrations only: Query first. Submit résumé or promotional literature or photocopies or tearsheets—no original work sent unsolicited. No phone calls. Responds only if interested.
**Terms** Pays authors royalty based on selling price. Advances vary. Pays illustrators by the project or royalty. Sends galleys to authors; dummies to illustrators. Manuscript guidelines for 1 first-class stamp and #10 SAE.
**Tips** "Material **must** pertain to Texas or the Southwest. Check all facts about historical figures and events in both fiction and nonfiction. Be accurate."

## HOLIDAY HOUSE INC.
425 Madison Ave., New York NY 10017. (212)688-0085. Fax: (212)421-6134. Website: www.holidayhouse.com. Estab. 1935. Book publisher. Vice President/Editor-in-Chief: Regina Griffin. **Acquisitions:** Acquisitions Editor. **Art Director:** Claire Counihan. Publishes 35 picture books/year; 3 young readers/year; 15 middle readers/year; 8 young adult titles/year. 20% of books by first-time authors; 10% from agented writers. Mission Statement: "To publish high-quality books for children."
**Fiction** All levels: adventure, contemporary, fantasy, folktales, ghost, historical, humor, multicultural, school,

suspense/mystery, sports. Recently published *In Defense of Liberty*, by Rurrell Freedman; *A Kenya Christmas*, by Tony Johnston, illustrated by Leonard Jenkins; *Uncommon Faith*, by Trudy Krisher.

**Nonfiction** All levels: animal, biography, concept, contemporary, geography, historical, math, multicultural, music/dance, nature/environment, religion, science, social issues.

**How to Contact/Writers** Send queries only to editor. Responds to queries in 3 months; mss in 4 months. "If we find your book idea suits our present needs, we will notify you by mail." Once a ms has been requested, the writers should send in the exclusive submission, with a SASE, otherwise the ms will not be returned.

**Illustration** Works with 35 illustrators/year. Reviews ms illustration packages from artists. Send ms with dummy. Do not submit original artwork or slides. Color photocopies or printed samples are preferred. Responds only if interested. Samples filed.

**Terms** Pays authors and illustrators an advance against royalties. Originals returned at job's completion. Book catalog, ms/artist's guidelines available for a SASE.

**Tips** "Fewer books are being published. It will get even harder for first timers to break in."

## HENRY HOLT & CO., LLC

175 Fifth Ave., New York NY 10011. (646)307-5282. Fax: (646)307-5247. Website: www.henryholtchildrensbooks .com. **Manuscript Acquisitions:** Laura Godwin, editor-in-chief/associate publisher of Books for Young Readers dept.; Nina Ignatowicz, executive editor; Reka Simonsen, editor; Kate Farrell, editor. **Art Acquisitions:** Patrick Collins, creative director. Publishes 20-40 picture books/year; 4-6 chapter books/year; 10-15 middle readers/year; 8-10 young adult titles/year. 15% of books by first-time authors; 40% of books from agented writers. "Henry Holt and Company Books for Young Readers is known for publishing quality books that feature imaginative authors and illustrators. We tend to publish many new authors and illustrators each year in our effort to develop and foster new talent."

**Fiction** Picture books: animal, anthology, concept, folktales, history, humor, multicultural, nature/environment, poetry, special needs, sports. Middle readers: adventure, contemporary, history, humor, multicultural, special needs, sports, suspense/mystery. Young adults: contemporary, multicultural, problem novel, sports.

**Nonfiction** Picture books: animal, arts/crafts, biography, concept, geography, history, hobbies, multicultural, music, dance, nature/environment, sports. Middle readers, young readers, young adult: biography, history, multicultural, sports.

**How to Contact/Writers** Fiction/nonfiction: Submit complete ms with SASE. Responds in 4 months. Will not consider simultaneous or multiple submissions.

**Illustration** Works with 50-60 illustrators/year. Reviews ms/illustration packages from artists. Random samples OK. Illustrations only: Submit tearsheets, slides. Do *not* send originals. Responds to art samples in 1 month. Samples returned with SASE; samples filed. If accepted, original artwork returned at job's completion. Portfolios are reviewed every Monday.

**Terms** Pays authors/illustrators royalty based on retail price. Sends galleys to authors; proofs to illustrators.

## HOUGHTON MIFFLIN CO.

Children's Trade Books, 222 Berkeley St., Boston MA 02116-3764. (617)351-5000. Fax: (617)351-1111. E-mail: childrens_books@hmco.com. Website: www.houghtonmifflinbooks.com. **Manuscript Aquisitions** Hannah Rodgers, editorial associate; Margaret Raymo, senior editors; Eden Edwards, Graphia senior editor; Walter Lorraine, books editor; Kate O'Sullivan, editor. **Art Acquisitions:** Sheila Smallwood, creative director. Imprints include Walter Lorraine Books, Clarion Books, and Graphia. Averages 60 titles/year. Publishes hardcover originals and trade paperback reprints and originals. "Houghton Mifflin gives shape to ideas that educate, inform, and above all, delight."

- Houghton Mifflin title *The Red Book*, by Barbara Lehmah, won a 2005 Caldecott Honor Award. Their title *Remember: The Journey to School Intergration*, by Toni Morrison, won a 2005 Coretta Scott King Author Award. Their title *Missy Violet and Me*, by Barbara Hathaway, won a 2005 Coretta Scott King/John Steptoe New Talent Award for text. Their titles *The Tarantual Scientist*, by Sy Montgomery, photos by Nic Bishop, and *Sequoyah: The Cherokee Man Who Gave His People Writing*, written and illustrated by James Rumford, translated into Cherokee by Anna Sixkiller Huckaby, won 2005 Robert F. Sibert Honor Awards.

**Fiction** All levels: all categories except religion. "We do not rule out any theme, though we do not publish specifically religious material." Recently published *Henry Climbs a Mountain*, by D.B. Johnson (ages 4-8, picture book); *Ollie*, by Oliver Donrea (ages 2-5, picture book); *Mosque*, by David Macaulay (all ages, picture book).

**Nonfiction** All levels: all categories except religion. Recently published *American Boy: The Adventures of Mark Twain*, by Don Brown (ages 4-8, picture book); *Actual Size*, by Steve Jenkin (picture book); *The Tarantula Scientist*, by Sy Montgomery, photographs by Nic Bishop (ages 7-12).

**How to Contact/Writers** Fiction: Submit complete ms. Nonfiction: Submit outline/synopsis and sample chapters. Responds within 4 months only if interested.

**Illustration** Works with 60 illustrators/year. Reviews ms/illustration packages from artists. Manuscript/illustration packages or illustrations only: Query with samples (colored photocopies are fine); provide tearsheets. Responds in 4 months. Samples returned with SASE; samples filed if interested.

**Terms** Pays standard royalty based on retail price; offers advance. Illustrators paid by the project and royalty. Manuscript and artist's guidelines available for SASE.

## HUNTER HOUSE PUBLISHERS

P.O. Box 2914, Alameda CA 94501-0914. (510)865-5282. Fax: (510)865-4295. E-mail: acquisitions@hunterhouse .com. Website: www.hunterhouse.com. **Manuscript Acquisitions:** Jeanne Brondino. Publishes 0-1 titles for teenage women/year. 50% of books by first-time authors; 5% of books from agented writers.

**Nonfiction** Young adults: self help, health, multicultural, violence prevention. ''We emphasize that all our books try to take multicultural experiences and concerns into account. We would be interested in a self-help book on multicultural issues.'' Books are therapy/personal growth-oriented. Does *not* want to see books for young children, fiction, illustrated picture books, autobiography. Published *Turning Yourself Around: Self-Help Strategies for Troubled Teens*, by Kendall Johnson, Ph.D.; *Safe Dieting for Teens*, by Linda Ojeda, Ph.D.

**How to Contact/Writers** Query; submit overview and chapter-by-chapter synopsis, sample chapters and statistics on your subject area, support organizations or networks and marketing ideas. ''Testimonials from professionals or well-known authors are crucial.'' Responds to queries in 3 months; mss in 6 months. Publishes a book 18 months after acceptance. Will consider simultaneous submissions.

**Terms** Payment varies. Sends galleys to authors. Book catalog available for 9×12 SAE and $1.25 postage; ms guidelines for standard SAE and 1 first-class stamp.

**Tips** Wants therapy/personal growth workbooks; teen books with solid, informative material. ''We do few children's books. The ones we do are for a select, therapeutic audience. No fiction! Please, no fiction.''

## A ⊠ HYPERION BOOKS FOR CHILDREN

114 Fifth Ave., New York NY 10011-5690. (212)633-4400. Fax: (212)633-4833. Website: www.hyperionbooksfor children.com. **Manuscript Acquisitions:** Editorial Director. **Art Acquisitions:** Anne Diebel, art director. 10% of books by first-time authors. Publishes various categories.

- Hyperion title *Knuffle Bunny: A Cautionary Tale*, written and illustrated by Mo Willems, won a 2005 Caldecott Honor Award. Their title *Who Am I Without Him?: Short Stories About Girls and the Boys in Their Lives*, by Sharon G. Flake, won a 2005 Coretta Scott King Author Honor Award.

**Fiction** Picture books, young readers, middle readers, young adults: adventure, animal, anthology (short stories), contemporary, fantasy, folktales, history, humor, multicultural, poetry, science fiction, sports, suspense/mystery. Middle readers, young adults: commercial fiction. Recently published *Emily's First 100 Days of School*, by Rosemary Wells (ages 3-6, *New York Times* bestseller); *Artemis Fowl*, by Eoin Colfer (YA novel, *New York Times* bestseller); *Dumpy The Dump Truck*, series by Julie Andrews Edwards and Emma Walton Hamilton (ages 3-7).

**Nonfiction** All trade subjects for all levels.

**How to Contact/Writers** Only interested in agented material.

**Illustration** Works with 100 illustrators/year. ''Picture books are fully illustrated throughout. All others depend on individual project.'' Reviews ms/illustration packages from artists. Submit complete package. Illustrations only: Submit résumé, business card, promotional literature or tearsheets to be kept on file. Responds only if interested. Original artwork returned at job's completion.

**Photography** Works on assignment only. Publishes photo essays and photo concept books. Provide résumé, business card, promotional literature or tearsheets to be kept on file.

**Terms** Pays authors royalty based on retail price. Offers advances. Pays illustrators and photographers royalty based on retail price or a flat fee. Sends galleys to authors; dummies to illustrators. Book catalog available for 9×12 SAE and 3 first-class stamps.

## IDEALS CHILDREN'S BOOKS AND CANDYCANE PRESS

Imprint of Ideals Publications, 535 Metroplex Dr., Suite 250, Nashville TN 37211. Website: www.idealsbooks.c om. **Manuscript Acquisitions:** Children's Editor. **Art Acquisitions:** Eve DeGrie, art director. Publishes 10 picture books/year; 40 board books/year. 50% of books by first-time authors.

**Fiction** Picture books: animal, concept, history, religion. Board books: animal, history, nature/environment, religion. Average word length: picture books—1,500; board books—200.

## ILLUMINATION ARTS

P.O. Box 1865, Bellevue WA 98009. (425)644-7185. Fax: (425)644-9274. E-mail: liteinfo@illumin.com. Website: www.illumin.com. **Manuscript Acquisitions :** Ruth Thompson, editorial director. **Art Acquisitions:** Carol Morris, publisher's assistant.

**Fiction** Word length: Prefers under 1,000, but will consider up to 1,500 words. Recently published *A Mother's*

*Promise*, by Lisa Humphrey, illustrated by David Danioth; *We Share One World*, by Jane E. Hoffelt, illustrated by Marty Husted; *Too Many Murkles*, by Heidi Charissa Schmidt, illustrated by Ann Richardson; *Little Ruth Reddingford*, by Hank Wesselman, illustrated by Raquel Abreu.

**How to Contact/Writers** Fiction: Submit complete ms. Responds to queries in 3 months with SASE only. No electronic or CD submissions for text or art. Publishes a book 1-2 years after acceptance. Will consider simultaneous submissions.

**Illustration** Works with 3-5 illustrators/year. Uses color artwork only. Reviews ms/illustration packages from artists. Query or send ms with dummy. Illustrations only: Query with color samples, résumé and promotional material to be kept on file or returned with SASE only. Responds in 3 months with SASE only. Samples returned with SASE or filed.

**Terms** Pays authors and illustrators royalty based on wholesale price. Book fliers available for SASE.

**Tips** "Read our books and follow our guidelines. Be patient. The market is competitive. We receive 2,000 submissions annually and publish 4-5 books a year. Sorry, we are unable to track unsolicited submissions."

## IMPACT PUBLISHERS, INC.

P.O. Box 6016, Atascadero CA 93423-6016. (805)466-5917. Fax: (805)466-5919. E-mail: info@impactpublishers. com. Website: www.impactpublishers.com. **Manuscript Acquisitions:** Melissa Froehner, children's editor. **Art Acquisitions:** Sharon Skinner, art director. Imprints: Little Imp Books, Rebuilding Books, The Practical Therapist Series. Publishes 1 young reader/year; 1 middle reader/year; 1 young adult title/year. 20% of books by first-time authors. "Our purpose is to make the best human services expertise available to the widest possible audience. We publish only popular psychology and self-help materials written in everyday language by professionals with advanced degrees and significant experience in the human services."

**Nonfiction** Young readers, middle readers, young adults: self-help. Recently published *The Divorce Helpbook for Kids*, by Cynthia MacGregor (ages 8-12, children's/divorce/emotions).

**How to Contact/Writers** Nonfiction: Query or submit complete ms, cover letter, résumé. Responds to queries in 12 weeks; mss in 3 months. Will consider simultaneous submissions or previously published work.

**Illustration** Works with 1 illustrator/year. Uses b&w artwork only. Reviews ms/illustration packages from artists. Query. Contact: Children's Editor. Illustrations only: Query with samples. Contact: Sharon Skinner, production manager. Responds only if interested. Samples returned with SASE; samples filed. Originals returned to artist at job's completion.

**Terms** Pays authors royalty of 10-12%. Offers advances. Pays illustrators by the project. Book catalog available for #10 SAE with 2 first-class stamps; ms guidelines available for SASE. All imprints included in a single catalog.

**Tips** "Please do not submit fiction, poetry or narratives."

## ☐ IMPERIAL INTERNATIONAL

30 Montauk Blvd., Oakdale NY 11769. (631)567-7227. Fax: (631)567-8745. E-mail: laura@edconpublishing.c om. Website: www.edconpublishing.com. **Manuscript Acquisitions:** Laura Solimene. Publishes 12 young readers/year, 12 middle readers/year, 12 young adult titles/year. 30% of books by first-time authors.

**Fiction** Young readers, middle readers, young adult/teens: hi-lo. Average word length: young readers—4,000; middle readers—6,000; young adults—8,000. Recently published *A Midsummer Night's Dream*, adaptation by Laura Algieri; *Twelfth Night*, adaptation by Julianne Davidow; *The Merchant of Venice*, adaptation by Rachel Armington.

**How to Contact/Writers** Fiction: Submit outline/synopsis and 1 sample chapter. Responds to queries/mss in 1 month. Publishes book 6 months after acceptance. Will consider simultaneous submissions.

**Illustration** Works with 6 illustrators/year. Reviews ms/illustration packages from artists. Query. Illustrations only: Send postcard sample with samples, SASE. Responds in 2 weeks. Samples returned with SASE; samples filed.

**Terms** Work purchased outright from authors for $1,000. Pays illustrators by the project (range: $250-$750). Book catalog available for $8 \times 1\frac{1}{2} \times 11$ SASE and $1.35 postage; ms and art guidelines available for SAE. Catalog available on website.

## ☐ INCENTIVE PUBLICATIONS, INC.

2400 Crestmoor Rd., Suite 211, Nashville TN 37215. (800)421-2830. Fax: (615)385-2967. E-mail: info@incentive publications.com. Website: www.incentivepublications.com. **Acquisitions:** Patience Camplair. Approximately 20% of books by first-time authors. "We publish only educational resource materials for teachers and parents of children from pre-school age through high school. We publish *no fiction*. Incentive endeavors to produce developmentally appropriate research-based educational materials to meet the changing needs of students, teachers and parents. Books are written by teachers for teachers for the most part."

**Nonfiction** Black & white line illustrated books, young reader, middle reader: activity books, arts/craft, multicultural, science, health, how-to, reference, animal, history, nature/environment, special needs, social issues, supplemental educational materials. "Any manuscripts related to child development or with content-based activities and innovative strategies will be reviewed for possible publication." Recently published Better Grades series (middle grade) and Ready to Learn series (8 books).

**How to Contact/Writers** Nonfiction: Submit outline/synopsis, sample chapters and SASE. Responds to queries in 6 weeks; mss in 2 months. Typically publishes a book 18 months after acceptance. Will consider simultaneous submissions.

**Illustration** Works with 2-6 illustrators/year. Responds in 1 month if reply requested (send SASE). Samples returned with SASE; samples filed. Need 4-color cover art; b&w line illustration for content.

**Terms** Pays authors in royalties (5-10% based on wholesale price) or work purchased outright (range: $500-1,000). Pays illustrators by the project (range: $200-1,500). Pays photographers by the project. Original artwork not returned. Book catalog and ms and artist guidelines for SAE with $1.78 postage.

**Tips** Writers: "We buy only educational teacher resource material that can be used by teachers and parents (home schoolers). Please do not submit fiction! Incentive Publications looks for a whimsical, warm style of illustration that respects the integrity and age of the child. We work primarily with local artists, but not exclusively."

## INNOVATIVE KIDS

18 Ann St., Norwalk CT 06854. (203)838-6400. Fax: (203)855-5582. E-mail: info@innovativekids.com. Website: www.innovativekids.com. **Manuscript Acquisitions:** Submissions Editor. **Art Acquisitions:** Art Director. Publishes 20 activity books/year; 10 young readers/year. 5% of books by first-time authors. "IKIDS knows kids! We make learning fun!"

**Nonfiction** Picture books: activity books, animal, arts/crafts, careers, concept, geography, health, hobbies, how-to, science. Young readers: activity books, animal, arts/craft, careers, concept, geography, history, hobbies, how-to, nature/environment, reference, science, sports, textbooks. Recently published *Flip-Flap Math* and *Big Book of Clues: A to Z.*

**How to Contact/Writers** Nonfiction: Submit complete ms.

**Illustration** Works with 30 illustrators/year. Uses color artwork only. Reviews ms/illustration packages from artists. Submit ms with dummy. Contact: Submissions Editor. Illustration only: Query with brochure, samples, photocopies, résumé or tearsheets. Contact: Art Director. Responds only if interested. Samples filed.

**Photography** Buys stock and assigns work. Contact: Art Director. Submit résumé, published samples, color promo pieces.

**Terms** Work purchased outright; payment varies. Book catalog available for $8 \times 10$ SASE with $1.07 postage. Catalog available on website.

**Tips** "Make sure your project is appropriate to IK prior to sending it. All IK titles are interactive and educational but above all else fun!"

## IPICTUREBOOKS

24 West 25th Street, 11th Floor, New York NY 10010. E-mail: info@ipicturebooks.com. Website: www.ipictureb ooks.com. **Art Director:** Matt Postawa. Online book publisher. "ipicturebooks is the #1 brand for children's e-books on the Internet. It is designed to appeal to parents, children, teachers and librarians seeking in-print, out-of print and original enhanced e-books for use on home computers, school and library networked computers, proprietary and open hand-helds and dedicated e-book readers. It will sell e-books by individual downloaded copy, site licenses and subscription models. ipicturebooks will also introduce a variety of 'enhanced' e-books, ranging from original ebooks illustrated digitally, to 'custom' e-books in which a child's name appears to 'e-pop up books' to e-books with spoken text to e-books with music and animation." See website for submission information for writers and illustrators, as well as sample e-books.

● ipicturebooks is temporarily closed to manuscript submissions, but is accepting illustration promo samples.

**Illustraition** Mail or e-mail promo cards to art director at mpostawa@bpvp.com.

## JALMAR PRESS

P.O. Box 1185, Torrance CA 90745-6329. (310)816-3085. Fax: (310)816-3092. E-mail: blwjalmar@att.net. Website: www.jalmarpress.com. **Acquisitions:** Bradley Winch, publisher; Cathy Winch, manager. Imprint: Person-hood Press. Does not publish children's picture books or books for young readers. 10% of books by first-time authors. Publishes self-esteem (curriculum content related), character education, drug and alcohol abuse prevention, peaceful conflict resolution, stress management, virtues whole-brain learning, accelerated learning and emotional intelligence materials for counselors, teachers, and other care givers. "Our goal is to empower children to become personally and socially responsible through activities presented by teachers, counselors and other caregivers that allow them to experience being both successful and responsible. Our titles are activity-driven and develop social, emotional and ethical skills that lead to academic achievements."

• Jalmar's catalog is found on their website. Jalmar is now the exclusive distributor for Innerchoice Publishing's entire line of school counselor-oriented material (K-12).

**Fiction** All levels: self-concept, self-esteem. Does not want to see "children's fiction books that have to do with cognitive learning (as opposed to affective learning) and autobiographical work." Published *Hilde Knows: Someone Cries for the Children*, by Lisa Kent, illustrated by Mikki Macklen (child abuse); *Scooter's Tail of Terror: A Fable of Addiction and Hope*, by Larry Shles (ages 5-105). "All submissions must teach (by metaphor) in the areas listed above."

**Nonfiction** All levels: activity books to develop social, emotional and ethical skills. Does not want to see autobiographical work. Published *Esteem Builders Program*, by Michele Borba, illustrated by Bob Burchett (for school use—6 books, tapes, posters).

**How to Contact/Writers** Fiction/nonfiction: Submit complete ms. Responds to queries/mss in 2 months. Publishes a book 12-18 months after acceptance. Will consider simultaneous submissions.

**Illustration** Works with 2 illustrators/year. Responds in 1 week. Samples returned with SASE; samples filed.

**Terms** Pays authors 7½-15% royalty based on net receipts. Average advance varies. Pays illustrators by the project on a bid basis. Pays photographers per photo on a bid basis. Book catalog/ms guidelines free on request.

**Tips** Wants "thoroughly researched, tested, practical, activity-oriented, curriculum content and grade/level correlated books on self-esteem, peaceful conflict resolution, stress management, emotional intelligence, and whole brain learning and books bridging self-esteem to various 'trouble' areas, such as 'at risk,' 'dropout prevention,' etc. Illustrators—make artwork that can be reproduced. Emotional intelligence is becoming a 'hot' category, as is character education and morality-based education."

## 🖸 🖵 JAYJO BOOKS, L.L.C.

A Guidance Channel Company, P.O. Box 9120, Plainview NY 11803-0760. (516)349-5520. Fax: (516)349-5521. E-mail: jayjobooks@guidancechannel.com. Website: www.jayjo.com. **Manuscript Acquisitions:** Sally Germain. Publishes 3-5 illustrated, young readers/year. 25% of books by first-time authors. "Our goal is to provide quality children's health education through entertainment and teaching, while raising important funds for medical research and education."

**Fiction** Young readers, middle readers: health, special needs, chronic conditions. Average word length: young readers—1,800; middle readers—1,800. Recently published *Taking Arthritis to School*, by Deedee L. Miller (ages 5-10); *Taking Depression to School*, by Kathy Khalsa (ages 5-10).

**Nonfiction** Young readers, middle readers: health, special needs, chronic conditions. Average word length: young readers—1,500; middle readers-1,500.

**How to Contact/Writers** Fiction/nonfiction: Send query. Responds in 3 months. Publishes a book 2 years after acceptance. Will consider simultaneous submissions.

**Illustration** Works with 2 illustrators/year. Uses color artwork only. Illustrations only: Query with samples. Responds in 3 months. Samples returned with SASE; samples filed.

**Terms** Work purchased outright from authors. Pays illustrators by the project. Book catalog and guidelines available for #10 SAE and 1 first-class stamp. Manuscript guidelines for SASE.

**Tips** "Send query letter. Since we only publish books adapted to our special format, we only read what fits our format and contact appropriate potential authors to work with them to customize manuscripts. Send letter with no more than 5 pages of writing samples."

## JEWISH LIGHTS PUBLISHING

P.O. Box 237, Rt. 4, Sunset Farm Offices, Woodstock VT 05091. (802)457-4000. Fax: (802)457-4004. E-mail: tholtz@jewishlights.com. Website: www.jewishlights.com. **Manuscript Acquisitions:** Submissions Editor. **Art Acquisitions:** Tim Holtz. Publishes 2 picture books/year; 1 young reader/year. 50% of books by first-time authors; 1% of books from agented authors. All books have spiritual/religious themes. "Jewish Lights publishes books for people of all faiths and all backgrounds who yearn for books that attract, engage, educate and spiritually inspire. Our authors are at the forefront of spiritual thought and deal with the quest for the self and for meaning in life by drawing on the Jewish wisdom tradition. Our books cover topics including history, spirituality, life cycle, children, self-help, recovery, theology and philosophy. We do *not* publish autobiography, biography, fiction, *haggadot*, poetry or cookbooks. At this point we plan to do only two books for children annually, and one will be for younger children (ages 4-10)."

**Fiction** Picture books, young readers, middle readers: spirituality. "We are not interested in anything other than spirituality." Recently published *God's Paintbrush*, by Sandy Eisenberg Sasso, illustrated by Annette Compton (ages 4-9).

**Nonfiction** Picture book, young readers, middle readers: activity books, spirituality. Recently published *When a Grandparent Dies: A Kid's Own Remembering Workbook for Dealing with Shiva and the Year Beyond*, by Nechama Liss-Levinson, Ph.D. (ages 7-11); *Tough Questions Jews Ask: A Young Adult's Guide to Building a Jewish Life*, by Rabbi Edward Feinstein (ages 12 and up).

**How to Contact/Writers** Fiction/nonfiction: Query with outline/synopsis and 2 sample chapters; submit complete ms for picture books. Include SASE. Responds to queries/mss in 4 months. Publishes a book 1 year after acceptance. Will consider simultaneous submissions and previously published work.

**Illustration** Works with 2 illustrators/year. Reviews ms/illustration packages from artists. Query. Illustrations only: Query with samples; provide résumé. Samples returned with SASE; samples filed.

**Terms** Pays authors royalty of 10% of revenue received; 15% royalty for subsequent printings. Offers advances. Pays illustrators by the project or royalty. Pays photographers by the project. Sends galleys to authors; dummies to illustrators. Book catalog available for 6½×9½ SAE and 59¢ postage; ms guidelines available for SASE.

**Tips** "Explain in your cover letter why you're submitting your project to *us* in particular. Make sure you know what we publish."

## Ⓝ JEWISH PUBLICATION SOCIETY

2100 Arch St., 2nd floor, Philadelphia PA 19103. (215)832-0600. Fax (215)568-2017. Website: www.jewishpub.o rg. Estab. 1888. Specializes in Judaica. **Writers contact:** Acquisitions. **Illustrators contact:** Robin Norman, production manager. Produces 1 middle reader/year; 1 young adult book/year. 50% of books by first-time authors. Jewish Publication Society's mission is "creating a shared Jewish literacy, since 1888."

**Fiction** Middle readers, young adults/teens: contemporary, folktales, history, short story collections, religion (Jewish). Recently published *Wise. and Not So Wise: 10 Tales from the Rabbis*, by Phillis Gershator, illustrated by Alexa Ginsburg (all ages).

**Nonfiction** Middle readers: biography (Jewish), religion. Young adults/teens: biography, religion. Recently published Kids' Catalog series (books for ages 8-12); *Ilan Ramon: Jewish Star*, by Devra Newberger Speregen.

**How to Contact/Writers** Accepts international submissions. Fiction: Submit outline/synopsis and 1 sample chapter. Nonfiction: Query. Responds to queries in 4 weeks; mss in 6 months. Publishes book 12-18 months after acceptance. Considers simultaneous submissions, electronic submissions, previously published work.

**Illustration** Accepts material from international illustrators. Works with 1 illustrator/year. Uses both color (for covers) and b&w. Reviews ms/illustration packages. For ms/illustration packages: Query. Submit ms/illustration packages to Acquisitions. Reviews work for future assignments. If interested in illustrating future titles, query with samples. Submit samples to Robin Norman.

**Terms** Author sees galleys for review. Originals returned to artist at job's completion. Catalog on website. See website for writer's guidelines.

**Tips** "We do not accept submissions for picture books for young children. While we will review all other types of children's book submissions, we are most interested in those for short story and folktale collections and for young adult novels—all with strong Jewish themes—and for new titles in our Kids' Catalog series. We generally do not acquire stories on immigrant themes or the Holocaust."

## JOURNEYFORTH

Imprint of Bob Jones University Press, 1700 Wade Hampton Blvd., Greenville SC 29614. (8 64)242-5100, ext. 4350. Fax: (864)298-0268. E-mail: jb@bjup.com. Website: www.bjup.co m. Estab. 1974. Specializes in trade books, Christian material, educational material. **Acquisitions Editor:** Nancy Lohr. Publishes 1 picture book/year; 2 young readers/year; 4 middle readers/year; 3 young adult titles/year. 10% of books by first-time authors. "We aim to produce well-written books for readers of varying abilities and interests—books excellent in every facet of their presentation and fully consistent with biblical truth."

**Fiction** Young readers, middle readers, young adults: adventure, animal, contemporary, fantasy, folktales, history, humor, multicultural, nature/environment, problem novels, suspense/mystery. Average word length: young readers—10,000-12,000; middle readers—10,000-40,000; young adult/teens—40,000-60,000. Recently published *Tommy's Race*, by Sharon Hambrick, illustrated by Maurie Manning (ages 6-7, contemporary fiction); *Regina Silsby's Secret War*, by Thomas J. Brodeur (young adult historical ficiton); *Two Sides to Everything*, by Deb Brammer (ages 9-12, contemporary fiction).

**Nonfiction** Young readers, middle readers, young adult: biography. Average word length: young readers—10,000-12,000; middle readers—10,000-40,000; young adult/teens—40,000-60,000. Recently published *George Mueller*, by Rebecca Davis (ages 7-9, Christian biography); *Children of the Storm*, by Natasha Vius (young adult autobiography); *Fanny Crosby*, by Rebecca Davis (Christian biography).

**How to Contact/Writers** Fiction: Query. "Do not send stories with magical elements. We are not currently accepting picture books. We do not publish these genres: romance, science fiction, poetry and drama." Nonfiction: Query or submit outline/synopsis and 5 sample chapters. Responds to queries in 4 weeks; mss in 3 months. Publishes book 12-15 months after acceptance. Will consider previously published work.

**Illustration** Works with 4-6 illustrators/year. Query with samples. Send promo sheet; will review website portfolio if applicable. Responds only if interested. Samples returned with SASE; samples filed.

**Terms** Pays authors royalty based on wholesale price or work purchased outright. Pays illustrators by the project. Originals returned to artist at job's completion. Book catalog and ms guidelines free on request. Send 9×12 SASE

with 2 first-class stamps for book catalog and mss guidelines. Writer's guidelines available on website.
**Tips** "Review our backlist and be sure your work is a good fit. Polish your manuscript; only the best writing is going to get our attention. If it reads like a rough draft, we will not be inclined to give it serious consideration."

## JUST US BOOKS, INC.
356 Glenwood Ave., East Orange NJ 07017. (973)676-4345. Fax: (973)677-7570. E-mail: cherylhudson@justusbooks.com. Website: www.justusbooks.com. **Acquisitions:** Cheryl Willis Hudson. Publishes 4-8 titles/year. 33% of books by first-time authors. Looking for "queries for YA and middle reader fiction and nonfiction."
**Fiction** Middle readers: contemporary (African-American themes). Young adults: concept, contemporary, history, humor, suspense/mystery. Average word length: "varies" per picture book; young reader—500-2,000; middle reader—5,000. Wants African-American themes. Gets too many traditional African folktales. Recently published *Kid Carame: Mess at Loch Ness, by Dwayne J. Ferguson; Follow Up Letters to Santa From Kids Who Never Got A Responce*, by Tony Medina (middle readers).
**Nonfiction** Young adult: biography, concept, social issues (African-American themes). Recently published *Reflections of a Black Cowboy*, by Robert Miller.
**How to Contact/Writers** Fiction/nonfiction: Query or submit outline/synopsis with SASE for proposed title. Responds to queries in 8-10 weeks only with SASE; no longer accepting unsolicited mss. Publishes a book 12-18 months after acceptance. Will consider simultaneous submissions (with prior notice). All submissions must be accompanied by a SASE and must be sent via U.S. mail only. *No faxes or e-mails*
**Illustration** Works with 4 illustrators/year. Reviews ms/illustration packages from artists ("but prefers to review them separately"). "Query first." Illustrations only: Query with samples; send résumé, promo sheet, slides, client list, tearsheets; arrange personal portfolio review. Responds only if interested. Samples not returned; samples filed. Original artwork returned at job's completion "depending on project."
**Photography** Purchases photos from freelancers. Buys stock and assigns work. Wants "African-American and multicultural themes—kids age 10-13 in school, home and social situations."
**Terms** Pays authors royalty and some work for hire depending on project. Pays illustrators by the project or royalty, or flat fee based on project. Sends galleys to authors; dummies to illustrators. Book catalog for business-size SASE and $1.06 postage; ms/artist's guidelines for business-size SASE and 37¢ postage.
**Tips** Writers: "Keep the subject matter fresh and lively. Avoid 'preachy' stories with stereotyped characters. Rely more on authentic stories with sensitive three-dimensional characters." Illustrators: "Submit 5-10 good, neat samples. Be willing to work with an art director for the type of illustration desired by a specific house and grow into larger projects. All queries and submissions must be accompanied by a SASE to receive a response. Please visit our website to familiarize yourself with Just Us Books *before* sending a query or manuscript."

## ☐ KAEDEN BOOKS
P.O. Box 16190, Rocky River OH 44116-6190. (440)617-1400. Fax: (440)617-1403. Website: kaeden.com. **Acquisitions:** Craig Urmston, Creative Vice President. 50% of books by first-time authors. "Kaeden Books produces high quality, emergent , early reader , and transitional books for classroom and reading program educators."
**Fiction** Young readers: adventure, animal, concept, contemporary, health, history, humor, multicultural, nature/environment, science fiction, sports, suspense/mystery. Average word length: picture books—20-150 words; young readers—20-300 words. Recently published *Moose's Loose Tooth*, by Nancy Louise Spinelle; *Another Sneeze, Louise!*, by Cheryl A. Potts; *Sammy's Moving*, by Kathleen Urmston and Karen Evans.
**Nonfiction** Young readers: activity books, animal, biography, careers, geography, health, history, hobbies, how-to, multicultural, music/dance, nature/environment, religion, science, sports. Multicultural needs include group and character diversity in stories and settings. Average word length: picture books—20-150 words; young readers—20-150 words.
**How to Contact/Writers** Fiction/nonfiction: Submit complete ms. Do not send original transcripts. Responds to mss in 1 year. Will consider simultaneous submissions, electronic submissions via disk or modem.
**Illustration** Works with 10 illustrators/year. Reviews ms/illustration packages from artists. Submit art samples in color. Can be photocopies or tearsheets. Illustrations only: Query with samples. Send résumé, promo sheet, tearsheets, photocopies of work, preferably in color. Responds only if interested. Samples are filed.
**Terms** Work purchased outright from authors. "Royalties to our previous authors." Pays illustrators by the project (range: $50-150/page). Book catalog available for 8½ × 11 SAE and 3 first-class stamps.
**Tips** " We are particularly interested in nonfiction social studies for grades 1, 2 and 3 only."

## ☐ KAMEHAMEHA SCHOOLS PRESS
1887 Makuakane St., Honolulu HI 96817. (808)842-8719. Fax: (808)842-8895. E-mail: kspress@ksbe.edu. Website: kspress.ksbe.edu. **Manuscript Acquisitions:** Acquisitions Editor. "Kamehameha Schools Press publishes in the areas of Hawaiian history, Hawaiian culture, Hawaiian language and Hawaiian studies."

# Linda Zinnen

*A small-town girl's publishing adventures*

think kids who read are very open to any sort of setting as long as the story is interesting and the characters are lively," says Linda Zinnen about her books *The Truth About Rats, Rules & Seventh Grade*; *Holding at Third*; and *The Dragons of Spratt, Ohio*, all three of which are set in small Ohio towns. "The main thing that interests kid readers is a rattling good story populated by amazing and animated characters," she says.

Zinnen, formerly of Zanesville, Ohio (population 25,586), broke into the children's publishing business in one of the few ways available to a small-town girl—she went to the library. "When I finished my fourth novel in 1996, it dawned on me that I really like to write, that I was probably going to go on writing, and that, after practicing for the past five years, I was getting discernibly better at it," she says. "Frankly, I'd never heard of the Society of Children's Book Writers and Illustrators (SCWBI), literary agents, critique groups, or even *Children's Writer's & Illustrator's Market*. I spent one rainy spring afternoon flipping through children's books, picking out the mid-grades with good cover art (embarrassing but true—I judge every book by its cover).

"About halfway through the afternoon, one of the reference librarians got involved. He handed me a stack of writer's books that discussed query letters, manuscript formatting, the crucial role of agents, and how the writer must thoroughly and earnestly research in order to find the perfect publishing house. Well, I'm terrible at being earnest. And thoroughness is hard. On the other hand, all that cover-art pondering had been great fun. Simon & Schuster had a nifty art department, so I wrote them a letter."

And the rest is children's book history . . . sort of. "After working for a year with my editor on the story, the book was ultimately rejected in acquisitions," Zinnen says. "During the next year, though, I wrote another book, my editor moved to HarperCollins, and our first book, *The Truth about Rats, Rules & Seventh Grade*, was published in 2001."

A book contract for an author from a tiny Ohio town may seem unlikely—after all, even writers living in New York or L.A. have an difficult time getting their work published. There is an unexpected juxtaposition in working from a small town and submitting to a place like New York, Zinnen admits, but she's constantly aware of the universal appeal of a compelling story and the, well, pedigrees of those acquiring and editing books.

"Now I've never actually tried it, being chicken," Zinnen says, "but I suspect that if you scratch a random bunch of New York editors, you'll find that among all those native New Yorkers there's at least one person who started out life in French Lick, Indiana, or Petosky, Michigan. Call it the James Thurber syndrome—the everyman from Ohio State who lands a staff job at *The New Yorker* and ends up paling around with E.B. White and Harold Ross."

In all, distance from an urban cultural center is one of the last things Zinnen thinks a burgeoning children's writer should worry about. A much more difficult obstacle you'll encounter, she believes, is the writing itself. Children are an insightful audience who will sense when an author is relying too heavily on prose and not enough on characterization and plot. Kids demand exciting story lines with enough realism to be relatable, which can be a difficult juggling act of interesting, farfetched plot lines with distinguishing yet universal characteristics.

Zinnen believes adventure is the heart and soul of any stand-out children's book. "By 'adventure,' I don't mean only what we normally think of as the adventure genre: discovering pirate treasure or diffusing nuclear warheads or driving off the edge of a planet, though I dearly love books like that and wish we had more of them," she says. "But falling in love is an adventure, don't you think? So is finding out your best friend cheated all year on Miss Finch's spelling tests. Learning how to parallel park? Now that's an adventure!"

If adventure is the cornerstone of excellent children's literature, building a believable character is the foundation of adventure—you can't know what a character is going to do or where it might take him if you don't know him well. "Whatever sort the

Jacket art © 2004 Mark Zug. Jacket design Nicole de las Heras.

Mid-grade novelist Linda Zinnen's sets her books, including *The Dragons of Spratt, Ohio*, in small Ohio towns. Spratt, however, is no ordinary small town—it's the home of the International Center for the Preservation of Wildlife, a facility that houses a clutch of dragon eggs. When these eggs hatch, it's up to young John Salt to protect the nine dragon babies in this "exciting fantasy with a subtle message about self-acceptance and individuality." (*School Library Journal*).

protagonist is," says Zinnen, "he needs to do something *he himself* considers meaningful or interesting or alarming, as opposed to simply having meaningful or interesting or alarming things happen to him in the first half of the book and then spending the last half thinking meaningful or interesting or alarming thoughts about his fate in life. Adventure is the stuff of interest and intelligence—it's what the protagonist does next that shows us who he is becoming. And giving the reader the chance to walk around in somebody else's skin—is that not juvenile literature's highest and most noble calling?"

Falling into the trap of writing beautiful prose without an exciting story behind it is something that happens to many writers, and Zinnen believes children's authors should stay as far away from it as possible. "It seems to me that we're in perilous danger of being snookered by the notion that, if one's characters are simply oozing singular voice and personhood, the story can be any old rag of a thing and the book will still be wrapped in glory," she explains. "But voice without story—without the right story, the most adventuresome story for this particular voice in its particular space-time continuum—makes the

Book Publishers

protagonist a spectator to his own life. Now that's boring,'' she says.

Create a bold, realistic, and believable character and give her something fabulously interesting to do—that's Linda Zinnen's key to writing exciting and publishable children's literature. Concoct an adventurous story that is also believable and the appeal will be so universal you can make the setting anywhere—and maybe intice a big-shot New York editor to remember his childhood in Brady, Nebraska. A piece of advice for future writers of stimulating, realistic literature: ''Take your writing seriously and yourself not seriously at all,'' she counsels, ''and you'll be fine.''

—*Erin Nevius*

**Fiction** Young reader, middle readers, young adults: biography, history, multicultural, Hawaiian folklore. Recently published *The Fish and Their Gifts/Nä Makana a Nä I'a*, written and illustrated by the students of the Kanuoka.
**Nonfiction** Young reader, m iddle readers, young adults: biography, history, multicultural, Hawaiian folklore.
**How to Contact/Writers** Query. Responds to queries in 2 months; mss in 3 months. Publishes a book 12-18 months after acceptance.
**Illustration** Uses color and b&w artwork. Illustrations only: Query with samples. Responds only if interested. Samples not returned.
**Terms** Work purchased outright from authors. Pays illustrators by the project. Sends galleys to authors. Book catalog available (call or write for copy). All imprints included in a single catalog. Catalog available on website.
**Tips** ''Writers and illustrators *must* be knowledgeable in Hawaiian history/culture and be able to show credentials to validate their proficiency. Greatly prefer to work with writers/illustrators available in the Honolulu area.''

## KAR-BEN PUBLISHING, INC.
A division of Lerner Publishing Group, 11430 Strand Drive, #2, Rockville MD 20852-4371. (301)984-8733. Fax: (301)881-9195. E-mail: karben@aol.com. Website: www.karben.com. **Manuscript Acquisitions:** Madeline Wikler and Judye Groner, editorial directors. Publishes 10-15 picture books/year; 20% of books by first-time authors. All of Kar-Ben Copies' books are on Jewish themes for young children and families.
● Also see listing for Lerner Publishing Group and Carolrhoda Books.
**Fiction** Picture books: adventures, concept, folktales, history, humor, multicultural, religion, special needs; *must be* on a Jewish theme. Average word length: picture books—1,500. Recently published *Noah and the Ziz*, by Jacqueline Jules, illustrated by Katherine Janus Kahn (ages 4-8); *Grandpa and Me on Tu B'Shevat*, by Marji E. Gold-Vukson, illustrated by Leslie Evans (ages 4-8).
**Nonfiction** Picture books, young readers: activity books, arts/crafts, biography, careers, concept, cooking, history, how-to, multicultural, religion, social issues, special needs; must be of Jewish interest. Recently published *Paper Clips—The Making of a Children's Holocaust Memorial*, by Peter and Dagmar Schroeder (ages 8-12); *It's Hanukkah Time*, by Latifa Berry Kropf, photos by Tod Cohen (ages 1-4); *Apples and Pomegranates—A Rosh Hashanah Seder*, by Rahel Musleah, illustrated by Judy Jarrett (all ages); *Where Do People Go When They Die?*, by Mindy Avra Portnoy, illustrated by Shelly O. Haas (ages 5-10).
**How to Contact/Writers** Fiction/nonfiction: Submit complete ms. Responds to queries/mss in 6 weeks. Publishes a book 24-36 months after acceptance. Will consider simultaneous submissions. **Illustration** Works with 6-8 illustrators/year. Prefers ''four-color art in any medium that is scannable.'' Reviews ms/illustration packages from artists. Submit whole ms and sample of art (no originals). Illustrations only: Submit tearsheets, photocopies, promo sheet ''which show skill in children's book illustration.'' Enclose SASE for response. Responds to art samples in 3-5 weeks.
**Terms** Pays authors royalties of 5-6% of net against advance of $500-1,000; or purchases outright (range: $2,000-3,000). Offers advance (average amount: $1,000). Pays illustrators by the project (range: $2,000-5,000). Sends galleys to authors. Original artwork returned at job's completion. Book catalog free on request. Manuscript guidelines on website.
**Tips** Looks for ''books for young children with Jewish interest and content, modern, non-sexist, not didactic. Fiction or nonfiction with a Jewish theme can be serious or humorous, life cycle, Bible story, or holiday-related. In particular, we are looking for stories that reflect the ethnic and cultural diversity of today's Jewish family.''

## Ⓐ KINGFISHER
Imprint of Houghton Mifflin Company, 215 Park Ave. South, New York NY 10003. (212)420-5800. Fax: (212)420-5899. Website: www.houghtonmifflinbooks.com/kingfisher. **Contact:** Kristen McLean. Kingfisher is an award-

winning publisher of nonfiction and fiction for children of all ages. They publish high-quality books with strong editorial content and world class illustration at a competitive price, offering value to parents and educators.

• Kingfisher is not currently accepting unsolicited manuscripts. All solicitations must be made by a recognized literary agent.

**Fiction** Recently published *The Kingfisher Book of Family Poems*, by Belinda Hollyer.

**Nonfiction** Recently published *Communications*, by Richard Platt.

## ALFRED A. KNOPF AND CROWN BOOKS FOR YOUNG READERS
Imprint of Random House Children's Books, 1745 Broadway, New York NY 10019. (212)782-9000. Website: www.randomhouse.com/kids. See Random House and Delacorte and Doubleday Books for Young Readers listings. Book publisher. "We publish distinguished juvenile fiction and nonfiction for ages 0-18."

• Knopf title *The People Could Fly: The Picture Book*, illustrated by Leo and Diane Dillon, written by Virginia Hamilton, won a 2005 Coretta Scott King Illustrator Honor Award.

**How to Contact/Writers** Query letter with SASE. Address envelope to: Acquisitions Editor, Knopf & Crown/Books for Young Readers, Random House, 1745 Broadway, 9-3, New York, NY 10019.

**Illustration** Contact: Isabel Warren-Lynch, executive director, art & design. Responds only if interested. Samples returned with SASE; samples filed.

**Terms** Pays illustrators and photographers by the project or royalties. Original artwork returned at job's completion.

## KRBY CREATIONS, LLC
P.O. Box 327, Bay Head NJ 08742. Fax: (815)846-0636. E-mail: info@KRBYCreations.com. Website: www.KRBYCreations.com. Estab. 2003. Specializes in trade books, nonfiction, fiction. **Writers contact:** Kevin Burton. 50% of books by first-time authors. 0% subsidy-published books.

**Fiction** Recently published *Mr. Georges and the Red Hat*, by Stephen Heigh (picture book); *Patch the Porcupine*, by Scott Nelson (picture book).

**How to Contact/Writers** Fiction/nonfiction: Query. Responds to queries in 1 months; mss in 1-3 months. Publishes book 1 year after acceptance. Considers simultaneous submissions, electronic submissions.

**Terms** Pays authors royalty of 6-15% based on wholesale price. Catalog on website. Offers writer's guidelines for SASE.

**Tips** "Submit as professionally as possible; make your vision clear to us about what you are trying to capture. Know your market/audience and identify it in your proposal. Tell us what is new/unique with your idea."

## WENDY LAMB BOOKS
Imprint of Random House, 1745 Broadway, New York NY 10019. Fax: (212)782-8234. Website: www.randomhouse.com. **Manuscript Acquisitions:** Wendy Lamb. Receives 300-400 submissions/year. Publishes 12 middle readers/year; 12 young adult titles/year. 15% of books by first-time authors and 10% unagented writers.

• Wendy Lamb Books title *How I Live Now*, by Meg Rosoff, won the 2005 Michael L. Printz Award.

**Fiction** Recently published *Island Boy*, by Graham Salisbury; *Brian's Hunt*, by Gary Paulsen; *Bucking the Sarge*, by Christopher Paul Curtis.

**How to Contact/Writers** Fiction/nonfiction: Query with SASE for reply or via e-mail. "A query letter should briefly describe the book you want to write, the intended age group, and your publishing credits, if any. If you like, you may send no more than 5 pages of the manuscript of shorter works (i.e. picture books) and a maximum of 10 pages for longer works (i.e. novels). *Please do not send more than the specified amount.* Also, do not send cassette tapes, videos, or other materials along with your query or excerpt. Manuscript pages sent will not be returned. Do not send original art."

**Illustration** Reviews ms/illustration packages from artists. Query with SASE for reply.

**Terms** Pays illustrators and photographers by project or royalties. Original artwork returned at job's completion.

## LARK BOOKS
Sterling Publishing, 67 Broadway, Ashville NC 28801. (828)253-0467. Fax: (828)253-7952. E-mail: joe@larkbooks.com. Website: www.larkbooks.com. Specializes in nonfiction. **Writers contact:** Joe Rhatigan, senior editor. **Illustrators contact:** Celia Naranjo, creative director. Produces 1 picture book/year; 2 young readers/year; 12 middle readers/year. 40% of books by first-time authors. "Lark Books' philisophy is to produce high-quality, content-oriented nonfiction title for ages 3-18 with a focus on art, science, nature, fun and games, crafts, and activity."

**Fiction** All levels: folktales. Picture books: folktales, nature/environment. Young readers, middle readers, young adults/teens: folktales.

**Nonfiction** All levels: activity books, animal, arts/crafts, cooking, hobbies, how-to, nature/environment, self help. Recently published *Gross Me Out*, by Joe Rhatigan, illustrated but Clay Meyer (ages 8 and up, activity/

craft/science); *Wild About Weather*, by Ed Brotak (ages 8 and up, science/activity); *Kids' Guide to Digital Photography*, by Jenni Bidner (ages 8 and up, hobbies).

**How to Contact/Writers** Accepts international submissions. Fiction: Submit complete ms. Nonfiction: Submit outline/synopsis and 1 sample chapter. Responds to queries in 3 weeks; mss in 3 months. Publishes book 1 year after acceptance. Considers simultaneous submissions, electronic submissions, previously published work.

**Illustration** Accepts material from international illustrators. Works with 5-7 illustrators/year. Reviews ms/ illustration packages. For ms/illustration packages: Send ms with dummy. Submit ms/illustration packages to Joe Rhatigan, senior editor. If interested in illustrating future titles, query with samples. Submit samples to Celia Naranjo, creative director. Samples returned with SASE.

**Terms** Offers advance against royalties. Author sees galleys for review. Illustrators see dummies for review. Originals not returned. Catalog on website. Individual catalogs for imprints. See website for writer's guidelines.

**Tips** "Study the market you're writing for. Let me know why you think now is the right time to publish your book idea. I'm always on the lookout for strong writers with an expertise in an area (science, art, etc.), and even through we publish a lot of books that appeal to teachers and parents, these books are for the kids. Our books have a lot of humor in them as well as a lot of things to do and learn."

## LEE & LOW BOOKS INC.

95 Madison Ave., New York NY 10016-7801. (212)779-4400. E-mail: info@leeandlow.com. Website: www.leea ndlow.com. **Acquisitions:** Louise May, editor-in-chief; Jennifer Fox, senior editor. Publishes 12-14 picture books/year. 25% of books by first-time authors. Lee & Low publishes only books with multicultural themes. "One of our goals is to discover new talent and produce books that reflect the multicultural society in which we live."

&bull; Lee & Low Books is dedicated to publishing culturally authentic literature. The company makes a special effort to work with writers and artists of color and encourages new voices. See listing for their imprint BeBop Books.

**Fiction** Picture books, young readers: anthology, contemporary, history, multicultural, poetry. "We are not considering folktales or animal stories." Picture book, middle reader: contemporary, history, multicultural, nature/environment, poetry, sports. Average word length: picture books—1,000-1,500 words. Recently published *Sky Dancers*, by Ann Kirk, illustrated by Christy Hale; *Poems to Dream Together*, by Francisco X. Alarcón, illustrated by Paula Barragán.

**Nonfiction** Picture books: concept. Picture books, middle readers: biography, history, multicultural, science and sports. Average word length: picture books—1,500-3,000. Recently published *Knockin' on Wood*, by Lynne Barasch; *Rattlesnake Mesa*, by Ednah New Rider Weber, photographed by Richela Renkun.

**How to Contact/Writers** Fiction/nonfiction: Submit complete ms. No e-mail submissions. Responds in 4 months. Publishes a book 1-2 years after acceptance. Will consider simultaneous submissions. Guidelines on website.

**Illustration** Works with 12-14 illustrators/year. Uses color artwork only. Reviews ms/illustration packages from artists. Contact: Louise May. Submit ms with dummy. Illustrations only: Query with samples, résumé, promo sheet and tearsheets. Responds only if interested. Samples returned with SASE; samples filed. Original artwork returned at job's completion.

**Photography** Buys photos from freelancers. Works on assignment only. Model/property releases required. Submit cover letter, résumé, promo piece and book dummy.

**Terms** Pays authors royalty. Offers advances against royalty. Pays illustrators royalty plus advance against royalty. Photographers paid royalty plus advance against royalty. Sends galleys to authors; proofs to illustrators. Book catalog available for 9×12 SAE and $1.75 postage; ms and art guidelines available via website or with SASE.

**Tips** "We strongly urge writers to visit our website and familiarize themselves with our list before submitting. Materials will only be returned with SASE."

## LEGACY PRESS

Imprint of Rainbow Publishers, P.O. Box 261129, San Diego CA 92196. (858)668-3260. **Manuscript/Art Acquisitions:** Christy Scannell, editorial director. Publishes 3 young readers/year; 3 middle readers/year; 3 young adult titles/year. Publishes nonfiction, Bible-teaching books. "We publish growth and development books for the evangelical Christian from a non-denominational viewpoint that may be marketed primarily through Christian bookstores."

**Nonfiction** Young readers, middle readers, young adults: reference, religion. Recently published *The Christian Girl's Guide to Friendship*, by Kathy Widenhouse, illustrated by Anita DuFalla.

**How to Contact/Writers** Nonfiction: Submit outline/synopsis and 3-5 sample chapters. Responds to queries in 6 weeks; mss in 3 months. Publishes a book 36 months after acceptance. Will consider simultaneous submissions and previously published work.

**Illustration** Works with 5 illustrators/year. Reviews ms/illustration packages from artists. Submit ms with 5-10 pieces of final art. Illustrations only: Query with samples to be kept on file.

**Terms** Pays authors royalty or work purchased outright. Offers advances. Pays illustrators per illustration. Sends galley to authors. Book catalog available for business size SASE; ms guidelines for SASE.

**Tips** "Get to know the Christian bookstore market. We are looking for innovative ways to teach and encourage children about the Christian life. No picture books please."

## LERNER PUBLISHING GROUP

241 First Ave. N., Minneapolis MN 55401. (612)332-3344. Fax: (612)332-7615. E-mail: info@lernerbooks.com. Website: www.lernerbooks.com. **Manuscript Acquisitions:** Jennifer Zimian, nonfiction submissions editor and Zelda Wagner, fiction submissions editor. Primarily publishes books for children ages 7-18. List includes titles encompassing nature, geography, natural and physical science, current events, ancient and modern history, world art, special interest, sports, world cultures, and numerous biography series.

- Lerner only accepts submissions during the month of November. See also listing for Carolrhoda Books, Kar-Ben Publishing, and The Millbrook Press.

**How to Contact/Writers** Submissions are accepted in the month of November only. Lerner Publishing Group does not publish alphabet books, puzzle books, song books, textbooks, workbooks, religious subject matter or plays. Work received in any month other than November will be returned unopened. "A SASE is required for authors who wish to have their materials returned. Please allow 8 months for a response. No phone calls please."

## ARTHUR A. LEVINE BOOKS

Imprint of Scholastic, Inc., 557 Broadway, New York NY 10012. (212)343-4436. Fax: (212)343-4890. **Acquisitions:** Arthur A. Levine, editorial director. Publishes 8 picture books/year; 1 middle reader/year; 7 young adult titles/year. 25% of books by first-time authors.

**Fiction** Recently published *Agent A to Agent Z*, by Andy Rash (alphabet picture books); *The Slightly True Story of Cedar B. Hartley*, by Martine Murray (middle grade); *The Guild of Geniuses*, by Dan Santat (picture book).

**Nonfiction** Recently published: *Confucius: the Golden Rule*, by Russell Freedman, illustrated by Frederic Clement; *Frida*, by Jonah Winter, illustrated by Ana Juan; *Ice-Cream Cones for Sale*, by Elaine Greenstein.

**How to Contact/Writers** Fiction/nonfiction: Accepts queries only. Responds to queries in 1 month; mss in 5 months. Publishes a book 1½ years after acceptance.

**Illustration** Works with 8 illustrators/year. Will review ms/illustration packages from artists. Query first. Illustrations only: Send postcard sample with tearsheets. Samples not returned.

## ⒶLITTLE, BROWN AND COMPANY CHILDREN'S BOOKS

Time Warner Book Group Company, Time-Life Bldg., 1271 Avenue of the Americas, New York NY 10020. (212)522-8700. Fax: (212)522-7997. **Editor-in-Chief:** Megan Tingley. Executive Editor: Andrea Spooner. Executive Editor: Cynthia Eagan. Senior Editor: Jennifer Hunt. **Creative Director:** Alyssa Morris. Editorial Director of Megan Tingley Books: Megan Tingley. Publishes picture books, board books, chapter books and general nonfiction and novels for middle and young adult readers.

- Little, Brown does not accept unsolicited manuscripts or unagented material.

**Fiction** Picture books: adventure, animal, contemporary, folktales, history, humor, multicultural, nature/environment. Young adults: contemporary, humor, multicultural, nature/environment, suspense/mystery, chick lit. Multicultural needs include "any material by, for and about minorities." Average word length: picture books—1,000; young readers—6,000; middle readers—15,000-25,000; young adults—20,000-40,000. Recently published *Gossip Girl: You're the One that I Want*, by Cecily von Ziegesar; *Toot & Puddle: The New Friend*, by Holly Hobbie; *The Secret of Castle Cant*, by K.P. Bath, *Leap Day*, by Wendy Mass, *How to Train your Dragon*, by Cressida Cowell, *The Not-So-Star Spangled Life of Sunita Sen*, by Mitali Perkins.

**Nonfiction** Middle readers, young adults: arts/crafts, history, multicultural, nature, self help, social issues, sports, science. Average word length: middle readers—15,000-25,000; young adults—20,000-40,000. Recently published *Harlem Stomp*, by Laban Carrick Hill; *Museum 1-2-3*, by the Metropolitan Museum of Art; *Rich Dad's Escape from the Rat Race: How Rich Dad's Advice Made a Poor Kid Rich*, by Robert T. Kiyosaki with Sharon. L. Lechter, C.P.A.

**How to Contact/Writers Only interested in solicited agented material.** Fiction: Submit complete ms. Nonfiction: Submit cover letter, previous publications, a proposal, outline and 3 sample chapters. Do not send originals. Responds to queries in 2 weeks. Responds to mss in 2 months.

**Illustration** Works with 40 illustrators/year. Illustrations only: Query art director with b&w and color samples; provide résumé, promo sheet or tearsheets to be kept on file. Does not respond to art samples. Do not send originals; copies only.

**Photography** Works on assignment only. Model/property releases required; captions required. Publishes photo essays and photo concept books. Uses 35mm transparencies. Photographers should provide résumé, promo sheets or tearsheets to be kept on file.

**Terms** Pays authors royalties based on retail price. Pays illustrators and photographers by the project or royalty based on retail price. Sends galleys to authors; dummies to illustrators.

**Tips** ''Publishers are cutting back their lists in response to a shrinking market and relying more on big names and known commodities. In order to break into the field these days, authors and illustrators should research their competition and try to come up with something outstandingly different.''

## LLEWELLYN WORLDWIDE LTD.

P.O. Box 64383, St. Paul MN 55164-0383. (651)291-1970. Fax: (651)291-1908. E-mail: childrensbooks@llewellyn.com. Website: http://teen.llewellyn.com. **Manuscript Acquisitions :** Megan C. Atwood. 60% of books by first-time authors. ''Our mission is to provide quality, well-written, edgy books with a paranormal/metaphysical slant for both the teen and middle grade demographics.''

**Fiction** Middle reader, young adult: paranormal/metaphysical slant. Recently published *L.O.S.T.*, by Debbie Federici and Susan Vaught (young adult); *White is for Magic*, by Laurie Stolarz (young adult) ; *Diadem: Worlds of Magic*, by John Peel (middle grade).

**Nonfiction** Proposals will be evaluated, but we are currently not seeking nonfiction at this time.

**How to Contact/Writers** Fiction: Query or submit complete ms. Submit outline/synopsis and 1-2 sample chapters. Nonfiction: Query or submit complete ms or submit outline/synopsis and 1-2 sample chapters. Responds to queries/mss in 2 months. Will consider simultaneous submissions, e-mail submissions only for queries and proposals, previously published work.

**Terms** Pays authors royalty of 10% based on wholesale price. Book catalog available for 9×12 SASE and 4 first-class stamps; ms guidelines available for SASE.

**Tips** ''Please be sure only to send those submissions that hit the Middle Grade (ages 8-12) and Young Adult (ages 12-18) markets. We do not accept any proposals for a younger audience at this time. We are interested in quality manuscripts specifically with a metaphysical or occult slant that fits our genre. Generally speaking, always request guidelines from a publishing company and follow the instructions before submitting. Also, be sure to familiarize yourself with a publishing company's repertoire of books to make sure that your proposal fits the company's genre.''

## ☐ LOLLIPOP POWER BOOKS

Imprint of Carolina Wren Press, 120 Morris Street, Durham NC 27701. (919)560-2738. Fax: (919)560-2759. E-mail: carolina@carolinawrenpress.org. Website: www.carolinawrenpress.org. **Manuscript Acquisitions:** Children's Book Editor. **Art Acquisitions:** Art Director. Publishes 1 picture book/year. 50% of books by first-time authors. ''Carolina Wren Press and Lollipop Power specialize in children's books that counter stereotypes or debunk myths about race, gender, sexual orientation, etc. We are also interested in books that deal with health or mental health issues—our two biggest sellers are *Puzzles* (about a young girl coping with Sickle Cell Disease) and *I like it when you joke with me, I don't like it when you touch me* (about inappropriate touching). Many of our children's titles are bilingual (English/Spanish).''

**Fiction** Average word length: picture books—500.

**How to Contact/Writers** Children's lit submissions are read February through June. (Illustrators may send samples any time.) Fiction: Submit outline/synopsis and 3 sample chapters. Responds to queries/mss in 3 months. Publishes book 2 years after acceptance. Will consider simultaneous submissions.

**Illustration** Works with 1 illustrator/year. Reviews ms/illustration packages from artists. Submit ms with 5 pieces of final art. Illustrations only: Send photocopies, résumé, samples, SASE. Responds only if interested. Samples returned with SASE; samples filed.

**Terms** Pays authors royalty of 10% minimum based on retail price or work purchased outright from authors (range: $500-$2,000). Pays illustrators by the project (range: $500-$2,000). Sends galleys to authors; dummies to illustrators. Originals returned to artist at job's completion. Manuscript and art guidelines available for SASE. Catalog available on website.

## LUCENT BOOKS

Imprint of The Gale Group, 15822 Bernard Center Dr., Suite C, San Diego CA 92127. Website: www.gale.com/lucent. E-mail: chandra.howard@thomson.com. **Acquisitions:** Chandra Howard. Series publisher of educational nonfiction for junior high school and library markets.

   • See also listing for Greenhaven Press.

**Nonfiction** Young adults: nature/environmental issues, science and technology, careers, geopolitics, history, reference, religion, contemporary social issues. Recently published *Women in the American Revolution*; *The Trial of Leopold and Loeb*; *Multicultural America*; *Civil Liberties and the War on Terrorism*.

**How to Contact/Writers** E-mail query with résumé or list of publications.

**Terms** Work purchased outright from authors; write-for-hire, flat fee.
**Tips** No unsolicited manuscripts.

## LUNA RISING

Imprint of Rising Moon, P.O. Box 1389, Flagstaff AZ 86002-1389. (928)774-5251. Fax: (928)774-0592. E-mail: editorial@northlandpub.com. Website: www.lunarisingbooks.com. Estab. 2004. Specializes in trade books, fiction. **Writers contact:** Theresa Howell. Produces 2-4 picture books/year. 20% of books by first-time authors. ''Luna Rising's objective is to provide children with high-quality bilingual picture books in Spanish and English.''
**Fiction** Picture books: multicultural.
**Nonfiction** Picture books: biography, multicultural. Recently published *My Name is Celia: The Life of Celia Cruz*, by Monica Brown, illustrated by Rafael Lopez; *Playing Loteria*, by Rene Colato Lainez, illustrated by Jill Arena.
**How to Contact/Writers** Fiction/nonfiction: Submit complete ms. Responds to queries in 3 months. Publishes book 1-2 years after acceptance. Considers simultaneous submissions.
**Terms** Authors paid royalty or flat fee. Offers advance against royalties. Offers writer's guidelines for SASE.
**Tips** ''We are looking for original bilingual stories and biographies of Latino role models. Call for book catalog.''

## MAGINATION PRESS

Washington DC 20002-2984. (202)218-3982. Fax: (202)336-5624. Website: www.maginationpress.com. **Acquisitions:** Darcie Conner Johnston, managing editor. Publishes 4 picture books/year; 4 young readers/year; 2 middle readers/year; 1 young adult title/year. 75% of books by first-time authors. ''We publish books dealing with the psycho/therapeutic resolution of children's problems and psychological issues with a strong self-help component.''
- Magination Press is an imprint of the American Psychological Association.
**Fiction** All levels: health, multicultural, special needs. Picture books, middle readers, some young adult titles. Recently published *Oh, Brother! Growing Up With a Special Needs Sibling*, by Natalie Hale, illustrated by Kate Sternberg (ages 8-13); *Blue Cheese Breath and Stinky Feet: How to Deal With Bullies*, by Catherine DePino, illustrated by Bonnie Matthews and Charles Beyl (ages 6-12); *Rising Above the Storm Clouds: What It's Like to Forgive*, by Robert Enright, PhD, illustrated by Kathryn Kunz Finney (ages 4-8).
**Nonfiction** All levels: psychological and social issues, special needs, self help. Picture books, young readers, middle readers: activity, workbooks. Recently published *All About Adoption: How Families Are Made & How Kids Feel About It*, by Marc Nemiroff and Jane Annunziata, illustrated by Carol Koeller (ages 4-8); *Breathe Easy: Young People's Guide to Asthma*, by Jonathan H. Weiss, PhD, illustrated by Michael Chesworth (ages 8-12); *Why Are You So Sad? A Child's Book About Parental Depression*, by Beth Andrews, illustrated by Nicole Wong (ages 3-8).
**How to Contact/Writers** Fiction/nonfiction: Submit complete ms. Responds to queries in 1-2 months; mss in 2-6 months. Will consider simultaneous submissions. Materials returned only with a SASE. Publishes a book 18-24 months after acceptance.
**Illustration** Works with 10-15 illustrators/year. Reviews ms/illustration packages. Will review artwork for future assignments. Responds only if interested, or immediately if SASE or response card is included. We keep all samples on file.
**How to Contact/Illustrators** Illustrations only: Query with samples. Original artwork returned at job's completion.
**Photography** Buys stock.
**Terms** Pays authors royalty of 5-15% based on actual revenues (net). Pays illustrators by the project. Book catalog and ms guidelines on request with SASE. Catalog available on website.

## MASTER BOOKS

Imprint of New Leaf Press, P.O. Box 726, Green Forest, AR 72638. (870)438-5288. Fax: (870)438-5120. E-mail: nlp@newleafpress.net. Website: www.masterbooks.net. **Manuscript Acquisitions:** Roger Howerton, acquisitions editor. **Art Acquisitions:** Brent Spurlock, art director. Publishes 2 picture books/year; 3 young readers/year; 3 middle readers/year; 2 young adult titles/year. 10% of books by first-time authors.
**Nonfiction** Picture books: activity books, animal, nature/environment, creation. Young readers, middle readers, young adults: activity books, animal, biography Christian, nature/environment, science, creation. Recently published *Whale of a Story*, by Buddy Davis (middle readers, Bible story); *Dinky Dinosaur*, by Darrell Wiskur (picture book, creation); *For Those Who Dare*, by John Hudson Tiner (young adult, biography).
**How to Contact/Writers** Nonfiction: Submit outline/synopsis and 3 sample chapters. Responds to queries/mss in 3 months. Publishes book 1 year after acceptance. Will consider simultaneous submissions.
**Illustration** We are not looking for illustrations.
**Terms** Pays authors royalty of 3-15% based on wholesale price. Sends galleys to authors. Book catalog available

for 9×12 SAE and $1.85 postage; ms guidelines available for SASE. Catalog available on website.

**Tips** "All of our children's books are creation-based, including topics from the Book of Genesis. We look also for homeschool educational material that would be supplementary to a homeschool curriculum."

## MARGARET K. MCELDERRY BOOKS

Imprint of Simon & Schuster Children's Publishing Division, 1230 Avenue of the Americas, New York NY 10020. (212)698-7000. Website: www.simonsayskids.com. Editor at Large: Margaret K. McElderry. **Manuscript Acquisitions:** Emma D. Dryden, vice president and editorial director; Karen Wojtyla, senior editor. **Art Acquisitions:** Ann Bobco, executive art director. Imprint of Simon & Schuster Children's Publishing Division. Publishes 10-12 picture books/year; 2-4 young readers/year; 8-10 middle readers/year; 5-7 young adult titles/year. 10% of books by first-time authors; 33% of books from agented writers. "Margaret K. McElderry Books publishes original hardcover trade books for children from pre-school age through young adult. This list includes picture books, easy-to-read books, fiction for eight to twelve-year-olds, poetry, fantasy and young adult fiction. The style and subject matter of the books we publish is almost unlimited. We do not publish textbooks, coloring and activity books, greeting cards, magazines, pamphlets, or religious publications."

• Margaret K. McElderry Books is not currently accepting unsolicited manuscripts. McElderry title *The Legend of Buddy Bush*, by Sheila P. Moss, won a 2005 Coretta Scott King Author Honor Award.

**Fiction** Young readers: adventure, contemporary, fantasy, history, poetry. Middle readers: adventure, contemporary, fantasy, humor, mystery. Young adults: contemporary, fantasy, mystery. "Always interested in publishing humorous picture books, original beginning reader stories, and strong poetry." Average word length: picture books—500; young readers—2,000; middle readers—10,000-20,000; young adults—45,000-50,000. Recently published *Bear Wants More*, by Karma Wilson, illustrated by Jane Chapman; *Mathmatickles*, by Betsy Franco, illustrated by Steven Salerno; *The Puppeteer's Apprentice*, by D. Anne Love; *Izzy's Place*, by Marc Kornblatt.

**Nonfiction** Young readers, young adult teens, biography, history. Average word length: picture books—500-1,000; young readers—1,500-3,000; middle readers—10,000-20,000; young adults—30,000-45,000. Recently published *Shout, Sister, Shout!*, by Roxane Orgill.

**How to Contact/Writers** Fiction/nonfiction: Submit query and 3 sample chapters with SASE; may also include brief résumé of previous publishing credits. Responds to queries in 1 month; mss in 3 months. Publishes a book 18 months after contract signing. Will consider simultaneous submissions (only if indicated as such).

**Illustration** Works with 20-30 illustrators/year. Query with samples; provide promo sheet or tearsheets; arrange personal portfolio review. Contact: Ann Bobco, executive art director. Responds to art samples in 3 months. Samples returned with SASE or samples filed.

**Terms** Pays authors and illustrators royalty based on retail price. Pays photographers by the project. Original artwork returned at job's completion. Manuscript guidelines free on request with SASE.

**Tips** "We're looking for strong, original fiction. We are always interested in picture books for the youngest age reader."

## MEADOWBROOK PRESS

5451 Smetana Dr., Minnetonka MN 55343-9012. (952)930-1100. Fax: (952)930-1940. Website: www.meadowbrookpress.com. **Manuscript Acquisitions:** Submissions Editor. **Art Acquisitions:** Art Director. Publishes 1-2 middle readers/year. 20% of books by first-time authors; 10% of books from agented writers. Publishes children's poetry books, activity books, arts-and-crafts books and how-to books.

• Meadowbrook does not accept unsolicited children's picture books, short stories or novels. They are primarily a nonfiction press. The publisher offers specific guidelines for children's poetry. Be sure to specify the type of project you have in mind when requesting guidelines.

**Nonfiction** Young readers, middle readers: activity books, arts/crafts, how-to. Average word length: varies. Recently published *Wiggle and Giggle Busy Book*, by Trish Kuffner (activity book); *Rolling in the Aisle*, by Bruce Lansky.

**How to Contact/Writers** Nonfiction: Query or submit outline/synopsis with SASE. Responds to queries in 4 months. Publishes a book 1-2 years after acceptance. Send a business-sized SASE and 2 first-class stamps for free writer's guidelines and book catalog before submitting ideas. Will consider simultaneous submissions.

**Illustration** Works with 2 illustrators/year. Reviews ms/illustration packages from artists. Submit ms with 2-3 pieces of nonreturnable samples. Illustrations only: Responds only if interested. Samples filed.

**Photography** Buys photos from freelancers. Buys stock. Model/property releases required. Submit cover letter.

**Terms** Pays authors royalty of 5-7% based on retail price. Offers average advance payment of $2,000-4,000. Pays illustrators per project. Pays photographers by the project. Book catalog available for 5×11 SASE and 2 first-class stamps; ms guidelines and artists guidelines available for SASE.

**Tips** "Illustrators and writers should send for our free catalog and guidelines before submitting their work to us. Also, illustrators should take a look at the books we publish to determine whether their style is consistent with ours. Writers should also note the style and content patterns of our books. Please correspond with us by mail before telephoning with questions about your submission. We work with the printed word and will respond more effectively to your questions if we have something in front of us.''

## Ⓝ MEDALION PRESS, INC.

27825 N. Forest Garden, Wauconda IL 60084. Website: www.medallionpress.com. Estab. 2003. Specializes in trade books, fiction. **Manuscript Acquisitions:** Wenda Burbank, acquisitions editor. Imprints: Bronze (YA), Wenda Burbank, acquisitions editor. Produces 11 young adult books/year. 80% of books by first-time authors.
**Fiction** Young adults/teens: adventure, contemporary, fantasy, history, humor, multicultural, nature/environment, problem novels, science fiction, special needs, sports, suspense. Average word length: young adult—55,000 minimum. Recently published *The Secret of the Shabaz*, by Jennifer Macaire (ages 9 and up, YA).
**How to Contact/Writers** Accepts international submissions. Fiction: Submit outline/synopsis and first 3 sample chapters. Responds to queries in up to 6 months; mss in up to 12 months. Publishes book up to 2 years after acceptance.
**Terms** Offers advance against royalties. Average advance: $1,000. Catalog on website.
**Tips** ''We cannot stress enough how important is is that a submission packet be edited properly. You may have the best book in the world in terms of a story idea, but if the book is grammatically poor, it will be rejected. Have an unbiased editor edit your manuscript before submitting. Lead/start trends rather than follow them. We are up to our ears in YA fantasty submissions and are not currently seeking anymore. Where are the action adventure, mystery, suspense, thriller stories for young adults?''

## MERIWETHER PUBLISHING LTD.

885 Elkton Dr., Colorado Springs CO 80907-3557. (719)594-9916. Fax: (719)594-9916. E-mail: merpcds@aol.com. Website: www.meriwetherpublishing.com. **Manuscript Acquisitions:** Ted Zapel, comedy plays and educational drama; Rhonda Wray, religious drama. ''We do most of our artwork in-house; we do not publish for the children's elementary market.'' 75% of books by first-time authors; 5% of books from agented writers. ''Our niche is drama. Our books cover a wide variety of theatre subjects from play anthologies to theatrecraft. We publish books of monologs, duologs, short one-act plays, scenes for students, acting textbooks, how-to speech and theatre textbooks, improvisation and theatre games. Our Christian books cover worship on such topics as clown ministry, storytelling, banner-making, drama ministry, children's worship and more. We also publish anthologies of Christian sketches. We do not publish works of fiction or devotionals.''
**Fiction** Middle readers, young adults: anthology, contemporary, humor, religion. ''We publish plays, not prose-fiction.'' Our emphasis is comedy plays instead of educational themes.
**Nonfiction** Middle readers: activity books, how-to, religion, textbooks. Young adults: activity books, drama/theater arts, how-to church activities, religion. Average length: 250 pages. Recently published *New 1-Act Plays for Acting Students*, by Deb Bert and Norman Bert; *Millenium Monologs*, by Gerald Lee Ratliff.
**How to Contact/Writers** Nonfiction: Query or submit outline/synopsis and sample chapters. Responds to queries in 3 weeks; mss in 2 months. Publishes a book 6-12 months after acceptance. Will consider simultaneous submissions.
**Illustration** Works with 2 illustrators/year. Query first. Query with samples; send résumé, promo sheet or tearsheets. Samples returned with SASE.
**Terms** Pays authors royalty of 10% based on retail or wholesale price. Book catalog for SAE and $2 postage; ms guidelines for SAE and 1 first-class stamp.
**Tips** ''We are currently interested in finding unique treatments for theater arts subjects: scene books, how-to books, musical comedy scripts, monologs and short comedy plays for teens.''

## MERKOS PUBLICATIONS

Imprint of Merkos L'Inyonei Chinuch, 291 Kingston Ave., Brooklyn NY 11213. (718)778-0226. Fax: (718)778-4148. E-mail: orders@kehotonline.com. Website: www.kehotonline.com. **Acquisitions:** Yonason Gordon, project coordinator. Imprints: Merkos Publications; Kehot Publication Society. Publishes 2 picture books/year; 2 young readers/year; 2 middle readers/year; 2 young adult titles/year. 30% of books by first-time authors. ''A Jewish book publisher dedicated to fine Chasidic literature.''
**Fiction** Picture books, young readers, middle readers, young adults: religion. Recently published *The Money in the Honey*, by Aidel Buckmon (ages 9-11, picture book); *The Bat Mitzvah Club: Debbie's Story*, by Shayna Meiseles (ages 9-12, novel); *A Touch of the High Holidays*, by Deborah Glazer (ages 0-3, board book).
**Nonfiction** Picture books, young readers, middle readers, young adults: religion.
**How to Contact/Writers** Fiction/nonfiction: Query. Responds to queries in 2 weeks; mss in 4 months. Responds only if interested. Publishes a book 6 months after acceptance.
**Illustration** Uses color artwork only. Reviews ms/illustration packages from artists. Query. Illustrations only: query with samples. Responds in 2 weeks. Samples not returned; samples filed.

# Peter McCarty

*Create the images you want to see*

**W**hen people describe Peter McCarty's drawings, they use words like "luminous," "shimmering," "nostalgic" and "glowing." When speaking about his writing, they praise his droll humor and understated wit. But more often than not they talk about the characters.

Whether a dog named Hondo, a cat named Fabian, a determined bunny rabbit or an introspective T-Rex, McCarty's characters strike a chord with people—and readers feel like they know each one personally. McCarty sends his characters on everyday adventures, inviting his readers along for the ride. By book's end, characters grow and learn—and readers never forget them. That so many people love his books is a mystery to the author/illustrator. And although he is a 2003 Caldecott Honor Medal winner and is a much-admired teacher at the School for Visual Arts, McCarty "still feels like I am setting up my life."

Here, he discusses his origins as an author/illustrator, his "style" and the people and animals who inspired him.

### How did you launch your career?

In 1992 I graduated from The School of Visual Arts with a portfolio that lent itself to picture books. A teacher named William Low recommended I see an editor at Henry Holt named Laura Godwin, who gave me the opportunity to illustrate *Night Driving*, by John Coy. I killed myself doing it. I worked way past the pay, which was a lot of money to me at the time.

### How did you go from illustrating other people's work, to illustrating your own books?

After I finished with *Night Driving*. Laura Godwin asked if I would like to write and illustrate my own story. It has been wonderful working with Laura all these years. She has actually written some of my best lines.

### Adults seem to love your books as much as children do. How do write stories that will appeal to grown-ups as well as children?

I try to write and draw books without being conscious of the audience. I just try to entertain myself so I hope children and adults will be entertained as well.

### Speaking of entertaining, *Hondo & Fabian* is one of your most entertaining books. How did you get the idea for that storyline?

Hondo and Fabian were my pets. They have both passed on. I used to take Hondo to the beach when I lived in New Jersey. The imagery of a yellow Lab diving into the waves gave me the idea. I threw Fabian in for a little comic relief.

### How did you get the idea for *T Is for Terrible*?

I was a huge dinosaur freak when I was a kid. I have always loved dinosaurs and have collected dinosaur books since my childhood. I would look at these books and try to copy the dinosaurs. I always believed that the measure of a good dinosaur book was how many Tyrannosaurus rexes were in it. I thought of *T Is for Terrible* as the book I would have always wanted.

### What advice do you have for illustrators who want to write their own books?

Any aspiring illustrator should be delighted to illustrate any material. You should first get

T Is for TERRIBLE

PETER McCARTY

As he created the artwork for *T Is for Terrible*, author/illustrator Peter McCarty was inspired by the work of dinosaur artists like Rudolph F. Zallinger. "In the 1940s he created a famous mural in the Peabody Museum at Yale University, which really established how people thought of dinosaurs back then and, to a certain extent, still think of them today," says McCarty. "He's the Michelangelo of dinosaur art. I really admire what he did and hope that some of his influence is visible in *T Is for Terrible*."

a lot of experience illustrating other people's writing. It is also good to do a book cover once in a while. I enjoy and respect the work. It is a pleasure to read the books and create a vision for them. Writing and illustrating your own book is a whole other ball game. When you are preparing your illustrator's portfolio be sure to include sequential images showing consistency.

### How did you develop your illustration style?

I don't like to think I work in a style. I know it looks that way, but I draw and paint as well as I can. As a boy I would draw pictures out of my head. I would create the images I wanted to see. I still do. I would recommend to any illustrator to make their pictures the best they can. Their own weirdness will take over.

### Could you describe something about your process—your daily life as an artist/writer?

I work in a corner bedroom in a house out in suburbia. I work with simple materials so I don't need much space. I probably spend too much time thinking. I try to get outside as much as I can. I am in search of another yellow Lab to walk.

I might make a sequel to *Hondo & Fabian* so I am going to need some new pets.

—*Mary Cox*

written and illustrated by

Peter McCarty

His own pets inspired Peter McCarty's delightful picture book *Hondo & Fabian*. "The colored-pencil, selectively realistic illustrations are velvet-warm and fog-fuzzy," says *School Library Journal* about the book. "Hondo and Fabian have a gentle charm, and this amiable slice of life is a nice choice for bedtimes, for libraries needing more pet books, and for McCarty fans."

**Terms** Payment negotiable. Originals returned at job's completion. Book catalog available online. All imprints included in a single catalog.

**Tips** "We are the publishing house of Chabad-Lubavitch. As such, it's best to familiarize yourself with the material we put out either through our website or your local Lubavitch emissary."

## Ⓝ METRON PRESS

American Bible Association, 1865 Broadway, New York NY 10023. (212)408-1345. Fax: (212)408-1562. E-mail: gayala@american bible.org. Website: www.metronpress.com. Estab. 2002. Specializes in mass market books, trade books, Christian material, fiction, multicultural material. **Writers contact:** Brian Augustyn, senior editor. **Illustrators contact:** Brian Augustyn, senior editor. "Metron Press is committed to bringing readers vibrant stories of the human experience, told in a variety of artistic styles, with the goal of empowering personal and community aspirations." Publishes graphic novels with a Christian/Biblical bent for a teen audience.

**Fiction** Young adults/teens: problem novels, religion. Recently published: *Unforgiven*, by Brian Augustyn, art by Dick Giordano (teen graphic novel); *Testament*, by Jim Krueger, art by a team of creators (teen graphic novel); *Samson*, by Mario Ruiz with Jerry Novick, art by Mario Ruiz and Kevin Conrad (teen graphic novel).

**How to Contact/Writers** Accepts international submissions. Fiction/nonfiction: Query or submit complete ms. Responds to queries in 10-20 weeks; to mss in 5 weeks. Publishes book 1 year after acceptance. No simultaneous, electronic, or previously published submissions.

**Illustration** Accepts material from international illustrators. Works with 25 illustrators/year. Uses both color and b&w. Reviews ms/illustration packages. For ms/illustration packages: Query. Reviews work for future assignments. If interested in illustrating future titles, query with samples. Responds in 2-3 weeks. Samples returned with SASE.

**Photography** Buys stock images and assigns work. Submit photos to: Robert Schwalb, director. Seeking inspirational and youth. For first contact, send cover letter, CD with low res images.

**Terms** Work purchased outright from authors (range: $5,000-250,000). Pays illustrators by the project (range: $75-500/page). Pays photographers by the project (range: $100-1,000). Illustrators see dummies for review. Originals returned to artist at job's completion. Catalog on website. Individual catalogs for imprints. See website for writer's, artist's, photographer's guidelines.

**Tips** "Looking for established comic trade experience—manga/anime a plus."

## MILKWEED EDITIONS

1011 Washington Ave. S., Suite 300, Minneapolis MN 55415-1246. (612)332-3192. Fax: (612)215-2550. E-mail: editor@milkweed.org. Website: www.milkweed.org. **Manuscript Acquisitions:** H. Emerson Blake, editor-in-chief. Publishes 3-4 middle readers/year. 25% of books by first-time authors. "Milkweed Editions publishes with the intention of making a humane impact on society, in the belief that literature is a transformative art uniquely able to convey the essential experiences of the human heart and spirit. To that end, Milkweed Editions publishes distinctive voices of literary merit in handsomely designed, visually dynamic books, exploring the ethical, cultural, and esthetic issues that free societies need continually to address."

**Fiction** Middle readers: adventure, contemporary, fantasy, multicultural, nature/environment, suspense/mystery. Does not want to see anthologies, folktales, health, hi-lo, picture books, poetry, religion, romance, sports. Average length: middle readers—90-200 pages. Recently published *Perfect*, by Natasha Friend (contemporary); *The Trouble with Jeremy Chance*, by George Harrar (historical); *The $66 Summer*, by John Armistead (multicultural, mystery).

**How to Contact/Writers** Fiction: Submit complete ms. Responds to mss in 6 months. Publishes a book 1 year after acceptance. Will consider simultaneous submissions.

**Illustration** Works with 2-4 illustrators/year. Reviews ms/illustration packages from artists. Query; submit ms with dummy. Illustrations only: Query with samples; provide résumé, promo sheet, slides, tearsheets and client list. Samples filed or returned with SASE; samples filed. Originals returned at job's completion.

**Terms** Pays authors royalty of 6% based on retail price. Offers advance against royalties. Illustrators' contracts are decided on an individual basis. Sends galleys to authors. Book catalog available for $1.50 to cover postage; ms guidelines available for SASE or at website. Must include SASE with ms submission for its return.

## Ⓒ THE MILLBROOK PRESS

A division of Lerner Publishing Group, 241 First Avenue North Minneapolis, MN 5540. (800)328-4929. Fax: (800)332-1132. Website: www.lernerbooks.com.

- Millbrook Press publishes supplementary series and individual titles for the K-8 School & Library market. Millbrook Press is now a division of Lerner Publishing Group, an independent publisher since 1959. See listing for Lerner for submission information.

## MIRRORSTONE

Imprint of Wizards of the Coast, P.O. Box 707, Renton WA 98057. (425)254-2287. Website: www.mirrorstonebo

oks.com. **Manuscript Acquisitions:** Nina Hess. **Art Acquisitions:** Matt Adelsperger, art director. Publishes 12 middle readers/year; 6 young adult titles/year. 25% of books by first-time authors. ''We publish series novels for young readers designed to spur the imagination.''

**Fiction** Young readers, middle readers, young adults: fantasy. Average word length: middle readers—50-55,000; young adults—70-75,000. Recently published *Temple of the Dragonslayer*, by Tim Waggoner (ages 10 and up); *Search for the Spiritkeeper*, by Matt Forbeck (ages 8 and up); *Riddle in Stone*, by Ree Soesbee (ages 8 and up).

**How to Contact/Writers** Fiction: Query with samples, résumé. ''No manuscripts, please.'' Responds to queries in 6-8 weeks. Publishes book 9 months after acceptance.

**Illustration** Works with 4 illustrators/year. Query. Contact: Matt Adelsperger, art director. Illustrations only: Query with samples, résumé.

**Terms** Pays authors royalty of 4-6% based on retail price. Offers advances (average amount: $4,000). Pays illustrators by the project. Book catalog available for SASE and 5 first-class stamps; ms guidelines available for SASE. All imprints included in a single catalog. Catalog available on website.

**Tips** Editorial staff attended or plans to attend the following conference: BEA.

## MITCHELL LANE PUBLISHERS, INC.

P.O. Box 196, Hockessin DE 19707. (302)234-9426. Fax: (302)234-4742. E-mail: mitchelllane@mitchelllane.com. Website: www.mitchelllane.com. **Acquisitons:** Barbara Mitchell, president. Publishes 80 young adult titles/ year. ''We publish nonfiction for children and young adults.''

**Nonfiction** Young readers, middle readers, young adults: biography, multicultural. Average word length: 4,000-50,000 words. Recently published *Clay Aiken*; *Alicia Keys* (both Blue Banner Biographies); *LeBron James*, by Joanne Mattern (A Robbie Reader).

**How to Contact/Writers** Most assignments are work-for-hire.

**Illustration** Works with 2-3 illustrators/year. Reviews ms/illustration packages from artists. Query. Illustration only: Query with samples; send résumé, portfolio, slides, tearsheets. Responds only if interested. Samples not returned; samples filed.

**Photography** Buys stock images. Needs photos of famous and prominent minority figures. Captions required. Uses color prints or digital images. Submit cover letter, résumé, published samples, stock photo list.

**Terms** Work purchased outright from authors (range: $350-2,000). Pays illustrators by the project (range: $40-250). Sends galleys to authors.

**Tips** ''Most of our assignments are work-for-hire. Submit résumé and samples of work to be considered for future assignments.''

## ☐ MONDO PUBLISHING

980 Avenue of the Americas, New York NY 10018. (212)268-3560. Fax: (212)268-3561. Website: www.mondopub.com. **Acquisitions:** editorial staff. Publishes 60 picture and chapter books/year. 10% of books by first-time authors. Publishes various categories. ''Our motto is 'creative minds creating ways to create lifelong readers.' We publish for both educational and trade markets, aiming for the highest quality books for both.''

**Fiction** Picture books, young readers, middle readers: adventure, animal, contemporary, fantasy, folktales, history, humor, multicultural, nature/environment, poetry, sports. Multicultural needs include: stories about children in different cultures or about children of different backgrounds in a U.S. setting. Recently published *Herbert Fieldmouse: Secret Agent*, by Kevin O'Malley (ages 6-12); *Blueberry Mouse*, by Alice Low (ages 4-6); *Eaglesmount: The Silver Horn*, by Cherith Baldry (ages 8-12); *Right Outside My Window*, by Mary Ann Hoberman; *Jake Greenthumb*, by Loki (ages 4-8).

**Nonfiction** Picture books, young readers, middle readers: animal, biography, geography, how-to, multicultural, nature/environment, science, sports. Recently published *Seahorses*, by Sylvia James; *How to Make a Collage*, by Sue and Will Johnson.

**How to Contact/Writers** Fiction/nonfiction: Query or submit complete ms. Responds to queries in 1 month; mss in 6 months. Will consider simultaneous submissions. Manuscripts returned with SASE. Queries must also have SASE.

**Illustration** Works with 40 illustrators/year. Reviews ms/illustration packages from illustrators. Illustration only: Query with samples, résumé, portfolio. Responds only if interested. Samples returned with SASE; samples filed. Send attention: Art Deptartment.

**Photography** Occasionally uses freelance photographers. Buys stock images. Uses mostly nature photos. Uses color prints, transparencies, slides or digital images.

**Terms** Pays authors royalty of 2-5% based on wholesale/retail price for trade titles. Offers advance based on project. Pays illustrators by the project (range: $3,000-9,000), royalty of 2-4% based on retail price. Pays photographers by the project or per photo. Sends galleys to authors depending on project. Originals returned to artists at job's completion. Book catalogs available for 9 × 12 SASE with $3.20 postage.

**Tips** ''Prefer illustrators with book experience or a good deal of experience in illustration projects requiring consistency of characters and/or setting over several illustrations. Prefer manuscripts targeted to trade market plus crossover to educational market.''

## ⓝ MOON MOUNTAIN PUBLISHING

P.O. Box 188, West Rockport ME 04865. (207)236-0958. E-mail: hello@moonmountainpub.com. Website: www. moonmountainpub.com. **Manuscript/Art Acquisitions:** Cate Monroe, publisher. Publishes 5 picture books/year. 50% of books by first-time authors. ''We are a publisher of children's picture books. We are open to submissions of fiction manuscripts (including complete text/illustration packages) that lend themselves to picture book illustration and design. We publish books with positive, life-affirming themes. We strive to encourage the following qualities in children: kindness, honor, love, respect, courge, dedication, comfort, contentment, hope, intelligence, talent, creativity and imagination.''

• Moon Mountain Publishing is not accepting manuscripts at this time, but will look at promo postcards from illustrators.

**Fiction** Picture books: adventure, animal, concept, contemporary, fantasy, folktales, humor, multicultural, nature/environment. Average word length: picture books—200-2,000 words. Recently published *Hamlet & the Magnificent Sandcastle*, by Brian Lies (ages 5-8, picture book fiction); *Petronella*, by Jay Williams, illustrated by Margaret Oryan-Kean (age 8-12, picture book fiction); *Hello Willow*, by Kimberly Poulton, illustrated by Jennifer O'Keefe (ages 0-5, picture book fiction).

**Illustration** Works with 9 illustrators/year. Uses color artwork only. Reviews ms/illustration packages from artists. Send ms with dummy or submit ms with 3-4 pieces of final art. Contact: Robert Holtzman, editor. Illustrations only: Query with samples; send promo sheet, portfolio and slides. Contact: Cate Monroe, publisher. Responds only if interested. Samples returned with SASE; samples filed.

**Photography** Works on assignment only.

**Terms** Pays authors royalty. Offers advances. Pays illustrators royalty and advance. Originals returned to artist at job's completion. Book catalog available for #10 SAE and 1 first-class stamp; ms guidelines available for SASE. Catalog available on website.

## MOREHOUSE PUBLISHING CO.

4775 Linglestown Rd., Harrisburg PA 17112. Website: www.morehousegroup.com.

• Morehouse is no longer publishing children's books.

## ⓒ MORGAN REYNOLDS PUBLISHING

620 S. Elm St., Suite 223, Greensboro NC 27406. (336)275-1311. Fax: (336)275-1152. E-mail: editorial@morganreynolds.com. Website: www.morganreynolds.com. **Acquisitions:** Casey Cornelius, editor. Book publisher. Publishes 25 young adult titles/year. 50% of books by first-time authors. Morgan Reynolds publishes nonfiction books for juvenile and young adult readers. ''We prefer lively, well-written biographies of interesting figures for our extensive biography series. Subjects may be contemporary or historical. Books for our Great Events series should take an insightful and exciting look at pivotal periods and/or events.''

**Nonfiction** Middle readers, young adults/teens: biography, history. Average word length: 25-35,000. Recently published *No Easy Answers: Bayard Rustin and the Civil Rights Movement*, by Calvin Craig Miller; *Empire in the East: The Story of Genghis Khan*, by Earle Rice, Jr.; *The Mail Must Go Through: The Story of the Pony Express*, by Margaret Rav; *Nikola Tesla and the Taming of Electricity*, by Lisa J. Aldrich.

**How to Contact/Writers** First-time authors submit entire ms. Query; submit outline/synopsis with at least 2 sample chapters and SASE. Responds to queries in 6 weeks; mss in 2 months. Publishes a book 1 year after acceptance. Will consider simultaneous submissions.

**Terms** Pays authors negotiated price. Offers advances and royalties. Sends galleys to authors. Manuscript guidelines available at our website or by mail with SASE and 1 first-class stamp. Visit website for complete catalog.

**Tips** Does not respond without SASE. ''Familiarize yourself with our titles before sending a query or submission, keeping in mind that we do *not* publish fiction, poetry, memoirs, picture books. We focus on serious-minded, well-crafted, nonfiction books for young adults that will complement school curriculums, namely biographies of significant figures.'' Editorial staff has attended or plans to attend the following conferences: ALA, TLA.

## MOUNT OLIVE COLLEGE PRESS

634 Henderson St., Mount Olive NC 28365. (919)658-2502. **Acquisitions:** Pepper Worthington, editor. Publishes 1 middle reader/year. 85% of books by first-time authors.

**Fiction** Middle readers: animal, humor, poetry. Average word length: middle readers—3,000 words.

**Nonfiction** Middle readers: nature/environment, religion, self help. Average word length: middle readers—3,000 words.

**How to Contact/Writers** Submit complete ms or outline/synopsis and 3 sample chapters. Responds to queries in 1-2 years.
**Illustration** Uses b&w artwork only. Submit ms with 50% of final art. Contact: Pepper Worthington, editor. Responds in 6-12 months if interested. Samples not returned.
**Terms** Payment negotiated individually. Book catalog available for SAE and 1 first-class stamp.

## NEW CANAAN PUBLISHING COMPANY INC.
P.O. Box 752, New Canaan CT 06840. (203)966-3408. Fax: (203)548-9072. E-mail: djm@newcanaanpublishing.com. Website: www.newcanaanpublishing.com. Book publisher. Vice President: Kathy Mittelstadt: Publishes 1 picture book/year; 1 young reader/year; 1 middle reader/year; 1 young adult title/year. 50% of books by first-time authors. "We seek books with strong educational or traditional moral content and books with Christian themes."
   • To curb the number of unsolicited submissions, New Cannan Books only accepts: 1—books for children of military families; 2—middle readers and young adult books addressing Christian themes (e.g., devotionals, books addressing teen or pre-teen issues with a Christian focus, whether in a fictional context or otherwise); and 3—historical fiction.
**Fiction** All levels: adventure, history, religion (Christianity), suspense/mystery. Picture books: phonics readers. "Stories about disfunctional families are not encouraged." Average word length: picture books—1,000-3,000; young readers—8,000-30,000; middle readers—8,000-40,000; young adult s—15,000-50,000. Recently published *My Daddy Is An Airman*, by Kirk and Sharron Hilbrecht; *It's Me Again, God*, by Mary Elizabeth Anderson.
**Nonfiction** All levels: geography, history, how-to, reference, religion (Christian only), textbooks. Average word length: picture books—1,000-3,000; young readers—8,000-30,000; middle readers—8,000-40,000; young adults—15,000-50,000.
**How to Contact/Writers** Submit outline/synopsis or complete ms with biographical information and writing credentials. Does not guarantee a response unless offer to publish is forthcoming. Responds to queries in 4-6 months; mss in 6 months. Publishes a book 12-18 months after acceptance.
**Illustration** Works with 3-5 illustrators/year. Reviews ms/illustration packages from artists. Query or send ms with dummy. Illustrations only: Query with samples; send résumé, promo sheet. Responds in 1-2 months if need exists.
**Terms** Pays authors royalty of 7-12% based on wholesale price. Royalty may be shared with illustrator where relevant. Pays illustrators royalty of 4-6% as share of total royalties. Book catalog available for SAE; ms guidelines available on website.
**Tips** "We are diligent but small, so please be patient."

## NEW VOICES PUBLISHING
Imprint of KidsTerrain, Inc., P.O. Box 560, Wilmington MA 01887. (978)658-2131. Fax: (978)988-8833. E-mail: rschiano@kidsterrain.com. Website: www.kidsterrain.com. Estab. 2000. Specializes in fiction. **Manuscript/Art Acquisitions:** Book Editor. Publishes 2 picture books/year. 95% of books by first-time authors.
**Fiction** Picture books, young readers: multicultural. Average word length: picture books—500; young readers—500-1,200. Recently published *Last Night I Left Earth for Awhile*, written and illustrated by Natalie L. Brown-Douglas (ages 4-8).
**How to Contact/Writers** Fiction: Not accepting unsolicited mss. Publishes book 12-18 months after acceptance. Will consider simultaneous submissions.
**Illustration** Works with 2 illustrators/year. Uses color artwork only. Reviews ms/illustration packages from artists. No queries accepted until 2005. Responds in 2 weeks. Samples returned with SASE.
**Terms** Pays authors royalty of 10-15% based on wholesale price. Pays illustrators by the project or royalty. Sends galleys to authors. Offers writer's guidelines for SASE.

## NOMAD PRESS
2456 Christain St., White River Junction NJ 05001. (802)649-1995. Fax: (802)649-2667. E-mail: lauri@nomadpress.net. Website: www.nomadpress.net. Estab. 2001. Specializes in nonfiction, educational material. **Writers contact:** Alex Kahan, publisher. **Illustrators contact:** Alex Kahan, publisher. Produces 6-8 young readers/year. 10% of books by first-time authors. "We produce nonfiction children's activity books that bring a particular science or cultural topic into sharp focus."
   • Nomad Press does not accept picture books or fiction.
**Nonfiction** Middle readers: activity books, history, science. Average word length: middle readers—30,000. Recently published *Tools of Navigation: A Kid's Guide to the History and Science of Finding Your Way*, by Rachel Dickinson (ages 9-12, activity); *Tools of Timekeeping: A Kid's Guide to the History and Science of Telling Time*, by Linda Formichelli and Eric Martin (agest 9-12, activity/education); *Great Civil War Projects You Can Build Yourself*, by Maxine Anderson (ages 8-12, activity/education resource).

**How to Contact/Writers** Accepts international submissions. Nonfiction: Query or submit complete ms. Responds to queries in 1-2 months. Publishes book 1 year after acceptance.

**Terms** Pays authors royalty based on retail price or work purchased outright. Offers advance against royalties. Catalog on website. All imprints included in single catalog. See website for writer's guidelines.

**Tips** "We publish a very specific kind of nonfiction children's activity book. Please keep this in mind when querying or submitting."

## ▲ NORTH-SOUTH BOOKS

350 Seventh Ave., Suite 1400, New York NY 10001. (212)706-4545. Website: www.northsouth.com. Imprint: Night Sky. U.S. office of Nord-Siid Verlag, Switzerland. Publishes 75 titles/year.

- North-South and its imprint do not accept queries or unsolicited manuscripts.

## NORTHWORD BOOKS FOR YOUNG READERS

Imprint of T&N Children's Publishing international, 11571 K-Tel Dr., Minnetonka MN 55343. (982)933-7537. Website: www.tnkidsbooks.com. Estab. 1984. Specializes in trade books, nonfiction. **Contact:** Submissions Editor. Produces 6-8 picture books/year; 5-10 young readers/year; 6 middle readers/year. 10-20% of books by first-time authors. NorthWord's mission is "to publish books for children that encourage a love for the natural world."

**Fiction** Picture books: animal, concept, history, nature/environment, poetry—all nature-related. Young readers: animal, history, nature/environment, poetry—all nature-related. Average word length: picture books—500-1,000; young readers—1,000-4,000. Recently published *Anna's Table*, by Eve Bunting, illustrated by Taia Morley (ages 5-8, picture book); *The Day I Could Fly*, by Lunn Crosbie Loux, illustrated by Guy Porfino (ages 5-8, picture book); *All Around Cats*, by Dolly Viscardi, illustrated by David Brooks (ages 5-8, picture book).

**Nonfiction** Picture books: activity books, animal, arts/crafts, biography, careers, concept, cooking, geography, history, hobbies, how-to, nature/environment, science, sports. Young readers: activity books, animal, arts/crafts, biography, careers, cooking, geography, history, hobbies, how-to, nature/environment, science, sports. Middle readers: activity books, animal, arts/crafts, biography, careers, cooking, history, hobbies, nature/environment, sports. Average word length picture books—500-1,000; young readers—1,000-4,000. Recently published *John Muir and Stickeen*, by Marybeth Loriecki and Julie Dunlap, illustrated by Bill Farnsworth (ages 5-8, nonfiction picture book); *Yoga Bear*, by Karen Pierce, illustrated by Paula Brinkman (ages 2-6, nonfiction picture book); *Everything Reptiles*, by Cherie Winner (ages 8-11, nonfiction series).

**How to Contact/Writers** Accepts international submissions. Fiction: Query. Nonfiction: Submit outline/synopsis. Responds to queries/mss in 3 months. Publishes book 2 years after acceptance. Considers simultaneous submissions, previously published work.

**Illustration** Accepts material from international illustrators. Works with 8-10 illustrators/year. Uses color artwork only. For ms/illustration packages: Send ms with dummy. Submit ms/illustration packages to Submission Editor. Reviews work for future assignments. If interested in illustrating future titles, query with samples. Submit samples to Submissions Editor. Responds in 3 months. Samples returned with SASE. Samples filed.

**Photography** Buys stock images. Submit photos to Submissions Editor. Looking for animal/nature photography. Model/property releases required. Photo captions required. Uses color prints. For first contact, send cover letter, client list, stock photo list, promo piece (color).

**Terms** Offers advance against royalties (average advance: $2,000-10,000). Pays illustrators royalty based on retail price. Pays photographers by the project (range: $100). Author sees galleys for review. Illustrators see dummies for review. Originals returned to artist at job's completion. Catalog available for 9×11 SASE and $1.29 postage. Individual catalogs for imprints. Offers writer's, artist's guidelines for SASE; see website for guidelines.

**Tips** "Know our material and mission and what we've recently published."

## ▣ THE OLIVER PRESS, INC.

Charlotte Square, 5707 W. 36th St., Minneapolis MN 55416-2510. (952)926-8981. Fax: (952)926-8965. E-mail: queries@oliverpress.com. Website: www.oliverpress.com. **Acquisitions:** Denise Sterling, Jenna Anderson, Megan Rocker. Publishes 8 young adult titles/year. 10% of books by first-time authors. "We publish collective biographies of people who made an impact in one area of history, including science, government, archaeology, business and crime.

**Nonfiction** Middle reader, young adults: biography, history, multicultural, social issues, history of science and technology. "Authors should only suggest ideas that fit into one of our existing series. We would like to add to our Innovators series on the history of technology and our Business Builders series on leaders of industry." Average word length: young adult—20,000 words. Recently published *Business Builders in Toys and Games*, by Nathan Aaseng (ages 10 and up, collective biography); *Women of Adventure*, by Jacqueline McLean (ages 10 and up, collective biography); *Meteorology: Predicting the Weather*, by Susan and Steven Wills (ages 10 and up, collective biography); *Voyageurs, Lumberjacks, and Farmers: Pioneers of the Midwest*, by Kieran Doherty (ages 10 and up, collective biography).

**How to Contact/Writers** Nonfiction: Query with outline/synopsis. Responds in 6 months. Publishes a book approximately 1 year after acceptance.

**Photography** Rarely buys photos from freelancers. Please do not send unsolicited materials.

**Terms** Pays authors flat fee or fee against negotiable royalty. Work purchased outright from authors (fee negotiable). Book catalog and ms guidelines available online or for SASE.

**Tips** "Authors should read some of the books we have already published before sending a query to The Oliver Press."

## ONSTAGE PUBLISHING

214 E. Moulton St. NE, Decatur AL 35601. (256)308-2300. (888)420-8879. Website: www.onstagebooks.com. **Manuscript Acquisitions:** Dianne Hamilton. Publishes 2-4 middle readers/year; 1-2 young adult titles/year. 80% of books by first-time authors.

**Fiction** Picture books: adventure, contemporary, history, nature/environment, suspense/mystery. Middle readers: adventure, contemporary, fantasy, history, nature/environment, science fiction, suspense/mystery. Young adults: adventure, contemporary, fantasy, history, humor, science fiction, suspense/mystery. Average word length: picture books—100-1,500; middle readers—5,000 and up; young adults—25,000 and up. Recently published *The Masterpiece*, by Darren Butler (a mystery book, ages 12 and up, the Abbie Girl Spy adventures); *Will Paris Burn?*, by Annie Laura Smith (middle grade fiction).

**Nonfiction** Query first; currently not producing nonfiction.

**How to Contact/Writers** Fiction: Send complete ms if under 20,000 words, otherwise send synopsis and first 3 chapters. Responds to queries/mss in 6 months. Publishes a book 1-2 years after acceptance. Will consider simultaneous submissions.

**Illustration** Reviews ms/illustration packages from artists. Submit ms with 3 pieces of final art. Contact: Dianne Hamilton, senior editor. Illustrations only: Arrange personal portfolio review. Responds in 6 weeks. Samples returned with SASE.

**Photography** Works on assignment only. Contact: Art Department. Model/property releases required; captions required. Uses color, 5×7, semi gloss prints. Submit cover letter, published samples, stock photo list.

**Terms** Pays authors/illustrators/photographers advance plus royalties. Sends galleys to authors; dummies to illustrators. Book catalog available on website. All imprints included in a single catalog. Catalog available on website.

**Tips** "Study our catalog and get a sense of the kind of books we publish, so that you know whether your project is likely to be right for us."

## ORCHARD BOOKS

Imprint of Scholastic, Inc., 557 Broadway, New York NY 10012. (212)343-6782. Fax: (212)343-4890. Website: www.scholastic.com. Book publisher. Editorial Director: Ken Geist. **Manuscript Acquisitions:** Amy Griffin, senior editor. **Art Acquisitions:** David Saylor, art director. "We publish approximately 55 books yearly including fiction, poetry, picture books, and young adult novels." 10% of books by first-time authors.

• Orchard is not accepting unsolicited manuscripts; query letters only.

**Fiction** All levels: animal, contemporary, history, humor, multicultural, nature/environment, poetry. Recently published *Stuart's Cape*, by Sara Pennypacker, illustrated by Martin Matje; *Where Are You Going? To See My Friend!*, by Eric Carle and Kazuo Iwamura (picture book); *Alice in Pop-Up Wonderland*, by J. otto Seibold (picture book).

**Nonfiction** "We rarely publish nonfiction." Recently published *Shutting Out the Sky*, by Deborah Hopkinson.

**How to Contact/Writers** Query only with SASE. Responds in 3 months.

**Illustration** Works with 15 illustrators/year. Art director reviews ms/illustration portfolios. Submit "tearsheets or photocopies or photostats of the work." Responds to art samples in 1 month. Samples returned with SASE. No disks or slides, please.

**Terms** Most commonly an advance against list royalties. Sends galleys to authors; dummies to illustrators. Original artwork returned at job's completion.

**Tips** "Read some of our books to determine first whether your manuscript is suited to our list."

## OUR CHILD PRESS

P.O. Box 4379, Philadelphia PA 19087-0074. Phone/fax: (610)308-8088. E-mail ourchildpress@aol.com. Website: www.ourchildpress.com. **Acquisitions:** Carol Perrott, president. 90% of books by first-time authors.

**Fiction/Nonfiction** All levels: adoption, multicultural, special needs. Published *Like Me*, written by Dawn Martelli, illustrated by Jennifer Hedy Wharton; *Is That Your Sister?*, by Catherine and Sherry Burin; *Oliver: A Story About Adoption*, by Lois Wichstrom.

**How to Contact/Writers** Fiction/ nonfiction: Query or submit complete ms. Responds to queries/mss in 6 months. Publishes a book 6-12 months after acceptance.

**Ilustration** Works with 1-5 illustrators/year. Reviews ms/illustration packages from artists. Manuscript/illustration packages and illustration only: Query first. Submit résumé, tearsheets and photocopies. Responds to art samples in 2 months. Samples returned with SASE; samples kept on file.

**Terms** Pays authors royalt y of 5-10% based on wholesale price. Pays illustrators royalt y of 5-10% based on wholesale price. Original artwork returned at job's completion. Book catalog for business-size SAE and 67¢ postage.

## ◘ OUR SUNDAY VISITOR, INC.

200 Noll Plaza, Huntington IN 46750. (260)356-8400. Fax: (260)359-9117. Website: www.osv.com. **Acquisitions:** Jacquelyn M. Lindsey, Michael Dubruiel, Kelly Renz. **Art Director:** Eric Schoenig. Publishes primarily religious, educational, parenting, reference and biographies. OSV is dedicated to providing books, periodicals and other products that serve the Catholic Church.

- Our Sunday Visitor, Inc., is publishing only those children's books that tie in to sacramental preparation and Catholic identity. Contact the acquisitions editor for ms guidelines.

**Nonfiction** Picture books, middle readers, young readers, young adults. Recently published *The Mass Book for Children*, by Rosemarie Gortler and Donna Piscitelli, illustrated by Mimi Sternhagen.

**How to Contact/Writers** Query, submit complete ms, or submit outline/synopsis and 2-3 sample chapters. Responds to queries/mss in 2 months. Publishes a book 18-24 months after acceptance. Will consider simultaneous submissions, electronic submissions via disk or modem, previously published work.

**Illustration** Reviews ms/illustration packages from artists. Illustration only: Query with samples. Contact: Acquisitions Editor. Responds only if interested. Samples returned with SASE; samples filed.

**Photography** Buys photos from freelancers. Contact: Acquisitions Editor.

**Terms** Pays authors royalty of 10-12% net. Pays illustrators by the project (range: $200-1,500). Sends galleys to authors; dummies to illustrators. Book catalog available for SASE; ms guidelines available for SASE.

**Tips** "Stay in accordance with our guidelines."

## THE OVERMOUNTAIN PRESS

P.O. Box 1261, Johnson City TN 37605. (423)926-2691. Fax: (423)929-2464. E-mail: submissions@overmtn.com. Website: www.overmountainpress.com. **Manuscript Acquisitions:** Jason Weems, senior editor. Publishes 3 picture books/year; 2 young readers/year; 2 middle readers/year. 50% of books by first-time authors. "We are primarily a publisher of southeastern regional history, and we have recently published several titles for children. We consider children's books about Southern Appalachia only!"

**Fiction** Picture books: folktales, history. Young readers, middle readers: folktales, history, suspense/mystery. Average word length: picture books—800-1,000; young readers—5,000-10,000; middle readers—20,000-30,000. Recently published *Bloody Mary: The Mystery of Amanda's Magic Mirror*, by Patrick Bone (young, middle reader); *Bark and Tim*, by Ellen Gidaro and Audrey Vernick; *Appalachian ABCs*, by Francie Hall, illustrated by Kent Oehm (pre-elementary, picture book).

**Nonfiction** Picture books, young readers, middle readers: biography (regional), history (regional). Average word length: picture books—800-1,000; young readers—5,000-10,000; middle readers—20,000-30,000. Recently published *The Little Squash Seed*, written and illustrated by Gayla Dowdy Seale (preschool-elementary, picture book).

**How to Contact/Writers** Fiction/nonfiction: Submit outline/synopsis and 2 sample chapters. Responds to queries in 2 months; mss in 6 months. Publishes book 1 year after acceptance. Will consider simultaneous submissions and previously published work.

**Illustration** Works with 4 illustrators/year. Uses color artwork only. Reviews ms/illustration packages from artists. Send ms with dummy with at least 3 color copies of sample illustrations. Illustrations only: Send résumé. Responds only if interested. Samples not returned; samples filed.

**Terms** Pays authors royalty of 5-15% based on wholesale price. Pays illustrators royalty of 5-10% based on wholesale price or by author/illustrator negotiations (author pays). Sends galleys to authors; dummies to illustrators. Originals sometimes returned to artist at job's completion. Book catalog available for 8½×11 SAE and 4 first-class stamps; ms guidelines available for SASE. All imprints included in a single catalog. Catalog available on website.

**Tips** "Because we are fairly new in the children's market, we will not accept a manuscript without complete illustrations. We are compiling a database of freelance illustrators which is available to interested authors. Please call if you have questions regarding the submission process or to see if your product is of interest. The children's market is huge! If the author can find a good local publisher, he or she is more likely to get published. We are currently looking for authors to represent our list in the new millennium. At this point, we are accepting regional (Southern Appalachian) manuscripts only. *Please* call if you have a question regarding this policy."

# Jarrett J. Krosoczka

*Showcasing work on the Web*

**W**hen I was 19 and a junior at the Rhode Island School of Design, I created a project called *'Hello,' said this Slug*. As I wanted to get all of my rejection letters out of the way while still a student, I sent the project to a number of publishers," says children's author and illustrator Jarrett J. Krosoczka. "Everyone who saw it rejected it, but I received a lot of positive feedback."

Positive feedback has graduated into a successful career for Krosoczka, the author and illustrator of picture books *Good Night, Monkey Boy*; *Bubble Bath Pirates*; *Annie Was Warned*; *Baghead*; and *Max for President*. The books create whimsical, somewhat ridiculous and yet relatable characters and situations, beautifully illustrated in acrylic paint. They are a lovely balance of punk rock rebelliousness, old-fashioned adventure, and a slight dash of the ancient morality tale that slides in a lesson without the notice of the young reader.

Children's books seemed a natural fit for Krosoczka. "I drew a lot when I was a kid. I mean, all the time—after school, on weekends, on road trips . . . even if my grandparents took me out to eat I would bring along a sketchbook and draw," he says. "My drawings were always character-based and I was constantly creating story lines for them. When I wasn't drawing, they lived in my head."

What wasn't so pre-ordained for Krosoczka's career is his intricate, elaborate, and amusing website, studiojjk.com. Far from the typical illustrator's website, functioning merely as a private art gallery, studiojjk.com is an interactive site where the viewer can not only read excerpts, purchase books, and evaluate his illustrations, but also play video games based on his books, view works-in-progress in his sketchbook, and download buddy icons for instant messaging or computer wallpaper.

"The first incarnation of what eventually became studiojjk.com was created when I was a junior at the Rhode Island School of Design. It started off as a simple vehicle to showcase my illustration work, and was just crude intro and portfolio pages. As my work has progressed, the site has progressed," he explains.

"I do all the design and programming for my site. I knew nothing about computers when I entered college and I've never taken a class on the subject. I'm completely self-taught, mostly by trial and error, but I've also read books and taken tutorials on various programs," he says. "The more unusual sections were created to help my site (and my work) stand above the crowd. The video games were created to draw people back to the site again and

Released during a presidential election year, Jarrett J. Krosoczka's *Max for President* teaches kids a little about the election process, the ups and downs of winning and losing, and that every president needs help to do the job. Visit www.studiojjk.com to see more examples of Krosoczka's work.

again. They were incredibly difficult to program—they're designed in Flash (as is the site) and involved a lot of math.''

As more and more people have begun purchasing books from online vendors, as well as learning about different artists and authors and deciding what they're interested in from the Internet, it's become increasingly important for authors and illustrators to have a presence on the Web. Krosoczka has faced this challenge head-on by creating a site where his fans (or soon-to-be fans) can explore his work in unique and interesting ways, such as the games and sketchbook, learn about him from his ''serious,'' ''fake,'' or ''short'' bio, and ultimately purchase his work—online or from a bookstore. ''I wouldn't say I'm selling a lot of books through my website, but I am selling a lot of books *because* of my website. It builds up my fan base, which in turn sells books,'' he says.

Another sales opportunity facilitated by the website are the visits Krosoczka makes to

What happens when a sheep, pig, chicken, goat, and cow are ready to ROCK? Find out in Jarrett J. Krosoczka's latest picture book *Punk Farm*—and be sure to visit the totally rockin' www.punkfarm.com, where you can get stickers and posters, download wallpaper and buddy icons, buy Punk Farm merchandize, load the band's ''barn blazing'' cover of ''Old McDonald Had a Farm'' into your MP3 player, and join the Punk Farm revolution e-mail list.

schools around the country, giving interactive presentations on how he came to be an author and illustrator and reading aloud from his books. "My site provides a detailed description of my presentation, has a Flash video, lets schools know what I expect from them, and has information on how they can order my books through the publisher," he says.

Throughout its incarnations from a mere gallery to an interactive, multi-functional marketing tool, studiojjk.com has remained true to its original intent: to showcase the work. "My main goal has always been for the reader to look at my site and recognize the personality and attitude that is present in the books," Krosoczka says. "I've also wanted to stay true to the look of my books, so everything on the site is painted." By sticking to his original purpose for the site and adding interesting, playful features, Krosoczka has created a site that is both a fitting and exemplary display of his work and a virtual playground that children and adults alike can enjoy.

So how did Krosoczka go from positive feedback to writing and illustrating success? Drive, hard work, and a little bit of good advice. "[Children's author and illustrator] Grace Lin helped me kick the door into publishing wide open," he explains. "It was November 1999 and she had just seen the release of her first book, *The Ugly Vegetables*. She suggested sending my postcards to the editors—I had been sending them to the art directors—because of their pull in the acquisitions process." Within four days, Krosoczka got the phone call that eventually led to the publication of his first book, *Good Night, Monkey Boy*, by Knopf in 2001.

Advice alone, however, will not that elusive book contract make. Krosoczka recommends a mixture of enthusiasm, individuality, and old-fashioned pride and enjoyment in your work. "Be insatiable," he says. "Constantly submit your work and then resubmit it. Work on your craft, improve on improvements, and continually set goals for yourself. Put yourself into your work as much as you can—the more you enjoy the process of creating, the better your story and illustrations will be." And always remember what makes a good book. "Publishers have their eyes on the immediate dollar with this whole celebrities-writing-children's books thing, but honestly, only well-crafted picture books will stand the test of time."

Next up for Krosoczka is *Punk Farm*, due for release in May 2005 from Knopf (check out the website at www.punkfarm.com). Following in spring 2006 is *Giddy Up, Cowgirl!* from Viking, about a well meaning girl who tries to help her mom run errands. And the pièce de résistance? "*Slug*, which is derived from that story I started back when I was a student at the Rhode Island School of Design, is due from Knopf in fall 2006! The publication of that book will truly be a dream come true," says Krosoczka.

*—Erin Nevius*

**Book Publishers**

## RICHARD C. OWEN PUBLISHERS, INC.

P.O. Box 585, Katonah NY 10536. (800)336-5588. Fax: (914)232-3977. Website: www.rcowen.com. **Acquisitions:** Janice Boland, children's books editor/art director. Publishes 20 picture story books/year. 90% of books by first-time authors. We publish "child-focused books, with inherent instructional value, about characters and situations with which five-, six-, and seven-year-old children can identify—books that can be read for meaning, entertainment, enjoyment and information. We include multicultural stories that present minorities in a positive and natural way. Our stories show the diversity in America." Is not interested in lesson plans, or books of activities for literature studies or other content areas.

**Fiction** Picture books, young readers: adventure, animal, contemporary, folktales, hi-lo, humor, multicultural, nature/environment, poetry, science fiction, sports, suspense/mystery. Does not want to see holiday, religious themes, moral teaching stories. "No talking animals with personified human characteristics, jingles and rhymes, alphabet books, stories without plots, stories with nostalgic views of childhood, soft or sugar-coated tales. No stereotyping." Average word length: under 500 words. Recently published *Caribbean Cats*, by Susan S. Giles;

*Freedom Quilts*, by Candy Grant Helmf, illustrated by Joanne Friar; *Dogs at School*, by Suzanne Hardin, illustrated by Jo-Ann Friar.

**Nonfiction** Picture books, young readers: animals, careers, hi-lo, history, how-to, music/dance, geography, multicultural, nature/environment, science, sports. Multicultural needs include: "Good stories respectful of all heritages, races, cultural—African-American, Hispanic, American Indian." Wants lively stories. No "encyclopedic" type of information stories. Average word length: under 500 words. Recently published *New York City Buildings*, by Ann Mace, photos by Tim Holmstron.

**How to Contact/Writers** Fiction/nonfiction: Submit complete ms and cover letter. Responds to mss in 1 year. Publishes a book 2-3 years after acceptance. See website for guidelines.

**Illustration** Works with 20 illustrators/year. Uses color artwork only. Illustration only: Send color copies/reproductions or photos of art or provide tearsheets; do not send slides or originals. Include SASE and cover letter. Responds only if interested; samples filed.

**Photography** Buys photos from freelancers. Contact: Janice Boland, art director. Include SASE and cover letter. Wants photos that are child-oriented; candid shots; not interested in portraits. "Natural, bright, crisp and colorful—of children and of interesting subjects and compositions attractive to children. If photos are assigned, we buy outright—retain ownership and all rights to photos taken in the project." Sometimes interested in stock photos for special projects. Uses 35mm, $2^1/4 \times 2^1/4$ color transparencies.

**Terms** Pays authors royalty of 5% based on wholesale price or outright purchase (range: $25-500). Offers no advances. Pays illustrators by the project (range: $100-2,500). Pays photographers by the project (range: $100-2,000) or per photo ($100-150). Original artwork returned 12-18 months after job's completion. Book brochure, ms/artists guidelines available for SASE.

**Tips** Seeking "stories (both fiction and nonfiction) that have charm, magic, impact and appeal; that children living in today's society will want to read and reread; books with strong storylines, child-appealing language, action and interesting, vivid characters. Write for the ears and eyes and hearts of your readers—use an economy of words. Visit the children's room at the public library and immerse yourself in the best children's literature."

## PACIFIC PRESS

P.O. Box 5353, Nampa ID 83653-5353. (208)465-2500. Fax: (208)465-2531. E-mail: booksubmissions@pacificpress.com. Website: www.pacificpress.com/writers/books.htm. **Manuscript Acquisitions:** Tim Lale. **Art Acquisitions:** Randy Maxwell, creative director. Publishes 1 picture book/year; 2 young readers/year; 2 middle readers/year. 5% of books by first-time authors. Pacific Press brings the Bible and Christian lifestyle to children.

**Fiction** Picture books, young readers, middle readers, young adults: religion. Average word length: picture books—100; young readers—1,000; middle readers—15,000; young adults—40,000. Recently published *I Miss Grandpa*, by Karen Holford; *The Secret of Scarlet Cove*, by Charles Mills.

**Nonfiction** Picture books, young readers, middle readers, young adults: religion. Average word length: picture books—100; young readers—1,000; middle readers—15,000; young adults—40,000. Recently published *Beanie: The Horse That Wasn't a Horse*, by Heather Grovet.

**How to Contact/Writers** Fiction/nonfiction: Query or submit outline/synopsis and 3 sample chapters. Responds to queries in 3 months; mss in 1 year. Publishes a book 6-12 months after acceptance. Will consider e-mail submissions.

**Illustration** Works with 2 illustrators/year. Uses color artwork only. Query. Responds only if interested. Samples returned with SASE.

**Photography** Buys stock and assigns work. Model/property releases required.

**Terms** Pays author royalty of 6-15% based on wholesale price. Offers advances (average amount: $1,500). Pays illustrators royalty of 6-15% based on wholesale price. Pays photographers royalty of 6-15% based on wholesale price. Sends galleys to authors. Originals returned to artist at job's completion. Manuscript guidelines for SASE. Catalog available on website (www.adventistbookcenter.com).

**Tips** Pacific Press is owned by the Seventh-day Adventist Church. The Press rejects all material that is not Bible-based.

## ◘ PARENTING PRESS, INC.

P.O. Box 75267, Seattle WA 98175-0267. (206)364-2900. Fax: (206)364-0702. E-mail: office@parentingpress.com. Website: www.parentingpress.com. Estab. 1979. Book publisher. Publisher: Carolyn Threadgill. **Acquisitions:** Elizabeth Crary (parenting) and Carolyn Threadgill (children and parenting). Publishes 4-5 books/year for parents or/and children and those who work with them. 40% of books by first-time authors. "Parenting Press publishes educational books for children in story format—no straight fiction. Our company publishes books that help build competence in parents and children. We are known for practical books that teach parents and can be used successfully by parent educators, teachers, and educators who work with parents. We are interested in books that help people feel good about themselves because they gain skills needed in dealing with others. We are particularly interested in material that provides 'options' rather than 'shoulds.' "

• Parenting Press's guidelines are available on their website.

**Fiction** Picture books: concept. Publishes social skills books, problem-solving books, safety books, dealing-with-feelings books that use a "fictional" vehicle for the information. "We rarely publish straight fiction." Recently published *The Way I Feel*, written and illustrated by Janan Cain, a book that promotes emotional literacy.

**Nonfiction** Picture books: health, social skills building. Young readers: health, social skills building books. Middle readers: health, social skills building. No books on "new baby; coping with a new sibling; cookbooks; manners; books about disabilities (which we don't publish at present); animal characters in anything; books that tell children what they should do, instead of giving options." Average word length: picture books—500-800; young readers—1,000-2,000; middle readers—up to 10,000. Published *25 Things to Do When Grandpa Passes Away, Mom and Dad Get Divorced, or the Dog Dies*, by Laurie Kanyer, illustrated by Jenny Williams (ages 2-12).

**How to Contact/Writers** Query. Responds to queries/mss in 3 months, "after requested." Publishes a book 18 months after acceptance. Will consider simultaneous submissions.

**Illustrations** Works with 3-5 illustrators/year. Reviews ms/illustration packages from artists. "We do reserve the right to find our own illustrator, however." Query. Illustrations only: Submit "résumé, samples of art/drawings (no original art); photocopies or color photocopies okay." Responds only if interested. Samples returned with SASE; samples filed, if suitable.

**Terms** Pays authors royalty of 3-12% based on wholesale price. Pays illustrators (for text) by the project; 3-6% royalty based on wholesale price. Pays illustrators by the project ($250-3,000). Sends galleys to authors; dummies to illustrators. Book catalog/ms/artist's guidelines for #10 SAE and 1 first-class stamp.

**Tips** "Make sure you are familiar with the unique nature of our books. All are aimed at building certain 'people' skills in adults or children. Our publishing for children follows no trend that we find appropriate. Children need nonfiction social skill-building books that help them think through problems and make their own informed decisions. The traditional illustrated story book does not *usually* fit our requirements because it does all the thinking for the child."

## PAULINE BOOKS & MEDIA

50 St. Paul's Ave., Jamaica Plain MA 02130-3491. (617)522-8911. E-mail: editorial@pauline.org. Website: www.pauline.org. **Manuscript Acquisitions:** Sr. Patricia Edward Jablonski, F.S.P. **Art Acquisitions:** Sr. Helen Rita Lane, FSP, art director. Publishes 2 picture books/year; 5 young readers/year; 3-5 middle readers/year; 1-2 young adult titles/year. 20% of books by first-time authors. "We communicate the Gospel message through our lives and all available forms of media, responding to the needs and hopes of all people in the spirit of St. Paul."

**Nonfiction** Picture books, young readers, middle readers, young adults: religion. Average word length: picture books—150-500; young readers—8,000-10,000; middle readers—15,000-25,000. Recently published *My Guardian Angel Coloring & Activity Book*, by D.Thomas Halpin, F.S.P., illustrated by Virginia Helen Richards, F.S.P. (ages 6-9); *The Rosary Comic Book*, written and illustrated by Gene Yang (ages 9-12); *When Should I Pray?*, by Nancy Pharr, illustrated by Heidi Rose (ages 4-7).

**How to Contact/Writers** Nonfiction: Submit query letter with outline/synopsis and 3 sample chapters. Responds to queries in 2 months; mss in 4 months. Publishes book 2-3 years after acceptance. Will consider simultaneous submissions, electronic submissions via disk or modem.

**Illustration** Works with 20-35 illustrators/year. Uses color artwork only. Illustrations only: Send résumé, promotional literature, client list or tearsheets. Responds only if interested. Samples returned with SASE only or samples filed.

**Photography** Buys stock and assigns work. Looking for children, animals and nature (not New England) photos. Model/property releases required; captions required. Uses color or b&w, 4×6, either matte or semigloss prints. Submit cover letter, résumé, client list, promo piece, published samples, stock photo list.

**Terms** Pays authors royalty of 5-10% based on wholesale price. Offers advances (average amount: $200). Pays illustrators by the project (range: $600-5,000) or royalty of 5-10% based on wholesale price. Pays photographers by the project, per photo or royalty depending on agreement. Sends galleys to authors. Book catalog available for 10½×13½ SAE and 7 first-class stamps; ms and art guidelines available for SASE. Catalog available on website.

**Tips** "Please be sure that all material submitted is consonant with Christian teaching and values. We generally do not accept anthropomorphic stories, fantasy or poetry."

## PAULIST PRESS

997 Macarthur Blvd., Mahwah NJ 07430. (201)825-7300. Website: www.paulistpress.com. **Acquisitions:** Children's Editor. Publishes 6 titles/year. 40% of books by first-time authors. "Our goal is to produce books on Catholic themes."

**Fiction** "No novels. Picture books must have explicitly Catholic themes. No picture books on angels, adoption, grandparents, death, sharing, prejudice, September 11th, or other general themes."

**Nonfiction** All levels: concept, social issues, Catholic doctrine, prayers or customs. Recently published *Hail Mary/Our Father*, illustrated by Vicki Pastore (picture book); *Great Women of Faith*, by Sue Stanton (young adult); *Dorothy Day*, by Elaine Murray Stone (young adult); *Child's Guide to First Holy Communion*, by Elizabeth Ficocelli, illustrated by Anne Catharine Blake; *My Catholic Lent and Easter Activity Book*, by Jennifer Galvin.

**How to Contact/Writers** Submit complete ms for picture books; query and sample for longer works; include SASE with all submissions. Responds to queries/mss in 6 months. Publishes a book 2-3 years after acceptance.

**Illustration** "Overstocked on samples right now. We tend to use artists we've used before."

**Terms** Pays authors royalty of 4-8% based on net sales. Average advance payment is $500. Pays illustrators by flat fee or advance and royalty, depending on the book.

**Tips** "We receive too many inappropriate manuscripts. Please know our books, know our market, and submit accordingly. There should be a reason why you're submitting to a Catholic publisher and not a trade house. Please note that we have several Child's Guide books in progress. Query first for topic. Our biggest need is for activity books that can be used in a home, school, or church setting. Query first, as we have many of these in progress, too."

## PEACHTREE PUBLISHERS, LTD.

1700 Chattahoochee Ave., Atlanta GA 30318-2112. (404)876-8761. Fax: (404)875-2578. E-mail: hello@peachtree-online.com. Website: www.peachtree-online.com. **Acquisitions:** Helen Harriss. **Art Director:** Loraine Joyner. Production Manager: Melanie McMahon Ives. Publishes 25-30 titles/year.

**Fiction** Picture books, young readers: adventure, animal, concept, history, nature/environment. Middle readers: adventure, animal, history, nature/environment, sports. Young adults: fiction, mystery, adventure. Does not want to see science fiction, romance.

**Nonfiction** Picture books: animal, history, nature/environment. Young readers, middle readers, young adults: animal, biography, nature/environment. Does not want to see religion.

**How to Contact/Writers** Fiction/nonfiction: Submit complete ms by postal mail only. Responds to queries/mss in 4 months. Publishes a book 1-2 years after acceptance. Will consider simultaneous submissions.

**Illustration** Works with 8-10 illustrators/year. Illustrations only: Query production manager or art director with samples, résumé, slides, color copies to keep on file. Responds only if interested. Samples returned with SASE; samples filed.

**Terms** "Manuscript guidelines for SASE, visit website or call for a recorded message. No fax or e-mail submittals or queries please."

## PEEL PRODUCTIONS

P.O. Box 546, Columbus NC 28722. (828)894-8838. Fax: (801)365-9898. E-mail: editor@peelbooks.com. Website: www.peelbooks.com. **Acquisitions:** Susan Dubosque, editor. Publishes 1 picture book/year; 4 how-to-draw books/year.

• Visit this company's website to see the types of books they publish.

**Nonfiction** Young readers, middle readers: activity books (how to draw).

**How to Contact/Writers** Nonfiction: Query first. Responds to queries in 2 months. Publishes a book 1 year after acceptance. Will consider simultaneous submissions.

**Terms** Pays authors royalty. Offers advances. Sends galleys to authors. Book catalog available for SAE and 2 first-class stamps.

## ☑ PELICAN PUBLISHING CO. INC.

1000 Burmaster St., Gretna LA 70053-2246. (504)368-1175. Website: www.pelicanpub.com. **Manuscript Acquisitions:** Nina Kooij, editor-in-chief. **Art Acquisitions:** Terry Callaway, production manager. Publishes 17 young readers/year; 8 middle readers/year. 10% of books from agented writers. "Pelican publishes hardcover and trade paperback originals and reprints. Our children's books (illustrated and otherwise) include history, biography, holiday, and regional. Pelican's mission is "to publish books of quality and permanence that enrich the lives of those who read them."

**Fiction** Young readers: folktales, history, holiday, multicultural and regional. Middle readers: Louisiana history. Multicultural needs include stories about African-Americans, Irish-Americans, Jews, Asian-Americans, Cajuns and Hispanics. Does not want animal stories, general Christmas stories, "day at school" or "accept yourself" stories. Maximum word length: young readers—1,100; middle readers—40,000. Recently published *The Principal's Night Before Christmas*, by Steven L. Layne (ages 5-8, fiction).

**Nonfiction** Young readers: biography, history, multicultural. Middle readers: Louisiana history, holiday, regional. Recently published *Halloween Alphabet* , by Beverly Barras Vidrine (ages 5-8, holiday).

**How to Contact/Writers** Fiction/nonfiction: Query. Responds to queries in 1 month; mss in 3 months. Publishes a book 9-18 months after acceptance.
**Illustration** Works with 15 illustrators/year. Reviews ms/illustration packages from artists. Query first. Illustrations only: Query with samples (no originals). Responds only if interested. Samples returned with SASE; samples kept on file.
**Terms** Pays authors in royalties; buys ms outright "rarely." Sends galleys to authors. Illustrators paid by "various arrangements." Book catalog and ms guidelines available on website or for SASE.
**Tips** "No anthropomorphic stories, pet stories (fiction or nonfiction), fantasy, poetry, science fiction or romance. Writers: be as original as possible. Develop characters that lend themselves to series and always be thinking of new and interesting situations for those series. Give your story a strong hook—something that will appeal to a well-defined audience. There is a lot of competition out there for general themes. We look for stories with specific 'hooks' and audiences, and writers who actively promote their work."

## PHILOMEL BOOKS
Penguin Putnam Inc., 345 Hudson St., New York NY 10014. (212)414-3610. Website: www.penguin.com. **Manuscript Acquisitions:** submissions editor. **Art Acquisitions:** Gina DiMassi, designer. Publishes 18 picture books/year; 2 middle-grades/year; 2 young readers/year; 4 young adult titles/year. 5% of books by first-time authors; 80% of books from agented writers. "We look for beautifully written, engaging manuscripts for children and young adults. "
- Philomel Books is not accepting unsolicited manuscripts.
**Fiction** All levels: adventure, animal, anthology, contemporary, fantasy, folktales, hi-lo, history, humor, poetry, sports, multicultural. Middle readers, young adults: problem novels, science fiction, suspense/mystery. No concept picture books, mass-market "character" books, or series. Average word length: picture books—1,000; young readers—1,500; middle readers—14,000; young adult—20,000.
**Nonfiction** Picture books, young readers, middle readers: hi-lo. "Creative nonfiction on any subject." Average word length: picture books—2,000; young readers—3,000; middle readers—10,000.
**How to Contact/Writers** Not accepting unsolicited mss. Fiction: Submit outline/synopsis and first two chapters. Nonfiction: Query. Responds to queries in 6 months; mss in 8 months. Must include SASE for response.
**Illustration** Works with 20-25 illustrators/year. Reviews ms/illustration packages from artists. Query with art sample first. Illustrations only: Query with samples. Send résumé and tearsheets. Responds to art samples in 1 month. Original artwork returned at job's completion. Samples returned with SASE or kept on file.
**Terms** Pays authors in royalties. Average advance payment "varies." Illustrators paid by advance and in royalties. Sends galleys to authors; dummies to illustrators. Book catalog, ms guidelines free on request with SASE (9×12 envelope for catalog).
**Tips** Wants "unique fiction or nonfiction with a strong voice and lasting quality. Discover your own voice and own story and persevere." Looks for "something unusual, original, well-written. Fine art. The genre (fantasy, contemporary, or historical fiction) is not so important as the story itself and the spirited life the story allows its main character. We are also interested in receiving adolescent novels, current, contemporary fiction with voice."

## ◻ PIANO PRESS
P.O. Box 85, Del Mar CA 92014-0085. (619)884-1401. Fax: (858)755-1104. E-mail: PianoPress@aol.com. Website: www.pianopress.com. **Manuscript Acquisitions:** Elizabeth C. Axford, M.A, editor. "We publish music-related books, either fiction or nonfiction, coloring books, songbooks and poetry."
**Fiction** Picture books, young readers, middle readers, young adults: folktales, multicultural, poetry, music. Average word length: picture books—1,500-2,000. Recently published *Strum a Song of Angels*, by Linda Oatman High and Elizabeth C. Axford; *Music and Me*, by Kimberly White and Elizabeth C. Axford.
**Nonfiction** Picture books, young readers, middle readers, young adults: multicultural, music/dance. Average word length: picture books—1,500-2,000. Recently published *The Musical ABC*, by Dr. Phyllis J. Perry and Elizabeth C. Axford; *Merry Christmas Happy Hanukkah—A Multilingual Songbook & CD*, by Elizabeth C. Axford.
**How to Contact/Writers** Fiction/ nonfiction: Query. Responds to queries in 3 months; mss in 6 months. Publishes a book 1 year after acceptance. Will consider simultaneous submissions, electronic submissions via disk or modem.
**Illustration** Works with 1 or 2 illustrators/year. Reviews ms/illustration packages from artists. Query. Illustrations only: Query with samples. Responds in 3 months. Samples returned with SASE; samples filed.
**Photography** Buys stock and assigns work. Looking for music-related, multicultural. Model/property releases required. Uses glossy or flat, color or b&w prints. Submit cover letter, résumé, client list, published samples, stock photo list.
**Terms** Pays authors, illustrators, and photographers royalty of 5-10% based on retail price. Sends galleys to authors; dummies to illustrators. Originals returned to artist at job's completion. Book catalog available for #10

SASE and 2 first-class stamps. All imprints included in a single catalog. Catalog available on website.

**Tips** ''We are looking for music-related material only for any juvenile market. Please do not send nonmusic-related materials. Query first before submitting anything.''

## PIÑATA BOOKS

Imprint of Arte Publico Press, University of Houston, 452 Cullen Performance Hall, Houston TX 77204-2004. (713)743-2843. Fax: (713)743-3080. Website: www.artepublicopress.com. **Manuscript Acquisitions:** Dr. Nicholas Kanellos; Gabriela Baeza Ventura, executive editor. **Art Acquisitions:** Linda Garza, production manager. Publishes 6 picture books/year; 2 young readers/year; 5 middle readers/year; 5 young adult titles/year. 80% of books are by first-time authors. ''Arte Publico's mission is the publication, promotion and dissemination of Latino literature for a variety of national and regional audiences, from early childhood to adult, through the complete gamut of delivery systems, including personal performance as well as print and electronic media.''

**Fiction** Recently published *My Tata's Guitar/La Guitarra De Mi Tata*, by Ethriam Cash Brammer, illustrated by Daniel Lechon (ages 3-7); *Lorenzo's Revolutionary Quest*, by Lila and Rick Guzman (ages 11 and up); *Teen Angel*, by Gloria Velasquez (ages 11 and up).

**Nonfiction** Recently published *Cesar Chavez: The Struggle for Justice/Cesar Chavez: La Lucha Por La Justicia*, by Richard Griswold del Castillo, illustrated by Anthony Accardo (ages 3-7).

**How to Contact/Writers** Accepts material from U.S./Hispanic authors only (living abroad OK). Manuscripts, queries, synopses, etc. are accepted in either English or Spanish. Fiction: Submit complete ms. Nonfiction: Query. Responds to queries in 2-4 months; mss in 3-6 months. Publishes a book 2 years after acceptance. Will sometimes consider previously published work.

**Illustration** Works with 6 illustrators/year. Uses color artwork only. Reviews ms/illustration packages from artists. Query or send portfolio (slides, color copies). Illustrations only: Query with samples or send résumé, promo sheet, portfolio, slides, client list and tearsheets. Responds only if interested. Samples not returned; samples filed.

**Terms** Pays authors royalty of 10% minimum based on wholesale price. Offers advances (average amount $2,000). Pays illustrators advance and royalties of 10% based on wholesale price. Sends galleys to authors. Catalog available on website: ms guidelines available for SASE.

## PINEAPPLE PRESS, INC.

P.O. Box 3889, Sarasota FL 34239. (941)739-2219. Fax: (941)739-2296. E-mail: info@pineapplepress.com. Website: www.pineapplepress.com. **Manuscript Acquisitions:** June Cussen. Publishes 1 picture book/year; 1 young reader/year; 1 middle reader/year; 1 young adult title/year. 50% of books by first-time authors. ''Our mission is to publish good books about Florida.''

**Fiction** Picture books, young readers, middle readers, young adults: animal, folktales, history, nature/environment. Recently published *A Land Remembered* (Student Edition), by Patrick Smith, (ages 9 up, Florida historical fiction).

**Nonfiction** Picture books: animal, history, nature/environmental, science. Young readers, middle readers, young adults: animal, biography, geography, history, nature/environment, science. Recently published *Those Funny Flamingos*, by Jan Lee Wicker, illustrated by Steve Weaver (ages 5-9); *The Gopher Tortoise, A Life History*, by Ray and Patricia Ashton (ages 9 up).

**How to Contact/Writers** Fiction: Query or submit outline/synopsis and 3 sample chapters. Nonfiction: Query or submit outline/synopsis and intro and 3 sample chapters. Responds to queries/samples in 2 months. Will consider simultaneous submissions.

**Illustration** Works with 2 illustrators/year. Reviews ms/illustration packages from artists. Query with nonreturnable samples. Contact: June Cussen, executive editor. Illustrations only: Query with brochure, nonreturnable samples, photocopies, résumé. Responds only if interested. Samples returned with SASE, but prefers nonreturnable; samples filed.

**Terms** Pays authors royalty of 10-15%. Pays illustrators royalties. Sends galleys to authors; dummies to illustrators. Originals returned to artist at job's completion. Book catalog available for 9×12 SAE with $1.06 postage; all imprints included in a single catalog. Catalog available on website at www.pineapplepress.com.

**Tips** ''Learn about publishing and book marketing in general. Be familiar with the kinds of books published by the publishers to whom you are submitting.''

## N: PITSPOPANY PRESS

40 E. 78th St., #16D, New York NY 10021. (212)472-4959. Fax: (212)472-6253. E-mail: pitspop@netvision.net.il. Website: www.pitspopany.com. Estab. 1992. Specializes in trade books, Judaica, nonfiction, fiction, multicultural material. **Manuscript Acquisitions:** Yaacov Peterseil, publisher. **Art Acquisitions:** Yaacov Peterseil, publisher. Produces 6 picture books/year; 4 young readers/year; 4 middle readers/year; 4 young adult books/year. 10% of books by first-time authors. ''Pitspopany Press is dedicated to bringing quality children' s books of

Jewish interest into the marketplace. Our goal is to create titles that will appeal to the esthetic senses of our readers and, at the same time, offer quality Jewish content to the discerning parent, teacher, and librarian. While the people working for Pitspopany Press embody a wide spectrum of Jewish belief and opinion, we insist that our titles be respectful of the mainstream Jewish viewpoints and beliefs. Most of all, we are committed to creating books that all Jewish children can read, learn from, and enjoy.''

**Fiction** Picture books: animal, anthology, fantasy, folktales, history, humor, multicultural, nature/environment, poetry. Young readers: adventure, animal, anthology, concept, contemporary, fantasy, folktales, health, history, humor, multicultural, nature/environment, poetry, religion, science fiction, special needs, sports, suspense. Middle readers: animal, anthology, fantasy, folktales, health, hi-lo, history, humor, multicultural, nature/environment, poetry, religion, science fiction, special needs, sports, suspense. Young adults/teens: animal, anthology, contemporary, fantasy, folktales, health, hi-lo, history, humor, multicultural, nature/environment, poetry, religion, science fiction, special needs, sports, suspense. Recently published *Hayyim's Ghost*, by Eric Kimmel, illustrated by Ari Binus (ages 6-9); *The Littlest Pair*, by Syliva Rouss, illustrated by Hally Hannan (ages 3-6); *The Converso Legacy*, by Sheldon Gardner (ages 10-14, historial fiction).

**Nonfiction** All levels: activity books, animal, arts/crafts, biography, careers, concept, cooking, geography, health, history, hobbies, how-to, multicultural, music/dance, nature/environment, reference, religion, science, self help, social issues, special needs, sports.

**How to Contact/Writers** Accepts international submissions. Fiction/nonfiction: Submit outline/synopsis. Responds to queries/mss in 6 weeks. Publishes book 9 months after acceptance. Considers simultaneous submissions, electronic submissions.

**Illustration** Accepts material from international illustrators. Works with 6 illustrators/year. Uses color artwork only. Reviews ms/illustration packages. For ms/illustration packages: Submit ms with 4 pieces of final art. Submit ms/illustration packages to Yaacov Peterseil, publisher. Reviews work for future assignments. If interested in illustrating future titles, send promo sheet. Submit samples to Yaacov Peterseil, publisher. Samples returned with SASE. Samples not filed.

**Photography** Works on assignment only. Submit photos to Yaacov Peterseil, publisher.

**Terms** Pays authors royalty or work purchased outright. Offers advance against royalties. Author sees galleys for review. Originals returned to artist at job's completion. Catalog on website. All imprints included in single catalog. Offers writer's guidelines for SASE.

## ◻ THE PLACE IN THE WOODS

Different Books, 3900 Glenwood Ave., Golden Valley MN 55422-5307. (763)374-2120. Fax: (952)593-5593. E-mail: placewoods@aol.com. **Acquisitions:** Roger Hammer, publisher/editor. Publishes 2 elementary-age titles/year; 1 middle reader/year; 1 young adult title/year. 100% of books by first-time authors. Books feature primarily diversity/multicultural/disability themes by first-time authors and illustrators.

**Fiction** All levels: adventure, animal, contemporary, fantasy, folktales, hi-lo, history, humor, poetry, multicultural, special needs. Recently published *Little Horse*, by Frank Minogue, illustrated by Beth Cripe (young adult fiction); *Smile, It's OK To Be You*, by Karen Foster French, illustrated by Susan Brados (grades preschool-8, self-esteem); *Mona & Friends in Land of Joan* (series), by Dawn Rosewitz (ages 5-11, adventure).

**Nonfiction** All levels: hi-lo, history, multicultural, special needs. Multicultural themes must avoid negative stereotypes. ''Generally, we don't publish nonfiction, but we would look at these.'' Recently published *African America*, by Roger Hammer, illustrated by Tacoumba Aiken (ages 12 and up, history); *American Woman*, by Roger Hammer, illustrated by Christie Nelson (history); *Hispanic America*, by Roger Hammer, illustrated by Paul Moran (history).

**How to Contact/Writers** Fiction/nonfiction: Submit complete ms. Responds to queries/mss in 1 month with SASE. ''No multiple or simultaneous submissions. Please indicate a time frame for response.''

**Illustration** Works with 4 illustrators/year. Uses primarily b&w artwork only. Reviews ms/illustration packages from authors. Query; submit ms. Contact: Roger Hammer, editor. Illustration only: Query with samples. Responds in 1 month. Include SASE. ''We buy all rights.''

**Photography** Buys photos from freelancers on assignment only. Uses photos that appeal to children. Model/property releases required; captions required. Uses any b &w prints. Submit cover letter and samples with SASE.

**Terms** Manuscripts purchased outright from authors ($250). Pays illustrators by the project ($10). Pays photographers per photo (range: $10-250). For all contracts, ''initial payment repeated with each subsequent printing.'' Original artwork not returned at job's completion. Guidelines available for SASE.

**Tips** ''Tell me about *who* you are, *how* you've come to be *where* you are, and *what* you want to accomplish. Don't waste our time telling me how good your work is it should speak for itself.''

## PLAYERS PRESS, INC.

P.O. Box 1132, Studio City CA 91614-0132. (818)789-4980. **Manuscript Acquisitions:** Robert W. Gordon, vice

# John Peters

*Librarian reveals what he and
young readers want*

I n the Central Children's Room at the New York Public Library, you will find 5-year-olds engrossed in story time, 10-year-olds checking out DVDs in the media center, and adults of all ages researching children's literature.

On most days, in the middle of this quiet chaos sits John Peters—supervising librarian for the children's section of the NYPL. Peters has been sharing the library's mission for 24 years throughout neighborhood branches, and now works in the main building with a staff of four professional librarians. Their task is to keep watch over the children's research and circulating collections, numbering up to about 110,000 items in all.

Trained as a rare books librarian at Columbia University, Peters has observed the evolution of libraries over the years. While they certainly have become more media-oriented with DVD rentals and kid-friendly websites, old-fashioned story time has remained a core element of their programming.

"In the end," says Peters, "our mission is to promote literacy so anyone can have an opportunity to listen to wisdom of the past, or join the great cultural conversation that goes on in books and media."

Unfortunately, Peters adds, "Even the richest libraries can't afford to buy everything." There are many choices on what to shelve, and often times the main decision-makers in that process are librarians. Peters offers some unique insight on what publishers and authors can do to get the best books on library shelves, and, ultimately, into the hands of young readers.

**Many librarians say they have tremendous purchasing power, but that publishers don't market to them enough. Do you agree?**
We are over marketed in some areas and under marketed in others. We are flooded with picture books and fiction. We do not see as much good nonfiction out there.

**What are some of the current trends in library purchasing?**
We are kind of fighting a two-front war here. On the one hand, it has always been our mission to provide the best in literature for our customers. On the other hand, we want to connect with them and acknowledge that there is a popular culture and to be part of that. We are forever agonizing over whether we should buy Little Golden Books or the latest movie tie-ins, or if we should stay away from those sorts of things and have the kind of material that people would not often buy for themselves, or even know to ask for. We do have to make choices somewhere. So far we have successfully managed to stay away from the most common kinds of tie-ins and stick with the books with what we consider lasting value.

**You mentioned that children's library use has been rising steadily during the last 10-15 years. What has been done to maintain this upward trend?**

I think there is a closer and closer connection between books and media. It seems as though every month at least one or two new films is originally based on a children's book. It works the other way, too. We had our first bonafide bestseller in Harry Potter. That was the first book that behaved the way that adult bestsellers do. It has bootstrapped a lot of other authors, titles, books and series along with it. The effect of that is really hard to underestimate.

**What do you think attracts kids to books—titles, illustrations, subject matter?**

There's some ineffable quality to a book that makes people choose it over all of the books that are to the right and to the left of it. Different people will be drawn by radically different things. We do look for books that have some sort of attractive quality to the cover art. However, we have found many examples of books that have cover art that doesn't capture your attention instantly, but actually grows on you over time as you read the book. It's the difference between grabbing a book because of what you see on the cover and then not finding the inside as memorable as you might have expected, and finding a book that really changes you and becomes a part of your mental set.

**What topics have stood the test of time for children?**

Truly funny books are always something we need more of. Books about children who undergo quests—who overcome some challenge or meet some kind of destiny in their lives, or are taken out of their normal lives and swept up in some sort of adventure that they never would have expected—are also good. I see lots and lots of new fantasy coming out and finding lots of eager readers. We are also seeing a more conscious acknowledgement on the parts of publishers that picture books need to appeal as much to grown-ups as to children.

**What problems do you see in the publishing industry?**

There are definitely too many hardcover picture books. There may be some dilution of general quality, too. There are only so many really good illustrators and writers of children's books.

**What is being done well in the publishing industry?**

It is always good to see publishers doing something adventuresome. Different publishers have come up with different ways of responding to economic pressures. Some become very conservative and will only publish TV tie-ins or something with sure-fire sales potential. Others will at least keep a little bit of experimentation going in hopes that their midlist will be able to support that. I think that's just a good thing to do. That's how many of our classics have come to be. They were strange and experimental when they were issued, but they have turned out to be some of the bedrock of children's literature.

**Do you have any tips/advice to help writers reach young readers?**

What we find, almost universally, is that many people feel that they should write for children in order to teach something. So they create these didactic stories, with less attention paid to the language and the character and the natural structure of the story, than the lesson that's implicit in them. My advice to new authors is to forget about that. It's all right if there is some sort of wisdom, but it should not be the biggest thing in the story. It's much more important to draw in your reader and have that conversation with your reader and find a way to engage the interests of your reader than to pound some lesson home.

—*Joanna Dower*

president/editorial director. **Art Acquisitions:** Attention: Art Director. Publishes 7-25 young readers, dramatic plays and musicals/year; 2-10 middle readers, dramatic plays and musicals/year; 4-20 young adults, dramatic plays and musicals/year. 35% of books by first-time authors; 1% of books from agented writers. Players Press philosophy: "To create is to live life's purpose."

**Fiction** All levels: plays. Recently published *Play From African Folktales*, by Carol Korty (collection of short plays); *Punch and Judy*, a play by William-Alan Landes; *Silly Soup!*, by Carol Korty (a collection of short plays with music and dance).

**Nonfiction** Picture books, middle readers, young readers, young adults. "Any children's nonfiction pertaining to the entertainment industry, performing arts and how-to for the theatrical arts only." Needs include activity books related to theatre: arts/crafts, careers, history, how-to, music/dance, reference and textbook. Recently published *Scenery*, by J. Stell (How to Build Stage Scenery); *Monologues for Teens*, by Vernon Howard (ideal for teen performers); *Humorous Monologues*, by Vernon Howard (ideal for young performers); *Actor's Resumes*, by Richard Devin (how to prepare an acting résumé).

**How to Contact/Writers** Fiction/nonfiction: Submit plays or outline/synopsis and sample chapters of entertainment books. Responds to queries in 1 month; mss in 1 year. Publishes a book 10 months after acceptance. No simultaneous submissions.

**Illustration** Works with 2-6 new illustrators/year. Use primarily b&w artwork. Illustrations only: Submit reésumeé, tearsheets. Responds to art samples in 1 week only if interested. Samples returned with SASE; samples filed.

**Terms** Pays authors royalty based on wholesale price. Pays illustrators by the project (range: $5-1,000). Pays photographers by the project (up to $1,000); royalty varies. Sends galleys to authors; dummies to illustrators. Book catalog and ms guidelines available for 9×12 SASE.

**Tips** Looks for "plays/musicals and books pertaining to the performing arts only. Illustrators: send samples that can be kept for our files."

## PLAYHOUSE PUBLISHING

1566 Akron-Peninsula Rd., Akron OH 44313. (330)926-1313. Fax: (330)926-1315. E-mail: webmaster@playhousepublishing.com. Website: www.playhousepublishing.com. **Acquisitions:** Submissions Editor. Imprints: Picture Me Books, Nibble Me Books. Publishes 10-15 novelty/board books/year. 25% of books by first-time authors. "Playhouse Publishing is dedicated to finding imaginative new ways to inspire young minds to read, learn and grow—one book at a time."

**Fiction** Picture books: adventure, animal, concept/novelty. Average word length: board books—75. Recently published *Pretend & Play Superhero*, by Cahty Hapka, illustrated by Hector Borlasca; *My Little Book of Blessings*, by Laurie Lazzaro Knowlton, illustrated by Nathan Szerdy; *My Little Doctor Bag*, by Cathy Hapka, illustrated by Paul Sharp; *Squeaky Clean & All Gone*, by Merry North, illustrated by Julia Woolf.

**How to Contact/Writers** Does not consider unsolicited mss.

**Terms** Catalog available online.

## PLUM BLOSSOM BOOKS

Parallax Press. P.O. Box 7355, Berkeley CA 94707. (510)525-0101. Fax: (510)525-7129. E-mail: rachel@parallax.org. Website: www.parallax.org. Estab. 1985. Specializes in nonfiction, fiction. **Writers contact:** Rachel Neuman, senior editor. Produces 2 picture books/year. 30% of books by first-time authors. "Plum Blossom Books publishes stories for children of all ages that focus on mindfulness in daily life, Buddhism, and social justice."

**Fiction** Picture books: adventure, contemporary, folktales, multicultural, nature/environment, religion. Young readers: adventure, contemporary, folktales, multicultural, nature/environment, religion. Middle readers: multicultural, nature/environment, religion. Young adults/teens: nature/environment, religion. Recently published *The Hermit and the Well*, by Thich Nhat Hanh, illustrated by Dinh Mai (ages 4-8, hardcover); *Each Breath a Smile*, by Sister Thuc Nghiem and Thich Nhat Hanh, illustrated by T. Hop (ages 2-5, paperback picture book); *Meow Said the Mouse*, by Beatrice Barbey, illustrated by Philippe Ames (ages 5-8, picture and activity book).

**Nonfiction** All levels: nature/environment, religion (Buddhist), Buddhist counting books.

**How to Contact/Writers** Accepts international submissions. Fiction/nonfiction: Query or submit complete ms. Responds to queries in 1-2 weeks. Responds to mss in 4 weeks. Publishes book 9-12 months after acceptance. Considers electronic submissions.

**Illustration** Accepts material from international illustrators. Works with 3 illustrators/year. Uses both color and b&w. Reviews ms/illustration packages. For ms/illustration packages: Query. Send ms with dummy. Reviews work for future assignments. If interested in illustrating future titles, query with samples. Responds in 4 weeks. Samples returned with SASE. Samples filed.

**Photography** Buys stock images and assigns work. Submit photos to Rachel Neuman, senior editor. Uses b&w prints. For first contact, send cover letter, published samples.

**Terms** Pays authors royalty of 20% based on wholesale price. Pays illustrators by the project. Author sees galleys for review. Illustrators see dummies for review. Originals returned to artist at job's completion. Catalog available for SASE. Offers writer's, artist's guidelines for SASE. See website for writer's, artist's, photographer's guidelines.

**Tips** "Read our books before approaching us. We are very specifically looking for mindfulness and Buddhist messages in high-quality stories where the Buddhist message is implied rather than stated outright."

## POLYCHROME PUBLISHING CORPORATION

4509 N. Francisco, Chicago IL 60625. (773)478-4455. Fax: (773)478-0786. E-mail: polypub@earthlink.net. Website: www.polychromebooks.com. **Contact:** Editorial Board. **Art Director:** Brian Witkowski. Publishes 2-4 picture books/year; 1-2 middle readers/year; 1-2 young adult titles/year. 50% of books are by first-time authors. Stories focus on children of Asian ancestry in the United States.

**Fiction** All levels: adventure, contemporary, history, multicultural, problem novels, suspense/mystery. Middle readers, young adults: anthology. Multicultural needs include Asian American children's experiences. Not interested in animal stories, fables, fairy tales, folk tales. Published *Nene and the Horrible Math Monster*, by Marie Villanueva; *Stella: On the Edge of Popularity*, by Lauren Lee.

**Nonfiction** All levels: multicultural. Multicultural needs include Asian-American themes.

**How to Contact/Writers** Fiction/nonfiction: Submit complete ms along with an author's bio regarding story background. Responds to queries in 4 months; mss in 6 months. Publishes a book 1-2 years after acceptance. Will consider simultaneous submissions.

**Illustration** Works with 4-6 illustrators/year. Reviews ms/illustration packages from artists. Submit ms with bio of author, story background and photocopies of sample illustrations. Contact: Editorial Board. Illustrations only: Query with résumé and samples (can be photocopies) of drawings of multicultural children. Responds only if interested. Samples returned with SASE; samples filed "only if under consideration for future work."

**Terms** Pays authors royalty of 2-10% based on wholesale price. Work purchased outright ($25 minimum). Pays illustrators 2-10% royalty based on wholesale price. Sends galleys to authors; dummies to illustrators. Book catalog available for #10 SAE and 34¢. Manuscript guidelines available for SASE.

**Tips** Wants "stories about experiences that will ring true with Asian Americans, including tolerance and anti-bias that people of *all* colors can identify with."

## PRICE STERN SLOAN, INC.

Penguin Group (USA), 345 Hudson St., New York NY 10014. (212)414-3590. Fax: (212)414-3396. Estab. 1963. **Acquisitions:** Debra Dorfman, president/publisher. "Price Stern Sloan publishes quirky mass market novelty series for children's as well as licensed movie tie-in books.

• Price Stern Sloan does not accept unsolicited manuscripts.

**Fiction** Picture books, young readers: humor. "We publish quirky, funny picture books, novelty books, and quirky full-color series." Recently published *Elf*; *Fear Factor Mad Libs*; *Super Silly Mad Libs Jr.*; *Justice League Mad Libs*; *Inside the Little Old Woman's Shoe*, by Chuck Reasoner.

**How to Contact/Writers** Query. Responds to queries in 3 weeks.

**Terms** Work purchased outright. Offers advance. Book catalog available for 9×12 SASE and 5 first-class stamps; address to Book Catalog. Manuscript guidelines available for SASE; address to Manuscript Guidelines.

**Tips** "Price Stern Sloan has a unique, humorous, off the wall feel. Most of our titles are unique in concept as well as execution."

## PROMETHEUS BOOKS

59 John Glenn Dr., Amherst NY 14228-2197. (800)421-0351 Fax: (716)564-2711. E-mail: SLMitchell@prometheusbooks.com. Website: www.PrometheusBooks.com. **Acquisitions:** Steven L. Mitchell, editor-in-chief. Publishes 1-2 titles/year. 50% of books by first-time authors; 30% of books from agented writers. "We hope more books will be published that focus on real issues children face and real questions they raise. Our primary focus is to publish children's books with alternative viewpoints: humanism, free thought, moral values, critical reasoning, human sexuality, and independent thinking based upon science and reasoning, skepticism toward the paranormal. Our niche is the parent who seeks informative books based on these principles. We are dedicated to offering customers the highest-quality books. We are also committed to the development of new markets both in North America and throughout the world."

**Nonfiction** All levels: sex education, moral education, critical thinking, nature/environment, science, self help, skepticism, social issues. Average word length: picture books—2,000; young readers—10,000; middle readers— 20,000; young adult/teens—60,000. Recently published *A Solstice Tree For Jenny*, by Karen Shrugg (ages 4 and up); *All Families Are Different*, by Sid Gordon (ages 7 and up); *Flat Earth? Round Earth?*, by Theresa Martin (ages 7 and up).

**How to Contact/Writers** Submit complete ms with sample illustrations (b&w). Responds to queries in 3 weeks; mss in 1-2 months. Publishes a book 12-18 months after acceptance. SASE required for return of ms/proposal.

**Book Publishers**

**Illustration** Works with 1-2 illustrators/year. "We will keep samples in a freelance file, but freelancers are rarely used." Reviews ms/illustration packages from artists. "Prefer to have full work (ms and illustrations); will consider any proposal." Include résumé, photocopies.

**Terms** Pays authors royalty of 5-15% based on wholesale price and binding. "Author hires illustrator; we do not contract with illustrators." Pays photographers per photo (range: $50-100). Sends galleys to author. Book catalog is free on request.

**Tips** "We do not accept projects with anthropomorphic characters. We stress realistic children in realistic situations. "Books should reflect secular humanist values, stressing nonreligious moral education, critical thinking, logic, and skepticism. Authors should examine our book catalog and website to learn what sort of manuscripts we're looking for."

## 🔼 PUFFIN BOOKS

Penguin Group (USA), Inc., 345 Hudson St., New York NY 10014-3657. (212)414-3600. Website: www.penguin.com/youngreaders. **Acquisitions:** Sharyn November, senior editor and editorial director of Firebird. Imprints: Speak, Firebird, Sleuth. Publishes trade paperback originals and reprints. Publishes 175-200 titles/year. Receives 600 queries and mss/year. 1% of books by first-time authors; 5% from unagented writers. "Puffin Books publishes high-end trade paperbacks and paperback originals and reprints for preschool children, beginning and middle readers, and young adults."

**Fiction** Picture books, young adult novels, middle grade and easy-to-read grades 1-3: fantasy and science fiction, graphic novels, classics. "We publish mostly paperback reprints. We publish some original fiction and nonfiction titles." Recently published *SASS: Westminster Abby*, by Micol Ostow; *Puffin Graphics: Frankenstein*.

**Nonfiction** Biography, illustrated book, young children's concept books (counting, shapes, colors). Subjects include education (for teaching concepts and colors, not academic), women in history. "Women in history books interest us." Publishes Alloy Books series.

**Illustration** Reviews artwork. Send color copies.

**Photography** Reviews photos. Send color copies.

**How to Contact/Writers** Fiction: Submit 3 sample chapters with SASE. Nonfiction: Submit 5 pages of ms with SASE. "It could take up to 5 months to get response." Publishes book 1 year after acceptance. Will consider simultaneous submissions, if so noted. Does not accept unsolicited picture book mss.

**Terms** Pays royalty. Offers advance (varies). Book catalog for 9 × 12 SASE with 7 first-class stamps; send request to Marketing Department.

## Ⓝ Ⓐ PUSH

Scholastic, 557 Broadway, New York NY 10012-3999. Website: www.thisispush.com. Estab. 2002. Specializes in fiction. Produces 6-9 young adult books/year. 50% of books by first-time authors. PUSH publishes new voices in teen literature.

- PUSH does not accept unsolicited manuscripts or queries, only agented or referred fiction/memoir. See Tackling Tough Topics in YA Lit to hear from PUSH editor David Levithan and PUSH author Billy Merrill.

**Fiction** Young adults: contemporary, multicultural, poetry. Recently published *Splintering*, by Eireann Corrigan; *Never Mind the Goldbergs*, by Matthue Roth; *Perfect World*, by Brian James.

**Nonfiction** Young adults: memoir. Recently published *Talking in the Dark*, by Billy Merrell; *You Remind Me of You*, by Eireann Corrigan.

**How to Contact/Writers Only interested in agented material.** Accepts international submissions. Fiction/nonfiction: Submit complete ms. Responds to queries in 2 months; mss in 4 months. No simultaneous, electronic, or previously published submissions.

**Tips** "We only publish first-time writers (and then their subsequent books), so authors who have published previously should not consider PUSH. Also, for young writers in grades 7-12, we run the PUSH novel Contest with the Scholastic Art & Writing Awards. Every year it begins in October and ends in March. Rules can be found on our website."

## 🔼 G.P. PUTNAM'S SONS

Penguin Putnam Books For Young Readers, 345 Hudson St., New York NY 10014. (212)414-3610. Website: www.penguinputnam.com. **Manuscript Acquisitions:** Kathy Dawson, executive editor; Susan Kochan, senior editor; John Rudolph, editor. **Art Acquisitions:** Cecilia Yung, art director, Putnam and Philomel. Publishes 30 picture books/year; 10 middle readers/year; 2 young adult titles/year. 5% of books by first-time authors; 50% of books from agented authors.

- G. Putnam's Sons title *Al Capone Does My Shirts*, by Gennifer Choldenko, won a 2005 Newbery Honor Award. Their title *Coming on Home Soon*, by Jacqueline Woodson, illustrated by E.B. Lewis won a 2005 Caldecott Honor Award.

**Fiction** Picture books: animal, concept, contemporary, humor, multicultural, special needs. Young readers:

adventure, contemporary, history, humor, multicultural, special needs, suspense/mystery. Middle readers: adventure, contemporary, history, humor, fantasy, multicultural, problem novels, special needs, sports, suspense/mystery. Young adults: contemporary, history, fantasy, problem novels, special needs. ''Multicultural books should reflect different cultures accurately but unobtrusively.'' Does not want to see series. Average word length: picture books—200-1,000; middle readers—10,000-30,000; young adults—40,000-50,000. Recently published *I Wanna Iguana*, by Karen Orloff, illustrated by Dave Catrow (ages 4-8); *I Was a Nonblond Cheerleader*, by Kieran Scott (ages 12 and up).

**Nonfiction** Picture books: animal, biography, concept, history, nature/environment, science. Subject s must have broad appeal but inventive approach. Average word length: picture books—200-1,500. Recently published *Atlantic*, by G. Brian Karas (ages 4-8, 32 pages).

**How to Contact/Writers** Fiction: Query with outline/synopsis and 1-3 sample chapters. Nonfiction: Query with outline/synopsis, 1 or 2 sample chapters and a table of contents. Unsolicited picture book mss only; do not send art unless requested. Responds to queries in 3 weeks; mss in 2 months. Publishes a book 2 years after acceptance. Will consider simultaneous submissions on queries only.

**Illustration** Write for illustrator guidelines. Works with 40 illustrators/year. Reviews ms/illustration packages from artists. Manuscript/illustration packages and illustration only: Query. Responds only if interested. Samples returned with SASE; samples filed.

**Terms** Pays authors royalty based on retail price. Pays illustrators by the project or royalty based on retail price. Sends galleys to authors. Original artwork returned at job's completion. Books catalog and ms and artist's guidelines available for SASE.

**Tips** ''Study our catalogs and get a sense of the kind of books we publish, so that you know whether your project is likely to be right for us.''

## RAINBOW PUBLISHERS

P.O. Box 261129, San Diego CA 92196. (858)668-3260. Website: www.rainbowpublishers.com. **Acquisitions:** Christy Scannell, editorial director. Publishes 5 young readers/year; 5 middle readers/year; 5 young adult titles/year. 50% of books by first-time authors. ''Our mission is to publish Bible-based, teacher resource materials that contribute to and inspire spiritual growth and development in kids ages 2-12.''

**Nonfiction** Young readers, middle readers, young adult/teens: activity books, arts/crafts, how-to, reference, religion. Does not want to see traditional puzzles. Recently published 5-Minute Sunday School Activities series, by Mary J. Davis (series of 2 books for ages 5-10).

**How to Contact/Writers** Nonfiction: Submit outline/synopsis and 3-5 sample chapters. Responds to queries in 6 weeks; mss in 3 months. Publishes a book 18 months after acceptance. Will consider simultaneous submissions, submissions via disk and previously published work.

**Illustration** Works with 2-5 illustrators/year. Reviews ms/illustration packages from artists. Submit ms with 2-5 pieces of final art. Illustrations only: Query with samples. Responds in 6 weeks. Samples returned with SASE; samples filed.

**Terms** For authors work purchased outright (range: $500 and up). Pays illustrators by the project (range: $300 and up). Sends galleys to authors. Book catalog available for 10×13 SAE and 2 first-class stamps; ms guidelines available for SASE.

**Tips** ''Our Rainbow imprint carries reproducible books for teachers of children in Christian ministries, including crafts, activities, games and puzzles. Our Legacy imprint (new in '97) handles nonfiction titles for children in the Christian realm, such as Bible story books, devotional books, and so on. Please write for guidelines and study the market before submitting material.''

## ☐ Ⓐ RANDOM HOUSE-GOLDEN BOOKS FOR YOUNG READERS GROUP

Random House, Inc., 1745 Broadway, New York NY 10019. (212)782-9000. Estab. 1935. Book publisher. ''Random House Books aims to create books that nurture the hearts and minds of children, providing and promoting quality books and a rich variety of media that entertain and educate readers from 6 months to 12 years.'' Publisher/Vice President: Kate Klimo. Associate Publisher/Art Director: Cathy Goldsmith. **Acquisitions:** Easy-to-Read Books (step-into-reading and picture books), color and activity books, board and novelty books, fiction and nonfiction for young and mid-grade readers: Heidi Kilgras, executive editor. Stepping Stones and middle grade fiction: Jennifer Dussling, senior editor. 100% of books published through agents; 2% of books by first-time authors.

 • Random House-Golden Books does not accept unsolicited manuscripts, only agented material. They reserve the right not to return unsolicited material.

**How to Contact/Writers Only interested in agented material.** Reviews ms/illustration packages from artists through agent only. Does not open or respond to unsolicited submissions.

**Terms** Pays authors in royalties; sometimes buys mss outright. Sends galleys to authors. Book catalog free on request.

## ▣ RAVEN TREE PRESS, LLC

200 S. Washington, Suite 306, Green Bay WI 54301. (920)438-1605. Fax: (920)438-1607. E-mail: dawn@raventre epress.com. Website: www.raventreepress.com. **Manuscript Acquisitions:** Amy Crane Johnson. Publishes 8-10 picture books/year. 50% of books by first-time authors. "We publish entertaining and educational bilingual materials for families."

**Fiction** Picture books, young readers: adventure, animal, concept, contemporary, fantasy, folktales, health, hi-lo, history, humor, multicultural, nature/environmental, poetry, science fiction, special needs, sports, suspense/mystery. Average word length: picture books/young readers—500.

**How to Contact/Writers** Fiction/nonfiction: Check website.

**Illustration** Check website.

**Terms** Pays authors royalty. Offers advances against royalties. Pays illustrators by the project or royalty. Originals returned to artist at job's completion. Catalog available on website.

**Tips** "Submit only based on guidelines. No queries please. Word count is a definite issue, since we are bilingual." Editorial staff attended or plans to attend the following conferences: BEA, ALA, and SCBIW.

## RED RATTLE BOOKS

Imprint of Soft Skull Press, 71 Bond St., Brooklyn NY 11217. Website: www.softskull.com. **Manuscript/Art Acquisitions:** Richard Eoin Nash, publisher. Publishes 4-6 children's books/year. Editorial philosophy: "to satisfy the need for socially aware, nondidactic, sophisticated children's literature that's in line with the ideals of a new generation of parents."

**Fiction** Picture books, young adult: graphic novels, poetry. Recently published *The Saddest Little Robot*, by Brian Gage.

**How to Contact/Writers** Fiction: Submit cover letter with address information, phone and e-mail, outline/synopsis and sample chapter (no more than 30 pages). Responds only if interested and SASE included. Poetry: Submit "cover letter and no more than 10 pages."

**Illustration** Accepts graphic novel submissions. Submit at least 5 "fully inked pages of art" with synopsis.

**Tips** Do not send full mss unless requested. "We do not accept phone calls or e-mail manuscripts."

## ▣ ▥ RENAISSANCE HOUSE

Imprint of Laredo Publishing, Beverly Hills CA 90210. (800)547-5113. Fax: (310)860-9902. E-mail: laredo@renai ssancehouse.net. Website: www.renaissancehouse.net. **Manuscript Acquisitions:** Raquel Benatar. **Art Acquisitions:** Sam Laredo. Publishes 5 picture books/year; 10 young readers/year; 10 middle readers/year; 5 young adult titles/year. 10% of books by first-time authors.

**Fiction** Picture books: animal, folktales, multicultural. Young readers: animal, anthology, folktales, multicultural. Middle readers, young adult/teens: anthology, folktales, multicultural, nature/environment. Recently published *Isabel Allende, Memories for a Story* (English-Spanish, age 9-12, biography); *Stories of the Americas*, a series of legends by several authors (ages 9-12, legend).

**How to Contact/Writers** Submit outline/synopsis. Responds to queries/mss in 3 weeks. Publishes a book 1 year after acceptance. Will consider simultaneous submissions, e-mail submissions.

**Illustration** Works with 25 illustrators/year. Uses color artwork only. Reviews ms/illustration packages from artists. Send ms with dummy. Contact: Sam Laredo. Illustrations only: Send tearsheets. Contact: Raquel Benatar. Responds in 3 weeks. Samples not returned; samples filed.

**Terms** Pays authors royalty of 5-10% based on retail price. Pays illustrators by the project. Sends galleys to authors; dummies to illustrators. Originals returned to artist at job's completion. Book catalog available for 9×12 SASE and $3 postage. All imprints included in a single catalog. Catalog available on website.

## RISING MOON

Imprint of Northland Publishing, Inc., P.O. Box 1389, Flagstaff AZ 86002-1389. (928)774-5251. Fax: (928)774-0592. E-mail: editorial@northlandpub.com. Website: www.risingmoonbooks.com. Estab. 1988. **Manuscript Acquisitions:** Theresa Howell, kids editor. Publishes hardcover and trade paperback originals. Publishes 8-10 titles/year. Receives 1,000 submissions/year. 20% of books by first-time authors; 20% from unagented writers. "Rising Moon's objective is to provide children with entertaining and informative books that follow the heart and tickle the funny bone."

**Fiction** "Rising Moon is no longer publishing middle-grade children's fiction. Needs fiction picture books with Southwest themes. We are looking for fractured fairy tales and original stories with Southwest themes." Recently published *Bedtime in the Southwest*, by Mona Hodgson, illustrated by Renee Graef.

**How to Contact/Writers** Call for book catalog; ms guidelines online. No e-mail submissions. Accepts simultaneous submissions. Responds in 3 months to queries.

**Terms** Pays authors royalty. Sometimes pays flat fee. Offers advance. Publishes book 1-2 years after acceptance.

**Tips** "Our audience is composed of regional Southwest-interest readers."

### 🅐 ROARING BROOK PRESS

143 West St., Suite W, New Milford, CT 06776. (860)350-4434. **Manuscript/Art Acquisitions**: Simon Boughton, publisher; Deborah Brodie, executive editor. Publishes approximately 40 titles/year. 1% of books by first-time authors. This publisher's goal is "to publish distinctive high-quality children's literature for all ages. To be a great place for authors to be published. To provide personal attention and a focused and thoughtful publishing effort for every book and every author on the list."

• Roaring Brook Press was recently purchased by Holtzbrinck Publishers, a group of companies that includes Henry Holt and Farrar, Straus & Giroux. Roaring Brook is not accepting unsolicited manuscripts.

**Fiction** Picture books, young readers, middle readers, young adults: adventure, animal, contemporary, fantasy, history, humor, multicultural, nature/environment, poetry, religion, science fiction, sports, suspense/mystery. Recently published *Stealing Henry*, by Carolyn MacCullough.

**How to Contact/Writer Primarily interested in agented material.** Not accepting unsolicited mss or queries. Will consider simultaneous agented submissions.

**Illustration Primarily interested in agented material.** Works with 25 illustrators/year. Illustrations only: Query with samples. Do not send original art; copies only through the mail. Samples returned with SASE.

**Photography** Works on assignment only.

**Terms** Pays authors royalty based on retail price. Pays illustrators royalty or flat fee depending on project. Sends galleys to authors; dummies to illustrators, if requested.

**Tips** "You should find a reputable agent and have him/her submit your work."

### THE ROSEN PUBLISHING GROUP INC.

29 E. 21st St., New York NY 10010. (212)777-3017. Fax: (212)777-0277. E-mail: info@rosenpub.com. Website: www.rosenpublishing.com. **Art Acquisitions:** Cindy Reiman, photo director. Imprints: Rosen (Young Adult) (Iris Rosoff, editorial director); Rosen Central (Iris Rosoff, editorial director); PowerKids Press (Joanne Randolph, editorial director).

**Nonfiction** Picture books: biography, health, hi-lo, nature/environment, science, self-help, social issues, special needs. Young readers: biography, health, hi-lo, multicultural, nature/environment, science, self-help, social issues, special needs. Middle readers: biography, careers, health, multicultural, nature/environment, science, self-help, social issues, special needs. Young adult: careers, health, multicultural, science, self-help, biography. Average word length: young readers—800-950; middle readers—5,000-7,500; young adults—between 8,000 and 30,000.

**How to Contact/Writers** Nonfiction: Query with outline/synopsis and sample chapter as well as SASE. No unsolicited mss, no phone calls.

**Photography** Buys stock and assigns work. Contact: Cindy Reiman, photo manager.

**Terms** Pays flat fee or royalty, depending on book.

**Tips** "Our list is specialized, and we publish only in series. Authors should familiarize themselves with our publishing program and policies before submitting."

### 🅓 RUNNING PRESS KIDS

Imprint of Running Press Book Publishers, 125 S. 22nd St., Philadelphia PA 19103-4399. (215)567-5080. Fax: (800)453-2884. Website: www.runningpress.com. **Manuscript Acquisitions:** Submissions Editor. **Art Acquisitions:** Associate Design Director. Publishes 10 picture books/year. 20% of books by first-time authors. "We want to publish the books and products that parents, teachers, and librarians want their kids to experience, and that kids can't wait to get their hands on."

**Fiction** Picture books: adventure, animal, anthology, concept, contemporary, fantasy, folktales, health, hi-lo, history, humor, multicultural, nature/environment, poetry, suspense/mystery. Average word length: picture books—5,000. Recently published *Halloween Night*, by Charles Gigna (picture book poetry); *The Three Funny Friends*, by Charlotte Zolotow (picture book); *The Thread of Life*, illustrated by Mary Grand Pre (picture book).

**Nonfiction** Picture books: activity books, animal, arts/crafts, biography, careers, concept, cooking, hi-lo, history, hobbies, how-to, science. Young readers, middle readers: activity books, animal, arts/crafts, biography, careers, concept, cooking, geography, health, hi-lo, history, hobbies, how-to, science.

**How to Contact/Writers** Fiction: Submit complete ms. Nonfiction: Query. Responds to queries in 1 month; mss in 2 months. Publishes book 2 years after acceptance. Will consider simultaneous submissions and previously published work.

**Illustration** Works with 30 illustrators/year. Reviews ms/illustration packages from artists. Send ms with dummy. Illustrations only: Send postcard sample. Responds only if interested. Samples not returned; samples filed.

**Terms** Pays authors royalty or work purchased outright from authors. Offers advances. Pays illustrators by the project or royalties. Sends galleys to authors; dummies to illustrators. Originals returned to artist at job's

# Deborah Brodie

*Says the seasoned editor:*
*Revision is the best part*

**Book Publishers**

t's a good thing for the children's book world that Deborah Brodie never became too enamored with wide skies and wheat fields. Otherwise, the Kansas native might never have made her move to the publishing capital of the world.

"Growing up my dream was to live in New York—I learned about the city from adult novels," says Brodie, Executive Editor of Roaring Brook Press. "At the age of 12, I decided I would go to New York and never leave. So I did. I graduated from high school early, just so I could get here."

Her grand plan? To become a "journalist."

"I really meant an editor, but I hadn't yet heard the term," Brodie says.

Today, Brodie, who spent 22 years at Viking before moving to Roaring Brook, is one of the most respected editors in the industry. Here she speaks about her job, the slush pile, revision, and the editing process.

### What is the easiest thing about your job?
Making a phone call to acquire a manuscript. Oh, that's a wonderful moment! The phone call that moves someone into the next stage, that opens doors. We've been able to do that for fourteen never-before-published writers at Roaring Brook, and it's exhilarating. Several of the writers who published their first books with us are now working on their third or fourth.

### Did you ever want to be a writer?
I am not a writer. I think I'm a better editor because I'm not.

### Why is that?
First, the impulse to write is so strong it overrides most other things. An editor who writes becomes a writer who edits, and the writing takes precedence. I only want to be the best editor I can. I get an idea and I give it away. This is what I do. A blank piece of paper sends me into a panic. I want you to put it on the paper and let me move it around.

When I teach or lead workshops, I start by saying, "I cannot teach you to write." Of course, everyone wants a refund. [laughs] But I do say that, if you do the work, we can make your writing better, bring it up another level or even more. Revising is the most interesting part of the process anyway.

### OK, let's talk about revision.
Revision? It's the best part! What is hard is keeping up with everything so you have time for the pure work. I would not be doing my job if I didn't do some of the peripheral

things—marketing, going to conferences, meeting agents, reading submissions, negotiating contracts, checking proofs, networking.

But the process of revising—that's the core of the work. I'm not the right editor for someone who thinks every word is sacred and [the writing] doesn't need work. I think everyone has ideas, many people can write, but what makes the difference is being willing to revise intelligently and revise vigorously. And more than once. I don't run out of energy for revising. I will go as far as the writer is willing to go.

### Can you give an example of a slush-pile discovery you have made?

In the 1980s, Barthe DeClements' *Nothing's Fair in Fifth Grade*, the book of that decade. It became a genuine bestseller, and is still in print. A slush pile success story is heartening, but in a way, it's deceptive.

We get hundreds of manuscripts a week. One day at Viking, I asked an assistant to actually count unsolicited manuscripts. It was 100 a week, 200 a week. In my 22 years at Viking, we probably published a dozen? And of those, only two were truly bestsellers. Statistically, [the number of accepted submissions] is minute. It's so hard for authors, I know. But it's hard on editors to say no, too, and keeping up with the workload is impossible. The happiest moment is a "yes" for both author and editor.

SPACER AND RAT

Margaret Bechard

Jacket photo © 2005 Michael Llewellyn. Jacket design by Patti Ratchford.

"Author Margaret Bechard thought she'd move *Treasure Island* to a space station, but her characters had plans of their own," says Roaring Brook Press editor Deborah Brodie of her October 2005 release. "*Spacer and Rat* is science fiction for those who love SF; riveting fiction for those who don't. Great for all sentient life forms!"

### What's the best thing about working at Roaring Brook Press?

We do something to promote every book. We're author-centered—authors come first. It means we're not looking to publish series. We don't do merchandise. We're not looking for some genre. The writing comes first. We're seeking long-term relationships with our authors.

### Sounds great from a writer's point of view.

On this side of the desk, it's pretty yummy.

### Can you give us some insight as to your taste in books?

It's really from one extreme to another. From young baby books that are deceptively simple, like *The Baby Goes Beep*, by Rebecca O'Connell; to middle grade fiction with humor, like *Busted!*, by Betty Hicks; to a teen novel with sex and violence, like *Target*, by Kathleen Jeffrie Johnson, that pushes the limit. We are known for not being afraid. I never say no to

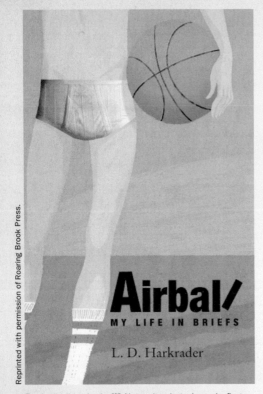

Reprinted with permission of Roaring Brook Press.

Basketball in the buff? Not quite, but close. In first-time novelist L.D. Harkrader's *Airball: My Life in Briefs*, a Deborah Brodie Book from Roaring Brook Press, Kirby Nickel loves *watching* basketball and he loves *talking about* basketball. The only problem is he can't *play* basketball. But Coach has a plan for Kirby and the supremely untalented seventh grade team. "Think: the Emperor's New Clothes," says Brodie.

anyone who says I want to write about "x." You just have to write it really well and with a point of view that is suitable.

## Can you take us through your thought process when editing?

When I look at a picture book text, I am not always 100 percent sure about what this book can become, so I'm fortunate to have an energetic and thoughtful designer, Jennifer Browne, to brainstorm with. When I look at the manuscript of a middle-grade or teen novel, I know what its potential is. I see what it could become. I'm more sure of my instincts. I'm about potential—that's what I'm about.

But it depends on the book. I try to work with the person the way the person needs to be worked with. Some people must have a deadline or else they can't manage. Others get too panicked with a deadline. One of my favorite things to do is brainstorm with an author or illustrator and find out what they're thinking about, even when they're not always sure themselves. It's a privilege to work with an author at an early stage.

It's a high-energy way of working. Sometimes I know something is there and sometimes I can pull it out of the author. Sometimes we discover it together. Sometimes we're both surprised. It's what I love. And I hope I'll be able to do it for a long time. I was born to do this work. If I weren't doing this, I'd be a teacher. The nurturing and helping people reach their potential. That's the heart of it.

—*Barb Odanaka*

completion. Book catalog available for 9 × 12 SAE; ms guidelines available for SASE. All imprints included in a single catalog. Catalog available on website.

## SALINA BOOKSHELF, INC.

1254 W. University Ave., Suite 130, Flagstaff AZ 86001. (928)773-0066. Fax: (928)526-0386. E-mail: sales@salin abookshelf.com. Website: www.salinabookshelf.com. **Manuscript Acquisitions:** Jessie Ruffenach. **Art Acquisitions:** Art Department. Publishes 10 picture books/year; 4 young readers/year; 1 young adult title/year. 50% of books are by first-time authors.

**Fiction** Picture books, young readers, middle readers, young adults: adventure, animal, contemporary, folktales, multicultural.

**Nonfiction** Picture books: multicultural. Young readers, middle readers, young adults: biography, history, multicultural.

**How to Contact/Writers** Fiction/nonfiction: Query or submit complete ms. Responds to queries in 1 month; mss in 2 months. Publishes a book 1 year after acceptance. Will consider simultaneous submissions and previously published work.

**Illustration** Works with 8 illustrators/year. Reviews ms/illustration packages from artists. Query. Illustrations only: Query with samples. Responds in 1 month. Samples returned with SASE; samples filed.

**Photography** Buys stock and assigns work.

**Terms** Pays authors royalty based on retail price. Offers advances (average amount varies). Pays illustrators and photographers by the project. Originals returned to artist at job's completion. Catalog available for SASE or on website; ms guidelines available for SASE.

**Tips** ''Please note that all our books are Navajo-oriented.''

## N SASQUATCH BOOKS
119 South Main St., Seattle WA 98104. (800)775-0817. Fax: (206)467-4301. Website: www.sasquatchbooks.com. Estab. 1986. Specializes in trade books, nonfiction, fiction. **Writers contact:** The Editors. **Illustrators contact:** Kate Basart, art director. Produces 5 picture books/year. 20% of books by first-time authors. ''We are seeking quality nonfiction works about the Pacific Northwest and West Coast regions (including Alaska and California). The literature of place includes how-to and where-to as well as history and narrative nonficiton.''

**Fiction** Young readers: adventure, animal, concept, contemporary, humor, nature/environment. Recently published *Alaska's Three Pigs*, by Arlene Laverde, illustrated by Mindy Dwyer (picture book); *Catwalk*, written and illustrated by Jasper Tomkins (picture book).

**Nonfiction** Picture books: activity books, animal, concept, nature/environment. Recently published *Northwest Animal Babies*, by Andrea Helman, photographs by Art Wolfe; *O is for Orca: An Alphabet Book,* by Andrea Helman, photographs by Art Wolfe.

**How to Contact/Writers** Accepts international submissions. Fiction: Query, submit complete ms, or submit outline/synopsis. Nonfiction: Query. Responds to queries in 3 months. Publishes book 6 months after acceptance. Considers simultaneous submissions.

**Illustration** Accepts material from international illustrators. Works with 5 illustrators/year. Uses both color and b&w. Reviews ms/illustration packages. For ms/illustration packages: Query. Submit ms/illustration packages to The Editors. Reviews work for future assignments. If interested in illustrating future titles, query with samples. Submit samples to Kate Basart, art director. Samples returned with SASE. Samples filed.

**Photography** Buys stock images and assigns work. Submit photos to: Kate Basart, art director.

**Terms** Pays authors royalty based on retail price. Offers advance against royalties. Offers a wide range of advances. Author sees galleys for review. Originals not returned. Catalog on website. See website for writer's guidelines.

## SCHOLASTIC INC.
557 Broadway, New York NY 10012. (212)343-6100. Website: www.scholastic.com. Imprints: Cartwheel Books, Orchard Books, Scholastic Press, Blue Sky Press, Scholastic Reference and Arthur A. Levine Books.
• Scholastic does not accept unsolicited manuscripts; writers may query.

**Illustration** Works with 50 illustrators/year. Does not review ms/illustration packages. Illustrations only: Send promo sheet and tearsheets. Responds only if interested. Samples not returned. Original artwork returned at job's completion.

**Terms** All contracts negotiated individually; pays royalty. Sends galleys to author; dummies to illustrators.

## N SCHOLASTIC LIBRARY PUBLISHING
(formerly Grolier Publishing), 90 Old Sherman Turnpike, Danbury CT 06816. (203)797-3500. Book publisher. Vice President/Publisher: Phil Friedman. **Manuscript Acquisitions:** Kate Nunn, editor-in-chief. **Art Acquisitions:** Marie O'Neil, art director. Imprints: Grolier, Children's Press, Franklin Watts. Publishes more than 400 titles/year. 5% of books by first-time authors; very few titles from agented authors. Publishes informational (nonfiction) for K-12; picture books for young readers, grades 1-3.

**Fiction** Publishes 1 picture book series, Rookie Readers, for grades 1-2. Does not accept unsolicited mss.

**Nonfiction** Photo-illustrated books for all levels: animal, arts/crafts, biography, careers, concept, geography, health, history, hobbies, how-to, multicultural, nature/environment, science, social issues, special needs, sports. Average word length: young readers—2,000; middle readers—8,000; young adult—15,000.

**How to Contact/Writers** Fiction: Does not accept fiction proposals. Nonfiction: Query; submit outline/synopsis, résumé and/or list of publications, and writing sample. SASE required for response. Responds in 3 months. Will consider simultaneous submissions. No phone or e-mail queries; will not respond to phone inquiries about submitted material.

**Illustration** Works with 15-20 illustrators/year. Uses color artwork and line drawings. Illustrations only: Query with samples or arrange personal portfolio review. Responds only if interested. Samples returned with SASE. Samples filed. Do not send originals. No phone or e-mail inquiries; contact only by mail.

**Photography** Contact: Caroline Anderson, photo manager. Buys stock and assigns work. Model/property releases and captions required. Uses color and b&w prints; $2^{1}/_{4} \times 2^{1}/_{4}$, 35mm transparencies, images on CD-ROM.
**Terms** Pays authors royalty based on net or work purchased outright. Pays illustrators at competitive rates. Photographers paid per photo. Sends galleys to authors; dummies to illustrators.

## SCHOLASTIC PRESS

557 Broadway, New York NY 10012. (212)343-6100. Website: www.scholastic.com. **Manuscript Acquisitions:** Dianne Hess, executive editor (picture book fiction/nonfiction, middle grade, YA); Lauren Thompson, senior editor (picture book fiction/nonfiction); Tracy Mack, executive editor (picture book, middle grade, YA); Elizabeth Szabla, editorial director (picture book fiction/nonfiction, middle grade, YA); Leslie Budnick, associate editor (picture books fiction/nonfiction, middle grade); Jennifer Rees, associate editor (picture book fiction/nonfiction, middle grade, YA). **Art Acquisitions:** David Saylor, all hardcover prints for Scholastic. Publishes 60 titles/year. 1% of books by first-time authors.
  • Scholastic Press title *Walt Whitman: Words for America*, by Barbara Kerley, illustrated by Brian Selznick, won a 2005 Robert F. Sibert Honor Award.
**Fiction** Looking for strong picture books, middle grade novels (ages 8-11) and interesting and well written young adult novels.
**Nonfiction** Interested in "unusual and interesting approaches to commonly dry subjects, such as biography, math, history and science."
**How to Contact/Writers** Fiction/nonfiction: "Send query with 1 sample chapter and synopsis. Don't call! Don't e-mail!" Picture books: submission accepted from agents or previously published authors only.
**Illustrations** Works with 30 illustrators/year. Uses both b&w and color artwork. Illustrations only: Query with samples; send tearsheets. Responds only if interested. Samples returned with SASE. Original artwork returned at job's completion.
**Terms** Pays advance against royalty.
**Tips** "Read *currently* published children's books. Revise, rewrite, rework and find your own voice, style and subject. We are looking for authors with a strong and unique voice who can tell a great story and have the ability to evoke genuine emotion. Children's publishers are becoming more selective, looking for irresistable talent and fairly broad appeal, yet still very willing to take risks, just to keep the game interesting."

## SEEDLING PUBLICATIONS

20 W. Kanawha Ave., Columbus OH 43214-1432. Phone/fax: (614)888-4140. E-mail: JStewart@JinL.com. Website: www.SeedlingPub.com. **Acquisitions:** Josie Stewart. 20% of books by first-time authors. Publishes books for the beginning reader in English. "Natural language and predictable text are requisite to our publications. Patterned text is acceptable, but must have a unique story line. Poetry, books in rhyme, full-length picture books or chapter books are not being accepted at this time. Illustrations are not necessary."
**Fiction** Young readers: adventure, animal, folktales, humor, multicultural, nature/environment. Multicultural needs include stories which include children from many cultures and Hispanic-centered storylines. Does not accept texts longer than 16 pages or over 150-200 words or stories in rhyme. Average word length: young readers—100. Recently published *Sherman in the Talent Show*, by Betty Erickson, illustrated by Kristine Dillard; *Moth or Butterfly?*, by Ryan Durney; *The Miller, His Son, and the Donkey*, by Lynn Salem and Josie Stewart (Legends, Fables & Folktales series).
**Nonfiction** Young readers: animal, arts/crafts, biography, careers, concept, multicultural, nature/environment, science. Does not accept texts longer than 16 pages or over 150-200 words. Average word length: young readers—100.
**How to Contact/Writers** Fiction/nonfiction: Submit complete ms. Responds in 9 months. Publishes a book 1-2 years after acceptance. Will consider simultaneous submissions. Prefers e-mail submissions from authors or illustrators outside the U.S.
**Illustration** Works with 8-9 illustrators/year. Uses color artwork only. Reviews ms/illustration packages from artists. Submit ms with dummy. Illustrations only: Send color copies. Responds only if interested. Samples returned with SASE only; samples filed if interested.
**Photography** Buys photos from freelancers. Works on assignment only. Model/property releases required. Uses color prints and 35mm transparencies. Submit cover letter and color promo piece.
**Terms** Work purchased outright from authors. Pays illustrators and photographers by the project. Original artwork is not returned at job's completion. Catalog available on website.
**Tips** "Study our website. Follow our guidelines carefully and test your story with children and educators."

## SHEN'S BOOKS

40951 Fremont Blvd., Fremont CA 94538. (510)668-1898. Fax: (510)668-1057. E-mail: info@shens.com. Website: www.shens.com. Estab. 1986. Specializes in multicultural material. **Acquisitions:** Renee Ting, president. Produces 2 picture books/year. 50% of books by first-time authors.

**Fiction** Picture books, young readers: folktales, multicultural. Middle readers: multicultural. Recently published *The Wishing Tree*, by Roseanne Thong, illustrated by Connie McLennan (ages 4-8); *The Magical Monkey King*, by Ji-li Jiang (ages 7-10, chapter book); *Many Ideas Open the Way*, by Randy Snook (picture books of proverbs).

**Nonfiction** Picture books, young readers: multicultural. Recently published *Land of Morning Calm*, by John Stickler, illustrated by Soma Han (ages 7-12, picture book).

**How to Contact/Writers** Accepts international submissions. Fiction/nonfiction: Submit complete ms. Responds to queries in 1-2 weeks; mss in 6-12 months. Publishes book 1 year after acceptance. Considers simultaneous submissions.

**Illustration** Accepts material from international illustrators. Works with 2 illustrators/year. Uses color artwork only. Reviews ms/illustration packages. For ms/illustration packages: Send ms with dummy. Submit ms/illustration packages to Renee Ting, president. Reviews work for future assignments. If interested in illustrating future titles, query with samples. Submit samples to Renee Ting, president. Samples not returned. Samples filed.

**Photography** Works on assignment only. Submit photos to Renee Ting, president.

**Terms** Authors pay negotiated by the project. Pays illustrators by the project. Pays photographers by the project. Illustrators see dummies for review. Catalog on website.

**Tips** "Be familiar with our catalog before submitting."

## SILVER MOON PRESS

160 Fifth Ave., New York NY 10010. (212)242-6499. Fax: (212)242-6799. E-mail: mail@silvermoonpress.com. Website: www.silvermoonpress.com. Publisher: David Katz. Managing Editor: Hope Killcoyne. **Marketing Co-ordinator:** Karin Lillebo Book publisher. Publishes 2 books for grades 4-6. 25% of books by first-time authors; 10% books from agented authors. "We publish books of entertainment and educational value and develop books which fit neatly into curriculum for grades 4-6. Silver Moon Press publishes mainly American historical fiction with a strong focus on the Revolutionary War and Colonial times. History comes alive when children can read about other children who lived when history was being made!"

**Fiction** Middle readers: historical, multicultural and mystery. Average word length: 14,000. Recently published *A Silent Witness in Harlem*, by Eve Creary; *In the Hands of the Enemy*, by Robert Sheely; *Ambush in the Wilderness*, by Kris Hemphill; *Race to Kitty Hawk*, by Edwina Raffa and Annelle Rigsby.

**How to Contact/Writers** Fiction: Query. Send synopsis and/or a few chapters, along with a SASE. Responds to queries in 1 month; mss in 2 months. Publishes a book 1-2 years after acceptance. Will consider simultaneous submissions, or previously published work.

**Illustration** Works with 2-3 illustrators/year. Reviews ms/illustration packages from artists. Query. Illustrations only: Query with samples, résumé, client list. Responds only if interested. Samples returned with SASE; samples filed. Original artwork returned at job's completion.

**Photography** Buys photos from freelancers. Buys stock and assigns work. Uses archival, historical, sports photos. Captions required. Uses color, b&w prints; 35mm, $2\frac{1}{4} \times 2\frac{1}{4}$, $4 \times 5$, $8 \times 10$ transparencies. Submit cover letter, résumé, published samples, client list, promo piece.

**Terms** Pays authors royalty or work purchased outright. Pays illustrators by the project, no royalty. Pays photographers by the project, per photo, no royalty. Sends galleys to authors; dummies to illustrators. Book catalog available for $8\frac{1}{2} \times 11$ SAE and 77¢ postage.

## SIMON & SCHUSTER BOOKS FOR YOUNG READERS

1230 Avenue of the Americas, New York NY 10020. (212)698-7000. Fax: (212)698-2796. Website: www.simonsayskids.com. **Manuscript Acquisitions:** Elizabeth Law, vice president and associate publisher; David Gael, editorial director; Kevin Lewis, executive editor; Paula Wiseman, vice president and editorial director, Paula Wiseman Books. **Art Acquisitions:** Dan Potash, creative director. Publishes 75 books/year. "We publish high-quality fiction and nonfiction for a variety of age groups and a variety of markets. Above all we strive to publish books that will offer kids a fresh perspective on their world."

- Simon & Schuster Books for Young Readers does not accept unsolicited manuscripts. Queries are accepted via mail. Simon & Schuster title *ellington was not a street*, illustrated by Kadir Nelson, written by Nzotake Shange, won the 2005 Coretta Scott King Illustrator Award. Their title *Worth*, by Alexandra LaFayer, won the 2005 Scott O'Dell Award.

**Fiction** Picture books: animal, minimal text/very young readers. Middle readers, young adult: fantasy, adventure, suspense/mystery. All levels: contemporary, history, humor. Recently published *Little Quack's Bedtime*, by Lauren Thompson, illustrated by Derek Anderson (picture book, ages 3-7); *Shrimp*, by Rachel Cohn (young adult fiction, ages 13 and up).

**Nonfiction** Picture books: concept. All levels: narrative, current events, biography, history. "We're looking for picture book or middle grade nonfiction that have a retail potential. No photo essays.'' Recently published *A Is For Abigail*, by Lynne Cheney, illustrated by Robin Preiss Glasser (picture book nonfiction, all ages).

**How to Contact/Writers** Accepting query letters only; please note the appropriate editor. Responds to queries/mss in 3-4 months. Publishes a book 2 years after acceptance. Will consider simultaneous submissions.

**Illustration** Works with 70 illustrators/year. Do not submit original artwork. Editorial reviews ms/illustration packages from artists. Submit query letter to Submissions Editor. Illustrations only: Query with samples; samples filed. Provide promo sheet, tearsheets. Responds only if interested.

**Terms** Pays authors royalty (varies) based on retail price. Pays illustrators or photographers by the project or royalty (varies) based on retail price. Original artwork returned at job's completion. Manuscript/artist's guidelines available via website or free on request. Call (212)698-2707.

**Tips** ''We're looking for picture books centered on a strong, fully-developed protagonist who grows or changes during the course of the story; YA novels that are challenging and psychologically complex; also imaginative and humorous middle-grade fiction. And we want nonfiction that is as engaging as fiction. Our imprint's slogan is 'Reading You'll Remember.' We aim to publish books that are fresh, accessible and family-oriented; we want them to have an impact on the reader.''

## Ⓐ SLEEPING BEAR PRESS

Imprint of Gale Group, 310 N. Main St., Suite 300, Chelsea MI 48118. (734)475-4411. Fax: (734)475-0787. Website: www.sleepingbearpress.com. **Manuscript Acquisitions:** Heather Hughes. **Art Acquisitions:** Jennifer Lundahl, creative director. Publishes 30 picture books/year. 50% of books by first-time authors.

**Fiction** Picture books: adventure, animal, concept, folktales, history, multicultural, nature/environment, religion, sports. Young readers: adventure, animal, concept, folktales, history, humor, multicultural, nature/environment, religion, sports. Average word length: picture books—1,800. Recently published *Cosmos Moon*, by Devin Scillian, illustrated by Mark Braught (ages 4-8); *Redheaded Robbie's Christmas Story*, by Bill Luttrell, illustrated by Luc Melanson (ages 4-10); *Penny: The Forgotten Coin*, by Denise Brennan-Nelson.

**Nonfiction** Average word length: picture books—1,800. Recently published *The Edmund Fitzgerald*; *Mercedes and the Chocolate Pilot*; *P is for Passport* .

**How to Contact/Writers Only interested in agented material.** Fiction/nonfiction: Submit complete ms. Responds to queries in 1 month; mss in 2 months. Publishes book 2 years after acceptance. Will consider e-mail submissions, simultaneous submissions.

**Illustration Only interested in agented material.** Works with 30 illustrators/year. Uses color artwork only. Reviews ms/illustration packages from artists. Send ms with dummy. Illustrations only: Send samples, SASE, URL. Responds in 1 month. Samples returned with SASE.

**Terms** Pays authors royalty. Offers advances. Pays illustrators royalty. Sends galleys to authors. Originals returned to artist at job's completion. Book catalog available. All imprints included in a single catalog. Catalog available on website.

**Tips** ''Please review our book on line before sending material or calling.'' Editorial staff attended or plans to attend the following conferences: BEA, IRA, Regional shows, UMBE, NEBA, AASL, ALA, and numerous local conferences.

## SMALLFELLOW PRESS

Imprint of Tallfellow Press, 1180 S. Beverly Dr., Suite 320, Los Angeles CA 90035. E-mail: asls@pacbell.net; tallfellow@pacbell.net. Website: www.smallfellow.com. **Manuscript/Art Acquisitions:** Claudia Sloan.

- Smallfellow no longer accepts manuscripts.

## SMOOCH

Imprint of Dorchester Publishing, 200 Madison Ave., Suite 2000, New York NY 10016. Fax: (203)846-1776. Website: www.smoochya.com. **Manuscript Acquisitions:** Kate Seaver, editor. **Art Acquisitions:** Chelsea Shriver, assistant editor. **Manuscript Acquisitions:** Brian Giblin. **Art Acquisitions:** Marcin Pilchowski. Publishes 12 picture books/year; 8 young readers/year. Soundprints publishes children's books accompanied by plush toys and read-along cassettes that deal with wildlife, history and nature. All content must be accurate and realistic and is curated by experts for veracity.

- Smooch does not accept unsolicited manuscripts.

**Fiction** Picture books: animal. Young readers: animal, multicultural, nature/environment. Middle readers: history, multicultural. Recently published My *Abnormal Life*, by Lee McClain; *Got Fangs?*, by Katie Maxwell.

**Nonfiction** Picture books: animals. Young readers: animal, multicultural, nature/environment. Middle readers: history, multicultural. Recently published *Swordfish Returns*, by Susan Korman; *Crocodile Crossing*, by Schuyler Bull; *Time to Eat, Panda*, by Ann Whitehead Nagda.

**How to Contact/Writers** Fiction/nonfiction: Submit published writing samples. Responds in 6-8 months. Publishes book 2 years after acceptance.

**Illustration** Works with 12 illustrators/year. Uses color artwork only. Query. Contact: Chelsea Shriver, assistant editor. Query with samples. Samples not returned.

**Terms** Work purchased outright from authors for $1,000-2,500. Pays illustrators by the project. Book catalog available for 8½×11 SASE; ms and art guidelines available for SASE. Catalog available on website.

**Tips** "As a small publisher with very specific guidelines for our well-defined series, we are not able to accept unsolicited manuscripts for publication. All of our authors are contracted on a 'work for hire basis,' meaning that they create manuscripts to our specifications, depending on our need. While we generally work with an established group of authors who know our needs as a publisher, we are always interested in reviewing the work of new potential authors. If you would like to submit some published writing samples, we would be happy to review them and keep them on file for future reference. Please send all writing samples to assistant editor."

## ST. ANTHONY MESSENGER PRESS

28 W. Liberty St., Cincinnati OH 45202-6498. (513)241-5615. Fax: (513)241-0399. E-mail: books@americancath olic.org. Website: www.AmericanCatholic.org. **Manuscript Acquisitions:** Lisa Biedenbach, editorial director. 25% of books by first-time authors. Imprints include Franciscan Communications (print and video) and Ikono-graphics (video). "Through print and electronic media marketed in North America and worldwide, we endeavor to evangelize, inspire and inform those who search for God and seek a richer Catholic, Christian, human life. We also look for books for parents and religious educators."

**Nonfiction** Picture books, young readers, middle readers, young adults: religion. "We like all our resources to include anecdotes, examples, etc., that appeal to a wide audience. All of our products try to reflect cultural and racial diversity. All our books must be explicitly Catholic." Recently published *Friend Jesus: Prayers for Children*, by Gaynell Bordes Cronin; *Can You Find Jesus? Introducing Your Child to the Gospel*, by Philip Gallery and Janet Harlow (ages 5-10); *People of the Bible: Their Life and Customs*, by Claire Musatti (ages 5-10).

**How to Contact/Writers** Query or submit outline/synopsis and sample chapters. Responds to queries in 6 weeks; mss in 2 months. Publishes a book 12-18 months after acceptance.

**Illustration** Works with 2 illustrators/year. "We design all covers and do most illustrations in-house, unless illustrations are submitted with text." Reviews ms/illustration packages from artists. Query with samples, résumé. Contact: Jeanne Kortekamp, art director. Responds to queries in 1 month. Samples returned with SASE; samples filed. Originals returned at job's completion.

**Photography** Purchases photos from freelancers. Contact: Jeanne Kortekamp, art director. Buys stock and assigns work.

**Terms** Pays authors royalty of 10-12% based on net receipts. Offers advances (average amount: $1,000). Pays illustrators by the project. Pays photographers by the project. Sends galleys to authors. Book catalog and ms guidelines free on request.

**Tips** "We do not publish fiction. We are slowing down publication of children's books. Know our audience—Catholic. We seek popularly written manuscripts that include the best of current Catholic scholarship. Parents, especially baby boomers, want resources for teaching children about the Catholic faith for passing on values. We try to publish items that reflect strong Catholic Christian values."

## STANDARD PUBLISHING

8121 Hamilton Ave., Cincinnati OH 45231. (513)931-4050. Fax: (513)931-0950. Website: www.standardpub.c om. **Manuscript Acquisitions:** Diane Stortz, director Family Resources; Ruth Frederick, director Children's Ministry. **Art Acquisitions:** Rob Glover, Family Resources lead designer; Sany Wimmer, Children's Ministry lead designer. Many projects are written in-house. No young adult novels. 25-40% of books by first-time authors; 10% of books from agented writers. Publishes picture books, board books, nonfiction, devotions and resources for teachers.

• Standard also has a listing in Greeting Cards, Puzzles & Games.

**Fiction** Recently published *Jesus Must Be Really Special*, by Jennie Bishop, illustrated by Amy Wummer.

**Nonfiction** Recently published *Through the Bible Devotions*, by Mark Littleton.

**How to Contact/Writers** Responds in 3-6 months.

**Illustration** Works with 20 new illustrators/year. Illustrations only: Submit cover letter and photocopies. Responds to art samples only if interested. Samples returned with SASE; samples filed.

**Terms** Pays authors royalty based on net price or work purchased outright (range varies by project). Pays photographers by the photo. Sends galleys to authors on most projects. Book catalog available for $2 and 8½×11 SAE; ms guidelines availbable on website.

**Tips** "We look for manuscripts that help draw children into a relationship with Jesus Christ, develop insights about Bible teachings, and make reading fun."

## STARSEED PRESS

Imprint of HJ Kramer, P.O. Box 1082, Tiburon CA 94920. (415)435-5367. Fax: (415)435-5364. **Manuscript**

**Acquisitions:** Jan Phillips. **Art Acquisitions:** Linda Kramer, vice president. Publishes 2 picture books/year. 50% of books by first-time authors. "We publish 4-color, 32-page children's picture books dealing with self-esteem and positive values, with a non-denominational, spiritual emphasis."
**Fiction** Picture books: self-esteem, multicultural, nature/environment. Average word length: picture books— 500-1,500. Recently published *Thank You God*, by Holly Bea, illustrated by Kim Howard (ages 3-7, picture book).
**Nonfiction** Picture books: multicultural, nature/environment.
**How to Contact/Writers** Fiction/nonfiction: Submit outline/synopsis. Responds to queries/mss in 10 weeks. Publishes a book 18 months after acceptance. Will consider simultaneous submissions, previously published work.
**Illustration** Works with 2 illustrators/year. Uses color artwork only. Illustrations only: Query with samples. Responds only if interested. Samples returned with SASE; samples filed.
**Terms** Negotiates based on publisher's net receipts. Split between author and artist. Originals returned to artist at job's completion. Book catalog available for 9×11 SAE with $1.98 postage; ms and art guidelines available for SASE. All imprints included in a single catalog.

## STEMMER HOUSE PUBLISHING

4 White Brook Rd., Gilsum NH 03448. (800)345-6665 or (603)357-0236. Fax: (603)357-2073. E-mail: pbs@pathw aybook.com. Website: www.stemmer.com. Estab. 1975. **Acquisitions:** Craig Thorn. Acquisitions Editors: Craig Thorn, Maressa Grieco. Publishes 2 picture books/year; 2 young readers/year; 1 middle reader/year. 90% of books by first-time authors.
**Fiction** Picture books, young readers, middle readres: animal, fantasy, folktales, nature/environment. Average word length: picture books—400; young readers—600; middle readers—800.
**Nonfiction** Picture books, young readers, middle readers: animal, arts/crafts, geography, history, nature/environ-ronment. Average word length: picture books—400; young readers—600; middle readers—800.
**How to Contact/Writers** Fiction/nonfiction: Query or submit outline/synopsis. Responds to queries in 1-2 months; mss in 4-8 weeks. Publishes book 2 years after acceptance. Will consider simultaneous submissions.
**Illustration** Works with 3-5 illustrators/year. Reviews ms/illustration packages from artists. Query or submit ms with 2-3 pieces of final art. Contact: Craig Thorn, editor-in-chief. Illustrations only: Query with samples, résumé, SASE, and tearsheets to be kept on file. Contact: Judith Peter. Responds only if interested. Samples returned with SASE; samples filed.
**Photography** Buys stock and assigns work. Uses nature, locations. Model/property releases required only upon use; captions not required. Submit cover letter and samples.
**Terms** Pays authors royalty of 10-15% based on wholesale price. Offers advances (average amount: $300-500). Pays illustrators and photographers royalty of 10-15% based on wholesale price. Sends galleys to authors; dummies to illustrators. Originals returned to artist at job's completion. Book catalog available for 6×9 SASE with postage.

## STERLING PUBLISHING CO., INC.

387 Park Ave. S., 10th Floor, New York NY 10016-8810. (212)532-7160. Fax: (212)981-0508. E-mail: info@sterlin gweb.com. Website: www.sterlingpublishing.com. **Manuscript Acquisitions:** Frances Gilbert. **Art Acquisitions:** Karen Nelson, creative director. Publishes 20 picture books/year; 50 young readers/year; 150 middle readers/year; 10 young adult titles/year. 15% of books by first-time authors.
**Fiction** Picture books.
**Nonfiction** Young readers: activity books, arts/crafts, cooking, hobbies, how-to, science. Middle readers, young adults: activity books, arts/crafts, hobbies, how-to, science, mazes, optical illusions, games, magic, math, puzzles.
**How to Contact/Writers** Nonfiction: Submit outline/synopsis and 1 sample chapter. Responds to queries/mss in 6 weeks. Publishes book 1 year after acceptance. Will consider simultaneous submissions, previously published work.
**Illustration** Works with 50 illustrators/year. Reviews ms/illustration packages from artists. Contact: Frances Gilbert, editorial director. Illustrations only: Send promo sheet. Contact: Karen Nelson, creative director. Responds in 6 weeks. Samples returned with SASE; samples filed.
**Photography** Buys stock and assigns work. Contact: Karen Nelson.
**Terms** Pays authors royalty or work purchased outright from authors. Offers advances (average amount: $2,000). Pays illustrators by the project. Pays photographers by the project or per photo. Sends galleys to authors; dummies to illustrators. Originals returned to artist at job's completion. Offers writer's guidelines for SASE. Catalog available on website.
**Tips** "We are primarily a nonfiction activities-based publisher. We do not publish fiction, but we are beginning to develop a picture book list. Our list is not trend-driven. We focus on titles that will backlist well."

## ☐ Ⓐ SUPER MANAGEMENT

Smarty Pants A/V, 15104 Detroit, Suite 2, Lakewood OH 44107-3916. (216)221-5300. Fax: (216)221-5348. **Acquisitions:** S. Tirk, CEO/President. Publishes 12 young readers/year. 5% of books by first-time authors. "We do mostly the classics or well known names such as Paddington Bear."

**Fiction** Picture books: adventure, animal, folktales, multicultural, nature/environment, poetry. Average word length: young readers—24 pages. Recently published *The Best of Mother Goose*, from the "Real M.G."; *Beatrix Potter, Paddington Bear*.

**Nonfiction** Picture books, young readers: activity books, animal, music/dance, nature/environment. Average word length: picture books—24 pages; middle readers—24 pages.

**How to Contact/Writers** Fiction: Submit complete ms. Responds in 3 weeks. Publishes a book 6-12 months after acceptance. Will consider simultaneous submissions and previously published work.

**Illustration Only interested in agented material.** Works with several illustrators/year. Uses color artwork only. Reviews ms/illustration packages from artists. Submit ms with dummy with return prepaid envelope. Contact: S. Tirk, CEO/President. Illustrations only: send promo sheet. Responds in 3 weeks to queries. Samples returned with SASE.

**Photography** Works on assignment only. Model/property releases required. Uses color prints. Submit color promo piece.

**Terms** Pays author negotiable royalty. Buys artwork and photos outright. Manuscript and art guidelines available for SASE.

**Tips** "We deal with mostly children's classics and well-known characters."

## Ⓝ TANGLEWOOD BOOKS

P.O. Box 3009, Terre Haute IN 47803. E-mail: ptierney@tanglewoodbooks.com. Website: www.tanglewoodbooks.com. Estab. 2003. Specializes in trade books. **Writers contact:** Peggy Tierney, publisher. **Illustrators contact:** Peggy Tierney, publisher. Produces 2-3 picture books/year, 1-2 middle readers/year, 1-2 young adult titles/year. 20% of books by first-time authors. "Tanglewood Press strives to publishh entertaining, kid-centric books."

**Fiction** Picture books: adventure, animal, concept, contemporary, fantasy, folktales, humor. Average word length: picture books—500. Recently published *Mystery at Blackbeard's Cove*, by Audrey Penn, illustrated by Josh Miller and Phillip Howard (ages 8-12, adventure); *It All Began with a Bean*, by Katie McKy, illustrated by Tracy Hill (ages 4-8, humorous); *You Can't Milk a Dancing Cow*, by Tom Dunsmuir, illustrated by Brain Jones (ages 4-8, humorous).

**How to Contact/Writers** Accepts international submissions. Fiction: Submit complete ms. Responds to mss in 6-9 months. Publishes book 2 years after acceptance. Considers simultaneous submissions.

**Illustration** Accepts material from international illustrators. Works with 3-4 illustrators/year. Uses both color and b&w. Reviews ms/illustration packages. For ms/illustration packages: Send ms with dummy. Submit ms/illustration packages to Peggy Tierney, publisher. If interested in illustrating future titles, query with samples. Submit samples to Peggy Tierney, publisher. Samples returned with SASE. Samples filed.

**Terms** Illustrators paid by the project for covers and small illustrations; royalty of 3-5% for picture books. Author sees galleys for review. Illustrators see dummies for review. Originals returned to artist at job's completion.

**Tips** "Please see lengthly 'Submissions' page on our website."

## Ⓝ TEORA USA

2 Wisconsin Circle, #870, Chevy Chase MD 20815. (301)986-6990. Fax: (301)986-6992. E-mail: info@teora.com. Website: www.teora.com. Estab. 2003. Specializes in mass market books, trade books, nonfiction, educational material. **Acquisitions:** Teora Raducanu, president. Produces 10 picture books/year, 2 young readers/year, 1 middle reader/year.

**Nonfiction** All levels: activity books, animal, careers, geography, health, history, hobbies. Recently published *1000 Games for Smart Kids*; *My First Words*; *Little Rabbits Have Fur*.

**How to Contact/Writers** Accepts international submissions. Submit outline/synopsis and 20% of the ms. Responds to queries/mss in 6 months. Publishes book 1 year after acceptance. Considers electronic submissions, previously published work.

**Illustration** Accepts material from international illustrators. Uses both color and b&w. Reviews ms/illustration packages. For ms/illustration packages: Submit ms with 20% of final art. Reviews work for future assignments. If interested in illustrating future titles, query with samples. Samples not returned.

**Photography** Buys stock images and assigns work. Model/property releases required. Photo captions required. For first contact, send published samples, portfolio.

**Terms** Author sees galleys for review. Illustrators see dummies for review. Originals not returned. Catalog on website.

## TILBURY HOUSE, PUBLISHERS

2 Mechanic St., #3, Gardiner ME 04345. (207)582-1899. Fax: (207)582-8227. E-mail: tilbury@tilburyhouse.com.

Website: www.tilburyhouse.com. **Publisher:** Jennifer Bunting. Children's Book Editor: Audrey Maynard. Publishes 1-3 young readers/year.

**Fiction** Picture books, young readers, middle readers: multicultural, nature/environment. Special needs include books that teach children about tolerance and honoring diversity. Recently published *Say Something*, by Peggy Moss; *The Goat Lady*, by Jane Bregoli.

**Nonfiction** Picture books, young readers, middle readers: multicultural, nature/environment. Recently published *Life Under Ice*, by Mary Cerullo, with photography by Bill Curtsinger; *Saving Birds*, by Pete Salmansohn and Steve Kress.

**How to Contact/Writers** Fiction/nonfiction: Submit outline/synopsis. Responds to queries/mss in 1 month. Publishes a book 1-2 years after acceptance. Will consider simultaneous submissions "with notification."

**Illustration** Works with 2 illustrators/year. Illustrations only: Query with samples. Responds in 1 month. Samples returned with SASE. Original artwork returned at job's completion.

**Photography** Buys photos from freelancers. Works on assignment only.

**Terms** Pays authors royalty based on wholesale price. Pays illustrators/photographers by the project; royalty based on wholesale price. Sends galleys to authors. Book catalog available for 6×9 SAE and 57¢ postage.

**Tips** "We are primarily interested in children's books that teach children about tolerance in a multicultural society, honor diversity, and make readers curious about the larger world. We are also interested in books that teach children about environmental issues."

## Ⓐ MEGAN TINGLEY BOOKS

Imprint of Little, Brown and Company, Time and Life Building, New York NY 10020. (212)522-8700. Fax: (212)522-7997. Website: www.lb-kids.com. **Manuscript Acquisitions:** Nancy Conescu, assistant editor. **Art Acquisitions:** Creative Director. Publishes 10 picture books/year; 1 middle reader/year; 2 young adult titles/year. 2% of books by first-time authors.

- Megan Tingley Books accepts agented material only.

**Fiction** Average word length: picture books—under 1,000 words. Recently published *You Read to Me, I'll Read to You: Very Short Fairy Tales to Read Together*, by Mary Ann Hoberman, illustrated by Michael Emberley (ages 4 and up, picture book); *The Peace Book*, by Todd Parr (all ages, picture book); *Luna*, by Julie Peters (ages 12 and up).

**Nonfiction** All levels: animal, arts/crafts, biography, concept, history, multicultural, music/dance, nature/environment, science, self help, social issues, special needs. Recently published *Look-Alikes Christmas*, by Joan Steiner (all ages); *My New York* (revised edition), by Kathy Jakobsen; *Harlem Stomp!*, by Carrick Hill (ages 10 and up).

**How to Contact/Writers Only interested in agented material only.** Query. Responds to mss in 2 months. Publishes a book 2 years after acceptance. Will consider simultaneous submissions, previously published work.

**Illustration** Works with 10 illustrators/year. Reviews ms/illustration packages from artists. Illustrations only: Query with samples. Contact: Editorial Assistant. Responds only if interested. Samples not returned; samples kept on file.

**Photography** Buys stock images. Contact: Editorial Assistant. Submit cover letter; samples are kept on file.

**Terms** Pays illustrators and photographers by the project or royalty based on retail price. Sends galleys to authors. Originals returned to artist at job's completion. All imprints included in a single catalog. Responds within 2 months only if interested.

## Ⓝ TOKYOPOP INC.

5900 Willshire Blvd., Los Angeles CA 90036. (323)692-6700. Fax: (323)692-6701. Website: www.tokyopop.com. Estab. 1996. Specializes in trade books, fiction, multicultural material. **Manuscript Acquisitions:** Jeremy Ross, editorial director; Nicole Monsastirsky, novels; Teresa Imperato, kids books. **Art Acquisitions:** Jeremy Ross, editorial director. Produces 75 picture books/year; 6 young readers/year; 6 young adult books/year. 25% of books by first-time authors. "We are the leading Asian popculture-influenced publisher in the world. Our product lines include manga, cine-manga™, young adult novels, chapter books, and merchandise."

**Fiction** Young readers: adventure, contemporary, humor, science fiction, suspense. Middle readers: adventure, contemporary, fantasy, humor, problem novels, science fiction. Young adults/teens: adventure, contemporary, fantasy, humor, problem novels, science fiction, suspense. Average word length: young readers—9,000; middle readers—9,000; young adult—50,000.

**Nonfiction** Middle readers, young adult/teens: activity books, arts/crafts, hobbies.

**How to Contact/Writers** Accepts international submissions. Fiction: Submit outline/synopsis and 2 sample chapters. Responds to queries/mss in 6 months. Publishes book 18 months after acceptance.

**Illustration** Accepts material from international illustrators. Works with 25 illustrators/year. Uses primarily b&w artwork. Reviews ms/illustration packages. Submit ms/illustration packages to Jeremy Ross, editorial director. Reviews work for future assignments. If interested in illustrating future titles, query with samples.

Submit samples to Jeremy Ross, editorial director. Responds in 3 months. Samples not returned.
**Terms** Pays authors royalty of 8% based on retail price. Pays illustrators by the project (range: $500-5,000). Author sees galleys for review. Illustrators see dummies for review. Originals not returned. Catalog on website. See website for artist's guidelines.
**Tips** "Submit cool, innovative, offbeat, cutting-edge material that captures the essence of teen pop culture."

## TOMMY NELSON®
Imprint of Thomas Nelson, Inc., P.O. Box 141000, Nashville TN 37214. (615)889-9000. Fax: (615)902-2219. Website: www.tommynelson.com.
- Tommy Nelson no longer accepts or reviews unsolicited queries, proposals, or manuscripts. Unsolicited material will be returned to sender.

## TOR BOOKS
175 Fifth Ave., New York NY 10010-7703. Fax: (212)388-0191. E-mail: Juliet.Pederson@Tor.com. Website: www.tor.com. **Contact:** Juliet Pederson, assistant to publisher, children's/YA division. Publisher: Kathleen Doherty; Senior Editor: Susan Chang. Imprints: Forge, Orb, Starscape, Tor Teen. Publishes 5-10 middle readers/year; 5-10 young adult titles/year.
- Tor Books is the "world's largest publisher of science fiction and fantasy, with strong category publishing in historical fiction, mystery, western/Americana, thriller, YA."
**Fiction** Middle readers, young adult titles: adventure, animal, anthology, concept, contemporary, fantasy, history, humor, multicultural, nature/environment, problem novel, science fiction, suspense/mystery. Average word length: middle readers—30,000; young adults—60,000-100,000. Published *Hidden Talents, Flip*, by David Lubar (ages 10 and up, fantasy); *Briar Rose*, by Jane Yolen (ages 12 and up).
**Nonfiction** Middle readers and young adult: geography, history, how-to, multicultural, nature/environment, science, social issues. Does not want to see religion, cooking. Average word length: middle readers—25,000-35,000; young adults—70,000. Published *Strange Unsolved Mysteries*, by Phyllis Rabin Emert; *Stargazer's Guide (to the Galaxy)*, by Q.L. Pearce (ages 8-12, guide to constellations, illustrated).
**How to Contact/Writers** Fiction/nonfiction: Submit outline/synopsis and complete ms. Responds to queries in 1 month; mss in 6 months for unsolicited work; 1 month or less for agented submissions.
**Illustration** Query with samples. Contact: Irene Gallo, art director. Responds only if interested. Samples kept on file.
**Terms** Pays authors royalty. Offers advances. Pays illustrators by the project. Book catalog available for 9x12 SAE and 3 first-class stamps. Submission guidelines available with SASE.
**Tips** "Know the house you are submitting to, familiarize yourself with the types of books they are publishing. Get an agent. Allow him/her to direct you to publishers who are most appropriate. It saves time and effort."

## TRICYCLE PRESS
Imprint of Ten Speed Press, P.O. Box 7123, Berkeley CA 94707. (510)559-1600. Website: www.tenspeed.com. **Acquisitions:** Nicole Geiger, publisher. Publishes 12-14 picture books/year; 2 middle readers/year; 1 'tween fiction/year; 3 board books/year. 25% of books by first-time authors. "Tricycle Press looks for something outside the mainstream; books that encourage children to look at the world from a different angle. Tricycle Press, like its parent company, Ten Speed Press, is known for its quirky, offbeat books. We publish high literary quality trade books."
**Fiction** Board books, picture books, middle grade: animal, contemporary, fantasy, history, multicultural, nature, poetry, suspense/mystery. Picture books, young readers: concept. Middle readers: anthology, novels. Average word length: picture books—800-1,000. Recently published *Finklehopper Frog*, by Irene Livingston, illustrated by Brian Lies (ages 5-8 picture book); *Yesterday I Had the Blues*, by Jeron Frame, illustrated by Gregory Christie.
**Nonfiction** Picture books, middle readers: animal, arts/crafts, biography, careers, concept, cooking, history, how-to, multicultural, music/dance, nature/environment, science. Recently published *Q is for Quark: A Science Alphabet Book*, by David M. Schwartz (ages 9 and up, picture book); *Honest Pretzels and 64 Other Amazing Recipes for Cooks Ages 8 & Up*, by Mollie Katzen; *The Young Adventurer's Guide to Everest*, by Jonathan Chester (ages 8 and up, nonfiction picture book).
**How to Contact/Writers** Fiction: Submit complete ms for picture books. Submit outline/synopsis and 2-3 sample chapters for chapter book. "No queries!" Nonfiction: Submit complete ms. Responds to mss in 4-6 months. Publishes a book 1-2 years after acceptance. Welcomes simultaneous submissions and previously published work. Do not send original artwork; copies only, please. No electronic or faxed submissions.
**Illustration** Works with 12 illustrators/year. Uses color and b&w. Reviews ms/illustration package from artists. Submit ms with dummy and/or 2-3 pieces of final art. Illustrations only: Query with samples, promo sheet, tearsheets. Responds only if interested. Samples returned with SASE; samples filed. Original artwork returned at job's completion unless work for hire.

**Photography** Works on assignment only. Uses 35mm transparencies or high resolution scans. Submit samples.
**Terms** Pays authors royalty of 7½-8½% based on net receipts. Offers advances. Pays illustrators and photographers royalty of 7½-8½% based on net receipts. Sends galleys of novels to authors. Book catalog for 9×12 SASE (3 first-class stamps). Manuscript guidelines for SASE (1 first-class stamp). Guidelines available at website.
**Tips** "We are looking for something a bit outside the mainstream and with lasting appeal (no one-shot-wonders)."

### A TROPHY/TEMPEST/EOS PAPERBACKS

1350 Avenue of the Americas, New York NY 10019. (212)261-6500. Fax: (212)261-6668. Website: www.harperc ollins.com and www.harperteen.com. Book publisher. Imprint of HarperCollins Children's Books Group. Publishes 20-25 chapter books/year, 70-75 middle grade titles/year, 25-30 reprint picture books/year, 10-15 teen titles/year; 40 young adult titles/year.

- Trophy is primarily a reprint imprint. Tempest is a teen imprint. Eos is a fantasy/science fiction imprint. Avon is a commercial paperback fiction imprint. Trophy and Tempest also publish a limited number of hardcover originals and paperback reprints each year.

**How to Contact/Writers** Does not accept unsolicited or unagented mss.

### TURTLE BOOKS

866 United Nations Plaza, Suite 525, New York NY 10017. (212)644-2020. Website: www.turtlebooks.com.
**Acquisitions:** John Whitman. "Turtle Books publishes only picture books for young readers. Our goal is to publish a small, select list of quality children's books each spring and fall season. As often as possible, we will publish our books in both English and Spanish editions."

- Turtle does a small number of books and may be slow in responding to unsolicited manuscripts.

**Fiction** Picture books: adventure, animal, concept, contemporary, fantasy, folktales, hi-lo, history, humor, multicultural, nature/environment, religion, sports, suspense/mystery. Recently published *The Legend of Mexicatl*, by Jo Harper, illustrated by Robert Casilla (the story of Mexicatl and the origin of the Mexican people); *Vroom, Chugga, Vroom-Vroom*, by Anne Miranda, illustrated by David Murphy (a number identification book in the form of a race car story); *The Crab Man*, by Patricia VanWest, illustrated by Cedric Lucas (the story of a young Jamaican boy who must make the difficult decision between making an income and the ethical treatment of animals); *Prairie Dog Pioneers*, by Jo and Josephine Harper, illustrated by Craig Spearing (the story of a young girl who doesn't want to move, set in 1870s Texas); *Keeper of the Swamp*, by Ann Garrett, illustrated by Karen Chandler (a dramatic coming-of-age story wherein a boy confronts his fears and learns from his ailing grandfather the secrets of the swamp); *The Lady in the Box*, by Ann McGovern, illustrated by Marni Backer (a modern story about a homeless woman named Dorrie told from the point of view of two children); *Alphabet Fiesta*, by Anne Miranda, illustrated by young schoolchildren in Madrid, Spain (an English/Spanish alphabet story).
**How to Contact/Writers** Send complete ms. "Queries are a waste of time." Response time varies.
**Illustrators** Works with 6 illustrators/year. Responds to artist's queries/submissions only if interested. Samples returned with SASE only.
**Terms** Pays royalty. Offers advances.

### TWO LIVES PUBLISHING

P.O. Box 736, Ridley Park PA 19078. (610)532-2024. Fax: (610)532-2790. E-mail: info@TwoLives.com. Website: www.TwoLives.com. **Manuscript Acquisitions:** Bobbie Combs. Publishes 1 picture book/year; 1 middle reader/year. 100% of books by first-time authors. "We create books for children whose parents are lesbian, gay, bisexual or transgender."
**Fiction** Picture books, young readers, middle readers: contemporary.
**How to Contact/Writers** Fiction: Query. Responds to queries/mss in 3 weeks. Publishes book 2-3 years after acceptance. Will consider e-mail submissions, simultaneous submissions, previously published work.
**Illustration** Works with 2 illustrators/year. Uses color artwork only. Query ms/illustration packages. Contact: Bobbie Combs, publisher. Illustrations only: Send postcard sample with brochure, photocopies. Contact: Bobbie Combs, publisher. Responds only if interested. Samples filed.
**Terms** Pays authors royalty of 5-10% based on retail price. Offers advances (average amount: $250). Pays illustrators royalty of 5-10% based on retail price. Sends galleys to authors. Originals returned to artist at job's completion. Catalog available on website.

### N TWO-CAN PUBLISHING

T & N Children's Publishing, 11571 K-Tel Drive, Minnetonka MN 55343. Website: www.two-canpublishing.com. Estab. 1990. Specializes in trade books, nonfiction. **Manuscript Acquisitions:** Jill Anderson, editorial director. Produces 10 young readers/year; 5 middle readers/year. 5% of books by first-time authors. "Two-Can's line of nonfiction children's books feature bright, appealing designs, well-researched facts, and fun-to-read texts. Nonfiction does not have to be boring!''

**Nonfiction** Picture books, young readers, middle readers: animal, geography, health, history, multicultural, nature/environment, reference, science. Average word length: picture books—400-800; young readers—800-3,000; middle readers—2,500-15,000. Recently published *The Trail West*, by Ellen Galford (ages 8-11, history/art history); *My First Trip Around the World* (ages 5-8, geography/culture); *The Little Book of Dinosaurs*, by Cherie Winner (ages 4-7, animals).

**How to Contact/Writers** Accepts international submissions. Fiction: Submit complete ms (preferred) or submit outline/sysnopsis and 2 sample chapters (acceptable for middle grade titles). Responds to queries/mss in 2 months. Publishes book 1-2 years after acceptance. Considers simultaneous submissions.

**Illustration** Works with 5 illustrators/year. Uses color artwork only. Reviews ms/illustration packages. For ms/illustration packages: Submit ms/illustration packages to Jill Anderson, editorial director. Reviews work for future assignments. If interested in illustrating future titles, query with samples, photocopies. Submit samples to Art Director. Samples not returned. Samples filed.

**Photography** Buys stock images; assigns work (rarely). Contact: Jill Anderson, editorial director. Photo needs ''depend on project we are working on—nature, culture, how-to. . . just about anything.'' Model/property releases required. Photo captions required. Uses color transparencies. For first contact, send cover letter, published samples, stock photo list, promo piece.

**Terms** Pays authors royalty based on retail price or work purchased outright. Pays illustrators by the project or royalty. Pays photographers by the project, per photo or royalty. Author sees galleys for review. Illustrators see dummies for review. See website for writer's and artist's guidelines.

### Ⓐ TYNDALE HOUSE PUBLISHERS, INC.

351 Executive Dr., P.O. Box 80, Wheaton IL 60189. (630)668-8300. **Manuscript Acquisitions** : Jan Axford. **Art Acquisitions** : Talinda Laubach. Publishes approximately 20 Christian children's titles/year.

• Tyndale House no longer reviews unsolicited manuscripts. Only accepts agented material.

**Fiction** Middle readers: adventure, religion, suspense/mystery.

**Nonfiction** Picture books: religion. Young readers: Christian living, Bible, devotionals.

**How to Contact/Writers Only interested in agented material.** ''Request children's writer's guidelines from (630)668-8310, ext. 836 for more information.''

**Illustration** Uses full-color for book covers, b&w or color spot illustrations for some nonfiction. Illustrations only: Query with photocopies (color or b&w) of samples, résumé.

**Photography** Buys photos from freelancers. Works on assignment only.

**Terms** Pay rates for authors and illustrators vary.

**Tips** ''All accepted manuscripts will appeal to Evangelical Christian children and parents.''

### URJ PRESS

(formerly UHAC Press), 633 Third Ave., New York NY 10017. (212)650-4120. Fax: (212)650-4119. E-mail: press@urj.org. Website: www.urj.press.com. **Manuscript/Art Acquisitions:** Rabbi Hara Person, editor-in-chief. Publishes 4 picture books/year; 2 young readers/year; 2 middle readers/year; 2 young adult titles; 4 textbooks/year. ''The URJ publishes textbooks for the religious classroom, children's tradebooks and scholarly work of Jewish education import—no adult fiction and no YA fiction.''

**Fiction** Picture books: religion. Average word length: picture books—1,500. Recently published *The Purim Costume*, by Peninnah Schram, illustrated by Tammy L. Keiser (ages 4-8, picture book); *A Year of Jewish Stories: 52 Tales for Children and Their Families*, by Grace Ragues Maisel and Samantha Shubert, illustrated by Tammy L. Keiser (ages 4-12, picture book).

**Nonfiction** Picture books, young readers, middle readers: religion. Average word length: picture books—1,500. Recently published *The Seven Species: Stories and Recipes Inspired by the Foods of the Bible*, by Matt Biers-Ariel, illustrated by Tama Goodman (story and recipe book).

**How to Contact/Writers** Fiction: Submit outline/synopsis and 2 sample chapters. Nonfiction: Submit complete ms. Responds to queries/mss in 4 months. Publishes a book 18-24 months after acceptance. Will consider simultaneous submissions.

**Illustration** Works with 5 illustrators/year. Reviews ms/illustration packages from artists. Send ms with dummy. Illustrations only: Send portfolio to be kept on file. Responds in 2 months. Samples returned with SASE. Looking specifically for Jewish themes.

**Photography** Buys stock and assigns work. Uses photos with Jewish content. Prefers modern settings. Submit cover letter and promo piece.

**Terms** Offers advances. Pays photographers by the project (range: $200-3,000) or per photo (range: $20-100). Book catalog free; ms guidelines for SASE.

**Tips** "Look at some of our books. Have an understanding of the Reform Jewish community. We sell mostly to Jewish congregations and day schools."

## VIEWPOINT PRESS

P.O. Box 430, Pleasant Garden NC 27313. (336)370-1600. E-mail: vpressbks@world.att.net. Website: http://membe rs.tripod.com/ ~ viewpointpress. **Writers contact:** M.E. Smith-Ankrom. **Illustrators contact:** Lloyd Oxendine, Art Editor. Produces 1 picture book/year. 65% of books by first-time authors. "Viewpoint Press aims to "produce quality literature for children's of all ages."

**Fiction** Picture books: animal, contemporary, history, nature/environment. Young readers: animal, contemporary, fantasy, folktales, history. Middle readers: contemporary, history, nature/environment, problem novels. Recently published *The Super, Stupendous, and Tremendously Terrific Show and Tell Day*, by Martha McFarland, illustrated by Dianne Ellis (contemporary picture book, for grades K-3); *Cowpath Days*, by Mary Alice Countess, illustrated by Susan Daggett (chapter book for grades 2-6); *Walking Ribbon*, by Julia T. Ebel, illustrated by Cheryl Powell (historically-based picture books for grades 1-5).

**Nonfiction** Picture books: animal, history, nature/environment, social issues, special needs. Young readers: history, nature/environment, social issues, special needs. Middle readers: history, nature/environment, social issues, special needs.

**How to Contact/Writers** Fiction/nonfiction: Query or submit complete ms. Responds to queries in 3 weeks; to mss in 3-4 months. Publishes book 2-3 years after acceptance. Considers simultaneous submissions.

**Illustration** Works with 1-2 illustrators/year. Uses both color and b&w. If interested in illustrating future titles, query with samples, arrange personal portfolio review, send promo sheet, portfolio, slides. Submit samples to Art Director, Lloyd Oxendine. Responds in 3 months. Samples not returned. Samples filed.

**Terms** Pays authors royalty of 6-11% based on net profit. Pays illustrators royalty of 3-6% based on net profit. Author sees galleys for review. Illustrators see dummies for review. Originals not returned. Catalog on website. Offers writer's, artist's guidelines for SASE.

**Tips** "Our main interest is in historically-based stories. We're looking for realistic, likable characters, accuracy in detail of period."

## VIKING CHILDREN'S BOOKS

Penguin Group Inc., 345 Hudson St., New York NY 10014-3657. (212)414-3600. Fax: (212)414-3399. Website: www.penguin.com. **Acquisitions:** Catherine Frank, editor, picture books, middle grade and young adult fiction; Tracy Gates, executive editor, picture books, middle grade, young adult fiction; Joy Peskin, senior editor, picture books, middle grade, young adult fiction; Jill Davis, senior editor picture books, middle grade, young adult, unique nonfiction; Anne Gunton, associate editor, picture books, middle grade, young adult. **Art Acquisitions:** Denise Cronin, Viking Children's Books. Publishes hardcover originals. Publishes 60 books/year. Receives 7,500 queries/year. 25% of books from first-time authors; 33% from unagented writers. "Viking Children's Books is known for humorous, quirky picture books, in addition to more traditional fiction and publishes the highest quality trade books for children including fiction, nonfiction, and novelty books for pre-schoolers through young adults." Publishes book 1-2 years after acceptance of artwork. Hesitantly accepts simultaneous submissions.

• Viking Children's Books is not accepting unsolicited submissions at this time.

**Fiction** All levels: adventure, animal, contemporary, fantasy, hi-lo, history, humor, multicultural, nature/environment, poetry, problem novels, religion, romance, science fiction, sports, suspense/mystery. Recently published *Llama Llama Red Pajama*, by Anna Dewdney (ages 2 up, picture book); *Prom*, by Laurie Halse Anderson (ages 12 and up).

**Nonfiction** Picture books: animal, biography, concept. Young readers, middle readers, young adult: animal, biography, concept, geography, hi-lo, history, multicultural, music/dance, nature/environment, science, sports. Recently published *Understanding the Holy Land*, by Mitch Frank (ages 11 up, nonfiction).

**Illustration** Works with 30 illustrators/year. Responds to artist's queries/submissions only if interested. Samples returned with SASE only or samples filed. Originals returned at job's completion.

**Terms** Pays 2-10% royalty on retail price or flat fee. Advance negotiable.

## VSP BOOKS

P.O. Box 17011, Alexandria VA 22302. (703)684-8142. Fax: (703)684-7955. E-mail: mail@VSPBooks.com. Website: www.VSPBooks.com. **Manuscript Acquisitions:** Peter Barnes. Imprints: VSP Books, Vacation Spot Publishing. Publishes 3 picture books/year. 50% of books by first-time authors. "We publish children's books about special and historic places."

**Fiction** Picture books: history. Average word length: picture books—1,000.

**How to Contact/Writers** Fiction: Query.

**Illustration** Works with 2-3 illustrators/year. Uses color artwork only. Reviews ms/illustration packages from artists. Query. Illustrations only: Query with photocopies. Contact: Peter Barnes, publisher. Samples not returned.

**Terms** Pays authors royalties based on retail price or work purchased outright. Pays illustrators by the project or royalties. Sends galleys to authors; dummies to illustrators. Originals returned to artist at job's completion. Book catalog available for SASE. Catalog available on website.

## ▨ WALKER & COMPANY

Books for Young Readers, 104 Fifth Ave., New York NY 10011. (212)727-8300. Fax: (212)727-0984. Website: www.walkeryoungreaders.com. **Manuscript Acquisitions:** Emily Easton, publisher. Beth Marhoffer, assistant editor. Publishes 20 picture books/year; 2-4 middle readers/year; 2-4 young adult titles/year. 5% of books by first-time authors; 65% of books from agented writers.

- *The Mysterious Collection of Dr. David Harleyson*, by Jean Cassells, received a 2005 Golden Kite Award.

**Fiction** Picture books: adventure, history, humor. Middle readers: adventure, contemporary, history, humor, multicultural. Young adults: adventure, contemporary, humor, historical fiction, suspense/mystery. Recently published *One Witch*, by Laura Leuck, illustrated by S.D. Schinder (ages 3-8, picture book); *Straight to the Pole*, Kevin O'Malley (ages 6-10, picture book); *All's Fair in Love, War, and High School*, by Janette Rallison (12 and up, teen/young adult novel).

**Nonfiction** Picture book, middle readers: biography, history. Recently published *Lonesome George the Giant Tortoise*, by Francine Jacobs, illustrated by Jean Cassels (ages 4-8, picture book, nature); *Fantastic Flights*, by Patrick O'Brien (ages 7-12, picture book history); *The Middle School Survival*, by Arlene Erlbach (10-14, illustrated nonfiction). Multicultural needs include "contemporary, literary fiction and historical fiction written in an authentic voice. Also high interest nonfiction with trade appeal."

**How to Contact/Writers** Fiction/nonfiction: Submit outline/synopsis and sample chapters; complete ms for picture books. Responds to queries/mss in 3-4 months. Send SASE for writer's guidelines.

**Illustration** Works with 10-12 illustrators/year. Editorial department reviews ms/illustration packages from artists. Query or submit ms with 4-8 samples. Illustrations only: Tearsheets. "Please do not send original artwork." Responds to art samples only if interested. Samples returned with SASE.

**Terms** Pays authors royalty of 5-10%; pays illustrators royalty or flat fee. Offers advance payment against royalties. Original artwork returned at job's completion. Sends galleys to authors. Book catalog available for 9×12 SASE; ms guidelines for SASE.

**Tips** Writers: "Make sure you study our catalog before submitting. We are a small house with a tightly focused list. Illustrators: Have a well-rounded portfolio with different styles." Does not want to see folktales, ABC books, paperback series, genre fiction. "Walker and Company is committed to introducing talented new authors and illustrators to the children's book field."

## ▢ WEIGL PUBLISHERS INC.

350 5th Ave. Suite 3304, New York NY 10118-0069. (866)649-3445. Fax: (866)449-3445. E-mail: info@weigl.com. Website: www.weigl.com. **Manuscript/Art Acquisitions:** Tine Schenberger. Publishes 25 young readers/year; 40 middle readers/year; 20 young adult titles/year. 15% of books by first-time authors. "Our mission is to provide innovative high-quality learning resources for schools and libraries worldwide at a competitive price."

**Nonfiction** Young readers: animal, biography, geography, history, multicultural, nature/environment, science. Middle readers: animal, biography, geography, history, multicultural, nature/environment, science, social issues, sports. Young adults: biography, careers, geography, history, multicultural, nature/environment, social issues. Average word length: young readers—100 words/page; middle readers—200 words/page; young adults—300 words/page. Recently published *Prehistoric Life* (ages 8 and up, science series); *Indigenous Peoples* (ages 8 and up, social studies series); *Natural Wonders* (ages 6 and up, social studies series).

**How to Contact/Writers** Nonfiction: Query. Responds to queries in 3 months. Publishes book 6-9 months after acceptance. Will consider e-mail submissions, simultaneous submissions.

**Illustration** Works with 3-6 illustrators/year. Reviews ms/illustration packages from artists. Query. Contact: Lee Schenkman, managing editor. Illustrations only: Query with brochure, résumé. Responds only if interested. Samples not returned; samples filed.

**Photography** Buys stock. Contact: Tina Schwartzenberger, photo editor. Uses animals, nature, history, geography. Model/property releases required. "We prefer slides or digital images." Submit cover letter, stock photo list.

**Terms** Work purchased outright from authors. Pays illustrators by the project. Pays photographers per photo. Originals returned to artist at job's completion. Book catalog available for 9½×11 SASE. Catalog available on website.

## ▨ ▢ WESTWINDS PRESS/ALASKA NORTHWEST BOOKS

Graphic Arts Center Publishing Company, P.O. Box 10306, Portland OR 97296-0306. (503)226-2402. Fax: (503)223-1410. E-mail: editorial@gacpc.com. Website: www.gacpc.com. Independent book packager/producer. **Writers contact:** Tricia Brown, acquisitions editor. **Illustrators contact:** same. Produces 4 picture books/year, 1-2 young readers/year. 10% of books by first-time authors. "Graphic Arts Center Publishing Company publishes and distributes regional titles through its three imprints: Graphic Arts Center Publishing, Alaska Northwest Books and WestWinds Press. GACP is known for its excellence in publishing high-end photo-essay books. Alaska Northwest, established in 1959, is the premier publisher of nonfiction Alaska books on subjects ranging from cooking, Alaska Native culture, memoir, history, natural history, reference, biography, humor and children's books. WestWinds Press, established in 1999, echoes those themes with content that focuses on the Western States."

**Fiction** Picture books: animal, folktales, nature/environment. Young readers: adventure, animal, folktales, nature/environment. Average word length: picture books—1,100; young readers—9,000. Recently published *Kumak's Fish*, by Michael Bania (folktale, ages 6 and up); *Sweet Dreams, Polar Bear*, by Mindy Dwyer (3 and up); *Seldovia Sam and the Sea Otter Rescue*, by Susan Springer, illustrated by Amy Meissner (adventure, beginning chapter book).

**Nonfiction** Picture books: animal, nature/environment. Young readers: animal, nature/environment. Middle readers: nature/environment. Average word length: picture books—1,100; young readers—9,000. Recently published *Sharkabet*, by Ray Troll (ages 5 and up); *Winter Is*, by Anne Dixon, illustrated by Mindy Dwyer (environment/nature, ages 3-6).

**How to Contact/Writers** Accepts international submissions. Fiction/nonfiction: Submit complete ms. Responds to queries in 3 months; mss in 6 months. Publishes book 1-2 years after acceptance. Considers simultaneous submissions, electronic submissions, previously published work.

**Illustration** Accepts material from international illustrators. Works with 4 illustrators/year. Uses both color and b&w. Reviews ms/illustration packages. For ms/illustration packages: Send ms with dummy. Submit ms/illustration packages to Tricia Brown, acquisitions editor. Reviews work for future assignments. If interested in illustrating future titles, query with samples. Samples returned with SASE. Samples not filed.

**Photography** Works on assignment only. Submit photos to Tim Frew, executive editor. Photo captions required. For first contact, send cover letter, portfolio, complete proposal.

**Terms** Offers advance against royalties. Originals returned to artist at job's completion. All imprints included in single catalog.

## WHITE MANE KIDS

Imprint of White Mane Publishing, P.O. Box 708, Shippensburg PA 17257. (717)532-2237. Fax: (717)532-6110. Website: www.whitemane.com. **Manuscript Acquisitions:** Harold Collier. Publishes middle readers and young adult titles.

**Fiction** Middle readers, young adults/teens: history. Recently published *Lottie's Courage: A Contraband Slave's Story*, by Phyllis Haislip; *Ghosts of Vicksburg*, by Kathleen Ernst; *Off to Fight* (#3 Young Heroes of History series), by Alan Kay.

**Nonfiction** Middle readers, young adults: history. Recently published *Slaves Who Dared: The Stories of 10 African American Heroes*, by Mary Garrison.

**How to Contact/Writers** Fiction/nonfiction: Query. Responds to queries in 1 month; mss in 3 months. Publishes book 12-18 months after acceptance. Will consider simultaneous submissions.

**Illustration** Works with 2-3 illustrators/year. Uses color artwork only. Artwork for book covers only. Reviews ms/illustration packages from artists. Query. Illustrations only: Query with samples. Responds only if interested. Samples not returned; samples filed.

**Terms** Pays authors royalties. Pays illustrators by the project. Sends galleys to authors. Originals returned to artist at job's completion. Book catalog available; ms guidelines available for SASE. All imprints included in a single catalog.

**Tips** "We are interested in historically accurate fiction for middle and young adult readers. We do *not* publish picture books."

## ALBERT WHITMAN & COMPANY

6340 Oakton St., Morton Grove IL 60053-2723. (847)581-0033. Fax: (847)581-0039. Website: www.albertwhitman.com. **Manuscript Acquisitions:** Kathleen Tucker, editor-in-chief. **Art Acquisitions:** Carol Gildar, art director. Publishes 30 books/year. 20% of books by first-time authors; 15% from agented authors.

**Fiction** Picture books, young readers, middle readers: adventure, concept (to help children deal with problems), fantasy, history, humor, multicultural, suspense. Middle readers: problem novels, suspense/mystery. "We are interested in contemporary multicultural stories—stories with holiday themes and exciting distinctive novels. We publish a wide variety of topics and are interested in stories that help children deal with their problems and concerns. Does not want to see "religion-oriented, ABCs, pop-up, romance, counting." Recently published *April Foolishness*, by Teresa Bateman, illustrated by Nadine Wescott; *Mabela the Clever*, by Margaret Read

MacDonald, illustrated by Tim Coffey; *Wanda's Monster*, by Eileen Spinelli, illustrated by Nancy Hayashi; *Doing Time On Line*, by Jan Siebold.

**Nonfiction** Picture books, young readers, middle readers: animal, arts/crafts, health, history, hobbies, multicultural, music/dance, nature/environment, science, sports, special needs. Does not want to see "religion, any books that have to be written in, or fictionalized biographies." Recently published *Shelter Dogs*, by Peg Kehret; *Apples Here!*, by Will Hubbell; *The Groundhog Day Book of Facts and Fun*, by Wendie Old, illustrated by Paige Billin-Frye.

**How to Contact/Writers** Fiction/nonfiction: Submit query, outline and sample chapter. For picture books send entire ms. Include cover letter. Responds to queries in 6 weeks; mss in 4 months. Publishes a book 18 months after acceptance. Will consider simultaneous submissions "if notified."

**Illustration** "We are not accepting illustration samples at this time. Submissions will not be returned."

**Photography** Publishes books illustrated with photos but not stock photos—desires photos all taken for project. "Our books are for children and cover many topics; photos must be taken to match text. Books often show a child in a particular situation (e.g., kids being home-schooled, a sister whose brother is born prematurely)." Photographers should query with samples; send unsolicited photos by mail.

**Terms** Pays authors, illustrators and photographers royalties. Book catalog for $8 \times 10$ SAE and 3 first-class stamps.

**Tips** "In both picture books and nonfiction, we are seeking stories showing life in other cultures and the variety of multicultural life in the U.S. We also want fiction and nonfiction about mentally or physically challenged children—some recent topics have been autism, stuttering, diabetes. Look up some of our books first to be sure your submission is appropriate for Albert Whitman & Co."

## JOHN WILEY & SONS, INC.

111 River St., Hoboken NJ 07030. (201)748-6000. Website: www.wiley.com. **Acquisitions:** Kate Bradford, senior editor. Publishes 18 middle readers/year; 2 young adult titles/year. 10% of books by first-time authors. Publishes educational nonfiction: primarily history, science, math, and other activities.

**Nonfiction** Middle readers: activity books, arts/crafts, biography, cooking, geography, health, history, hobbies, how-to, nature/environment, reference, science, self help. Young adults: activity books, arts/crafts, health, hobbies, how-to, nature/environment, reference, science, self help. Average word length: middle readers—20,000-40,000. Recently published *World Ward and the Modern Age*, by David King (ages 8-12, US history); *Janice VanCleave's Super Science Models* (ages 8-12, science/activity).

**How to Contact/Writers** Query. Submit outline/synopsis, 2 sample chapters and an author bio. Responds to queries in 1 month; mss in 3 months. Publishes a book 1 year after acceptance. Will consider simultaneous and previously published submissions.

**Illustration** Works with 6 illustrators/year. Uses primarily b&w artwork. Reviews ms/illustration packages from artists. Query. Illustrations only: Query with samples, résumé, client list. Responds only if interested. Samples filed. Original artwork returned at job's completion. No portfolio reviews.

**Photography** Buys photos from freelancers.

**Terms** Pays authors royalty of 10-12% based on wholesale price, or by outright purchase. Offers advances. Pays illustrators by the project. Photographers' pay negotiable. Sends galleys to authors. Book catalog available for SASE.

**Tips** "We're looking for topics and writers that can really engage kids' interest, plus we're always interested in a new twist on time-tested subjects." Nonfiction submissions only; no picture books.

## WINDSTORM CREATIVE LTD.

P.O. Box 28, Port Orchard WA 98366. E-mail: wsc@windstormcreative.com. Website: www.windstormcreative. com. **Acquisitions:** Ms. Cris DiMarco, senior editor, young adult; Jennifer Anna, children's. Publishes trade paperback originals and reprints. Publishes 10 titles/year. 50% of books from first-time authors; 50% from unagented writers. WSC consists of the following imprints: Blue Works—Children's titles and young adult novels released in paper and on multimedia CD-ROM; Lightning Rod Ltd—Internet & Episode Guides; WSC—Cutting-edge fiction. Publishes genre fiction and poetry primarily in paper and on multimedia CD-ROM; RAMPANT Gaming—Role-playing and other games for ages 14 and Paper Frog—theater and film, Orchard Academy—nonfiction, home school-based books and CD-ROMs; Full Spectrum—nonfiction. "We do not backlist. Ninety-five percent of our titles are still in print. We are an independent press with corporate synergy. We do not publish work that is racist, homophobic, sexist or graphically violent in content. All of our authors and artists should expect to be proactive in marketing their work. If you do not wish to read from and/or sign your books and/or artwork, you should not submit work to us."

**Fiction** All levels: adventure, animal, fantasy, folktales, history, nature/environment, science fiction, suspense/mystery. Recently published *Yen Shei and the American Bonsai*, by Jennifer Anna/Karen Hallion (middle reader, Cris DiMarco, pre-chapter); *Mrs. Estronsky and the UFO*, by Pat Schmatz (junior high, Jennifer Anna).

**Nonfiction** All levels: activity books, animal, how-to, multicultural.

**How to Contact/Writers** ''You must use the submission form plus label from the website. All queries or submissions *without* the label will be destroyed.''

**Illustration** Works with 20 illustrators/year. Visit website for guidelines. Responds to queries in 4 months, only if interested. Samples returned with SASE; samples filed. Originals returned at job's completion.

**Photography** Buys photos from freelancers. See website.

**Terms** Pays authors at least 15% royalty based on retail price. Will consider simultaneous submissions. Artists and photographers are paid flat fee for covers only. All other work is paid by the project ($200-1,000) or royalty basis. Royalty payment is 15% of gross monies received.''

**Tips** ''We reserve the right to destroy any submissions that deviate from our format.''

## WINDWARD PUBLISHING

An imprint of the Finney Company, 3943 Meadowbrook Rd., Minneapolis MN 55426. (952)938-9330. Fax: (952)938-7353. E-mail: feedback@finney-hobar.com. Website: www.finney-hobar.com. **Manuscript/Art Acquisitions:** Alan E. Krysan. Publishes 2 picture books/year; 4-6 young readers, middle readers, young adult titles/year. 50% of books by first-time authors.

**Fiction** Young readers, middle readers, young adults: adventure, animal, nature/environment. Recently published *Nightlight*, by Jeannine Anderson (ages 4-8, picture book); *Daddy Played Music for the Cows*, by Maryann Weidt (ages 4-8, picture book).

**Nonfiction** Young readers, middle readers, young adults: activity books, animal, careers, nature/environment, science. Young adults: textbooks. Recently published *My Little Book of Collection*, by Hope Irvin Marston (ages 4-8, introductions to the wonders of nature); *Space Station Science*, by Marianne Dyson (ages 8-13, science).

**How to Contact/Writers** Fiction: Query. Nonfiction: Submit outline/synopsis and 3 sample chapters. Responds to queries in 1 month; mss in 2 months. Publishes book 6-12 months after acceptance. Will consider simultaneous submissions and previously published work.

**Illustration** Reviews ms/illustration packages from artists. Send ms with dummy. Query with samples. Responds in 2 months. Samples returned with SASE; samples filed.

**Photography** Buys stock and assigns work. Photography needs depend on project—mostly ocean and beach subject matter. Uses color, 4×6, glossy prints. Submit cover letter, résumé, stock photo list.

**Terms** Author's payment negotiable by project. Offers advances (average amount: $500). Illustrators and photographers payment negotiable by project. Sends galleys to authors; dummies to illustrators. Originals returned to artist at job's completion. Book catalog available for 6×9 SAE and 3 first-class stamps; ms guidelines available for SASE. Catalog mostly available on website.

## PAULA WISEMAN BOOKS

Imprint of Simon & Schuster, 1230 Sixth Ave., New York NY 10020. (212)698-7272. Fax: (212)698-2796. E-mail: paulawiseman@simonandschuster.com. Website: www.simonsays.com. Publishes 10 picture books/year; 2 middle readers/year; 2 young adult titles/year. 10% of books by first-time authors.

**Fiction** Considers all categories. Average word length: picture books—500; others standard length. Recently published *Mighty Jackie: The Strike-Out Queen*, by Marissa Moss, illustrated by C.F. Payne.

**Nonfiction** Picture books: animal, biography, concept, history, nature/environment. Young readers: animal, biography, history, multicultural, nature/environment, sports. Average word length: picture books—500; others standard length.

**How to Contact/Writers** Submit complete ms.

**Illustration** Works with 15 illustrators/year. Uses color artwork only. Will review ms/illustration packages from artists. Prefers e-mail for initial contact. Send ms with dummy.

## WM KIDS

Imprint of White Mane Publishing Co., Inc., P.O. Box 708, 73 W. Burd St., Shippensburg PA 17257. (717)532-2237. Fax : (717)532-6110. E-mail: marketing@whitemane.com. Website: www.whitemane.com. **Acquisitions:** Harold Collier, acquisitions editor. Imprints: White Mane Books, Burd Street Press, White Mane Kids, Ragged Edge Press. Publishes 10 middle readers/year. 50% of books are by first-time authors.

**Fiction** Middle readers, young adults: history. Average word length: middle readers—30,000. Does not publish picture books. Recently published *Lottie's Courage*, by Phyllis Haislip (historical fiction, grades 5 and up); Young Heroes of History series, by Alan Kay (grades 5 and up).

**Nonfiction** Middle readers, young adults: history. Average word length: middle readers—30,000. Does not publish picture books. Recently published *Slaves Who Dared: The Story of Ten African American Heroes*, by Mary Garrison (young adult).

**How to Contact/Writers** Fiction: Query. Nonfiction: Submit outline/synopsis and 2-3 sample chapters. Responds to queries in 1 month; mss in 3 months. Publishes a book 12-18 months after acceptance. Will consider simultaneous submissions.

**Illustration** Works with 3 illustrators/year. Illustrations used for cover art only. Responds in 1 month. Samples returned with SASE.

**Photography** Buys stock and assigns work. Submit cover letter and portfolio.

**Terms** Pays authors royalty of 7-10%. Pays illustrators and photographers by the project. Sends galleys for review. Originals returned to artist at job's completion. Book catalog and writer's guidelines available for SASE. All imprints included in a single catalog.

## ☐ WORLD BOOK, INC.

233 N. Michigan Ave., Suite 2000, Chicago IL 60601. (312)729-5800. Fax: (312)729-5612. Website: www.worldb ook.com. **Manuscript Acquisitions:** Paul A. Kobasa, editor-in-chief. **Art Acquisitions:** Sandra Dyrlund, art/ design manager. World Book, Inc. (publisher of *The World Book Encyclopedia*), publishes reference sources and nonfiction series for children and young adults in the areas of science, mathematics, English-language skills, basic academic and social skills, social studies, history, and health and fitness. We publish print and nonprint material appropriate for children ages 3-18. WB does not publish fiction, poetry, or wordless picture books.''

**Nonfiction** Young readers: animal, arts/crafts, careers, concept, geography, health, reference. Middle readers: animal, arts/crafts, careers, geography, health, history, hobbies, how-to, nature/environment, reference, science. Young adult: arts/crafts, careers, geography, health, history, hobbies, how-to, nature/environment, reference, science.

**How to Contact/Writers** Nonfiction: Submit outline/synopsis only; no mss. Responds to queries/mss in 2 months. Unsolicited mss will not be returned. Publishes a book 18 months after acceptance. Will consider simultaneous submissions.

**Illustration** Works with 10-30 illustrators/year. Illustrations only: Query with samples. Responds only if interested. Samples returned with SASE; samples filed ''if extra copies and if interested.''

**Photography** Buys stock and assigns work. Needs broad spectrum; editorial concept, specific natural, physical and social science spectrum. Model/property releases required; captions required. Uses color $8 \times 10$ glossy and matte prints, 35mm, $2^{1}/_{4} \times 2^{1}/_{4}$, $4 \times 5$, $8 \times 10$ transparencies. Submit cover letter, résumé, promo piece (color and b&w).

**Terms** Payment negotiated on project-by-project basis. Sends galleys to authors. Book catalog available for $9 \times 12$ SASE. Manuscript and art guidelines for SASE.

## ☐ THE WRIGHT GROUP/MCGRAW HILL

19201 120th Ave. NE, Suite 100, Bothell WA 98011. Fax: (800)543-7323. Website: www.wrightgroup.com. **Manuscripts Acquisitions:** Judy Sommer, vice president marketing. **Art Acquisitions:** Vicky Tripp, director of design. Publishes over 100 young readers/year, over 50 middle readers/year. ''The Wright Group is dedicated to improving literacy by providing outstanding tutorials for students and teachers.''

**Fiction** Picture books, young readers: adventure, animal, concept, contemporary, fantasy, folktales, hi-lo, history, humor, multicultural, nature/environment, poetry, sports, suspense/mystery. Middle readers: adventure, animal, contemporary, fantasy, folktales, hi-lo, history, humor, multicultural, nature/environment, poetry, problem novels. Average word length: young readers—50-5,000; middle readers—3,000-10,000. Recently published *Wild Crayons*, by Joy Cowley (young reader fantasy); *The Gold Dust Kids*, by Michell Dionetti (historical fiction chapter book for young readers); *Watching Josh*, by Deborah Eaton (middle reader, mystery).

**Nonfiction** Picture books, young readers, middle readers: animal, biography, careers, concept, geography, health, hi-lo, history, how-to, multicultural, nature/environment, science, sports. Average word length: young readers—50-3,000. Recently published *Iditarod*, by Joe Ramsey (young reader); *The Amazing Ant*, by Sara Sams (young reader); *Chameleons*, by Nic Bishop (young reader).

**How to Contact/Writers** Fiction/nonfiction: Submit complete ms or submit outline/synopsis and 3 sample chapters. Responds to queries in 1 month; mss in 5 months. Publishes a book 8 months after acceptance. Will consider previously published work.

**Illustration** Query with samples. Responds only if interested. Samples kept on file.

**Photography** Buys stock and assigns work. Model/property release and captions required. Uses $8^{1}/_{2} \times 11$ color prints. Submit published samples, promo pieces.

**Terms** Work purchased outright from authors ($500-2,400). Illustrators paid by the project. Photographers paid by the project ($3,500-5,000) or per photo ($300-350). Book catalog available online.

**Tips** ''Much of our illustration assignments are being done by offsite developers, so our level of commission in this area is minimal.''

# Canadian & International Book Publishers

W hile the United States is considered the largest market in children's publishing, the children's publishing world is by no means strictly dominated by the U.S. After all, the most prestigious children's book extravaganza in the world occurs each year in Bologna, Italy, at the Bologna Children's Book Fair and some of the world's most beloved characters were born in the United Kingdom (i.e., Winnie-the-Pooh and Mr. Potter).

In this section you'll find book publishers from English-speaking countries around the world from Canada to Australia and New Zealand to the United Kingdom. The listings in this section look just like the U.S. Book Publishers section; and the publishers listed are dedicated to the same goal—publishing great books for children.

Like always, be sure to study each listing and research each publisher carefully before submitting material. Determine whether a publisher is open to U.S. or international submissions, as many publishers accept submissions only from residents of their own country. Some publishers accept illustration samples from foreign artists, but do not accept manuscripts from foreign writers. Illustrators do have a slight edge in this category as many illustrators generate commissions from all around the globe. Visit publishers' websites to be certain they publish the sort of work you do. Visit online bookstores to see if publishers' books are available there. Write or e-mail to request catalogs and submission guidelines.

When mailing requests or submissions out of the United States, remember that U.S. postal stamps are useless on your SASE. Always include International Reply Coupons (IRCs) with your SAE. Each IRC is good for postage for one letter. So if you want the publisher to return your manuscript or send a catalog, be sure to enclose enough IRCs to pay the postage. For more help visit the United State Postal Service website at www.usps.com/global. Visit www.timeanddate.com/worldclock and American Computer Resources, Inc.'s International Calling Code Directory at www.the-acr.com/codes/cntrycd.htm before calling or faxing internationally to make sure you're calling at a reasonable time and using the correct numbers.

**Useful Websites**

As in the rest of *Children's Writer's & Illustrator's Market*, the maple leaf 🍁 symbol identifies Canadian markets. Look for the Canadian 🍁 and International 🌐 symbols throughout *Children's Writer's & Illustrator's Market* as well. Several of the Society of Children's Book Writers and Illustrator's (SCBWI) international conferences are listed in the Conferences & Workshops section along with other events in locations around the globe. Look for more information about SCBWI's international chapters on the organization's website, www.scbwi.org. You'll also find international listings in Magazines and Young Writer's & Illustrator's Markets. See Useful Online Resources on page 371 for sites that offer additional international information.

Information on Canadian and international book publishers listed in the previous edition but not included in this edition of *Children's Writer's & Illustrator's Market* may be found in the General Index.

### ALLEN & UNWIN

406 Albert St., East Melbourne VIC 3002 Australia. E-mail: frontdesk@allenandunwin.com. Website: www.allen andunwin.com. **Contact:** Children's Editor.

• Allen & Unwin was voted Publisher of the Year by Australian booksellers in 1992, 1996, 2001, 2002. They do not accept unsolicited picture book manuscripts.

**Fiction** Junior novels: For beginner readers ages 5-8, word length: 5,000-10,000; for confident readers ages 7-10, word length: 10,000-20,000. "Looking for fresh original storylines, strong engaging characters, a flair for language and an authentic voice." Inbetween novels: for middle readers ages 11-14, word length: 35,000-55,000. "Looking for great storytelling, popular or literary. Highly entertaining narratives avoiding heavy teenage issues preferred." Young adult novels: for teenage readers ages 13-16, word length: 40,000-60,000; for mature teenagers and older readers, ages 15+, word length: 40,000-100,000. "Need to be extremely well-written and engrossing. Looking for stories which are groundbreaking, challenging and experimental."

**Nonfiction** Considers nonfiction for children and teenagers "if it is imaginative, timely and authoritative."

**How to Contact/Writers** Fiction: Submit complete ms (5,000 words or more) and SASE "of suitable size." Nonfiction: Send proposal, detailed chapter outline and 3 sample chapters. Responds to mss in 4 months.

**Tips** "Do not send e-mail submissions."

### ANNICK PRESS LTD.

15 Patricia Ave., Toronto ON M2M 1H9 Canada. (416)221-4802. Fax: (416)221-8400. E-mail: annickpress@annic kpress.com. Website: www.annickpress.com. **Creative Director:** Sheryl Shapiro. Publishes 8 picture books/year; 3 young readers/year; 3 middle readers/year; 8 young adult titles/year. 25% of books by first-time authors. "Annick Press maintains a commitment to high-quality books that entertain and challenge. Our publications share fantasy and stimulate judgment and abilities."

• Annick Press does not accept unsolicited manuscripts.

**Fiction** No unsolicited mss. Recently published *The Mole Sisters and the Fairy Ring*, by Roslyn Schwartz (ages 2-4, picture book); *The Dirt Eaters*, by Dennis Foon (ages 11 and up, young adult novel); *Cabbagehead*, by Loris Lesynski (ages 4-8, illustrated poetry collection).

**Nonfiction** Recently published *Archers, Alchemists, and 98 other Medieval Jobs You Might Have Loved or Loathed*, by Priscilla Galloway, illustrated by Martha Newbigging (ages 8-12); *Escapes!*, by Laura Scandiffio, illustrated by Stephen MacEachern (ages 8 and up); *Made You Look: How Advertising Works and Why You Should Know*, by Shari Graydon, illustrated by Warren Clark (ages 8 and up).

**Illustration** Works with 20 illustrators/year. Illustrations only: Query with samples. Contact: Creative Director. Responds in 6 months with SASE. Samples returned with SASE or kept on file.

**Terms** Pays authors royalty of 5-12% based on retail price. Offers advances (average amount: $3,000). Pays illustrators royalty of 5% minimum. Originals returned to artist at job's completion. Book catalog available on website.

### BEACH HOLME PUBLISHERS

409 Granville St., Suite 1010, Vancouver BC V6J (V6C, NOT V6J) 1T2 Canada. (604)733-4868. (888)551-6655 (orders). Fax: (604)733-4860. E-mail: bhp@beachholme.bc.ca. Website: www.beachholme.bc.ca. Manuscript Acquisitions: Michael Carroll, publisher. Art Acquisitions: Michael Carroll. Publishes 5-6 young adult titles/year; 7-8 adult literary titles/year. 25% of books by first-time authors. "We publish primarily regional historical fiction. We publish young adult novels for children aged 8-13 and black-and-white illustrated chapter books for children aged 7-10). We are particularly interested in works that have a historical basis and are set in the Pacific Northwest, or northern Canada. Include ideas for teacher's guides or resources and appropriate topics for a classroom situation if applicable."

• Beach Holme only accepts work from Canadian writers.

**Fiction** Young adults: contemporary, folktales, history, multicultural, nature/environment, poetry. Multicultural needs include themes reflecting cultural heritage of the Pacific Northwest, i.e., first nations, Asian, East Indian, etc. Does not want to see generic adventure or mystery with no sense of place. Average word length: middle readers—15,000-20,000; young adults/teens—30,000-40,000. Recently published *Chasing the Arrow*, by Charles Reid (ages 9-13); *Death by Exposure*, by Eric Walters and Kevin Spreekmeester (ages 8-12); *Pomiuk, Prince of the North*, by Alica Walsh (ages 7-10).

**How to Contact/Writers** Fiction: Submit outline/synopsis and 3 sample chapters. Responds to queries/mss in 6 months. Publishes a book 6 months-1 year after acceptance. No electronic or multiple submissions.

**Illustration** Works with 4-5 Canadian illustrators/year. Responds to submissions in 2 months if interested. Samples returned with SASE; samples filed. Originals returned at job's completion. Works mainly with Canadian illustrators.

**Terms** Pays illustrators by the project (range: $500-1,000). Pays photographers by the project (range: $100-300). Sends galleys to authors.Book catalog available for 9×12 SAE and 3 first-class Canadian stamps; ms guidelines available online at website.

**Tips** "Research what we have previously published and view our website to familiarize yourself with what we are looking for. Please, be informed."

## ☒ BOARDWALK BOOKS

Imprint of The Dundurn Group, 8 Market St., Suite 200, Toronto ON M5E 1M6 Canada. (416)214-5544. Fax: (416)214-5556. E-mail: infol@dundurn.com. Website: www.dundurn.com. **Manuscript Acquisitions:** Barry Jowett. Boardwalk Books is the YA imprint of The Dundurn Group. Publishes 6 young adult titles/year. 25% of books by first-time authors. "We aim to publish sophisticated literary fiction for youths aged 12 to 16."

**Fiction** Young adults: contemporary, history, suspense/mystery. Average word length: young adults—40,000-45,000. Recently published *Sam's Light*, by Valerie Sherrard (ages 12-16, fiction), *Smoke and Mirrors*, by Lesley Choyce (ages 12-16, fiction), *Mercury Man*, by Tom Henighan (ages 12-16, fiction).

**How to Contact/Writers** Accepts material from residents of Canada only. Fiction: Submit outline/synopsis and 3 sample chapters (or approximately 50 pages). Responds to queries/mss in 3 months. Publishes book 1 year after acceptance. Will consider simultaneous submissions.

**Terms** Offers advances. Sends galleys to authors. Book catalog available for 9×12 SAE with sufficient Canadian postage or international coupon. All imprints included in a single catalog. Writer's guidelines available on website.

**Tips** "Be sure your submission suits our list. We do not accept picture books."

## ☒ BUSTER BOOKS

Imprint of Michael O'Mara Books, 9 Lion Yard, Tremadoc Rd., London SW4 7NQ United Kingdom. 020 7720 8643. Fax: 022 7819 5934. E-mail: busterbooks@michaelomarabooks.com. Website: www.mombooks.com/busterbooks. "We are dedicated to providing irresistible and fun books for children of all ages. We typically publish novelty books, sets of board books for preschoolers, and a variety of nonfiction for children ages 8-12."

**Nonfiction** Picture books, young readers, middle readers.

**How to Contact/Writers** Prefers synopsis and sample text over complete mss. Responds to queries/mss in 6 weeks. Will consider e-mail submissions.

**Tips** "Please do not submit fiction. We do not accept it." Visit website before submitting.

## ☒ ☒ CHILD'S PLAY (INTERNATIONAL) LTD.

Children's Play International, Ashworth Rd., Bridgemean, Swindon, Wiltshire SN5 7YD United Kingdom. 01793 616286. Fax: 01793 512795. E-mail: allday@childs-play.com. Website: www.childs-play.com. Estab. 1972. Specializes in nonfiction, fiction, educational material, multicultural material. **Manuscript Acquisitions:** Sue Baker, Neil Burden. **Art Acquisitions:** Annie Kubler, art director. Produces 30 picture books/year; 10 young readers/year; 2 middle readers/year. 20% of books by first-time authors. "A child's early years are more important than any other. This is when children learn most about the world around them and the language they need to survive and grow. Childn's Play aims to create exactly the right material for this all-important time."

**Fiction** Picture books: adventure, animal, concept, contemporary, folktales, multicultural, nature/environment. Young readers: adventure, animal, anthology, concept, contemporary, folktales, humor, multicultural, nature/environment, poetry. Average word length: picture books-0-1,500; young readers-2,000. Recently published *Goldilocks and the Three Bears*, by Estelle Corke (ages 3-6, fairy tale); *Tiger and the Wiseman*, by A. Fusek-Peters, illustrated by Diana Mayo (ages 4-8, traditional tale); *Twinkle Twinkle Little Star*, by A. Kubler (ages 0-3, nursery rhyme).

**Nonfiction** Picture books: activity books, animal, concept, multicultural, music/dance, nature/environment, science. Young readers: activity books, animal, concept, multicultural, music/dance, nature/environment, science. Average word length: picture books-2000; young readers-3000. Recently published *Proud Parents-Penguin*, by Pam Adams (ages 2-5, animal); *My First Signs*, by A. Kubler (ages 0-3, sign language for hearing babies); *Chameleon*, by R. Hatfield (ages 3-8, animal pop-up book).

**How to Contact/Writers** Accepts international submissions. Fiction/nonfiction: Query or submit complete ms. Responds to queries in 10 weeks; mss in 15 weeks. Publishes book 2 years after acceptance. Considers simultaneous submissions, electronic submissions.

**Illustration** Accepts material from international illustrators. Works with 10 illustrators/year. Uses color artwork only. Reviews ms/illustration packages. For ms/illustration packages: Query or submit ms/illustration packages to Sue Baker, editor. Reviews work for future assignments. If interested in illustrating future titles, query with samples, CD, website address. Submit samples to Annie Kubler, art director. Responds in 10 weeks. Samples not returned. Samples filed.

**Terms** Work purchased outright from authors (range: $500-15,000). Pays illustrators by the project (range: $500-15,000). Author sees galleys for review. Originals not returned. Catalog on website. Offers writer's, artist's guidelines for SASE.

**Tips** "Look at our website to see the kind of work we do before sending. Do not send cartoons. We do not publish novels. We do publish lots of books with pictures of babies/toddlers."

## COTEAU BOOKS LTD.

401-2206 Dewdney Ave., Regina SK S4R 1H3 Canada. (306)777-0170. E-mail: coteau@coteaubooks.com. Website: www.coteaubooks.com. **Acquisitions:** Barbara Sapergia, children's editor. Publishes 8-10 juvenile and/or young adult books/year; 18-20 books/year; 40% of books by first-time authors. "Coteau Books publishes the finest Canadian fiction, poetry, drama and children's literature, with an emphasis on western writers."

- Coteau Books publishes Canadian writers and illustrators only; manuscripts from the U.S. are returned unopened.

**Fiction** Young readers, middle readers, young adults: adventure, contemporary, fantasy, history, humor, multicultural, nature/environment, science fiction, suspense/mystery. "No didactic, message pieces, nothing religious. No picture books. Material should reflect the diversity of culture, race, religion, creed of humankind—we're looking for fairness and balance." Recently published *Peacekeepers*, by Dianne Linden (ages 10 and up); *The Star-Glass*, by Duncan Thornton (ages 10 and up); *The Innocent Polly McDoodle*, by Mary Woodbury (ages 9 and up).

**Nonfiction** Young readers, middle readers, young adult/teen: biography, history, multicultural, nature/environment, social issues.

**How to Contact/Writers** Fiction: Submit complete ms or sample chapters to acquisitions editor. Include SASE. Responds to queries/mss in 4 months. Publishes a book 1-2 years after acceptance.

**Illustration** Works with 1-4 illustrators/year. Illustrations only: Submit nonreturnable samples. Responds only if interested. Samples returned with SASE; samples filed.

**Photography** "Very occasionally buys photos from freelancers." Buys stock and assigns work.

**Terms** Pays authors royalty based on retail price. Pays illustrators and photographers by the project. Sends galleys to authors; dummies to illustrators. Original artwork returned at job's completion. Book catalog free on request with 9×12 SASE.

**Tips** "Truthfully, the work speaks for itself! Be bold. Be creative. Be persistent! There is room, at least in the Canadian market, for quality novels for children, and at Coteau, this is a direction we will continue to take."

## EMMA TREEHOUSE

Treehouse Children's Books, Little Orchard House, Mill Lane, Beckington, Somerset BA11 6SN United Kingdom. +44 (0)1373 831215. Fax: +44 (0)1373 831216. E-mail: sales@emmatreehouse.com. Website: www.emmatreehouse.com. Estab. 1992. Publishes mass market books, trade books. We are an independent book packager/producer. **Manuscript Acquisitions:** David Bailey, director. **Art Acqusitions** Richard Powell, creative director. Imprints: Treehouse Children's Books. Produces 100 young readers/year.

**Fiction** Picture books: adventure, animal, concept, folktales, humor.

**Nonfiction** Picture books: activity books, animal, concept.

**How to Contact/Writers** Only interested in agented material. Accepts international submissions. Fiction: Submit outline/synopsis. Nonfiction: Submit complete ms. Responds to queries in 3 weeks. No simultaneous, electronic, or previously published submissions.

**Illustration** Only interested in agented illustration submissions. Accepts material from international illustrators. Works with 10 illustrators/year. Uses color artwork only. Reviews ms/illustration packages. For ms/illustration packages: Send ms with dummy. Submit ms/illustration packages to Richard Powell, creative director. Reviews work for future assignments. If interested in illustrating future titles, arrange personal portfolio review. Submit samples to Richard Powell, creative director. Responds in 3 weeks. Samples returned with SASE. Samples not filed.

**Terms** Work purchased outright. Pays illustrators by the project. Illustrators see dummies for review. Catalog available for SASE. All imprints included in single catalog.

## FABER AND FABER

3 Queen Square, London WC1N 3AU United Kingdom. Website: www.faber.co.uk. **Contact:** The Editorial Department.

**Fiction** Recently published *Heir of Mystery*, by Philip Ardagh (ages 8-11, fiction); *Virtutopia*, by Russell Stannard (ages 12 and up); *Rocket Science*, by Jeanne Willis (ages 8-11).

**Nonfiction** Recently published *The Spy's Handbook*, by Herbie Brennan; *The Hieroglyph's Handbook*, by Philip Ardagh.

**How to Contact/Writers** Submit synopsis and 20 pages of sample text with SASE. Responds in 8-10 weeks.

**Tips** "Try to discern whether or not your work is suitable for our list by looking on our website or in bookshops at the types of books we publish. We do not, for example, publish in fields such as fantasy, science fiction, or photography, all of which we regularly receive."

## FENN PUBLISHING CO.

34 Nixon Rd., Bolton ON L7E-1W2 Canada. (905)951-6600. Fax: (905)951-6601. E-mail: fennpubs@hbfenn.com. Website: www.hbfenn.com. **Manuscript/Art Acquisitions:** C. Jordan Fenn, publisher. Publishes 35 books/year.

**Fiction** Picture books: adventure, animal, folktales, multicultural, religion, sports. Young readers: adventure, animal, folktales, multicultural, religion. Middle readers: adventure, animal, health, history, multicultural, religion, special needs, sports. Young adults: adventure, animal, contemporary, folktales, health, history, multicultural, nature/environment, religion, science fiction, sports.

**Nonfiction** Picture books, young readers, middle readers: activity books, animal, arts/crafts, geography, health, history, hobbies, how-to, multicultural, nature/environment, religion.

**How to Contact/Writers** Fiction/nonfiction: Query or submit complete ms. Responds to queries/mss in 2 months.

**Illustration** Reviews ms/illustration packages from artists. Responds only if interested. Samples not returned or filed.

## DAVID FICKLING BOOKS

Random House Children's Books, 31 Beamont St., Oxford OX1 2NP United Kingdom. (018)65-339000. Fax: (018)65-339009. E-mail: lsoar@randomhouse.co.uk. Publishes 12 fiction titles/year.

**Fiction** Considers all categories.

**How to Contact/Writers** Submit outline/synopsis and 3 sample chapters. Responds to mss in 2-3 months.

**Illustration** Reviews ms/illustration packages from artists. Illustrations only: query with samples.

**Photography** Submit cover letter, résumé, promo pieces.

## FITZHENRY & WHITESIDE LTD.

195 Allstate Pkwy., Markham ON L3R 4T8 Canada. (905)477-9700. Fax: (905)477-9179. E-mail: fitzkids@fitzhenry.ca. Website: www.fitzhenry.ca/. Book publisher. President: Sharon Fitzhenry; Children's Publisher: Gail Winskill; Nonfiction children's editor: Linda Biesenthal. Publishes 10 picture books/year; 5 early readers and early chapter books/year; 6 middle novels/year; 7 young adult titles/year. 10% of books by first-time authors. Publishes fiction and nonfiction—social studies, visual arts, biography, environment. Emphasis on Canadian authors and illustrators, subject or perspective.

**How to Contact/Writers** Fiction/nonfiction. Publishes a book 12-18 months after acceptance. Will consider simultaneous submissions.

**Illustration** Works with 15 illustrators/year. Reviews ms/illustration packages from artists. Submit outline and sample illustration (copy). Illustrations only: Query with samples and promo sheet. Responds in 3 months. Samples returned with SASE; samples filed if no SASE.

**Photography** Buys photos from freelancers. Buys stock and assigns work. Captions required. Uses b&w 8×10 prints; 35mm and 4×5 transparencies. Submit stock photo list and promo piece.

**Terms** Pays authors royalty of 10%. Offers "respectable" advances for picture books, 5% to author, 5% to illustrator. Pays illustrators by the project and royalty. Pays photographers per photo. Sends galleys to authors; dummies to illustrators.

**Tips** "We respond to quality."

## GROUNDWOOD BOOKS

720 Bathurst St., Suite 500, Toronto ON M5S 2R4 Canada. (416)537-2501. Fax: (416)537-4647. Website: www.groundwoodbooks.com. **Manuscript Acquisitions:** Acquisitions Editor. **Art Acquisitions:** Art Director. Publishes 10 picture books/year; 3 young readers/year; 5 middle readers/year; 5 young adult titles/year. 10% of books by first-time authors.

**Fiction** Recently published *Boy O'Boy*, by Brian Doyle (middle reader); *A Thief in the House of Memory*, by Tim Wynne-Jones (young adult); *Stella, Princess of the Sky*, by Marie-Louise Gay (picture book).

**How to Contact/Writers** Fiction: Submit synopsis and sample chapters. Responds to mss in 4-6 months. Will consider simultaneous submissions.

**Illustration** Works with 10-15 illustrators/year. Reviews ms/illustration packages from artists. Illustrations only: Send résumé, promo sheet, slides, color or b&w copies, and tearsheets. Responds only if interested. Samples not returned.

**Terms** Offers advances. Pays illustrators by the project for cover art; otherwise royalty. Sends galleys to authors; dummies to illustrators. Originals returned to artist at job's completion. Book catalog available for SASE. "Visit our website for guidelines." Backlist available on website.

**Tips** "Try to familiarize yourself with our list before submitting to judge whether or not your work is appropriate for Groundwood."

## HYPERION PRESS LIMITED

300 Wales Ave., Winnipeg MB R2M 2S9 Canada. (204)256-9204. Fax: (204)255-7845. E-mail: tamos@escape.ca. Website: www.escape.ca/~tamos. **Acquisitions:** Dr. M. Tutiah, editor. Publishes authentic-based, retold folktales/legends for ages 4-9. "We are interested in a good story that is well researched and how-to craft material."

**Fiction** Recently published *The Little Match Girl*, written and digitally illustrated by Helena Maria Stankiewicz; *Cossack Tales*, illustrated by Stefan Czernecki.

**Nonfiction** Recently published *Making Drums*, by Dennis Waring.

**How to Contact/Writers** Fiction/nonfiction: Query. Responds usually within 3 months.

**Illustration** Reviews ms/illustration packages from artists. Manuscript/illustration packages and illustration only: Query. Samples returned with SASE.

**Terms** Pays authors royalty. Pays illustrators by the project. Sends galleys to authors; dummies to illustrators. Book catalog available for SAE and $2 postage (Canadian).

## KEY PORTER BOOKS

6 Adelaide St. E, Toronto ON M5C 1H6 Canada. (416)862-7777. Fax: (416)862-2304. E-mail: info@keyporter.com. Website: www.keyporter.com. Book publisher. Publishes 4 picture books/year; 4 young readers/year. 30% of books by first-time authors. "Key Porter Books is the largest independent, 100% Canadian-owned trade publisher."

**Fiction** Picture books, young readers, middle readers, young adult: adventure, animal, anthology, fantasy, folktales, sports. Average word length: picture books—1,500; young readers—5,000. Recently published *The Goodfellows Chronicles, Book 1: The Sacred Seal, Book 2: The Messengers, Book 3: The Book of the Sage*, by J.C. Mills (young adult fiction); *Rosie in Los Angeles: Action!*, by Carol Matas (young adult); *Last Sam's Cage*, by David A. Poulson.

**Nonfiction** Picture books: animal, arts/crafts, cooking, geography, nature/environment, reference, science. Middle readers: animal, nature/environment, reference, science. Average word length: picture books—1,500; middle readers—15,000. Recently published *The Dinosaur Atlas*, by Don Lessem (ages 8-12); *So Cool*, by Dennis Lee; *Coyote's New Suit, by Thomas King; Bashful Bob and Doleful Dorinda*, by Margaret Atwood.

**How to Contact/Writers** Only interested in agented material; *no unsolicited mss.* "Although Key Porter Books does not review unsolicited manuscript submissions, we do try and review queries and proposals." Responds to queries/proposals in 6 months.

**Photography** Buys photos from freelancers. Buys stock and assigns work. Captions required. Uses 35mm transparencies. Submit cover letter, résumé, duplicate slides, stock photo list.

**Tips** "Please note that all proposals and accompanying materials will be discarded unless sufficient postage has been provided for their return. Please do not send any original artwork or other irreplaceable materials. We do not accept responsibility for any materials you submit."

## KIDS CAN PRESS

29 Birch Ave., Toronto ON M4V 1E2 Canada. (800)265-0884. E-mail: info@kidscan.com. Website: www.kidscanpress.com. **Manuscript Acquisitions:** Acquisitions Editor. **Art Acquisitions:** Art Director. Publishes 6-10 picture books/year; 10-15 young readers/year; 20-30 middle readers/year; 2-3 young adult titles/year. 10-15% of books by first-time authors.

• Kids Can Press is currently accepting unsolicited manuscripts from Canadian authors only.

**Fiction** Picture books, young readers: concept. All levels: adventure, animal, contemporary, fantasy, folktales, history, humor, multicultural, nature/environment, poetry, special needs, sports, suspense/mystery. Average word length: picture books—1,000-2,000; young readers—750-1,500; middle readers—10,000-15,000; young adults—over 15,000. Recently published *Suki's Kimono*, by Chieri Ugaki, illustrated by Stephane Jorlisch (picture book); *The Secret of Sagawa Lake*, by Mary Labatt (early novel-mystery); *Stanley's Party*, by Linda Bailey, illustrated by Bill Slavin.

**Nonfiction** Picture books: activity books, animal, arts/crafts, biography, careers, concept, health, history, hobbies, how-to, multicultural, nature/environment, science, social issues, special needs, sports. Young readers: activity books, animal, arts/crafts, biography, careers, concept, history, hobbies, how-to, multicultural. Middle readers: cooking, music/dance. Average word length: picture books—500-1,250; young readers—750-2,000; middle readers—5,000-15,000. Recently published *The Kids Winter Handbook*, by Jane Drake and Ann Love, illustrated by Heather Collins (informational activity); *Animals at Work*, by Etta Kaner, illustrated by Pat Stephens (animal/nature); *Quilting*, by Biz Storms, illustrated by June Bradford (craft book).

**How to Contact/Writers** Fiction/nonfiction: Submit outline/synopsis and 2-3 sample chapters. For picture books submit complete ms. Responds in 6 months. Publishes a book 18-24 months after acceptance.

**Illustration** Works with 40 illustrators/year. Reviews ms/illustration packages from artists. Send color copies of illustration portfolio, cover letter outlining other experience. Contact: Art Director. Illustrations only: Send tearsheets, color photocopies. Contact: Art Director, Kids Can Press, 2250 Military Rd., Tonawanda NY 14150. Responds only if interested. Samples returned with SASE; samples filed.

### 🌐 KOALA BOOKS

P.O. Box 626, Mascot NSW 1460 Australia. (61)02 9667-2997. Fax: (61)02 9667-2881. E-mail: admin@koalabooks.com.au. Website: www.koalabooks.com.au. **Manuscript Acquisitions:** Children's Editor. **Art Acquisitions:** Children's Designer, deb@koalabooks.com.au. "Koala Books is an independent wholly Australian-owned children's book publishing house. Our strength is providing quality books for children at competitive prices."

**Fiction** Picture books.

**Nonfiction** Looks for quirky nonfiction for younger readers.

**How to Contact/Writers** Accepts material from residents of Australia only. Fiction and picture books only: Submit complete ms, blurb, synopsis, brief author biography, list of author's published works. Also SASE large enough for ms return. Responds to mss in 3 months.

**Illustration** Accepts material from residents of Australia only. Illustrations only: Send cover letter, brief bio, list of published works and samples (color photographs or photocopies) in "an A4 folder suitable for filing." Contact: Children's Designer. Responds only if interested. Samples not returned; samples filed.

**Terms** Pays authors royalty of 10% based on retail price or work purchased outright occasionally (may be split with illustrator).

**Tips** "Take a look at our website to get an idea of the kinds of books we publish. A few hours research in a quality children's bookshop would be helpful when choosing a publisher."

### 📭 📖 LIGHTWAVE PUBLISHING

26275 98th Ave., Maple Ridge BC V2W 1K3 Canada. (604)462-7890. Fax: (604)462-8208. E-mail: mikal@lightwavepublishing.com. Website: www.lightwavepublishing.com. Estab. 1991. **Assistant:** Mikal Marrs. Independent book packager/producer specializing in Christian material. Publishes over 15 titles/year. "Our mission is helping parents pass on their Christian faith to their children."

**Fiction** Picture books: religion adventure, concept. Young readers: concept, religion. Middle readers: adventure, religion. Young adults: religion.

**Nonfiction** Picture books, young readers: activity books, concept, religion. Middle readers, young adults: concept, religion. Average word length: young readers—2,000; middle readers—20,000; young adults—30,000. Recently published *Focus On The Family's Guide to Spiritual Growth of Children*, edited by Osborne, Bruner, Trent.

**How to Contact/Writers** No longer accepts work-for-hire writers, queries or mss.

### 🌐 LION HUDSON PLC

(formerly Lion Publishing PLC), Mayfield House, 256 Banbury Rd., Oxford OX2 7DH England. (44)1865 302750. Fax: (44)1865 302757. E-mail: enquires@lionhudson.com. Website: www.lionhudson.com. Imprint: Lion Children's Books.

● Lion's children's fiction and poetry lists are limited to previously published authors.

**Fiction** Picture books, young readers, middle readers: concept, fantasy, folktales, religion (Christian). Middle readers: adventure. Recently published *The Wolf Who Cried Boy*, by Bob Hartman, illustrated by Tim Raglin (ages 5-8, picture books); *Telling the Sea*, by Pauline Fisk (ages 10-14); *The Life Shop*, by Margaret McAllister (ages 10-14); *Saint Nicholas*, by Mary Joslin.

**Nonfiction** Picture books, young readers, middle readers: religion (Christian). Recently published *The Story of the Cross*, by Mary Joslin, illustrated by Gail Newey (ages 4-8); *The Jesus Encyclopedia*, by Lois Rock (ages 7-12); *The Lion Book of Five-Minute Bible Stories*, by Lois Rock, illustrated by Richard Johnson (ages 4-8).

**How to Contact/Writers** Fiction/nonfiction: Submit outline/synopsis with cover letter (include background information, previously published work, qualifications and experience). Responds to queries in 3 months.

**Illustration** Accepts material from residents of England only. Manuscript/illustration packages should be submitted to Art Director at jacquic@lionhodson.com. Illustrations only: E-mail or query with samples. Responds only if interested. Samples not returned.

**Tips** "Online manuscript submissions are not accepted. We are not publishing fiction for teenagers. Please look through the Lion site. If the genre of book you have in mind does not appear on our site, then there is no point in submitting to us."

## ⊕ LITTLE TIGER PRESS

Imprint of Magi Publications, 1 The Coda Centre, 189 Munster Rd., London SW6 6AW United Kingdom. (44)20-7385 6333. Fax: (44)20 7385 7333. Website: www.littletigerpress.com. "Our aim is to create books that our readers will love as much as we do—helping them develop a passion for books that offer laughter, comfort, learning or exhilarating flights of the imagination!"

**Fiction** Picture books: animal, concept, contemporary, humor. Average word length: picture books—1,000 words or less. Recently published *Cuddly Cuffs*, by Lucy Richards (ages 0-3, cloth, chewable, washable books); *Quiet!*, by Paul Bright and Guy Parker-Rees (ages 3-7, picture book).

**Nonfiction** Picture books. Average word length: picture books—1,000 words or less.

**How to Contact/Writers** Fiction/nonfiction: Submit complete ms. Responds to queries/mss in 2 months.

**Illustration** Illustrations only: Query with samples (include SASE with IRCs). Do not send originals. Color photocopies are best. Responds only if interested. Samples returned with SASE.

**Tips** "Every reasonable care is taken of the manuscripts and samples we receive, but we cannot accept responsibility for any loss or damage. Try to read or look at as many books a publisher has published before sending in your material."

## ⊡ LOBSTER PRESS

1620 Sherbrooke St. W., Suites C&D, Montreal QC H3H 1C9 Canada . (514)904-1100. Fax: (514)904-1101. E-mail: editorial@lobsterpress.com. Website: www.lobsterpress.com. **Editorial Assistant:** Karen Li. Publishes 4 picture books/year; 4 young readers/year. "Driven by a desire to produce quality books that bring families together."

● Lobster Press is not currently accepting manuscripts or queries.

**Fiction** Picture books, young readers, middle readers, young adults: adventure, animal, contemporary, health, history, multicultural, nature/environment, special needs, sports, suspense/mystery. Average word length: picture books—200-1,000. Recently published *Penelope and the Monsters*, by Sheri Radford, illustrated by Christine Tripp (picture book); *Fighting the Current*, by Heather Waldorf (Young Adult novel).

**Nonfiction** Young readers, middle readers and adults/teens: animal, biography, Canadian history/culture, careers, geography, hobbies, how-to, multicultural, nature/environment, references, science, self-help, social issues, sports, travel. Average word length: middle readers—40,000. Recently published *A Bloom of Friendship: The Story of the Canadian Tulip Festival*, by Anne Renaud, illustrated by Ashley Spires; *What Color is Your Piggy Bank? Entrepreneurial Ideas for Self-Starting Kids*, by Adelia Cellini Linecker.

**How to Contact/Writers** "We are not accepting manuscripts at the moment. Please refer to our website for updates."

**Illustration** Works with 5 illustrators/year. Uses line drawings and color artwork. Reviews ms/illustration packages from artists. Query with samples. Illustrations only: query with samples. Samples not returned; samples kept on file.

**Terms** Pays authors 5-10% royalty based on retail price. Offers advances (average amount: $2,000-4,000). Pays illustrators by the project (range: $1,000-2,000) or 2-7% royalty based on retail price. Sends galleys to authors; dummies to illustrators. Originals returned to artist at job's completion. Writer's and artist's guidelines available on website.

**Tips** "Please do not call and ask for an appointment. We do not meet with anyone unless we are going to use their work."

## ⊕ MANTRA LINGUA

Global House, 303 Ballards Lane, London N12 8NP United Kingdom. (44)0208 445 5123. Website: www.mantralingua.com. **Manuscript Acquisitions:** Series Editor. Mantra Lingua "connects and transcends national differences in a way that is respectful and appreciative of local cultures."

● Mantra Lingua publishes books in English and more than 42 languages, including sign language. They are currently seeking myths and folklore for picture books only.

**Fiction** Picture books, young readers, middle readers: folktales, multicultural, myths. Average word length: picture books—1,000-1,500; young readers—1,000-1,500. Recently published *Beowulf—An Anglo-Saxon Epic*, retold by Henriette Barkow, illustrated by Alan Down (ages 9-13); *Jill and the Beanstalk*, by Manju Gregory (ages 3-8).

**How to Contact/Writers** Accepts material from residents of United Kingdom only. Fiction: Myths only. Submit outline/synopsis (250 words, describe myth, "where it is from, whether it's famous or unknown, and why it would make a great picture book.") Will consider e-mail submissions only.

**Illustration** Uses 2D animations for CD-ROMs. Query with samples. Responds only if interested. Samples not returned; samples filed.

## ⊕ ⊡ MILES KELLY PUBLISHING

The Bardfield Centre, Great Bardfield, Essex CM7 4SL 811309 United Kingdom. (44)1371 811309. Fax: (44)1731

811393. E-mail: info@mileskelly.net. Website: www.mileskelly.net. **Art Acquisitions:** Jim Miles, director. Publishes 6 picture books/year; 30-40 young readers/year; 40-50 middle readers/year; 3-6 young adult titles/year. Produces "top-quality illustration and design complementing sound and well-written information."
**How to Contact/Writers** Responds to queries in 2 weeks.
**Illustration** Works with 100 illustrators/year. Illustrations only. Contact: Jim Miles, director. Responds in 3 weeks only if interested.
**Terms** Pays authors by the word only. Pays Illustrators 30 minimum. Catalog available online.
**Tips** "Check our website first. Be aware that most UK publishers need international sales to make books viable—so appeal to international tastes."

## Ⓝⓐ MILET PUBLISHING LTD.

6 North End Parade, London W14 0SJ United Kingdom. +44 20 7603 5477. Fax: +44 20 7610 5475. E-mail:info@milet.co. Website: www.milet.com. Estab. 1995. Specializes in trade books, nonfiction, fiction, multicultural material. **Writers contact:** Editorial Director. **Illustrators contact:** Editorial Director. Produces 30+ picture books, 2 middle readers/year. "Milet publishes the leading list of bilingual children's books, featuring hundreds of popular and original titles in English with over 20 languages; a celebrated range of artistic, innovative and award-winning children's books in English; an outstanding, growing World Literature list, featuring works translated from Turkish; and a line of contemporary, definitive English-Turkish dictionaries. Milet is dedicated to introducing the work of innovative, international authors and artists—our children's books match fresh and bold artistic styles with meaningful and entertaining stories. Milet's bilingual children's books celebrate multiculturalism and multilingualism. With our bilingual books, bilingual and monolingual children alike can enjoy stories in English with languages like Albanian, Arabic, Bengali, Chinese, French, German, Kurdish, Russian, Somali, Spanish, Turkish, Urdu and Vietnamese."
**Fiction** Picture books: adventure, animal, concept, contemporary, hi-lo, humor, multicultural, poetry. Young readers: adventure, animal, concept, contemporary, fantasy, hi-lo, multicultural, nature/environment, poetry. Middle readers: adventure, animal, contemporary, fantasy, multicultural, nature/environment, poetry, problem novels. Young adults/teens: contemporary, fantasy, multicultural, nature/environment, poetry, problem novels. Recently published *Alphabet Poem*, by Michael Rosen and Herve Tullet (ages 3 and up, picture books); *Bella Balistaica and the Temple of Tikal*, by Adam Guillain (ages 8-12, novel).
**Nonfiction** All levels: activity books, animal, arts/crafts, concept, hi-lo, multicultural, nature/environment, social issues. Recently published *Milet Picture Dictionary*, by Sedat Turhan & Sally Hagin (in English and 18 bilingual editions).
**How to Contact/Writers** Accepts international submissions. Fiction/nonfiction: Submit outline/synopsis and 2-3 sample chapters. Responds to queries in 1 weeks; mss in 1-2 months. Publishes book 12-18 months after acceptance. Considers simultaneous submissions.
**Illustration** Accepts material from international illustrators. Works with 4-5 illustrators/year. Uses both color and b&w. Reviews ms/illustration packages. For ms/illustration packages: Submit ms with 2-3 pieces of final art. Reviews work for future assignments. If interested in illustrating future titles, send résumé, promo sheet, client list. Submit samples to Editorial Director. Samples returned with SASE.
**Terms** Authors paid all terms negotiated depending on type of project. Author sees galleys for review. Illustrators see dummies for review. Catalog on website. All imprints included in single catalog. See website for writer's, artist's guidelines.
**Tips** "Please check our list on our website to see if your work will be suitable. We are interested only in fresh, imaginative, non-traditional work."

## ⓜ MOOSE ENTERPRISE BOOK & THEATRE PLAY PUBLISHING

Imprint of Moose Hide Books, 684 Walls Rd., Sault Ste. Marie ON P6A 5K6 Canada. E-mail: mooseenterprises@on.aibn.com. **Manuscript Acquisitions:** Edmond Alcid. Publishes 2 middle readers/year; 2 young adult titles/year. 75% of books by first-time authors. Editorial philosophy: "To assist the new writers of moral standards."
  • This publisher does not offer payment for stories published in its anthologies and/or book collections. Be sure to send a SASE for guidelines.
**Fiction** Middle readers, young adults: adventure, fantasy, humor, suspense/mystery, story poetry. Recently published *Realm of the Golden Feather*, by C.R. Ginter (ages 12 and up, fantasy); *Tell Me a Story*, short story collection by various authors (ages 9-11, humor/adventure); *Spirits of Lost Lake*, by James Walters (ages 12 and up, adventure).
**Nonfiction** Middle readers, young adults: biography, history, multicultural.
**How to Contact/Writers** Fiction/nonfiction: Query. Responds to queries in 1 month; mss in 3 months. Publishes book 1 year after acceptance. Will consider simultaneous submissions.
**Illustration** Uses primarily b&w artwork. Illustrations only: Query with samples. Responds in 1 month, if interested. Samples returned with SASE; samples filed.

**Terms** Originals returned to artist at job's completion. Manuscript and art guidelines available for SASE.

**Tips** "Do not copy trends, be yourself, give me something new, something different."

## NOVALIS

Imprint of Saint Paul University, 223 Main Street, Ottawa ON K15 1C4 Canada. (613)782-3039. Fax: (613)751-4020. E-mail: kburns@ustpaul.ca. Website: www.novalis.ca. **Manuscript Acquisitions:** Kevin Burns. Publishes 1 picture book/year; 1 young reader/year; 1 middle reader/year; 1 young adult title/year. 15% of books by first-time authors.

**Nonfiction** Picture books, young readers: biography, religion. Middle readers, young adults: biography, religion, social issues. Recently published *The Wonderful Story of Christmas*, by Claude Lafortune;*The Adventures of Fergie the Frog*, by Nancy Cocks, illustrated by Jirina Marton.

**How to Contact/Writers** Nonfiction: Submit outline/synopsis and 2 sample chapters. Responds to queries in 1 month; mss in 2 months. Publishes book 12-18 months after acceptance. Will consider e-mail submissions, simultaneous submissions.

**Illustration** Works with in-house and up to 3 illustrators/year. Reviews ms/illustration packages from artists. Submit ms with representative selection of final art. Contact: Kevin Burns, commissioning editor. Illustrations only: Query with samples, SASE, résumé. Responds in 3 weeks. Samples returned with SASE (use International Reply Coupons from your national postal service mailing from outside of Canada; samples not filed.

**Photography** Buys stock and occasionally assigns work. Model/property releases required; captions required.

**Terms** Pays authors royalty of 10% based on retail price. Offers advances (amount negotiated). Pays illustrators by the project (fees negotiated). Pays photographers per photo (fee negotiated). Sends galleys to authors. Originals returned to artist at job's completion. Book catalog available at no cost; ms guidelines available for SASE. All imprints included in a single catalog.

## ORCA BOOK PUBLISHERS

1016 Balmoral St., Victoria BC V8T 1A8 Canada. (250)380-1229. Fax: (250)380-1892. Website: www.orcabook.com. **Acquisitions:** Maggie deVries, children's book editor (young readers); Andrew Woolridge, editor (Orca Soundings); Bob Tyrrell, editor (teen fiction). Publishes 7 picture books/year; 16 middle readers/year; 10 young adult titles/year. 25% of books by first-time authors.

• Orca only considers authors who are Canadian or who live in Canada.

**Fiction** Picture books: animals, contemporary, history, nature/environment. Middle readers: contemporary, history, fantasy, nature/environment, problem novels. Young adults: adventure, contemporary, hi-lo (Orca Soundings), history, multicultural, nature/environment, problem novels, suspense/mystery. Average word length: picture books—500-1,500; middle readers—20,000-35,000; young adult—25,000-45,000; Orca Soundings—13,000-15,000. Published *Tall in the Saddle*, by Anne Carter, illustrated by David McPhail (ages 4-8, picture book); *Me and Mr. Mah*, by Andrea Spalding, illustrated by Janet Wilson (ages 5 and up, picture book); *Alone at Ninety Foot*, by Katherine Holubitsky (young adult).

**How to Contact/Writers** Fiction: Submit complete ms if picture book; submit outline/synopsis and 3 sample chapters. "All queries or unsolicited submissions should be accompanied by a SASE." Responds to queries in 2 months; mss in 3 months. Publishes a book 18-36 months after acceptance. Submission guidelines available online.

**Illustration** Works with 8-10 illustrators/year. Reviews ms/illustration packages from artists. Submit ms with 3-4 pieces of final art. "Reproductions only, no original art please." Illustrations only: Query with samples; provide résumé, slides. Responds in 2 months. Samples returned with SASE; samples filed.

**Terms** Pays authors royalty of 5% for picture books, 10% for novels, based on retail price. Offers advances (average amount: $2,000). Pays illustrators royalty of 5% minimum based on retail price and advance on royalty. Sends galleys to authors. Original artwork returned at job's completion if picture books. Book catalog available for legal or 8½×11 SAE and $2 first-class postage. Manuscript guidelines available for SASE. Art guidelines not available.

**Tips** "We are not seeking seasonal stories, board books, or 'I Can Read' Books. Orca Sounding line offers high interest teen novels aimed at reluctant readers. The story should reflect the universal struggles young people face, but need not be limited to 'gritty' urban tales. Can include adventure, mystery/suspense, fantasy, etc. There's a definite need for humorous stories that appeal to boys and girls. Protagonists are between 14 and 17 years old."

## PICCADILLY PRESS

5 Castle Rd., London NW1 8PR United Kingdom. (44)20 7267 4492. Fax: (44)20 7267 4493. E-mail: books@piccadillypress.co.uk. Website: www.piccadillypress.co.uk.

**Fiction** Picture books: animal, contemporary, fantasy, nature/environment. Young adults: contemporary, humor, problem novels. Average word length: picture books—500-1,000; young adults—25,000-35,000. Recently published *Soul Love*, by Lynda Waterhouse (young adult); *Mates, Dates and Great Escapes*, by Cathy Hopkins (young adult); *Hamish and the Missing Teddy*, by Moira Munro (picture book).

**Nonfiction** Young adults: self help (humorous). Average word length: young adults—25,000-35,000. Recently published *Don't Blame Me, I'm a Gemini!*, by Reina James Reinstein & Mike Reinstein.

**How to Contact/Writers** Fiction: Submit complete ms for picture books or submit outline/synopsis and 2 sample chapters for YA. Enclose a brief cover letter and SASE for reply. Nonfiction: Submit outline/synopsis and 2 sample chapters. Responds to mss in approximately 6 weeks.

**Illustration** Illustrations only: Query with samples (do not send originals).

**Tips** "Keep a copy of your manuscript on file."

### 🌐 PIPERS' ASH LTD.

Church Rd., Christian Malford, Chippenham Wiltshire SN15 4BW United Kingdom. (44)1249 720563. Fax: (44)8700 568916. E-mail: pipersash@supamasu.com. Website: www.supamasu.com. **Manuscript Acquisitions :** Manuscript Evaluation Desk. Publishes 1 middle reader/year; 2 young adult titles/year. 90% of books by first-time authors. Editorial philosophy is "to discover new authors with talent and potential."

**Fiction** Young readers, middle readers: adventure. Young adults: problem novels. Average word length: young readers—10,000; middle readers—20,000; young adults—30,000. Visit website or send for catalog for published titles.

**Nonfiction** Young readers: history, multicultural, nature/environment. Middle readers: biography, history, multicultural, nature/environment, sports. Young adults: self help, social issues, special needs. Average word length: young readers—10,000; middle readers—20,000; young adults—30,000.

**How to Contact/Writers** Fiction/nonfiction: Query. Responds to queries in 1 week; mss in 3 months. Publishes book 2 months after acceptance. Will consider e-mail submissions, previously published work.

**Terms** Pays authors royalty of 10% based on wholesale price. Sends galleys to authors. Book catalog available for A5 SASE. Offers ms guidelines for SASE. "Include adequate postage for return of manuscript plus publisher's guidelines."

**Tips** "Visit our website —note categories open to writers and word link to pages of su bmission guidelines."

### 🌐 MATHEW PRICE LTD.

The Old Glove Factory, Bristol Rd., Sherborne Dorset DT9 4HP United Kingdom. (44)19 35 81-6010. Fax: (44)19 35 81-6310. E-mail: mathewp@mathewprice.com. Website: www.mathewprice.com. **Manuscript Acquisitions:** Mathew Price, chairman. Publishes 10 picture books/year; 2 young readers/year; 3 novelties/year; 4 board books/ year ; 3 gift books/year. "Mathew Price Ltd. works to bring to market talented authors and artists profitably by publishing books for children that lift the hearts of people young and old all over the world."

**Fiction/Nonfiction** Will consider any category.

**Illustration** Accepts material from artists in other countries. Uses color artwork only. Reviews ms/illustration packages from artists. Send ms with dummy or submit ms with 2 pieces of final art. Will review the work of illustrators interested in receiving future assignments.

**Terms** Originals returned to artist at job's completion. Book catalog available. All imprints included in a single catalog. Catalog available on website.

**Tips** "Study the market, keep a copy of all your work, and include a SAE if you want materials returned."

### Ⓝ 🌐 QED PUBLISHING

Quarto, 226 City Road, London EC1V 2TT United Kingdom. +44 (0)20 7812 8631. Fax: +44 (0)20 7253 4370. E-mail: stevee@quarto.com. Website: www.quarto.com. Estab. 2003. Specializes in trade books, educational material, multicultural material. **Manuscripts Acquisitions:** Steve Evans, publisher. **Art Acquisitions:** Steve Evans, publisher. Produces 12 picture books/year; 20 young readers/year. Strives for "editorial excellence with ground-breaking design."

**Fiction** Average word length: picture books—500; young readers—3,000; middle readers—3,500. Recently published *Said Mouse to Mole*, by Clare Bevan, illustrated by Sanja Resacek (ages 4 and up); *Lenny's Lost Spots*, by Caia Warren, illustrated by Genny Maines (ages 2 and up); *Stroke the Cat*, by Wes Magee, illustrated by Pauline Jiewert (ages 5 and up, poetry).

**Nonfiction** Picture books: animal, arts/crafts, biography, geography, reference, science. Young readers: activity books, animal, arts/crafts, biography, geography, reference, science. Middle readers: activity books, animal, arts/crafts, biography, geography, science. Average word length: picture books—500; young readers—3,000; middle readers—3,500. Recently published *You and Your Pa Kitten*, by Jean Coppendale (ages 7 and up, animal); *Travel Through India*, by Elaine Jackson (ages 7 and up, geography); *Cartooning*, by Dori Roberts (ages 7 and up, art).

**How to Contact/Writers** Fiction/nonfiction: Query.

**Illustration** Accepts material from international illustrators. Works with 25 illustrators/year. For ms/illustration packages: Submit ms with 2 pieces of final art. Submit ms/illustration packages to Louise Morley, creative director. Reviews work for future assignments. Submit samples to Louise Morley, creative director. Responds in 2 weeks. Samples filed.

**Photography** Buys stock images and assigns work. Submit photos to: Louise Morley, creative director. Uses step-by-step photos. For first contact, send CD of work.

**Tips** ''Be persistent.''

## ⊕ ☐ ▭ QUARTZ EDITIONS

Premier House, 112 Station Rd., Edgware, Middlesex HA8 7BJ United Kingdom. (44)208 951 5656. Fax: (44)208 381 2588. E-mail: quartzeditions@btconnect.com. **Manuscript/Art Acquisitions:** Susan Pinkus, managing director. Publishes more than 20 titles/year, but varies. ''We aim to produce high-quality, lavishly illustrated titles for the international market, including translated editions for many countries—viz. France, Mexico, Russia, China, Japan, etc.''

**Fiction** Picture books: adventure, animal, fantasy, folktales, humor. Young readers, middle readers: adventure, animal, fantasy, folktales, humor, suspense/mystery. Young adults: adventure, animal, fantasy, folktales, humor, suspense/mystery, teen romance. Average word length: varies. Recently published *The Haunted School*, by C. Rose, illustrated by M. Dorey (ages 8-12).

**Nonfiction** Picture books, young readers, middle readers, young adults: animal, careers, geography, health, history, how-to, nature/environment, religion, science, textbooks. Recently published *Insects* (8 titles), by T. Green (ages 9-14).

**How to Contact/Writers** Fiction/nonfiction: Submit complete ms. Responds to queries/mss in 1 month. Will consider simultaneous submissions.

**Illustration** Works with 6-10 illustrators/year. Reviews ms/illustration packages from artists. Submit ms/illustration package as complete as possible. Illustration only: send résumé, client list, tearsheets. Responds in 1 month. Samples filed.

**Photography** Buys stock and assigns work. Uses mostly natural history. Model/property releases required; captions required. Uses color prints and transparencies. Submit cover letter, résumé, published samples, client list, stock photo list.

**Terms** Work purchased outright from authors. Pays illustrators by the project. Pays photographers by the project. Book catalog available for 10×8 SASE. All imprints included in a single catalog.

**Tips** ''All submissions must be accompanied by stamped addressed envelope/packaging for return; otherwise no responsibility accepted. Please relate nonfiction titles to school curriculum as far as possible. Please do not send us the only copy of your manuscript. All manuscripts must be typed with double spacing.''

## ▚ RAINCOAST BOOKS

9050 Shaughnessy St., Vancouver BC V6P 6E5 Canada. (604)323-7100. Fax: (604)323-2600. E-mail: info@raincoast.com. Website: www.raincoast.com. **Manuscript Acquisitions:** Editorial Department. Imprints: Polestar, Press Gang. Publishes 4 picture books/year; 4 young adult titles/year

- Raincoast Books does not accept unsolicited manuscripts or e-mail queries. They accept material from Canadian residents only.

**Fiction** Picture books, young readers, young adults: contemporary, history. Recently published *Chimp and Zee and the Big Storm*, by Catherine and Laurence Anholt (picture book); *The Song within My Heart*, by David Bouchard, paintings by Allen Sapp (picture book); *Tess*, by Jocelyn Reekie (juvenile fiction).

**Nonfiction** Picture books, young readers: science, sports, natural history. Recently published *Albertosaurus Death of a Predator*, by Monique Keiran; *A Young Dancer's Apprenticeship*, by Olympia Dowd.

**How to Contact/Writers** Fiction/nonfiction: query letter with ''details about the work including word count, subject matter and your publication history for picture books and young readers.'' For young adult fiction submit query letter with list of publication credits plus 1-page outline of the plot. Responds to queries in 4 months. Will consider simultaneous submissions (indicate in query letter).

**Illustration** Illustrations only: Query with samples; ''no more than 10, nonreturnable color photocopies. Do not send original artwork or slides. Submit new samples to us as they become available.'' Contact: Creative Director. Responds only if interested. Samples not returned.

**Terms** Book catalog available online.

**Tips** ''For older (teen readers) we're looking for subject matter that pushes the boundaries a little. For children's illustrative work, we are interested in illustrators who can successfully convey an artistic, painterly, whimsical style. Please refer to our catalogue for examples.''

## ⊕ RANDOM HOUSE CHILDREN'S BOOKS

61-63 Uxbridge Rd., London W5 5SA England. (0208)231-6000. Fax: (0208)231-6737. E-mail: enquiries@randomhouse.co.uk. Website: www.kidsatrandomhouse.co.uk. Book publisher. **Manuscript Acquisitions:** Philippa

Dickinson, managing director. Imprints: Doubleday, Corgi Pups (ages 5-8), Young Corgi (ages 6-9), Corgi Yearling (ages 8-11), Corgi (ages 10 and up). Publishes 120 picture books/year; 120 fiction titles/year.

**Fiction** Picture books: adventure, animal, anthology, contemporary, fantasy, folktales, humor, multicultural, nature/environment, poetry, suspense/mystery. Young readers: adventure, animal, anthology, contemporary, fantasy, folktales, humor, multicultural, nature/environment, poetry, sports, suspense/mystery. Middle readers: adventure, animal, anthology, contemporary, fantasy, folktales, humor, multicultural, nature/environment, problem novels, romance, sports, suspense/mystery. Young adults: adventure, contemporary, fantasy, humor, multicultural, nature/environment, problem novels, romance, science fiction, suspense/mystery. Average word length: picture books—800; young readers—1,500-6,000; middle readers—10,000-15,000; young adults—20,000-45,000.

**How to Contact/Writers** Strongly prefers agented material. Accepts submissions addressed to Editorial Department of specific imprints.

**Illustration** Works with 50 illustrators/year. Reviews ms/illustration packages from artists. Submit ms with dummy. Contact: Penny Walker. Illustrations only: Query with samples. Responds in 12 weeks. Samples are returned with SASE (IRC).

**Photography** Buys photos from freelancers. Contact: Tracey Hurst, art department. Buys stock images. Photo captions required. Uses color or b&w prints. Submit cover letter, published samples.

**Terms** Pays authors royalty. Offers advances. Pays illustrators by the project or royalty. Pays photographers by the project or per photo.

**Tips** "Although Random House is a big publisher, each imprint only publishes a small number of books each year. Our lists for the next few years are already full. Any book we take on from a previously unpublished author has to be truly exceptional, so we strongly prefer to consider manuscripts sent to us by literary agents."

### RED DEER PRESS

Rm. 813, MacKimmie Library Tower, 2500 University Dr. NW, Calgary AB T2N 1N4 Canada. (403)220-4334. Fax: (403)210-8191. E-mail: rdp@ucalgary.ca. Website: www.reddeerpress.com. **Manuscript/Art Acquisitions:** Peter Carver, children's editor. Publishes 3 picture books/year; 4 young adult titles/year. 20% of books by first-time authors. Red Deer Press is known for their "high-quality international children's program that tackles risky and/or serious issues for kids."

• Red Deer only publishes books written and illustrated by Canadians and books that are about or of interest to Canadians.

**Fiction** Picture books, young readers: adventure, contemporary, fantasy, folktales, history, humor, multicultural, nature/environment, poetry. Middle readers, young adult/teens: adventure, contemporary, fantasy, folktales, hi-lo, history, humor, multicultural, nature/environment, problem novels, suspense/mystery. Recently published *Courage to Fly*, by Troon Harrison, illustrated by Zhong-Yang Huung (ages 4-7, picture book); *Amber Waiting*, by Nan Gregory, illustrated by Macdonald Denton (ages 4-7, picture book); *Tom Finder*, by Martine Leavitt (ages 14 and up).

**How to Contact/Writers** Fiction/nonfiction: Query or submit outline/synopsis. Responds to queries in 6 months; mss in 8 months. Publishes a book 18 months after acceptance. Will consider simultaneous submissions.

**Illustration** Works with 4-6 illustrators/year. Illustrations only: Query with samples. Responds only if interested. Samples not returned; samples filed for six months. Canadian illustrators only.

**Photography** Buys stock and assigns work. Model/property releases required. Submit cover letter, résumé and color promo piece.

**Terms** Pays authors royalty (negotiated). Occasionally offers advances (negotiated). Pays illustrators and photographers by the project or royalty (depends on the project). Sends galleys to authors. Originals returned to artist at job's completion. Guidelines not available.

**Tips** "Our publishing program is full for the next several years in the children's picture book, juvenile and teen fiction categories, thus we are only accepting manuscripts with exceptional potential. Writers, illustrators, and photographers should familiarize themselves with Red Deer Press's children's publishing program."

### RONSDALE PRESS

3350 W. 21st Ave., Vancouver BC V6S 1G7 Canada. (604)738-4688. Fax: (604)731-4548. E-mail: ronhatch@pinc.com. Website: ronsdalepress.com. Estab. 1988. Book publisher. **Manuscript/Art Acquisitions:** Veronica Hatch, children's editor. Publishes 2 children's books/year. 40% of titles by first-time authors. "Ronsdale Press is a Canadian literary publishing house that publishes 8-10 books each year, two of which are children's titles. Of particular interest are books involving children exploring and discovering new aspects of Canadian history."

**Fiction** Young adults: Canadian historical novels. Average word length: middle readers and young adults—50,000. Recently published *Adrift In Time*, by John Wilson (ages 9-14); *The Tenth Pupil*, by Constance Horne (ages 9-14); *Beginnings*, edited by Ann Walsh (anthology of short stories, ages 9 and up); *Eyewitness*, by Margaret Thompson (ages 8-14); *Hurricanes over London*, by Charles Reid (ages 8-14).

**Nonfiction** Middle readers, young adults: animal, biography, history, multicultural, social issues. Average word length: young readers—90; middle readers—90.

**How to Contact/Writers** Accepts material from residents of Canada only. Fiction/nonfiction: Submit complete ms. Responds to queries in 2 weeks; mss in 2 months. Publishes a book 1 year after acceptance. Will consider simultaneous submissions.

**Illustrations** Works with 2 illustrators/year. Reviews ms/illustration packages from artists. Requires only cover art. Responds in 2 weeks. Samples returned with SASE. Originals returned to artist at job's completion.

**Terms** Pays authors royalty of 10% based on retail price. Pays illustrators by the project $800-1,200. Sends galleys to authors. Book catalog available for 8½×11 SAE and $1 postage; ms and art guidelines available for SASE.

**Tips** "Ronsdale Press publishes well-written books that have a new slant on things and that can take an age-old story and give it a new spin. We are particularly interested in novels for young adults with a historical component that offers new insights into a part of Canada's history. We publish only Canadian authors."

## 🌐 SCHOLASTIC AUSTRALIA

Scholastic Press and Margaret Hamilton Books, P.O. Box 579, Lindfield NSW 2070 Australia. Website: www.sch olastic.com.au. **Manuscript Acquisitions:** Megan Fauvet, publishing secretary, Scholastic Press and Margaret Hamilton Books; Dyan Blacklock, publisher Omnibus Books. **Art Acquisitions:** Megan Fauvet, publishing secretary, Scholastic Press and Margaret Hamilton Books; Dyan Blacklock, publisher, Omnibus Books. Imprints: Scholastic Press (Margrete Lamond, acquisitions editor); Margaret Hamilton Books (Margrete Lamond, acquisitions editor); Omnibus Books (Dyan Bladdock). "Communicating with children around the world."

• Scholastic Australia accepts material from residents of Australia only.

**Fiction** Picture books, young readers. Recently published *After Alice*, by Jane Carroll (ages 8-12, fiction); *Amelia Ellicott's Garden*, by Lilianna Stafford, illustrated by Stephen Michael King (ages 5-7, picture book); *An Ordinary Day*, by Libby Gleeson, illustrated by Armin Greder (ages 5-15, picture book).

**Nonfiction** Omnibus and Scholastic Press will consider nonfiction. Recently published *Bass and Flinders*, by Cathy Dodson, illustrated by Roland Harvey (ages 9-12, history); *The Cartoon Faces Book*, by Robert Ainsworth (ages 7-14, art & craft); *Excuse Me, Captain Cook, Who Did Discover Australia?*, by Michael Salmon (ages 7-12, history).

**How to Contact/Writers** Fiction/nonfiction: Submit complete ms. For picture books, submit only ms, no art. Responds to mss in 2 months.

**Illustration** Illustrations only: Send portfolio. Contact appropriate office for more information on what to include with portfolio.

**Tips** "Scholastic Australia publishes books for children under three publishing imprints—Scholastic Press, Omnibus Books and Margaret Hamilton Books. To get a more specific idea of the flavor of each list, you will need to visit your local bookstore. Don't be too surprised or disappointed if your first attempts are not successful. Children's book publishing is a highly competitive field, and writing children's books is not quite as easy as some might imagine. But we are always ready to find the next Harry Potter or Paddington Bear, so if you believe you can write it, we're ready to hear from you."

## 🔲 SCHOLASTIC CANADA LTD.

175 Hillmount Rd., Markham ON L6C 1Z7 Canada. (905)887-READ. Fax: (905)887-1131. Website: www.scholas tic.ca; for ms/artist guidelines: www.scholastic.ca/guideline.html. **Acquisitions:** Editor, children's books. Publishes hardcover and trade paperback originals. Imprints: Scholastic Canada; North Winds Press; Les Editions Scholastic. Publishes 30 titles/year; imprint publishes 4 titles/year. 3% of books from first-time authors; 50% from unagented writers. Canadian authors, theme or setting required.

• At presstime Scholastic Canada was not accepting unsolicited manuscripts. For up-to-date information on their current submission policy, call their publishing status line at (905)887-7323, ext. 4308 or view their submission guidelines on their website.

**Fiction** Picture books, young readers, young adult. Average word length: picture books—under 1,000; young readers—7,000-10,000; young adult—25,000-40,000. Recently published *Dear Canada: With Nothing but Our Courage*, by Karleen Bradford (ages 9 and up); *After the War*, by Carol Matas (novel).

**Nonfiction** Animals, biography, history, hobbies, nature, recreation, science, sports. Reviews artwork/photos as part of ms package. Send photocopies. Recently published *Whose Bright Idea Was It?*, by Larry Verstraete (about amazing inventions).

**How to Contact/Writers** Query with synopsis, 3 sample chapters and SASE. Nonfiction: Query with outline, 1-2 sample chapters and SASE (IRC or Canadian stamps only). Responds in 3 months. Publishes book 1 year after acceptance.

**Illustration** Illustrations only: Query with samples; send résumé. Never send originals. Contact: Ms. Yuksel Hassan.
**Terms** Pays authors royalty of 5-10% based on retail price. Offers advances (range: $1,000-5,000, Canadian). Book catalog for 8½×11 SAE with $2.05 postage stamps (IRC or Canadian stamps only).

### 🌐 SCHOLASTIC CHILDREN'S BOOKS UK

1-19 New Oxford St., London WC1A 1NU United Kingdom. Website: www.scholastic.co.uk. **Manuscript Acquisitions:** The Editorial Department.
**Fiction** Recently published *Dudley Top Dog*, by Jo Davies; *Partytime*, by Maureen Roffey; *Catch*, by Trish Cooke.
  • Scholastic UK accepts material from residents of United Kingdom only.
**Nonfiction** Recently published *My Story: Waterloo*, by Bryan Perrett; *Pickle Hill Primary: Miss Niles Mummy Lessons*, by Alan MacDonald; *Horrible Histories: Ruthless Romans*, by Terry Deary.
**How to Contact/Writers** Fiction/nonfiction: Query or submit complete ms and SASE. Responds to queries/mss in 6 months.
**Tip** "Do not be depressed if your work is not accepted. Getting work published can be a frustrating process, and it's often best to be prepared for disappointment."

### 📛 SECOND STORY PRESS

20 Maud St., Suite 401, Toronto ON M5V 2M5 Canada. (416)537-7850. Fax: (416)537-0588. E-mail: info@secondstorypress.ca. Website: www.secondstorypress.on.ca.
**Fiction** Considers nonsexist, nonracist, and nonviolent stories, as well as historical fiction, chapter books, picture books. Recently published *Mom and Mum Are Getting Married!*, by Ken Setterington.
**Nonfiction** Picture books: biography. Recently published *The Underground Reporters: A True Story*, by Kathy Kacer (a new addition to our holocause remembrance series for young readers).
**How to Contact/Writers** Accepts appropriate material from residents of Canada only. Fiction and nonfiction: Submit complete ms or submit outline and sample chapters by postal mail only. No electronic submissions or queries.

### 🌐 TAFELBERG PUBLISHERS

Imprint of NB Publishers, 40 Heerengracht, Cape Town, Western Cape 8001 South Africa. (+27) (21)406-3033. Fax: (+27) (21)406-3812. E-mail: lsteyn@tafelberg.com. Website: www.tafelberg.com. **Manuscript Acquisitions:** Louise Steyn, publisher. Publishes 3 picture books/year; 2 young readers/year; 2 middle readers/year; 4 young adult titles/year. 40% of books by first-time authors.
**Fiction** Picture books, young readers: animal, anthology, contemporary, fantasy, folktales, hi-lo, humor, multicultural, nature/environment, scient fiction, special needs. Middle readers, young adults: animal (middle reader only), contemporary, fantasy, hi-lo, humor, multicultural, nature/environment, problem novels, science fiction, special needs, sports, suspense/mystery. Average word length: picture books—1,500-7,500; young readers—25,000; middle readers—15,000; young adults—40,000. Recently published *Because Pula Means Rain*, by Jenny Robson (ages 12-15, realism); *Die Geel Komplot*, by George Weidenau (ages 8-11, fantasy); *Welcome to the Martin Tudhope Show*, by Sarah Britten (ages 12-15, realism/humor).
**How to Contact/Writers** Fiction: Query or submit complete ms. Responds to queries in 2 weeks; mss in 2-6 months. Publishes book 1 year after acceptance. Will consider e-mail submissions.
**Illustration** Works with 2-3 illustrators/year. Reviews ms/illustration packages from artists. Send ms with dummy or e-mail and jpegs. Contact: Louise Steyn, publisher. Illustrations only: Query with brochure, photocopies, résumé, URL, JPEGs. Responds only if interested. Samples not returned.
**Terms** Pays authors royalty of 15-18% based on wholesale price. Pays illustrators by the project or royalty of 7½% based on wholesale price. Sends galleys to authors. Originals returned to artist at job's completion.
**Tips** "Writers: Story needs to have a South African or African style. Illustrators: I'd like to look, but the chances of getting commissioned are slim. The market is small and difficult. Do not expect huge advances. Editorial staff attended or plans to attend the following conferences: PBBY, Frankfurt, SCBWI Bologna.

### 📛 THISTLEDOWN PRESS LTD.

633 Main St., Saskatoon SK S7H 0J8 Canada. (306)244-1722. Fax: (306)244-1762. E-mail: tdpress@thistledown.sk.ca. Website: www.thistledown.sk.ca. **Acquisitions:** Allan Forrie, publisher. Publishes numerous middle reader and young adult titles/year. "Thistledown originates books by Canadian authors only, although we have co-published titles by authors outside Canada. We do not publish children's picture books."
  • Thistledown publishes books by Canadian authors only.
**Fiction** Middle readers, young adults: adventure, anthology, contemporary, fantasy, humor, poetry, romance, science fiction, suspense/mystery, short stories. Average word length: young adults—40,000. Recently published *Up All Night*, edited by R.P. MacIntyre (young adult, anthology); *Offside*, by Cathy Beveridge (young adult, novel); *Cheeseburger Subversive*, by Richard Scarsbrook; *The Alchemist's Daughter*, by Eileen Kernaghan.

**How to Contact/Writers** Submit outline/synopsis and sample chapters. "We do not accept unsolicted full-length manuscripts. These will be returned." Responds to queries in 4 months. Publishes a book about 1 year after acceptance. No simultaneous submissions.

**Illustration** Prefers agented illustrators but "not mandatory." Works with few illustrators. Illustrations only: Query with samples, promo sheet, slides, tearsheets. Responds only if interested. Samples returned with SASE; samples filed.

**Terms** Pays authors royalty of 10-12% based on retail price. Pays illustrators and photographers by the project (range: $250-750). Sends galleys to authors. Original artwork returned at job's completion. Book catalog free on request. Manuscript guidelines for #10 envelope and IRC.

**Tips** "Send cover letter including publishing history and SASE."

## TORMONT PUBLICATIONS
338 Saint Antoine St. E., Montreal QC H2Y 1A3 Canada. E-mail: info@tormont.ca. Website: www.tormont.com. Estab. 1984. **Manuscript Acquisitions:** Diane Mineau, director, editorial and creation. **Art Acquisitions:** Helene Cousineau, art director. "We specialize in children's mass market books as well as novelty books, games, and activity kits."

**Fiction** Considers mass market books.

**Nonfiction** Picture books, young readers, middle readers, young adults: activity books. Considers novelty books, games.

**How to Contact/Writers** Accepts material from residents of Canada only. Fiction/nonfiction: Submit complete ms. Responds to mss in 2 months.

**Illustration** Illustrations only: Send portfolio. Contact: Helene Cousineau, art director. Responds in 2 months. Samples returned with SASE.

**Tips** "Work submitted should be of the highest quality and the subject matter should 'travel well," that is, it should be of broad interest and relevance to the world children's market, since we publish internationally in well over a dozen languages. Please do not send any originals of your manuscripts, illustrations or prototypes, since we cannot be held responsible for lost or damaged materials. Send only photocopies. For U.S. and international/submissions, include a Universal Postal Order for the cost of return postage."

## TRADEWIND BOOKS
202-1807 Maritime Mews, Vancouver BC V6H 3W7 Canada. (604)662-4405. Fax: (604)730-0154. E-mail: tradewindbooks@mail.lycos.com. Website: www.tradewindbooks.com. **Manuscript Acquisitions:** Michael Katz, publisher. **Art Acquisitions:** Carol Frank, art director. Senior Editor: R. David Stephens. Publishes 3 picture books; 2 young adult titles/year. 15% of books by first-time authors.

**Fiction** Picture books: adventure, animal, multicultural, folktales. Average word length: 900 words. Recently published *The Clone Conspiracy*, by Simon Rose; *Bamboo*, by Paul Yee; *A Telling Time*, by Irene Watts, illustrated by Kathryn Shoemaker.

**How to Contact/Writers** Picture books: Submit complete ms. YA novels by Canadian authors only. Will consider simultaneous submissions. Do not send query letter. Responds to mss in 6 weeks. Unsolicited submissions accepted only if authors have read a selection of books published by Tradewind Books. Submissions must include a reference to these books.

**Illustration** Works with 3-4 illustrators/year. Uses color artwork only. Reviews ms/illustration packages from artists. Send ms with dummy. Illustrations only: Query with samples. Responds only if interested. Samples returned with SASE; samples filed.

**Terms** Royalties negotiable. Offers advances against royalties. Originals returned to artist at job's completion. Book catalog available for 8×10 SAE and 3 first-class Canadian stamps. Catalog available on website.

## USBORNE PUBLISHING
83-85 Saffron Hill, London EC1N 8RT United Kingdom. Fax: (020)7430 1562. Website: www.usborne.com. **Manuscript Acquisitions:** Fiction Editorial Director. **Art Acquisitions:** Usborne Art Department. "Usborne Publishing is a multiple-award winning, world-wide children's publishing company specializing in superbly researched and produced information books with a unique appeal to young readers."

**Fiction** Young readers, middle readers: adventure, contemporary, fantasy, history, humor, multicultural, nature/environment, science fiction, suspense/mystery. Average word length: young readers—3,500-8,000; middle readers—10,000-30,000. Recently published *Lift-the-Flap Dinosaurs*, by Alastair Smith (preschool); Fame School Series, by Cindy Jefferies (ages 8 and up).

**How to Contact/Writers** Refer to guidelines on website or request from above address. Fiction: Submit 3 sample chapters and a full synopsis with SASE. Does not accept submissions for nonfiction. Responds to queries in 1 month; mss in 4 months.

**Illustration** Works with 30 illustrators per year. Illustrations only: Query with samples. Samples not returned; samples filed.

**PhotographyContact:** Usbourne Art Department. Submit samples.

**Terms** Pays authors royalty of 7½-10% based on retail price.

**Tips** "Do not send any original work and, sorry, but we cannot guarantee a reply."

## WHITECAP BOOKS

351 Lynn Ave., North Vancouver BC V7J 2C4 Canada. (604)980-9852. Fax: (604)980-8197. E-mail: whitecap@w hitecap.ca. Website: www.whitecap.ca. **Manuscript Acquisitions:** Helen Stortini. **Illustration Acquisitions:** Roberta Batchelor, art director. Publishes 2 picture books/year; 2 young readers/year; 2 middle readers/year; 2 young adult/year.

**Fiction** Picture books: humor. Middle readers: adventure, animal, suspense/mystery. Young adult: adventure, suspense/mystery. Recently published *Eleven Lazy Llamas*, by Dianna Bonder (ages 4-6); *Take It to the Extreme/Skater Stuntboys*, by Pam Withers (ages 14-16); *Mustang Mountain/Swift Horse*, by Sharon Siamon (ages 8-12).

**Nonfiction** Young readers: animal, science. Does not want to see text that writes down to children. Recently published *Welcome to the World of Kangaroos*, by Diane Swanson (ages 5-7); *Lupé*, by Rebecca Grambo (ages 5-7).

**How to Contact/Writers** Fiction/nonfiction: Query. Responds to queries/ms in 6 months. Publishes a book 1 year after acceptance. Please send international postal voucher if submission is from U.S. Mark envelopes "submissions." No e-mail submissions.

**Illustration** Works with 1-2 illustrators/year. Uses color artwork only. Reviews ms/illustration packages from artists. Query. Contact: Helen Stortini, acquisitions. Illustrations only: Send postcard sample with tearsheets. Contact: Roberta Batchelor, art director. Responds only if interested.

**Photography** Buys stock and assigns work. Model/property releases required; captions required. "Mostly work with digital images." Submit stock photo list.

**Terms** Pays authors a negotiated royalty or purchases work outright. Offers advances. Pays illustrators and photographers negotiated amount. Originals returned to artist at job's completion. Manuscript guidelines available on website.

**Tips** "Check our website before submitting. Please indicate if you want the manuscript returned and supply a large enough envelope and sufficient postage. Don't send U.S. postage SASE to Canada. It can't be used. Check out current children's books to see what is appropriate. Do research on a company before submitting."

# Magazines

WOMEN IN SCIENCE

C hildren's magazines are a great place for unpublished writers and illustrators to break into the market. Writers, illustrators and photographers alike may find it easier to get book assignments if they have tearsheets from magazines. Having magazine work under your belt shows you're professional and have experience working with editors and art directors and meeting deadlines.

But magazines aren't merely a breaking-in point. Writing, illustration, and photo assignments for magazines let you see your work in print quickly, and the magazine market can offer steady work and regular paychecks (a number of them pay on acceptance). Book authors and illustrators may have to wait a year or two before receiving royalties from a project. The magazine market is also a good place to use research material that didn't make it into a book project you're working on. You may even work on a magazine idea that blossoms into a book project.

## TARGETING YOUR SUBMISSIONS

It's important to know the topics typically covered by different children's magazines. To help you match your work with the right publications, we've included several indexes in the back of this book. The **Subject Index** lists both book and magazine publishers by the fiction and nonfiction subjects they're seeking.

**If you're a writer**, use the Subject Index in conjunction with the **Age-Level Index** to narrow your list of markets. Targeting the correct age group with your submission is an important consideration. Many rejection slips are sent because a writer has not targeted a manuscript to the correct age. Few magazines are aimed at children of all ages, so you must be certain your manuscript is written for the audience level of the particular magazine you're submitting to. Magazines for children (just as magazines for adults) may also target a specific gender.

**If you're a poet**, refer to the **Poetry Index** to find which magazines publish poems.

Each magazine has a different editorial philosophy. Language usage also varies between periodicals, as does the length of feature articles and the use of artwork and photographs. Reading magazines *before* submitting is the best way to determine if your material is appropriate. Also, because magazines targeted to specific age groups have a natural turnover in readership every few years, old topics (with a new slant) can be recycled.

**If you're a photographer**, the Photography Index lists children's magazines that use photos from freelancers. Using it in combination with the subject index can narrow your search. For instance, if you photograph sports, compare the Magazine list in the Photography Index with the list under Sports in the Subject Index. Highlight the markets that appear on both lists, then read those listings to decide which magazines might be best for your work.

Since many kids' magazines sell subscriptions through direct mail or schools, you may not be able to find a particular publication at bookstores or newsstands. Check your local library, or send for copies of the magazines you're interested in. Most magazines in this section have sample copies available and will send them for a SASE or small fee.

Also, many magazines have submission guidelines and theme lists available for a SASE. Check magazines' websites, too. Many offer excerpts of articles, submission guidelines, and theme lists and will give you a feel for the editorial focus of the publication.

Watch for the Canadian ⊞ and International ⊕ symbols. These publications' needs and requirements may differ from their U.S. counterparts.

For tips on writing for the magazine market, see the Insider Report with **Mireille Messier** on page 248.

**Information on magazines listed in the previous edition but not included in this edition of** *Children's Writer's & Illustrator's Market* **may be found in the General Index.**

### ADVENTURES

WordAction Publishing Company, 6401 The Paseo, Kansas City MO 64131. (816)333-7000. Fax: (816)333-4439. E-mail: jjsmith@nazarene.org. **Articles Editor:** Julie J. Smith. Weekly magazine. "Adventures is a full-color story paper for first and second graders. It is designed to connect Sunday School learning with the daily living experiences of the early elementary child. The reading level should be beginning. The intent of Adventures is to provide a life-related paper that will promote Christian values, encouraging good choices and providing reinforcement for biblical concepts taught in Faith Connections curriculum published by WordAction Publishing." Entire publication aimed at juvenile market.

● Adventures is not accepting new submissions until September 2006.

### ADVOCATE, PKA'S PUBLICATION

PKA Publication, 1881 Little Westkill Rd., Prattsville NY 12468. (518)299-3103. **Publisher:** Patricia Keller. Bimonthly tabloid. Estab. 1987. Circ. 12,000. "Advocate advocates good writers and quality writings. We publish art, fiction, photos and poetry. Advocate's submitters are talented people of all ages who do not earn their livings as writers. We wish to promote the arts and to give those we publish the opportunity to be published."

● Gaited Horse Association newsletter is included in this publication. Horse-oriented stories, poetry, art and photos are currently needed.

**Fiction** Middle readers, young adults/teens: adventure, animal, contemporary, fantasy, folktales, health, humorous, nature/environment, problem-solving, romance, science fiction, sports, suspense/mystery. Looks for "well written, entertaining work, whether fiction or nonfiction." Buys approximately 42 mss/year. Average word length: 1,500. Byline given. Wants to see more humorous material, nature/environment and romantic comedy.

**Nonfiction** Middle readers, young adults/teens: animal, arts/crafts, biography, careers, concept, cooking, fashion, games/puzzles, geography, history, hobbies, how-to, humorous, interview/profile, nature/environment, problem-solving, science, social issues, sports, travel. Buys 10 mss/year. Average word length: 1,500. Byline given.

**Poetry** Reviews poetry any length.

**How to Contact/Writers** Fiction/nonfiction: send complete ms. Responds to queries in 6 weeks; mss in 2 months. Publishes ms 2-18 months after acceptance.

**Illustration** Uses b&w artwork only. Uses cartoons. Reviews ms/illustration packages from artists. Submit a photo print (b&w or color), an excellent copy of work (no larger than 8×10) or original. Illustrations only: "Send previous unpublished art with SASE, please." Responds in 2 months. Samples returned with SASE; samples not filed. Credit line given.

**Photography** Buys photos from freelancers. Model/property releases required. Uses color and b&w prints. Send unsolicited photos by mail with SASE. Responds in 2 months. Wants nature, artistic and humorous photos.

**Terms** Pays on publication with contributor's copies. Acquires first rights for mss, artwork and photographs. Pays in copies. Original work returned upon job's completion. Sample copies for $4. Writer's/illustrator/photo guidelines with sample copy.

**Tips** "Artists and photographers should keep in mind that we are a b&w paper. Please do not send postcards. Use envelope with SASE."

### AIM MAGAZINE, America's Intercultural Magazine

P.O. Box 1174, Maywood IL 60153-8174. Website: www.aimmagazine.org. **Contact:** Ruth Apilado (nonfiction),

Mark Boone (fiction). Quarterly magazine. Circ. 8,000. "Readers are high school and college students, teachers, adults interested in helping to purge racism from the human blood stream by the way of the written word—that is our goal!" 15% of material aimed at juvenile audience.

**Fiction** Young adults/teens: adventure, folktales, humorous, history, multicultural, "stories with social significance." Wants stories that teach children that people are more alike than they are different. Does not want to see religious fiction. Buys 20 mss/year. Average word length: 1,000-4,000. Byline given.

**Nonfiction** Young adults/teens: biography, interview/profile, multicultural, "stuff with social significance." Does not want to see religious nonfiction. Buys 20 mss/year. Average word length: 500-2,000. Byline given.

**How to Contact/Writers** Fiction: Send complete ms. Nonfiction: Query with published clips. Responds to queries/mss in 1 month. Will consider simultaneous submissions.

**Illustration** Buys 6 illustrations/issue. Preferred theme: Overcoming social injustices through nonviolent means. Reviews ms/illustration packages from artists. Query first. Illustrations only: Query with tearsheets. Responds to art samples in 1 month. Samples filed. Original artwork returned at job's completion "if desired." Credit line given.

**Photography** Wants "photos of activists who are trying to contribute to social improvement."

**Terms** Pays on acceptance. Buys first North American serial rights. Pays $15-25 for stories/articles. Pays in contributor copies if copies are requested. Pays $25 for b&w cover illustration. Photographers paid by the project. Sample copies for $5.

**Tips** "Write about what you know."

## AMERICAN CAREERS

Career Communications, Inc., 6701 W. 64th St., Overland Park KS 66202. (913)362-7788. Fax: (913)362-4864. Website: www.carcom.com. **Articles Editor:** Mary Pitchford. **Art Director:** Jerry Kanabel. Published 1 time/year. Estab. 1990. Circ. 400,000. Publishes career and education information for students in grades 8-10.

**Nonfiction** Buys 20 mss/year. Average word length: 300-800. Byline given.

**How to Contact/Writers** Nonfiction: Query with résumé and published clips. Responds to queries in 2 years. Will consider simultaneous submissions.

**Terms** Pays on acceptance. Pays writers variable amount.

**Tips** Send a query in writing with résumé and clips.

## AMERICAN CHEERLEADER

Lifestyle Ventures LLC, 250 W. 57th St., Suite 420, New York NY 10107. (212)265-8890. Fax: (212)265-8908. E-mail: editors@americancheerleader.com. Website: www.americancheerleader.com. **Editorial Director:** Sheila Noone. **Managing Editor:** Marisa Walker. Bimonthly magazine. Estab. 1995. Circ. 200,000. Special interest teen magazine for kids who cheer.

**Nonfiction** Young adults: biography, interview/profile (sports personalities), careers, fashion, beauty, health, how-to (cheering techniques, routines, pep songs, etc.), problem-solving, sports, cheerleading specific material. "We're looking for authors who know cheerleading." Buys 20 mss/year. Average word length: 750-2,000. Byline given.

**How to Contact/Writers** Query with published clips. Responds to queries/mss in 3 months. Publishes ms 3 months after acceptance. Will consider electronic submission via disk or e-mail.

**Illustration** Buys 2 illustrations/issue; 12-20 illustrations/year. Works on assignment only. Reviews ms/illustration packages from artists. Illustrations only: Query with samples; arrange portfolio review. Responds only if interested. Samples filed. Originals not returned at job's completion. Credit line given.

**Photography** Buys photos from freelancers. Looking for cheerleading at different sports games, events, etc. Uses 35mm, $2\frac{1}{4} \times 2\frac{1}{4}$ transparencies and $5 \times 7$ prints. Query with samples; provide résumé, business card, tearsheets to be kept on file. "After sending query, we'll set up an interview." Responds only if interested.

**Terms** Pays on publication. Buys all rights for mss, artwork and photographs. Pays $100-500 for stories. Pays illustrators $50-200 for b&w inside, $100-300 for color inside. Pays photographers by the project $300-750; per photo (range: $25-100). Sample copies for $4.

**Tips** "Authors: We invite proposals from freelance writers who are involved in or have been involved in cheerleading—i.e. coaches, sponsors or cheerleaders. Our writing style is upbeat, and 'sporty' to catch and hold the attention of our teen readers. Articles should be broken down into lots of sidebars, bulleted lists, etc. Photographers and illustrators must have teen magazine experience or high profile experience."

## AMERICAN GIRL, INC.

8400 Fairway Place, Middleton WI 53562-0984. (608)836-4848. Website: www.americangirl.com. **Executive Editor:** Editorial Dept. Assistant. Bimonthly magazine. Estab. 1992. Circ. 750,000. "For girls ages 8-12. We use fiction and nonfiction."

**Fiction** Middle readers: contemporary, multicultural, suspense/mystery, good fiction about anything. No romance, science fiction or fantasy. No preachy, moralistic tales or stories with animals as protagonists. Only girl characters—no boys. Buys approximately 2 mss/year. Average word length: 2,300. Byline given.

**Nonfiction** How-to, interview/profile, history. Any articles aimed at girls ages 8-12. Buys 3-10 mss/year. Average word length: 600. Byline sometimes given. No historical profiles about obvious female heroines—Annie Oakley, Amelia Earhart; no romance or dating.

**How to Contact/Writers** Fiction: Query with published clips. Nonfiction: Query. Responds to queries/mss in 3 months. Will consider simultaneous submissions.

**Illustration** Works on assignment only.

**Terms** Pays on acceptance. Buys first North American serial rights. Pays $500 minimum for stories; $300 minimum for articles. Sample copies for $3.95 and 9×12 SAE with $1.93 in postage (send to Magazine Department Assistant). Writer's guidelines free for SASE.

**Tips** "Keep (stories and articles) simple but interesting. Kids are discriminating readers, too. They won't read a boring or pretentious story. We're looking for short (maximum 175 words) how-to stories and short profiles of girls for 'Girls Express' section, as well as word games, puzzles and mazes."

## APPLESEEDS, The Magazine for Young Readers

Cobblestone Publishing, A Division of Carus Publishing, 140 E. 83rd St., New York NY 10028. E-mail: swbuc@aol.com. Website: www.cobblestonepub.com/pages/writersAPPguides.html. **Editor:** Susan Buckley. Magazine published monthly except June, July and August. *AppleSeeds* is a 36-page, multidisciplinary, nonfiction social studies magazine from Cobblestone Publishing for ages 8-10. Published 9 times/year.

• Above address is for *AppleSeeds* submissions only. Cobblestone address is: 30 Grove St., Petersborough NH 03458. *AppleSeeds* is aimed toward readers ages 8-10. See website for current theme list.

**How to Contact/Writers** Nonfiction: Query only. Send all queries to Susan Buckley. See website for submission guidelines and theme list. E-mail queries are preferred.

**Tips** "Submit queries specifically focused on the theme of an upcoming issue. We generally work 6 months ahead on themes. We look for unusual perspectives, original ideas, and excellent scholarship. We accept **no unsolicited manuscripts** Writers should check our website at cobblestonepub.com/pages/writersAPPguides/html for current guidelines, topics, and query deadlines. We use very little fiction. Illustrators should not submit unsolicited art."

## Ⓝ 🌐 AQUILA

New Leaf Publishing, P.O Box 2518, Eastbourne BN21 2BR United Kingdom. (01323)431313. Fax: (01323)731136. E-mail: info@aquila.co.uk. Website: www.aquila.co.uk. **Submissions Editor:** Jackie Berry and Karen Lutener. Monthly magazine. Estab. 1993. "Aquila is an educational magazine for readers ages 8-13 including factual articles (no pop/celebrity material), arts/crafts and puzzles." Entire publication aimed at juvenile market.

**Fiction** Young readers: animal, contemporary, fantasy, folktales, health, history, humorous, multicultural, nature/environment, problem solving, religious, science fiction, sports, suspense/mystery. Middle readers: animal, contemporary, fantasy, folktales, health, history, humorous, multicultural, nature/environment, problem solving, religious, romance, science fiction, sports, suspense/mystery. Buys 6-8 mss/year. Byline given.

**Nonfiction** Considers young readers: animal, arts/crafts, concept, cooking, games/puzzles, health, history, how-to, interview/profile, math, nature/environment, science, sports. Middle readers: animal, arts/crafts, concept, cooking, games/puzzles, health, history, interview/profile, math, nature/environment, science, sports. Buys 48 mss/year. Average word length: 350-750.

**How To Contact/Writers** Fiction: Query with published clips. Nonfiction: Query with published clips. Responds to queries in 6-8 weeks. Publishes ms 1 year after acceptance. Considers electronic submissions via disk or e-mail, previously published work.

**Illustration** Color artwork only.Works on assignment only. For first contact, query with samples. Submit samples to Jackie Berry, Editor. Responds only if interested. Samples not returned. Samples filed.

**Terms** Buys exclusive magazine rights. Buys exclusive magazine rights rights for artwork. Pays 150-200 for stories; 50-100 for articles. Additional payment for ms/illustration packages. Additional payment for ms/photo packages. Pays illustrators $130-150 for color cover. Sample copies free for SASE. Writer's guidelines free for SASE. Publishes work by children.

**Tips** "We only accept a high level of educational material for children ages 8-13 with a good standard of literacy and ability."

## ASK, Arts and Sciences for Kids

Carus Publishing, 140 S. Dearborn, Suite 1450, Chicago IL 60603. (312)701-1720. E-mail: ask@caruspub.com. Website: www.cricketmag.com. **Editor:** Lonnie Plecha. **Art Director:** Karen Kohn. Magazine published 9 times/year. Estab. 2002. "Ask encourages children between the ages of 7 and 10 to inquire about the world around them."

**Nonfiction** Young readers, middle readers: animal, history, nature/environment, science. Average word length: 150-1,500. Byline given.

**How to Contact/Writers** *Ask* does not accept unsolicited mss or queries. All articles are commissioned. To be considered for assignments, experienced science writers may send a résumé and 3 published clips.

**Illustration** Buys 10 illustrations/issue; 60 illustrations/year. Works on assignment only. Illustrations only: Query with samples.

## BABAGANEWZ

Jewish Family & Life, 11141 Georgia Ave. #406, Wheaton MD 20902. (301)962-9636. Fax: (301)962-9635. Website: www.babaganewz.com. **Articles Editor:** Mark Levine. **Production Editor:** Aviva Werner. Monthly magazine. Estab. 2001. Circ. 30,000. *"BabagaNewz* helps middle school students explore Jewish values that are at the core of Jewish beliefs and practices.''

**Fiction** Middle readers: religious, Jewish themes. Buys 1 ms/year. Average word length: 1,000-1,500. Byline given.

**Nonfiction** Middle readers: arts/crafts, concept, games/puzzles, geography, history, humorous, interview/profile, nature/environment, religion, science, social issues. Most articles are written by assignment. Average word length: 350-1,000. Byline given.

**How to Contact/Writers** Nonfiction: Queires only for ficiton; queries preferred for nonfiction. **No unsolicited mss.**

**Illustration** Uses color artwork only. Works on assignment only. Illustrations only: Send postcard sample with promo sheet, résumé, URL. Responds only if interested. Credit line given.

**Photography** Photos by assigment.

**Terms** Pays on acceptance. Usually buys all rights for mss. Original artwork returned at job's completion. Sample copies free for SAE 9×12 and 4 first-class stamps.

**Tips** ''Most work is done on assignment. We are looking for freelance writers with experience writing nonfiction for 9- to 13-year-olds, especially on Jewish-related themes. No unsolicited manuscripts.''

## BABYBUG

Carus Publishing Company, P.O. Box 300, Peru IL 61354. (815)224-5803, ext. 656. **Editor:** Paula Morrow. **Art Director:** Suzanne Beck. Published 10 times/year (monthly except for combined May/June and July/August issues). Estab. 1994. ''A listening and looking magazine for infants and toddlers ages 6 to 24 months, *Babybug* is 6×7, 24 pages long, printed in large type on high-quality cardboard stock with rounded corners and no staples.''

**Fiction** Looking for very simple and concrete stories, 4-6 short sentences maximum.

**Nonfiction** Must use very basic words and concepts, 10 words maximum.

**Poetry** Maximum length 8 lines. Looking for rhythmic, rhyming poems.

**How to Contact/Writers** ''Please do not query first.'' Send complete ms with SASE. ''Submissions without SASE will be discarded.'' Responds in 3 months.

**Illustration** Uses color artwork only. Works on assignment only. Reviews ms/illustration packages from artists. ''The manuscripts will be evaluated for quality of concept and text before the art is considered.'' Contact: Suzanne Beck. Illustrations only: Send tearsheets or photo prints/photocopies with SASE. ''Submissions without SASE will be discarded.'' Responds in 3 months. Samples filed.

**Terms** Pays on publication for mss; after delivery of completed assignment for illustrators. Rights purchased vary. Original artwork returned at job's completion. Rates vary ($25 minimum for mss; $250 minimum for art). Sample copy for $5. Guidelines free for SASE or available on web site, FAQ at www.cricketmag.com.

**Tips** ''*Babybug* would like to reach as many children's authors and artists as possible for original contributions, but our standards are very high, and we will accept only top-quality material. Before attempting to write for *Babybug*, be sure to familiarize yourself with this age child.''

## N BLACKGIRL MAGAZINE

The Destiny Agency, P.O. Box 90429, Atlanta GA 30364. (404)840-9957, (404)762-0282. Fax: (404)762-0283. E-mail:kenyajames@mac.co. Website: www.blackgirlmagazine.com. **Articles Editor:** Tishenna Brown. **Fiction Editor:** Kenya James. **Art Director:** Fahamu Pecon. **Photo Editor:** Delphine Fawandu. Estab. 2002. ''We are focused on hightlighting the interest of girls as well as focusing on topics such as history, education, and style.'' Entire publication aimed at juvenile market.

**Fiction** Young adults/teens: contemporary, folktales, history, humorous, multicultural, problem solving, religious, sports. Buys 10-15 mss/year. Average word length: 600-1,200. Byline given.

**Nonfiction** Considers young adults/teens: arts/crafts, biography, careers, cooking, fashion, games/puzzles, health, history, humorous, interview/profile, math, multicultural, science. Buys 10-15 mss/year. Average word length: 600-1,200. Byline given.

**Poetry** Maximum length: 150.

**How To Contact/Writers** Fiction/nonfiction: Send complete ms. Considers simultaneous submissions, electronic submissions via disk or e-mail.

**Illustration** Both b&w and color artwork. Works on assignment only. Reviews ms/illustration packages from artists. Ms/illustration packages: Send ms with dummy, presskit. Submit package to Kenya James, Editor-in-Chief. For first contact, query with samples, arrange a portfolio review, send portfolio, slides, tearsheets. Submit samples to Doaimah Zaakee, Assistant Art Director. Samples not returned. Samples filed. Credit line given.

**Photography** Purchases photos both separately and with accompanying mss. Needs African-America girls and teens. Model/property releases required. Photo captions required. Uses color prints. Submit portfolio for review.

**Terms** Originals returned to artist at job's completion. Sample copies available for $4. Writer's guidelines free for SASE. Illustrator's guidelines free for SASE. Photographer's guidelines free for SASE. Publishes work by children.

## BOYS' LIFE

Boy Scouts of America, 1325 W. Walnut Hill Lane, Irving TX 75015-2079. (972)580-2366. Fax: (972)580-2079. Website: www.boyslife.org. **Managing Editor:** W. Butterworth, IV. **Senior Editor:** Michael Goldman. **Fiction Editor:** Rich Haddaway. **Director of Design:** Joseph P. Connolly. **Art Director:** Scott Feaster. Monthly magazine. Estab. 1911. Circ. 1,300,000. *Boys' Life* is "a 4-color general interest magazine for boys 8 to 18 who are members of the Cub Scouts, Boy Scouts or Venturers."

**Fiction** Young readers, middle readers, young adults: adventure, animal, contemporary, history, humor, multicultural, nature/environment, problem-solving, sports, science fiction, spy/mystery. Does not want to see "talking animals and adult reminiscence." Buys only 12-16 mss/year. Average word length: 1,000-1,500. Byline given.

**Nonfiction** Young readers, middle readers, young adult: animal, arts/crafts, biography, careers (middle readers and young adults only), cooking, health, history, hobbies, how-to, interview/profile, multicultural, nature/environment, problem-solving, science, sports. "Subject matter is broad. We cover everything from professional sports to American history to how to pack a canoe. A look at a current list of the BSA's more than 100 merit badge pamphlets gives an idea of the wide range of subjects possible. Even better, look at a year's worth of recent issues. Column subjects are science, nature, earth, health, sports, space and aviation, cars, computers, entertainment, pets, history, music and others." Average word length: 500-1,500. Columns 300-750 words. Byline given.

**How to Contact/Writers** Fiction: Send complete ms with cover letter and SASE to fiction editor. Nonfiction: Major articles query senior editor. Columns query associate editor with SASE for response. Responds to queries/mss in 2 months.

**Illustration** Buys 10-12 illustrations/issue; 100-125 illustrations/year. Works on assignment only. Reviews ms/illustration packages from artists. "Query first." Illustrations only: Send tearsheets. Responds to art samples only if interested. Samples returned with SASE. Original artwork returned at job's completion. Credit line given.

**Terms** Pays on acceptance. Buys first rights. Pays $750 and up for fiction; $400-1,500 for major articles; $150-400 for columns; $250-300 for how-to features. Pays illustrators $1,500-3,000 for color cover; $100-1,500 color inside. Pays photographers by the project. Sample copies for $3.60 plus 9×12 SASE. Writer's/illustrator's/photo guidelines available for SASE.

**Tips** "We strongly urge you to study at least a year's issues to better understand the type of material published. Articles for *Boys' Life* must interest and entertain boys ages 8 to 18. Write for a boy you know who is 12. Our readers demand crisp, punchy writing in relatively short, straightforward sentences. The editors demand well-reported articles that demonstrate high standards of journalism. We follow *The New York Times* manual of style and usage. All submissions must be accompanied by SASE with adequate postage."

## BOYS' QUEST

P.O. Box 227, Bluffton OH 45817-0227. (419)358-4610. Fax: (419)358-5027. Website: www.boysquest.com. **Articles Editor:** Marilyn Edwards. Bimonthly magazine. Estab. 1995. "*Boys' Quest* is a magazine created for boys from 6 to 13 years, with youngsters 8, 9 and 10 the specific target age. Our point of view is that every young boy deserves the right to be a young boy for a number of years before he becomes a young adult. As a result, *Boys' Quest* looks for articles, fiction, nonfiction, and poetry that deal with timeless topics, such as pets, nature, hobbies, science, games, sports, careers, simple cooking, and anything else likely to interest a young boy."

**Fiction** Picture-oriented material, young readers, middle readers: adventure, animal, history, humorous, multicultural, nature/environment, problem-solving, sports. Does not want to see violence, teenage themes. Buys 30 mss/year. Average word length: 200-500. Byline given.

**Nonfiction** Picture-oriented material, young readers, middle readers: animal, arts/crafts, cooking, games/puzzles, history, hobbies, how-to, humorous, math, problem-solving, sports. Prefer photo support with nonfiction. Buys 30 mss/year. Average word length: 200-500. Byline given.

**Poetry** Reviews poetry. Maximum length: 21 lines. Limit submissions to 6 poems.

**How to Contact/Writers** All writers should consult the theme list before sending in articles. To receive current theme list, send a SASE. Fiction/Nonfiction: Query or send complete ms (preferred). Send SASE with correct postage. No faxed or e-mailed material. Responds to queries in 2 weeks; mss in 2 weeks (if rejected); 5 weeks (if scheduled). Publishes ms 3 months-3 years after acceptance. Will consider simultaneous submissions and previously published work.

**Illustration** Buys 10 illustrations/issue; 60-70 illustrations/year. Uses b&w artwork only. Works on assignment only. Reviews ms/illustration packages from artists. Illustrations only: Query with samples, tearsheets. Responds in 1 month only if interested and a SASE. Samples returned with SASE; samples filed. Credit line given.

**Photography** Photos used for support of nonfiction. "Excellent photographs included with a nonfiction story is considered very seriously." Model/property releases required. Uses b&w, 5×7 or 3×5 prints. Query with samples; send unsolicited photos by mail. Responds in 3 weeks.

**Terms** Pays on publication. Buys first North American serial rights for mss. Buys first rights for artwork. Pays 5/word for stories and articles. Additional payment for ms/illustration packages and for photos accompanying articles. Pays $150-200 for color cover; $25-35 for b&w inside. Pays photographers per photo (range: $5-10). Originals returned to artist at job's completion. Sample copies for $5 (includes postage); $6 outside U.S. Writer's/illustrator's/photographer's guidelines and theme list are free for SASE.

**Tips** "First be familiar with our magazines. We are looking for lively writing, most of it from a young boy's point of view—with the boy or boys directly involved in an activity that is both wholesome and unusual. We need nonfiction with photos and fiction stories—around 500 words—puzzles, poems, cooking, carpentry projects, jokes and riddles. Nonfiction pieces that are accompanied by black and white photos are far more likely to be accepted than those that need illustrations. We will entertain simultaneous submissions as long as that fact is noted on the manuscript."

## BREAD FOR GOD'S CHILDREN

Bread Ministries, Inc., P.O. Box 1017, Arcadia FL 34265-1017. (863)494-6214. Fax: (863)993-0154. E-mail: bread@sunline.net. Website: www.breadministries.org. **Editor:** Judith M. Gibbs. Bimonthly magazine. Estab. 1972. Circ. 10,000 (U.S. and Canada). "*Bread* is designed as a teaching tool for Christian families." 85% of publication aimed at juvenile market.

**Fiction** Young readers, middle readers, young adult/teen: adventure, religious, problem-solving, sports. Looks for "teaching stories that portray Christian lifestyles without preaching." Buys approximately 20 mss/year. Average word length: 900-1,500 (for teens); 600-900 (for young children). Byline given.

**Nonfiction** All levels: how-to. "We do not want anything detrimental to solid family values. Most topics will fit if they are slanted to our basic needs." Buys 3-4 mss/year. Average word length: 500-800. Byline given.

**Illustration** "The only illustrations we purchase are those occasional good ones accompanying an accepted story."

**How to Contact/Writers** Fiction/nonfiction: Send complete ms. Responds to mss in 6 months "if considered for use." Will consider simultaneous submissions and previously published work.

**Terms** Pays on publication. Pays $30-50 for stories; $30 for articles. Sample copies free for 9×12 SAE and 5 first-class stamps (for 2 copies).

**Tips** "We want stories or articles that illustrate overcoming obstacles by faith and living solid, Christian lives. Know our publication and what we have used in the past. Know the readership and publisher's guidelines. Stories should teach the value of morality and honesty without preaching. Edit carefully for content and grammar."

## BRILLIANT STAR

National Spiritual Assembly of the Báhas'ís of the U.S., 1233 Central St., Evanston IL 60201. (847)853-2354. Fax: (847)256-1372. E-mail: brilliantstar@usbnc.org. Website: www.brilliantstar.org. **Associate Editor:** Susan Engle. **Art Director:** Amethel Parel-Sewell. Publishes 6 issues/year. Estab. 1969. "Our magazine is designed for children ages 8-12. *Brilliant Star* presents Baha history and principles through fiction, non-fiction, activities, interviews, puzzles, cartoons, games, music, and art. Universal values of good character, such as kindness, courage, creativity, and helpfulness are incorporated into the magazine.

**Fiction** Middle readers: contemporary, fantasy, folktale, multicultural, nature/environment, problem-solving, religious. Average word length: 700-1,400. Byline given.

**Nonfiction** Middle readers: arts/crafts, games/puzzles, geography, how-to, humorous, multicultural, nature/environment, religion, social issues. Buys 6 mss/year. Average word length: 300-700. Byline given.

**Poetry** "We only publish poetry written by children at the moment."

**How to Contact/Writers** Fiction: Send complete ms. Nonfiction: Query. Responds to queries/mss in 6 weeks. Publishes ms 6 months-1 year after acceptance. Will consider e-mail submissions.

**Illustration** Works on assignment only. Reviews ms/illustration packages from artists. Illustrations only: Query with samples. Contact: Aaron Kreader, graphic designer. Responds only if interested. Samples kept on file. Credit line given.

**Photography** Buys photos with accompanying ms only. Model/property release required; captions required. Responds only if interested.

**Terms** Pays 2 copies of issue. Buys first rights and reprint rights for mss. Buys first rights and reprint rights for artwork; first rights and reprint rights for photos. Sample copies for $3. Writer's/illustrator's/photo guidelines for SASE.

**Tips** *"Brilliant Star's* content is developed with a focus on children in their 'tween' years, ages 8-12. This is a period of intense emotional, physical, and psychological development. Familiarize yourself with the interests and challenges of children in this age range. Keep your language and concepts age-appropriate. Use short words, sentences, and paragraphs. Activities and games may be submitted in rough or final form. Send us a description of your activity along with short, simple instructions. We avoid long, complicated activities that require adult supervision. If you think they will be helpful, please try to provide step-by-step rough sketches of the instructions. You may also submit photographs to illustrate the activity."

## CADET QUEST

Calvinist Cadet Corps, P.O. Box 7259, Grand Rapids MI 49510. (616)241-5616. E-mail: submissions@calvinistcadets.org. Website: www.calvinistcadets.org. **Editor:** G. Richard Broene. Magazine published 7 times/year. Circ. 10,000. "Our magazine is for members of the Calvinist Cadet Corps—boys aged 9-14. Our purpose is to show how God is at work in their lives and in the world around them. Our magazine offers nonfiction articles and fast-moving fiction—everything to appeal to the interests and concerns of boys and teach Christian values subtly."

**Fiction** Middle readers, boys/early teens: adventure, humorous, multicultural, problem-solving, religious, sports. Buys 12 mss/year. Average word length: 900-1,500.

**Nonfiction** Middle readers, boys/early teens: arts/crafts, games/puzzles, hobbies, how-to, humorous, interview/profile, problem-solving, science, sports. Buys 6 mss/year. Average word length: 400-900.

**How to Contact/Writers** Fiction/nonfiction: Send complete ms by mail with SASE or by e-mail. "Please note: e-mail submissions must have material in the body of the e-mail. We do not open attachments." Responds to queries in 1 month; mss in 2 months. Will consider simultaneous submissions.

**Illustration** Buys 1 illustration/issue; buys 6 illustrations/year. Works on assignment only. Reviews ms/illustration packages from artists. Responds in 5 weeks. Samples returned with SASE. Originals returned to artist at job's completion. Credit line given.

**Photography** Buys photos from freelancers. Wants nature photos and photos of boys.

**Terms** Pays on acceptance. Buys first North American serial rights; reprint rights. Pays 4-5¢/word for stories/articles. Pays illustrators $50-200 for b&w/color cover or b&w inside. Sample copy free with 9 × 12 SAE and 4 first-class stamps.

**Tips** "Our publication is mostly open to fiction; look for new themes at our website. We use mostly fast-moving fiction that appeals to a boy's sense of adventure or sense of humor. Avoid preachiness, simplistic answers to complicated problems and long dialogue with little action. Articles on sports, outdoor activities, science, crafts, etc. should emphasize a Christian perspective but avoid simplistic moralisms."

## CALLIOPE, Exploring World History

Cobblestone Publishing Company, 30 Grove St., Suite C, Peterborough NH 03458. (603)924-7209. Fax: (603)924-7380. Website: www.cobblestonepub.com. **Managing Editor:** Lou Waryncia. **Co-editors:** Rosalie Baker and Charles Baker. **Art Director:** Ann Dillon. Magazine published 9 times/year. *"Calliope* covers world history (East/West), and lively, original approaches to the subject are the primary concerns of the editors in choosing material."

- *Calliope* themes for 2005-2006 include the Aztecs, Medieval Japan, the Spice Trade, Rembrandt, the Irish Potato Famine, Charles Dickens. For additional themes and time frames, visit their website.

**Fiction** Middle readers and young adults: adventure, folktales, plays, history, biographical fiction. Material must relate to forthcoming themes. Word length: up to 800.

**Nonfiction** Middle readers and young adults: arts/crafts, biography, cooking, games/puzzles, history. Material must relate to forthcoming themes. Word length: 300-1,000.

**How to Contact/Writers** "A query must consist of the following to be considered (please use nonerasable paper): a brief cover letter stating subject and word length of the proposed article; a detailed one-page outline explaining the information to be presented in the article; an bibliography of materials the author intends to use in preparing the article; a self-addressed stamped envelope. Writers new to *Calliope* should send a writing sample with query. In all correspondence, please include your complete address as well as a telephone number where you can be reached. A writer may send as many queries for one issue as he or she wishes, but each query must have a separate cover letter, outline, bibliography and SASE. Telephone and e-mail queries are not accepted. Handwritten queries will not be considered. Queries may be submitted at any time, but queries sent well in advance of deadline *may not be answered for several months.* Go-aheads requesting material proposed in queries are usually sent five months prior to publication date. Unused queries will be returned approximately three to four months prior to publication date.''

**Illustration** Illustrations only: Send tearsheets, photocopies. Original work returned upon job's completion (upon written request).

**Photography** Buys photos from freelancers. Wants photos pertaining to any forthcoming themes. Uses b&w/color prints, 35mm transparencies. Send unsolicited photos by mail (on speculation).

**Terms** Buys all rights for mss and artwork. Pays 20-25/word for stories/articles. Pays on an individual basis for poetry, activities, games/puzzles. ''Covers are assigned and paid on an individual basis.'' Pays photographers per photo ($15-100 for b&w; $25-100 for color). Sample copy for $4.95 and SAE with $2 postage. Writer's/illustrator's/photo guidelines for SASE.

## CAMPUS LIFE

Christianity Today, International, 465 Gundersen Dr., Carol Stream IL 60188. (630)260-6200. Fax: (630)260-0114. E-mail: clmag@campuslife.net. Website: www.campuslife.net. **Articles and Fiction Editor:** Chris Lutes. Bimonthly magazine. Estab. 1944. Circ. 100,000. ''Our purpose is to help Christian high school students navigate adolescence with their faith intact.''

**Fiction** Young adults: humorous, problem-solving. Buys 5-6 mss/year. Byline given.

**Poetry** Reviews poetry.

**How to Contact/Writers** Fiction/nonfiction: Query only.

**Terms** Pays on acceptance. Writer's guidelines available for SASE.

## CAREER WORLD

Weekly Reader Corp., 200 First Stamford Place, P.O. Box 120023, Stamford CT 06912-0023. careerworld@weeklyreader.com. **Articles Editor:** Anne Flounders. **Art Director:** Kimberly Shake. Monthly (school year) magazine. Estab. 1972. A guide to careers, for students grades 6-12.

**Nonfiction** Young adults/teens: education, how-to, interview/profile, career awareness and development. Byline given.

**How to Contact/Writers** Nonfiction: Query with published clips and résumé. ''We do not want any unsolicited manuscripts.'' Responds to queries in 2 weeks.

**Illustration** Buys 5-10 illustrations/year. Works on assignment only. Reviews ms/illustration packages from artists. Manuscript/illustration packages and illustration only: Query; send promo sheet and tearsheets. Credit line given.

**Photography** Purchases photos from freelancers.

**Terms** Pays on publication. Buys all rights for mss. Pays $150 and up for articles. Pays illustrators by the project. Writer's guidelines free, but only on assignment.

## CAREERS & COLLEGES

Chalkboard Communications, LLC, P.O. Box 22, Keyport NJ 07735. (212)563-4688. Website: www.careersandcolleges.com. **Editorial Director:** Don Rauf. Magazine published 4 times during school year (September, November, January, March). Circ. 750,000. ''*Careers & Colleges* provides juniors and seniors in high school with useful, thought-provoking, and hopefully entertaining reading on career choices, higher education and other topics that will help prepare them for life after high school. Each issue focuses on a specific single theme: How to Get Into College; How to Pay for College; Careers; and Life After High School.''

**Nonfiction** Young adults/teens: careers, college, health, how-to, humorous, interview/profile, personal development, problem-solving, social issues, sports, travel. Buys 10-20 mss/year. Average word length: 1,000-1,500. Byline given.

**How to Contact/Writers** Nonfiction: Query. Responds to queries in 6 weeks. Will consider electronic submissions.

**Illustration** Buys 5 illustrations/issue; buys 20 illustrations/year. Works on assignment only. Reviews ms/illustration packages from artists. Query first. Illustrations only: Send tearsheets, cards. Responds to art samples in 3 weeks if interested. Credit line given.

**Terms** Pays on acceptance plus 45 days. Buys all rights. Pays $100-600 for assigned/unsolicited articles. Additional payment for ms/illustration packages ''must be negotiated.'' Pays $300-1,000 for color illustration; $200-700 for b&w/color inside illustration. Pays photographers by the project. Sample copy $5, writer's guidelines with SASE or via website.

**Tips** "We look for articles with great quotes, good reporting, good writing. Articles must be rich with examples and anecdotes, and must tie in with our mandate to help our teenaged readers plan their futures. We are especially looking for the most current trends, policy changes and information regarding college admissions, financial aid, and career opportunities. Visit our website for a good sense of our magazine."

## CARUS PUBLISHING COMPANY
P.O. Box 300, Peru IL 61354.
- See listings for *Babybug*, *Cicada*, *Click*, *Cricket*, *Ladybug*, *Muse*, *Spider* and *ASK* Carus. Publishing owns Cobblestone Publishing, publisher of *AppleSeeds*, *Calliope*, *Cobblestone*, *Dig*, *Faces*, *Footsteps* and *Odyssey*.

## CATHOLIC FORESTER
Catholic Order of Foresters, P.O. Box 3012, 355 Shuman Blvd., Naperville IL 60566-7012. (630)983-4900. E-mail: magazine@CatholicForester.com. Website: www.chatholicforester.com. **Articles Editor:** Patricia Baron. **Assistant V.P Communication:** Mary Ann File. **Art Director:** Keith Halla. Quarterly magazine. Estab. 1883. Circ. 85,000. Targets members of the Catholic Order of Foresters. In addition to the organization's news, it offers general interest pieces on health, finance, family life. Also use inspirational and humorous fiction.
**Fiction** Buys 6-10 mss/year. Average word length: 500-1,500.
**How to Contact/Writers** Fiction: Submit complete ms. Responds in 4 months. Will consider previously published work.
**Illustration** Buys 2-4 illustrations/issue. Uses color artwork only. Works on assignment only.
**Photography** Buys photos with accompanying ms only.
**Terms** Pays on acceptance. Buys first North American serial rights, reprint rights, one-time rights. Sample copies for 9×12 SAE and 3 first-class stamps. Writer's guidelines free for SASE.

## CELEBRATE
Word Action Publishing Co., Church of the Nazarene, 6401 The Paseo, Kansas City MO 64131. (816)333-7000, ext. 2487. (816)333-4439. E-mail: dwillemin@nazarene.org. Website: www.wordaction.com. **Editor:** Melissa Hammer. **EditorialAssistant:** Denise Willemin. Weekly publication. Estab. 2001. Circ. 30,000. "This weekly take-home paper connects Sunday School learning to life for preschoolers (age 3 and 4), kindergartners (age 5 and 6) and their families." 75% of publication aimed at juvenile market; 25% parents.
**Nonfiction** Picture-oriented material: arts/crafts, cooking, poems, action rhymes, piggyback songs (theme based). 50% of mss nonfiction. Byline given.
**Poetry** Reviews poetry. Maximum length: 4-8 lines. Unlimited submissions.
**How to Contact/Writers** Nonfiction: query. Responds to queries in 1 month. Responds to mss in 6 weeks. Publishes ms 1 year after acceptance. Will accept electronic submission via e-mail.
**Terms** Pays on acceptance. Buys all rights, multi-use rights. Pays a minimum of $2 for songs and rhymes; 25¢/line for poetry; $15 for activities, crafts, recipes. Compensation includes 2 contributor copies. Sample copy for SASE.
**Tips** "Limited acceptance at this time."

## 🌐 CHALLENGE
Pearson Education Australia, P.O. Box 1024, South Melbourne VIC 3205 Australia. (61)03 9811 2800. Fax: (61)03 981 2999. E-mail: magazines@pearsoned.com.au. Website: www.pearsoned.com.au/schools. **Articles Editor:** Petra Poupa. **Fiction Editor:** Meredith Costain. Quarterly Magazine. Circ. 20,000. "Magazines are educational and fun. We publish mainly nonfiction articles in a variety of genres and text types. They must be appropriate, factually correct, and of high interest. We publish interviews, recounts, informational and argumentative articles."
- *Challenge* is a theme-based publication geared to ages 11-14. Check the website to see upcoming themes and deadlines.
**Fiction** Middle readers, young adults: adventure, animal, contemporary, fantasy, folktale, humorous, multicultural, problem-solving, science fiction, sports, suspense/mystery. Buys 12 mss/year. Average word length: 400-1,000. Byline given.
**Nonfiction** Middle readers, young adults: animal, arts/crafts, biography, careers, cooking, fashion, geography, health, history, hobbies, how-to, humorous, interview/profile, math, multicultural, nature/environment, problem-solving, science, social issues, sports, travel (depends on theme of issue). Buys 100 ms/year. Average word length: 200-600. Byline given.
**Poetry** Reviews poetry.
**How to Contact/Writers** Fiction/nonfiction: Send complete ms. Responds to queries in 4-5 months; mss in 3 months. Publishes ms 3 months after acceptance. Will consider simultaneous submissions and electronic submissions via disk or e-mail.

**Photography** Looking for photos to suit various themes; photos needed depend on stories. Model/property release required; captions required. Uses color, standard sized, matte prints and 35mm transparencies. Provide résumé, business card, promotional literature and tearsheets to be kept on file. Responds only if interested.

**Terms** Pays on publication. Buys first Australian serial rights. Pays $80-200 (Australian) for stories; $100-220 (Australian) for articles. Additional payment for ms/illustration packages. Sample copies free for SAE. Writer's guidelines free for SASE.

**Tips** "Check out our website for information about our publications." See listings for *Comet* and *Explore.*

## ▢ CHEMMATTERS

American Chemical Society, 1155 16th Street, NW, Washington DC 20036. (202)872-6164. Fax: (202)833-7732. E-mail: chemmatters@acs.org. Website: www.chemistry.org/education/chemmatters.html. **Articles Editor:** Kevin McCue. **Art Director:** Cornithia Harris. Quarterly magazine. Estab. 1983. Circ. 35,000. "*ChemMatters*is a magazine for connecting high school readers with the fascinating chemistry of their everyday lives."

**Nonfiction** Young adults: biography, health, history, nature/environment, problem-solving, science. Must be related to chemistry. Buys 20 mss/year. Average word length: 1,400-2,100. Byline given.

**How to Contact/Writers** Nonfiction: Query with published clips. Responds to queries/mss in 2 weeks. Publishes ms 6 months after acceptance. Will consider simultaneous submissions, e-mail submissions.

Illustration Buys 3 illustrations/issue; 12 illustrations/year. Uses color artwork only. Works on assignment only. Reviews ms/illustration packages from artists. Query. Contact: Cornithia Harris, art director *ChemMatters.* Illustrations only: Query with promo sheet, résumé. Responds in 2 weeks. Samples returned with SASE; samples not filed. Credit line given.

**Photography** Looking for photos of high school students engaged in science-related activities. Model/property release required; captions required. Uses color prints, but prefers high-res PDFs. Query with samples. Responds in 2 weeks.

**Terms** Pays on acceptance. Minimally buys first North American serial rights, but prefers to buy all rights, reprint rights, electronic rights for mss. Buys all rights for artwork; non exclusive first rights for photos. Pays $500-$1,000 for articles. Additional payment for ms/illustration packages and for photos accompanying articles. Sample copies free for SAE 10×13 and 3 first-class stamps. Writer's guidelines free for SASE (available as e-mail attachment upon request).

**Tips** "Be aware of the content covered in a standard high school chemistry textbook. Choose themes and topics that are timely, interesting, fun, mystifying, AND that relate to the content and concepts of the first-year chemistry course. Articles should describe real people involved with real science. Best articles feature young people making a difference or solving a problem."

## CHILDREN'S BETTER HEALTH INSTITUTE

1100 Waterway Blvd., P.O. Box 567, Indianapolis IN 46206. See listings for *Children's Digest*, *Children's Playmate*, *Humpty Dumpty's Magazine*, *Jack and Jill*, *Turtle* and *U*S* Kids.*

## CHILDREN'S DIGEST

Children's Better Health Institute, 1100 Waterway Blvd., P.O. Box 567, Indianapolis IN 46206. (317)634-1100. Fax: (317)684-8094. Website: www.childrensdigestmag.org. For children ages 10-12.

- See website for submission guidelines.

## CHILDREN'S PLAYMATE

Children's Better Health Institute, 1100 Waterway Blvd., Box 567, Indianapolis IN 46206. (317)634-1100. Fax: (317)684-8094. Website: www.childrensplaymatemag.org. **Editor:** Terry Harshman. **Art Director:** Rob Falco. Magazine published 6 times/year. Estab. 1929. Circ. 135,000. For children ages 6-8 years; approximately 50% of content is health-related.

**Fiction** Average word length: 100-300. Byline given.

**Nonfiction** Young readers: easy recipes, games/puzzles, health, medicine, safety, science. Buys 16-20 mss/ year. Average word length: 300-500. Byline given.

**Poetry** Maximum length: 20-25 lines.

**How to Contact/Writers** Fiction/nonfiction: Send complete ms. Responds to mss in 3 months. Do not send queries.

**Illustration** Works on assignment only. Reviews ms/illustration packages from artists. Query first.

**Terms** Pays on publication for illustrators and writers. Buys all rights for mss and artwork. Pays 17¢/word for stories. Pays minimum $25 for poems. Pays $275 for color cover illustration; $90 for b&w inside; $70-155 for color inside. Sample copy $1.75. Writer's/illustrator's guidelines for SASE.

## CICADA

Carus Publishing Company, P.O. Box 300, 315 Fifth St., Peru IL 61354. (815)224-5803, ext. 656. Fax: (815)224-

6615. E-mail: CICADA@caruspub.com. Website: www.cricketmag.com. **Editor-in-Chief:** Marianne Carus. **Executive Editor:** Deborah Vetter. **Senior Editor:** Tracy C. Schoenle. **Senior Art Director:** Ron McCutchan. Bimonthly magazine. Estab. 1998. *Cicada* publishes fiction and poetry with a genuine teen sensibility, aimed at the high school and college-age market. The editors are looking for stories and poems that are thought-provoking but entertaining.

**Fiction** Young adults: adventure, animal, contemporary, fantasy, history, humorous, multicultural, nature/environment, romance, science fiction, sports, suspense/mystery, stories that will adapt themselves to a sophisticated cartoon, or graphic novel format. Buys up to 60 mss/year. Average word length: about 5,000 words for short stories; up to 15,000 for novellas (one novella per issue).

**Nonfiction** Young adults: first-person, coming-of-age experiences that are relevant to teens and young adults (example: life in the Peace Corps). Buys 6 mss/year. Average word length: about 5,000 words. Byline given.

**Poetry** Reviews serious, humorous, free verse, rhyming (if done well) poetry. Maximum length: up to 25 lines. Limit submissions to 5 poems.

**How to Contact/Writers** Fiction/nonfiction: send complete ms. Responds to mss in 3 months. Publishes ms 1-2 years after acceptance. Will consider simultaneous submissions if author lets us know.

**Illustration** Buys 20 illustrations/issue; 120 illustrations/year. Uses color artwork for cover; b&w for interior. Works on assignment only. Reviews ms/illustration packages from artists. Send ms with 1-2 sketches and samples of other finished art. Illustrations only: Query with samples. Responds in 6 weeks. Samples returned with SASE; samples filed. Credit line given.

**Photography** Wants documentary photos (clear shots that illustrate specific artifacts, persons, locations, phenomena, etc., cited in the text) and "art" shots of teens in photo montage/lighting effects etc. Uses b&w 4×5 glossy prints. Submit portfolio for review. Responds in 6 weeks.

**Terms** Pays on publication. Rights purchased vary. Pays up to 25¢/word for mss; up to $3/line for poetry. Pays illustrators $750 for color cover; $50-150 for b&w inside. Pays photographers per photo (range: $50-150). Sample copies for $8.50. Writer's/illustrator's/photo guidelines for SASE.

**Tips** "Please don't write for a junior high audience. We're looking for complex character development, strong plots, and thought-provoking themes for young people in high school and college. Don't forget humor! We're getting too many cancer-related stories and too much depressing fiction in general."

## THE CLAREMONT REVIEW

4980 Wesley Road, Victoria BC V8Y 1Y9 Canada. (250)685-5221. Fax: (250)658-5387. E-mail: editor@theClaremontReview.ca. Website: www.theClaremontReview.ca. Magazine 2 times/year. Estab. 1992. Circ. 500. "Publish quality fiction and poetry of emerging writers aged 13 to 19."

**Fiction** Young adults: multicultural, problem-solving, social issues, relationships. Average word length: 1,500-3,000.

**Poetry** Maximum length: 60 lines. No limit on submissions.

**How to Contact/Writers** Fiction: Send complete ms. Responds to queries in 2 weeks; mss in 2 months. Publishes ms 6 months after acceptance.

**Illustration** Illustrations only: Send postcard sample with samples, SASE. Contact: Janice McCachen, editor. Responds in 2 months. Samples returned with SASE. Credit line given.

**Terms** Buys first North American rights for mss. Pays contributor's copies when published. Sample copies for $8.00. Writer's guidelines for SASE.

**Tips** "Looking for good, concrete narratives with credible dialogue and solid use of original detail. It must be unique, honest and have a glimpse of some truth. Send an error-free final draft with a short covering letter and bio. Read our magazine first to familiarize yourself with what we publish."

## CLASS ACT

Class Act, Inc., P.O. Box 802, Henderson KY 42419-0802. E-mail: classact@lightpower.net. Website: www.classactpress.com. **Editor:** Mary Anderson. **Articles Editor:** Susan Thurman. Monthly, September-May. Newsletter. Estab. 1993. Circ. 300. "We are looking for practical, ready-to-use ideas for the English/language arts classroom (grades 6-12)."

**Nonfiction** Young adults/teens: games/puzzles. Does not want to see esoteric material; no master's thesis; no poetry (except articles about how to write poetry). Buys 20 mss/year. Average word length: 200-2,000. Byline given.

**How to Contact/Writers** Send complete ms. E-mail submissions (no attachments) and submissions on disk using Word encouraged. Responds to queries/mss in 1 month. Usually publishes ms 3-12 months after acceptance. Will consider simultaneous submissions. Must send SASE.

**Terms** Pays on acceptance. Pays $10-40 per article. Buys all rights. Sample copy for $3 and SASE.

**Tips** "We're interested only in language arts-related articles for teachers and students. Writers should realize teens often need humor in classroom assignments. In addition, we are looking for teacher-tested ideas that have already worked in the classroom. We currently have more puzzles than we need and are looking for prose rather than puzzles. Be clever. We've already seen a zillion articles on homonyms and haikus. If a SASE isn't sent, we'll assume you don't want a response.''

## Ⓝ CLICK

140 S. Dearborn, Suite 1450, Chicago IL 60603. (312)701-1720. Fax: (312)701-1728. E-mail: click@caruspub.com. Website: www.cricketmag.com. **Editor:** Lonnie Plecha. **Art Director:** Deb Porter. Magazine published 9 times/year. Estab. 1998. *''Click* is a science and exploration magazine for children ages 3-7. Designed and written with the idea that it's never too early to encourage a child's natural curiosity about the world, *Click's* 40 full-color pages are filled with amazing photographs, beautiful illustrations, and stories and articles that are both entertaining and thought-provoking.''

**Nonfiction** Young readers: animals, nature/environment, science. Average word length: 300-1,000. Byline given.

**How to Contact/Writers** *Click* does not accept unsolicited mss or queries. All articles are commissioned. To be considered for assignments, experienced science writers may send a résumé and 3 published clips.

**Illustration** Buys 10 illustrations/issue; 60 illustrations/year. Works on assignment only. Query with samples. Responds only if interested. Credit line given.

## CLUB CONNECTION

Gospel Publishing House, 1445 N. Boonville, Springfield MO 65807. (417)862-2781. E-mail clubconnection@ag.org. Website: www.clubconnection.ag.org. **Articles Editor:** Kelly Kirksey. Quarterly magazine. Estab. 1996. Circ. 11,000. ''A Christian magazine for girls clubs with a leaders' insert. We publish materials of a Christian nature.''

**Fiction** Young readers, middle readers: adventure, health, history, humorous, multicultural, nature/environment, problem-solving, religious, sports. Buys 15 mss/year. Average word length: 250-750. Byline given.

**Nonfiction** Young readers, Middle readers: arts/crafts, biography, concept, cooking, fashion, games/puzzles, geography, health, hobbies, how-to, humorous, interview/profile, multicultural, problem-solving, religion, social issues, sports, travel. Buys 8 mss/year. Average word length: 250-750. Byline given.

**How to Contact/Writers** Fiction/Nonfiction: Send complete ms. Responds to mss in 1 month. Publishes ms 9-12 months after acceptance. Will consider simultaneous submissions, e-mail submissions, previously published work.

**Illustration** Uses color artwork only. Works on assignment only.

**Photography** Buys photos with accompanying ms only. Uses color prints 3×5.

**Terms** Pays on publication. Buys first rights for mss. Original artwork returned at job's completion. Pays $25-40 for stories and articles. Additional payment for ms/illustration packages and for photos accompanying articles. Pays photographers $10 per photo. Sample copies for $2.00. Writer's guidelines for SASE.

## COBBLESTONE: Discover American History

Cobblestone Publishing, 30 Grove St., Suite C, Peterborough NH 03458. (603)924-7209. Fax: (603)924-7380. Website: www.cobblestonepub.com. **Editor:** Meg Chorlian. **Art Director:** Ann Dillon. **Editorial Director:** Lou Waryncia. Magazine published 9 times/year. Circ. 30,000. *''Cobblestone* is theme-related. Writers should request editorial guidelines which explain procedure and list upcoming themes. Queries must relate to an upcoming theme. It is recommended that writers become familiar with the magazine (sample copies available).''

• *Cobblestone* themes for 2005-2006 are available on website or with SASE.

**Fiction** Middle readers, young adults: folktales, history, multicultural.

**Nonfiction** Middle readers (school ages 8-14): arts/crafts, biography, geography, history (world and American), multicultural, social issues. All articles must relate to the issue's theme. Buys 120 mss/year. Average word length: 600-800. Byline given.

**Poetry** Up to 100 lines. ''Clear, objective imagery. Serious and light verse considered.'' Pays on an individual basis. Must relate to theme.

**How to Contact/Writers** Fiction/nonfiction: Query. ''A query must consist of all of the following to be considered: a brief cover letter stating the subject and word length of the proposed article, a detailed one-page outline explaining the information to be presented in the article, an extensive bibliography of materials the author intends to use in preparing the article, a SASE. Writers new to *Cobblestone* should send a writing sample with query. If you would like to know if your query has been received, please also include a stamped postcard that requests acknowledgment of receipt. In all correspondence, please include your complete address as well as a telephone number where you can be reached. A writer may send as many queries for one issue as he or she wishes, but each query must have a separate cover letter, outline, bibliography and SASE. Telephone queries are not accepted. Handwritten queries will not be considered. Queries may be submitted at any time, but queries sent well in advance of deadline *may not be answered for several months.* Go-aheads requesting material proposed in queries are usually sent five months prior to publication date. Unused queries will be returned approximately three to four months prior to publication date."

**Illustration** Buys 5 color illustrations/issue; 45 illustrations/year. Preferred theme or style: Material that is simple, clear and accurate but not too juvenile. Sophisticated sources are a must. Works on assignment only. Reviews ms/illustration packages from artists. Query. Illustrations only: Send photocopies, tearsheets, or other nonreturnable samples. "Illustrators should consult issues of *Cobblestone* to familiarize themselves with our needs." Responds to art samples in 1 month. Samples are not returned; samples filed. Original artwork returned at job's completion (upon written request). Credit line given.

**Photography** Photos must relate to upcoming themes. Send transparencies and/or color prints. Submit on speculation.

**Terms** Pays on publication. Buys all rights to articles and artwork. Pays 20-25¢/word for articles/stories. Pays on an individual basis for poetry, activities, games/puzzles. Pays photographers per photo ($50-100 for color). Sample copy $4.95 with $7\frac{1}{2} \times 10\frac{1}{2}$ SAE and 5 first-class stamps; writer's/illustrator's/photo guidelines free with SAE and 1 first-class stamp.

**Tips** Writers: "Submit detailed queries which show attention to historical accuracy and which offer interesting and entertaining information. Study past issues to know what we look for. All feature articles, recipes, activities, fiction and supplemental nonfiction are freelance contributions." Illustrators: "Submit color samples, not too juvenile. Study past issues to know what we look for. The illustration we use is generally for stories, recipes and activities." (See listings for *AppleSeeds*, *Calliope*, *Dig*, *Faces*, *Footsteps*, and *Odyssey*.)

## COLLEGEBOUND TEEN MAGAZINE

Ramholtz Publishing, Inc., 1200 South Ave., Suite 202, Staten Island NY 10314. (718)761-4800. Fax: (718)761-3300. E-mail: editorial@collegebound.net. Website: www.collegebound.net. **Articles Editor:** Gina LaGuardia. **Art Director:** Suzanne Vidal. Monthly magazine and website. Estab. 1987. Circ. 75,000 (regionals); 725,000 (nationals). *CollegeBound Teen Magazine* is written by college students (and those "young at heart") for high school juniors and seniors. It is designed to provide an inside view of college life, with college students from around the country serving as correspondents. The magazine's editorial content offers its teen readership personal accounts on all aspects of college, from living with a roommate, choosing a major, and joining a fraternity or sorority, to college dating, interesting courses, beating the financial aid fuss, and other college-bound concerns. *CollegeBound Teen Magazine* is published six times regionally throughout the tri-state area. Special issues include the National Editions (published each September and February) and Spring California, Illinois, Texas, Florida and New England issues. The magazine offers award-winning World Wide Web affiliates starting at *CollegeBound.NET*, at www.collegebound.net.

**Nonfiction** Young adults: careers, college prep, fashion, health, how-to, interview/profile, problem-solving, social issues, college life. Buys 70 mss/year. Average word length: 400-1,100 words. Byline given.

**How to Contact/Writers** Nonfiction: Query with published clips. Responds to queries in 2 months; mss in 10 weeks. Publishes ms 3-4 months after acceptance. Will consider electronic submission via disk or modem, previously published work (as long as not a competitor title).

**Illustration** Buys 2-3 illustrations/issue. Uses color artwork only. Works on assignment only. Reviews ms/illustration packages from artists. Query. Illustrations only: Query with samples. Responds in 2 months. Samples kept on file. Credit line given.

**Terms** Pays on publication. Buys first North American serial rights, all rights or reprint rights for mss. Buys first rights for artwork. Originals returned if requested, with SASE. Pays $25-100 for articles 30 days upon publication. All contributors receive 2 issues with payment. Pays illustrators $25-125 for color inside. Sample copies free for #10 SASE and $3 postage. Writer's guidelines for SASE.

**Tips** "Review the sample issue and get a good feel for the types of articles we accept and our tone and purpose."

## 🌐 COMET

Pearson Education Australia, 95 Coventry St., South Melbourne VIC Australia. (61)03 9697 0666. Fax: (61)03 9699 2041. E-mail: magazines@pearsoned.com.au. Website: www.pearsoned.com.au/schools. **Articles Editor:** Petra Poupa. **Fiction Editor:** Meredith Costain. Quarterly Magazine. Circ. 20,000. "Magazines are educational and fun. We publish mainly nonfiction articles in a variety of genres and text types. They must be appropriate, factually correct, and of high interest. We publish interviews, recounts, informational and argumentative articles."

● *Comet* is a theme based publication. Check their website to see upcoming themes and deadlines.

**Fiction** Picture-oriented material, young readers: adventure, animal, contemporary, folktale, multicultural, nature/environment, problem solving. Young readers: fantasy, humorous, suspense/mystery. Average word length: 400-1,000. Byline given.

**Nonfiction** Picture-oriented material, young readers: animal, arts/crafts, biography, careers, cooking, health, hobbies, how-to, interview/profile, math, multicultural, nature/environment, problem-solving, science, social issues, sports, travel. Picture-oriented material: geography. Young readers: games/puzzles, humorous. Average word length: 200-600. Byline given.

**Poetry** Reviews poetry.

**How to Contact/Writers** Fiction/nonfiction: Send complete ms. Responds to queries in 1 month; mss in 3 months. Publishes ms 3 months after acceptance. Will consider simultaneous submissions and electronic submissions via disk or e-mail.

**Photography** Looking for photos to suit various themes; photos needed depend on stories. Model/property release required; captions required. Uses color, standard sized, matte prints and 35mm transparencies. Provide résumé, business card, promotional literature and tearsheets to be kept on file. Responds only if interested.

**Terms** Pays on publication. Buys first Australian rights. Pays $80-200 (Australian) for stories; $100-220 (Australian) for articles. Additional payment for ms/illustration packages. Sample copies free for SAE. Writer's guidelines free for SASE.

**Tips** ''Check out our website for information about our publications.'' See listings for *Challenge* and *Explore.*

## COUSTEAU KIDS

(formerly *Dolphin Log*), The Cousteau Society, 710 Settlers Landing Rd., Hampton VA 23669. (757)722-9300. Fax: (757)722-8185. E-mail: mnorkin@ilsweb.com. Website: www.cousteaukids.org. **Articles Editor:** Melissa Norkin, editor. ''Entirely nonfiction subject matter encompasses all areas of science, natural history, marine biology, ecology, and the environment as they relate to our global water system. The philosophy of the magazine is to delight, instruct, and instill an environmental ethic and understanding of the interconnectedness of living organisms, including people. Of special interest are articles on ocean- or water-related themes which develop reading and comprehension skills.'' Entire publication aimed at juvenile market.

**Nonfiction** Considers Young Readers: animal, games/puzzles, geography, interview/profile, nature/environment, ocean, science. Middle Readers: animal, games/puzzles, geography, interview/profile, nature/environment, ocean, science. Multicultural needs include indigenous peoples, lifestyles of ancient peoples, etc. Does not want to see talking animals. No dark or religious themes. Average word length: 500-700. Byline given.

**How To Contact/Writers** Fiction: Query. Unsolicited mss returned unopened. Responds to queries in 3 months; mss in 6 months.

**Illustration** Buys 6 illustrations/year. Preferred theme: biological illustration. Reviews ms/illustration packages from artists. For first contact, query with samples, send résumé, promo sheet. Responds only if interested. Credit line given.

**Photography** Wants ''sharp, colorful pictures of sea creatures. The more unusual the better.'' Submit duplicate slides only. Query fo submissions/rates.

**Terms** Pays on publication. Buys first North American serial rights, reprint rights. Pays $75-250 for articles. Pays $100-400 for illustrations. Pays illustrators $75-200 for color photos. Sample copies available for $2.50 with 9×12 SEA and 3 first-class stamps. Writer's/illustrator's guidelines free for SASE.

**Tips** ''Writers: Write simply and clearly and don't anthropomorphize. Illustrators: Be scientifically accurate and don't anthropomorphize. Some background in biology is helpful, as our needs range from simple line drawings to scientific illustrations which must be researched for biological and technical accuracy.''

## CRICKET MAGAZINE

Carus Publishing, Company, P.O. Box 300, Peru IL 61354. (815)224-5803, ext. 656. Website: www.cricketmag.c om. **Editor-in-Chief:** Marianne Carus. **Executive Editor:** Deborah Vetter. **Senior Editor:** Tracy Schoenle. **Assistant Editor:** Adam Oldaker. **Senior Art Director:** Ron McCutchan. Monthly magazine. Estab. 1973. Circ. 72,000. Children's literary magazine for ages 9-14.

**Fiction** Middle readers, young adults/teens: contemporary, fantasy, folk and fairy tales, history, humorous, science fiction, suspense/mystery. Buys 140 mss/year. Maximum word length: 2,000. Byline given.

**Nonfiction** Middle readers, young adults/teens: adventure, architecture, archaeology, biography, foreign culture, games/puzzles, geography, natural history, science and technology, social science, sports, travel. Multicultural needs include articles on customs and cultures. Requests bibliography with submissions. Buys 40 mss/year. Average word length: 200-1,500. Byline given.

**Poetry** Reviews poems, 1-page maximum length. Limit submission to 5 poems or less.

**How to Contact/Writers** Send complete ms. Do not query first. Responds to mss in 3 months. Does not like but will consider simultaneous submissions. SASE required for response.

**Illustration** Buys 35 illustrations (14 separate commissions)/issue; 425 illustrations/year. Preferred theme for style: ''strong realism; strong people, especially kids; good action illustration; no cartoons. All media, but prefer other than pencil.'' Reviews ms/illustration packages from artists, ''but reserves option to re-illustrate.'' Send complete ms with sample and query. Illustrations only: Provide tearsheets or good quality photocopies to be kept on file. SASE required for response/return of samples. Responds to art samples in 2 months.

**Photography** Purchases photos with accompanying ms only. Model/property releases required. Uses color transparencies, b&w glossy prints.

**Terms** Pays on publication. Rights purchased vary. Do not send original artwork. Pays up to 25¢/word for unsolicited articles; up to $3/line for poetry. Pays $750 for color cover; $75-150 for b&w, $150-250 for color inside. Writer's/illustrator's guidelines for SASE.

**Tips** Writers: "Read copies of back issues and current issues. Adhere to specified word limits. *Please* do not query." Illustrators: "Edit your samples. Send only your best work and be able to reproduce that quality in assignments. Put name and address on *all* samples. Know a publication before you submitis your style appropriate?"

### N CURRENT SCIENCE

Weekly Reader Corp., 200 First Stanford Place, Stanford CT 06912-0034. (203)705-3500. Fax: (203)705-1661. E-mail: science@weeklyreader.com. Website: www.weeklyreader.com. **Submissions Editor:** Hugh Westrup. 16 times/year magazine. Estab. 1927. "Current Science uses today's new to make science relevant to students in grades 6-10. Each issue covers every area of the science curriculum—life, earth, and physical science, plus health and technology." Entire publication aimed at juvenile market.

**Nonfiction** Considers young adults/teens: health, nature/environment, science. Buys 30-40 mss/year. Average word length: 800-1600. Byline given.

**How To Contact/Writers** Nonfiction: Query with published clips. Responds to queries in 1. Considers electronic submissions via e-mail.

**Terms** Pays on publication. Sample copies free for SASE. Writer's guidelines free for SASE.

### DANCE MAGAZINE

333 Seventh Ave., 11th Floor, New York NY 10001. (212)979-4803. Fax: (646)674-0102 Website: www.dancemagazine.com. **Editor-in-Chief:** Wendy Perron. **Art Director:** Ragnar Johnson. Monthly magazine. Estab. 1927. Circ. 45,000. Covers "all things dance—features, news, reviews, calendar. We have a Young Dancer section." Byline given.

**How to Contact** Query with published clips.

**Photography** Uses dance photos.

**Terms** Pays on publication. Buys first rights. Additional payment for ms/illustration packages and for photos accompanying articles. Pays photographers per photo. Sample copies for $4.95.

**Tips** "Study the magazine for style."

### DAVEY AND GOLIATH

(formerly *Christ in Our Home for Families with Children*), Augsburg Fortress, 100 S. Fifth St., Suite 700, Minneapolis MN 55440. E-mail: dg@augsburgfortress.org. Website: www.augsburgfortress.org. **Editor:** Arlene Flancher. Quarterly magazine. Circ. approximately 50,000. This is a booklet of interactive conversations and activities related to daily devotional material. Used primarily by Lutheran families with elementary school-aged children.

**Fiction** Young readers, middle readers: adventure, contemporary, faith-related conversations, holidays and church seasons, nature/environment, problem-solving, religious, service activities. Byline given.

**Nonfiction** Young readers, middle readers: devotional, faith-related conversations and activities, narrative, nature/environment, problem-solving, religious, social issues. Byline given.

**How to Contact/Writers** Fiction/nonfiction: Query with published clips. Responds to unsolicited mss in 3 months. Manuscripts are accepted for review only. Published material is 100% assigned.

**Terms** Pays on acceptance of final ms assignment. Buys all rights. Pays $40/printed page on assignment. Free sample and information for prospective writers. Include 6×9 SAE and postage.

**Tips** "Pay attention to details in the sample devotional. Follow the process laid out in the information for prospective writers. Ability to interpret Bible texts appropriately for children is required."

### DIG

Cobblestone Publishing, 30 Grove St., Suite C, Peterburough NH 03450. (603)924-7209. Fax: (603)924-7380. E-mail: cfbakeriii@meganet.net. Website: www.digonsite.com. **Editor:** Rosalie Baker. **Editorial Director:** Lou Waryncia. **Art Director:** Ann Dillon. Magazine published 9 times/year. Estab. 1999. Circ. 20,000. An archaeology magazine for kids ages 8-14. Publishes entertaining and educational stories about discoveries, artifacts, archaeologists.

• *Dig* was purchased by Cobblestone Publishing, a division of Carus Publishing.

**Nonfiction** Middle readers, young adults: biography, games/puzzles, history, science, archaeology. Buys 50 mss/year. Average word length: 400-800. Byline given.

**How to Contact/Writers** Fiction/nonfiction: Query. "A query must consist of all of the following to be considered: a brief cover letter stating the subject and word length of the proposed article, a detailed one-page outline explaining the information to be presented in the article, a bibliography of materials the author intends to use in preparing the article, and a SASE. Writers new to *Dig* should send a writing sample with query. If you would like to know if a query has been received, include a stamped postcard that requests acknowledgement of receipt.'' Multiple queries accepted (include separate cover letter, outline, bibliography, SASE)may not be answered for many months. Go-aheads requesting material proposed in queries are usually sent 5 months prior to publication date. Unused queries will be returned approximately 3-4 months prior to publication date.

**Illustration** Buys 10-15 illustrations/issue; 60-75 illustrations/year. Prefers color artwork. Works on assignment only. Reviews ms/illustration packages from artists. Query. Illustrations only: Query with samples. Arrange portfolio review. Send tearsheets. Responds in 2 months only if interested. Samples not returned; samples filed. Credit line given.

**Photography** Uses anything related to archaeology, history, artifacts, and current archaeological events that relate to kids. Uses color prints and 35mm transparencies. Provide résumé, promotional literature or tearsheets to be kept on file. Responds only if interested.

**Terms** Pays on publication. Buys all rights for mss. Buys first North American rights for photos. Original artwork returned at job's completion. Pays 20-25¢/word. Additional payment for ms/illustration packages and for photos accompanying articles. Pays per photo.

**Tips** ''We are looking for writers who can communicate archaeological concepts in a conversational, interesting, informative and *accurate* style for kids. Writers should have some idea where photography can be located to support their work.''

## DISCOVERIES

Children's Ministries, Sunday School Curriculum, 6401 The Paseo, Kansas City MO 64131. (816)333-7000. Fax: (816)333-4439. E-mail: vfolsom@nazarene.org. **Editor:** Virginia L. Folsom. **Executive Editor:** Donna L. Fillmore. **Assistant Editor:** Sarah Weatherwax. Take-home paper. ''*Discoveries* is a leisure-reading piece for third- and fourth-graders. It is published weekly by WordAction Publishing. The major purpose of the magazine is to provide a leisure-reading piece which will build Christian behavior and values and provide reinforcement for Biblical concepts taught in the Sunday School curriculum. The focus of the reinforcement will be life-related, with some historical appreciation. *Discoveries'* target audience is children ages eight to ten in grades three and four. The readability goal is third to fourth grade.''

**Fiction** Middle readers: adventure, contemporary, humorous, religious. ''Fiction stories should vividly portray definite Christian emphasis or character-building values, without being preachy. The setting, plot and action should be realistic.'' 500-word maximum. Byline given.

**Nonfiction** Puzzles that fit the theme list and trivia (150 words) about any miscellaneous area of interest to 8 to 10-year olds (hobbies, fun activities, to do in your spare time, interesting facts). Please document sources.

**How to Contact/Writers** Fiction: Send complete ms. Responds to queries/mss in 1 month.

**Terms** Pays ''approximately one year before the date of issue.'' Buys multi-use rights. Pays $25 for stories; $15 for trivia, puzzles, and cartoons. Contributor s receive 2 complimentary copies of publication. Sample copy free for #10 SASE with 1 first-class stamp. Writer's/artist's guidelines free with #10 SAE.

**Tips** ''*Discoveries* is committed to reinforcement of the Biblical concepts taught in the Sunday School curriculum. Because of this, the themes needed are mainly as follows: faith in God, obedience to God, accepting Jesus as Savior, finding God's will, choosing to do right, trusting God in hard times, prayer, importance of Bible memorization, appreciation of Bible as God's Word to man, Christians working together, showing kindness to others, witnessing. Because of this stories must follow our theme list. Please request one before attempting to submit copy.'' (See listing for *Passport*.)

## DRAMATICS MAGAZINE

Educational Theatre Association, 2343 Auburn Ave., Cincinnati OH 45219. (513)421-3900. E-mail: dcorathers@ edta.org. Website: www.edta.org. **Articles Editor:** Don Corathers. **Art Director:** William Johnston. Published monthly September-May. Estab. 1929. Circ. 35,000. ''Dramatics is for students (mainly high school age) and teachers of theater. Mix includes how-to (tech theater, acting, directing, etc.), informational, interview, photo feature, humorous, profile, technical. ''We want our student readers to grow as theater artists and become a more discerning and appreciative audience. Material is directed to both theater students and their teachers, with strong student slant.''

**Fiction** Young adults: drama (one-act and full-length plays.) Does not want to see plays that show no understanding of the conventions of the theater. No plays for children, no Christmas or didactic ''message'' plays. ''We prefer unpublished scripts that have been produced at least once.'' Buys 5-9 plays/year. Emerging playwrights have better chances with résumé of credits.

**Nonfiction** Young adults: arts/crafts, careers, how-to, interview/profile, multicultural (all theater-related). ''We try to portray the theater community in all its diversity.'' Does not want to see academic treatises. Buys 50 mss/year. Average word length: 750-3,000. Byline given.

**How to Contact/Writers** Send complete ms. Responds in 3 months (longer for plays). Published ms 3 months after acceptance. Will consider simultaneous submissions and previously published work occasionally.

**Illustration** Buys 0-2 illustrations/year. Works on assignment only. Arrange portfolio review; send résumé, promo sheets and tearsheets. Responds only if interested. Samples returned with SASE; sample not filed. Credit line given.

**Photography** Buys photos with accompanying ms only. Looking for "good-quality production or candid photography to accompany article. We very occasionally publish photo essays." Model/property release and captions required. Uses $5 \times 7$ or $8 \times 10$ b&w glossy prints and 35mm transparencies. Also uses high resolution digital files or Zip disk or CD (JPEG or TIFF files). Query with résumé of credits. Responds only if interested.

**Terms** Pays on acceptance. Buys one-time print and short term web rights. Buys one-time rights for artwork and photos. Original artwork returned at job's completion. Pays $100-500 for plays; $50-500 for articles; up to $100 for illustrations. Pays photographers by the project or per photo. Sometimes offers additional payment for ms/illustration packages and photos accompanying a ms. Sample copy available for $9 \times 12$ SAE with 4 ounces first-class postage. Writer's and photo guidelines available for SASE or via website.

**Tips** "Obtain our writer's guidelines and look at recent back issues. The best way to break in is to know our audience—drama students, teachers and others interested in theaterand write for them. Writers who have some practical experience in theater, especially in technical areas, have an advantage, but we'll work with anybody who has a good idea. Some freelancers have become regular contributors."

## DYNAMATH

Scholastic Inc., 557 Broadway, Room 4052, New York NY 10012-3999. (212)343-6458. Fax: (212)343-4459. E-mail: dynamath@scholastic.com. Website: www.scholastic.com/dynamath. **Editor:** Matt Friedman. **Art Director:** Vanessa Frazier. Monthly magazine. Estab. 1982. Circ. 200,000. Purpose is "to make learning math fun, challenging and uncomplicated for young minds in a very complex world."

**Nonfiction** Middle readers: animal, arts/crafts, cooking, fashion, games/puzzles, health, history, hobbies, how-to, humorous, math, multicultural, nature/environment, problem-solving, science, social issues, sports—all must relate to math and science topics and end with a 5 question math or science activity. Average length: 600 words.

**How to Contact/Writers** Nonfiction: Query with published clips, send ms. Responds to queries in 1 month; mss in 6 weeks. Publishes ms 4 months after acceptance. Will consider simultaneous submissions.

**Illustration** Buys 4 illustrations/issue. Illustration only: Query first; send résumé and tearsheets. Responds on submissions only if interested. Credit line given.

**Terms** Pays on acceptance. Buys all rights for mss, artwork, photographs. Originals returned to artist at job's completion. Pays $50-450 for stories.

## ⊕ EXPLORE

Pearson Education Australia, 95 Coventry St., South Melbourne VIC Australia. (61)03 9697 0666. Fax: (61)03 9699 2041. E-mail: magazines@pearsoned.com.au. Website: www.pearsoned.com.au/schools. **Articles Editor:** Petra Poupa. **Fiction Editor:** Meredith Costain. Quarterly Magazine. Circ. 20,000. "Magazines are educational and fun. We publish mainly nonfiction articles in a variety of genres and text types. They must be appropriate, factually correct, and of high interest. We publish interviews, recounts, informational and argumentative articles."

• *Explore* is a theme based publication. Check the website to see upcoming themes and deadlines.

**Fiction** Young readers, middle readers: adventure, animal, contemporary, fantasy, folktale, humorous, multicultural, nature/environment, problem-solving, suspense/mystery. Middle readers: science fiction, sports. Average word length: 400-1,000. Byline given.

**Nonfiction** Young readers, middle readers: animal, arts/crafts, biography, careers, cooking, health, history, hobbies, how-to, interview/profile, math, multicultural, nature/environment, problem-solving, science, social issues, sports, travel. Young readers: games/puzzles. Middle readers: concept, fashion, geography. Average word length: 200-600. Byline given.

**Poetry** Reviews poetry.

**How to Contact/Writers** Fiction/nonfiction: Send complete ms. Responds to queries in 1 month; mss in 3 months. Publishes ms 3 months after acceptance. Will consider simultaneous submissions and electronic submissions via disk or e-mail.

**Photography** Looking for photos to suit various themes; photos needed depend on stories. Model/property release required; captions required. Uses color, standard sized, matte prints and 35mm transparencies. Provide résumé, business card, promotional literature and tearsheets to be kept on file. Responds only if interested.

**Terms** Pays on publication. Buys first Australian rights. Pays $80-200 (Australian) for stories; $100-220 (Australian) for articles. Additional payment for ms/illustration packages. Sample copies free for SAE. Writer's guidelines free for SASE.

**Tips** "Check out our website for information about our publications." (See listings for *Challenge* and *Comet*.)

## FACES, People, Places & Cultures

Cobblestone Publishing, 30 Grove St., Peterborough NH 03458. (603)924-7209. Fax: (603)924-7380. E-mail: facesmag@yahoo.com. Website: www.cobblestonepub.com. **Editor:** Elizabeth Crooker Carpentiere. **Editorial Director:** Lou Warnycia. **Art Director:** Ann Dillon. Magazine published 9 times/year (September-May). Circ. 15,000. *Faces* is a theme-related magazine; writers should send for theme list before submitting ideas/queries. Each month a different world culture is featured through the use of feature articles, activities and photographs and illustrations.

- See website for 2005-2006 theme list for *Faces*.

**Fiction** Middle readers, young adults/teens: adventure, folktales, history, multicultural, plays, religious, travel. Does not want to see material that does not relate to a specific upcoming theme. Buys 9 mss/year. Maximum word length: 800. Byline given.

**Nonfiction** Middle readers and young adults/teens: animal, anthropology, arts/crafts, biography, cooking, fashion, games/puzzles, geography, history, how-to, humorous, interview/profile, nature/environment, religious, social issues, sports, travel. Does not want to see material not related to a specific upcoming theme. Buys 63 mss/year. Average word length: 300-600. Byline given.

**Poetry** Clear, objective imagery; up to 100 lines. Must relate to theme.

**How to Contact/Writers** Fiction/nonfiction: Query with published clips and 2-3 line biographical sketch. "Ideas should be submitted six to nine months prior to the publication date. Responses to ideas are usually sent approximately four months before the publication date." Guidelines on website.

**Illustration** Buys 3 illustrations/issue; buys 27 illustrations/year. Preferred theme or style: Material that is meticulously researched (most articles are written by professional anthropologists); simple, direct style preferred, but not too juvenile. Works on assignment only. Roughs required. Reviews ms/illustration packages from artists. Illustrations only: Send samples of b&w work. "Illustrators should consult issues of *Faces* to familiarize themselves with our needs." Responds to art samples only if interested. Samples returned with SASE. Original artwork returned at job's completion (upon written request). Credit line given.

**Photography** Wants photos relating to forthcoming themes.

**Terms** Pays on publication. Buys all rights for mss and artwork. Pays 20-25¢/word for articles/stories. Pays on an individual basis for poetry. Covers are assigned and paid on an individual basis. Pays illustrators $50-300 for color inside. Pays photographers per photo ($25-100 for color). Sample copy $4.95 with 7½×10½ SAE and 5 first-class stamps. Writer's/illustrator's/photo guidelines via website or free with SAE and 1 first-class stamp.

**Tips** "Writers are encouraged to study past issues of the magazine to become familiar with our style and content. Writers with anthropological and/or travel experience are particularly encouraged; *Faces* is about world cultures. All feature articles, recipes and activities are freelance contributions." Illustrators: "Submit b&w samples, not too juvenile. Study past issues to know what we look for. The illustration we use is generally for retold legends, recipes and activities."

## FLORIDA LEADER, for high school students

Oxendine Publishing, Inc., P.O. Box 14081, Gainesville FL 32604-2081. (352)373-6907. Fax: (352)373-8120. E-mail: stephanie@studentleader.com. Website: www.floridaleader.com. **Articles Editor:** Stephanie Reck. **Art Director:** Jeff Riemersma. Published 2 times/year. Estab. 1992. Circ. 25,000. "Magazine features articles focused on student leadership, current financial aid and admissions information, and stories on other aspects of college life for prospective college students. *Florida Leader* highlights achievements of Florida students and helps them make college decisions." Audience includes ages 14-17.

**Nonfiction** Young adult/teens: interview/profile (with student leaders), problem-solving. Looking for "more advanced pieces on college preparation—academic skills, career exploration and general motivation for college." Buys 6-8 mss/year. Average word length: 800-1,000. 200-300 for columns.

**How to Contact/Writers** Nonfiction: Query with published clips. Responds to queries/mss in 5 weeks. Publishes ms 3-5 months after acceptance. Will consider electronic submissions, previously published work. Responds only if interested. Samples returned with SASE.

**Illustration** Buys 5 illustrations/issue; 20 illustrations/year. Uses color artwork only. Works on assignment only. Reviews ms/illustration packages from artists. Query. Illustrations only: query with samples; send résumé, promo sheet, tearsheets. Responds only if interested. Samples returned with SASE; samples filed. Credit line given.

**Photography** Buys photos from freelancers. Buys photos separately. Works on assignment only. Model/property release required. Uses color prints and 35mm, 2¼×2¼, 4×5 transparencies. Query with samples. Responds only if interested.

**Terms** Pays on publication. Buys first North American serial rights, reprint rights for mss. Buys first-time rights for artwork and photos. Originals returned at job's completion. Pays illustrators $75 for color inside. Pays photographers by the project (range: $150-300). Sample copies for $3.50. Writer's guidelines for SASE, e-mail, or on website.

**Tips** "Query first and review past issues for style and topics."

## Focus on the Family CLUBHOUSE; Focus on the Family CLUBHOUSE JR.

Focus on the Family, Colorado Springs CO 80920. (719)531-3400. Website: www.clubhousemagazine.org. **Editor:** Jesse Florea, *Clubhouse*; Annette Bourland, editor *Clubhouse Jr.* Art Director: Mike Harrigan. Monthly magazine. Estab. 1987. Combined circulation is 175,000. "*Focus on the Family Clubhouse* is a 24-page Christian magazine, published monthly, for children ages 8-12. Similarly, *Focus on the Family Clubhouse Jr.* is published for children ages 4-8. We want fresh, exciting literature that promotes biblical thinking, values and behavior in every area of life."

**Fiction** Young readers, middle readers: adventure, contemporary, multicultural, nature/environment, religious. Middle readers: history, sports, science fiction. Multicultural needs include: "interesting, informative, accurate information about other cultures to teach children appreciation for the world around them." Buys approximately 6-10 mss/year. Average word length: *Clubhouse*, 500-1,400; *Clubhouse Jr.*, 250-1,100. Byline given on all fiction and puzzles.

**Nonfiction** Young readers, middle readers: arts/crafts, cooking, games/puzzles, how-to, multicultural, nature/environment, religion, science. Young readers: animal. Middle readers, young adult/teen: interview/profile. Middle readers: sports. Buys 3-5 mss/year. Average word length: 200-1,000. Byline given.

**Poetry** *Clubhouse Jr.* wants to see "humorous or biblical" poetry for 4-8 year olds. Maximum length: 250 words. *Clubhouse* does not want poetry.

**How to Contact/Writers** Fiction/nonfiction: send complete ms with SASE. Responds to queries/mss in 6 weeks.

**Illustration** Buys 8 illustrations/issue. Uses color artwork only. Works on assignment only. Reviews ms/illustration packages from artists. Submit ms with rough sketches. Illustrations only: Query with samples, arrange portfolio review or send tearsheets. Responds in 3 months. Samples returned with SASE; samples kept on file. Credit line given.

**Photography** Buys photos from freelancers. Uses 35mm transparencies. Photographers should query with samples; provide résumé and promotional literature or tearsheets. Responds in 2 months.

**Terms** Pays on acceptance. Buys first North American serial rights for mss. Buys first rights or reprint rights for artwork and photographs. Original artwork returned at job's completion. Additional payment for ms/illustration packages. Pays writers $150-300 for stories; $50-150 for articles. Pays illustrators $300-700 for color cover; $200-700 for color inside. Pays photographers by the project or per photo. Sample copies for 9×12 SAE and 3 first-class stamps.

**Tips** "Test your writing on children. The best stories avoid moralizing or preachiness and are not written *down* to children. They are the products of writers who share in the adventure with their readers, exploring the characters they have created without knowing for certain where the story will lead. And they are not always explicitly Christian, but are built upon a Christian foundation (and, at the very least, do not contradict biblical views or values)."

## FOOTSTEPS, The Magazine of African American History

Cobblestone Publishing Co., 30 Grove St., Suite C, Peterborough NH 03458. (603)924-7204 , (800)821-0115. Fax: (608)924-7380. Website: www.cobblestonepub.com. **Editor:** Charles F. Baker. Magazine on African American history and heritage for readers ages 8-14.

- *Footsteps* themes for 2004-2005 include Black Inventors, Women Writers, and The Blues. For additional themes and time frames, visit the website.

**Nonfiction** Middle readers: history, interviews/profile. Word length: 300-750 words.

**How to Contact/Writers** Query with cover letter, outline, bibliography and SASE. "All material must relate to the theme of a specific upcoming issue in order to be considered."

**Terms** Writer's guidelines available on website.

**Tips** "We are looking for articles that are lively, age-appropriate, and exhibit an original approach to the theme of the issue. Cultural sensitivity and historical accuracy are extremely important."

## THE FRIEND MAGAZINE

The Church of Jesus Christ of Latter-day Saints, 50 E. North Temple, Salt Lake City UT 84150-3226. (801)240-2210. **Editor:** Vivian Paulsen. **Art Director:** Mark Robison. Monthly magazine for 3-11 year olds. Estab. 1971. Circ. 275,000.

**Nonfiction** Publishes children's/true stories —adventure, ethnic, some historical, humor, mainstream, religious/inspirational, nature. Length: 1,000 words maximum.

**Poetry** Reviews poetry. Maximum length: 20 lines.

**How to Contact/Writers** Send complete ms. Responds to mss in 2 months.

**Illustration** Illustrations only: Query with samples; arrange personal interview to show portfolio; provide résumé and tearsheets for files.

**Terms** Pays on acceptance. Buys all rights for mss. Pays $100 for unsolicited nonfiction articles , 200-300 words; $250 for 400 words and up; $50 for poems ; $ 15 for recipes, activities and games. Contributors are encouraged to send for sample copy for $1.50, 9 x11 envelope and four 37 -cent stamps. Free writer's guidelines.

**Tips** "*The Friend* is published by The Church of Jesus Christ of Latter-day Saints for boys and girls up to eleven years of age. All submissions are carefully read by the *Friend* staff, and those not accepted are returned within two months for SASE. Submit seasonal material at least one year in advance. Query letters and simultaneous submissions are not encouraged. Authors may request rights to have their work reprinted after their manuscript is published."

## FUN FOR KIDZ

P.O. Box 227, Bluffton OH 45817-0227. (419)358-4610. Fax: (419)358-5027. Website: www.funforkidz.com. **Articles Editor:** Marilyn Edwards. Bimonthly magazine. Estab. 2002. "*Fun for Kidz* is a magazine created for boys and girls ages 6-13, with youngsters 8, 9, and 10 the specific target age. The magazine is designed as an activity publication to be enjoyed by both boys and girls on the alternative months of *Hopscotch* and *Boys' Quest* magazines."

• *Fun for Kidz* is theme-oriented. Send SASE for theme list and writer's guidelines.

**Fiction** Picture-oriented material, young readers, middle readers: adventure, animal, history, humorous, problem-solving, multicultural, nature/environment, sports. Average word length: 300-700.

**Nonfiction** Picture-oriented material, young readers, middle readers: animal, arts/crafts, cooking, games/puzzles, history, hobbies, how-to, humorous, problem-solving, sports, carpentry projects. Average word length: 300-700. Byline given.

**Poetry** Reviews poetry.

**How to Contact/Writers** Fiction/nonfiction: Send complete ms. Responds to queries in 2 weeks; mss in 5 weeks. Will consider simultaneous submissions. "Will not respond to faxed/e-mailed queries, mss, etc."

**Illustration** Works on assignment mostly. "We are anxious to find artists capable of illustrating stories and features. Our inside art is pen & ink." Query with samples. Samples kept on file.

**Photography** "We use a number of back & white photos inside the magazine; most support the articles used."

**Terms** Pays on publication. Buys first American serial rights. Buys first American serial rights and photos for artwork. Pays 5/word; $10/poem or puzzle; $35 for art (full page); $25 for art (partial page). Pays illustrators $5-10 for b&w photos. Sample copies available for $5 (includes postage); $6 outside U.S.

**Tips** "Our point of view is that every child deserves the right to be a child for a number of years before he or she becomes a young adult. As a result, *Fun for Kidz* looks for activities that deal with timeless topics, such as pets, nature, hobbies, science, games, sports, careers, simple cooking, and anything else likely to interest a child."

## GIRLS' LIFE

Monarch, 4517 Harford Rd., Baltimore MD 21214. (410)426-9600. Fax: (410)254-0991. E-mail: lizzie@girlslife.com. Website: www.girlslife.com. **Associate Editor:**Lizzie Skurnick. Bimonthly magazine. Estab. 1994. General interest magazine for girls, ages 10-15.

**Fiction** Teen and 'tween.

**Nonfiction** Arts/crafts, fashion, interview/profile, social issues, sports, travel, hobbies, relationships. Buys appoximately 25 mss/year. Word length varies. Byline given.

**How to Contact/Writers** Nonfiction: Query with descriptive story ideas, résumé and published writing samples. Responds in 6 weeks. Publishes ms 3 months after acceptance. Will consider simultaneous submissions. No phone calls. No e-mails.

**Illustration** Uses color artwork only. Works on assignment only. Reviews ms/illustration packages from artists. Send ms with dummy. Illustration only: Query with samples; send tearsheets. Contact: Chun Kim, creative director. Responds only if interested. Samples returned with SASE; samples filed. Credit line given.

**Photography** Hires photographers. Send portfolio. Responds only if interested.

**Terms** Pays on publication. Original artwork returned at job's completion. Pays $500-800 for features; $150-350 for departments. Sample copies available for $5. Writer's guidelines for SASE or via website.

**Tips** "Don't call with queries. Make query short and punchy."

## GUIDE MAGAZINE

Review and Herald Publishing Association, 55 W. Oak Ridge Dr., Hagerstown MD 21740. (301)393-4038. Fax: (301)393-4055. E-mail: guide@rhpa.org. Website: www.guidemagazine.org. **Editor:** Randy Fishell. **Designer:** Brandon Reese. Weekly magazine. Estab. 1953. Circ. 32,000. "Ours is a weekly Christian journal written for middle readers and young teens (ages 10-14), presenting true stories relevant to the needs of today's young person, emphasizing positive aspects of Christian living."

**Nonfiction** Middle readers, young adults/teens: adventure, animal, character-building, contemporary, games/puzzles, humorous, multicultural, problem-solving, religious. "We need true, or based on true, happenings, not merely true-to-life. Our stories and puzzles must have a spiritual emphasis." No violence. No articles. "We always need humor and adventure stories.'' Buys 150 mss/year. Average word length: 500-600 minimum, 1,200-1,300 maximum. Byline given.

**How to Contact/Writers** Nonfiction: Send complete ms. Responds in 1 month. Will consider simultaneous submissions. ''We can only pay half of the regular amount for simultaneous submissions.'' Responds to queries/mss in 6 weeks. Credit line given. ''We encourage e-mail submissions.''

**Terms** Pays on acceptance. Buys first North American serial rights; first rights; one-time rights; second serial (reprint rights); simultaneous rights. Pays 6-12¢/word for stories and articles. ''Writer receives several complimentary copies of issue in which work appears.'' Sample copy free with 6×9 SAE and 2 first-class stamps. Writer's guidelines for SASE.

**Tips** ''Children's magazines want mystery, action, discovery, suspense and humor—no matter what the topic. For us, truth is stronger than fiction.''

## ▣ GUIDEPOSTS FOR KIDS

1050 Broadway, Suite 6, Chesterton IN 46304. Fax: (219)926-3839. E-mail: gp4k@guideposts.org. Website: www.gp4k.com. **Editor-in-Chief:** Mary Lou Carney. **Managing Editor:** Rosanne Tolin. **Art Director:** Mike Lyons. **Art Coordinator:** Rose Pomeroy. Electronic magazine. Estab. 1998. 95,000 plus unique visitors/month. ''*Guideposts for Kids* online by Guideposts for kids 6-13 years old (emphasis on upper end of that age bracket). It is a value-centered, electronic magazine that is *fun* to visit. The site hosts a long list of interactive and editorial features including games, puzzles, how-tos, stories, poems, facts and trivia.

• *Guideposts for Kids* is online only.

**Fiction** Middle readers: adventure, animal, contemporary, fantasy, folktales, historical, humorous, multicultural, nature/environment, problem-solving, science fiction, sports, suspense/mystery. Multicultural needs include: Kids in other cultures—school, sports, families. Does not want to see preachy fiction. ''We want real stories about real kids doing real things—conflicts our readers will respect; resolutions our readers will accept. Problematic. Tight. Filled with realistic dialogue and sharp imagery. No stories about 'good' children always making the right decision. If present at all, adults are minor characters and *do not* solve kids' problems for them.'' Buys approximately 25 mss/year. Average word length: 200-900. Byline given.

**Nonfiction** Middle readers: animal, current events, games/puzzles, history, how-to, humorous, interview/profile, multicultural, nature/environment, problem-solving, profiles of kids, science, seasonal, social issues, sports. ''Make nonfiction issue-oriented, controversial, thought-provoking. Something kids not only *need* to know but *want* to know as well.'' Buys 20 mss/year. Average word length: 200-1,300. Byline usually given.

**How to Contact/Writers** Fiction: Send complete ms. Nonfiction: Query or send ms. Responds to queries/mss in 6 weeks.

**Photography** Looks for ''spontaneous, *real* kids in action shots.''

**Terms** Pays on acceptance. Buys electronic and nonexclusive print rights. ''Features range in payment from $50-200; fiction from $75-250. We pay higher rates for stories exceptionally well-written or well-researched. Regular contributors get bigger bucks, too.'' Writer's guidelines free for SASE.

**Tips** ''Make your manuscript good, relevant and playful. No preachy stories about Bible-toting children. *Guideposts for Kids* is not a beginner's market. Study our e-zine magazine. (Sure, you've heard that before—but it's *necessary*!) Neatness *does* count. So do creativity and professionalism. SASE essential if sending a query by snail mail.''

## GUIDEPOSTS SWEET 16

(formerly *Guideposts for Teens*), 1050 Broadway, Suite 6, Chesterton IN 46304.(219)929-4429. Fax: (219)926-3839. E-mail: gp4t@guideposts.org. Website: www.gp4teens.com. E-mail: writers@guidepostssweet16mag.com. Website: www.guidepostssweet16mag.com. **Editor-in-Chief:** Mary Lou Carney. **Art Director:** Meghan McPhail. **Art Coordinator:** Rose Pomeroy. Bimonthly magazine. Estab. 1998. ''*Guideposts Sweet 16* is a general-interest magazine for teenage girls, ages 11-17. We are an inspirational publication that offers true, first-person stories about real teens. Our watchwords are 'wholesome', 'current, 'fun', and 'inspiring'. We also publish shorter pieces on fashion, beauty, celebrity, boys, embarrassing moments, and advice columns.''

**Nonfiction** Young adults: quizzes, celebrity interviews, true stories, fashion and beauty. Average word length: 200-1,500. Byline sometimes given.

**How to Contact/Writers** Nonfiction: Query. Responds to queries/mss in 6 weeks. Will consider simultaneous submissions or electronic submission via disk or modem. Send SASE for writer's guidelines.

**Illustration** Uses color artwork only. Works on assignment only. Reviews ms/illustration packages from artists. Query. Contact: Rose Pomeroy, art coordinator. Illustrations only: Query with samples. Responds only if interested. Samples kept on file. Credit line given.

**Photography** Buys photos separately. Wants location photography and stock; digital OK. Uses color prints and 35mm, 2¼×2¼, or 8×10 transparencies. Query with samples; provide web address. Responds only if interested.

**Terms** Pays on acceptance. Buys all rights for mss. Buys one-time rights for artwork. Original artwork returned at job's completion. Pays $300-500 for true stories; $100-300 for articles. Additional payment for photos accompanying articles. Pays illustrators $125-1,500 for color inside (depends on size). Pays photographers by the project (range: $100-1,000). Sample copies for $4.50 from: Guideposts, 39 Seminary Hill Rd., Carmel NY 10512. Attn: Special Handling.

**Tips** ''Study our magazine! Language and subject matter should be current and teen-friendly. No preaching, please! (Your 'takeaway' should be inherent.) We are most in need of inspirational action/adventure, and relationship stories written in first-person and narrated by teenage girls. We need 'light' stories about finding a date and learning to drive, as well as catch-in-the-throat stories. We also need short (250-word) true stories with a miracle/'aha' ending for our 'Mysterious Moments' department. For illustrators: We get illustrators from two basic sources: submissions by mail and submissions by Internet. We also consult major illustrator reference books. We prefer color illustrations, 'on-the-edge' style. We accept art in almost any digital or reflective format.''

## HIGH ADVENTURE

Assemblies of God, 1445 N. Boonville Ave., Springfield MO 65802. (417)862-2781, ext. 4177. (417)831-8230. E-mail: rangers@ag.org. Website: www.royalrangers.ag.org. **Editor:** Jerry Parks. Quarterly magazine. Circ. 100,000. Estab. 1971. Magazine is designed to provide boys from kindergarten through high school age with worthwhile, enjoyable, leisure reading; to challenge them in narrative form to higher ideals and greater spiritual dedication; and to perpetuate the spirit of Royal Rangers through stories, ideas and illustrations. 75% of material aimed at juvenile audience.

**Fiction** Adventure, humorous, problem solving, religious, sports, travel. Maximum word length: 1,000. Byline given.

**Nonfiction** Articles: Christian living, devotional, Holy Spirit, salvation, self-help, biography, missionary stories, news items, testimonies, inspirational stories based on true-life experiences; arts/crafts, games/puzzles, geography, health, hobbies, how-to, humorous, nature/environment, problem-solving, sports, travel.

**How to Contact/Writers** Fiction/nonfiction: Send complete ms. Will consider simultaneous submissions. Samples returned with SASE by request. Prefer hardcopy and media (3.5, CD or via e-mail).

**Terms** Pays on publication. Buys first or all rights. Pays 6¢/word for articles ($30-35 for one page; $60-65 for two pages); $25-30 for cartoons; $15 for puzzles, $5 for jokes. Sample copy free with 9×12 SASE. Free writer's/ illustrator's guidelines with SASE.

**Tips** Obtain writer's guidelines. Articles are not subject to a theme-associated listing, but can be seasonal in nature or as described above.

## HIGHLIGHTS FOR CHILDREN

803 Church St., Honesdale PA 18431. (570)253-1080. E-mail: eds@highlights-corp.com. Website: www.highlights.com. **Contact:** Manuscript Coordinator. Editor: Christine French Clark. **Art Director:** Cindy Smith. Monthly magazine. Estab. 1946. Circ. 2.5 million. ''Our motto is 'Fun With a Purpose.' We are looking for quality fiction and nonfiction that appeals to children, encourages them to read, and reinforces positive values. All art is done on assignment.''

**Fiction** Picture-oriented material, young readers, middle readers: adventure, animal, contemporary, fantasy, folktales, history, humorous, multicultural, problem-solving, sports. Multicultural needs include first person accounts of children from other cultures and first-person accounts of children from other countries. Does not want to see war, crime, violence. ''We see too many stories with overt morals.'' Would like to see more contemporary, multicultural and world culture fiction, mystery stories, action/adventure stories, humorous stories, and fiction for younger readers. Buys 150 mss/year. Average word length: 500-800. Byline given.

**Nonfiction** Picture-oriented material, young readers, middle readers: animal, arts/crafts, biography, careers, games/puzzles, geography, health, history, hobbies, how-to, interview/profile, multicultural, nature/environment, problem-solving, science, sports. Multicultural needs include articles set in a country *about* the people of the country. Does not want to see trendy topics, fads, personalities who would not be good role models for children, guns, war, crime, violence. ''We'd like to see more nonfiction for younger readers—maximum of 500 words. We still need older-reader material, too—500-800 words.'' Buys 200 mss/year. Maximum word length: 800. Byline given.

**How to Contact/Writers** Send complete ms. Responds to queries in 1 month; mss in 6 weeks.

**Illustration** Buys 25-30 illustrations/issue. Preferred theme or style: Realistic, some stylization. Works on assignment only. Reviews ms/illustration packages from artists. Illustrations only: photocopies, promo sheet, tearsheets, or slides. Resume optional. Portfolio only if requested. Contact: Art Director. Responds to art samples in 2 months. Samples returned with SASE; samples filed. Credit line given.

**Terms** Pays on acceptance. Buys all rights for mss. Pays $50 and up for unsolicited articles. Pays illustrators $1,000 for color cover; $25-200 for b&w inside, $100-500 for color inside. Sample copies $3.95 and 9×11 SASE with 4 first-class stamps. Writer's/illustrator's guidelines free with SASE.

**Tips** "Know the magazine's style before submitting. Send for guidelines and sample issue if necessary." Writers: "At *Highlights* we're paying closer attention to acquiring more nonfiction for young readers than we have in the past." Illustrators: "Fresh, imaginative work encouraged. Flexibility in working relationships a plus. Illustrators presenting their work need not confine themselves to just children's illustrations as long as work can translate to our needs. We also use animal illustrations, real and imaginary. We need crafts, puzzles and any activity that will stimulate children mentally and creatively. We are always looking for imaginative cover subjects. Know our publication's standards and content by reading sample issues, not just the guidelines. Avoid tired themes, or put a fresh twist on an old theme so that its style is fun and lively. We'd like to see stories with subtle messages, but the fun of the story should come first. Write what inspires you, not what you think the market needs."

## HOPSCOTCH, The Magazine for Girls,

The Bluffton News Publishing and Printing Company, P.O. Box 164, Bluffton OH 45817-0164. (419)358-4610. Fax: (419)358-5027. Website: hopscotchmagazine.com. **Editor:** Diane Winebar, editorial assistant. Bimonthly magazine. Estab. 1989. Circ. 14,000. For girls from ages 6-12, featuring traditional subjects—pets, games, hobbies, nature, science, sports, etc.—with an emphasis on articles that show girls actively involved in unusual and/or worthwhile activities."

**Fiction** Picture-oriented material, young readers, middle readers: adventure, animal, history, humorous, nature/environment, sports, suspense/mystery. Does not want to see stories dealing with dating, sex, fashion, hard rock music. Buys 30 mss/year. Average word length: 300-700. Byline given.

**Nonfiction** Picture-oriented material, young readers, middle readers: animal, arts/crafts, biography, cooking, games/puzzles, geography, hobbies, how-to, humorous, math, nature/environment, science. Does not want to see pieces dealing with dating, sex, fashion, hard rock music. "Need more nonfiction with quality photos about a *Hopscotch*-age girl involved in a worthwhile activity." Buys 46 mss/year. Average word length: 400-700. Byline given.

**Poetry** Reviews traditional, wholesome, humorous poems. Maximum word length: 300; maximum line length: 20. Will accept 6 submissions/author.

**How to Contact/Writers** All writers should consult the theme list before sending in articles. To receive a current theme list, send a SASE. Fiction: Send complete ms. Nonfiction: Query or send complete ms. Responds to queries in 2 weeks; mss in 5 weeks. Will consider simultaneous submissions.

**Illustration** Buys approximately 10 illustrations/issue; buys 60-70 articles/year. "Generally, the illustrations are assigned after we have purchased a piece (usually fiction). Occasionally, we will use a painting—in any given medium—for the cover, and these are usually seasonal." Uses b&w artwork only for inside; color for cover. Reviews ms/illustration packages from artists. Query first or send complete ms with final art. Illustrations only: Send résumé, portfolio, client list and tearsheets. Responds to art samples only if interested and SASE in 1 month. Samples returned with SASE. Credit line given.

**Photography** Purchases photos separately (cover only) and with accompanying ms only. Looking for photos to accompany article. Model/property releases required. Uses 5×7, b&w prints; 35mm transparencies. Black & white photos should go with ms. Should show girl or girls ages 6-12.

**Terms** For mss: pays on publication. For mss, artwork and photos, buys first North American serial rights; second serial (reprint rights). Original artwork returned at job's completion. Pays 5¢/word and $5-10/photo. "We always send a copy of the issue to the writer or illustrator." Text and art are treated separately. Pays $200 maximum for color cover; $25-35 for b&w inside. Sample copy for $4 and 8×12 SASE. Writer's/illustrator's/photo guidelines, theme list free for #10 SASE.

**Tips** "Remember we publish only six issues a year, which means our editorial needs are extremely limited. Please look at our guidelines and our magazine . . . and remember, we use far more nonfiction than fiction. If decent photos accompany the piece, it stands an even better chance of being accepted. We believe it is the responsibility of the contributor to come up with photos. Please remember, our readers are 6-12 years—most are 8-10—and your text should reflect that. Many magazines try to entertain first and educate second. We try to do the reverse. Our magazine is more simplistic, like a book to be read from cover to cover. We are looking for wholesome, non-dated material."

## HORSEPOWER, Magazine for Young Horse Lovers

Horse Publications Group, P.O. Box 670, Aurora ON L4G 4J9 Canada. (800)505-7428. Fax: (905)841-1530. E-mail: info@horse-canada.com. Website: www.horse-canada.com. **Editor:** Susan Stafford. Bimonthly 16-page magazine, bound into Horse Canada, a bimonthly family horse magazine. Estab. 1988. Circ. 17,000. "*Horsepower* offers how-to articles and stories relating to horse care for kids ages 6-16, with a focus on safety."

**Fiction** Middle readers, young adults: adventure, health, history, humorous, problem-solving. Buys 2-3 mss/year. Average word length: 500-1,000.

**Nonfiction** Middle readers, young adults: arts/crafts, biography, careers, fashion, games/puzzles, health, history, hobbies, how-to, humorous, interview/profile, problem-solving, travel. Buys 6-10 mss/year. Average word length: 500-1,200. Byline given.

**How to Contact/Writers** Fiction: query. Nonfiction: send complete ms. Responds to queries in 6 months; mss in 3 months. Publishes ms 6 months after acceptance. Will consider simultaneous submissions, electronic submission via disk or email, previously published work.

**Illustration** Buys 3 illustrations/year. Reviews ms/illustration packages from artists. Contact: Editor. Query with samples. Responds only if interested. Samples returned with SASE; samples kept on file. Credit line given.

**Photography** Look for photos of kids and horses, instructional/educational, relating to riding or horse care. Uses b&w and color $4\times6$, $5\times7$, matte or glossy prints. Query with samples. Responds only if interested. Accepts TIFF or JPEG 300 dpi, disk or e-mail.

**Terms** Pays on publication. Buys one-time rights for mss. Original artwork returned at job's completion if SASE provided. Pays $50-75 for stories. Additional payment for ms/illustration packages and for photos accompanying articles. Pays illustrators $25-50 for color inside. Pays photographers per photo (range: $10-15). Sample copies for $4.50. Writer's/illustrator's/photo guidelines for SASE.

**Tips** "Articles must be easy to understand, yet detailed and accurate. How-to or other educational features must be written by, or in conjunction with, a riding/teaching professional. Fiction is not encouraged, unless it is outstanding and teaches a moral or practical lesson."

## HUMPTY DUMPTY'S MAGAZINE

Children's Better Health Institute, 1100 Waterway Blvd., Indianapolis IN 46206. (317)636-8881. Fax: (317)684-8094. Website: www.humptydumptymag.org. **Editor:** Phyllis Lybarger. **Art Director:** Rob Falco. Magazine published 6 times/year. *HDM* is edited for children ages 4-6. It includes fiction (easy-to-reads; read alouds; rhyming stories; rebus stories), nonfiction articles (some with photo illustrations), poems, crafts, recipes, and puzzles. Content encourages development of better health habits.

- *Humpty Dumpty's* publishes material promoting health and fitness with emphasis on simple activities, poems and fiction.

**Fiction** Picture-oriented stories: adventure, animal, contemporary, fantasy, folktales, health, humorous, multicultural, nature/environment, problem-solving, science fiction, sports. Also, talking inanimate objects are very difficult to do well. Beginners (and maybe everyone) should avoid these." Buys 8-10 mss/year. Maximum word length: 300. Byline given.

**Nonfiction** Picture-oriented articles: animal, arts/crafts, concept, games/puzzles, health, how-to, humorous, nature/environment, no-cook recipes, science, social issues, sports. Buys 6-10 mss/year. Prefers very short nonfiction pieces—200 words maximum. Byline given. Send ms with SASE if you want ms returned.

**How to Contact/Writers** Send complete ms. Nonfiction: Send complete ms with bibliography if applicable. "No queries, please!" Responds to mss in 3 months. Send seasonal material at least 8 months in advance.

**Illustration** Buys 5-8 illustrations/issue; 30-48 illustrations/year. Preferred theme or style: Realistic or cartoon. Works on assignment only. Illustrations only. Query with slides, printed pieces or photocopies. Samples are not returned; samples filed. Responds to art samples only if interested. Credit line given.

**Terms** Writers: Pays on publication. Artists: Pays within 2 months. Buys all rights. "One-time book rights may be returned if author can provide name of interested book publisher and tentative date of publication." Pays up to 22¢/word for stories/articles; payment varies for poems and activities. 10 complimentary issues are provided to author with check. Pays $275 for color cover illustration; $35-90 per page b&w inside; $70-155 for color inside. Sample copies for $1.75. Writer's/illustrator's guidelines free with SASE.

## I.D.

Cook Communications Ministries, 4050 Lee Vance View, Colorado Springs CO 80918-7102. (719)536-0100. Fax: (719)536-3296. Website: www.cookministries.org. **Editor:** Gail Rohlfing. **Designer:** Kelly Robinson. Weekly magazine. Estab. 1991. Circ. 100,000. "*I. D.* is a class-and-home paper for senior high Sunday school students. Stories relate to Bible study."

**Fiction** Young adults: religious.

**How to Contact/Writers** Currently not accepting new submissions.

**Illustrations** Buys 5 illustrations/year. Uses b&w and color artwork. Illustrations only: Query. Works on assignment only. Responds in 6 months.

**Terms** Pays on acceptance. Pays $50-300 for stories and articles.

**Tips** "Samples copies of product are not available. *I.D.* is sold in Christian bookstores."

## INSIGHT

Because Life is Full of Decisions, 55 W. Oak Ridge Dr., Hagerstown MD 21740. (301)393-4038. Fax: (301)393-4055. E-mail: insight@rhpa.org. Website: www.insightmagazine.org. **Contact:** Dwain Nielson Esmond. Weekly magazine. Estab. 1970. Circ. 14,000. "Our readers crave true stories written by teens or written about teens that convey a strong spiritual point or portray a spiritual truth." 100% of publication aimed at teen market.

**Nonfiction** Young adults: animal, biography, fashion, health, humorous, interview/profile, multicultural, nature/environment, problem-solving, social issues, sports, travel: first-person accounts preferred. Buys 200 mss/year. Average word length: 500-1,500. Byline given.

**Poetry** Publishes poems written by teens. Maximum length: 250-500 words.

**How to Contact/Writers** Nonfiction: Send complete ms. Responds to queries in 2 months. Publishes ms 6-12 months after acceptance. Will consider simultaneous submissions, electronic submission via disk or modem, previously published work.

**Illustration** Works on assignment only. Reviews ms/illustration packages from artists. Query. Illustrations only: Query with samples. Samples kept on file. Credit line given.

**Photography** Looking for photos that will catch a young person's eye with unique elements such as juxtaposition. Model/property release required; captions not required but helpful. Uses color prints and 35mm, $2^{1}/_{4} \times 2^{1}/_{4}$, $4 \times 5$, $8 \times 10$ transparencies. Query with samples; provide business card, promotional literature or tearsheets to be kept on file. Responds only if interested.

**Terms** Pays on publication. Buys first North American serial rights for mss. Buys one-time rights for artwork and photos. Original artwork returned at job's completion. Pays $10-100 for stories/articles. Pays illustrators $100-300 for b&w (cover), color cover, b&w (inside), or color inside. Pays photographers by the project. Sample copies for $9 \times 14$ SAE and 4 first-class stamps.

**Tips** "Do your best to make your work look 'hip,' 'cool,' appealing to young people."

## INTEEN

Urban Ministries, Inc., 1551 Regency Ct., Calumet City IL 60409. (708)868-7100, ext. 239. Fax: (708)868-7105. E-mail: kawashington@urbanministries.com. **Editor:** Aja M. Carr. **Art Acquisitions:** Trinidad Zavala. Quarterly magazine. Estab. 1970. "We publish Sunday school lessons and features for urban teens."

- Contact *Inteen* for guidelines. They work on assignment only—do not submit work.

**Nonfiction** Young adults/teens: careers, games/puzzles, how-to, interview/profile, religion. "We make 40 assignments/year."

**Terms** Pays $75-150 for stories.

## JACK AND JILL

Children's Better Health Institute, 1100 Waterway Blvd., P.O. Box 567, Indianapolis IN 46206. (317)634-1100. Fax: (317)684-8094. Website: www.cbhi.org/magazines/jackandjill/index.shtml. **Editor:** Daniel Lee. **Art Director:** Jennifer Webber. Magazine published 6 times/year. Estab. 1938. Circ. 360,000. "Write entertaining and imaginative stories *for* kids, not just *about* them. Writers should understand what is funny to kids, what's important to them, what excites them. Don't write from an adult 'kids are so cute' perspective. We're also looking for health and healthful lifestyle stories and articles, but don't be preachy."

**Fiction** Young readers and middle readers: adventure, contemporary, folktales, health, history, humorous, nature, sports. Buys 30-35 mss/year. Average word length: 700. Byline given.

**Nonfiction** Young readers, middle readers: animal, arts/crafts, cooking, games/puzzles, history, hobbies, how-to, humorous, interview/profile, nature, science, sports. Buys 8-10 mss/year. Average word length: 500. Byline given.

**Poetry** Reviews poetry.

**How to Contact/Writers** Fiction/nonfiction: Send complete ms. Queries not accepted. Responds to mss in 3 months. Guidelines by request with a #10 SASE.

**Illustration** Buys 15 illustrations/issue; 90 illustrations/year. Responds only if interested. Samples not returned; samples filed. Credit line given.

**Terms** Pays on publication; up to 17/word. Pays illustrators $275 for color cover; $35-90 for b&w, $70-155 for color inside. Pays photographers negotiated rate. Sample copies $1.25. Buys all rights to mss and one-time rights to photos.

**Tips** Publishes writing/art/photos by children.

## KEYS FOR KIDS

CBH Ministries, Box 1, Grand Rapids MI 49501. (616)647-4500. Fax: (616)647-4950. E-mail: hazel@cbhministries.org. Website: www.cbhministries.org. **Fiction Editor:** Hazel Marett. Bimonthly devotional booklet. Estab. 1982. "This is a devotional booklet for children and is also widely used for family devotions."

**Fiction** Young readers, middle readers: religious. Buys 60 mss/year. Average word length: 400.

**How to Contact/Writers** Fiction: Send complete ms. Will consider simultaneous submissions, e-mail submissions, previously published work.

**Terms** Pays on acceptance. Buys reprint rights or first rights for mss. Pays $25 for stories. Sample copies free for SAE $6 \times 9$ and 3 first-class stamps. Writer's guidelines for SASE.

**Tips** "Follow guidelines after studying sample copy of the publication."

## ℕ KID ZONE
Scott Magazines, LLC, 450 Benson Bldg., Sioux City IA 51101. (712)255-0288. Fax: (712)255-0576. E-mail: JWinquist@scottpublications.com. Website: www.scottpublications.com. **Articles Editor:** Jennifer Winquist. Bi-monthly magazine. Estab. 2000. Circ. 80,000. Kid Zone is a crafts and activities magazine for 4-12 year olds. ''We publish projects, trivia, recipes, original stories, games, puzzles, and kid-friendly features on a variety of topics.''

**Nonfiction** Picture-oriented material, middle readers: animal, arts/crafts, cooking, how-to, multicultural, nature/environment, science. Buys 20 mss/year. Average word length: 300-700. Byline given.

**How to Contact/Writers** Nonfiction: Send complete ms. Responds to queries/mss in 2 months. Publishes ms 6-12 months after acceptance. Will consider simultaneous submissions, e-mail submissions.

**Illustration** Buys 6 illustrations/issue. Uses color artwork only. Works on assignment only. Illustrations only: Send postcard sample. Contact: Jennifer Winquist, editor. Responds only if interested. Samples filed. Credit line sometimes given.

**Photography** Buys photos with accompanying ms only. Model/property release required. Uses color prints. Responds only if interested.

**Terms** Pays on publication. Buys world rights for mss. Buys first world rights for artwork. Pays $10-$50 for stories. Sample copies for $4.95. Writer's guidelines for SASE.

**Tips** ''Non-fiction writers who can provide extras to coincide with their submission (photos, games, project ideas, recipes) are more likely to be selected.''

## THE KIDS HALL OF FAME NEWS
The Kids Hall of Fame, 3 Ibsen Court, Dix Hills NY 11746. (631)242-9105. Fax: (631)242-8101. E-mail: VictoriaNesnick@TheKidsHallofFame.com. Website: www.TheKidsHallofFame.com. **Publisher:** Victoria Nesnick. **Art/Photo Editor:** Amy Gilvary. Quarterly magazine. Estab. 1998. ''We spotlight and archive extraordinary positive achievements of contemporary and historical kids internationally under age 20. These inspirational stories are intended to provide positive peer role models and empower others to say, 'If that kid can do it, so can I,' or 'I can do better.' Our magazine is the prelude to The Kids Hall of Fame set of books (one volume per age) and museum.''

**How to Contact/Writers** Query with published clips or send complete mss with SASE for response. Go to website for sample stories and for The Kids Hall of Fame nomination form.

**Tips** ''Nomination stories must be positive and inspirational, and whenever possible, address the 7 items listed in the 'Your Story and Photo' page of our website. Request writers' guidelines and list of suggested nominees. Day and evening telephone queries acceptable.''

## LADYBUG, The Magazine for Young Children
Carus Publishing Company, P.O. Box 300, Peru IL 61354. (815)224-5803 , ext. 656. **Editor:** Paula Morrow. **Art Director:** Suzanne Beck. Monthly magazine. Estab. 1990. Circ. 130,000. Literary magazine for children 2-6, with stories, poems, activities, songs and picture stories.

**Fiction** Picture-oriented material: adventure, animal, fantasy, folktales, humorous, multicultural, nature/environment, problem-solving, science fiction, sports, suspense/mystery. ''Open to any easy fiction stories.'' Buys 50 mss/year. Story length: limit 800 words. Byline given.

**Nonfiction** Picture-oriented material: activities, animal, arts/crafts, concept, cooking, humorous, math, nature/environment, problem-solving, science. Buys 35 mss/year. Story length: limit 800 words.

**Poetry** Reviews poems, 20-line maximum length; limit submissions to 5 poems. Uses lyrical, humorous, simple language.

**How to Contact/Writers** Fiction/nonfiction: Send complete ms. Queries not accepted. Responds to mss in 3 months. Publishes ms up to 3 years after acceptance. Will consider simultaneous submissions if informed. Submissions without SASE will be discarded.

**Illustration** Buys 12 illustrations/issue; 145 illustrations/year. Prefers ''bright colors; all media, but use watercolor and acrylics most often; same size as magazine is preferred but not required.'' To be considered for future assignments: Submit promo sheet, slides, tearsheets, color and b&w photocopies. Responds to art samples in 3 months. Submissions without SASE will be discarded.

**Terms** Pays on publication for mss; after delivery of completed assignment for illustrators. Rights purchased vary. Original artwork returned at job's completion. Pays 25¢/word for prose; $3/line for poetry. Pays $750 for color (cover) illustration, $50-100 for b&w (inside) illustration, $250/page for color (inside). Sample copy for $5. Writer's/illustrator's guidelines free for SASE or available on website, FAQ at www.cricketmag.com.

**Tips** Writers: ''Get to know several young children on an individual basis. Respect your audience. We want less cute, condescending or 'preachy-teachy' material. Less gratuitous anthropomorphism. More rich, evocative language, sense of joy or wonder. Keep in mind that people come in all colors, sizes, physical conditions. Be inclusive in creating characters. Set your manuscript aside for at least a month, then reread critically.'' Illustrators: "Include examples, where possible, of children, animals, and—most important—action and narrative (i.e., several scenes from a story, showing continuity and an ability to maintain interest)." (See listings for *Babybug*, *Cicada*, *Cricket*, *Muse* and *Spider*.)

## LEADING EDGE

3146 JKHB, Provo UT 84602. (801)378-3553. E-mail: tle@byu.edu. Website: http://tle.byu.edu. **Nonfiction Director:** Matthew Gibbbins. **Fiction Director:** Jillena O'Brien. **Art Director:** Amanda Wallace. Twice yearly magazine. Estab. 1981. Circ. 500. "We general publish fantasy and science fiction." 20% of publication aimed at juvenile market.
**Fiction** Young adults: fantasy, science fiction. Buys 16 mss/year. Average word length: up to 17,000. Byline given.
**Nonfiction** Young adults: science. Buys 2-3 mss/year. Average word length: up to 17,000. Byline given.
**How to Contact/Writers** Fiction/Nonfiction: Send complete ms. Responds to queries/mss in 2 months. Publishes ms 2-6 months after acceptance.
**Illustration** Buys 24 illustrations/issue; 48 illustrations/year. Uses b&w artwork only. Works on assignment only. Send ms with dummy. Contact: Paige Owen, art director. Illustrations only: Send postcard sample with portfolio, samples, SASE, URL. Responds only if interested. Samples returned with SASE; samples filed. Credit line given.
**Terms** Pays on publication. Buys first North American serial rights for mss. Buys first North American serial rights for artwork. Original artwork returned at job's completion. Pays $10-$100 for stories. Additional payment for ms/illustration packages. Pays illustrators $50 for color cover, $30 for b&w inside. Sample copies for $4.95. Writer's/illustrator's guidelines for SASE.

## MUSE

Carus Publishing, 140 S. Dearborn, Suite 1450, Chicago IL 60603. (312)701-1720. Fax: (312)701-1728. E-mail: muse@caruspub.com. Website: www.cricketmag.com. **Editor:** Diana Lutz.**Art Director:** Karen Kohn. **Photo Editor:** Carol Parden. Estab. 1996. Circ. 50,000. "The goal of *Muse* is to give as many children as possible access to the most important ideas and concepts underlying the principal areas of human knowledge. Articles should meet the highest possible standards of clarity and transparency aided, wherever possible, by a tone of skepticism, humor, and irreverence."
**Nonfiction** Middle readers, young adult: animal, arts, history, math, nature/environment, problem-solving, science, social issues.
**How to Contact/Writers** *Muse* is not accepting unsolicited mss or queries. All articles are commissioned.
**Illustration** Buys 6 illustrations/issue; 40 illustrations/year. Uses color artwork only. Works on assignment only. Query with samples. Responds only if interested. Samples returned with SASE. Credit line given.
**Photography** Needs vary. Query with samples to photo editor.

## NATIONAL GEOGRAPHIC KIDS

National Geographic Society, 1145 17th St. NW, Washington DC 20036-4688. (202)857-7000. Fax: (202)775-6112. Website: www.nationalgeographic.com/ngkids. **Editor:** Melina Bellows. **Art Director:** Jonathan Halling. **Photo Director:** Jay Sumner. Monthly magazine. Estab. 1975. Circ. 900,000.

## NATURE FRIEND MAGAZINE

2673 Twp. Rd., Sugarcreek OH 44681. (330)852-1900. Fax: (330)852-3285. **Articles Editor:** Marvin Wengerd. Monthly magazine. Estab. 1983. Circ. 13,000.
**Fiction** Picture-oriented material, conversational, no talking animal stories.
**Nonfiction** Picture-oriented material: animal, how-to, nature, photo-essays. No talking animal stories. No evolutionary material. Buys 50 mss/year. Average word length: 500. Byline given.
**Photography** Pays $75 for front cover, $50 for back cover, $75 for centerfold, $15-30 for text photos. Submit slides, transparencies or CD with color printout. Photo guidelines free with SASE.
**Terms** Pays on publication. Buys one-time rights. Pays $15 minimum. Payment for illustrations: $15-80/b&w, $50-100/color inside. Two sample copies and writer's guidelines for $5 with 9×12 SAE and $2 postage.
**Tips** Needs stories about unique animals or nature phenomena. "Please examine samples and writer's guide before submitting." Current needs: science and nature experiments (for ages 8-12) with art of photographs for the Learning by Doing feature; hands-on material.

## NEW MOON: The Magazine for Girls & Their Dreams

New Moon Publishing, Inc., 34 E. Superior St., #200, Duluth MN 55802. (218)728-5507. Fax: (218)728-0314. E-mail: girl@newmoon.org. Website: www.newmoon.org. **Managing Editor:** Kate Freeborn. Bimonthly magazine. Estab. 1992. Circ. 30,000. *"New Moon* is for every girl who wants her voice heard and her dreams taken seriously. *New Moon* portrays strong female role models of all ages, backgrounds and cultures now and in the past."

**Fiction** Middle readers, young adults: adventure, contemporary, fantasy, folktales, history, humorous, multicultural, nature/environment, problem-solving, religious, science fiction, sports, suspense/mystery, travel. Buys 6 mss/year. Average word length: 900-1,200. Byline given.

**Nonfiction** Middle readers, young adults: animal, arts/crafts, biography, careers, cooking, games/puzzles, health, history, hobbies, humorous, interview/profile, math, multicultural, nature/environment, problem-solving, science, social issues, sports, travel, stories about real girls. Does not want to see how-to stories. Wants more stories about real girls doing real things written *by girls*. Buys 6-12 adult-written mss/year; 30 girl-written mss/year. Average word length: 600. Byline given.

**How to Contact/Writers** Fiction/Nonfiction: Does not return or acknowledge unsolicited mss. Send only copies. Responds only if interested. Will consider simultaneous and e-mail submissions.

**Illustration** Buys 6-12 illustrations/year from freelancers. *New Moon* seeks 4-color cover illustrations as well as b&w illustrations for inside. Reviews ms/illustrations packages from artists. Query. Submit ms with rough sketches. Illustration only: Query; send portfolio and tearsheets. Samples not returned; samples filed. Responds in 6 months only if interested. Credit line given.

**Terms** Pays on publication. Buys all rights for mss. Buys one-time rights, reprint rights, for artwork. Original artwork returned at job's completion. Pays 6-12¢/word for stories and articles. Pays in contributor's copies. Pays illustrators $400 for color cover; $50-300 for b&w inside. Sample copies for $6.50. Writer's/cover art guidelines for SASE or available on website.

**Tips** "Please refer to a copy of *New Moon* to understand the style and philosophy of the magazine. Writers and artists who understand our goals have the best chance of publication. We're looking for stories about real girls, women's careers, and historical profiles. We publish girl's and women's writing only." Publishes writing/art/photos by girls.

## NICK JR. FAMILY MAGAZINE

Nickelodeon Magazine Group, 1633 Broadway, 7th Floor, New York NY 10019. (212)654-7707. Fax: (212)654-4840. Website: www.nickjr.com/magazine. **Deputy Editor:** Wendy Smolen. **Creative Director:** Don Morris. Published 9 times/year. Estab. 1999. Circ. 1,000,000. A magazine where kids play to learn and parents learn to play. 30% of publication aimed at juvenile market.

**Fiction** Picture-oriented material: adventure, animal, contemporary, humorous, multicultural, nature/environment, problem-solving, sports. Byline sometimes given.

**Nonfiction** Picture-oriented material: animal, arts/crafts, concept, cooking, games/puzzles, hobbies, how-to, humorous, math, multicultural, nature/environment, problem-solving, science, social issues, sports. Byline sometimes given.

**How to Contact/Writers** Fiction/nonfiction: Query or submit complete ms. Responds to queries/mss in 3-12 weeks. **Illustration Only interested in agented material.** Works on assignment only. Reviews ms/illustration packages from artists. Query or send ms with dummy. Contact: Don Morris, creative director. Illustrations only: arrange portfolio review; send résumé, promo sheet and portfolio. Responds only if interested. Samples not returned; samples kept on file. Credit line sometimes given.

## ODYSSEY, Adventures in Science

Cobblestone Publishing Company, 30 Grove St., Suite C, Peterborough NH 03458. (603)924-7209. Fax: (603)924-7380. E-mail: odyssey@cobblestonemv.com. Website: www.odysseymagazine.com. **Editor:** Elizabeth E. Lindstrom. **Executive Director:** Lou Waryncia. **Art Director:** Ann Dillon. Magazine published 9 times/year. Estab. 1979. Circ. 22,000. Magazine covers earth, general science and technology, astronomy and space exploration for children ages 10-16. All material must relate to the theme of a specific upcoming issue in order to be considered.

 • *Odyssey* themes can be found on website: www.odysseymagazine.com.

**Fiction** Middle readers and young adults/teens: science fiction, science, astronomy. Does not want to see anything not theme-related. Average word length: 900-1,200 words.

**Nonfiction** Middle readers and young adults/teens: interiors, activities. Don't send anything not theme-related. Average word length: 750-1,200, depending on section article is used in.

**How to Contact/Writers** Prefers hard copy queries to e-mail. "A query must consist of all of the following to be considered (please use nonerasable paper): a brief cover letter stating the subject and word length of the proposed article; a detailed one-page outline explaining the information to be presented in the article; an extensive bibliography of materials the author intends to use in preparing the article; a SASE. Writers new to *Odyssey* should send a writing sample with query. If you would like to know if your query has been received, please also include a stamped postcard that requests acknowledgment of receipt. In all correspondence, please

# Mireille Messier

*Always be on the lookout for ideas*

Freelance writer Mireille Messier's words reach into almost every corner of children's writing. Television, magazine articles, corporate gigs for Kool-Aid and Jell-O (those are her funny words under the pudding lids), nonfiction books, and novels—she's done it all, and in less than ten years, too. What is her key to success? Messier will modestly tell you she leads a charmed life. Indeed, she does make it look easy, but her success is due to way more than sheer happenstance. Her hard work gaining experience and honing her craft in English and French, combined with a brain that's always on the lookout for new ideas, allowed her to seize the opportunities that came her way. If, as the old saying goes, luck is merely preparation meeting opportunity, then Messier had a big hand in making her own luck.

Messier's interest in children's stories began at an early age. Outnumbered by much younger sisters, Messier spent her teen years amid television programs and books that were intended for a much younger audience than herself. Not only was she surprised to discover she enjoyed them, but she also realized that being older gave her a critical perspective her younger siblings didn't have. "I remember mentally re-writing endings that I thought were lame or creating my own episodes of popular television shows," she says. (For more on Messier—if you can read French—visit her her website, www.mireille.ca/).

## How did you break into children's writing?

Even as a child, I always enjoyed writing but I never set out to be a writer—I kind of stumbled into it. During a brainstorming session at the television station where I worked as a children's program co-host, I innocently suggested that we should have a segment of short stories read by a character. The team loved the idea and, by default, nominated me to write the stories. AAAAh! What had I done? Thirty-some odd stories later I realized I actually enjoyed writing for children and that I had a natural flair for it. That was almost ten years ago. I've never looked back.

## How did your television work segue into other kinds of children's writing?

Writing for television was all good and well until I realized I wasn't enjoying the "television" part of writing for television. It's then that I decided to take the plunge and become a full-time freelance writer. An English-language children's magazine based in Toronto decided to launch a French-language sister magazine, but didn't have anyone who knew the Quebec market, could write in French or adapt English copy to make it appealing to Quebec kids. *Planète 912* hired me as an editorial assistant. As I gained confidence, I pitched story ideas to other children's magazines—*Owl*, *Les débrouillards*, *YES Mag*, *What*, etc. My story ideas often got rejected, but once in a blue moon one made it through. The editors, for the most part, were very supportive and kept prompting me to keep the ideas coming, which is exactly what I did.

### What do you find to be the most challenging part of writing for children?

The most challenging part of writing for children is to find the right voice for your age group. You can't write the same way for a 7-year-old as you would for an 11-year-old. What's funny when you're a kid is quite suddenly laughable when you're a tween. As children's writers, we always have to be able to make that connection, to walk that proverbial tightrope, and to do it with ease. (Kids can spot a fake at a mile!) This is a challenge that other kinds of writers never have to deal with.

### How important is it to come up with a ''fresh'' approach? How do you find something ''fresh'' to write about?

Some wise author once said that there are thousands of ideas all around us and that the true writers are the ones that manage to recognize a handful of them. I feel the same way— I get my ideas from my day-to-day experiences. Almost anything can be made into an idea for a children's magazine. There's a story in the local newspaper about a new company raising ants for the sole purpose of selling them to landscapers dealing with aphid infestation. I see a story about ''Bugs With Jobs.'' A friend tells me about a family whose houseboat just docked next to his. I see a story about kids that live in unconventional houses. The key to keeping ideas fresh is to always be ''on,'' to be looking for ideas at all times, to ask questions, to be curious and to see the world through a child's eyes.

### You have two small children. How have they affected your writing?

Being around kids 24 hours a day has mostly changed the way I write novels. Kids are an endless source of inspiration and entertainment. Entire characters have sprung up from things my daughters do or say. For example, my eldest is going through a phase where she starts every single sentence with ''Ya know what?''. In my next novel there is an aggravating little neighbor girl who starts every single sentence with that same question. It's art imitating life at it's grandest!

I've also learned to work at strange hours, to carry a notepad wherever I go and not to take on more work than I realistically know I can do and do well.

### What advice do you have for new writers trying to break into children's magazine writing?

Aside from the basics—read the magazines you want to break into, analyze their content and style, replicate it in your query—don't put all your eggs in one basket. By that I mean that if you're serious about freelance writing you should have at least a half dozen ideas out there. There's nothing more demoralizing than waiting with bated breath on the outcome of one query. If you have many out, your chances of getting a positive response are increased and your wait time will seem shorter. Freelance writing is like baseball—the more often you're at bat, the greater your chances of hitting a homerun.

—Fiona Bayrock

include your complete address as well as a telephone number and e-mail address where you can be reached. A writer may send as many queries for one issue as he or she wishes, but each query must have a separate cover letter, outline, bibliography, and SASE. Telephone queries are not accepted. Handwritten queries will not be considered. Queries may be submitted at any time, but queries sent well in advance of deadline *may not be answered for several months*. Go-aheads requesting material proposed in queries are usually sent four months prior to publication date. Unused queries will be returned approximately three to four months prior to publication date."

**Illustration** Buys 3 illustrations/issue; 27 illustrations/year. Works on assignment only. Reviews ms/illustration packages from artists. Query. Contact: Beth Lindstrom, editor. Illustration only: Query with samples. Send tearsheets, photocopies. Responds in 2 weeks. Samples returned with SASE; samples not filed. Original artwork returned upon job's completion (upon written request).

**Photography** Wants photos pertaining to any of our forthcoming themes. Uses b&w and color prints; 35mm transparencies. Photographers should send unsolicited photos by mail on speculation.

**Terms** Pays on publication. Buys all rights for mss and artwork. Pays 20-25¢/word for stories/articles. Covers are assigned and paid on an individual basis. Pays photographers per photo ($15-100 for b&w; $25-100 for color). Sample copy for $4.95 and SASE with $2 postage. Writer's/illustrator's/photo guidelines for SASE. (See listings for *AppleSeeds*, *Calliope*, *Cobblestone*, *Dig*, *Faces* and *Footsteps*.)

### ON COURSE, A Magazine for Teens

General Council of the Assemblies of God, 1445 Boonville Ave., Springfield MO 65802-1894. (417)862-2781. Fax: (417)862-1693. E-mail: oncourse@ag.org. **Editor:** Amber Weigand-Buckley. **Art Director:** Jeff Fulton. Quarterly magazine. Estab. 1991. Circ. 180,000. *On Course* is a magazine to empower students to grow in a real-life relationship with Christ.

**Fiction** Young adults: Christian discipleship, contemporary, humorous, multicultural, problem-solving, sports. Average word length: 800. Byline given.

**Nonfiction** Young adults: careers, interview/profile, multicultural, religion, social issues, college life, Christian discipleship.

**How to Contact/Writers** Works on assignment basis only. Resumes and writing samples will be considered for inclusion in Writer's File to receive story assignments.

**Illustration** Buys 2 illustrations/issue; 8 illustrations/year. Uses color artwork only. Reviews ms/illustration packages from artists. Query. Illustration only: Query with samples or send résumé, promo sheet, slides, client list and tearsheets. Contact: Amber Weigand-Buckley. Responds only if interested. Originals not returned at job's completion. Credit line given.

**Photography** Buys photos from freelancers. "Teen life, church life, college life; unposed; often used for illustrative purposes." Model/property releases required. Uses color glossy prints and 35mm or 2¼×2¼ transparencies. Query with samples; send business card, promotional literature, tearsheets or catalog. Responds only if interested.

**Terms** Pays on acceptance. Buys first or reprint rights for mss. Buys one-time rights for photographs. Pays 10¢/word for stories/articles. Pays illustrators and photographers "as negotiated." Sample copies free for 9×11 SAE. Writer's guidelines for SASE.

### ON THE LINE

Mennonite Publishing Network, 616 Walnut Ave., Scottdale PA 15683. (724)887-8500. Fax: (724)887-3111. E-mail: otl@mph.org. **Editor:** Mary Clemens Meyer. Magazine published monthly. Estab. 1970. Circ. 4,500. "*On The Line* is a children's magazine for ages 9-14, emphasizing self-esteem and Christian values. Also emphasizes multicultural awareness, peacemaking, care of the earth and accepting others with differences."

**Fiction** Middle readers: contemporary, history, humorous, nature/environment, problem-solving, religious, sports. "No fantasy or fiction with animal characters." Buys 36 mss/year. Average word length: 1,000-1,800. Byline given.

**Nonfiction** Middle readers: arts/crafts, biography, cooking, games/puzzles, health, history, hobbies, how-to, humorous, sports. Does not want to see articles written from an adult perspective. Average word length: 200-600. Byline given.

**Poetry** Wants to see light verse, humorous poetry.

**How to Contact/Writers** Fiction/nonfiction: Send complete ms. "No queries, please." Responds to mss in 1 month. Will consider simultaneous submissions. Prefers e-mail submissions.

**Illustration** Buys 3-4 illustrations/issue; buys 45 illustrations/year. "Inside illustrations are done on assignment only to accompany our stories and articles; our need for new artists is limited." Illustrations only: "Prefer samples they do not want returned; these stay in our files." Responds to art samples only if interested.

**Terms** Pays on acceptance. For mss buys one-time rights; second serial (reprint rights). Buys one-time rights for artwork and photos. Pays 4-5¢/word for assigned/unsolicited articles. Pays $50 for full-color inside illustration.

Photographers are paid per photo, $25-50. Original artwork returned at job's completion. Sample copy $2 plus 7×10 SAE. Writer's guidelines (SASE).

**Tips** "We focus on the age 12-13 group of our age 9-14 audience."

## ⬛ PARENTS AND CHILDREN TOGETHER ONLINE, A magazine for parents and children on the World Wide Web

EDINFO Family Literary Center, 2805 East 10th St., Suite 140, Bloomington IN 47408. (800)759-4723. E-mail: erices@indiana.edu. Website: http://reading.indiana.edu/www/indexpcto.html. **Editor-in-Chief:** Mei-Yu Lu. Quarterly online magazine. Estab. 1990 (in print format). Circ. 250,000 via worldwide web. "Our magazine seeks to promote family literacy by presenting original articles, stories and literacy activities for parents and children via the worldwide web." More than 75% of publication aimed at juvenile market.

**Fiction** "We accept all categories. Would like to see stories on issues children are facing today. We welcome stories from all cultural backgrounds." Publishes 32 mss/year. Byline given.

**Nonfiction** "All categories are examined and considered. We especially look for articles with photographs and/or illustrations included. We welcome articles about and of interest to children that reflect diverse cultural backgrounds." Publishes 24 mss/year. Byline given.

**Poetry** Reviews poetry. "We accept poems written for children that they will enjoy—not poems about childhood by an adult looking back nostalgically." Publishes 32 mss/year. Byline given.

**How to Contact/Writers** Fiction/nonfiction: Send complete ms. Responds to queries in 1 week; mss in 1 week. Publishes ms 3-9 months after acceptance. Will consider simultaneous submissions, electronic submissions via e-mail and previously published work.

**Illustration** Publishes 20 illustrations/issue; 80 illustrations/year. Reviews ms/illustration packages from artists. Query with ms dummy. Contact: Editor. Illustrations only: Query with samples. Contact: Editor. Responds to art samples within 1 month. Samples returned with SASE. Credit line given.

**Photography** Looking for children and parents together, either reading together or involved in other literacy-related activities. Also, children with adults or other children. Uses color prints and 35mm transparencies. Query with samples. Send unsolicited photos by mail. Responds in 1 month.

**Terms** Art/photos use on web with copyright retained by artist/photographer. "We are a free online publication, and cannot afford to pay our contributors at present." Sample copies for $9. Writer's guidelines free for SASE, or on the PCTO website.

**Tips** "We are a good market for writers, artists and photographers who want their material to reach a wide audience. Since we are a free publication, available without charge to anyone with a web browser, we cannot offer our contributors anything more than a large, enthusiastic audience for their work. Our stories and articles are read by thousands of children and parents every month. Many works originally published by us have also been selected to be included in textbooks, test passages, and other databases."

## Ⓝ PASSPORT

Sunday School Curriculum, 6401 The Paseo, Kansas City MO 64131-1284. (816)333-7000. Fax: (816)333-4439. E-mail: sweatherwax@nazarene.org. Website: www.nazarene.org. **Editor:** Mike Wonch. Weekly take-home paper. "*Passport* looks for a casual, witty approach to Christian themes. We want hot topics relevant to preteens."

● Not accepting submissions at this time.

## POCKETS, Devotional Magazine for Children

The Upper Room, 1908 Grand Ave., P.O. Box 340004, Nashville TN 37203-0004. (615)340-7333. Fax: (615)340-7267. E-mail: pockets@upperroom.org. Website: www.pockets.org. **Articles/Fiction Editor:** Lynn W. Gilliam. **Art Director:** Chris Schechner, 408 Inglewood Dr., Richardson TX 75080. Magazine published 11 times/year. Estab. 1981. Circ. 99,000. "*Pockets* is a Christian devotional magazine for children ages 6-11. Stories should help children experience a Christian lifestyle that is not always a neatly wrapped moral package but is open to the continuing revelation of God's will."

**Fiction** Picture-oriented, young readers, middle readers: adventure, contemporary, occasional folktales, multicultural, nature/environment, problem-solving, religious. Does not accept violence or talking animal stories. Buys 25-30 mss/year. Average word length: 600-1,400. Byline given.

**Nonfiction** Picture-oriented, young readers, middle readers: cooking, games/puzzles. "*Pockets* seeks biographical sketches of persons, famous or unknown, whose lives reflect their Christian commitment, written in a way that appeals to children." Does not accept how-to articles. "Our nonfiction reads like a story." Multicultural needs include: stories that feature children of various racial/ethnic groups and do so in a way that is true to those depicted. Buys 10 mss/year. Average word length: 400-1,000. Byline given.

**How to Contact/Writers** Fiction/nonfiction: Send complete ms. "Do not accept queries." Responds to mss in 6 weeks. Will consider simultaneous submissions.

**Illustration** Buys 40-50 illustrations/issue. Preferred theme or style: varied; both 4-color. Works on assignment only. Illustrations only: Send promo sheet, tearsheets.

## Ⓝ POGO STICK

Stone Lightning Press, 1300 Kicker Rd., Tuscaloosa AL 35404. (205)553-2284. E-mail: lillskm@gmail.com. **Articles Editor:** Lillian Kopaska-Merkel. **Art Director:** Rain Kennedy. Quarterly digest-sized with saddle stitching. Estab. 2004. Publishes "fantasy and realistic fiction, poems, short stories, jokes, riddles, and art for and by kids under 17." Entire publication aimed at juvenile market.
**Fiction** Young readers: adventure, animal, fantasy, humorous, multicultural, nature/environment, problem-solving, suspense/mystery. Middle readers: adventure, animal, fantasy, humorous, multicultural, nature/environment, suspense/mystery. Young adults/teens: adventure, animal, fantasy, humorous, multicultural, nature/environment, suspense/mystery. Average word length: 50-2,000. Byline given.
**Nonfiction** Young readers, middle readers, young adults/teens: arts/crafts, games/puzzles.
**Poetry** Seeks fantasy, child-appropriate poetry. Max length: 100 words. Max of 6 poems/submission.
**How To Contact/Writers** Fiction: Send complete ms. Responds to queries in 2 months. Considers simultaneous submissions.
**Illustration** Black & white artwork only. For first contact, query with samples. Contact: Rain Kennedy, art director. Responds in 2 months. Samples returned with SASE. Credit line given.
**Terms** Pays on publication. Buys first North American serial rights. Buys first North American serial rights rights for artwork. Pays with contributor copies. Sample copies available for $3.50. Writer's guidelines free for SASE. Illustrator's guidelines free for SASE. Publishes work by children.
**Tips** "Always read guidelines first."

## PRIMARY STREET

Urban Ministries, Inc., 1551 Regency Ct., Columet City IL 60409. (708)868-7100. **Articles Editor:** Judith St. Clair Hull, Ph.D. Quarterly. Estab. 1975. Circ. 50,000. "We are looking for Sunday school curriculum that is relevant for African American children."
**Fiction** Young readers: religious.
**Nonfiction** Young readers: religious. Buys 12 lesson mss/year. Average length: 5,800-5,900 characters.
**How to Contact/Writers** Nonfiction: Query with published clips. Responds to queries in 3 months. Publishes ms 1 year after acceptance.
**Terms** Pays on acceptance. Buys all rights for mss.
**Tips** "We are looking for born again African-American writers who are able to convey the way of salvation to children."

## RANGER RICK

National Wildlife Federation, 11100 Wildlife Center Dr., Reston VA 20190. (703)438-6000. Website: www.nwf.org/rangerrick. **Editor:** Gerald Bishop. **Design Director:** Donna Miller. Monthly magazine. Circ. 600,000. "Our audience ranges from ages 7 to 12, though we aim the reading level of most material at 9-year-olds or fourth graders."
   • Ranger Rick does not accept submissions or queries.
**Fiction** Middle readers: animal (wildlife), fables, fantasy, humorous, multicultural, plays, science fiction. Average word length: 900. Byline given.
**Nonfiction** Middle readers: animal (wildlife), conservation, humorous, nature/environment, outdoor adventure, travel. Buys 15-20 mss/year. Average word length: 900. Byline given.
**How to Contact/Writers** No longer accepting unsolicited queries/mss.
**Illustration** Buys 5-7 illustrations/issue. Preferred theme: nature, wildlife. Works on assignment only. Illustrations only: Send résumé, tearsheets. Responds to art samples in 2 months.
**Terms** Pays on acceptance. Buys exclusive first-time worldwide rights and non-exclusive worldwide rights thereafter to reprint, transmit, and distribute the work in any form or medium. Original artwork returned at job's completion. Pays up to $700 for full-length of best quality. For illustrations, buys one-time rights. Pays $150-250 for b&w; $250-1,200 for color (inside, per page) illustration. Sample copies for $2.15 plus a 9×12 SASE.

## READ

Weekly Reader Corporation, 200 First Stamford Place, P.O. Box 120023, Stamford CT 06912-0023. Fax: (203)705-1661. Website: www.weeklyreader.com. **Senior Editor:** Debra Nevins. Magazine published 18 times during the school year. Language arts periodical for use in classrooms for students ages 12-16; motivates students to read and teaches skills in listening, comprehension, speaking, writing and critical thinking.
**Fiction** Wants short stories, narratives and plays to be used for classroom reading and discussions. Middle

readers, young adult/teens: adventure, animal, contemporary, fantasy, folktales, history, humorous, multicultural, nature/environment, sports. Average word length: 1,000-2,500.

**Nonfiction** Middle readers, young adult/teen: animal, games/puzzles, history, humorous, problem solving, social issues.

**How to Contact** Responds to queries/mss in 6 weeks.

**Tips** "We especially like plot twists and surprise endings. Stories should be relevant to teens and contain realistic conflicts and dialogue. Plays should have at least 12 speaking parts for classroom reading. Avoid formula plots, trite themes, underage material, stilted or profane language, and sexual suggestion. Get to know the style of our magazine as well as our teen audience. They are very demanding and require an engaging and engrossing read. Grab their attention, keep the pace and action lively, build to a great climax, and make the ending satisfying and/or surprising. Make sure characters and dialogue are realistic. Do not use cliché. Make the writing fresh—simple, yet original. Obtain guidelines first. Be sure submissions are relevant."

## READ AMERICA (The Quarterly Newsletter for Reading Coordinators)

The Place in the Woods, 3900 Glenwood Ave., Golden Valley MN 55422-5302. (763)374-2120. **Articles Editor:** Roger Hammer. **Fiction Editor:** Susan Brudos. **Art Director:** Alisa Rubino. Quarterly newsletter. Estab. 1979. Circ. 10,000+. "Two sections: one is news about reading; the other is stories and poetry for children (to read or be read to)." 50% of publication aimed at juvenile market.

**Fiction** Picture-oriented material, young readers, middle readers, young adults: adventure, animal, fantasy, folktale, history, humorous, multicultural, sports, suspense/mystery, main characters with disabilities who overcome adversity. Average word length: 300-1,500. Byline given.

**Nonfiction** Picture-oriented material, young readers, middle readers, young adults: animal, biography, humorous, multicultural, sports. Buys 6 mss/year. Average word length: 500-1,500. Byline given.

**Poetry** "No restrictions other than it needs to communicate with the reader—not be just purging of author's issues." Maximum length: 300-500 lines. Limit submissions to 3-6 poems.

**How to Contact/Writers** Fiction/Nonfiction: Send complete ms. Responds to queries/mss in 6-12 months. Publishes ms 6 months to 1 year after acceptance.

**Illustration** Buys 100% illustrations/issue; 100% illustrations/year. Reviews ms/illustration packages from artists. Query or a ms with dummy. Contact: Roger Hammer, publisher. Illustrations only: Send postcard sample with samples, SASE. Contact: Roger Hammer. Responds only if interested. Samples returned with SASE; samples filed. Credit line given.

**Photography** Buys photos with accompanying ms only. Model/property release required. Uses b&w prints. Query with samples. Responds only if interested.

**Terms** Pays on acceptance. Buys all rights for mss. Buys all rights for artwork. Liberal reprint permission. Pays $50-$250 for stories; $50 for articles. Pays photographers per photo (range: $10 flat). Sample copies for $7.50. Writer's/illustrator's/photo guidelines for SASE.

**Tips** "No e-mail queries. No multiple submissions. Put enough postage to cover return if you want manuscript back. Indicate when you need a response (return deadline). If you have an illustrator in mind, send examples and contact data. Nonfiction: Indicate your particular qualifications for the subject about which you write."

## SCIENCE WEEKLY

Science Weekly Inc., P.O. Box 70638, Chevy Chase MD 20813. (301)680-8804. Fax: (301)680-9240. E-mail: scienceweekly@erols.com. Website: www.scienceweekly.com. **Publisher:** Dr. Claude Mayberry. Magazine published 14 times/year. Estab. 1984. Circ. 200,000.

• *Science Weekly* uses freelance writers to develop and write an entire issue on a single science topic. Send résumé only, not submissions. Authors must be within the greater D.C., Virginia, Maryland area. *Science Weekly* works on assignment only.

**Nonfiction** Young readers, middle readers, (K- 6th grade): science/math education, education, problem-solving.

**Terms** Pays on publication. Prefers people with education, science and children's writing background. *Send résumé only.* Samples copies free with SAE and 3 first-class stamps.

## SCIENCE WORLD

Scholastic Inc., 557 Broadway, New York NY 10012-3999. (212)343-6100. Fax: (212)343-6945. E-mail: sciencew orld@scholastic.com. **Editor:** Patty Janes. **Art Director:** Felix Batcup. Magazine published biweekly during the school year. Estab. 1959. Circ. 400,000. Publishes articles in Life Science/Health, Physical Science/Technology, Earth Science/Environment/Astronomy for students in grades 7-10. The goal is to make science relevant for teens.

• *Science World* publishes a separate teacher's edition with lesson plans and skills pages to accompany feature articles.

**Nonfiction** Young adults/teens: animal, concept, geography, health, nature/environment, science. Multicultural needs include: minority scientists as role models. Does not want to see stories without a clear news hook. Buys 20 mss/year. Average word length: 800-1,000. Byline given. Currently does not accept unsolicited mss.

**How to Contact/Writers** Nonfiction: Query with published clips and/or brief summaries of article ideas. Responds only if interested. No unsolicited mss.

**Illustration** Buys 2 illustrations/issue; 28 illustrations/year. Works on assignment only. Illustration only: Query with samples, tearsheets. Responds only if interested. Samples returned with SASE; samples filed "if we use them." Credit line given.

**Photography** Model/property releases required; captions required including background information. Provide résumé, business card, promotional literature or tearsheets to be kept on file. Responds only if interested.

**Terms** Pays on acceptance. Buys all rights for mss/artwork. Originals returned to artist at job's completion. For stories/articles, pays $200. Pays photographers per photo.

## ⓐ SEVENTEEN MAGAZINE

Hearst Magazines, 1440 Broadway, 13th Floor, New York NY 10018. (917)934-6500. Fax: (917)934-6574. Website: www.seventeen.com. **Features Editor:** Sarah Nanus. **Features Assistant:** Melanie Abrahams. **Photo Editor:** Elizabeth Kildahl. Monthly magazine. Estab. 1944. "We reach 14.5 million girls each month. Over the past five decades, *Seventeen* has helped shape teenage life in America. We represent an important rite of passage, helping to define, socialize and empower young women. We create notions of beauty and style, proclaim what's hot in popular culture and identify social issues."

**Nonfiction** Young adults: careers, cooking, hobbies, how-to, humorous, interview/profile, multicultural, social issues. Buys 7-12 mss/year. Word length: Varies from 200-2,000 words for articles. Byline sometimes given.

**Illustration Only interested in agented material.** Buys 10 illustrations/issue; 120 illustrations/year. Works on assignment only. Reviews ms/illustration packages. Illustrations only: Query with samples. Responds only if interested. Samples not returned; samples filed. Credit line given.

**Photography** Looking for photos to match current stories. Model/property releases required; captions required. Uses color, 8×10 prints; 35mm, 2¼×2¼, 4×5 or 8×10 transparencies. Query with samples or résumé of credits, or submit portfolio for review. Responds only if interested.

**Terms** Pays on publication. Buys first North American serial rights, first rights or all rights for mss. Buys exclusive rights for 3 months; online rights for photos. Original artwork returned at job's completion. Pays $1/word for articles/stories (varies by experience). Additional payment for photos accompanying articles. Pays illustrators/photographers $150-500. Sample copies not available. Writer's guidelines for SASE.

**Tips** Send for guidelines before submitting.

## SHARING THE VICTORY, Fellowship of Christian Athletes

8701 Leeds, Kansas City MO 64129. (816)921-0909. Fax: (816)921-8755. Website: www.fca.org. **Articles/Photo Editor:** Jill Ewert. **Art Director:** Frank Grey. Magazine published 9 times a year. Estab. 1982. Circ. 80,000. "Purpose is to present to coaches and athletes, and all whom they influence, the challenge and adventure of receiving Jesus Christ as Savior and Lord."

**Nonfiction** Young adults/teens: religion, sports. Buys 30 mss/year. Average word length: 500-1,200. Byline given.

**How to Contact/Writers** Nonfiction: Query with published clips. Responds in 6 weeks. Publishes ms 3 months after acceptance. Will consider simultaneous submissions, electronic submissions via disk or modem and previously published work.

**Photography** Purchases photos separately. Looking for photos of sports action. Uses color prints and 35mm transparencies. E-mail electronic submissions.

**Terms** Pays on publication. Buys first rights and second serial (reprint) rights. Pays $150-400 for assigned and unsolicited articles. Photographers paid per photo. Sample copies for 9×12 SASE and $1. Writer's/photo guidelines for SASE.

**Tips** "Be specific—write short. Take quality, sharp photos. Everything must be tied to FCA ministry." Interested in colorful sports photos.

## SHINE brightly

GEMS Girls' Clubs, Box 7259, Grand Rapids MI 49510. (616)241-5616. Fax: (616)241-5558. E-mail: christina@gemsgc.org. Website: www.gems.org. **Editor:** Jan Boone. **Managing Editor:** Christina Malone. Monthly (with combined June/July/August summer issue) magazine. Circ. 16,000. "*SHINE brightly* is designed to help girls ages 9-14 see how God is at work in their lives and in the world around them."

**Fiction** Middle readers: adventure, animal, contemporary, health, history, humorous, multicultural, nature/environment, problem-solving, religious, sports. Does not want to see unrealistic stories and those with trite, easy endings. Buys 30 mss/year. Average word length: 400-900. Byline given.

**Nonfiction** Middle readers: animal, arts/crafts, careers, cooking, fashion, games/puzzles, health, hobbies, how-to, humorous, nature/environment, multicultural, problem-solving, religious, social issues, sports, travel, also movies, music and musicians. Buys 9 mss/year. Average word length: 100-400. Byline given.

**How to Contact/Writers** Send for annual update for publication themes. Fiction/nonfiction: Send complete ms. Responds to mss in 1 month. Will consider simultaneous submissions. Guidelines on website.

**Illustration** Buys 3 illustrations/year. Prefers ms/illustration packages. Works on assignment only. Responds to submissions in 1 month. Samples returned with SASE. Credit line given.

**Terms** Pays on publication. Buys first North American serial rights, first rights, second serial (reprint rights) or simultaneous rights. Original artwork not returned at job's completion. Pays 3-5¢/word, up to $35 for stories, assigned articles and unsolicited articles. Poetry is $5-15. Games and Puzzles are $5-10. "We send complimentary copies in addition to pay." Pays up to $125 for color cover illustration; $25-50 for color inside illustration. Pays photographers by the project ($20-50 per photo). Writer's guidelines for SASE.

**Tips** Writers: "The stories should be current, deal with adolescent problems and joys, and help girls see God at work in their lives through humor as well as problem-solving."

## SKATING

U.S. Figure Skating, 20 First St., Colorado Springs CO 80906. (719)635-5200. Fax: (719)635-9548. E-mail: skating magazine@usfsa.org. Website: www.usfigureskating.org/magazine.asp. **Articles Editor:** Amy Partain. Magazine published 10 times/year. Estab. 1923. Circ. 45,000. "The mission of *SKATING* is to communicate information about the sport (figure skating) to the U.S. Figure Skating membership and figure skating fans, promoting U.S. Figure Skating programs, personalities, events and trends that affect the sport."

**Nonfiction** Young readers, middle readers, young adults: biography, health, sports. Buys 30 mss/year. Average word length: 750-2,000. Byline given.

**How to Contact/Writers** Nonfiction: Query with published clips. Responds to queries/mss in 1 month. Publishes ms 2 months after acceptance. Prefers electronic submissions via disk or e-mail.

**Illustration** Buys 1 illustration/year. Works on assignment only. Reviews ms/illustration packages from artists. Query. Illustrations only: Query with samples. Responds only if interested. Samples returned with SASE; or filed. Credit line given.

**Photography** Uses photos of kids learning to skate on ice. Model/property release required; captions required. Uses color most sizes glossy prints, 35mm transparencies. Contact by e-mail if interested in submitting. Responds only if interested.

**Terms** Pays on publication. Buys first rights for mss, artwork and photos. Original artwork returned at job's completion. Pays $75-150 for stories and articles. Additional payment if photos are used. Pays photographers per photo (range: $15-35). Sample copies for SAE. Writer's/photo guidelines for SASE.

**Tips** "*SKATING* covers Olympic-eligible skating, primarily focusing on the U.S. We do *not* cover professional skating. We are looking for fun, vibrant articles on U.S. Figure Skating members of all age levels and skills, especially synchronized skaters and adult skaters."

## SKIPPING STONES

A Multicultural Children's Magazine, P.O. Box 3939, Eugene OR 97403. (541)342-4956. E-mail: editor@skipping stones.org. Website: www.skippingstones.org. **Articles/Photo/Fiction Editor:** Arun N. Toke. Bimonthly magazine. Estab. 1988. Circ. 2,500. "*Skipping Stones* is an award-winning multicultural, nonprofit children's magazine designed to encourage cooperation, creativity and celebration of cultural and ecological richness. We encourage submissions by minorities and under-represented populations."

- Send SASE for *Skipping Stones* guidelines and theme list for detailed descriptions of the topics they want. *Skipping Stones* has won awards from Ed Press, NAME (National Association for Multicultural Education) and Parent's Choice.

**Fiction** Middle readers, young adult/teens: contemporary, meaningful, humorous. All levels: folktales, multicultural, nature/environment. Multicultural needs include: bilingual or multilingual pieces; use of words from other languages; settings in other countries, cultures or multi-ethnic communities.

**Nonfiction** All levels: animal, biography, cooking, games/puzzles, history, humorous, interview/profile, multicultural, nature/environment, creative problem-solving, religion and cultural celebrations, sports, travel, social and international awareness. Does not want to see preaching, violence or abusive language; no poems by authors over 18 years old; no suspense or romance stories. Average word length: 500-750. Byline given.

**How to Contact/Writers** Fiction: Query. Nonfiction: Send complete ms. Responds to queries in 1 month; mss in 4 months. Will consider simultaneous submissions; reviews artwork for future assignments. Please include your name on each page.

**Illustration** Prefers illustrations by teenagers and young adults. Will consider all illustration packages. Manuscript/illustration packages: Query; submit complete ms with final art; submit tearsheets. Responds in 4 months. Credit line given.

**Photography** Black & white photos preferred, but color photos with good contrast are welcome. Needs: youth 7-17, international, nature, celebration.

**Terms** Acquires first and reprint rights for mss and photographs. Pays in copies for authors, photographers and illustrators. Sample copies for $5 with SAE and 4 first-class stamps. Writer's/illustrator's guidelines for 4×9 SASE.

**Tips** "We want material meant for children and young adults/teenagers with multicultural or ecological awareness themes. Think, live and write as if you were a child, 'tween or teen." Wants "material that gives insight to cultural celebrations, lifestyle, custom and tradition, glimpse of daily life in other countries and cultures. Photos, songs, artwork are most welcome if they illustrate/highlight the points. Translations are invited if your submission is in a language other than English. Upcoming themes will include cultural celebrations, living abroad, disability, hospitality customs of various cultures, cross-cultural understanding, African, Asian and Latin American cultures, humor, international, turning points and magical moments in life, caring for the earth, spirituality, and Multicutural Awareness."

## SPARKLE

GEMS Girls' Clubs, P.O. Box 7259, Grand Rapids MI 49510. (616)241-5616. Fax: (616)241-5558. E-mail: christina@gemsgc.org. Website: www.gemsgc.org. **Articles/Fiction Editor:** Christina Malone. **Art Director/Photo Editor:** Tina DeKam. Magazine published 3 times/year. Estab. 2002. "We are a Christian magazine geared toward girls in the 1st-3rd grades. *Sparkle* prints stories, articles, crafts, recipes, games and more. The magazine is based on an annual theme."

**Fiction** Young readers: adventure, animal, contemporary, health, humorous, multicultural, nature/environment, problem-solving, religious, sports, suspense/mystery. Buys 8 mss/year. Average word length: 100-400. Byline given.

**Nonfiction** Young readers, middle readers: animal, arts/crafts, biography, careers, cooking, concept, fashion, games/puzzles, geography, health, history, hobbies, how-to, interview/profile, math, multicultural, nature/environment, problem-solving, science, social issues, sports, travel. Average word length: 100-400. Byline given.

**How to Contact/Writers** Fiction/nonfiction: Send complete ms. Responds to ms in 1 month. Publishes ms 4-6 months after acceptance. Will consider previously published work.

**Illustration** Buys 2 illustrations/issue; 6 illustrations/year. Uses color artwork only. Works on assignment only. Reviews ms/illustration packages from artists. Send ms with dummy. Contact: Christina Malone, managing editor. Illustrations only: send promo sheet. Responds only if interested. Samples returned with SASE; samples filed. Credit line given.

**Photography** Looking for close-up photos of girls, grades 1-3. Uses color prints. Send unsolicited photos by mail. Responds only if interested.

**Terms** Pays on publication. Buys first North American serial rights for mss, artwork and photos. Pays $20 minimum for stories and articles. Pays illustrators $50-100 for color cover; $25-100 for color inside. Pays photographers per photo (range: $25-100). Additional payment for ms/illustration packages and for photos accompanying articles. Sample copies for $1. Writer's/illustrator/photo guidelines free for SASE.

## SPIDER, The Magazine for Children

Carus Publishing Company, P.O. Box 300, Peru IL 61354. (815)224-5803, ext. 656. Website: www.cricketmag.com. **Editor-in-Chief:** Marianne Carus. **Editor:** Heather Delabre. **Art Director:** Sue Beck. Monthly magazine. Estab. 1994. Circ. 70,000. *Spider* publishes high-quality literature for beginning readers, primarily ages 6-9.

**Fiction** Young readers: adventure, contemporary, fantasy, folktales, science fiction. "Authentic, well-researched stories from all cultures are welcome. No didactic, religious, or violent stories, or anything that talks down to children." Average word length: 300-1,000. Byline given.

**Nonfiction** Young readers: animal, arts/crafts, cooking, games/puzzles, geography, history, math, multicultural, nature/environment, problem-solving, science. "Well-researched articles on all cultures are welcome. Would like to see more games, puzzles and activities, especially ones adaptable to *Spider*'s takeout pages. No encyclopedic or overtly educational articles." Average word length: 300-800. Byline given.

**Poetry** Serious, humorous. Maximum length: 20 lines.

**How to Contact/Writers** Fiction/nonfiction: Send complete ms with SASE. Do not query. Responds to mss in 3 months. Publishes ms 2-3 years after acceptance. Will consider simultaneous submissions and previously published work.

**Illustration** Buys 20 illustrations/issue; 240 illustrations/year. Uses color artwork only. "Any medium—preferably one that can wrap on a laser scanner—no larger than 20×24. We use more realism than cartoon-style art." Works on assignment only. Reviews ms/illustration packages from artists. Illustrations only: Send promo sheet and tearsheets. Responds in 6 weeks. Samples returned with SASE; samples filed. Credit line given.

**Photography** Buys photos from freelancers. Buys photos with accompanying ms only. Model/property releases and captions required. Uses 35mm or $2^1/_4 \times 2^1/_4$ transparencies. Send unsolicited photos by mail; provide résumé and tearsheets. Responds in 6 weeks.

**Terms** Pays on publication for text; within 45 days from acceptance for art. Rights purchased vary. Buys first and promotional rights for artwork; one-time rights for photographs. Original artwork returned at job's completion. Pays up to 25¢/word for previously unpublished stories/articles. Authors also receive 2 complimentary copies of the issue in which work appears. Additional payment for ms/illustration packages and for photos accompanying articles. Pays illustrators $750 for color cover; $200-300 for color inside. Pays photographers per photo (range: $25-75). Sample copies for $5. Writer's/illustrator's guidelines for SASE.

**Tips** Writers: "Read back issues before submitting." (See listings for *Babybug*, *Cicada*, *Cricket*, *Muse*, *Ladybug* and *ASK*.)

## ⓐ SPORTS ILLUSTRATED FOR KIDS

135 W. 50th St., New York NY 10020-1393. (212)522-4876. Fax: (212)467-4247. Website: www.sikids.com. **Managing Editor:** Neil Cohen. **Art Director:** Beth Bugler. **Photo Editor:** Andrew McCloskey. Monthly magazine. Estab. 1989. Circ. 1,000,000. Each month *SI Kids* brings the excitement, joy, and challenge of sports to life for boys and girls ages 8-14 via: action photos, dynamic designs, interactive stories; a spectrum of sports: professional, extreme, amateur, women's and kids; profiles, puzzles, playing tips, sports cards; posters, plus drawings and writing by kids. 100% of publication aimed at juvenile and teen market.

**Nonfiction** Middle readers, young adults: biography, games/puzzles, interview/profile, sports. Buys less than 20 mss/year. Average word length: 500-700. Byline given.

**How to Contact/Writers** Nonfiction: Query. Responds in 6 weeks. Will consider simultaneous submissions.

**Illustration Only interested in agented material.** Buys 50 illustrations/year. Works on assignment only. Reviews ms/illustration packages from artists. Submit ms/illustration package with SASE. Contact: Beth Bugler, art director. Illustrations only: Send promo sheet and samples. Contact: Beth Bugler, art director. Responds in 1 month. Samples kept on file. Credit line given.

**Photography** Looking for action sports photography. Uses color prints and 35mm transparencies. Submit portfolio for review. Responds in 1 month.

**Terms** Pays on acceptance. Buys all rights for mss. Buys all rights for artwork. Buys all rights for photos. Original artwork returned at job's completion. Pays $500 for 500-600 word articles. by the project—$400; $500/day; per photo (range: $75-1,000). Sample copies free for $9 \times 12$ SASE. Writer's guidelines for SASE or via website.

## STORY FRIENDS

Mennonite Publishing Network, 616 Walnut Ave., Scottdale PA 15683. (724)887-8500. Fax: (724)887-3111. E-mail: storyfriends@mph.org. **Editor:** Susan Reith Swan. Estab. 1905. Circ. 6,000. Monthly magazine that reinforces Christian values for children ages 4-9.

**Fiction** Picture-oriented material: contemporary, humorous, multicultural, nature/environment, problem-solving, religious, relationships. Multicultural needs include fiction or nonfiction pieces which help children be aware of cultural diversity and celebrate differences while recognizing similarities. Buys 45 mss/year. Average word length: 300-800. Byline given.

**Nonfiction** Picture-oriented: animal, humorous, interview/profile, multicultural, nature/environment. Buys 10 mss/year. Average word length: 300-800. Byline given.

**Poetry** Average length: 4-12 lines.

**How to Contact/Writers** Fiction/nonfiction: Send complete ms. Responds to mss in 10 weeks. Will consider simultaneous submissions.

**Illustration** Works on assignment only. Send tearsheets with SASE. Responds in 2 months. Samples returned with SASE; samples filed. Credit line given.

**Terms** Pays on acceptance. Buys one-time rights or reprint rights for mss and artwork. Original artwork returned at job's completion. Pays 3-5¢/word for stories and articles. Pays photographers $15-30 per photo. Writer's guidelines $2; SAE and 2 first-class stamps.

**Tips** "Become immersed in high quality children's literature."

## TEEN MAGAZINE

Hearst Magazines, 3000 Ocean Park Blvd., Suite 3048, Santa Monica CA 90405. (310)664-2950. Fax: (310)664-2959. Website: www.teenmag.com. **Contact:** Jane Fort, editor-in-chief (fashion, beauty, TeenPROM) ; Damon Romine, deputy editor (entertainment, movies, TV, music, books, covers, photo editor, intern coordinator) ; Heather Hewitt, managing editor (manufacturing, advertising, new products, what's hot). Quarterly magazine. Estab. 1957. "We are a pure junior high school female (ages 10-15) audience. *TEEN*'s audience is upbeat and wants to be informed."

**Fiction** Young adults: romance. Does not want to see ''that which does not apply to our market , i.e., science fiction, history, religious, adult-oriented.''

**Nonfiction** Young adults: how-to, arts/crafts, fashion, interview/profile, games/puzzles. Does not want to see adult-oriented, adult point of view.

**How to Contact/Writers No unsolicited materials accepted.**

**Illustration** Buys 10 illustrations/issues; 50 illustrations/year. Uses various styles. ''Light, upbeat.'' Illustrations only: ''Want to see samples whether it be tearsheets, slides, finished pieces showing the style.'' Responds only if interested. Credit line given.

**Terms** Pays on acceptance. Buys all rights. Pays $ 500-1,000 for illustrations.

**Tips** Illustrators: ''Present professional finished work. Get familiar with our magazine and send samples that would be compatible with the style of publication.'' There is a need for artwork with ''fiction/specialty articles. Send samples or promotional materials on a regular basis.''

## TEENAGE CHRISTIAN E-MAGAZINE

Christian Publishing Inc., P.O. Box 2227, Brentwood TN 37024-2227. (800)637-2613. E-mail: teenagechristian@ bellsouth.net. Website: www.teenagechristian.net. **Articles Editor:** Ben Forrest. Monthly magazine. Estab. 1961. Circ. 5,000. ''We provide inspirational articles and stories that help teenagers grow in their relationship with God.''

**Fiction** Young adults: adventure, contemporary, health, humorous, problem-solving, religious, sports. Buys 15 mss/year. Byline sometimes given.

**Nonfiction** Young adults: biography, careers, concept, games/puzzles, health, hobbies, how-to, humorous, interview/profile, problem-solving, religion, social issues, sports, travel. Buys 12 mss/year. Average word length: 500-1,000. Byline sometimes given.

**Poetry** Maximum length: 200 words. Limit submissions to 5 poems.

**How to Contact/Writers** Fiction/Nonfiction: Send complete ms. Responds to queries/mss in 3 weeks. Publishes ms 2 months after acceptance. Will consider simultaneous submissions, e-mail submissions, previously published work.

**Illustration** Works on assignment only. Send ms with dummy. Illustrations only: URL. Responds only if interested.

**Photography** Buys photos separately. Model/property release required. Uses color prints and $2\frac{1}{4} \times 2\frac{1}{4}$ , $4 \times 5$ or $8 \times 10$ transparencies. E-mail or URL. Responds only if interested.

**Terms** Pays on publication. Buys one-time rights for mss. Buys all rights for artwork; all rights for photos. Pays $25 for stories; $25 for articles.

## THREE LEAPING FROGS, (Northern Nevada's Fun Newspaper for Kids)

Juniper Creek Publishing Inc., P.O. Box 2205, Carson City NV 89702. (775)849-1637. Fax: (775)849-1707. Website: www.junipercreekpubs.com. **Articles/Fiction Editor:** Ellen Hopkins. Bimonthly tabloid. Estab. 2001. Circ. 30,000. ''Three Leaping Frogs is a regional, themed publication. All articles/stories should be aimed at children ages 8-13 and adhere to our themes.''

**Fiction** Middle readers, young adults: adventure, animal, contemporary, folktale, health, history, humorous, multicultural, nature/environment, problem-solving, sports (middle reader only). Buys 5 mss/year. Average word length: 300-600. Byline given.

**Nonfiction** Middle readers: animal, art/crafts, biography, cooking, games/puzzles, geography, health, history, how-to, humorous, interview/profile, math, multicultural, nature/environment, problem-solving, science, social issues, sports. Buys 50 mss/year. Average word length: 350-600. Byline given.

**Poetry** Maximum length: 20 lines. Limit submissions to 5 poems.

**How to Contact/Writers** Fiction/Nonfiction: Send complete ms. Responds to queries/mss in 6 weeks or less. Publishes ms 3 months after acceptance. Will consider simultaneous submissions, e-mail submissions, previously published work.

**Photography** Buys photos with accompanying ms only. Model/property release required. ''Digital images only.''

**Terms** Pays on publication. Buys one-time rights for mss. Buys one-time rights for photos. Pays copies—$25 for stories and articles. Additional payment for ms/illustration packages and for photos accompanying articles. Pays writers with contributor's copies in lieu of cash for games, crafts, and puzzles. Sample copies for $1.00. Writer's guidelines for SASE.

**Tips** ''Three Leaping Frogs is a regional publication. Please review guidelines before submitting.''

## TURTLE MAGAZINE, For Preschool Kids

Children's Better Health Institute, 1100 Waterway Blvd., Indianapolis IN 46206-0567. (317)636-8881. Fax: (317)684-8094. Website: www.turtlemag.org. **Editor:** Terry Harshman. **Art Director:** Bart Rivers. Monthly/ bimonthly magazine published 6 times/year. Circ. 300,000. *Turtle* uses read-aloud stories, especially suitable for bedtime or naptime reading, for children ages 2-5. Also uses poems, simple science experiments, easy recipes and health-related articles.

**Fiction** Picture-oriented material: health-related, medical, history, humorous, multicultural, nature/environment, problem-solving, sports, recipes, simple science experiments. Avoid stories in which the characters indulge in unhealthy activities. Buys 20 mss/year. Average word length: 150-300. Byline given. Currently accepting submissions for Rebus stories only.

**Nonfiction** Picture-oriented material: cooking, health, sports, simple science. "We use very simple experiments illustrating basic science concepts. These should be pretested. We also publish simple, healthful recipes." Buys 24 mss/year. Average word length: 100-300. Byline given.

**Poetry** "We're especially looking for short poems (4-8 lines) and slightly longer action rhymes to foster creative movement in preschoolers. We also use short verse on our inside front cover and back cover."

**How to Contact/Writers** Fiction/nonfiction: Send complete mss. Queries are not accepted. Responds to mss in 3 months.

**Terms** Pays on publication. Buys all rights for mss. Pays up to 22¢/word for stories and articles (depending upon length and quality) and 10 complimentary copies. Pays $25 minimum for poems. Sample copy $1.75. Writer's guidelines free with SASE and on website.

**Tips** "Our need for health-related material, especially features that encourage fitness, is ongoing. Health subjects must be age-appropriate. When writing about them, think creatively and lighten up! Always keep in mind that in order for a story or article to educate preschoolers, it first must be entertaining—warm and engaging, exciting, or genuinely funny. Here the trend is toward leaner, lighter writing. There will be a growing need for interactive activities. Writers might want to consider developing an activity to accompany their concise manuscripts." (See listings for *Child Life, Children's Digest, Children's Playmate, Humpty Dumpty's Magazine, Jack and Jill* and *U*S* Kids.*)

## [N] U MAG

USAA, 9800 Fredericksburg Rd., San Antonio TX 78285. (210)498-4302. Fax: (210)498-0030. E-mail: sharibiediger@usaa.com. **Submissions Editor:** Shari Biediger. Quarterly magazine. Estab. 1995. "*U Mag* is intended to educate USAA's young members about topic that interest them now and will affect them in the future. Content is organized by theme (such as family, citizenship, money smarts, the future, safety, and communication). It encourages readers age 9-12 to think, laugh, learn, and interact with parents and others." Entire publication aimed at juvenile market.

**Fiction** Middle readers: adventure, contemporary. Buys 1 mss/year. Sometimes gives byline.

**Nonfiction** Considers middle readers: arts/crafts, careers, games/puzzles, geography, history, how-to, interview/profile, math, problem-solving, travel. Buys 8 mss/year. Average word length: 500.

**How To Contact/Writers** Fiction: Send complete ms. Nonfiction: Query with published clips. Responds to queries in 3 weeks. Publishes ms 6 after acceptance. Considers simultaneous submissions.

**Terms** Pays on acceptance. Buys all rights. Pays 150-500 for stories; 150-500 for articles. Sample copies free for SASE (9 × 12 size envelope and $1.80 first-class stamps). Writer's guidelines free for SASE.

**Tips** "Each issue of *U Mag* is organized by theme. We use these themes to develop more targeted topics, such as communication, relationships, money, and setting goals. We often profile readers' stories. We prefer that profile subjects be young USAA members and their families, but it is not mandatory. Profiles don't have to be super-kids. Instead we aim to profile children that our readers—who are mostly current and former military dependents—can relate to. We rarely feature celebrities, but would consider them if a writer has access and a story that fits one of our themes. USSA also publishes *U-Turn* magazine for readers 13-17."

## U*S* KIDS

Children's Better Health Institute, 1100 Waterway Blvd., P.O. Box 567, Indianapolis IN 46206. (317)636-8881. Website: www.uskidsmag.org. **Editor:** Daniel Lee. **Art Director:** Greg Vanzo. Magazine published 6 times a year. Estab. 1987. Circ. 230,000.

**Fiction** Young readers: adventure, animal, contemporary, health, history, humorous, multicultural, nature/environment, problem-solving, sports, suspense/mystery. Buys limited number of stories/year. Query first. Average word length: 500-800. Byline given.

**Nonfiction** Young readers: animal, arts/crafts, cooking, games/puzzles, health, history, hobbies, how-to, humorous, interview/profile, multicultural, nature/environment, science, social issues, sports, travel. Wants to see interviews with kids ages 5-10, who have done something unusual or different. Buys 30-40 mss/year. Average word length: 400. Byline given.

**Poetry** Maximum length: 8-24 lines.

**How to Contact/Writers** Fiction: Send complete ms. Responds to queries and mss in 3 months.

**Illustration** Buys 8 illustrations/issue; 70 illustrations/year. Color artwork only. Works on assignment only. Reviews ms/illustration packages from artists. Query. Illustrations only: Send résumé and tearsheets. Responds only if interested. Samples returned with SASE; samples kept on file. Does not return originals. Credit line given.

**Photography** Purchases photography from freelancers. Looking for photos that pertain to children ages 5-10. Model/property release required. Uses color and b&w prints; 35mm, $2\frac{1}{4} \times 2\frac{1}{4}$, $4 \times 5$ and $8 \times 10$ transparencies. Photographers should provide résumé, business card, promotional literature or tearsheets to be kept on file. Responds only if interested.

**Terms** Pays on publication. Buys all rights for mss. Purchases all rights for artwork. Purchases one-time rights for photographs. Pays 17¢/word minimum. Additional payment for ms/illustration packages. Pays illustrators $155/page for color inside. Photographers paid by the project or per photo (negotiable). Sample copies for $2.95. Writer's/illustrator/photo guidelines for #10 SASE.

**Tips** "Write clearly and concisely without preaching or being obvious." (See listings for *Child Life*, *Children's Digest*, *Children's Playmate*, *Humpty Dumpty's Magazine*, *Jack and Jill* and *Turtle Magazine*.)

## U-TURN

USAA, 9800 Fredericksburg, San Antonio TX 78288. (210)498-0030. Fax: (210)498-0300. E-mail: shari.biediger @ussa.com. **Editor:** Shari Biediger. Quarterly magazine. Estab. 1999. "*U-Turn* is intended to educate USAA's young members about topics that interest them now and will affect them in the future; focusing on driving, money, relationships, safety, college, and career planning to strengthem the character and knowledge of forward-thinking readers age 13-17." Entire publication aimed at juvenile market.

**Nonfiction** Considers young adults/teens: careers, how-to, humorous, interview/profile, math, problem-solving, social issues, sports, travel. Buys 4 mss/year. Average word length: 250-800.

**How to Contact/Writers** Fiction: Query with published clips.

**Terms** Pays on acceptance. Buys all rights. No additional payment for ms/illustration packages. No additional payment for ms/photo packages. Sample copies free for SASE ($9 \times 12$ size envelope and $1.80 postage). Writer's guidelines free for SASE. Publishes work by children.

**Tips** "While most of the topics covered in *U-Turn* are assigned by the editor, ideas for articles are welcome and encouraged. After articles are assigned, the editor and writer work closely to develop the direction of the article as it is researched. *U-Turn* reinforces the importance of its readers' voices and ideas by publishing their submissions in each issue. In addition, a large and active teen panel comprised of readers is vital to *U-Turn*'s editorial mission. While *U-Turn* has rarely published fiction, poetry, or prose, we would consider pieces such as this if they are high quality and applicable to a topic covered in an issue—please submit completed stories for consideration rather than queries. USAA also publishes *U Mag* for ages 9-12."

## WEE ONES E-MAGAZINE

1011 Main St., Darlington MD 21034. E-mail:info@weeonesmag.co. Website: www.weeonesmag.com. **Editor:** Jennifer Reed. Online magazine. Estab. 2001. "We are an online children's magazine for children ages 5-10. Our mission is to use the Internet to encourage kids to read. We promote literacy and family unity." 100% of publication aimed at juvenile market.

**Fiction** Picture-oriented material: adventure, contemporary, health, history, humorous, multicultural, nature/environment, problem-solving, sports, rebus with illustrations. Buys 40 mss/year. Average word length: up to 500. Byline given.

**Nonfiction** Picture-oriented material: animal, arts/crafts, biography, concept, cooking, games/puzzles, geography, health, history, hobbies, how-to, humorous, multicultural, nature/environment, problem-solving, science, sports, travel. Buys over 60 mss/year. Average word length: up to 600. Byline given.

**Poetry** Uses rhyming poetry. Limit submissions to 3 poems. Up to twenty lines.

**How to Contact/Writers** Fiction/nonfiction: Send complete ms via e-mail. Responds to mss in 1-2 months. Publishes ms 6-12 months after acceptance. Will consider simultaneous submissions, electronic submissions via e-mail. No attachments please!

**Illustration** Buys 6 illustrations/issue. Works on assignment only. Reviews ms/illustration packages from artists. Query. Illustrations only: Query with samples. Contact: Jeff Reed, art editor. Responds only if interested. Samples returned with SASE or kept on file. Credit line given.

**Photography** Uses photos of children in various activities. Uses color b&w $4 \times 6$ prints. Responds only if interested.

**Terms** Pays on publication. Buys nonexclusive worldwide electronic and reprint rights for mss, artwork and photos. Pays 5¢/word for stories and articles. Additional payment for ms/illustration packages and for photos accompanying articles. Pays $5-20 for b&w and color inside. Pays photographers per photo (range: $3). Writer's/illustrator/photo guidelines for SASE.

**Tips** "*Wee Ones* is a growing online children's magazine. We are not in print-yet! We reach over 90 countries and receive 50,000 hits per month. Study our magazine before submitting. Our guidelines are located on our site. Your chance for acceptance depends widely on how well you know our magazine and follow our guidelines. We do not publish stories with monsters, witches, ghosts or Halloween themes."

## ⬛ WHAT IF?, Canada's Fiction Magazine for Teens

What If Publications, 19 Lynwood Place, Guelph ON N1G 2V9 Canada. (519)823-2941. Fax: (519)823-8081. E-mail: editor@whatifmagazine.com. Website: www.whatifmagazine.com. **Articles/Fiction Editor:** Mike Leslie. **Art Director:** Jean Leslie. Bimonthly magazine. Estab. 2003. Circ. 25,000. "The goal of *What If?* is to help young adults get published for the first time in a quality literary setting alongside more experienced and well-known Canadian writers."

**Fiction** Young adults: adventure, contemporary, fantasy, folktale, health, humorous, multicultural, nature/environment, problem-solving, science fiction, sports, suspense/mystery. Buys 48 mss/year. Average word length: 500-3,000. Byline given.

**Nonfiction** Young adults: editorial. "We publish editorial content from young adult writers only—similar to material seen on newspapers op-ed page." Average word length: 100-500. Byline given.

**Poetry** Reviews poetry: all styles. Maximum length: 20 lines. Limit submissions to 4 poems.

**How to Contact/Writers** Fiction/Nonfiction: Send complete ms. Responds to mss in 2 months. Publishes ms 4 months after acceptance. Will consider e-mail submissions, previously published work if the author owns all rights.

**Illustration** Buys approximately 150 illustrations/year. Reviews ms/illustration packages from artists. Send ms with dummy. Query with samples. Contact: Jean Leslie, production manager. Responds in 1 month. Samples returned with SASE. Credit line given.

**Terms** Pays on publication. Buys first rights for mss and artwork. Original artwork returned at job's completion. Pays 3 copies for stories; 1 copy for articles. "We are a new magazine and, until we build our subscription and advertising base, we pay in contributor's copies only." Pays illustrators 3 copies. Sample copies for $7.50. Writer's/illustrator's guidelines for SASE or available by e-mail.

**Tips** "Read our magazine. The majority of the material we publish (90%) is by Canadian young adults. Another 10% is by Canadian Adults. We are currently accepting material from Canadian teens only. The majority of material we receive from young adults is contemporary, science fiction and fantasy. As an adult, avoid these genres."

## ⬛ WHAT'S HERS/WHAT'S HIS

(formerly *What Magazine*), What! Publishers Inc., 108-93 Lombard Ave., Winnipeg MB R3B 3B1 Canada. (204)985-8160. Fax: (204)957-5638. E-mail: lalkin@m2ci.mb.ca. Website: www.whatmagnet.com. **Editor-in-Chief:** Barbara Chabai. Magazine published 6 times/year. Estab. 1987. Circ. 280,000—180,000, *Hers*; 100,000, *His*. "Informative and entertaining teen magazine for both genders ages 13-19. Articles deal with issues and ideas of relevance to Canadian teens. Articles must include Canadian references. The magazine is distributed through schools so we aim to be cool and responsible at the same time."

**Nonfiction** Young adults (13 and up): biography, careers, concept, health, how-to, humorous, interview/profile, nature/environment, science, social issues, sports. "No cliché teen stuff. Absolutely no fiction. Also, we're getting too many heavy pitches lately on teen pregnancy, AIDS, etc." Buys 8 mss/year. Average word length: 400-1,800. Byline given.

**How to Contact/Writers** Nonfiction: Query with published clips. Responds to queries/mss in 2 months. Publishes ms 2 months after acceptance.

**Terms** Pays on publication plus 30 days. Buys first rights for mss. Pays $100-500 (Canadian) for articles. Sample copies available for 9×12 SASE and $1.45 (Canadian). Writer's guidelines free for SASE.

**Tips** "Teens are smarter today than ever before. Respect that intelligence in queries and articles. Aim for the older end of our age-range (14-19) and avoid cliché. Humor works for us almost all the time."

## WINNER

The Health Connection, 55 W. OakRidge Dr., Hagerstown MD 21740. (301)393-4010. Fax : (301)393-3294. E-mail: Winner@healthconnection.org. Website: www.winnermagazine.org. **Articles Editor:** Anita Jacobs. **Art Director:** In transition at press time. Monthly magazine (September-May). Estab. 1958. Publishes articles that will promote choosing a positive lifestyle for children in grades 4-6.

**Fiction** Young readers, middle readers: contemporary, health, nature/environment, problem-solving, anti-to-bacco, alcohol, and drugs. Byline sometimes given.

**Nonfiction** Young readers, middle readers: biography, games/puzzles, health, hobbies, how-to, problem-solving, social issues. Buys 20 mss/year. Average word length: 600-650. Byline sometimes given.

**How to Contact/Writers** Fiction/nonfiction: Query. Responds in 6 weeks. Publishes ms 6-12 months after acceptance. Will consider simultaneous and e-mail submissions.

**Illustration** Buys 3 illustrations/issue; 30 illustrations/year. Uses color artwork only. Works on assignment only. Reviews ms/illustration packages from artists. Send ms with dummy. Responds only if interested. Samples returned with SASE.

**Terms** Pays on acceptance. Buys first rights for mss. Original artwork returned at job's completion. Additional payment for ms/illustration packages. Sometimes additional payment when photos accompany articles. Pays $200-400 for color inside. Writer's and illustrator's guidelines free for SASE. Sample magazine $2; include 9 × 12 envelope with 2 first-class stamps.

**Tips** Keep material upbeat and positive for elementary age children.

### WITH, The Magazine for Radical Christian Youth

Faith & Life Resources, 722 Main, Newton KS 67114. Fax: (316)283-0454. E-mail: carold@mennoniteusa.org. Wedsite: www.withonline.org. **Editor:** Carol Duerksen. Published 6 times a year. Circ. 5,800. Magazine published for Christian teenagers, ages 15-18. "We deal with issues affecting teens and try to help them make choices reflecting a radical Christian faith."

**Fiction** Young adults/teens: contemporary, fantasy, humorous, multicultural, problem-solving, religious, romance. Multicultural needs include race relations, first-person stories featuring teens of ethnic minorities. Buys 15 mss/year. Average word length: 1,000-2,000. Byline given.

**Nonfiction** Young adults/teens: first-person teen experience (as-told-to), how-to, humorous, multicultural, problem-solving, religion, social issues. Buys 15-20 mss/year. Average word length: 1,000-2,000. Byline given.

**Poetry** Wants to see religious, humorous, nature. "Buys 1-2 poems/year." Maximum length: 50 lines.

**How to Contact/Writers** Send complete ms. Query on first-person teen experience stories and how-to articles. (Detailed guidelines for first-person stories, how-tos, and fiction available for SASE.) Responds to queries in 3 weeks; mss in 6 weeks. Will consider simultaneous submissions.

**Illustration** Buys 6-8 assigned illustrations/issue; buys 64 assigned illustrations/year. Uses b&w and 2-color artwork only. Preferred theme or style: candids/interracial. Reviews ms/illustration packages from artists. Query first. Illustrations only: Query with portfolio (photocopies only) or tearsheets. Responds only if interested. Credit line given.

**Photography** Buys photos from freelancers. Looking for candid photos of teens (ages 15-18), especially ethnic minorities. Uses 8 × 10 b&w glossy prints. Photographers should send unsolicited photos by mail.

**Terms** Pays on acceptance. For mss buys first rights, one-time rights; second serial (reprint rights). Buys one-time rights for artwork and photos. Original artwork returned at job's completion upon request. Pays 6¢/word for unpublished mss; 4¢/word for reprints. Will pay more for assigned as-told-to stories. Pays $10-25 for poetry. Pays $50-60 for b&w cover illustration and b&w inside illustration. Pays photographers per project (range: $120-180). Sample copy for 9 × 12 SAE and 4 first-class stamps. Writer's/illustrator's guidelines for SASE.

**Tips** "We want stories, fiction or nonfiction, in which high-school-age youth of various cultures/ethnic groups are the protaganists. Stories may or may not focus on cross-cultural relationships. We're hungry for stuff that makes teens laugh—fiction, nonfiction and cartoons. It doesn't have to be religious, but must be wholesome. Most of our stories would not be accepted by other Christian youth magazines. They would be considered too gritty, too controversial, or too painful. Our regular writers are on the *With* wavelength. Most writers for Christian youth magazines aren't. Fiction and humor are the best places to break in. Send SASE and request guidelines." For photographers: "If you're willing to line up models and shoot to illustrate specific story scenes, send us a letter of introduction and some samples of your work."

### ◼ YES MAG, Canada's Science Magazine for Kids

Peter Piper Publishing Inc., 3968 Long Gun Place, Victoria BC V8N 3A9 Canada. Fax: (250)477-5390. E-mail: editor@yesmag.ca. Website: www.yesmag.ca. **Editor:** Shannon Hunt. **Art/Photo Director:** David Garrison. Managing Editor: Jude Isabella. Bimonthly magazine. Estab. 1996. Circ. 22,000. "*YES Mag* is designed to make science accessible, interesting, exciting, and FUN. Written for children ages 8 to 14, *YES Mag* covers a range of topics including science and technology news, environmental updates, do-at-home projects and articles about Canadian s cience and scientists."

**Nonfiction** Middle readers: animal, health, math, nature/environment, science. Buys 70 mss/year. Average word length: 250-1,250. Byline given.

**How to Contact/Writers** Nonfiction: Query with published clips or send complete ms (on spec only). Responds to queries/mss in 6 weeks. Generally publishes ms 3 months after acceptance. Will consider simultaneous submissions, previously published work.

**Illustration** Buys 2 illustrations/issue; 10 illustrations/year. Uses color artwork only. Works on assignment only. Reviews ms/illustration packages from artists. Query. Illustration only: Query with samples. Responds in 6 weeks. Samples filed. Credit line given.

**Photography** "Looking for science, technology, nature/environment photos based on current editorial needs." Photo captions required. Uses color prints. Provide résumé, business card, promotional literature, tearsheets if possible. Responds in 3 weeks.

**Terms** Pays on publication. Buys one-time rights for mss. Buys one-time rights for artwork/photos. Original artwork returned at job's completion. Pays $25-125 for stories and articles. Sample copies for $4. E-mail for writer's guidelines.

**Tips** "We do not publish fiction or science fiction. Visit our website for more information and sample articles. We prefer e-mail queries. Articles relating to the physical sciences and mathematics are encouraged."

## YOUNG & ALIVE
P.O. Box 6097, Lincoln NE 68506. (402)488-0981. Fax: (402)488-7582. E-mail: editorial@christianrecord.org. Website: www.christianrecord.org. **Articles Editor:** Ms. Gaylena Gibson. Quarterly magazine. Estab. 1976. Circ. 28,000. "We seek to provide wholesome, entertaining material for young adults ages 12 through age 25."
 • *Young & Alive* is not accepting submissions until 2009.

## YOUNG RIDER, The Magazine for Horse and Pony Lovers
Fancy Publications, P.O. Box 8237, Lexington KY 40533. (859)260-9800. Fax: (859)260-9814. Website: www.youngrider.com. **Editor:** Lesley Ward. Bimonthly magazine. Estab. 1994. "*Young Rider* magazine teaches young people, in an easy-to-read and entertaining way, how to look after their horses properly, and how to improve their riding skills safely."
**Fiction** Young adults: adventure, animal, horses, horse celebrities, famous equestrians. Buys 10 mss/year. Average word length: 1,500 maximum. Byline given.
**Nonfiction** Young adults: animal, careers, health (horse), sports, riding. Buys 20-30 mss/year. Average word length: 1,000 maximum. Byline given.
**How to Contact/Writers** Fiction/nonfiction: Query with published clips. Responds to queries in 2 weeks. Publishes ms 6-12 months after acceptance. Will consider simultaneous submissions, electronic submissions via disk or modem, previously published work.
**Illustration** Buys 2 illustrations/issue; 10 illustrations/year. Works on assignment only. Reviews ms/illustration packages from artists. Query. Contact: Lesley Ward, editor. Illustrations only: Query with samples. Contact: Lesley Ward, editor. Responds in 2 weeks. Samples returned with SASE. Credit line given.
**Photography** Buys photos with accompanying ms only. Uses color, slides, photos—in focus, good light. Model/property release required; captions required. Uses color 4×6 prints, 35mm transparencies. Query with samples. Responds in 2 weeks. Digital images must be high-res.
**Terms** Pays on publication. Buys first North American serial rights for mss, artwork, photos. Original artwork returned at job's completion. Pays $150 maximum for stories; $250 maximum for articles. Additional payment for ms/illustration packages and for photos accompanying articles. Pays $70-140 for color inside. Pays photographers per photo (range: $65-155). Sample copies for $3.50. Writer's/illustrator's/photo guidelines for SASE.
**Tips** "Fiction must be in third person. Read magazine before sending in a query. No 'true story from when I was a youngster.' No moralistic stories. Fiction must be up-to-date and humorous, teen-oriented. Need horsey interest or celebrity rider features. No practical or how-to articles—all done in-house."

## YOUNG SALVATIONIST
The Salvation Army, 615 Slaters Lane, Alexandria VA 22314-1112. (703)684-5500. Fax: (703)684-5534. E-mail: ys@usn.salvationarmy.org. Website: www.salpubs.com. **Editor-in-Chief:** Lt. Colonel Marlene Chase. **Editor:** Capt. Curtis Hartley. "We accept material with clear Christian content written for high school age teenagers. *Young Salvationist* is published for teenage members of The Salvation Army, an evangelical part of the Christian Church that focuses on living the Christian life."
**Fiction** Young adults/teens: contemporary, humorous, problem-solving, religious. Buys 10-11 mss/year. Average word length: 750-1,200. Byline given.
**Nonfiction** Young adults/teens: religious—careers, concept, interview/profile, how-to, humorous, multicultural, problem-solving, social issues, sports. Buys 40-50 mss/year. Average word length: 750-1,200. Byline given.
**How to Contact/Writers** Fiction/nonfiction: Query with published clips or send complete ms. Responds to queries/mss in 1 month. Will consider simultaneous submissions.
**Illustrations** Buys 3-5 illustrations/issue; 20-30 illustrations/year. Reviews ms/illustration packages from artists. Send ms with art. Illustrations only: Query; send résumé, promo sheet, portfolio, tearsheets. Responds only if interested. Samples returned with SASE; samples filed. Credit line given.
**Photography** Purchases photography from freelancers. Looking for teens in action.
**Terms** Pays on acceptance. Buys first North American serial rights, first rights, one-time rights or second serial (reprint) rights for mss. Purchases one-time rights for artwork and photographs. Original artwork returned at job's completion "if requested." For mss, pays 10-15¢/word; 10¢/word for reprints. Pays $60-150 color (cover) illustration; $60-150 b&w (inside) illustration; $60-150 color (inside) illustration. Pays photographers per photo (range: $60-150). Sample copy for 9×12 SAE and 4 first-class stamps. Writer's guidelines for #10 SASE.
**Tips** "Ask for theme list/sample copy! Write 'up,' not down to teens. Aim at young *adults*, not children." Wants "less fiction, more 'journalistic' nonfiction."

# Greeting Cards, Puzzles & Games

I n this section you'll find companies that produce puzzles, games, greeting cards, and other items (like coloring books, stickers, and giftwrap) especially for kids. These are items you'll find in children's sections of bookstores, toy stores, department stores, and card shops.

Because these markets create an array of products, their needs vary greatly. Some may need the service of freelance writers for greeting card copy or slogans for buttons and stickers. Others are in need of illustrators for coloring books or photographers for puzzles. Artists should send copies of their work that art directors can keep on file—never originals. Carefully read through the listings to find companies' needs, and send for guidelines and catalogs if they're available, just as you would for book or magazine publishers.

If you'd like to find out more about the greeting card industry beyond the market for children, there are a number of resources to help you. The Greeting Card Association is a national trade organization for the industry. For membership information, contact the GCA at 1156 15th St. NW, Suite 900, Washington DC 20005, (202)393-1778, www.greetingcard.org. *Greetings Etc.* (Edgel Communications), a quarterly trade magazine covering the greeting card industry, is the official publication of the Greeting Card Association. For information call (973)252-0100 or visit www.greetingsmagazine.com. For a complete list of companies, consult the latest edition of *Artist's & Graphic Designer's Market* (Writer's Digest Books). Writers should see *You Can Write Greeting Cards*, by Karen Ann Moore (Writer's Digest Books).

**Information on greeting card, puzzle, and game companies listed in the previous edition but not included in this edition of *Children's Writer's & Illustrator's Market* may be found in the General Index.**

## ABBY LOU ENTERTAINMENT
1411 Edgehill Place, Pasadena CA 91103. (612)795-7334. Fax: (626)795-4013. E-mail: ale@full-moon.com. **President:** George LeFave. Estab. 1985. Animation production company and book publisher. "We are looking for top creative children's illustrators with classic artwork. We are a children's book publisher moving into greeting cards—nature illustrations with characters." Publishes greeting cards (Whispering Gardens), coloring books, puzzles, games, posters, calendars, books (Adventures in Whispering Gardens). 100% of products are made for kids or have kid's themes.
**Writing** Needs freelance writing for children's greeting cards and other children's products. Makes 6 writing assignments/year. For greeting cards, accepts both rhymed and unrhymed verse ideas. Other needs for freelance writing include the theme of "Listen to your heart and you will hear the whispers." To contact, send cover letter, résumé, client list, writing samples. Responds in 2 weeks. Materials not returned; materials filed. For greeting cards, pays flat fee of $500, royalty of 3-10%; negotiable or negotiable advance against royalty. For other writing, payment is negotiated. Pays on acceptance. Buys one-time rights; negotiable. Credit line given.
**Illustration** Need freelance illustration for children's greeting cards, posters and TV related property. Makes 12 illustration assignments/year. Prefers a "classical look—property that needs illustration is Adventures in Whispering Gardens and multidimentional entertainment." Uses color artwork only. To contact send cover letter, published samples, slides, color photocopies and color promo pieces. Materials not returned; materials filed. For greeting cards and other artwork, payment is negotiable. Pays on acceptance or publication. Rights purchased are negotiable. Credit line given.
**Tips** "Give clear vision of what you want to do in the business and produce top quality, creative work."

## ARISTOPLAY, LTD.
202 Huron View Blvd., Ann Arbor MI 48103. (734)213-1617. Website: www.aristoplay.com. **Art Director:** Doreen Consiglio. Estab. 1979. Produces educational board games and card decks, activity kits—all educational subjects. 100% of products are made for kids or have kids' themes.
**Illustration** Needs freelance illustration and graphic designers (including art directors) for games, card decks and activity kits. Makes 2-4 illustration assignments/year. To contact, send cover letter, résumé, published samples or color photocopies. Responds back in 1 month if interested. For artwork, pays by the project, $500-5,000. Pays on acceptance (½-sketch, ½-final). Buys all rights. Credit line given.
**Photography** Buys photography from freelancers. Wants realistic, factual photos.
**Tips** "Creating board games requires a lot of back and forth in terms of design, illustration, editorial and child testing; the more flexible you are, the better. Also, factual accuracy is important." Target age group 4-14. "We are an educational game company. Illustrators working for us must be willing to research the subject and period of focus."

## AVANTI PRESS, INC.
6 W. 18th St., 12th Floor, New York NY 10011. (212)414-1025. Fax: (212)414-1055. Website: www.avantipress.com. **Photo Editors:** Bridget Hoyle and Judith Rosenbaum. Estab. 1979. Greeting card company. Publishes photographic greeting cards—non-seasonal and seasonal.
**Photography** Purchases photography from freelancers. Buys stock and assigns work. Buys approximately 150 stock images/year. Makes approximately 150 assignments/year. Wants "narrative, storytelling images, graphically strong and colorful!" Accepts only photographs. Does not return images or photographs. Uses b&w/color prints; any size or format. Pays either a flat fee or a royalty which is discussed at time of purchase." Pays on acceptance. Buys exclusive product rights (world-wide card rights). Credit line given. Photographer's guidelines for SASE or via website.
**Tips** At least 75% of products have kids' and pets themes. Submit seasonal material 9 months-1 year in advance. "All images submitted should express some kind of sentiment which either fits an occasion or can be versed and sent to the recipient to convey some feeling."

## AVONLEA TRADITIONS, INC.
17075 Leslie St., Units 12-15, Newmarket ON L3Y 8E1 Canada. (905)853-1777. Fax: (905)853-1763. Website: www.avonlea-traditions.com and www.maplelea.com. **President:** Kathryn Morton. Estab. 1988. Giftware and doll designer, importer and distributor. Designs, imports and distributes products related to Canada's famous storybook, *Anne of Green Gables*, and other Canadian themes. Creators of the new Maplelea Girls™, 18" vinyl doll play system which includes chapter books, journals, and accessories.
**Writing** (Girls) fiction.
**Illustration** Needs freelance illustration for books, stationery and packaging. Makes 2-3 illustration assignments/ month; 24/year. Prefers realistic style of artwork for chapter books. Also uses other youthful artwork styles. To contact, send color photocopies and promo pieces. Responds only if interested. Materials not returned;

materials filed. For other artwork, pays by the hour (range: $20-30). Pays on publication. Buys all rights. Credit line sometimes given.
**Photography** Sometimes uses stock photography of Canadian people and places.
**Tips** "We only use artists/writers who are Canadian."

### THE BEISTLE COMPANY

P.O. Box 10, Shippensburg PA 17257. (717)532-2131. Fax: (717)532-7789. E-mail: sales@beistle.com. Website: www.beistle.com. **Product Manager:** Rick Buterbaugh, art director. Estab. 1900. Paper products company. Produces decorations and party goods, posters—baby, baptism, birthday, holidays, educational, wedding/anniversary, graduation, ethnic themes, and New Year parties. 50% of products are made for kids or have kids' themes.
**Illustration** Needs freelance illustration for decorations, party goods, school supplies, point-of-purchase display materials and gift wrap. Makes 100 illustration assignments/year. Prefers fanciful style, cute 4- to 5-color illustration in gouache and/or computer illustration. To contact, send cover letter, résumé, client list, promo piece. To query with specific ideas, phone, write or fax. Responds only if interested. Materials returned with SASE; materials filed. Pays by the project or by contractual agreement; price varies according to type of project. Pays on acceptance. Buys all rights. Artist's guidelines available for SASE.
**Tips** Submit seasonal material 6 months in advance.

### CARDMAKERS

P.O. Box 236, Lyme NH 03768-0236. (603)795-4422. Fax: (603)795-4222. E-mail: info@cardmakers.com. Website: www.cardmakers.com. **Owner:** Peter Diebold. Estab. 1978. "We publish whimsical greeting cards with an emphasis on Christmas and business-to-business."
**Writing** To contact, send cover letter and writing samples with SASE. Responds in 3 months. Returns materials if accompanied by SASE. Pays on acceptance. Buys all rights. Credit line given. Writer's guidelines available for SASE.
**Illustration** Needs freelance illustration for greeting cards. Makes 30-50 illustration assignments/year. Looking for happy holidays, "activity" themes—nothing with an "edge." To contact, send cover letter, published samples, color photocopies, promo pieces and SASE. Query with specific ideas, keep it simple. Responds in 3 months. Materials returned with SASE. For greeting cards, pays flat fee of $100-400. Pays on acceptance. Credit line given. Artist's guidelines available for SASE.
**Photography** Buys stock images. Wants humor. To contact, send cover letter, published samples, SASE. Responds in 3 months. Returns material with SASE. Pays per photo (range: $100-400 for b&w, $100-400 for color). Pays on acceptance. Buys exclusive product rights. Credit line given. Guidelines available for SASE.
**Tips** Submit seasonal material 9 months in advance. "Be brief. Be polite. We look at all our mail. No calls, no fax, no e-mails. E-mails, requests for catalogs will get no response. Contact us through the U.S. Postal Service only! Worst times to submit—September-December. The best submissions we see are simple, right to the point, color samples with a 'check-off' stamped, return postcard eliciting comments/expression of interest."

### COURAGE CARDS

3915 Golden Valley Rd., Minneapolis MN 55422. (763)520-0211. Fax: (763)520-0299. E-mail: artsearch@courage.org. Website: www.couragecards.org. **Art and Production:** Laura Brooks. Estab. 1959. Not-for-profit greeting card company. Courage Cards helps support Courage Center, a not-for-profit provider of rehabilitation and independent living services for children and adults with disabilities. Publishes holiday greeting cards.
**Illustration** Needs freelance illustration for holiday greeting cards. Makes 40 illustration assignments/year. Prefers colorful traditional Christmas, peace, international and fall/winter seasonal art for holiday cards. Uses color artwork only. To contact, download guidelines from website or request via e-mail or phone. Responds to submissions in 6 months. Returns materials if accompanied by SASE. For greeting cards, pays flat fee of $350. Pays on publication. Buys reprint rights. Artist photo and promotion on the back of every card; credit line given for artists. Guidelines and application for the annual art search available on website.
**Tips** "We encourage artists to send in art entries through the art search. Please contact us for specific guidelines."

### CREATE-A-CRAFT

P.O. Box 941293, Plano TX 75094-1293. **Contact:** Editor. Estab. 1967. Greeting card company. Produces greeting cards (create-a-card), giftwrap, games (create-a-puzzle), coloring books, calendars (create-a-calendar), posters, stationery and paper tableware products for all ages.
**Writing** Needs freelance writing for children's greeting cards and other children's products. Makes 5 writing assignments/year. For greeting cards, accepts both rhymed and unrhymed verse ideas. Other needs for freelance writing include rhymed and unrhymed verse ideas on all products. To contact, send via recognized agent only.

Responds only if interested. Material not returned. For greeting cards, payment depends on complexity of project. Pays on publication. Buys all rights. Writer's guidelines available for SASE and $2.50—includes sample cards.

**Illustration** Works with 3 freelance artists/year. Buys 3-5 designs/illustrations/year. Primary age concentration is 4-8 year old market. Prefers artists with experience in cartooning. Works on assignment only. Buys freelance designs/illustrations mainly for greetings cards and T-shirts. Also uses freelance artists for calligraphy, P-O-P displays, paste-up and mechanicals. Considers pen & ink, watercolor, acrylics and colored pencil. Prefers humorous and ''cartoons that will appeal to families. Must be cute, appealing, etc. No religious, sexual implications or off-beat humor.'' Produces material for all holidays and seasons. Contact only through artist's agent. Some samples are filed; samples not filed are not returned. Responds only if interested. Write for appointment to show portfolio of original/final art, final reproduction/product, slides, tearsheets, color and b&w. Original artwork is not returned. ''Payment depends upon the assignment, amount of work involved, production costs, etc. involved in the project.'' Pays after all sales are tallied. Buys all rights. For guidelines and sample cards, send $2.50 and #10 SASE.

**Tips** Submit 6 months in advance. ''Demonstrate an ability to follow directions exactly. Too many submit artwork that has no relationship to what we produce. No phone calls accepted. Follow directions given. Do not ignore them. We do not work with anyone who does not follow them.''

### CREATIF LICENSING CORP.
31 Old Town Crossing, Mt. Kisco NY 10549. (914)241-6211. E-mail: art@creatifusa.com. Website: www.creatifu sa.com. **President:** Paul Cohen. Estab. 1975. Gift industry licensing agency. Publishes greeting cards, puzzles, posters, calendars, fabrics, home furnishings, all gifts. 50% of products are made for kids or have kids' themes.

**Illustration** Needs freelance illustration for children's greeting cards, all gift and home furnishings. Makes many illustration assignments/month. To contact, send cover letter, résumé, client list, published samples, photocopies, portfolio, promo piece and SASE. Responds in 2 month only if interested. Materials returned with SASE only; materials filed only if interested. For greeting cards, pays royalty and advance. For other artwork, pays royalty and advance. Pays on acceptance or publication. Artists and submission guidelines are available on website. Does not accept images via e-mail.

**Tips** Submit seasonal material 8-12 months in advance.

### DESIGN DESIGN INC.
P.O. Box 2266, Grand Rapids MI 49501. (616)774-2448. Fax: (616)774-4020. **Creative Director:** Tom Vituj. Estab. 1986. Greeting card company. 5% of products are made for kids or have kids themes.

**Writing** Needs freelance writing for children's greeting cards. Prefers both rhymed and unrhymed verse ideas. To contact, send cover letter and writing samples. Materials returned with SASE; materials not filed. For greeting cards, pays flat fee. Buys all rights or exclusive product rights; negotiable. No credit line given. Writer's guidelines for SASE.

**Illustration** Needs freelance illustration for children's greeting cards and related products. To contact, send cover letter, published samples, color or b&w photocopies, color or b&w promo pieces or portfolio. Returns materials with SASE. Pays by royalty. Buys all rights or exclusive product rights; negotiable. Artist's guidelines available for SASE. Do not send original art.

**Photography** Buys stock and assigns work. Looking for the following subject matter: babies, animals, dog, cats, humorous situations. Uses $4 \times 5$ transparencies or high quality 35mm slides. To contact, send cover letter with slides, stock photo list, color copies, published samples and promo piece. Materials returned with SASE; materials not filed. Pays royalties. Buys all rights or exclusive product rights; negotiable. Photographer's guidelines for SASE. Do not send original photography.

**Tips** Seasonal material must be submitted 1 year in advance.

### FAX-PAX USA, INC.
37 Jerome Ave., Bloomfield CT 06002. (860)242-3333. Fax: (860)242-7102. **Editor:** Stacey L. Savin. Estab. 1990. Buys 1 freelance project/year. Publishes art and history flash cards. Needs include U .S. history, natural history.

**Writing/Illustration** Buys all rights. Pays on publication. Cannot return material.

**Tips** ''We need concise, interesting, well-written 'mini-lessons' on various subjects including U.S. and natural history.''

### GALLERY GRAPHICS, INC.
P.O. Box 502, 20136 State Hwy. 59, Noel MO 64854-0502. (417)475-6191. Fax: (417)475-6494. E-mail: jacob@gal lerygraphics.com. Website: www.gallerygraphics.com. **Marketing Director:** Olivia Jacob. Estab. 1979. Greeting card, paper products company. Specializes in products including prints, cards, calendars, stationery, magnets,

framed items, books, flue covers and sachets. We market towards all age groups. Publishes reproductions of children's books from the 1800s. 10% of products are made for kids or have kid's themes.

**Illustration** Needs freelance illustration for children's greeting cards, other children's products. Makes 8 illustration assignments/year. Prefers children, angels, animals in any medium. Uses color artwork only. To contact, send cover letter, published samples, photocopies (prefer color), promo pieces. Responds in 3 weeks. "We'll return materials if a SASE is included. If artist can send something we can file, that would be ideal. I'll usually make copies." For greeting cards, pays flat fee of $100-700, or royalty of 5-7% for life of card. Pays on sales. Buys exclusive product rights. Credit line sometimes given.

**Tips** "We've significantly increased our licensing over the last year. Most of these are set up on a 5% royalty basis. Submit various art subjects."

## GLOBAL GRAPHICS & GIFTS, LCC

16781 Chagrin Blvd. #333, Cleveland OH 44120. E-mail: fredw@globalgraphics-gifts.com. Website: www.global graphics-gifts.com. **Contact:** Fred Willingham, president. Estab. 1995. Greeting card company. "Products include cards, gift bags, wrapping paper, party supplies, and stationery products." Produces greeting cards. 15% products for kids.

**Writing** Needs freelancers for children's greeting cards. For greeting cards, uses rhymed and unrhymed verse. For first contact, send cover letter, writing samples. Does not return materials. Samples filed. For children's greeting cards, pays writers flat fee of $25. For other assignments, pays by the project $25. Pays on acceptance. Buys all rights. Credit line sometimes given. Writer's guidelines on website.

**Illustration** Needs freelance illustration for children's greeting cards. Gives varied number of assignments/year. "We only accept wholesome subjects and themes. We like fun, loose and colorful styles. Animals always work well. Also, animals with human characteristics." Uses color artwork only. For first contact, send published samples, color photocopies, color promo pieces, unpublished samples. Responds only if interested. Does not return materials. Samples filed. For children's greeting card art, pays flat fee of $150-$400. For artwork for children's products, pays by the project: $150-$400. Pays on acceptance. Buys all rights. Sometimes gives credit line. Artist's guidelines on website.

**Photography** Buys stock and assigns work. Buys varied amount of stock images/year. Gives varied amount of assignments/year. "Seeking photos of animals and children, humorous, cute. Wholesome only. Images should tell a story." Accepts 4×5 transparencies. For first contact, send cover letter, résumé, stock photo list. Responds only if interested. Does not return materials. Promo materials filed. Pays by the project, a minimum of $150. **Pays on acceptance.** Buys all rights. Credit line sometimes given. Guidelines on website. Submit seasonal material 12 months in advance.

## GREAT AMERICAN PUZZLE FACTORY, INC.

16 S. Main St., Norwalk CT 06854. (203)838-4240. Fax: (203)866-9601. E-mail: Frankd@greatamericanpuzzle.com. Website: www.greatamericanpuzzle.com. **Art Director:** Frank DeStefano. Estab. 1976. Produces puzzles and games. 50% of products are made for kids or have kids' themes.

**Illustration** Needs freelance illustration for puzzles. Makes over 20 freelance assignments/year. To contact, send cover letter, color photocopies and color promo pieces (no slides or original art) with SASE. Responds in 1-2 months. Artists guidelines available for SASE. Rights purchased vary. Buys all rights to puzzles. Pays on publication. Payment varies. Also can contact via e-mail with website address or samples.

**Photography** Needs local cityscapes for regional puzzles. "Photos that we have used have been of wildlife. We do occasionally use city skylines. These are only for custom jobs, though, and must be 4×5 or larger format."

**Tips** Targets ages 4-12 and adult. "Go to a toy store and look at puzzles. See what is appropriate. No slides. Send color copies (3-4) for style. Looking for whimsical, fantasy and animal themes with a bright, contemporary style. Not too washy or cute. No people, babies, abstracts, landscapes or still life. We often buy reprint rights to existing work." Submit seasonal material 1 year in advance.

## INTERCONTINENTAL GREETINGS LTD.

176 Madison Ave., New York NY 10016. (212)683-5830. Fax: (212)779-8564. **Art Director:** Thea Groene . Estab. 1964. 100% of material freelance written and illustrated. Intended for greeting cards, scholastic products (notebook covers, pencil cases), novelties (gift bags, mugs), tin gift boxes, shower and bedding curtains. 30-40% of products are made for kids or have kids' themes.

**Illustration** Needs illustrations for children's greeting cards, notebook covers, photo albums, gift products. Prefers primarily greeting card subjects, suitable for gift industry. To contact, send cover letter, client list and published samples (if available), photocopies, slides and/or CDs with SASE. Pays percentage on publication. Clients purchase temporary exclusive product rights for contract period of 3 years. Credit line sometimes given.

**Photography** Needs stylized and interesting still lifes, studio florals, all themed toward the paper and gift industry. Guidelines available for SASE.

**Tips** Target group for juvenile cards: ages 1-10. Illustrators: Use clean colors, not muddy or dark. Send a neat, concise sampling of your work. Include a SASE to issue return of your samples if wanted.

## INTERNATIONAL PLAYTHINGS, INC.

75D Lackawanna Ave., Parsippany NJ 07054-1712. (973)316-2500. Fax: (973)316-5883. E-mail: info@intplay.com. Website: www.intplay.com. Estab. 1968. Toy/game company. Distributes and markets children's toys, games in specialty toy markets. 100% of products are made for kids or have kids' themes.

**Illustration** Needs freelance illustration for children's puzzles and games. Makes 10-20 illustration assignments/year. Prefers fine-quality, original illustration for children's puzzles. Uses color artwork only. To contact, send published samples, slides, portfolio, color photocopies or promo pieces. Responds in 1 month only if interested. Materials filed. For artwork, pays by the project (range: $500-2,000). Pays on publication. Buys one-time rights, negotiable.

**Tips** "Mail correspondence only, please. Sent to the attention of the Art Director. No phone calls. Send child-themed art, not cartoon-y. Use up-to-date themes and colors."

## JILLSON & ROBERTS

3300 W. Castor St., Santa Ana CA 92704-3908. (714)424-0111. Fax: (714)424-0054. Website: www.jillsonroberts.com. **Art Director:** Shawn Doll. Estab. 1973. Paper products company. Makes gift wrap/gift bags. 20% of products are made for kids or have kids' themes.

**Illustration** Needs freelance illustration for children's gift wrap. Makes 6-12 illustration assignments/year. Wants children/baby/juvenile themes. To contact, send cover letter. Responds in 1 month. Returns material with SASE; materials filed. For wrap and bag designs, pays flat fee (varies). Pays on publication. Rights negotiable. Artist's guidelines for SASE.

**Tips** Seasonal material should be submitted up to 3½ months in advance. "We produce two lines of gift wrap per year: one everyday line and one Christmas line. The closing date for everyday is July 1 and Christmas is September 1."

## MEADWESTVACO

(formerly AMCAL, Inc.), Courthouse Plaza NE, Dayton OH 45463. (800)345-6323. Website: www.meadweb.com. **Contact:** Richard Mallow, licensing account manager. Estab. 1975. Cards, calendars, desk diaries, boxed Christmas cards, journals, mugs, and other high quality gift and stationery products.

**Illustration** Receives over 150 submissions/year. "MeadWestvaco publishes high quality full color, narrative and decorative art for a wide market from traditional to contemporary. "Currently we are seeking updated interpretations of classic subjects such as florals and animals, strong decorative icons that are popular in the market place as well as in country folk art and decorative styles. Know the trends and the market. Juvenile illustration should have some adult appeal. We sell to small, exclusive gift retailers and large chains. Submissions are always accepted for future lines." To contact, send samples, photocopies, slides and SASE for return of submission. Responds in approximately 1 month. Rights purchased negotiable. Guideline sheets for #10 SASE and 1 first-class stamp.

**Tips** "To learn more about MeadWestvaco and our products, please visit our website."

## NRN DESIGNS

5142 Argosy Ave., Long Beach CA 92649. (714)898-6363. Fax: (714)898-0015. Website: www.nrndesigns.com. **Art Director:** Linda Braun. Estab. 1984. Prints invitations and scrapbook products, including stickers and albums. Themes include everyday, holiday, baby, wedding and birthdays.

**Illustration** Needs freelance illustration for children's imprintables. Uses color artwork only. To contact, send published samples. Materials filed.

**Tips** Submit seasonal material anytime. May also submit artwork to director at Linda@NRNDesigns.com.

## P.S. GREETINGS/FANTUS PAPER PRODUCTS

5730 North Tripp Ave., Chicago IL 60646. (773)267-6069. Fax: (773)267-6055. Website: www.psgreetings.com. **Contact:** Design Director. Greeting card company. Publishes boxed and individual counter greeting cards. Seasons include: Christmas, every major holiday and everyday. 20% of products are made for kids or have kid's themes. No phone calls please.

**Writing** Needs freelance writing for children's greeting cards. Makes 10-20 writing assignments/year. To contact, send writing samples. Responds in 1 month. Material returned only if accompanied with SASE. For greeting cards, pays flat fee/line. Pays on acceptance. Buys exclusive greeting card rights. Writer's guidelines free for SASE.

**Illustration** Needs freelance illustration for children's greeting cards. Makes about 30-50 illustration assignments/year. Open to all mediums, all themes. Uses primarily commissioned artwork. To contact, send published samples, color promo pieces and color photocopies only. Responds in 1 month. Material returned only if accompanied with SASE. Pays flat fee upon acceptance. Buys exclusive greeting card rights. Artist's guidelines free for SASE (speculative and on assignment).

**Photography** Buys photography from freelancers. Speculative and on assignment. Prefers finished digital files. To contact, send slides or CD of work. Responds in 1 month. Materials returned only for SASE; materials filed. Pays flat fee upon acceptance. Buys exclusive greeting card rights. Photographer's guidelines free for SASE.

**Tips** Seasonal material should be submitted 8 months in advance.

## PANDA INK

Woodland Hills CA 91367. (818)340-8061. Fax: (818)883-6193. E-mail: RuthLuuph@socal.r.r.com.Net. **Owner, Art/Creative Director:** Ruth Ann Epstein. Estab. 1981. Greeting card company and producer of clocks, magnets, bookmarks and miscellaneous gifts. Produces Judaica—whimsical, metaphysical, general, everyday. Publishes greeting cards. 15% of products are made for kids or have kids' themes.

**Writing** Needs freelance writing for children's greeting cards. Makes 1-2 writing assignments/year. For greeting cards, accepts both rhymed and unrhymed verse ideas. Looks for greeting card writing which is Judaica or metaphysical. To contact, send cover letter and SASE. To query with specific ideas, write to request disclosure form first. Responds in 1 month. Materials returned with SASE; materials filed. Pays on acceptance. Rights negotiable. Credit line sometimes given.

**Illustration** Needs freelance illustration for children's greeting cards, magnets, bookmarks. Makes 1-2 illustration assignments/year. Needs Judaica (Hebrew wording), metaphysical themes. Uses color artwork only. To contact, send cover letter. Query with specific ideas. Responds in 2 months. Materials returned with SASE; materials filed. Payment is negotiable. Pays on acceptance. Rights negotiable. Credit line sometimes given. Submit seasonal material 1 year in advance.

**Tips** "Always send SASE. Don't write for guidelines—we have no guidelines available. Send brightly colored, whimsical, good art."

## PEACEABLE KINGDOM PRESS

950 Gilman, Suite 200, Berkeley CA 94710. (510)558-2051. Fax: (510)558-2052. E-mail: pkp@pkpress.com. Website: www.pkpress.com. **Editors, Creative Development:** Helen Ring; Margaret Garrou. **Creative Director:** Suellen Ehnebuske. Estab. 1983. Produces posters, greeting cards, bookmarks and related products. Uses children's book illustrators exclusively, but not necessarily targeted only to children. 98% of products are made for kids or have kids' themes.

**Writing** Needs freelance writing for children's greeting cards. Makes approximately 300 writing assignments/year. To contact, send cover letter, client list, writing samples. Responds in 2 months. Materials not returned; materials filed. For greeting cards, pays a flat fee of $50.

**Illustration** Needs freelance illustration for children's greeting cards and posters. Makes 75 illustration assignments/year. "For specific occasions—Christmas, Valentine's Day, Mother's and Father's Days, etc., we look for visually sophisticated work with a narrative element." To contact, send cover letter, slides, promo pieces, published books or f&g's. and color photocopies. To query with specific ideas, submit 5×7 of same dimensions enlarged, vertical, plus ⅛, if full bleed color. Materials returned with SASE; materials not filed. Responds in 2 months. Pays on publication with advance and royalties. Buys first rights and reprint rights; negotiable for greeting cards. Buys rights to distribution worldwide. Artist's guidelines available for SASE.

**Tips** "We only choose from illustrations that are from published children's book illustrators, or commissioned art by established children's book illustrators. Submit seasonal and everyday greeting cards one year in advance."

## RED FARM STUDIO

1135 Roosevelt Ave., P.O. Box 347, Pawtucket RI 02862. (401)728-9300. **Contact:** Production Coordinator. Estab. 1949. Greeting card company. Publishes coloring books and paintables. 20% of products are made for kids or have kids' themes.

**Illustration** Needs freelance illustration for tweens' and teens' greeting cards, coloring books and paintables. Makes 1 illustration assignment/month; 6-12/year. Any medium accepted. For first contact, request art guidelines with SASE. Responds in 1 month. Returns materials with SASE. Appropriate materials are kept on file. "We work on assignment using ink line work (coloring books) or pencil renderings (paintables)." Buys all rights. Credit line given, and artist may sign artwork. Artist's guidelines for SASE.

**Tips** Majority of freelance assignments made during January-May/yearly. "Research companies before sending submissions to determine whether your styles are compatible."

## SHULSINGER JUDAICA, LTD.

799 Hinsdale St., Brooklyn NY 11207. (718)345-3300. Fax: (718)345-1540. **Merchandiser:** Raizy Lasker. Estab.

1979. Greeting card, novelties and paper products company. "We are a Judaica company, distributing products such as greeting cards, books, paperware, puzzles, games, novelty items—all with a Jewish theme." Publishes greeting cards, novelties, coloring books, children's books, giftwrap, party goods, tableware and puzzles. 60% of products are made for kids or have kids' themes to party stories, temples, bookstores, supermarkets and chain stores.

**Writing** Looks for greeting card writing which can be sent by children to adults and sent by adults to children (of all ages). Makes 5-10 freelance writing assignments/year. To contact, send cover letter. To query with specific ideas, write to request disclosure form first. Responds in 2 weeks. Materials returned with SASE; materials filed. For greeting cards, pays flat fee (this includes artwork). Pays on acceptance. Buys exclusive product rights.

**Illustration** Needs freelance illustration for children's greeting cards, books, novelties, games. Makes 15-25 illustration assignments/year. "The only requirement is a Jewish theme." To contact, send cover letter and photocopies, color if possible. To query with specific ideas, write to request disclosure form first. Responds in 2 weeks. Returns materials with SASE; materials filed. For children's greeting cards, pays flat fee (this includes writing). For other artwork, pays by the project. Pays on acceptance. Buys exclusive product rights. Credit line sometimes given. Artist's guidelines not available. Submit artwork via e-mail at mail@shulsinger.com.

**Tips** Seasonal material should be submitted 6 months in advance. "An artist may submit an idea for any item that is related to our product line. Generally, there is an initial submission of a portfolio of the artist's work, which will be returned at the artist's expense. If the art is appropriate to our specialized subject matter, then further discussion will ensue regarding particular subject matter. We request a sampling of at least 10 pieces of work, in the form of tearsheets, or printed samples, or high quality color copies that can be reviewed and then kept on file if accepted. If art is accepted and published, then original art will be returned to artist. Shulsinger Judaica, Ltd. maintains the right to re-publish a product for a mutually agreed upon time period. We pay an agreed upon fee per project."

## STANDARD PUBLISHING

8121 Hamilton Ave., Cincinnati OH 45231. (513)931-4050. Fax: (513)931-0950. E-mail: tneunschwander@standardpub.com. Website: www.standardpub.com. **Directors:** Paul Learned (youth-adult) and Ruth Frederick (children's resources). **Art Director:** Coleen Davis. Estab. 1866. Publishes children's books and teacher helps for the religious market. 75% of products are made for kids or have kids' themes.
• Standard also has a listing in Book Publishers.

**Writing** Responds in 3 months. Payment method varies. Credit line given.

**Illustration** Needs freelance illustration for puzzle, activity books, teacher guides. Makes 6-10 illustration assignments/year. To contact, send cover letter and photocopies. Responds in 3 months if interested. Payment method varies. Credit line given.

**Photography** Buys a limited amount of photos from freelancers. Wants mature, scenic and Christian themes.

**Tips** "Many of our projects are developed in-house and assigned. Study our catalog and products; visit Christian bookstores. We are currently looking for Bible-based word puzzles and activities."

## N THE STRAIGHT EDGE INC.

296 Court St., Brooklyn NY 11231. (718)643-2794. Fax: (718)403-9582. E-mail: straedge@aol.com. Website: www.straightedgeinc.com. **Contact:** Amy Epstein, president. Estab. 1983. Editorial products manufacturer, children's book publisher. The Straight Edge "designs and manufactures educational place mats and puzzles and interactive children's books." Produces puzzles, other books/booklets. 100% of products for kids.

**Writing** Needs freelancers for books. "Uses freelancers for books for readers ages 3-5." For first contact, send cover letter, résumé, client list, writing samples. To propose specific ideas, write to request a disclosure form first. Responds only if interested. Returns materials if accompanied by SASE. For other assignments, pays by the project; varies. **Pays on acceptance.** Buys all rights. Credit line given. Writer's guidelines not available.

**Illustration** Needs freelance illustration for other children's products (placemats, puzzles). Gives 4-8 assignments/year. Uses color artwork only. For first contact, send cover letter, résumé, client list, color photocopies. Returns materials if accompanied by SASE. For artwork for children's products, pays by the project; varies. Sometimes gives credit line. Artist's guidelines not available.

## TALICOR, INC.

14175 Telephone Ave., Suite A, Chino CA 91710. (909)517-1962. Fax: (909)517-1962. E-mail: webmaster@talicor.com. Website: www.talicor.com. **President:** Lew Herndon. Estab. 1971. Game and puzzle manufacturer. Publishes games and puzzles (adults' and children's). 70% of products are made for kids or have kids' themes.

**Writing** Makes 1 writing assignment/month.

**Illustration** Needs freelance illustration for games and puzzles. Makes 12 illustration assignments/year. To contact, send promo piece. Responds in 6 months. Materials returned for SASE; materials filed. For artwork, pays by the hour, by the project or negotiable royalty. Pays on acceptance. Buys negotiable rights.

**Photography** Buys stock and assigns work. Buys 6 stock images/year. Wants photos with wholesome family subjects. Makes 6 assignments/year. Uses 4×5 transparencies. To contact, send color promo piece. Responds only if interested. Materials returned for SASE; materials filed. Pays per photo, by the hour, by the day or by the project (negotiable rates). Pays on acceptance. Buys negotiable rights.

**Tips** Submit seasonal material 6 months in advance.

### WARNER PRESS

P.O. Box 2499, Anderson IN 46018-9988. Fax: (765)640-8005. E-mail: krhodes@warnerpress.org. Website: www.warnerpress.com. **Senior Editor:** Karen Rhodes. **Creative Director:** John Silvey. Estab. 1880. Publishes church resources, coloring and activity books and children's supplies, all religious-oriented. 15% of products are made for kids.

**Writing** To contact, request guidelines first (available for church resource products only). Contact: Jennie Bishop, senior editor. Responds in 2 months. Limited purchases of children's material right now. Materials may be kept on file for future use. Pays on acceptance. Buys all rights. Credit line sometimes given. E-mail for writer's guidelines or send SASE.

**Illustration** We purchase a very limited amount of freelance art at this time, but we are always looking for excellent coloring book artists.

**Photography** Buys photography from freelancers for church bulletin covers. Contact: John Silvey, creative director.

**Tips** "Writers request guidelines for church resource products before submitting. No guidelines available for children's products at present. We purchase a very limited amount of children's material, but we may grow into more children's products and opportunities. Make sure to include SASE. Solicited material will not be returned without SASE. Unsolicited material that does not follow guidelines will not be reviewed."

# Play Publishers & Producers

Writing plays for children and family audiences is a special challenge. Whether creating an original work or adapting a classic, plays for children must hold the attention of audiences that often include children and adults. Using rhythm, repetition, and dramatic action are effective ways of holding the attention of kids. Pick subjects children can relate to, and never talk down to them.

Theater companies often have limited budgets so plays with elaborate staging and costumes often can't be produced. Touring companies want simple sets that can be moved easily. Keep in mind that they may have as few as three actors, so roles may have to be doubled up.

Many of the companies listed here produce plays with roles for adults and children, so check the percentage of plays written for adult and children's roles. Most importantly, study the types of plays a theater wants and doesn't want. Many name plays they've recently published or produced, and some have additional guidelines or information available. For more listings of theaters open to submissions of children's and adult material and information on contests and organizations for playwrights, consult *Dramatists Sourcebook* (Theatre Communications Group, Inc.).

**Information on play publishers listed in the previous edition but not included in this edition of *Children's Writer's & Illustrator's Market* may be found in the General Index.**

## A.D. PLAYERS

2710 W. Alabama, Houston TX 77098. (713)521-1475. Fax: (713)522-5475. E-mail: adplayer@hearn.org. Website: www.adplayers.org. Estab. 1967. Produces 4-5 children's plays/year in new Children's Theatre Series. Produces children's plays for professional productions.

**Needs** 99-100% of plays/musicals written for adult roles; 0-1% for juvenile roles. "Cast must utilize no more than five actors. Need minimal, portable sets for arena stage with no fly space and no wing space." Does not want to see large cast or set requirements or New Age themes. Recently produced plays: *The Magician's Nephew*, by Aurand Harris; *Ruth*, by Jeannette Cliftgeorge (a new play on the Old Testament story of Ruth, musical).

**How to Contact** See website for submission guidelines.

**Terms** Buys some residual rights. Pay negotiated. Submissions returned with SASE.

**Tips** "Children's musicals tend to be large in casting requirements. For those theaters with smaller production capabilities, this can be a liability for a script. Try to keep it small and simple, especially if writing for theaters where adults are performing for children. We are interested in material that reflects family values, emphasizes the importance of responsibility in making choices, encourages faith in God and projects the joy and fun of telling a story."

## ALABAMA SHAKESPEARE FESTIVAL

#1 Festival Dr., Montgomery AL 36117. (334)271-5300. Fax: (334)271-5348. E-mail: asf@asf.net. Website: www.asf.net. **Literary Manager:** Gwen Orel. Estab. 1972. Produces 1 children's play/year.

**Needs** Produces children's plays for professional LORT (League of Regional Theaters) theatre. 90% of plays/ musicals written for adult roles; 10% for juvenile roles. Must have moderate sized casts (2-10 characters); have two stages (750 seat house/250 seat house). Interested in works for the Southern Writers' Project (contact ASF for information). Does not want to see plays exclusively for child actors. Recently produced plays: *Cinderella*, by Lynn Stevens (fairytale for elementary ages); *Wiley and the Hairy Man*, by Susan Zeder (southern folk tale for elementary ages).

**How to Contact** Send full mss which meet/address the focus of the Southern Writers' Project. Musicals: Query with synopsis, character breakdown and set description; scripts which meet/address the focus of the Southern Writers' Project. Will consider simultaneous submissions and previously performed work. Responds in 1 year. Send submissions to Literary Manager.

**Terms** Submissions returned with SASE.

**Tips** "Created in 1991 by Artistic Director Kent Thompson, the Alabama Shakespeare Festival's Southern Writers' Project is an exploration and celebration of its rich Southern cultural heritage. In an attempt to reach this goal the project seeks to provide for the growth of a 'new' voice for Southern writers and artists; to encourage new works dealing with Southern issues and topics including those that emphasize African-American experiences; to create theatre that speaks in a special way to ASF's unique and racially diverse audiences. In this way the Southern Writers' Project strives to become a window to the complexities and beauty found in this celebrated region of our country, the South."

## AMERICAN STAGE

P.O. Box 1560, St. Petersburg FL 33731-1560. (727)823-1600. Fax: (727)821-2444. E-mail: info@americanstage.o rg. Website: www.americanstage.org. **Producing Artistic Director:** Todd Olson. Estab. 1977. Produces 3 children's plays/year. Produces children's plays for professional children's theater programs, mainstage, school tours, performing arts halls.

**Needs** Limited by "Small mainstage venue, 1 touring production conducive to small cast, light technical pieces." Subject matter: classics and original work for children (ages K-12) and families. Recently produced plays: *King Island Christmas for the Mainstage* and *Alexander and the Terrible, Horrible, No Good Very Bad Day* for the School Tour and Mainstage; co-produced short plays for Theatre For Families with the Open Circle Players: *Who Put the Sea Serpent in My Soup*, for The City of St. Petersburg's First Night Celebration. Does not want to see plays that look down on children. Approach must be that of the child, fictional beings or animals.

**How to Contact** Query with synopsis, character breakdown and set description. Will consider simultaneous submissions and previously performed work.

**Terms** Purchases "professional rights." Pays writers in royalties (6-8%); $25-35/performance. SASE for return of submission.

**Tips** Sees a move in plays toward basic human values, relationships and multicultural communities.

## ANCHORAGE PRESS PLAYS, INC.

P.O. Box 2901, Louisville KY 40201-2901. Phone/fax: (502)583-2288. E-mail: applays@bellsouth.net. Website: www.applays.com. **Publisher:** Marilee Miller. Estab. 1935. Publishes 4-6 plays/year.

**Needs** Seeking theatrical play scripts suitable for K-12 audience and family audience with timeless themes and well told stories. We publish plays and plays with music. Recently produced plays: *The Rose of Treason*, by James Devita; *The Pied Piper of Hamelin*, by Tim Wright; *Bless Cricket, Crest Toothpaste and Tommy Tune*, by Linda Daugerty; *Hey Diddle Diddle!*, by Marilee Hebert Miller.

**How to Contact** Query for guidelines first. Will consider simultaneous submissions and previously performed work "essential to be proven." Responds in 1 year.

**Terms** Buys all stage rights. Pays royalty (varies extensively from 50% minimum to 75%). Submissions returned with SASE.

**Tips** "The plays we publish are chosen for their suitability to be produced for a youth or family audience. We are less interested in classroom teaching aids."

## APPLE TREE THEATRE

595 Elm Place, Suite 210, Highland Park IL 60035. (847)432-8223. Fax: (847)432-5214. E-mail: msage@appletree theatre.com. Website: www.appletreetheatre.com. **Contact:** Education Director. Produces 3 children's plays/year.

**Needs** Produces professional, daytime and educational outreach programs for grades 4-9. 98% of plays written for adult roles; 2% for juvenile roles. Uses a unit set and limited to 9 actors. No musicals. Straight plays only. Does not want to see: "children's theater," i.e. Peter Rabbit, Snow White. Material *must* be based in social issues. Recently produced plays: *Diary of Anne Frank*, by Frances Goodrich and Albert Hackett (about the Holocaust, ages 10-up); *Roll of Thunder, Hear My Cry*, adapted from the novel by Mildred Taylor (about civil rights, racial discrimination in Mississippi in 1930s, ages 10-up).

**How to Contact** Query for guidelines first. Query with synopsis, character breakdown and set description. Will consider simultaneous submissions and previously performed work. Responds in 2 months.

**Terms** Payment negotiated per contract. Submissions returned with SASE.

**Tips** "Never send an unsolicited manuscript. Include reply postcard for queries."

## BAKER'S PLAYS

P.O. Box 699222, Quincy MA 02269-9222. (617)745-0805. Fax: (617)745-9891. E-mail: info@bakersplays.com. Website: www.bakersplays.com. **Associate Editor:** Kurt Gombar. Estab. 1845. Publishes 20 plays/year; 2 musicals/year.

**Needs** Adaptations of both popular and lesser known folktales. Subject matter: "full lengths for family audience and full lengths and one act plays for teens." Recently published plays: *Fairy Tale Courtroom*, by Dana Proulx; *More Aesop's (oh so slightly) Updated Fables*, by Kim Esop-Wylie.

**How to Contact** Submit complete ms, score and tape or CD of songs. Responds in 8 months.

**Terms** Obtains worldwide rights. Pays writers in production royalties (amount varies) and book royalties.

**Tips** "Know the audience you're writing for before you submit your play anywhere. 90% of the plays we reject are not written for our market. When writing for children, never be afraid to experiment with language, characters or story. They are fertile soil for fresh, new ideas."

## BARTER THEATRE EDUCATION WING

P.O. Box 867, Abingdon VA 24212. (276)628-2281, ext. 318. Fax: (276)619-3335. E-mail: education@bartertheat re.com. Website: www.bartertheatre.com. **Artistic Director:** Richard Rose. **Education Director:** Tere Land. Estab. 1933. Produces 2-4 children's plays and 1 children's musical/year.

**Needs** "We produce 'By Kids for Kids' productions as well as professional and semi-professional children's productions. 5-10% of plays/musicals written for adult roles; 90% written for juvenile roles. Recently produced plays: *Barnum* (musical); and *The Hobbit* (musical).

**How to Contact** Query with synopsis, character breakdown and set description. Will consider simultaneous submissions and previously performed work. Responds only if interested.

**Terms** Pays for performance ($20-60). Submissions returned with SASE.

**Tips** "Find creative, interesting material for children K-12. Don't talk below the audience."

## BILINGUAL FOUNDATION OF THE ARTS

421 N. Avenue 19th, Los Angeles CA 90031. (323)225-4044. Fax: (323)225-1250. E-mail: bfa99@earthlink.net. Website: www.bfatheatre.org. **Contact:** Estela Saarlata, production manager. Estab. 1973. Produces 1 children's play/year.

**Needs** Produces children's plays for professional productions. 60% of plays/musicals written for adult roles; 40% for juvenile roles. No larger than 8 member cast. Recently produced plays: *Second Chance*, by A. Cardona and A. Weinstein (play about hopes and fears in every teenager for teenagers); *Choices*, by Gannon Daniels (violence prevention, teens); *Fool 4 Kool*, Leane Schirmer and Guillermo Reyes.

**How to Contact** Plays: Query with synopsis, character breakdown and set description and submit complete ms. Musicals: Query with synopsis, character breakdown and set description and submit complete ms with score. Will consider simultaneous submissions and previously performed work. Responds in 6 months.

**Terms** Pays royalty; per performance; buys material outright; "different with each play."

**Tips** "The plays should reflect the Hispanic experience in the U.S."

## BIRMINGHAM CHILDREN'S THEATRE

P.O. Box 1362, Birmingham AL 35201-1362. (205)458-8181. Fax: (205)458-8895. E-mail: bertb@bct123.org. Website: www.bct123.org. **Managing Directors:** Bert Brosowsky, Pat Anderson-Flowers. Estab. 1947. Produces 8-10 children's plays/year; some children's musicals/year.

**Needs** "BCT is an adult professional theater performing for youth and family audiences September-May." 99% of plays/musicals written for adult roles; 1% for juvenile roles. "Our Wee Folks Series is limited to 4-5 cast members and should be written with preschool-grade 1 in mind. We prefer interactive plays for this age group. We commission plays for our Wee Folks Series (preschool-grade 1), our Children's Series (K-6) and our Young Adult Series (6-12)." Recently produced plays: *Our Town*, by Thornton Wilder (YA series); *The Wizard of Oz*, by L. Frank Baum, adapted by R. Eugene Jackson (children's series); *Three Billy Goats Gruff*, by Jean Pierce (Wee Folks Series). No adult language. Will consider musicals, interactive theater for Wee Folks Series. Prefer children's series and young adult series limited to 4-7 cast members.

**How to Contact** Query first with synopsis, character breakdown and set description. Responds in 4 months.

**Terms** Buys negotiable rights. Submissions returned with SASE.

**Tips** "We would like our commissioned scripts to teach as well as entertain. Keep in mind the age groups (defined by each series) that our audience is composed of. Send submissions to the attention of Bert Brosowsky, managing director."

## CALIFORNIA THEATRE CENTER

P.O. Box 2007, Sunnyvale CA 94087. (408)245-2979. Fax: (408)245-0235. E-mail: ctc@ctcinc.org. E-mail: ctc@ct cinc.org. Website: www.ctcinc.org. **Resident Director:** Will Huddleston. Estab. 1975. Produces 15 children's plays and 1 musical for professional productions.

**Needs** 75% of plays/musicals written for adult roles; 20% for juvenile roles. Prefers material suitable for professional tours and repertory performance; one-hour time limit, limited technical facilities. Recently produced *Brave Irene*, adapted by Joan Cushing (children's lit, for grades K and up); *The Little Mermaid*, by Gayle Cornelison (children's classic, for ages K-4).

**How to Contact** Query with synopsis, character breakdown and set description. Send to: Will Huddleston. Will consider previously performed work. Responds in 6-12 months.

**Terms** Rights negotiable. Pays writers royalties; pays $35-50/performance. Submissions returned with SASE.

**Tips** "We sell to schools, so the title and material must appeal to teachers who look for things familiar to them. We look for good themes, universality. Avoid the cute. We also do a summer conservatory that requires large cast plays."

## CIRCA '21 DINNER THEATRE

P.O. Box 3784, Rock Island IL 61204-3784. (309)786-2667. Fax: (309)786-4119. Website: http://circa21.com. **Producer:** Dennis Hitchcock. Estab. 1977. Produces 3 children's musicals/year.

**Needs** Produces children's plays for professional productions. 95% of musicals written for adult roles; 5% written for juvenile roles. "Prefer a cast of four to eight—no larger than ten. Plays are produced on mainstage sets." Recently produced plays: *Little Red Riding Hood's Big Adventure*, by Marc Pence (ages 4-adult); *Cinderella*, by Prince Street Players (ages 4-adult).

**How to Contact** Send complete script with audiotape of music. Responds in 3 months.

**Terms** Payment negotiable.

## I.E. CLARK PUBLICATIONS

P.O. Box 246, Schulenburg TX 78956-0246. (979)743-3232. Fax: (979)743-4765. E-mail: ieclark@cvtv.net. Website: www.ieclark.com. **General Manager:** Lila Clark. Estab. 1956. Publishes 3 or more children's plays/year; 1 or 2 children's musicals/year.

**Needs** Publishes plays for all ages. Published plays: *Little Women*, by Thomas Hischak (dramatization of the Alcott novel for family audiences); *Heidi*, by Ann Pugh, music by Betty Utter (revision of our popular musical dramatization of the Johanna Spyri novel). Does not want to see plays that have not been produced.

**How to Contact** Submit complete ms and audio or video tape. Will consider simultaneous submissions and previously performed work. Responds in 4 months.

**Terms** Pays writers in negotiable royalties. SASE for return of submission.

**Tips** "We publish only high-quality literary works. Request a copy of our writer's guidelines before submitting. Please send only one manuscript at a time and be sure to include videos and audiotapes."

## COLUMBIA ENTERTAINMENT COMPANY

% Betsy Phillips, 309 Parkade, Columbia MO 65202-1447. (573)874-5628. Website: www.cectheatre.org. **Contest Director:** Betsy Phillips. Estab. 1988. Produces 0-2 children's plays/year; 0-1 children's musicals/year.
**Needs** "We produce children's theatre plays. Our theatre school students act all the roles. We cast adult and children roles with children from theatre school. Each season we have 5 plays done by adults (kid parts possible)—up to 3 theatre school productions. We need large cast plays—more than 20, as plays are produced by theater school classes (ages 5-14). We also consider small cast (7 characters) plays that might work with an individual class. Any set changes are completed by students in the play." Musical needs: Musicals must have songs written in ranges children can sing. Recently produced: *Mississippi Odyssey*, by Mary Barile (retelling of story set in Lewis & Clark era, family audience 5-100).
**How to Contact** Plays: Submit complete ms; use SASE to get form. Musicals: Submit complete ms and lead sheets. Score required if play is produced. CD or tape of music must be included, use SASE to get entry form. Will consider simultaneous submissions and previously performed work. Responds within 3 months of June 1st deadline. All scripts are read by a minimum of 3 readers. The authors will receive a written evaluation of the strengths and weaknesses of the play.
**Terms** "We have production rights sans royalties for one production. Production rights remain with author." Pays $500 1st prize. Submissions returned with SASE.
**Tips** "Please write a play/musical that appeals to all ages. We like plays that audiences of all ages will enjoy. We always need lots of parts, especially for girls."

## COLUMBUS CHILDREN'S THEATRE

372 W. Nationwide Blvd., Columbus OH 43215. (614)224-6672. Fax: (614)224-8844. E-mail: bgshows@aol.com. Website: www.colschildrenstheatre.org. **Artistic Director:** William Goldsmith. Estab. 1963. Produces 14 children's plays/year; 2-4 children's musicals/year.
**Needs** Produces Semi-Professional Children's Theatre Series, professional touring company (4 actors), Academy summer productions for ages 10-16 and ages 16-21. 60% of plays/musicals written for adult roles; 40% for juvenile roles. "Have some scenic limitations—a 175 seat thrust stage, very little backstage." Musical needs: "Always looking for a new holiday show." Recently produced plays: *Green Gables* (world premiere musical), by Janet Vogt & Mark Friedman (based upon the book by L.L. Montgomery for ages 6 and up); *The Best Christmas Pagent Ever,* by Barbara Robinson (Christmas story for ages 4 and up).
**How to Contact** Plays/musicals: Query with synopsis, character breakdown and set description. Will consider simultaneous submissions, e-mail submissions, previously performed work. Responds in 4-6 months.
**Terms** Rights on mss and scores negotiable. Pays 8% royalties; pays $35-$350/performance. Submissions returned with SASE.
**Tips** "Be careful of 'dark' stories. No matter how good they are, a parent doesn't want to bring their 4 or 5 year old to watch a play about a child dying. They can have serious subjects, but don't treat them darkly."

## CONTEMPORARY DRAMA SERVICE

Division of Meriwether Publishing Ltd., 885 Elkton Dr., Colorado Springs CO 80907-3557. (719)594-4422. Fax: (719)594-9916. E-mail: merpcds@aol.com. Website: www.meriwetherpublishing.com. **Associate Editor:** Arthur L. Zapel. Estab. 1979. Publishes 60 children's plays/year; 15 children's musicals/year.
**Needs** Prefer shows with a large cast. 50% of plays/musicals written for adult roles; 50% for juvenile roles. Recently published plays: *Pecos Bill, Slue Foot Sue and the Wing Dang Doo!*, by Arthur Zapel and Bill Francoeur (a musical); *Cinderella*, by Kirk Buis (a comedy spoof); *The Night the Animals Sang*, by Katherine Babb (a Christmas play). "We publish church plays for elementary level for Christmas and Easter. Most of our secular plays are for teens or college level." Does not want to see "full-length, three-act plays unless they are adaptations of classic works or have unique comedy appeal."
**How to Contact** Query with synopsis, character breakdown and set description; "query first if a musical." Will consider simultaneous submissions or previously performed work. Responds in 1 month.
**Terms** Purchases first rights. Pays writers royalty (10%) or buys material outright for $200-1,000. SASE for return of submission.
**Tips** "If the writer is submitting a musical play, a CD of the music should be sent. We prefer plays with humorous action. We like comedies, spoofs, satires and parodies of known works. A writer should provide credentials of plays published and produced. Writers should not submit items for the elementary age level."

## DALLAS CHILDREN'S THEATER

5938 Skillman, Dallas TX 75231-7608. Fax: (214)978-0118. E-mail: family@dct.org. Website: www.dct.org. **Artistic Associate:** Artie Olaisen. Estab. 1984. Produces 8-10 children's plays/year. Produces 1-2 children's musicals/year.
**Needs** Produces children's plays for professional theater. 80% of plays/musicals written for adult roles; 20%

for juvenile roles. Prefer cast size between 8-12. Musical needs: "We do produce musical works, but prefer nonmusical. Availability of music tracks is a plus." Does not want to see: anything not appropriate for a youth/family audience. Recently produced plays: *Holes*, by Louis Sachar (based on popular book, darkly humorous tale of crime, punishment and redemption for ages 8 and older); *Coyote Tales*, by Linda Daugherty (lively telling of traditional folk stories of Mexico for all ages). Does not accept unsolicited mss.

**How to Contact** Plays and musicals: Query with synopsis, character breakdown and set description. Will consider previously performed work. Responds in up to 1 year. Please, no phone calls; **no unsolicited scripts**.

**Terms** Rights and payment are negotiable. Submissions returned with SASE. All scripts should be sent to the attention of Artie Olaisen.

**Tips** "We are only interested in full-length substantive works. Please no classroom pieces. Our mainstage season serves a multi-generational family audience."

## DRAMATIC PUBLISHING, INC.

311 Washington St., Woodstock IL 60098. (815)338-7170. Fax: (815)338-8981. E-mail: plays@dramaticpublishing.com. Website: www.dramaticpublishing.com. **Acquisitions Editor:** Linda Habjan. Estab. 1885. Publishes 10-15 children's plays/year; 4-6 children's musicals.

**Needs** Recently published: *Redwall: The Legend of Redwall Abbey*, by Evelyn Swensson, based on the book by Brian Jacques. *Alexander and the Terrible, Horrible, No Good, Very Bad Day*, by Judith Viorst and Shelly Markham; *Anastasia Krupnik*, by Meryl Friedman, based on the book by Lois Lowry; *A Village Fable*, by James Still, adapted from *In the Suicide Mountain*, by John Gardner; *The Little Prince*, adapted by Rick Cummins and John Scoullar.

**How to Contact** Submit complete ms/score and CD/videotape (if a musical); include SASE if materials are to be returned. Responds in 3 months. Pays writers in royalties.

**Tips** "Original plays dealing with hopes, joys and fears of today's children are preferred to adaptations of old classics. No more adapted fairytales."

## DRAMATICS MAGAZINE

2343 Auburn Ave., Cincinnati OH 45219-2815. (513)421-3900. Fax: (513)421-7077. Website: www.edta.org. **Editor:** Don Corathers. Publishes 7 young adult plays/year.

**Needs** Most of plays written for high school actors. 14-18 years old (grades 9-12) appropriate for high school production and study. "We prefer not to receive plays geared for young children." Recently produced plays: *Korczak's Children*, by Jeffrey Hatcher (about the final days of the orphanage in the Warsaw Ghetto); *Governing Alice*, by C. Denby Swanson (a young woman breaks all the rules to honor her brother, who was killed in a botched holdup of a conveneince store, ages 15 and up.)

**How to Contact** Plays: Submit complete ms. Musicals: Not accepted. Will consider simultaneous submissions, electronic submissions via disk/modem, previously performed work. Responds in 6 months.

**Terms** Buys one-time publication rights. Payment varies. Submissions returned with SASE.

**Tips** Our readers are savvy theater makers. Give them more than stereotypes and fairy tales to work with.

## EARLY STAGES CHILDREN'S THEATRE @ STAGES REPERTORY THEATRE

3201 Allen Parkway, Suite 101, Houston TX 77019. (713)527-0220. Fax: (713)527-8669. E-mail: rbundy@stagestheatre.com. Website: www.stagestheatre.com. **Artistic Director:** Rob Bundy. Estab. 1978. Produces 5 children's plays/year.

**Needs** In-house professional children's theatre. 100% of plays/musicals written for adult roles. Cast size must be 8 or less. Performances are in 2 theaters—Arena has 230 seats; Thrust has 180 seats. Musical needs: Shows that can be recorded for performance; no live musicians. Touring Needs: Small cast (no more than 5) addressing relevant issues for middle and high school students and teachers—2003 tour of *In Between*, by R.N. Sandberg. Recently produced plays: *Cinderella*, by Sidney Berger, music by Rob Laudes, *The Courage of Mandy Kate Brown*, by Kate Pogue (a tale of the Underground Railroad).

**How to Contact** Plays/musicals: Query with synopsis, character breakdown and set description. Will consider simultaneous submissions and previously performed work. Responds only if interested.

**Terms** Manuscripts optioned exclusively. Pays 3-8% royalties. Submissions returned with SASE.

**Tips** "Select pieces that are intelligent, as well as entertaining, and that speak to a child's potential for understanding. We are interested in plays/musicals that are imaginative and open to full theatrical production."

## EL CENTRO SU TEATRO

4725 High, Denver CO 80216. (303)296-0219. Fax: (303)296-4614. E-mail: elcentro@suteatro.org. Website: www.suteatro.org. **Artistic Director:** Anthony J. Garcia. Estab. 1971. Produces 2 children's plays/year.

**Needs** "We are interested in plays by Chicanos or Latinos that speak to that experience. We do not produce standard musicals. We are a culturally specific company." Recently produced *Joaquim's Christmas*, by Anthony

J. Garcia (children's Christmas play for ages 7-15); and *The Dragonslayer*, by Silviana Woods (young boy's relationship with grandfather for ages 7-15); *And Now Miguel*, by Jim Krungold. Does not want to see "cutesy stuff."

**How to Contact** Query with synopsis, character breakdown and set description. Will consider simultaneous submissions and previously performed work. Responds in 9 months. Buys regional rights.

**Terms** Pays writers per performance: $35 1st night, $25 subsequent. Submissions returned with SASE.

**Tips** "People should write within their realm of experience but yet push their own boundaries. Writers should approach social issues within the human experience of their character."

## ELDRIDGE PUBLISHING CO. INC.

P.O. Box 14367, Tallahassee FL 32317. (800)447-8243. Fax: (800)453-5179. E-mail: info@histage.com. Website: www.histage.com or www.95church.com. **Editor:** Nancy Vorhis. Estab. 1906. Publishes approximately 25 children's plays/year; 2-3 children's musicals/year.

**Needs** "We publish for junior and high school, community theater and children's theater (adults performing for children), all genres, also religious plays." Recently published plays: *A Midsummer Night's Dream—A Musical*, adapted by Wade Bradford with music by Rachel Greenlee. Prefers work which has been performed or at least had a staged reading.

**How to Contact** Submit complete ms, sample or score and tape or CD of songs (if a musical). Will consider simultaneous submissions if noted. Responds in 3 months.

**Terms** Purchases all dramatic rights. Pays writers royalties of 50%; 10% copy sales; buys material outright for religious market.

**Tips** "Try to have your work performed, if at all possible, before submitting. We're always on the lookout for comedies which provide a lot of fun for our customers. But other more serious topics that concern teens, as well as intriguing mysteries and children's theater programs are of interest to us as well. We know there are many new talented playwrights out there, and we look forward to reading their fresh scripts."

## ENCORE PERFORMANCE PUBLISHING

P.O. Box 692, Orem UT 84059. (902)527-3524. Fax: (902)543-6156. E-mail: encoreplay@aol.com. Website: www.Encoreplay.com. **Contact:** Mike Perry. Estab. 1978. Publishes 20-30 children's plays/year; 10-20 children's musicals/year.

**Needs** Prefers close to equal male/female ratio if possible. Adaptations for K-12 and older. 60% of plays written for adult roles; 40% for juvenile roles. Recently published plays: *Boy Who Knew No Fear*, by G. Riley Mills/ Mark Levenson (adaptation of fairy tale, ages 8-16); *Two Chains*, by Paul Burton (about drug abuse, ages 11-18).

**How to Contact** Query first with synopsis, character breakdown, set description, production history, and song list if musical. Will only consider previously performed work. Responds in 2 months.

**Terms** Purchases all publication and production rights. Author retains copyright. Pays writers in royalties (50%). SASE for return of submission.

**Tips** "Give us issue and substance, be controversial without offense. Use a laser printer! Don't send an old manuscript. Make yours look the most professional."

## THE ENSEMBLE THEATRE

3535 Main, Houston TX 77002. (713)520-0055, ext. 317. Fax: (713)520-1269. Jackson Randolph. Estab. 1976. Produces 4 children's plays/year; 1 children's musical/year.

**Needs** Produces children's plays for professional productions (in-house and touring). 70% of plays/musicals written for adult roles; 30% for juvenile roles. Limited to cast of 6 or less, with limited staging, costuming and props. Musical needs: appropriate for limited or recorded accompaniment. Recently published *Coolsuit*, by Lauren Mayer; *On Stage*, by Nancy Zelenak, music and lyrics by C. Michael Perry.

**How to Contact** Plays: Query with synopsis, character breakdown and set description; submit complete ms. Musicals: Query with synopsis, character breakdown and set description. Will consider simultaneous submissions and previously performed work. Responds only if interested.

**Terms** Pays $20-75/performance.

**Tips** "Entertain, educate and enlighten."

## FLORIDA STUDIO THEATRE

1241 N. Palm Ave., Sarasota FL 34236. (941)366-9017. Fax: (941)955-4137. E-mail: james@fst2000.org. Website: www.fst2000.org. **Artistic Director:** Richard Hopkins. **Casting and Literary Coordinator:** James Ashford. Estab. 1973. Produces 3 children's plays/year.

**Needs** Produces children's plays for professional productions. "Prefer small cast plays (5-8 characters) that use imagination more than heavy scenery." Will consider new plays and previously performed work.

**How to Contact** Query with synopsis, character breakdown, 5 pages of sample dialogue; Attn: James Ashford. Responds in 1 month to queries. Rights negotiable. Payment negotiable. Submissions returned with SASE.
**Tips** "Children are a tremendously sophisticated audience. The material should respect this."

## THE FOOTHILL THEATRE COMPANY

P.O. Box 1812, Nevada City CA 95959-1812. (530)265-9320. Fax: (530)265-9325. E-mail: info@foothilltheatre.org. Website: www.foothilltheatre.org. **Literary Manager:** Gary Wright. Estab. 1977. Produces 0-2 children's plays/year; 0-1 children's musicals/year. Professional nonprofit theater.
**Needs** 95% of plays/musicals written for adult roles; 5% for juvenile roles. "Small is better, but will consider anything." Produced *Peter Pan*, by J.M. Barrie (kids vs. grownups, for all ages); *Six Impossible Things Before Breakfast*, by Lee Potts & Marilyn Hetzel (adapted from works of Lewis Carroll, for all ages). Does not want to see traditional fairy tales.
**How to Contact** Query with synopsis, character breakdown and set description. Will consider simultaneous submissions and previously performed work. Responds in 6 months.
**Terms** Buys negotiable rights. Payment method varies. Submissions returned with SASE.
**Tips** "Trends in children's theater include cultural diversity, real life issues (drug use, AIDS, etc.), mythological themes with contemporary resonance. Don't talk down to or underestimate children. Don't be preachy or didactic—humor is an excellent teaching tool."

## THE FREELANCE PRESS

P.O. Box 548, Dover MA 02030. (508)785-8250. **Managing Editor:** Narcissa Campion. Estab. 1979.
**Needs** Casts are comprised of young people, ages 8-15, and number 25-30. "We publish original musicals on contemporary topics for children and adaptations of children's classics (e.g., Rip Van Winkle)." Published plays: *The Tortoise and the Hare* (based on story of same name, for ages 8-12); *Monopoly*, (3 young people walk through board game, for ages 11-15).
  ● The Freelance Press does not accept plays for adult performers.
**How to Contact** Submit complete ms and score with SASE. Will consider simultaneous submissions and previously performed work. Responds in 3 months.
**Terms** Pays writers 10% royalties on book sales, plus performance royalties. SASE for return of submission.

## SAMUEL FRENCH, INC.

45 W. 25th St., New York NY 10010. (212)206-8990. Fax: (212)206-1429. **Senior Editor:** Lawrence Harbison. Estab. 1830. Publishes very few children's plays/year; "variable number of musicals."
**Needs** Subject matter: "all genres, all ages. No puppet plays. No adaptations of any of those old 'fairy tales.' No 'Once upon a time, long ago and far away.' No kings, princesses, fairies, trolls, etc."
**How to Contact** Submit complete ms and demo tape (if a musical). Responds in "minimum of 2 months."
**Terms** Purchases "publication rights, amateur and professional production rights, option to publish next 3 plays." Pays writers "book royalty of 10%; variable royalty for professional and amateur productions. SASE for return of submissions.
**Tips** "Most of our recent children's plays have been published by our London affiliate, Samuel French, Ltd., or by our subsidiary, Baker's Plays."

## THE GROWING STAGE THEATRE

In Residence at the Palace, Rt. 183, Netcong NJ 07857. (973)347-4946. Fax: (973)691-7069. Website: www.growingstage.com. **Executive Director:** Stephen L. Fredericks. Estab. 1982. Produces 5 mainstage children's shows (including musicals). Holds classes throughout the year and a summer day camp. Equity touring production to schools and other organizations. Professional actors work with community actors.
**Needs** 60% of plays/musicals written for adult roles; 40% for juvenile roles.
**How to Contact** Query with synopsis, character breakdown and set description. Will consider previously performed work. Responds in 2 months.
**Terms** "Contracts are developed individually." Pays $25-75/performance. Submissions returned with SASE.
**Tips** "There's an overabundance on issue-oriented plays. Creativity, quality, the standards we place on theater aimed at adults should not be reduced in preparing a script for young people. We, together, are forming the audience of tomorrow. Don't repel young people by making the theater another resource for the infomercial—nurture, challenge and inspire them. Never write down to your intended audience."

## HANGAR THEATRE

P.O. Box 205, Ithaca NY 14851. (607)273-8588. Fax: (607)273-4516. E-mail: playwrights@hangartheatre.org. Website: www.hangartheatre.org. **Artistic Director:** Kevin Moriarty. Estab. 1975. Produces 7 children's plays/year; 2 children's musicals/year.

**Needs** Produces summer season of children's plays performed by the Lab Company. 100% of plays/musicals written for adult roles. Musical needs: "No new musicals accepted." Recently produced plays: *Jack and the Beanstalk*, by Marjorie Sokoloff (play about a boy's coming of age including deaf and hearing actors for ages 5-10); *Pinocchio, A Musical About Adoption*, by Susan DiLallo and Jeffrey Harris (ages 4-10).

**How to Contact** Plays: Submit complete ms. Responds only if interested.

**Terms** Royalties negotiable. Submissions returned with SASE.

**Tips** "Children's plays should be under 60 minutes, with a recognizable title, character, or theme, and have less than 10 characters."

## HAYES SCHOOL PUBLISHING CO. INC.

321 Pennwood Ave., Pittsburgh PA 15221. (412)371-2373. Fax: (800)543-8771. E-mail: chayes@hayespub.com. Website: www.hayespub.com. **President:** Mr . Clair N. Hayes III. Estab. 1940.

**Needs** Wants to see supplementary teaching aids for grades K-12. Interested in all subject areas, especially music, foreign language (French, Spanish, Latin), early childhood education.

**How to Contact** Query first with table of contents or outline and 3-4 sample pages. Will consider simultaneous and e-mail submissions. Responds in 2 months.

**Terms** Purchases all rights. Work purchased outright. SASE for return of submissions.

## HEUER PUBLISHING COMPANY

P.O. Box 248, Cedar Rapids IA 52406.(319)364-6311. Fax: (319)364-1771. E-mail: editor@hitplays.com. Website: www.heuerpublishing.com. Estab. 1928. **Editor in Chief:** Geri Albrecht. Publishes 30+ plays/year. 5+ musicals/year. Serves the educational and community theater markets.

**Needs** Heuer is a pioneer in commissioning and publishing unique works from a broad range of playwrights and composers for schools and community theatres. We are interested in shows that are entertaining, yet thought-provoking, family appropriate yet edgy. Our new genre of plays and musicals address such areas as Multi-Cultural Awareness, Interactive Plays, Creative Dramatics and dramas that address a broad range of social challenges in the Social Scene. Recently published plays/musicals: *Sleeping Beauty & the Beast*, by Wade Bradford (a dazzling fractured fairy tale); *Virgil's Family Reunion*, by Eddie McPherson (charming characters, non-stop laughter); *Gina and The Prince of Mintz*, book and lyrics by Charles Kondek, music by Steve Liebman; *Mindboggling*, by Laura Woebbeking (over the top, high comedy).

**How to Contact** Submissions accepted online at www.heuerpublishing.com or through the mail. Will consider simultaneous submissions and welcomes previously performed work. Responds in 2 months.

**Terms** Contracts amateur and professional rights. Pays royalty or purchases work outright. Submissions returned with SASE.

**Tips** "We will continue to deepen our product offering and will expand our genre for 2005-06 to include classic literature, Shakespeare with a twist, operas/operettas, musicals in a box, historical enlightenment, curriculum-based plays and duets."

## HONOLULU THEATRE FOR YOUTH

2846 Ualena Street, Honolulu HI 96822. (808)839-9885. Fax: (808)839-7018. E-mail: hyt@hytweb.org. Website: www.htyweb.org. **Artistic Director:** Mark Lutwak. Estab. 1955. Produces 8 children's plays/year (1 or 2 may be musicals).

**Needs** Produces professional theatre company for professional productions. 100% of plays/musicals written for adult roles. "We use adults to play children's parts." "Many of our shows tour by air to five other islands. We try to keep shows simple, small-cast (7 or fewer actors), and under 75 minutes." Musical needs: "Live music, simple enough for the actors to perform themselves." Recently produced plays: *When Tiger Smoked His Pipe*, by Nora Okja Keller (play about Korean folktales for ages 7-10); *The Garden of Rikki Tikki Tavi*, by Y. York (loose adaptation from Kipling/friendship for ages 5-8).

**How to Contact** Plays/musicals: Query with synopsis, character breakdown and set description. Will consider simultaneous submissions, e-mail submissions, previously performed work. Responds in 1-3 months.

**Terms** Buys nonexclusive stock rights on mss and scores. Pays 6-8% royalties. Submissions returned with SASE.

**Tips** "We serve a specific community: Hawaii. The cultural/ethnic blend if very different here from the rest of mainland U.S. The history is different. The sensibility is different. Our plays reflect this. Study our website, past productions, think about what it might mean to be a child on Hawaii."

## MERRY-GO-ROUND YOUTH THEATRE

P.O. Box 506, Auburn NY 13021. (315)255-1305. Fax: (315)252-3815. E-mail: youthmgr@dreamscape.com. Website: www.merry-go-round.com. **Producing Director:** Ed Sayles. Estab. 1958. Produces 10 children's productions/year (some of which are musicals).

**Needs** 100% of plays/musicals written for adult roles. Cast maximum, 4 and staging must be tourable. Recently produced plays: *The Gifts of Obidiah Oak*, by David Eliet and Nancy Rosenburg (Musical Fable); *There Once Was a Longhouse, Where Now There is Your House*, by Rick Balian (Native Americans of New York state).

**How to Contact** Plays/musicals: query with synopsis, character breakdown and set description; submit complete ms and score. Will consider simultaneous submissions, electronic submissions via disk/e-mail and previously performed work. Responds in 2 months.

**Terms** ''Realize that our program is grade/curriculum specific. And understanding of the NYS Learning Standards may help a writer to focus on a point of curriculum that we would like to cover.''

## NEBRASKA THEATRE CARAVAN

6915 Cass St., Omaha NE 68132. (402)553-4890, ext. 154. Fax: (402)553-6288. E-mail: caravan@omahaplayhouse.com. Website: www.omahaplayhouse.com. **Producing Director:** Jerry O'Connor. Estab. 1976. Produces 3-4 children's plays/year; 1-2 children's musicals/year.

**Needs** Produces children's plays for professional productions with a company of 5-6 actors touring. 100% of plays/musicals written for adult roles; setting must be adaptable for easy touring. 65 minute show for grades 7-12; 60 minutes for elementary. Musical need: 1 piano or keyboard accompaniment. Recently produced plays: *A Thousand Cranes*, by Kathryn Schultz Miller (Sadako Susaki, for ages K-8).

**How to Contact** Plays: query with synopsis, character breakdown and set description. Musicals: query first. Will consider simultaneous submissions and previously performed work. Responds in 3 months.

**Terms** Pays $35-40/performance; pays commission—option 1: own outright; option 2: have right to produce at any later date—playwright has right to publish and produce. Submissions returned with SASE.

**Tips** ''Be sure to follow guidelines.''

## THE NEW CONSERVATORY THEATRE CENTER

25 Van Ness Ave., San Francisco CA 94102-6033. (415)861-4914. Fax: (415)861-6988. E-mail: email@nctcsf.org. Website: www.nctcsf.org. **Executive Director:** Ed Decker. Estab. 1981. Produces 3-5 children's plays/year; 1 children's musical/year.

**Needs** Limited budget and small casts only. Produces children's plays as part of ''a professional theater arts training program for youths ages 8-19 during the school year and 2 summer sessions. The New Conservatory also produces educational plays for its touring company. We do not want to see any preachy or didactic material.'' Recently produced plays: *Gary Grinkles Battles With Wrinkles*, by Stefan Lafer (ages 6-9); *And Then They Came For Me: Remembering the World of Anne Frank*, by James Still (ages 12 and up).

**How to Contact** Query with synopsis, character breakdown and set description, or submit complete ms and score. Responds in 3 months.

**Terms** Rights purchased negotiable. Pays writers in royalties. SASE for return of submission.

**Tips** ''Wants plays with name recognition, i.e., *The Lion, the Witch and the Wardrobe* as well as socially relevant issues. Plays should be under 50 minutes in length.''

## NEW PLAYS INCORPORATED

P.O. Box 5074, Charlottesville VA 22905-0074. (434)979-2777. Fax: (434)984-2230. E-mail: patwhitton@aol.com. Website: www.newplaysforchildren.com. **Publisher:** Patricia Whitton Forrest. Estab. 1964. Publishes 3-4 plays/year; 1 or 2 children's musicals/year.

**Needs** Publishes ''generally material for kindergarten through junior high.'' Recently published: *Everyman in the Circus of Life*, by Travis Tyre (contemporary adaptation of the medieval classic); *Buried Treasure*, by Tom Ballmar (adventure play for upper elementary/junior high).

**How to Contact** Submit complete ms and score. Will consider simultaneous submissions and previously performed work. Responds in 2 months (usually).

**Terms** Purchases exclusive rights to sell acting scripts. Pays writers in royalties (50% of production royalties; 10% of script sales). SASE for return of submission.

**Tips** ''Write the play you really want to write (not what you think will sell) and find a director to put it on.''

## NEW YORK STATE THEATRE INSTITUTE

37 First St., Troy NY 12180. (518)274-3200. Fax (518)274-3815. E-mail nysti@capital.net. Website: www.nysti.org. **Artistic Director:** Patricia B. Snyder. **Associate Artistic Director:** Ed Lange. Estab. 1976. Produces 5 children's plays/year; 1-2 children's musicals/year.

**Needs** Produces full-length family plays for professional theater. 90% of plays/musicals are written for adult roles; 10% for juvenile roles. Does not want to see plays for children only. Produced plays: *A Tale of Cinderella*, by Will Severin, W.A. Frankonis and George David Weiss (all ages); *Miracle On 34th Street*, by Valentine Davies.

**How to Contact** Query with synopsis, character breakdown and set description; submit tape of songs (if a musical). Will consider simultaneous submissions and previously performed work. Responds in 1 month for queries. SASE for return of submission.

**Tips** Writers should be mindful of "audience *sophistication*. We do not wish to see material that is childish. Writers should submit work that is respectful of young people's intelligence and perception—work that is appropriate for families, but that is also challenging and provocative."

## THE OPEN EYE THEATER
P.O. Box 959, Margaretville NY 12455. Phone/fax: (845)586-1660. E-mail: openeye@catskill.net. Website: www .theopeneye.org. **Producing Artistic Director:** Amie Brockway. Estab. 1972 (theater). Produces 3 plays/year for a family audience. Most productions include music but are not musicals.

**Needs** "Casts of various sizes. Technical requirements are kept to a minimum." Produces professional productions combining professional artists and artists-in-training (actors of all ages). Recently produced plays: *Freddy, The King of Detectives*, by Sandra Fenichel Asher, with music by Robert Cucinnota; *John Chapman and the Devil*, by Mary Barile; *The Wide Awake Princess*, by David Paterson, music by Steve Liebman; *Pixies, Kings and Magical Things*, by Ric Averil.

**How to Contact** "No videos or cassettes. Letter of inquiry only. Will consider previously performed work." Responds in 6 months.

**Terms** Rights agreement negotiated with author. Pays writers one-time fee or royalty negotiated with publisher. SASE for return of submission.

**Tips** "Send letter of inquiry only. We are interested in plays for a multigenerational audience (8-adult)."

## PHOENIX THEATRE'S COOKIE COMPANY
100 E. McDowell, Phoenix AZ 85004. (602)258-1974. Fax: (602)253-3626. E-mail: A-Prewitt@phxtheatre.org. Website: phxtheatre.org. **Artistic Director:** Alan J. Prewitt. Estab. 1980. Produces 4 children's plays/year.

**Needs** Produces theater with professional adult actors performing for family audiences. 95% of plays/musicals written for adult roles; 5% for juvenile roles. Requires small casts (4-7), small stage, mostly 1 set, flexible set or ingenious sets for a small space. Short musicals accepted. Does not want to see larger casts, multiple sets, 2 hour epics. Recently produced *The Quiltmaker's Gift* by Alan J. Prewitt (from the best selling children's books by Jeff Brumbeau); *The Sleeping Beauty*, by Alan J. Prewitt (classic tale gets "truthful parent" twist, for ages 4-12).

**How to Contact** Plays/musicals: Query with synopsis, character breakdown and set description. Will consider simultaneous submissions. Responds only if interested within 1 month.

**Terms** Submissions returned with SASE.

**Tips** "Only submit innovative, imaginative work that stimulates imagination and empowers the child. We specialize in producing original scripts based on classic children's literature."

## PIONEER DRAMA SERVICE
P.O. Box 4267, Englewood CO 80155-4267. (303)779-4035. Fax : (303)779-4315. E-mail: editors@pioneerdrama. com. Website: www.pioneerdrama.com. **Submissions Editor:** Lori Conary. **Publisher:** Steven Fendrich. Estab. 1960. Publishes more than 10 new plays and musicals/year.

**Needs** "We are looking for plays up to 90 minutes long, large ensemble casts with plenty of female and/or flexible roles and simple sets." Publishes plays for ages upper elementary school/high school, children's and community theatre. Recently published plays/musicals: *Lady Pirates of Captain Bree*, by Martin Follose, music and lyrics by Bill Francoeur; *Jolly Roger and the Pirate Queen*, by Craig Sodaro. Wants to see "script, CD/tape of music, pics and reviews."

**How to Contact** Query with synopsis, character breakdown, running time and set description or submit complete ms and CD/cassette of music (if a musical) with SASE. Will consider simultaneous submissions, e-mail submissions, previously performed work. Contact submissions editor. Responds in 4 months. Send SASE for writer's guidelines.

**Terms** Purchases all rights. Pays writers in royalties (10% on sales, 50% royalties on productions). Research Pioneer through catalog and website.

**Tips** "Research the company. Include a cover letter and a SASE."

## PLAYERS PRESS, INC.
P.O. Box 1132, Studio City CA 91614-0132. (818)789-4980. **Vice President:** R.W. Gordon. Estab. 1965. Publishes 10-20 children's plays/year; 3-12 children's musicals/year.

**Needs** Subject matter: "We publish for all age groups." Recently published: *African Folk Tales*, by Carol Korty (for ages 10-14).

**How to Contact** Query with synopsis, character breakdown and set description; include #10 SASE with query. Considers previously performed work only. Responds to query in 1 month; submissions in 1 year.

**Terms** Purchases stage, screen, TV rights. Payment varies; work purchased possibly outright upon written request. Submissions returned with SASE.

**Tips** "Submit as requested—query first and send only previously produced material. Entertainment quality is on the upswing and needs to be directed at the world, no longer just the U.S. Please submit with two #10 SASEs plus manuscript-size SASE. Please do not call."

## PLAYS, The Drama Magazine for Young People

P.O. Box 600160, Newton MA 02460. E-mail: lpreston@playsmag.com. Website: www.playsmag.com. **Editor:** Elizabeth Preston. Estab. 1941. Publishes 70-75 children's plays/year.

**Needs** "Props and staging should not be overly elaborate or costly. There is little call among our subscribers for plays with only a few characters; ten or more (to allow all students in a class to participate, for instance) is preferred. Our plays are performed by children in school from lower elementary grades through junior/senior high." 100% of plays written for juvenile roles. Subject matter: Audience is lower grades through junior/senior high. Recently published plays: *The Three-Sided Coin*, by John Tissot (Will a first-year teacher be able to stand his ground against a powerful parent with political connections?); *To Dine Alone*, by Martin A. Follose (Grandma plays matchmaker); *Besieged*, by Craig Sodaro (The attack on Vicksburg forces a family underground . . . and one of them faces harsh truths about herself); *The Red Door*, by Kevin Stone (Strange noises, a door that won't stay shut, ghostly figures give Joanna's birthday party a spooky feel); *Catch the Morning*, by Eric Alter (Young medical student tries to make sense of the world, post-September 11th). "Send nothing downbeat—no plays about drugs, sex or other 'heavy' topics."

**How to Contact** Query first on adaptations of folk tales and classics; otherwise submit complete ms. Responds in 3 weeks.

**Terms** Purchases all rights. Pay rates vary. Guidelines available; send SASE. Sample copy $4.

**Tips** "Get your play underway quickly. Keep it wholesome and entertaining. No preachiness, heavy moral or educational message. Any 'lesson' should be imparted through the actions of the characters, not through unbelievable dialogue. Use realistic situations and settings without getting into downbeat, depressing topics. No sex, drugs, violence, alcohol."

## RIVERSIDE CHILDREN'S THEATRE

3280 Riverside Park Dr., Vero Beach FL 32963. (561)234-8052. Fax: (561)234-4407. E-mail: rct@riversidetheatre. com. Website: www.riversidetheatre.com. **Education Director:** Linda Downey. Estab. 1980. Produces 4 children's plays/year; 2 children's musicals/year.

**Needs** Produces amateur youth productions. 100% of plays/musicals written for juvenile roles. Musical needs: For children ages 6-18. Produced plays: *The Beloved Dently*, by Dory Cooney (pet bereavement, general); *Taming of the Shrew*, by Shakespeare (general).

**How to Contact** Plays/musicals: Query with synopsis, character breakdown and set description. Will consider simultaneous submissions, electronic submissions via disk/modem and previously performed work. Responds only if interested.

**Terms** Pays royalty or $40-60 per performance. Submissions returned with SASE.

**Tips** "Interested in youth theatre for children ages 6-18 to perform."

## SEATTLE CHILDREN'S THEATRE

201 Thomas St., Seattle WA 98109. Fax: (206)443-0442. Website: www.sct.org. **Literary Manager:** Rita Giomi. Estab. 1975. Produces 5 full-length children's plays/year; 1 full-length children's musical/year. Produces children's plays for professional productions (September-June).

**Needs** "We generally use adult actors even for juvenile roles." Produced plays: *The King of Ireland's Son*, by Paula Wing (mythology and Hero Quest for ages 8 and older); *Pink and Say*, by Oyamo (adaptation from Patricia Polacco's book); *Holes*, by Louis Sacher. Does not want to see anything that condescends to young people— anything overly broad in style.

**How to Contact** Accepts agented scripts or those accompanied by a professional letter of recommendation (director or dramaturg). Responds in 1 year.

**Terms** Rights vary. Payment method varies. Submissions returned with SASE.

**Tips** "Please *do not* send unsolicited manuscripts. We prefer sophisticated material (our weekend performances have an audience that is half adults)."

## TADA!

15 W. 28th St., 3rd Floor, New York NY 10001. (212)252-1619. Fax: (212)252-8763. E-mail: tada@tadatheater.c om. Website: www.tadatheater.com. **Artistic/Literary Director:** Emmanuel Wilson. Estab. 1984. Produces 5 staged readings of children's plays and musicals/year; 0-5 children's plays/year; 2-3 children's musicals/year.

**Needs** "All actors are children, ages 8-17." Produces children's plays for professional, year-round theater.

100% of plays/musicals written for juvenile roles. Recently produced musicals: *Sleepover,* by Phillip Freedman and James Belloff (peer acceptance, for ages 3 and up); *The Little House of Cookies,* by Janine Nina Trevens and Joel Gelpe (international communication and friendship). Does not want to see fairy tales or material that talks down to children.
**How to Contact** Query with synopsis, character breakdown and set description; submit complete ms, score and tape of songs (if a musical). Responds in 1 year "or in October following the August deadline for our Annual Playwriting Competition. (Send two copies of manuscript if for competition)."
**Terms** Rights purchased "depend on the piece." Pays writers in royalties of 6% and/or pays commissioning fee. SASE a must for return of submissions.
**Tips** "For plays for our Annual Playwriting Competition, submit between January and August 15. We're looking for plays with current topics that specific age ranges can identify with, with a small cast of children and one or two adults. Our company is multiracial and city-oriented. We are not interested in fairy tales. We like to produce material that kids relate to and that touches their lives today."

### THEATER MU
2700 NE Winter St. #1A, Minneapolis MN 55413. (612)824-4804. Fax: (612)824-3396. E-mail: ricks@theatermu. org. Website: www.theatermu.org. **Artistic Director:** Rick Shiomi. Estab. 1992. Produces 1 children's play/ year.
**Needs** Produces professional (nonequity) regular seasons of 4 productions per year plus various development festivals. 90% of plays/musicals written for adult roles; 10% for juvenile roles. Musical needs: "Asian and Asian American subject matter." Recently produced plays: *Tiger Tales: Hmong Folktales,* by R.A. Shiomi & Cha Yang (play of Hmong folktales about tigers for elementary through middle school); *The Magic Bus to Asian Folktales,* by R.A. Shiomi, Cha Yang & Jaz Canlas (play about Asian folktales told by school bus driver for ages elementary through middle school).
**How to Contact** Plays: Query with synopsis, character breakdown and set description; submit complete ms. Musicals: Query with synopsis, character breakdown and set description. Will consider simultaneous submissions, previously performed work. Responds only if interested.
**Terms** Buys all rights on mss, production, and scores. Pays royalties; pays/performance.
**Tips** "Send synopsis and script and if you hear from us, we are interested."

### THEATRE FOR YOUNG AMERICA
5909 Johnson Dr., Mission KS 66202. (913)831-2131. **Artistic Director:** Gene Mackey. Estab. 1974. Produces 9 children's plays/year; 3-5 children's musicals/year.
**Needs** "We use a small cast (4-7), open thrust stage." Theatre for Young America is a professional equity company. 90% of plays/musicals written for adult roles; 10% for juvenile roles. Produced plays: *The Wizard of Oz,* by Jim Eiler and Jeanne Bargy (for ages 6 and up); *A Partridge in a Pear Tree,* by Lowell Swortzell (deals with the 12 days of Christmas, for ages 6 and up); *Three Billy Goats Gruff,* by Gene Mackey and Molly Jessup (Norwegian folk tales, for ages 6 and up).
**How to Contact** Query with synopsis, character breakdown and set description. Will consider simultaneous submissions and previously performed work. Responds in 2 months.
**Terms** Purchases production rights, tour rights in local area. Pays writers in royalties or $10-50/performance.
**Tips** Looking for "cross-cultural material that respects the intelligence, sensitivity and taste of the child audience."

# Young Writer's & Illustrator's Markets

The listings in this section are special because they publish work of young writers and artists (under age 18). Some of the magazines listed exclusively feature the work of young people. Others are adult magazines with special sections for the work of young writers. There are also a few book publishers listed that exclusively publish the work of young writers and artists. Many of the magazines and publishers listed here pay only in copies, meaning authors and illustrators receive one or more free copies of the magazine or book to which they contributed.

As with adult markets, markets for children expect writers to be familiar with their editorial needs before submitting. Many of the markets listed will send guidelines to writers. Guidelines state exactly what a publisher accepts and how to submit it. You can often get these by sending a request with a self-addressed, stamped envelope (SASE) to the magazine or publisher, or by checking a publication's website (a number of listings include web addresses). In addition to obtaining guidelines, read through a few copies of any magazines you'd like to submit to—this is the best way to determine if your work is right for them.

A number of kids' magazines are available on newsstands or in libraries. Others are distributed only through schools, churches or home subscriptions. If you can't find a magazine you'd like to see, most editors will send sample copies for a small fee.

Before you submit your material to editors, take a few minutes to read Before Your First Sale on page 8 for more information on proper submission procedures. You may also want to check out two other sections—Contests, Awards & Grants and Conferences & Workshops. Some listings in these sections are open to students (some exclusively)—look for the phrase **Open to students** in bold. Additional opportunities and advice for young writers can be found in *The Young Writers Guide to Getting Published* (Writer's Digest Books) and *A Teen's Guide to Getting Published: the only writer's guide written by teens for teens*, by Danielle and Jessica Dunn (Prufrock Press). More information on these books are given in the Helpful Books & Publications section in the back of this book.

**Information on companies listed in the previous edition but not included in this edition of *Children's Writer's & Illustrator's Market* may be found in the General Index.**

## THE ACORN

1530 Seventh St., Rock Island IL 61201. (309)788-3980. **Editor:** Betty Mowery. Audience consists of "teachers, parents, young authors." Purpose in publishing works of children: "to provide a showcase for young authors. We hope to publish material other publications won't." Children must be K-12 (put name, address, grade on mss). Guidelines and contest rules available for SASE.

**Magazines** 100% of magazine written by children. Uses 6 fiction pieces (500 words); 20 pieces of poetry (32 lines). No personal essays. No payment; purchase of a copy isn't necessary to be printed. Sample copy $3. Subscription $10 for 4 issues. Submit mss to Betty Mowery, editor. Send complete ms. Will accept typewritten, legibly handwritten and/or computer printout. Include SASE. Responds in 1 week. Will not respond without SASE.

**Artwork** Publishes artwork by children. Looks for "all types; size $4 \times 5$. Use black ink in artwork." No cash payment or copy. Submit artwork either with ms or separately to Betty Mowery. Include SASE. Responds in 1 week.

**Tips** "Always include SASE and put name on manuscripts. When submitting to contests send SASE plus entry fee of 6 37¢ stamps. Also publishes *The Shepherd.*"

## AMERICAN GIRL

8400 Fairway Place, Middleton WI 53562. (608)836-4848. Fax: (608)831-7089. Website: www.americangirl.com. **Contact:** Magazine Department Assistant. Bimonthly magazine. Audience consists of girls ages 8-12 who are joyful about being girls. Purpose in publishing works by young people: "self-esteem boost and entertainment for readers. *American Girl* values girls' opinions and ideas. By publishing their work in the magazine, girls can share their thoughts with other girls! Young writers should be 8-12 years old. We don't have writer's guidelines for children's submissions. Instruction for specific solicitations appears in the magazine."

**Magazines** 20% of magazine written by young people. "A few pages of each issue feature articles that include children's answers to questions or requests that have appeared in a previous issue of *American Girl* ." Pays in copies. Submit to address listed in magazine. Will accept legibly handwritten ms s. Include SASE. Responds in 3 months.

**Tips** "Please, no stories, poems, etc. about American Girls Collection Characters (Felicity, Samantha, Molly, Kirsten, Addy, Josefina or Kit). Inside *American Girl*, there are several departments that call for submissions. Read the magazine carefully and submit your ideas based on what we ask for."

## BEYOND WORDS PUBLISHING, INC.

20827 NW Cornell Rd., Suite 500, Hillsboro OR 97124-9808. (503)531-8700. Fax: (503)531-8773. Website: www.beyondwords.com. **Managing Editor of Children's Division:** Summer Steele. Publishes 2-3 picture books/year; 2-3 YA nonfiction books. Looks for "books that encourage creativity and inspire integrity in children ages 5-15." Wants to "encourage children to write, create, dream and believe in the possibilities of all life has to offer. The books must be unique, be of national interest, and the author must be personable and promotable." Writer's guidelines available with SASE or on website.

**Books** Publishes historical fiction, inspiring, and/or multicultural picture books. Also publishes nonfiction advice books for children, such as guides for kids about present-day issues and concerns. Responds in 6-9 months.

**Artwork/Photography** Submit artwork to Managing Editor.

**Tips** "We do not accept any submissions electronically and will not respond to submissions that do not include a SASE. Write about issues that affect your life. Trust your own instincts. You know best!"

## CHILD LIFE

Children's Better Health Institute, P.O. Box 567, Indianapolis IN 46206. Parcels and packages: please send to 1100 Waterway Blvd., Indianapolis IN 46202. (317)634-1100. Fax: (317)684-8094. Website: www.childlifemag.org. **Editor:** Jack Gramling. **Art Director:** Rob Falco. Magazine published 6 times/year. Estab. 1921. Circ. 30,000. Targeted toward kids ages 9-11. Focuses on health, sports, fitness, nutrition, safety, academic excellence, general interests, and the nostalgia of *Child Life's* early days. "We publish jokes, riddles and poems by children." Kids should include name, address, phone number (for office use) and school photo. "No mass duplicated, multiple submissions."

- Child Life is no longer accepting manuscripts for publication.

**Tips** "We use submissions from kids ages 9-11. Those older or younger should try one of our sister publications: *Children's Digest, Children's Playmate, Humpty Dumpty's Magazine, Jack and Jill, Turtle Magazine, U\*S\*Kids.*"

## CHIXLIT, the literary 'zine for chicks ages 7 to 17

P.O. Box 12051, Orange CA 92859. E -mail: submit@chixlit.com. Website: www.chixlit.com. Bimonthly magazine ("more of a 'zine , really.") *chixLIT* is a place for girls ages 7-17 to express themselves. "We coax emerging talent and emotions; share writing techniques and feelings; and let each other know we are not alone. There are plenty of places for grownups, but we wanted a place for chix like us! Writers must be female and ages 7-

17. From anywhere in the world is OK, but writing must be in English. We like a parent or adult guardian to tap with us and let us know it's honest work and OK to print. Writer's guidelines available on request and on website. Our audience is also teachers, librarians and scout leaders who want to encourage writing and confidence-building, as well as children's book authors who want to know what's going on in our heads!"

**Magazines** 95% of magazine written by young people. "We publish poems, short stories, reviews, rants, raves, love letters, song lyrics, journal entries and more. Always looking for regular contributors, critics, editors." Pays 1 free copy of the 'zine and discount on subscription rate. Prizes for contest s. Submit complete ms. Will accept typewritten form. Accepts e-mail submissions "in the body of an e-mail (no attachments!). Must be in English. We are planning a Spanish-language edition for 200 6." Include SASE if you want your submission back or an answer by snail mail ( but we prefer e-mail). Responds in 4 weeks , usually faster.

**Artwork** Publishes artwork and photography by girls ages 7-17. Looks for "photos of chix or things that chix like, artwork of chix or things that make you think of chix. We are open to individual expression, but it has to be by girls, and it has to be flat and scannable and look decent in b&w." Pays 1 free issue for any artwork used and a small gift for any chosen for the cover. "We prefer submission of a piece of work (or a good color or b&w copy) in an envelope (not rolled) and sent to our P.O. Box (so not too big)."

**Tips** "We dare you to dare. Our motto is, 'Words are powerful, and they can make you powerful too.' Buy a subscription and back issues to see what we're about and what other chix are up to."

## CICADA

Carus Publishing Company, P.O. Box 300, 315 Fifth St., Peru IL 61354. (815)224-5803, ext. 656. Fax: (815)224-6615. E-mail: www.cricketmag.com. Website: www.cicadamag.com. **Editor-in-Chief:** Marianne Carus. **Executive Editor:** Deborah Vetter. **Associate Editor:** Tracy Schoenle. Senior Art Director: Ron McCutchan. Bimonthly magazine.

- *Cicada* publishes work of writers and artists of high-school age (must be at least 14 years old). See the *Cicada* listing in the magazines section for more information, or check their website or copies of the magazine.

## THE CLAREMONT REVIEW

4980 Wesley Rd., Victoria BC V8Y 1Y9 Canada. (250)658-5221. Fax: (250)658-5387. E-mail: susan_field@sd63.bc.ca. Website: www.theClaremontReview.com. Magazine. Publishes 2 books/year by young adults. Publishes poetry and fiction with literary value by students aged 13-19 anywhere in English-speaking world. Purpose in publishing work by young people: to provide a literary venue. Sponsors annual poetry contest.

**Magazines** Uses 10-12 fiction stories (200-2,500 words); 30-40 poems. Pays in copies. Submit mss to editors. Submit complete ms. Will accept typewritten mss. SASE. Responds in 6 weeks (except during the summer).

**Artwork** Publishes artwork by young adults. Looks for b&w copies of imaginative art. Pays in copies. Send picture for review. Negative may be requested. Submit art and photographs to editors. SASE. Responds in 6 weeks.

**Tips** "Read us first—it saves disappointment. Know who we are and what we publish. We're closed July and August. SASE a must. American students send I.R.C.'s as American stamps *do not* work in Canada."

## CREATIVE KIDS

P.O. Box 8813, Waco TX 76714-8813. (800)998-2208. Fax: (254)756-3339. E-mail: ck@prufrock.com. Website: www.prufrock.com. **Editor:** Libby Goolsby. Magazine published 4 times/year. Estab. 1979. "All material is by children, for children." Purpose in publishing works by children: "to create a product that provides children with an authentic experience and to offer an opportunity for children to see their work in print. *Creative Kids* contains the best stories, poetry, opinion, artwork, games and photography by kids ages 8-14." Writers ages 8-14 must have statement by teacher or parent verifying originality. Writer's guidelines available on request with SASE.

**Magazines** Uses "about 6" fiction and nonfiction stories (800-900 words); poetry, plays, ideas to share (200-750 words) per issue. Pays "free magazine." Submit mss to submissions editor. Will accept typewritten mss. Include SASE. Responds in 1 month.

**Artwork/Photography** Publishes artwork and photos by children. Looks for "any kind of drawing, cartoon, or painting." Pays "free magazine." Send color copy of the work to submissions editor. Include SASE. Responds in 1 month.

**Tips** "*Creative Kids* is a magazine by kids, for kids. The work represents children's ideas, questions, fears, concerns and pleasures. The material never contains racist, sexist, or violent expression. A person may submit one piece of work per envelope. Each piece must be labeled with the student's name, birth date, grade, school, home address and school address. Include a photograph, if possible. Recent school pictures are best. Material submitted to *Creative Kids* must not be under consideration by any other publication. Items should be carefully prepared, proofread and double checked (perhaps also by a parent or teacher). All activities requiring solutions must be accompanied by the correct answers. Young writers and artists should always write for guidelines and then follow them."

## CREATIVE WITH WORDS, Thematic anthologies

Creative with Words Publications, P.O. Box 223226, Carmel CA 93922. Fax: (831)655-8627. E -mail: cwwpub@usa.net. Website: http://members.tripod.com/CreativeWithWords. **Editor:** Brigitta Geltrich. **Nature Editor:** Bert Hower. Publishes 10 anthologies/year. Estab. 1975. "We publish the creative writing of children (2 anthologies written by children; 2 anthologies written by adults; 6-8 anthologies written by all ages)." Audience consists of children, families, schools, libraries, adults, reading programs. Purpose in publishing works by children: to offer them an opportunity to get started in publishing. "Work must be of quality, typed, original, unedited, and not published before; age must be given (up to 19 years old) and home address." SASE must be enclosed with all correspondence and mss. Writer's guidelines and theme list available on request with SASE, via e-mail or on website.

**Books** Considers all categories except those dealing with sensationalism, death, violence, pornography and over tly religious themes. Uses fairy tales, folklore items (up to 800 words) and poetry (not to exceed 20 lines, 46 characters across). Published Nature Series: Seasons, Nature, School, Love and Relationships (all children and adults). Offers 20% discount on each copy of publication in which fiction or poetry by children appears. Submit mss to editor. Query; child, teacher or parent can submit; teacher and/or parents must verify originality of writing. Will accept typewritten and/or legibly handwritten mss sent with SASE. "Will not go through agents or over-protective 'stage mothers.' " Responds in 1 month after deadline of any theme.

**Artwork/Photography** Publishes b&w artwork, b&w photos and computer artwork created by children (language art work). No already existing computer artwork. Offers 20% discount on every copy of publication in which work by children appears. Submit artwork to editor, and request info on payment.

**Tips** "Enjoy the English language, life and the world around you. Look at everything from a different perspective. Look at the greatness inside all of us. Be less descriptive and use words wisely. Let the reader experience a story through a viewpoint character, don't be overly dramatic. Match illustrations/photos to the meaning of the story or poem."

## FREE SPIRIT PUBLISHING

217 Fifth Ave. North, Suite 200, Minneapolis MN 55401-1299. (612)338-2068. Fax: (612)337-5050. E-mail: acquisitions@freespirit.com. Website: www.freespirit.com. **Acquisitions:** Douglas Fehlan. Publishes 16-22 titles/year for children and teens, teachers, and parents. "Free Spirit Publishing is the home of SELF-HELP FOR KIDS® and SELF-HELP FOR TEENS®, nonfiction, issue-driven, solution-focused books and materials for children and teens and the parents and teachers who care for them."

● Free Spirit no longer accepts fiction or storybook submissions.

**Books** Publishes nonfiction. "Submissions are accepted from prospective authors, including youth ages 16 and up, or through agents. Please review our catalog and author guidelines (both available online) before submitting proposal." Responds to queries/mss in 4 months. "If you'd like materials returned, enclose a SASE with sufficient postage." Write, call, or e-mail for catalog and submission guidelines before sending submission. Accepts queries only by e-mail. Submission guidelines available online.

**Tips** "We do not publish fiction or picture storybooks, books with animal or mythical characters, books with religious or New Age content, or single biographies, autobiographies, or memoirs. We prefer books written in a natural, friendly style."

## GREEN KNEES

Imprint of Azro Press, PMB 342, 1704 Llano St. B, Santa Fe NM 87505. (505)989-3272. Fax: (505)989-3832. E-mail: books@azropress.com. Website: www.greenknees.com. Book publisher. Publishes 1 book/year by children. "Green Knees is primarily interested in picture books and easy readers written and illustrated by children who are 13 years old or younger." Writer's guidelines available on request.

**Books** Interested in animal stories and humor. Length: 1,000 words for fiction. Submit mss to Jaenet Guggenheim. Query or submit complete ms or synopsis and sample illustration (if longer than 40 pages). Send a copy of the ms, do not send original material. Will accept typewritten or electronic submissions (disk or e-mail). Include SASE. Responds in 2 months.

## HIGHLIGHTS FOR CHILDREN

803 Church St., Honesdale PA 18431. (570)253-1080. Magazine. Published monthly. "We strive to provide wholesome, stimulating, entertaining material that will encourage children to read. Our audience is children ages 2-12." Purpose in publishing works by young people: to encourage children's creative expression.

**Magazines** 15-20% of magazine written by children. Uses stories and poems. Also uses jokes, riddles, tongue twisters. Features that occur occasionally: "What Are Your Favorite Books?" (8-10/year), Recipes (8-10/year), "Science Letters" (15-20/year). Special features that invite children's submissions on a specific topic occur several times per year. Recent examples include "Pet Stories," "Best Costume Ever," "Your Dream Job," and

"Help the Cartoonists." Pays in copies. Submit complete ms to the editor. Will accept typewritten, legibly handwritten and computer printout mss. Responds in 6 weeks.

**Artwork** Publishes artwork by children. Pays in copies. No cartoon or comic book characters. No commercial products. Submit b&w or color artwork on unlined paper for "Our Own Pages." Features include "Creatures Nobody Has Ever Seen" (5-8/year) and "Illustration Job" (18-20/year). Responds in 6 weeks.

**Tips** "Remember to keep a photocopy of your work because we cannot return it. When submitting your work, please include your name, age, and full address."

### INSIGHT, Teens Meeting Christ

55 W. Oak Ridge Dr., Hagerstown MD 21740. (301)393-4038. Fax: (301)393-4055. E-mail: insight@rhpa.org. Website: www.insightmagazine.org. **Contact:** Dwain Nielson Esmond. Weekly magazine. Estab. 1970. Circ. 20,000. "Our readers crave true stories written by teens or written about teens that convey a strong spiritual point or portray a spiritual truth." 100% of publication aimed at teen and college-age market.

**Nonfiction** Young adults: animal, biography, fashion, health, humorous, interview/profile, multicultural, nature/environment, problem-solving, social issues, sports, travel: first-person accounts preferred. Buys 200 mss/year. Average word length: 500-1,500. Byline given.

### ⚡ KWIL KIDS PUBLISHING, The Little Publishing Company That Kwil Built

Kwilville, P.O. Box 29556, Maple Ridge BC V2X 2V0 Canada. E-mail: kmarquis@sd42.ca. Publishes weekly column in local paper, four quarterly newsletters. "*Kwil Kids* come in all ages, shapes and sizes—from 4-64 and a whole lot more! Kwil does not pay for the creative work of children but provides opportunity/encouragement. We promote literacy, creativity and creative 'connections' through written and artistic expression and publish autobiographical, inspirational, stories of gentleness, compassion, truth and beauty. Our purpose is to foster a sense of pride and enthusiasm in young writers and artists, to celebrate the voice of youth and to encourage growth through joy-filled practice and cheerleading, not criticism." Must include name, age, address and parent signature (if a minor). Will send guidelines upon request."

**Books** Publishes autobiographical, inspirational, creative stories (alliterative, rhyming refrains, juicy words), short rhyming and nonrhyming poems (creative, fun, original, expressive). Length: 500 words for fiction; 8-16 lines for poetry. No payments; self-published and sold "at cost" only (1 free copy). Submit mss to Kwil or Mr. Marquis. Submit complete ms. Send copy only; expect a reply but will not return ms. Will accept typewritten and legibly handwritten mss and e-mail. Include SASE or enclose IRC or $1 for postage, as U.S. stamps may not be used **from** Canada. Responds in April, August and December.

**Newsletter** 95% of newsletter written by young people. Uses 15 short stories, poems (20-100 words). No payment; free newsletters only. Submit complete ms. Will accept typewritten and legibly handwritten mss and e-mail. Kwil answers every letter in verse. Responds in April, August and December.

**Artwork** Publishes artwork and photography by children with writing. Looks for black ink sketches to go with writing and photos to go with writing. Submit by postal mail only; white background for sketches. Submit artwork/photos to Kwil publisher. Submit holiday/seasonal work 4 months in advance. Include SASE. Responds in 3 months.

**Tips** "We love stories that teach a lesson or encourage peace, love and a fresh, new understanding. Just be who you are and do what you do. Then all of life's treasures will come to you."

### MERLYN'S PEN: Fiction, Essays, and Poems by America's Teens

P.O. Box 910, East Greenwich RI 02818. (800)247-2027. Fax: (401)885-5199. Website: www.merlynspen.org. Magazine. Published annually. "By publishing student writing, *Merlyn's Pen* seeks to broaden and reward the young author's interest in writing, strengthen the self-confidence of beginning writers and promote among all students a positive attitude toward literature. We publish 75 manuscripts annually by students in grades 6-12. The entire magazine is dedicated to young adults' writing. Our audience is classrooms, libraries and students from grades 6-12." Writers must submit via website only. When a student is accepted, he/she, a parent and a teacher must sign a statement of originality. Writer's guidelines available at website.

**Magazines** Published authors receive $10-100. Submit 1 title at a time. Responds in 6 weeks.

**Tips** "You must visit our website and use the form there to submit."

### NEW MOON: The Magazine for Girls & Their Dreams

New Moon Publishing, Inc., 34 E. Superior St., Duluth MN 55802. (218)728-5507. Fax: (218)728-0314. E-mail: girl@newmoon.org. Website: www.newmoon.org. **Managing Editor:** Kate Freeborn. Bimonthly magazine. *New Moon* 's primary audience is girls ages 8-14. "We publish a magazine that listens to girls." More than 70% of *New Moon* is written by girls. Purpose in publishing work by children/teens: "We want girls' voices to be heard. *New Moon* wants girls to see that their opinions, dreams, thoughts and ideas count." Writer's guidelines available for SASE or online.

● See *New Moon*'s listing in Magazines section.
**Magazine** Buys 6 fiction mss/year (900-1,200 words); 30 nonfiction mss/year (600 words). Submit to Editorial Department. Submit query or complete mss for nonfiction; complete ms only for fiction. "We do not return or acknowledge unsolicited material. Do not send originals—we will not return any materials." Responds in 6 months if interested.
**Artwork/Photography** Publishes artwork and photography by girls. "We do not return unsolicited material."
**Tips** "Read *New Moon* to completely understand our needs."

## Ⓝ THE SHEPHERD

1530 7th St., Rock Island IL 61201. (309)788-3980. Magazine. **Editor:** Betty Mowery. "An inspirational publication including work by children K-12."
**Magazines** Publishes fiction up to 500 words and poetry up to 35 lines. No payment offered. Manuscripts: SASE must be included.
**Tips** "Guidelines and contest rules are available with SASE. A sample copy is available for $3. Also publishes *The Acorn*."

## Ⓢ SKIPPING STONES

Multicultural Children's Magazine, P.O. Box 3939, Eugene OR 97403-0939. (541)342-4956. E-mail: editor@Skipp ingStones.org. Website: www.SkippingStones.org. **Articles/Poems/Fiction Editor:** Arun N. Toke. 5 issues a year. Estab. 1988. Circulation 2,500. "*Skipping Stones* is a multicultural, nonprofit, children's magazine to encourage cooperation, creativity and celebration of cultural and environmental richness. It offers itself as a creative forum for communication among children from different lands and backgrounds. We prefer work by children under 18 years old. International, minorities and under-represented populations receive priority, multilingual submissions are encouraged." Guidelines for children's work available on request with SASE.

● *Skipping Stones'* theme for the 2004 Youth Honor Awards is multicultural/international understanding and nature awareness. Send SASE for guidelines and more information on the awards. *Skipping Stones* is winner of the NAME, Parents' Choice, and Ed Press awards.

**Magazines** 50% written by children and teenagers. Uses 5-10 fiction short stories and plays (500-750 words); 5-10 nonfiction articles, interviews, letters, history, descriptions of celebrations (500-750 words); 15-20 poems, jokes, riddles, proverbs (250 words or less) per issue. Pays in contributor's copies. Submit mss to editor. Submit complete ms for fiction or nonfiction work; teachers and parents can also submit their contributions. Submissions should include "cover letter with name, age, address, school, cultural background, inspiration piece, dreams for future." Will accept typewritten, legibly handwritten and computer/word processor mss. Include SASE. Responds in 4 months. Accepts simultaneous submissions.
**Artwork/Photography** Publishes artwork and photography for children. Will review all varieties of ms/illustration packages. Wants comics, cartoons, b&w photos, paintings, drawings (preferably ink & pen or pencil), 8×10, color photos OK. Subjects include children, people, celebrations, nature, ecology, multicultural. Pays in contributor's copies.
**Terms** "*Skipping Stones* is a labor of love. You'll receive complimentary contributor's (up to 4) copies depending on the extent/length of your contribution. We may allow others to reprint articles and art or photographs." Responds to artists in 4 months. Sample copy for $5 and 4 first-class stamps.
**Tips** "Let the 'inner child' within you speak out—naturally, uninhibited." Wants "material that gives insight on cultural celebrations, lifestyle, custom and tradition, glimpse of daily life in other countries and cultures. Please, no mystery for the sake of mystery! Photos, songs, artwork are most welcome if they illustrate/highlight the points. Upcoming features: Living abroad, turning points, inspirations and magical moments in life, cultural celebrations around the world, folktales, caring for the earth, endangered species, your dreams and visions, heroes, kid-friendly analysis of current events, resolving conficts, summer experiences, poetry, and minority experiences."

## SPRING TIDES

824 Stillwood Dr., Savannah GA 31419. (912)925-8800. Annual magazine. Audience consists of children 5-12 years old. Purpose in publishing works by young people: to promote and encourage writing. Requirements to be met before work is published: must be 5-12 years old. Writers guidelines available on request.
**Magazines** 100% of magazine written by young people. Uses 5-6 fiction stories (1,200 words maximum); autobiographical experiences (1,200 words maximum); 15-20 poems (20 lines maximum) per issue. Writers are not paid. Submit complete ms or teacher may submit. Will accept typewritten mss. SASE.
**Artwork** Publishes artwork by children. "We have so far used only local children's artwork because of the complications of keeping and returning pieces."

## STONE SOUP, The Magazine by Young Writers and Artists

Children's Art Foundation, P.O. Box 83, Santa Cruz CA 95063-0083. (831)426-5557. Fax: (831)426-1161. E-mail: editor@stonesoup.com. Website: www.stonesoup.com. **Articles/Fiction Editor, Art Director:** Ms. Gerry Mandel. Magazine published 6 times/year. Circ. 20,000. "We publish fiction, poetry and artwork by children through age 13. Our preference is for work based on personal experiences and close observation of the world. Our audience is young people through age 13, as well as parents, teachers, librarians." Purpose in publishing works by young people: to encourage children to read and to express themselves through writing and art. Writer's guidelines available upon request with a SASE.

**Magazines** Uses animal, contemporary, fantasy, history, problem-solving, science fiction, sports, spy/mystery/adventure fiction stories. Uses 5-10 fiction stories (100-2,500 words); 5-10 nonfiction stories (100-2,500 words); 2-4 poems per issue. Does not want to see classroom assignments and formula writing. Buys 65 mss/year. Byline given. Pays on publication. Buys all rights. Pays $40 each for stories and poems, $40 for book reviews. Contributors also receive 2 copies. Sample copy $4. Free writer's guidelines. "We don't publish straight nonfiction, but we do publish stories based on real events and experiences." Send complete ms to editor. Will accept typewritten and legibly handwritten mss. Do not include SASE. Send copies, not originals. "If we are interested in publishing your work, you will hear from us in 6 weeks. If you don't hear from us, it means we could not use your work. Don't be discouraged. Try again."

**Artwork/Photography** Does not publish artwork other than illustrations. Pays $25 for color illustrations. Contributors receive 2 copies. Sample copy $4. Free illustrator's guidelines. Send color copies, not originals. If you would like to illustrate for *Stone Soup*, send us 2 or 3 samples (color copies) of your work, along with a letter telling us what kinds of stories you would like to illustrate. We are looking for artists who can draw complete scenes, including the background. Send submissions to editor. Include SASE. Responds in 6 weeks. All artwork must be by children through age 13.

**Tips** "Only work by young people through age 13 is considered. Whether your work is about imaginary situations or real ones, use your own experiences and observations to give your work depth and a sense of reality. Read a few issues of our magazine to get an idea of what we like."

### TEEN VOICES

80 Summer St., Boston MA 02110. (617)426-5505. Fax: (617)426-5577. Website: www.teenvoices.com. Magazine. Published quarterly. Teen writers only. Writer's guidelines available on request with SASE.

**Magazines** Submit mss to Chianti Cleggett, articles editor. Submit complete mss. Include SASE. Responds in 3-6 months.

**Artwork/Photography** Publishes artwork and photography by children. Looks for both b&w and color artwork; works on assignment only. Include SASE.

**Tips** "Check out teenvoices.com and view our topics. Almost anything a 13-19 year old teen is interested in is what we publish."

### WHAT IF?, Canada's Fiction Magazine for Teens

19 Lynwood Place, Guelph ON N1G 2V9 Canada . (519)823-2941. Fax: (519)823-8081. E-mail: Whatif@rogers.com . Magazine. Published bimonthly. Writer's guidelines available on request.

● See full listing for *What If?* in Magazines section.

**Magazines** 75% of magazine written by young people. Pays in copies. Submit mss to Mike Leslie, managing editor. Submit complete ms. Responds in 3 months.

**Artwork** Publishes artwork by young adults. Submit artwork to Jean Leslie, production manager. Include SASE for return of samples. Responds in 1 month.

**Tips** "Your chances for publication are better if you submit work other than contemporary fiction. We would like to see more science-fiction, fantasy, and other genres."

### THE WRITERS' SLATE

The Writing Conference, Inc., P.O. Box 669, Ottawa KS 66067. Phone/fax: (785)242-1995. E-mail: jbushman@writingconference.com. Website: www.writingconference.com. Magazine. Publishes 3 issues/year. *The Writers' Slate* accepts original poetry and prose from students enrolled in kindergarten-12th grade. The audience is students, teachers and librarians. Purpose in publishing works by young people: to give students the opportunity to publish and to give students the opportunity *to read* quality literature written by other students. Writer's guidelines available on request.

**Magazines** 90% of magazine written by young people. Uses 10-15 fiction, 1-2 nonfiction, 10-15 other mss per issue. Submit mss to Shelley McNerney, editor, 7619 Hemlock St., Overland Park KS 66204. Submit complete ms. Will accept typewritten mss. Responds in 1 month. Include SASE with ms if reply is desired.

**Artwork** Publishes artwork by young people. Bold, b&w, student artwork may accompany a piece of writing. Submit to Shelley McNerney, editor. Responds in 1 month.

**Tips** "Always accompany submission with a letter indicating name, home address, school, grade level and teacher's name. If you want a reply, submit a SASE."

# Agents & Art Reps

his section features listings of literary agents and art reps who either specialize in, or represent a good percentage of, children's writers and/or illustrators. While there are a number of children's publishers who are open to non-agented material, using the services of an agent or rep can be beneficial to a writer or artist. Agents and reps can get your work seen by editors and art directors more quickly. They are familiar with the market and have insights into which editors and art directors would be most interested in your work. Also, they negotiate contracts and will likely be able to get you a better deal than you could get on your own.

Agents and reps make their income by taking a percentage of what writers and illustrators receive from publishers. The standard percentage for agents is 10 to 15 percent; art reps generally take 25 to 30 percent. We have not included any agencies in this section that charge reading fees.

## WHAT TO SEND

When putting together a package for an agent or rep, follow the guidelines given in their listings. Most agents open to submissions prefer initially to receive a query letter describing your work. For novels and longer works, some agents ask for an outline and a number of sample chapters, but you should send these only if you're asked to do so. Never fax or e-mail query letters or sample chapters to agents without their permission. Just as with publishers, agents receive a large volume of submissions. It may take them a long time to reply, so you may want to query several agents at one time. It's best, however, to have a complete manuscript considered by only one agent at a time. Always include a self-addressed, stamped envelope (SASE).

For initial contact with art reps, send a brief query letter and self-promo pieces, following the guidelines given in the listings. If you don't have a flier or brochure, send photocopies. Always include a SASE.

For those who both write and illustrate, some agents listed will consider the work of author/illustrators. Read through the listings for details.

As you consider approaching agents and reps with your work, keep in mind that they are very choosy about who they take on to represent. Your work must be high quality and presented professionally to make an impression on them. For additional listings of art reps see *Artist's & Graphic Designer's Market* (Writer's Digest Books).

For an agent's perspective on children's publishing, see the Insider Report with **Jennie Dunham** of Dunham Literary on page 298.

**Information on agents and art reps listed in the previous edition but not included in this edition of *Children's Writer's & Illustrator's Market* may be found in the General Index.**

## AGENTS

### ADAMS LITERARY
295 Greenwich St., #260, New York NY 10007. (212)786-9140. Fax: (212)786-9170. E-mail: info@adamsliterary. com. Website: www.adamsliterary.com. **Contact:** Tracey Adams. Estab. 2004. Member of AAR and SCBWI. 20% of clients are new/previously unpublished writers. 100% of material handled is books for young readers.
- Prior to becoming an agent, Tracey Adams worked in the editorial and marketing departments at several children's publishing houses.

**Represents** Considers fiction, nonfiction, picture books, middle grade, young adult. "We place authors' work based on insight and experience. Adams Literary offers editorial guidance and marketing knowledge."

**How to Contact** Adams Literary is closed to unsolicited queries and submissions. Considers both new and established writers by referral or conferences only.

**Terms** Agent receives 15% commission on domestic sales; 20% on foreign sales. Offers written contract.

**Writers' Conferences** Will attend Bologna Book Fair in Bologna, Italy, in April 2006. Other conferences listed on website.

**Tips** "We represent authors, not books, so we enjoy forming long-term relationships with our clients. We work hard to be sure we are submitting work which is ready to be considered, but we respect the role of editors and don't over-edit manuscripts ourselves. Our style is assertive yet collaborative."

### BOOKS & SUCH
4788 Carissa Ave., Santa Rosa CA 95405. (707)538-4184. Fax: (707)538-4184. E-mail: janet@janetgrant.com. Website: www.janetgrant.com. **Contact:** Janet Kobobel Grant. Estab. 1996. Associate member of CBA. Represents 50 clients. 1% of clients are new/unpublished writers. Specializes in "the Christian booksellers market but places some projections in the general market."
- Before becoming an agent, Janet Kobobel Grant was an editor for Zondervan and managing editor for *Focus on the Family*.

**Represents** 8% juvenile books. Considers: nonfiction, fiction, picture books, young adult.

**How to Contact** Prefers e-mail queries (no attachments) and queries via postal mail with SASE. Considers simultaneous queries. Responds in 1 month to queries; 6 weeks to mss. Returns material only with SASE.

**Recent Sales** *Landon Snow and the Auctor's Riddle* (Barbour); *God Called a Girl* (Bethany); *Ten Minutes to Showtime* (Tommy Nelson).

**Needs** Actively seeking "material that delights and charms the reader. A fresh approach to a perennial topic is always of interest." Obtains new clients through recommendations and conferences.

**Terms** Agent receives 15% commission on domestic and foreign sales. Offers written contract. 2 months notice must be given to terminate contract. Charges for postage, photocopying, fax and express mail.

## An Organization for Agents

In some listings of agents you'll see references to AAR (The Association of Authors' Representatives). This organization requires its members to meet an established list of professional standards and code of ethics.

The objectives of AAR include keeping agents informed about conditions in publishing and related fields; encouraging cooperation among literary organizations; and assisting agents in representing their author-clients' interests. Officially, members are prohibited from directly or indirectly charging reading fees. They offer writers a list of member agents on their website. They also offer a list of recommended questions an author should ask an agent. They can be contacted at AAR, P.O. Box 237201, Ansonia Station NY 10003. E-mail: info@aar-online.org. Website: www.aar-online.org.

**Tips** "The heart of my motivation is to develop relationships with the authors I serve, to do what I can to shine the light of success on them, and to help be a caretaker of their gifts and time."

## BOOKSTOP LITERARY AGENCY
67 Meadow View Rd., Orinda CA 94563. Website: www.bookstopliterary.com. Seeking both new and established writers. Estab. 1983. 100% of material handled is books of young readers.
**Represents** Considers fiction, nonfiction, picture books, middle grade, young adult. "Special interest in Hispanic writers and illustrators for children."
**How to Contact** Send entire ms with SASE. Considers simultaneous submissions. Responds in 6 weeks. Responds and returns material only with SASE.
**Terms** Agent receives 15% commission on domestic sales. Offers written contract, binding for 1 year.

## ANDREA BROWN LITERARY AGENCY, INC.
1076 Eagle Dr., Salinas CA 93905. (831)422-5925. Website: www.andreabrownlit.com. **President:** Andrea Brown. Estab. 1981. Member of SCBWI and WNBA. 10% of clients are new/previously unpublished writers. Specializes in "all kinds of children's books—illustrators and authors."
- Prior to opening her agency, Andrea Brown served as an editorial assistant at Random House and Dell Publishing and as an editor with Alfred A. Knopf.
**Member Agents** Andrea Brown, president; Laura Rennert, senior agent; Caryn Wiseman, Jennifer Jaeger, Rob Welsh, associate agents.
**Represents** 98% juvenile books. Considers: nonfiction (animals, anthropology/archaeology, art/architecture/design, biography/autobiography, current affairs, ethnic/cultural interests, history, how-to, nature/environment, photography, popular culture, science/technology, sociology, sports); fiction (historical, science fiction); picture books, young adult.
**How to Contact** Query. Responds in 3 months to queries and mss. E-mail queries only.
**Needs** Mostly obtains new clients through recommendations, editors, clients and agents.
**Recent Sales** *Fire on Ice*, autobiography of Sasha Cohen (HarperCollins); Five Ancestors series, by Jeff Stone (Random House); *Downside Up*, by Neal Shusterman (Simon & Schuster).
**Terms** Agent receives 15% commission on domestic sales; 20% on foreign sales. Written contract.
**Writers' Conferences** Agents at Andrea Brown Literary Agency attend Austin Writers League; SCBWI; Columbus Writers Conference; Willamette Writers Conference; Orange County Conferences; Mills College Childrens Literature Conference (Oakland CA); Asilomar (Pacific Grove CA); Maui Writers Conference; Southwest Writers Conference; San Diego State University Writer's Conference; Big Sur Children's Writing Workshop (Director); BookExpo America/Writer's Digest Books Writing Conference.
**Tips** Query first. "Taking on very few picture books. Must be unique—no rhyme, no anthropomorphism. Do not call or fax queries or manuscripts. E-mail queires accepted. Check website for details."

## CURTIS BROWN, LTD.
Ten Astor Place., New York NY 10003. (212)473-5400. Fax: (212)598-0917. Seeking both new and established writers. Estab. 1914. Member of AAR. Signatory of WGA. SCBWI. **Staff:** Elizabeth Harding and Ginger Knowlton.
**Represents** Considers fiction, nonfiction, picture books, middle grade, young adult.
**How to Contact** Query with SASE. If a picture book, send only one picture book ms. Considers simultaneous queries. Returns material only with SASE. Obtains clients through recommendations from others, queries/solicitations, conferences.
**Terms** Agent receives 15% commission on domestic sales; 20% on foreign sales. Offers written contract. 75 days notice must be given to terminate contract.

## BROWNE & MILLER LITERARY ASSOCIATES, LLC
410 S. Michigan Ave., Suite 460, Chicago IL 60605. (312)922-3063. Fax: (312)922-1905. E-mail: mail@brownean dmiller.com. Website: www.browneandmiller.com. **Contact:** Danielle Egan-Miller, president. Prefers to work with established writers. Handles only certain types of work. Estab. 1971. Member of AAR, RWA, MWA. Represents 85+ clients. 5% of clients are new/previously unpublished writers. 15% of material handled is books for young readers.
- Prior to opening the agency, Danielle Egan-Miller worked as an editor.
**Represents** Considers primarily YA fiction, fiction, young adult. "We love great writing and have a wonderful list of authors writing YA in particular." Not looking for picture books, middle grade.
**How to Contact** Query with SASE. Accepts queries by e-mail. Considers simultaneous queries. Responds in 2-4 weeks to queries; 4-6 months to mss. Returns material only with SASE. Obtains clients through recommendations from others.
**Recent Sales** Sold 10 books for young readers in the last year.

**Terms** Agent receives 15% commission on domestic sales; 20% on foreign sales. Offers written contract. Offers written contract, binding for 2 years. 30 days notice must be given to terminate contract.

**Tips** ''We are very hands-on and do much editorial work with our clients. We are passionate about the books we represent and work hard to help clients reach their publishing goals.''

### DUNHAM LITERARY, INC.

156 Fifth Ave., Suite 625, New York NY 10010-7002. Website: www.dunhamlit.com. **Contact:** Jennie Dunham. Seeking both new and established writers but prefers to work with established writers. Estab. 2000. Member of AAR, signatory of SCBWI. Represents 50 clients. 15% of clients are new/previously unpublished writers. 50% of material handled is books of young readers.

**Represents** Considers fiction, picture books, middle grade, young adult. Most agents represent children's books or adult books, and this agency represents both. Actively seeking mss with great story and voice. Not looking for activity books, workbooks, educational books, poetry.

**How to Contact** Query with SASE. Consider simultaneous queries and submissions. Responds in 1 week to queries; 2 months to mss. Returns material only with SASE. Obtains clients through recommendations from others.

**Recent Sales** Sold 30 books for young readers in the last year. *Alice in Wonderland*, by Robert Sabuda (Little Simon); *If I Were A Lion*, illustrated by Heather Solomon (Atheneum); *Dahlia*, by Barbara McClintock (Farrar, Straus & Giroux); *Who Will Tell My Brother?*, by Marlene Carvell (Hyperion); *While You Were Out*, by Judy Irvin Kuns; *How I Found the Strong*, by Margaret McMullan.

**Terms** Agent receives 15% commission on domestic sales; 20-25% on foreign sales. Offers written contract. 60 days notice must be given to terminate contract.

**Fees** The agency takes expenses from the clients' earnings for specific expenses documented during the marketing of a client's work in accordance with the AAR (Association of Authors' Representatives) Canon of Ethics. For example, photocopying, messenger, express mail, UPS, etc. The client is not asked to pay for these fees up front.

### DWYER & O'GRADY, INC.

P.O. Box 790, Cedar Key FL 32625. (352)543-9307. Fax: (603)375-5373. **Contact:** Elizabeth O'Grady. Estab. 1990. Member of SCBWI. Represents 25 clients. Represents both writers and illustrators.

● Dwyer & O'Grady is currently not accepting new clients.

**Member Agents** Elizabeth O'Grady (children's books); Jeff Dwyer (children's books).

**Represents** 95% juvenile books. Considers: nonfiction, fiction, picture books, young adult.

**How to Contact** Does not accept unsolicited mss.

**Needs** Obtains new clients through referrals or direct approach from agent to writer whose work they've read.

**Recent Sales** Clients include: Kim Ablon Whitney, Tom Bodett, Odds Bodkin, James Rumford, Nat Tripp, Geoffrey Norman, Clemence McLaren, Lita Judge, Steve Schuch, Virginia Stroud, Natasha Tarpley, Zong-Zhou Wang, Peter Sylvada, Mary Azarian, E.B. Lewis, Rich Michelson, Barry Moser, Stan Fellows, Lynda Jones, Irving Toddy and Tom Sanders.

**Terms** Agent receives 15% commission on domestic sales; 20% on foreign sales. Offers written contract. Thirty days notice must be given to terminate contract. Charges for ''photocopying of longer manuscripts or mutually agreed upon marketing expenses.''

**Writers' Conferences** Agents from Dwyer & O'Grady attend Book Expo; American Library Association; Society of Children's Book Writers & Illustrators conferences.

### 🗍 EDUCATIONAL DESIGN SERVICES INC.

7238 Treviso Lane, Boynton Beach FL 33437. E-mail: linder.eds@juno.com. **Contact:** B. Linder. Handles only certain types of work. Estab. 1981. 80% of clients are new/previously unpublished writers.

**Represents** Considers text materials for K-12 market. ''We specialize in educational materials to be used in classrooms, in class sets.'' Actively seeking educational, text materials. Not looking for picture books, story books, fiction; no illustrators.

**How to Contact** Query with SASE or send outline and 1 sample chapter. Considers simultaneous queries and submissions if so indicated. Responds in 608 weeks to queries/mss. Returns material only with SASE. Obtains clients through recommendations from others, queries/solicitations, or through conferences.

**Recent Sales** *How to Solve Word Problems in Mathematics*, by Wayne (McGraw-Hill); *Reviewing U.S. & New York State History*, by Farran-Paci (Amsco); *Minority Report*, by Gunn-Singh (Scarecrow Education).

**Terms** Agent receives 15% commission on domestic sales; 25% on foreign sales. Offers written contract, binding until any party opts out. Terminate contract through certified letter.

### ETHAN ELLENBERG LITERARY AGENCY

548 Broadway, #5-E, New York NY 10012. (212)431-4554. Fax: (212)941-4652. E-mail: agent@ethanellenberg.c

om. Website: EthanEllenberg.com. **Contact:** Ethan Ellenberg or Michael Psaltis. Estab. 1983. Represents 80 clients. 10% of clients are new/previously unpublished writers. Children's books are an important area for us.
- Prior to opening his agency, Ethan Ellenberg was contracts manager of Berkley/Jove and associate contracts manager for Bantam.

**Represents** "We do a lot of children's books." Considers: nonfiction, fiction, picture books, young adult.

**How to Contact** Children's submissions—send full ms. Young adults—send outline plus 3 sample chapters. Accepts queries by e-mail; does not accept attachments to e-mail queries or fax queries. Considers simultaneous queries and submissions. Responds in 10 days to queries; 1 month to mss. Returns materials only with SASE . "See website for detailed instructions, please follow them carefully."

**Terms** Agent receives 15% on domestic sales; 20% on foreign sales. Offers written contract, "flexible." Charges for "direct expenses only: photocopying, postage."

**Tips** "We do consider new material from unsolicited authors. Write a clear letter with a succinct description of your book. We prefer the first three chapters when we consider fiction, but for children's book submissions, we prefer the full manuscript. For all submissions you must include SASE for return or the material is discarded. It's always hard to break in, but talent will find a home. We continue to seek natural storytellers and nonfiction writers with important books." This agency sold over 100 titles per year in the last 4 years, including the 2003 Caldecott winner *My Friend Rabbit*, by Eric Rohman.

## FLANNERY LITERARY
1155 South Washing St., Suite 202, Naperville IL 60540-3300. (630)428-2682. Fax: (630)428-2683. **Contact:** Jennifer Flannery. Estab. 1992. Represents 40 clients. 95% of clients are new/previously unpublished writers. Specializes in children's and young adult, juvenile fiction and nonfiction.
- Prior to opening her agency, Jennifer Flannery was an editorial assistant.

**Represents** 100% juvenile books. Considers: nonfiction, fiction, picture books, middle grade, young adult.

**How to Contact** Query. "No e-mail or fax queries, please." Responds in 2 weeks to queries; 5 weeks to mss.

**Needs** Obtains new clients through referrals and queries.

**Terms** Agent receives 15% commission on domestic sales; 20% on foreign sales. Offers written contract, binding for life of book in print, with 30-day cancellation clause. 100% of business is derived from commissions on sales.

**Tips** "Write an engrossing succinct query describing your work." Flannery Literary sold 20 titles in the last year.

## BARRY GOLDBLATT LITERARY AGENCY INC.
320 Seventh Ave., #266, Brooklyn NY 11215. (718)832-8787. Fax: (718)832-5558. E-mail: bgliterary@earthlink.net. **Contact:** Barry Goldblatt. Estab. 2000. Member of AAR, SCBWI. Represents 35 clients. 40% of clients are new/previously unpublished writers. 100% of material handled is books for young readers. Staff includes Barry Goldblatt (picture books, middle grade, and young adult novels).

**Represents** Considers picture books, fiction, middle grade, young adult.

**How to Contact** Send queries only; no longer accepting unsolicited ms submissions. Prefers to read material exclusively. Responds in 3 weeks to queries; 2 months to mss. Returns material only with SASE. Obtains clients through recommendations from others.

**Recent Sales** *Spy Mice: The Black Paw*, by Heather Vogel Frederick; *Funny Little Monkey*, by Andrew Auseon; *TTFN*, by Lauren Myracle.

**Terms** Agent receives 15% commission on domestic sales; 20% on foreign and dramatic sales.

**Tips** "I structure my relationship with each client differently, according to their wants and needs. I'm mostly hands-on, but some want more editorial input, others less. I'm pretty aggressive in selling work, but I'm fairly laid back in how I deal with clients. I'd say I'm quite friendly with most of my clients, and I like it that way. To me this is more than just a simple business relationship."

## ASHLEY GRAYSON LITERARY AGENCY
1342 18th St., San Pedro CA 90732. (310)514-0267. Fax: (310)514-1148. Seeking both new and established writers. Estab. 1976. Agency is member of AAR, SCBWI, SFWA, RWA. Represents 75 clients. 5-10% new writers. 25% books for young readers. Staff includes Ashley Grayson, young adult and middle grade; Carolyn Grayson, young adult and middle grade; Dan Hooker, young adult and middle grade.

**Represents** Handles nonfiction, fiction, middle grade, young adult. "We represent top authors in the field and we market their books to publishers worldwide." Actively seeking fiction of high commercial potential.

**How to Contact** Query with SASE. Accepts queries by mail. Considers sumultaneous queries. Responds 1-2 months after query, 2-3 months after ms. Returns mss only with SASE. Obtains new clients through recommendations from others, queries/solicitations, conferences.

**Recent Sales** Sold 25+ books last year. *Juliet Dove, Queen of Love*, by Bruce Coville (Harcourt); *Alosha*, by

Resources

# Jennie Dunham

*Stewarding good books through the business of publishing*

E very book lover remembers that special moment in her life when the magic took hold. For literary agent Jennie Dunham, that moment occurred when she was a child in Connecticut—and best-selling author Mary Higgins Clark visited her school.

"Not knowing about publishers and editors, I told her that I wanted to create books when I was older," Dunham says. "She inscribed the book of hers I bought, 'See you on the bestseller list.' Now as an agent, I've had several bestselling books. I happened to be at a conference where she spoke a few years ago, and I got to tell her that her encouragement helped lead me to publishing and that I have in my own way fulfilled her nurturing dream for me."

Today, her New York-based Dunham Literary represents a diverse list of clients, from pop-up wizard Robert Sabuda to adult novelist (and recent mid-grade novelist) Margaret McMullan. A collector of first edition children's books, Dunham believes in cultivating dreams for others.

"I believe that when we hear or read these stories as children, we carry them with us for the rest of our lives," Dunham says. "And that means we can access them whenever we need to inside of us throughout life. That's very important, so I feel like a steward caring for these books and acknowledging their worth."

Here Dunham offers her take on agenting and getting published in today's children's book business. For more on Jennie Dunham, pleasevisit www.dunhamlit.com.

**How is your agenting style different, if at all, from others in the children's book field?**
Some people think it's really important to go to the right parties. I'm all about really good writing: believable characters, engaging stories, distinct voice.

**You ask to be contacted first by query, even for picture books. What percentage of your query letters, would you guess, inspire you to ask to see the manuscript?**
My agency receives over 10,000 query letters per year, and there is no way that I can read that many manuscripts. I request less than 1% of those. I end up reading about 500-700 manuscripts per year, and of these I offer less than 1% representation. When I turn down an author, I'm not trying to say that the writing is bad. What I'm saying is that I don't have the passion to take this project on. It's a business of having a few clients who are lucrative rather than a lot of clients who each earn a small amount. So, one of the things I look for is an author who is a strong writer and who, as far as I can tell, will develop by concentrating on writing one truly remarkable book at a time. Previous experience with children or publica-

tion credentials get me interested in a children's book writer, and fresh story ideas and interesting, believable characters also pique my interest.

**Most authors, especially first-timers, shudder at the thought of going through all that fine print and legalese on book contracts. As an agent, do you actually look forward to this part of your job, or do your eyes glaze over like the rest of us?**
A contract states which rights for the book the author and publisher will each control. It's significant to both parties. While it doesn't have quite the thrill of making a deal, I derive satisfaction from protecting writers by negotiating a good contract. One way of thinking about a contract is that it's a puzzle and all the pieces have to fit together.

**What are the mistakes new authors or illustrators make when first breaking into the business? What advice can you offer?**
Trying to get a book published too soon, before the manuscript is really ready to go. Thinking that the agent or editor will fix it for the writer. Neglecting to research properly before submitting a manuscript.

While writing may be worthwhile, fun, cathartic (or not) for writers, publishing is a business, and writers should keep this in mind when pursuing publication.

Remember to accept criticism kindly. You might not like what you hear, but an editor or agent is taking time and energy to give you an opinion that comes with professional expertise. Learn how to be equally gracious when accepting praise. Whatever you hear, the focus is about making your book better, not about judging you or your writing talent.

If an editor cannot offer you more money or grant the terms you're requesting for the contract or send you on a 30-store tour (or whatever), don't take it personally. You may be the editor's favorite author or illustrator, but the editor must deliver a business decision made by the publisher.

Consider what is important to you and act on it in a level-headed way. When writing letters, remember to put your name and contact details on the letter as well as the date. Be clear and concise.

**A lot has been said about how the children's book field has gotten more and more like its older counterpart—books for grown-ups. What's your take on this? Did Harry Potter really change everything?**
Some of the changes have come from Harry Potter, but the trend to take children's books more seriously as a business had been coming for a while. One thing that Harry Potter has done is to make other agents think that the children's book market is big, so when I meet other agents who handle only adult books, I hear them say, "I'm thinking of getting into that area" a lot. Of course, Harry Potter has not changed the size of the average first-time picture book or middle grade advance, so I smile when agents say this to me. The difference is when someone tells me that they love children's books and how do they add that to their agency.

**You've been in the industry long enough to see some changes. How is the field different than when you first became an agent? What do you expect will be different about it in 10 or 15 years?**
Tightening each year. More and more it's important for an author to develop an identity and name recognition. It used to be fine to be "a children's book writer" and now I find myself pitching authors with more specific descriptions such as "a humorous picture book writer" or "an edgy young adult writer." I think this trend will continue.

*—Barb Odanaka*

Christopher Pike (TOR); *Across Amphitar*, by David Lubar (TOR); *Three Stones Back*, by Matt dela Pena (Delacorte). Also represents: J.B. Cheaney, Pam Smallcomb, Bruce Wetter.
**Terms** Agent receives 15% on domestic sales, 20% on foreign sales. Offers written contract. Contract binding for 1 year. 30 days notice must be given for termination of contract.
**Tips** "We do request revisions as they are required. We are long-time agents, professional and known in the business. We perform professionally for our clients and we ask the same of them."

## KIRCHOFF/WOHLBERG, AUTHORS' REPRESENTATION DIVISION
866 United Nations Plaza, #525, New York NY 10017. (212)644-2020. Fax: (212)223-4387. Website: www.kirchoffwohlberg.com. **Director of Operations:** John R. Whitman. Estab. 1930s. Member of AAR. Represents 50 authors. 10% of clients are new/previously unpublished writers. Specializes in juvenile through young adult trade books and textbooks.
**Member Agents** Liza Pulitzer-Voges (juvenile and young adult authors).
**Represents** 80% juvenile books, 20% young adult. "We are interested in any original projects of quality that are appropriate to the juvenile and young adult trade book markets. But we take on very few new clients as our roster is full."
**How to Contact** "Send a query that includes an outline and a sample; SASE required." Responds in 1 month to queries; 2 months to mss. Please send queries to the attention of Liza Pulitzer-Voges.
**Needs** "Usually obtains new clients through recommendations from authors, illustrators and editors."
**Terms** Agent receives standard commission "depending upon whether it is an author only, illustrator only, or an author/illustrator book." Offers written contract, binding for not less than 1 year.
**Tips** "Kirchoff/Wohlberg has been in business since 1930 and sold over 50 titles in the last year."

## BARBARA S. KOUTS, LITERARY AGENT
P.O. Box 560, Bellport NY 11713. (631)286-1278. **Contact:** Barbara Kouts. Currently accepting new clients. Estab. 1980. Member of AAR. Represent 50 clients. 10% of clients are new/previously unpublished writers. Specializes in children's books.
**Represents** 100% juvenile books. Considers: nonfiction, fiction, picture books, ms/illustration packages, middle grade, young adult.
**How to Contact** Accepts queries by mail only. Responds in 1 week to queries; 6 weeks to mss.
**Needs** Obtains new clients through recommendations from others, solicitation, at conferences, etc.
**Recent Sales** *Sacajawea*, by Joseph Bruchac (Harcourt); *Born Blue*, by Han Nolan (Harcourt); *Froggy Plays in the Band*, by Jonathan London (Viking).
**Terms** Agent receives 1 0% commission on domestic sales; 20% on foreign sales. Charges for photocopying.
**Tips** "Write, do not call. Be professional in your writing."

## GINA MACCOBY LITERARY AGENCY
P.O. Box 60, Chappaqua NY 10514. (914)238-5630. **Contact:** Gina Maccoby. Estab. 1986. Represents writers and illustrators of children's books.
**Represents** 50% juvenile books. Considers: nonfiction, fiction, young adult.
**How to Contact** Query with SASE. "Please, no unsolicited manuscripts." Considers simultaneous queries and submisssions. Responds to queries in 2 months. Returns materials only with SASE.
**Needs** Usually obtains new clients through recommendations from own clients and/or editors.
**Terms** Agent receives 15% commission on domestic sales; 25% on foreign sales. Charges for photocopying. May recover certain costs such as airmail postage to Europe or Japan or legal fees.
**Tips** This agency sold 15-20 titles last year including *Scorpia*, by Anthony Horowitz.

## BARBARA MARKOWITZ LITERARY AGENCY
P.O. Box 41709, Los Angeles CA 90041. **Contact:** Barbara Markowitz. Seeking both new and established writers. Estab. 1980. Member of SCBWI. Represents 12 clients. 80% of clients are new/previously unpublished writers. 50% of material handled is books for 8-11 year old, mid-level readers. Staff includes Judith Rosenthal (young adult, historical fiction); Barbara Markowitz (mid-level and young adult, contemporary fiction).
• Prior to opening her agency, Ms. Markowitz owned Barbara Bookstores in Chicago.
**Represents** Considers fiction, middle grade, young adult (11-15 year olds) historical fiction. Actively seeking contemporary and historical fiction no more than 35,000 words for 8-11 year olds and 11-15 year olds. Not looking for fable, fantasy, fairytales; no illustrated; no science fiction; no books about dogs, cats, pigs.
**How to Contact** Query with SASE or send outline and 3 sample chapters. Considers simultaneous queries and submissions. Responds in 1 week to queries; 6 weeks to mss. Returns material only with SASE. "If no SASE provided, I discard." Obtains new clients through recommendations from others, queries/solicitations.

**Recent Sales** *Letting Go of Bobby James*, by Valerie Hobbs (Frances Foster/FSG); *My Father Was a Corporate Werewolf*, by Henry Garfield (Richard Jackson/Atheneum).

**Terms** Agent receives 15% commission on domestic sales; 15% on foreign sales. Offers written contract, binding for 1 year. 1-month notice must be given to terminate contract. Charges clients for postage only.

**Tips** Markowitz agenting style is "very hands on. Yes, I read, critique, light edit, make/request revisions. It's a very personal small agency."

## MCINTOSH & OTIS, INC.

353 Lexington Ave., New York NY 10016. (212)687-7400. Fax: (212)687-6894. **Contact:** Edward Necarsulmer IV. Seeking both new and established writers. Estab. 1927. Member of AAR and SCBWI. 20% of clients are new/previously unpublished writers. 100% of material handled is books for young readers.

**Represents** Considers fiction, middle grade, young adult. "McIntosh & Otis has a long history of representing authors of adult and children's books. The children's department is a separate division." Actively seeking "books with memorable characters, distinctive voice, and a great plot." Not looking for educational, activity books, coloring books.

**How to Contact** Query with SASE. Exclusive submission only. Responds in 6 weeks. Returns material only with SASE. Obtains clients through recommendations from others or through conferences.

**Terms** Agent receives 15% commission on domestic sales; 20% on foreign sales.

**Writers' Conferences** Attends Bologna Book Fair, in Bologna Italy in April, SCBWI Conference in New York in February, and regularly attends other conferences and industry conventions.

**Tips** "No e-mail or phone calls!"

## MEWS BOOKS

20 Bluewater Hill, Westport CT 06880. (203)227-1836. Fax: (203)227-1144. E-mail: mewsbooks@aol.com. **Contact:** Sidney B. Kramer. Seeking both new and established writers. Estab. 1974. 50% of material handled is books for young readers. Staff includes Sidney B. Kramer and Fran Pollak.

- Previously Sidney Kramer was Senior Vice President and founder of Bantam Books, President of New American Library, Director and Manager of Corgi Books in London, and attorney.

**Represents** Considers nonfiction, fiction, picture books, middle grade, young adult. Actively seeking books that have continuity of character and story. Not looking for unedited, poorly written mss by authors seeking learning experience.

**How to Contact** Query with SASE, send outline and 2 sample chapters. Accepts queries by e-mail—no attachments. Prefers to read material exclusively. Responds in a few weeks to queries. Returns material only with SASE. Obtains clients through recommendations from others, clients through conferences.

**Recent Sales** Sold 10 books for young readers in the last year.

**Terms** Agent receives 15% commission on domestic sales; 20% on foreign sales. Offers written contract, binding for 1-2 years. "We never retain an unhappy author, but we cannot terminate in the middle of activity. If submission is accepted, we ask for $100 against all expenses. We occasionally make referrals to editing services."

## ERIN MURPHY LITERARY AGENCY

2700 Woodlands Village, #300-458, Flagstaff AZ 86001-7127. (928)525-2056. Closed to unsolicited queries and submissions. Considers both new and established writers, by referral or personal contact (such as conferences) only. Estab. 1999. Member of SCBWI. Represents 50 clients. 50% of clients are new/previously unpublished writers. 100% of material handled is books of young readers.

- Prior to opening her agency, Erin Murphy was editor-in-chief at Northland Publishing/Rising Moon. Agency is not currently accepting unsolicited queries or submissions.

**Represents** Fiction, nonfiction, picture books, middle grade, young adult.

**Terms** Agent receives 15% commission on domestic sales; 20% on foreign sales. Offers written contract. 30 days notice must be given to terminate contract.

**Recent sales** Sold 30 books for young readers in the last year. Recent sales: *The Boy Returns*, by Clay Morgan (Dutton); *Timothy Cox Will Not Change His Sox*, by Robert Kinerk (S&S/Paula Wiseman Books); *Not Norman*, by Kelly Bennett (Candlewick); *The Forging of the Blade*, by R.L. La Fevers (Dutton); *Life, Love, and the Pursuit of Freethrows*, by Janette Rallison (Walker); *L.O.S.T*, by Debbie Federveu and Susan Vaught (Llewellyn); *Stormwitch*, by Susan Vaught (Bloomsbury); *Mirror, Mirror*, by Dotti Enderle (Llewellyn).

## ALISON PICARD, LITERARY AGENT

P.O. Box 2000, Cotuit MA 02635. Phone/fax: (508)477-7192. E-mail: ajpicard@aol.com. **Contact:** Alison Picard. Seeking both new and established writers. Estab. 1985. Represents 50 clients. 40% of clients are new/previously unpublished writers. 20% of material handled is books for young readers.

• Prior to opening her agency, Alison Picard was an assistant at a large New York agency before co-founding Kidde, Hoyt & Picard in 1982. She became an independent agent in 1985.

**Represents** Considers nonfiction, fiction, a very few picture books, middle grade, young adult. "I represent juvenile and YA books. I do not handle short stories, articles, poetry or plays. I am especially interested in commercial nonfiction, romances and mysteries/suspense/thrillers. I work with agencies in Europe and Los Angeles to sell foreign and TV/film rights." Actively seeking middle grade fiction. Not looking for poetry or plays.

**How to Contact** Query with SASE. Accepts queries by e-mail with no attachments. Considers simultaneous queries and submissions. Responds in 2 weeks to queries; 4 months to mss. Returns material only with SASE. Obtains clients through queries/solicitations.

**Recent Sales** *Funerals and Fly Fishing*, by Mary Bartek (Henry Holt & Co.), *Stage Fright*, by Dina Friedman (Farrar Straus & Giroux), *The Lucky Stone*, by Dina Friedman (Simon & Schuster), *Celebritrees* and *The Peace Bell*, by Margi Preus (Henry Holt & Co.)

**Terms** Receives 15% commission on domestic sales; 20-25% on foreign sales. Offers written contract, binding for 1 year. 1-week notice must be given to terminate contract.

**Tips** "We currently have a backlog of submissions."

## PUBLISHERS GRAPHICS INC.

231 Judd Rd., Easton CT 06612-1025. (203)445-1511. Fax: (203)445-1411. Website: www.publishersgraphics.c om. **Contact:** Paige Gillies. Not currently seeking new clients. Estab. 1972. Member of SCBWI. Represents 10 clients. 100% of material handled is books for children.

**Represents** Illustrators. "Our specialty is honest service to clients and publishers. We have thirty years experience and know that personal contact beats hundreds of thousands in ad and marketing dollars."

**How to Contact** "My portfolio is closed. Do not send queries or mss."

**Recent Sales** *Runaway Pumpkin*, illustrated by S.D. Schindier (Scholastic); *Oh No, Gotta Go*, illustrated by G. Brian Karas (Putnam); *Pearl and Wagner*, illustrated by R.W. Alley (Dial).

**Terms** Agent receives 25% commission on domestic sales; 25% on foreign sales. Offers written contract, binding for 3 years with automatic renewal. 1 month notice must be given to terminate contract.

**Tips** "My interest is in the artistic development of individual artists to enhance their satisfaction with their work and the assignments they receive. The clients determine my level of involvement in their process and in their life. I am straightforward and pragmatic."

## WENDY SCHMALZ AGENCY

P.O. Box 831, Hudson NY 12534. (518)672-7697. Fax: (518)672-7662. E-mail: wendy@schmalzagency.com. **Contact:** Wendy Schmalz. Seeking both new and established writers. Estab. 2001. Member of AAR. Represents 30 clients. 10% of clients are new/previously unpublished writers. 50% of material handled is books for young readers.

• Prior to opening her agency, Wendy Schmalz was an agent for 23 years at Harold Ober Associates.

**Represents** Considers nonfiction, fiction, middle grade, young adult. Actively seeking young adult novels, middle grade novels. Not looking for picture books, science fiction or fantasy.

**How to Contact** Query with SASE. Accepts queries by e-mail. Considers simultaneous queries. Responds in 2 weeks to queries; 4-6 weeks to mss. Returns material only with SASE. Obtains clients through recommendations from others.

**Recent Sales** Sold 15 books for young readers in the last year.

**Terms** Agent receives 15% commission on domestic sales; 20% on foreign sales. Fees for photocopying and FedEx.

## STIMOLA LITERARY STUDIO

308 Chase Court, Edgewater NJ 07020. Phone/fax: (201)945-9353. E-mail: LtryStudio@aol.com. **Contact:** Rosemary B. Stimola. Seeking both new and established writers. Estab. 1997. Member of AAR, SCBWI, ALA. Represents 50+ clients. 40% of clients are new/previously unpublished writers. 85% of material handled is books for young readers.

• Prior to opening her agency Rosemary Stimola was an independent children's bookseller.

**Represents** Preschool through young adult, fiction and nonfiction. "Agency is owned and operated by a former educator and children's bookseller with a Ph.D. in Linguistics." Actively seeking "remarkable young adult fiction." Not looking for novelty books.

**How to Contact** Query with SASE or e-mail. Considers simultaneous queries. Responds in 3 weeks to queries; 4-6 weeks to mss. Returns material only with SASE. While unsolicited queries are welcome, most clients come through editor, agent, client referrals.

**Recent Sales** Sold 18 books for young readers in the last year. *Black & White*, by Paul Volponi (Viking/Penguin);

*Queen of Twilight*, by Lisa Papademetriou (Razorbill/Penguin); *A Grape and a Raisin*, by James Proimos (Dial/Penguin); *Julep O'Toole: Confessions of a Middle Child*, by Trudi Trueit (Dutton, Puffin/Penguin); *Mama Outside, Mama Inside*, by Dianna Hutts Aston (Henry Holt); *Gregor and the Curse of the Warmbloods*, by Suzanne Collins (Scholastic).

**Terms** Agent receives 15% commission on domestic sales; 20% on foreign sales (if subagents used). Offers written contract, binding for all children's projects. 60 days notice must be given to terminate contract. "Charges $85 one-time fee to cover expenses. Client provides all copies of submission. Fee is taken from first advance payment and is payable *only* if manuscript is sold."

**Writers' Conferences** Will attend: ALA Midwinter, BEA, London Book Fair, SCBWI-NJ Regional, SCBWI-Iowa Regional.

**Tips** "Agent is hands-on, no-nonsense. May request revisions. Does not edit but may offer suggestions for improvement. Well-respected by clients and editors. A firm but reasonable deal negotiator."

## ANN TOBIAS—A LITERARY AGENCY FOR CHILDREN'S BOOKS

520 E. 84th St., Apt. 4L, New York NY 10028. **Contact:** Ann Tobias. Seeking both new and established writers. Handles only certain types of work. Estab. 1988. Represents 25 clients. 50% of clients are new/previously unpublished writers. 100% of material handled is books for children.

- Prior to opening her agency, Ann Tobias worked as a children's book editor at Harper, William Morrow, Scholastic.

**Represents** Fiction, nonfiction, middle grade, picture books, poetry, young adult, young readers.

**How to Contact** Send entire ms for picture books; 30 pages and synopsis for longer works. No e-mail, fax or phone queries. Accepts simultaneous submissions. Responds to all queries accompanied by SASE; 2 months to mss. Returns material only with SASE. Obtains clients through recommendations from editors.

**Recent Sales** Sold 12 titles in the last year.

**Terms** Agent receives 15% commission on domestic sales; 20% on foreign sales.

**Tips** "Read at least 200 children's books in the age group and genre in which you hope to be published. Follow this by reading another 100 children's books in other age groups and genres so you will have a feel for the field as a whole."

## SCOTT TREIMEL NY

434 Lafayette St., New York NY 10003. (212)505-8353. Fax: (212)505-0664. E-mail: STY@Verizon.net. **Contact:** Scott Treimel. Estab. 1995. Represents 33 clients. 10% of clients are new/unpublished writers. Specializes in children's books, all genres: tightly focused segments of the trade. Member AAR, Author's Guild, SCBWI.

- Prior to opening his agency, Scott Treimel was an assistant to Marilyn E. Marlow of Curtis Brown; a rights agent for Scholastic, Inc.; a book packager and rights agent for United Feature Syndicate; the founding director of Warner Bros. Worldwide Publishing; a freelance editor; and a rights consultant for HarperCollins Children's Books.

**Represents** 100% juvenile books. Considers middle grade, young adult novels and ms/illustration packages. No religious books.

**How to Contact** Accepts queries by postal mail only. Query with SASE. For picture books, send entire ms (no more than 2). Does not accept queries by fax or e-mail. **No multiple submissions.** Requires "90-day exclusivity on all submissions." Responds to queries or submissions only with SASE, otherwise discards.

**Needs** Interested in seeing first chapter books, middle-grade fiction and teen fiction. Obtains most clients through recommendations. Prefers published authors and illustrators.

**Recent Sales** Sold 23 titles in the last year. *My Life as a Chicken*, by Ellen Kelley (Harcourt); *Dodgeball*, by Janice Repka (Dutton). *Please is a Good Word to Say*, by Barbara Joosse (Philomel); *A Pieplate in the Sky*, by Alice Low (Holiday House); *Playing in Traffic*, by Gail Giles (Roaring Brook Press).

**Terms** Agent receives 15-20% commission on domestic sales; 20-25% on foreign sales. Offers verbal or written contract, binding on a "contract-by-contract basis." Charges for photocopying, overnight/express postage, messengers and books ordered for subsidiary rights sales. Offers editorial guidance, if extensive charges higher commission.

**Writer's Conferences** Speaks at Society of Children's Book Writers & Illustrators Conferences, SouthWest Writers Workshop, Pike's Peak Writers Conference, Kindling Words Retreat, participates in local and national panel discussions.

**Tips** "Do not pitch; do not 'explain' the book market; do not call; let your work speak for itself."

## WECKSLER-INCOMCO

170 West End Ave., New York NY 10023. (212)787-2239. Fax: (212)496-7035. E-mail: jacinny@aol.com. **Contact:** Sally Wecksler. Estab. 1971. Represents 30 clients. 50% of clients are new/previously unpublished writers.

"However, I prefer writers who have had something in print." Specializes in nonfiction with illustrations (photos and art).

- Prior to becoming an agent, Sally Wecksler was an editor at *Publishers Weekly*; publisher with the international department of R.R. Bowker; international director at Baker & Taylor; and head of the international department at the Association of American Publishers.

**Member Agents** Joann Amparan-Close (general, children's books), S. Wecksler (general, foreign rights/co-editions, fiction, illustrated books, children's books).

**Represents** 25% juvenile books. Considers: nonfiction, fiction, picture books.

**How to Contact** Query with outline plus 3 sample chapters. Include brief bio. Responds in 1 month on queries; 3 months on mss.

**Needs** Actively seeking "illustrated books for adults or children with beautiful photos or artwork." Does not want to receive "science fiction or books with violence." Obtains new clients through recommendations from others and solicitations.

**Terms** Agent receives 15% commission on domestic sales; 20% on foreign sales. Offers written contract, binding for 3 years.

**Tips** "Make sure a SASE is enclosed. Send three chapters and outline, clearly typed or word processed manuscript, double-spaced, written with punctuation and grammar in approved style. *We do not want to receive presentations by fax or e-mail.*"

## WRITERS HOUSE

21 W. 26th St., New York NY 10010. (212)685-2400. Fax: (212)685-1781. Website: www.writershouse.com. Estab. 1974. Member of AAR. Represents 280 clients. 50% of clients were new/unpublished writers. Specializes in all types of popular fiction and nonfiction. No scholarly, professional, poetry or screenplays.

**Member Agents** Amy Berkower (major juvenile authors); Merrilee Heifetz (quality children's fiction); Susan Cohen (juvenile and YA authors and illustrators), Jodi Reamer (juvenile and young adult fiction and nonfiction); Steven Malk (quality YA fiction and picture books); Robin Rue (YA fiction); Rebecca Sherman (middle grad and YA fiction); Ginger Clark (children's fiction).

**Represents** 35% juvenile books. Considers: nonfiction, fiction, picture books, young adult.

**How to Contact** Query. Responds in 4-6 weeks on queries.

**Needs** Obtains new clients through recommendations from others.

**Terms** Agent receives 15% commission on domestic sales; 20% on foreign sales. Offers written contract, binding for 1 year.

**Tips** "Do not send manuscripts. Write a compelling letter. If you do, we'll ask to see your work."

## WRITERS HOUSE

(West Coast Office), 3368 Governor Dr., Suite 224F, San Diego CA 92122. (858)678-8767. Fax: (858)678-8530. **Contact:** Steven Malk.

- See Writers House listing above for more information.

**Represents** Nonfiction, fiction, picture books, young adult.

## WYLIE-MERRICK LITERARY AGENCY

1138 S. Webster St., Kokomo IN 46902. (765)459-8258. E-mail: smartin@wylie-merrick.com or rbrown@wylie-merrick.com. Website: www.wylie-merrick.com. **Contact:** Sharene Martin or Robert Brown. Works with new and established writers. Estab. 1999. Member of SCBWI and Romance Writers of America (RWA). Represents 22 clients. 20% of clients are new/previously unpublished writers. 30% of material handled is books for young readers. Staff includes Sharene Martin (children's and adult fiction and selected commercial nonfiction), Robert Brown (adult and young adult novels).

- Wylie-Merrick is currently not accepting queries from writers unless one of their member agents has met with the writer at a conference or unless he or she has been referred by an editor or another agent Wylie-Merrick has worked with in the past. Please visit www.wylie-merrick.com for updated submission policies, as they do change.

**Represents** Considers mainstream and genre fiction, nonfiction, picture books, middle grade, young adult.

**How to Contact** Currently obtaining clients through recommendations from other agent/editors and conferences only.

**Recent Sales** *Whiskey on the Rocks* (Llewellyn); *Blackbelly* (Bridge Works); *If You Were Not You* (Roaring Brook).

**Terms** Agent receives 15% commission on domestic sales; 20% on foreign sales. Offers written contract. Charges no fees prior to sale.

**Writers' Conferences** Attended in 2005: Willamette Writers Conference; SCBWI Southwest Texas Writers

Cruise; Oklahoma Writers' Federation Conference; Las Vegas Writers Conference; SCBWI Southern Breeze Writers Conference.

**Tips** "If you are writing for publication, you must always remember that the reader is king. If you are writing for yourself, we can't help you build your career in this industry."

## ART REPS

### ART FACTORY

(formerly Nachreiner Boie Art Factory), 925 Elm Grove Rd., Elm Grove WI 53122. (262)785-1940. Fax: (262)785-1611. E-mail: tstocki@artfactoryltd.com. Website: www.artfactoryltd.com. **Contact:** Tom Stocki. Commercial illustration representative. Estab. 1978. Represents 9 illustrators. 10% of artwork handled is children's book illustration. Currently open to illustrators seeking representation. Open to both new and established illustrators.
**Handles** Illustration.
**Recent Sales** Represents Tom Buchs, Tom Nachreiner, Todd Dakins, Linda Godfrey, Larry Mikec, Bill Scott, Amanda Aquino, Gary Shea, Terry Herman, Troy Allen.
**Terms** Receives 25-30% commission. Offers written contract. Advertising costs are split: 75% paid by illustrators; 25% paid by rep. "We try to mail samples of all our illustrators at one time and we try to update our website; so we ask the illustrators to keep up with new samples." Advertises in *Picturebook*, *Workbook*.
**How to Contact** For first contact, send query letter, tearsheets. Responds only if interested. Call to schedule an appointment. Portfolio should include tearsheets. Finds illustrators through queries/solicitations.
**Tips** "Have a unique style."

### ASCIUTTO ART REPS., INC.

1712 E. Butler Circle, Chandler AZ 85225. (480)899-0600. Fax: (480)899-3636. **Contact:** Mary Anne Asciutto. Children's illustration representative. Estab. 1980. Member of SPAR, Society of Illustrators. Represents 12 illustrators. 99% of artwork handled is children's book illustration. Specializes in children's illustration for books, magazines, posters, packaging, etc. Markets include: publishing/packaging/advertising.
**Recent Sales** *Bats*, *Sharks*, *Whales*, *Snakes*, illustrated by Henderson (Boyd's Mill's Press).
**Terms** Rep receives 25% commission. No geographic restrictions. Advertising costs are split: 75% paid by talent; 25% paid by representative. For promotional purposes, talent should provide "prints (color) or originals within an 8½×11 size format."
**How to Contact** Send printed materials, tearsheets, photocopies and/or ms in a SASE. Responds in 2 weeks. After initial contact, send appropriate materials if requested. Portfolio should include original art on paper, tearsheets, photocopies or color prints of most recent work. If accepted, materials will remain for assembly.
**Tips** In obtaining representation "be sure to connect with an agent who handles the kind of accounts you (the artist/writer) *want*."

### CAROL BANCROFT & FRIENDS

4 Old Millplain Rd., Danbury CT 06811. (203)730-8270. Fax: (203)730-8275. E-mail: artists@carolbancroft.com. Website: www.carolbancroft.com. **Owner:** Carol Bancroft. Illustration representative for children's publishing. Estab. 1972. Member of SPAR, Society of Illustrators, Graphic Artists Guild, SCBWI. Represents 40 illustrators. Specializes in illustration for children's publishing—text and trade; any children's-related material. Clients include Scholastic, Houghton Mifflin, HarperCollins, Dutton, Harcourt Brace.
**Handles** Illustration for children of all ages. Recently sold *Two Fools and a Horse*, by Sally Derby, illustrated by Robert Rayevsky (Marshal Cavendish); *Tanuki's Gift*, by Tim Myers, illustrated by Robert Roth (Marshal Cavendish); and *Sidewalk Chalk*, by Jamie McGillian, illustrated by Blanche Sims (Sterling Publishing Company).
**Terms** Rep receives 25-30% commission. Advertising costs are split: 75% paid by talent; 25% paid by representative. For promotional purposes, talent must provide "laser copies (not slides), tearsheets, promo pieces, good color photocopies, etc.; 6 pieces or more is best; narrative scenes and children interacting." Advertises in *RSVP*, *Picture Book*, *Directory of Illustration* .
**How to Contact** "Send 2-3 samples by e-mail only and include website address."

### SHERYL BERANBAUM

75 Scenic Dr., Warwick RI 02886. (401)737-8591. Fax: (401)739-5189. E-mail: sheryl@beranbaum.com. Website: www.beranbaum.com. Commercial illustration representative. Estab. 1985. Member of Graphic Artists Guild. Represents 17 illustrators. 75% of artwork handled is children's book illustration. Currently open to

illustrators seeking representation. Open to both new and established illustrators. Submission guidelines available by phone.

**Handles** Illustration. "My illustrators are diversified and their work comes from a variety of the industry's audiences."

**Terms** Receives 30% commission. Charges marketing-plan fee or Web-only fee. Offers written contract. Advertising costs are split: 75% paid by illustrators; 25% paid by rep. Requires Itoya portfolio; postcards only for promotion.

**How to Contact** For first contact, send direct mail flier/brochure, tearsheets, photocopies. Responds only if interested. Portfolio should include photocopies.

## SAM BRODY, ARTISTS & PHOTOGRAPHERS CONSULTANT

77 Winfield St., Apt. 4, E. Norwalk CT 06855-2138. Phone/fax: (203)854-0805 (for fax, add 999). E-mail: sambrody@bigplanet.com. **Contact:** Sam Brody. Commercial illustration and photography broker. Estab. 1948. Member of SPAR. Markets include: advertising agencies; corporations/client direct; design firms; editorial/magazines; publishing/books; sales/promotion firms.

**Handles** Consultant.

**Terms** Agent receives 30% commission. For promotional purposes, talent must provide back-up advertising material, i.e., cards (reprints, *Workbook*, etc.) and self-promos.

**How to Contact** For first contact, send bio, direct mail flier/brochure, tearsheets. Responds in 3 days or within 1 day if interested. After initial contact, call for appointment or drop off or mail in appropriate materials for review. Portfolio should include tearsheets, slides, photographs. Obtains new talent through recommendations from others, solicitation.

**Tips** Considers "past performance for clients that I check with and whether I like the work performed."

## PEMA BROWNE LTD.

11 Tena Place, Valley Cottage NY 10989. (845)268-0029. **Contact:** Pema Browne. Estab. 1966. Represents 4 illustrators. 15% of artwork handled is children's book illustration. Specializes in general commercial. Markets include: all publishing areas; children's picture books; advertising agencies. Clients include HarperCollins, Thomas Nelson, Bantam Doubleday Dell, Nelson/Word, Hyperion, Putnam. Client list available upon request.

**Handles** Fiction, nonfiction, picture books, middle grade, young adult, ms/illustration packages. Looking for "professional and unique" talent.

**Recent Sales** *Sweet Potato Pie*, by Kathleen Lindsey (Lee & Low); *Is a Worry Worrying You*, by Ferida Wolff (Tanglewood Press).

**Terms** Rep receives 30% illustration commission; 15% author commission. Exclusive area representation is required. For promotional purposes, talent must provide color mailers to distribute. Representative pays mailing costs on promotion mailings.

**How to Contact** For first contact, send query letter, direct mail flier/brochure and SASE. If interested will ask to mail appropriate materials for review. Portfolios should include tearsheets and transparencies or good color photocopies, plus SASE. Accepts queries by mail only. Obtains new talent through recommendations and interviews (portfolio review).

**Tips** "We are doing more publishing—all types—less advertising." Looks for "continuity of illustration and dedication to work."

## CATUGEAU: ARTIST AGENT, LLC

3009 Margaret Jones Lane, Williamsburg VA 23185. (757)221-0666. Fax: (757)221-6669. E-mail: chris@catugeau.com. Website: www.CATugeau.com. **Owner/Agent:** Chris Tugeau. Children's publishing trade book, mass market, educational. Estab. 1994. Member of SPAR, SCBWI, Graphic Artists Guild. Represents 40 illustrators. 95% of artwork handled is children's book illustration.

- Not actively accepting new artists.

**Handles** Illustration ONLY.

**Terms** Receives 25% commission. "Artists responsible for providing samples for portfolios, promotional books and mailings." Exclusive representation required in educational. Trade "house accounts" acceptable. Offers written contract. Advertises in *Picturebook*, *RSVP*, *Directory of Illustration*.

**How to Contact** For first contact, send SASE for sample return, direct mail flier/brochure, photocopies. No CDs. Responds ASAP. Finds illustrators through recommendations from others, conferences, personal search.

**Tips** "Do research, look at artists' websites, talk to other artists and buyers. Do make sure you're comfortable with personality of rep. Be professional yourse . . . know what you do best, and be prepared to give rep what they need to present you! Do have e-mail and scanning capabilities, too."

## CORNELL & MCCARTHY, LLC

2-D Cross Hwy., Westport CT 06880. (203)454-4210. Fax: (203)454-4258. E-mail: cmartreps@aol.com. Website:

www.cornellandmccarthy.com. **Contact:** Merial Cornell. Children's book illustration representatives. Estab. 1989. Member of SCBWI and Graphic Artists Guild. Represents 30 illustrators. Specializes in children's books: trade, mass market, educational.

**Handles** Illustration.

**Terms** Agent receives 25% commission. Advertising costs are split: 75% paid by talent; 25% paid by representative. For promotional purposes, talent must provide 10-12 strong portfolio pieces relating to children's publishing.

**How to Contact** For first contact, send query letter, direct mail flier/brochure, tearsheets, photocopies and SASE. Responds in 1 month. Obtains new talent through recommendations, solicitation, conferences.

**Tips** "Work hard on your portfolio."

## CREATIVE FREELANCERS, INC.

4 Greenwich Hills Drive, Greenwich CT 06831 (800)398-9541. Fax: (203)532-2927. Website: www.freelancers.c om. **Contact:** Marilyn Howard. Commercial illustration representative. Estab. 1988. Represents over 30 illustrators. "Our staff members have art direction, art buying or illustration backgrounds." Specializes in children's books, advertising, architectural, conceptual. Markets include: advertising agencies; corporations/client direct; design firms; editorial/magazines; paper products/greeting cards; publishing/books; sales/promotion firms.

**Handles** Illustration. Artists must have published work.

**Terms** Rep receives 30% commission. Exclusive area representation is preferred. Advertising costs are split: 75% paid by talent; 25% paid by representative. For promotional purposes, talent must provide "printed pages to leave with clients. Must provide scans of artwork." Advertises in *American Showcase, Workbook*.

**How to Contact** For first contact, send tearsheets or "whatever best shows work." Responds back only if interested.

**Tips** Looks for experience, professionalism and consistency of style. Obtains new talent through "word of mouth and website."

## DIMENSION

1500 McAndrews Rd. W, #217, Burnsville MN 55337. (952)201-3981. Fax: (952)892-1722. E-mail: jkeltes@dime nsioncreative.com. Website: www.dimensioncreative.com. **Contact:** Joanne Koltes. Commercial illustration representatiave. Estab. 1982. Member of MN Book Builder. Represents 12 illustrators. 45% of artwork handled is children's book illustration. Staff includes Joanne Koltes.

**Terms** Advertises in *Picturebook* and *Minnesota Creative*.

**How to Contact** Contact via phone or e-mail. Responds only if interested.

## DWYER & O'GRADY, INC.

P.O. Box 790, Cedar Key FL 32625-0790. (352)543-9307. Fax: (603)375-5373. E-mail: eogrady@dwyerogrady.c om. Website: www.dwyerogrady.com. **Contact:** Elizabeth O'Grady. Agents for children's artists and writers , "small career development agents." Estab. 1990. Member of Society of Illustrators, SCBWI, ABA. Represents 18 illustrators and 7 writers. Staff includes Elizabeth O'Grady, Jeffrey Dwyer. Specializes in children's books (middle grade and young adult). Markets include: publishing/books, audio/film.

● Dwyer & O'Grady is currently not accepting new clients.

**Handles** Illustrators and writers of children's books.

**Recent Sales** *See You Down the Road*, by Kim Ablon Whitney (Knopf Books for Young Readers); *Norman On the Last Frontier*, by Tom Bodett (Knopf); *Happy Feet*, by R. Michelson, illustrated by E.B. Lewis (Harcourt).

**Terms** Receives 15% commission domestic, 20% foreign. Additional fees are negotiable. Exclusive representation is required (world rights). Advertising costs are paid by representative.

**How to Contact** For first contact, send query letter by postal mail only.

## PAT HACKETT/ARTIST REP

7014 N. Mercer Way, Mercer Island WA 98040-2130. (206)447-1600. Fax: (206)447-0739. Website: www.pathac kett.com. **Contact:** Pat Hackett. Commercial illustration representative. Estab. 1979. Member of Graphic Artists Guild. Represents 12 illustrators. 10% of artwork handled is children's book illustration. Currently open to illustrators seeking representation. Open to both new and established illustrators.

**Handles** Illustration. Looking for illustrators with unique, strong, salable style.

**Recent Sales** Represents Bryan Ballinger, Kooch Campbell, Jonathan Combs, Eldon Doty.

**Terms** Receives 25-33% commission. Advertising costs are split: 75% paid by illustrators; 25% paid by rep. Illustrator must provide portfolios (2-3) and promotional pieces. Advertises in *Picturebook, Workbook*.

**How to Contact** For first contact, send query letter, tearsheets, SASE, direct mail flier/brochure. Responds only if interested. Wait for response. Portfolio should include tearsheets. Lasers OK. Finds illustrators through recommendations from others, queries/solicitations.

**Tips** "Send query plus 1-2 samples, either by regular mail or e-mail. I don't have time to visit websites at first contact."

## HANNAH REPRESENTS

14431 Ventura Blvd., #108, Sherman Oaks CA 91423. (818)378-1644. E-mail: hannahrepresents@yahoo.com. **Contact:** Hannah Robinson. Literary representative for illustrators. Estab. 1997. 100% of artwork handled is children's book illustration. Looking for established illustrators only.

**Handles** Manuscript/illustration packages. Looking for illustrators with book already under contract.

**Terms** Receives 15% commission. Offers written contract.

**How to Contact** For first contact, send SASE and tearsheets. Responds only if interested. Call to schedule an appointment. Portfolio should include photocopies. Finds illustrators through recommendations from others, conferences, queries/solicitations, international.

**Tips** "Present a carefully developed range of characterization illustrations that are world-class enough to equal those in the best children's books."

## HERMAN AGENCY

350 Central Park West, New York NY 10025. (212)749-4907. Fax: (212)662-5151. E-mail: HermanAgen@aol.com. Website: www.hermanagencyinc.com. **Contact:** Ronnie Ann Herman. Literary and artistic agency. Estab. 1999. Member of SCBWI. Represents 30 illustrators, 7 authors. 90% of artwork handled is children's book illustration and related markets. Currently open to illustrators and authors seeking representation who are widely published by trade publishing houses.

• Looking for established illustrators and authors only.

**Handles** Illustration, ms/illustration packages and mss.

**Recent Sales** Represents illustrators: Joy Allen, Dawn Apperley, Tom Arma, Durga Bernhard, Ann Catherine Blake, Mary Bono, Seymour Chwast, Pascale Constantin, Rebecca Dickinson, Doreen Gay-Kassel, Jan Spivey Gilchrist, Barry Gott, Steve Haskamp, Aleksey Ivanov, Gideon Kendall, Ana Martin Larranaga, Mike Lester, Scott McDougall, Bob McMahon, Alexi Natchev, Jill Newton, John Nez, Anna Nilsen, Betina Ogden, Tamara Petrosino, Lynn Rowe Reed, Michael Rex, Pete Whitehead, Wendy Rouillard, David Sheldon, Mark Weber, Nick Zarin-Ackerman, Deborah Zemke. Represents authors: Robin Friedman, Anne Foster, Deloris Jordan, Bobbi Miller, Jill Robinson, Brian Yansky.

**Terms** Receives 25% commission for illustration assignments; 15% for ms assignments. Artists pay 75% of costs for promotional materialabout $300 a year. Exclusive representation usually required. Offers written contract. Advertising costs are split: 75% paid by illustrator; 25% paid by rep. Advertises in *Picturebook*, *Directory of Illustration*, *Promo Pages*.

**How to Contact** For first contact, send samples, SASE, direct mail flier/brochure, tearsheets, photocopies. Responds in 1 month or less. I will contact you if I like your samples. Portfolio should include tearsheets, photocopies, books, dummies. Finds illustrators and authors through recommendations from others, conferences, queries/solicitations.

## HK PORTFOLIO

10 E. 29th St., 40G, New York NY 10016. (212)689-7830. E-mail: mela@hkportfolio.com. Website: www.hkportfolio.com. **Contact:** Mela Bolinao. Commercial illustration representative. Estab. 1986. Member of SPAR, Society of Illustrators and Graphic Artists Guild. Represents 43 illustrators. Specializes in illustration for juvenile markets. Markets include: advertising agencies; editorial/magazines; publishing/books.

**Handles** Illustration.

**Recent Sales** *Sweet Tooth*, illustrated by Jack E. Davis (Simon & Schuster); *Humprey, Albert, and the Flying Machine*, illustrated by John Manders (Harcourt); *Bubble Gum, Bubble Gum*, illustrated by Laura Huliska Beith (Little Brown/Megan Tingley); *Pajamas Anytime*, illustrated by Hiroe Nakata (Putnam); *Luther's Halloween*, (illustrated by Valeria Petrone (Viking).

**Terms** Rep receives 25% commission. No geographic restrictions. Advertising costs are split: 75% paid by talent; 25% paid by representative. Advertises in *Picturebook* and *Workbook*.

**How to Contact** No geographic restrictions. For first contact, send query letter, direct mail flier/brochure, tearsheets, slides, photographs or color copies and SASE. Responds in 1 week. After initial contact, send in appropriate materials for review. Portfolio should include tearsheets, slides, photographs or photocopies.

## KIRCHOFF/WOHLBERG, ARTISTS' REPRESENTATION DIVISION

866 United Nations Plaza, #525, New York NY 10017. (212)644-2020. Fax: (212)223-4387. Website: www.kirchoffwohlberg.com. **Director of Operations:** John R. Whitman. **Artist's Representative:** Elizabeth Ford. Estab. 1930. Member of SPAR, Society of Illustrators, AIGA, Association of American Publishers, Bookbuilders of Boston, New York Bookbinders' Guild. Represents over 50 illustrators. Specializes in juvenile and young adult trade books and textbooks. Markets include: publishing/books.

**Handles** Illustration (juvenile and young adult).

**Terms** Rep receives 25% commission. Exclusive representation to book publishers is usually required. Advertising costs paid by representative ("for all Kirchoff/Wohlberg advertisements only"). Keeps some original work on file. Advertises in *Art Directors' Index*, *Society of Illustrators Annual*, children's book issues of *Publishers Weekly*.

**How to Contact** Please send all correspondence to the attention of Elizabeth Ford. For first contact, send query letter, "any materials artists feel are appropriate." Responds in 6 weeks. "We will contact you for additional materials." Portfolios should include "whatever artists feel best represents their work. We like to see children's illustration in any style. To see illustrators currently represented, visit website."

## LEVY CREATIVE MANAGEMENT
300 E. 46th St., Suite 8E, New York NY 10017. (212)687-6465. Fax: (212)661-4839. E-mail: info@levycreative.com. Website: www.levycreative.com. **Contact:** Sari Levy. Estab. 1998. Member of Society of Illustrators, Graphic Artists Guild, Art Directors Club. Represents 13 illustrators. 30% of artwork handled is children's book illustration. Currently open to illustrators seeking representation. Open to both new and established illustrators. Submission guidelines available on website.
**Handles** Illustration, ms/illustration packages.
**Recent Sales** Represents Alan Dingman, Marcos Chin, Thomas Fluharty, Max Gafe, Liz Lomax, Oren Sherman, Jason Tharp.
**Terms** Exclusive representation required. Offers written contract. Advertising costs are split: 75% paid by illustrators; 25% paid by rep. Advertises in *Picturebook*, *American Showcase*, *Workbook*, *Alternative Pick*, *Contact* .
**How to Contact** For first contact, send tearsheets, photocopies, SASE. "See website for submission guidelines." Responds only if interested. Portfolio should include professionally presented materials. Finds illustrators through recommendations from others, word of mouth, competitions.

## LINDGREN & SMITH
630 Ninth Ave., New York NY 10036. (212)397-7330. Fax: (212)397-7334. E-mail: inquiry@lindgrensmith.com. Website: www.redpaintbox.com. **Contact:** Pat Lindgren, Piper Smith. Illustration representative. Estab. 1984. Member of SCBWI. Markets include children's books, advertising agencies; corporations; design firms; editorial; publishing.
**Handles** Illustration.
**Terms** Exclusive representation is required. Advertises in *The Workbook*, *The Black Book* , *Picture Book*. .
**How to Contact** For first contact, send postcard or e-mail a link to a website or send one JPEG file. Responds only if interested via e-mail or phone.
**Tips** "Check to see if your work seems appropriate for the group. We only represent experienced artists who have been professionals for some time. Only author/illustrators manuscripts."

## MARLENA AGENCY, INC.
145 Witherspoon St., Princeton NJ 08542. (609)252-9405. Fax: (609)252-1949. E-mail: marlena@verizon.net. Website: www.marlenaagency.com. Commercial illustration representative. Estab. 1990. Member of Society of Illustrators. Represents 30 illustrators. Staff includes Marlena Torzecka, Greta T'Jonck, Ella Lupo. Currently open to illustrators seeking representation. Open to both new and established illustrators. Submission guidelines available for #10 SASE.
**Handles** Illustration.
**Recent Sales** *Pebble Soup*, by Marc Mongeau (Rigby); *Sees Behind Trees*, by Linda Helton (Harcourt Brace & Company); *New Orleans Band*, by Marc Mongeau (Scott Foresman); and *My Cat*, by Linda Helton (Scholastic). Represents a group of 30 international artists including Marc Mongeau, Gerard Dubois, Linda Helton, Paul Zwolak, Martin Jarrie, Serge Bloch, Hadley Hooper and Ferrucio Sardella.
**Terms** Exclusive representation required. Offers written contract. Requires printed portfolios, transparencies, direct mail piece (such as postcards) printed samples. Advertises in *Creative Blackbook*, *Work Book*.
**How to Contact** For first contact, send tearsheets, photocopies. Responds only if interested. Drop off or mail portfolio, photocopies. Portfolio should include tearsheets, photocopies. Finds illustrators through queries/solicitations, magazines and graphic design.
**Tips** "Be creative and persistent."

## THE NEIS GROUP
P.O. Box 174, 11440 Oak Dr., Shelbyville MI 49344. (269)672-5756. Fax: (269)672-5757. E-mail: neisgroup@wmis.net. Website: www.neisgroup.com. **Contact:** Judy Neis. Commercial Illustration representative. Estab. 1982. Represents 45 illustrators. 60% of artwork handled is children's book illustration. Currently open to illustrators seeking representation. Looking for established illustrators only.
**Handles** Illustration, photography and calligraphy/ms packages.

**Recent Sales** Represents Lyn Boyer, Pam Thomson, Dan Sharp, Terry Workman, Liz Conrad, Garry Colby, Clint Hansen, Don McLean, Julie Borden, Margo Burian, Eri ka LeBarre, Joel Spector, John White, Neverne Covington , Ruth Pettis , Matt LeBarres.

**Terms** Receives 25% commission. Advertising costs are split: 75% paid by illustrator; 25% paid by rep. "I prefer porfolios on CD, color printouts and e-mail capabilities whenever possible." Advertises in *Picturebook*, *American Showcase* , *Creative Black Book*, and *Directory of Illustration*.

**How to Contact** For first contact, send bio, tearsheets, direct mail flier/brochure. Responds only if interested. After initial contact, drop off portfolio of nonreturnables. Portfolio should include tearsheets, photocopies. Obtains new talent through recommendations from others and queries/solicitations.

## WANDA NOWAK/CREATIVE ILLUSTRATORS AGENCY

231 E. 76th St., 5D, New York NY 10021. (212)535-0438, ext. 1624. Fax: (212)535-1629. E-mail: wandanowak@a ol.com. Website: www.wandanow.com. **Contact:** Wanda Nowak. Commercial illustration representative. Estab. 1996. Member of Graphic Artists Guild. Represents 20 illustrators. 50% of artwork handled is children's book illustration. Staff includes Wanda Nowak. Open to both new and established illustrators.

**Handles** Illustration. Looking for "unique, individual style."

**Recent Sales** Represents Martin Matje, Emilie Chollat, Herve Blandon, Thea Kliros, Pierre Pratt, Frederique Bertrand, Ilja Bereznickas, Boris Kulikov, Yayo, Laurence Cleyet-Merle, E. Kerner, Ellen Usdin, Marie Lafrance.

**Terms** Receives 30% commission. Exclusive representation required. Offers written contract. Advertising costs are split: 70% paid by illustrators; 30% paid by rep. Advertises in *Picturebook*, *Workbook*, *The Alternative Pick*, *Black Book*.

**How to Contact** For first contact, send SASE. Responds only if interested. Drop off portfolio. Portfolio should include tearsheets. Finds illustrators through recommendations from others, sourcebooks like *CA*, *Picture Book*, *Black Book*, exhibitions.

**Tips** "Develop your own style. Send a little illustrated story, which will prove you can carry a character in different situations with facial expressions, etc."

## THE PENNY & STERMER GROUP

2031 Holly Dr., Prescott AZ 86305. (928)708-9446 (West Coast); (212)505-9342 (East Coast). Fax: (928)708-9447. Website: www.pennystermergroup.com. **Contact:** Carol Lee Stermer. Commercial illustration representative. Estab. 1978.

## REMEN-WILLIS DESIGN GROUP

2964 Colton Rd., Pebble Beach CA 93953. (831)655-1407. Fax: (831)655-1408. E-mail: AnnRWillis@aol.com. Websites: www.annremenwillis.com or www.Picture-book.com. Specializes in childrens' book illustration trade/education. Estab. 1984. Member of SCBWI. Represents 15 illustrators. 100% of artwork handled is children's book illustration.

**Recent Sales** List of illustrators represented available upon request.

**Terms** Offers written contract. Advertising costs are split: 50% paid by illustrators; 50% paid by rep. Illustrator must provide small precise portfolio for promotion. Advertises in *Picturebook*, *Workbook*.

**How to Contact** For first contact, send tearsheets, photocopies. Responds in 1 week. Mail portfolio to set up an interview or portfolio review. Portfolio should include tearsheets, photocopies.

**Tips** "Send samples of only the type of work you are interested in receiving. Check out rep's forte first."

## RENAISSANCE HOUSE

9400 Lloydcrest Dr., Beverly Hills CA 90210. (800)547-5113. Fax: (310)860-9902. E-mail: info@renaissancehous e.net. Website: www.renaissancehouse.net. **Contact:** Raquel Benatar. Children's, educational, multicultural, and textbooks, advertising rep. Estab. 1991. Represents 80 illustrators. 95% of artwork handled is children's book illustration. Currently open to illustrators seeking representation. Open to both new and established illustrators.

**Handles** Illustration.

**Recent Sales** Maribel Suarez (Little Brown, Hyperion); Ana Lopez (Scholastic); Ruth Araceli (Houghton Mifflin); Vivi Escriva (Albert Whitman); Marie Jara (Sparknotes); Sheli Petersen (McGraw-Hill).

**Terms** Exclusive representation required. Illustrators must provide scans of illustrations. Advertises in *Picturebook*, *Directory of Illustration*, own website and *Catalog of Illustrators*.

**How to Contact** For first contact send tearsheets. Responds in 2 weeks. Finds illustrators through recommendations from others, conferences, direct contact.

## S.I. INTERNATIONAL

43 E. 19th St., New York NY 10003. (212)254-4996. Fax: (212)995-0911. E-mail: info@si-i.com. Website: www

.si-i.com. Commercial illustration representative. Estab. 1983. Member of SPAR, Graphic Artists Guild. Represents 50 illustrators. Specializes in license characters, educational publishing and children's illustration, digital art and design, mass market paperbacks. Markets include design firms; publishing/books; sales/promotion firms; licensing firms; digital art and design firms.
**Handles** Illustration. Looking for artists "who have the ability to do children's illustration and to do license characters either digitally or reflectively."
**Terms** Rep receives 25-30% commission. Advertising costs are split: 70% paid by talent; 30% paid by representative. "Contact agency for details. Must have mailer." Advertises in *Picturebook*.
**How to Contact** For first contact, send query letter, tearsheets. Responds in 3 weeks. After initial contact, write for appointment to show portfolio of tearsheets, slides.

## LIZ SANDERS AGENCY

2415 E. Hangman Creek Lane, Spokane WA 99224-8514. E-mail: liz@lizsanders.com. Website: www.lizsanders. com. Commercial illustration representative. Estab. 1985. Currently open to illustrators seeking representation. Open to both new and established illustrators.
**Handles** Illustration. Markets include publishing, entertainment, giftware and advertising.
**Recent Sales** Represents Craig Orback, Amy Ning, Tom Pansini, Chris Lensch, Kate Endle, Susan Synarski, Sue Rama, Suzanne Beaky, and more.
**Terms** Receives 30% commission against pro bono mailing program. Offers written contract. Advertises in *Picturebook, American Showcase, Workbook, Directory of Illustration*. No geographic restrictions.
**How to Contact** For first contact, send tearsheets, direct mail flier/brochure, color copies, non-returnables or e-mail. Responds only if interested. After initial contact, submit portfolio. Portfolio should include tearsheets, photocopies. Obtains new talent through recommendations from others, conferences and queries/solicitations, Literary Market Place.

## THOROGOOD KIDS

5 Dryden Street, Covent Garden, London WC2E 9NW England. +44(0) 20 8859 7507. Fax: +44(0) 20 8333 7677. E-mail: kids@thorogood.net. Website: www.thorogood.net/kids. Commercial illustration representative. Estab. 1978. Represents 30 illustrators. 50% of artwork is children"s book illustration. Staff includes Doreen Thorogood, Steve Thorogood, Tom Thorogood. Open to illustrators seeking representation. Accepting both new and established illustrators. Guidelines not available.
**Handles** Accepts illustration, illustration/ms packages.
**Recent Sales** Recent sales: Princess Diaries Series, (UK Editions) illustrated by Nicola Slater (Macmillan); *Night Before Christmas*, illustrated by Anne Yvonne Gilbert (Dorling Kindersley); *Goldilocks and The Three Bears*, illustrated by Anne Yvonne Gilbert (Ladybird); *Have You Seen Elvis?*, illustrated by Nicola Slater (Pan Macmillan); *Marsha Mellow & Me*, illustrated by Kanako Yuzuru (Random House); *Louis & Bobo Are Moving*, illustrated by Christiane Engel (Topaz Books); The Five Ancestors Series, illustrated by Kanako and Yuzuru (Hodder). Represents Nicola Slater, Anne Yvonne Gilbert, Olivier Latyk, Sophie Allsopp, Carol Morley, Philip Nicholson, Dan Hambe, Bill Dare, Christiane Engel, Robin Heighway-Bury.
**How to Contact** For first contact, send tearsheets, photocopies, SASE, direct mail flyer/brochure. After initial contact, we will contact the illustrator if we want to see the portfolio. Portfolio should include tearsheets, photocopies. Finds illustrators through queries/solicitations, conferences.
**Tips** "Be unique and research your market. Talent will win out!"

## GWEN WALTERS ARTIST REPRESENTATIVE

1801 S. Flagler Dr., #1202, W. Palm Beach FL 33401. (561)805-7739. E-mail: artincgw@aol.com. Website: www.gwenWaltersartrep.com. Commercial illustration representative. Estab. 1976. Represents 18 illustrators. 90% of artwork handled is children's book illustration. Currently open to illustrators seeking representation. Looking for established illustrators only.
**Handles** Illustration.
**Recent Sales** Sells to "All major book publishers."
**Terms** Receives 30% commission. Artist needs to supply all promo material. Offers written contract. Advertising costs are split: 70% paid by illustrator; 30% paid by rep. Advertises in *Picturebook, RSVP, Directory of Illustration*.
**How to Contact** For first contact, send tearsheets. Responds only if interested. Finds illustrators through recommendations from others.
**Tips** "Go out and get some first-hand experience. Learn to tell yourself to understand the way the market works."

## WENDYLYNN & CO.

504 Wilson Rd., Annapolis MD 21401. (401)224-2729. Fax: (410)224-2183. E-mail wendy@wendylynn.com.

Website: wendylynn.com. **Contact:** Wendy Mays. Children's illustration representative. Estab. 2002. Member of SCBWI. Represents 16 illustrators. 100% of artwork handled is children's illustration. Staff includes Wendy Mays, Janice Onken. Currently open to illustrators seeking representation. Open to both new and established illustrators. Submission guidelines available on website.

**Handles** Illustration.

**Terms** Receives 25% commission. Exclusive representation required. Offers written contract. Requires 15-20 images submitted on disk. Advertises in *Picturebook*.

How to Contact For first contact, e-mail or send color photocopies or tearsheets with bio; e-mail is preferred. Responds ASAP. After initial contact mail artwork on CD and send tearsheets. Portfolio should include a minimum of 15 images. Finds illustrators through recommendations from others and from portfolio reviews.

**Tips** "Show a character developed consistently in different settings in a series of illustrations interacting with other children, animals or adults ."

## DEBORAH WOLFE LTD.

731 N. 24th St., Philadelphia PA 19130.(215)232-6666. Fax: (215)232-6585. E-mail: inquiry@illustrationOnline.com. Website: www.illustrationOnline.com. **Contact:** Deborah Wolfe. Commercial illustration representative. Estab. 1978. Member of Graphic Artist Guild. Represents 30 illustrators. Currently open to illustrators seeking representation.

**Handles** Illustration.

**Terms** Receives 25% commission. Exclusive representation required. Offers written contract. Advertising costs are split: 75% paid by illustrators; 25% paid by rep. Advertises in *Picturebook, American Showcase, Directory of Illustration, The Workbook, The Black Book*.

**How to Contact** Responds in 2 weeks. Portfolio should include "anything except originals." Finds illustrators through queries/solicitations.

# Clubs & Organizations

C ontacts made through organizations such as the ones listed in this section can be quite beneficial for children's writers and illustrators. Professional organizations provide numerous educational, business, and legal services in the form of newsletters, workshops, or seminars. Organizations can provide tips about how to be a more successful writer or artist, as well as what types of business records to keep, health and life insurance coverage to carry, and competitions to consider.

An added benefit of belonging to an organization is the opportunity to network with those who have similar interests, creating a support system. As in any business, knowing the right people can often help your career, and important contacts can be made through your peers. Membership in a writer's or artist's organization also shows publishers you're serious about your craft. This provides no guarantee your work will be published, but it gives you an added dimension of credibility and professionalism.

Some of the organizations listed here welcome anyone with an interest, while others are only open to published writers and professional artists. Organizations such as the Society of Children's Book Writers and Illustrators (SCBWI, www.scbwi.org) have varying levels of membership. SCBWI offers associate membership to those with no publishing credits, and full membership to those who have had work for children published. International organizations such as SCBWI also have regional chapters throughout the U.S. and the world. Write or call for more information regarding any group that interests you, or check the websites of the many organizations that list them. Be sure to get information about local chapters, membership qualifications, and services offered.

**Information on organizations listed in the previous edition but not included in this edition of _Children's Writer's & Illustrator's Market_ may be found in the General Index.**

Resources

## AMERICAN ALLIANCE FOR THEATRE & EDUCATION

7475 Wisconsin Avenue, Suite 300A Bethesda, MD 20814. (301) 951-7977. E-mail: info@aate.com. Website: www.aate.com. Purpose of organization: to promote standards of excellence in theatre and drama education. We achieve this by assimilating quality practices in theater and theater education, connecting artists, educators, researchers and scholars with each other, and by providing opportunities for our members to learn, exchange and diversify their work, their audiences and their perspectives. Membership cost: $110 annually for individual in U .S . and Canada, $160 annually for organization, $60 annually for students, $70 annually for retired people; add $30 outside Canada and U .S. Annual conference. Newsletter published quarterly (on website only). Contests held for unpublished play reading project and annual awards in various categories. Awards plaque and stickers for published playbooks. Publishes list of unpublished plays deemed worthy of performance in newsletter and press release and staged readings at conference.

**How to Contact/Writers** Manuscripts should be 8-10 pages, or 2,000 words. Manuscripts may include lesson plans, interviews, Coda Essays, and reviews of computer software, books, and plays (as scripts or in performance). A three-sentence biographical statement should also be included with a SASE.

## AMERICAN SOCIETY OF JOURNALISTS AND AUTHORS

1501 Broadway, Suite 302, New York NY 10036. Website: www.asja.org. **Executive Director:** Brett Harvey. Qualifications for membership: "Need to be a professional nonfiction writer. Refer to website for further qualifications." Membership cost: Application fee—$25; annual dues—$195. Group sponsors national conferences; monthly workshops in New York City. Workshops/conferences open to nonmembers. Publishes a newsletter for members that provides confidential information for nonfiction writers.

## ARIZONA AUTHORS ASSOCIATION

P.O. Box 87857, Phoenix AZ 85080-7857. Fax: (623)780-0468. E-mail: info@azauthors.com. Website: www.aza uthors.com. **President:** Vijaya Schartz. Purpose of organization: to offer professional, educational and social opportunities to writers and authors, and serve as a network. Members must be authors, writers working toward publication, agents, publishers, publicists, printers, illustrators, etc. Membership cost: $45/year writers; $30/year students; $60/year other professionals in publishing industry. Holds regular workshops and meetings. Publishes bimonthly newsletter and Arizona Literary Magazine. Sponsors Annual Literary Contest in poetry, essays, short stories, novels, and published books with cash prizes and awards bestowed at a public banquet in Phoenix. Winning entries are also published or advertised in the *Arizona Literary Magazine.* Send SASE or view website for guidelines.

## ASSITEJ/USA

724 Second Ave South, Nashville, TN 37210. (615)254-5719. Fax: (615)254-3255. E-mail: usassitej@aol.com. Website: www.assitej-usa.org. Purpose of organization: to promote theater for children and young people by linking professional theaters and artists together; sponsoring national, international and regional conferences and providing publications and information. Also serves as U .S . Center for International Association of Theatre for Children and Young People. Different levels of membership include: organizations, individuals, students, retirees, libraries. *TYA Today* includes original articles, reviews and works of criticism and theory, all of interest to theater practitioners (included with membership). Publishes journal that focuses on information on field in U .S . and abroad.

## THE AUTHORS GUILD

31 E. 28th St., 10th Floor, New York NY 10016. (212)563-5904. Fax: (212)564-8363. E-mail: staff@authorsguild.o rg. Website: www.authorsguild.org. **Executive Director:** Paul Aiken. Purpose of organization: to offer services and materials intended to help authors with the business and legal aspects of their work, including contract problems, copyright matters, freedom of expression and taxation. Guild has 8,000 members. Qualifications for membership: Must be book author published by an established American publisher within 7 years or any author who has had 3 works (fiction or nonfiction) published by a magazine or magazines of general circulation in the last 18 months. Associate membership also available. Annual dues: $90. Different levels of membership include: associate membership with all rights except voting available to an author who has a firm contract offer or is currently negotiating a royalty contract from an established American publisher. "The Guild offers free contract reviews to its members. The Guild conducts several symposia each year at which experts provide information, offer advice and answer questions on subjects of interest and concern to authors. Typical subjects have been the rights of privacy and publicity, libel, wills and estates, taxation, copyright, editors and editing, the art of interviewing, standards of criticism and book reviewing. Transcripts of these symposia are published and circulated to members. The *Authors Guild Bulletin,* a quarterly journal, contains articles on matters of interest to writers, reports of Guild activities, contract surveys, advice on problem clauses in contracts, tran-

scripts of Guild and League symposia and information on a variety of professional topics. Subscription included in the cost of the annual dues.''

## CANADIAN SOCIETY OF CHILDREN'S AUTHORS, ILLUSTRATORS AND PERFORMERS, (CANSCAIP)

104-40 Orchard View Blvd., Toronto ON M4R 1B9 Canada. (416)515-1559. Fax: (416)515-7022. E-mail: office@canscaip.org. Website: www.canscaip.org. **Office Manager:** Lena Coakley. Purpose of organization: development of Canadian children's culture and support for authors, illustrators and performers working in this field. Qualifications for membership: Members—professionals who have been published (not self-published) or have paid public performances/records/tapes to their credit. Friends—share interest in field of children's culture. Membership cost: $75 ( Members dues), $35 ( Friends dues), $45 ( Institution dues). Sponsors workshops/conferences. Publishes newsletter: includes profiles of members; news round-up of members' activities countrywide; market news; news on awards, grants, etc; columns related to professional concerns.

## LEWIS CARROLL SOCIETY OF NORTH AMERICA

P.O. Box 204, Napa CA 94559. E-mail: hedgehog@napanet.net. Website: www.lewiscarroll.org/lcsna.html. **Secretary:** Cindy Watter. ''We are an organization of Carroll admirers of all ages and interests and a center for Carroll studies.'' Qualifications for membership: ''An interest in Lewis Carroll and a simple love for Alice (or the Snark for that matter).'' Membership cost: $20 (regular membership), $50 (contributing membership). The Society meets twice a year—in spring and in fall; locations vary. Publishes a quarterly newsletter, *Knight Letter*, and maintains an active publishing program.

## THE CHILDREN'S BOOK COUNCIL, INC.

12 W. 37th St., 2nd Floor, New York NY 10018. (212)966-1990. Fax: (212)966-2073. E-mail: info@cbcbooks.org. Website: www.cbcbooks.org. **President:** Paula Quint. Purpose of organization: A nonprofit trade association of children's and young adult publishers and packagers, CBC promotes the enjoyment of books for children and young adults and works with national and international organizations to that end. The CBC has sponsored Children's Book Week since 1945 and Young People's Poetry Week since 1999. Qualifications for membership: trade publishers and packagers of children's and young adult books and related literary materials are eligible for membership. Publishers wishing to join should contact the CBC for dues information. Sponsors workshops and seminars for publishing company personnel. Individuals wishing to receive the CBC semi-annual journal, *CBC Features* with articles of interest to people working with children and books and materials brochures, may be placed on CBC's mailing list for a one-time-only fee of $60. Sells reading encouragement posters and graphics and informational materials suitable for libraries, teachers, booksellers, parents, and others working with children.

## FLORIDA FREELANCE WRITERS ASSOCIATION

Cassell Network of Writers, P.O. Box A, North Stratford NH 03590. (603)922-8338. E-mail: FFWA@Writers-Editors.com. **Executive Director:** Dana K. Cassell. Purpose of organization: To act as a link between Florida writers and buyers of the written word; to help writers run more effective communications businesses. Qualifications for membership: ''None. We provide a variety of services and information, some for beginners and some for established pros.'' Membership cost: $90/year. Publishes a newsletter focusing on market news, business news, how-to tips for the serious writer. Annual *Directory of Florida Markets* included in FFWA newsletter section and electronic download. Publishes annual *Guide to CNW/Florida Writers*, which is distributed to editors around the country. Sponsors contest: annual deadline March 15. Guidelines on website. Categories: juvenile, adult nonfiction, adult fiction and poetry. Awards include cash for top prizes, certificate for others. Contest open to nonmembers.

## GRAPHIC ARTISTS GUILD

90 John St., Suite 403, New York NY 10038. (212)791-3400. E-mail: membership@gag.org. Website: www.gag.org. **President:** Molly Knappen. Purpose of organization: ''To promote and protect the economic interests of member artists. It is committed to improving conditions for all creators of graphic arts and raising standards for the entire industry.'' Qualification for full membership: 50% of income derived from the creation of artwork. Associate members include those in allied fields, students and retirees. Initiation fee: $25. Full memberships: $130, $175, $230, $290 (fees based on annual adjusted gross income); student membership: $55/year. Associate membership: $140/year. Publishes *Graphic Artists Guild Handbook, Pricing and Ethical Guidelines* (free to members, $34.95 retail). ''The Guild UAW Local 3030 is a national union that embraces all creators of graphic arts intended for presentation as originals or reproductions at all levels of skill and expertise. The long-range goals of the Guild are: to educate graphic artists and their clients about ethical and fair business practices; to educate graphic artists about emerging trends and technologies impacting the industry; to offer programs and

services that anticipate and respond to the needs of our members, helping them prosper and enhancing their health and security; to advocate for the interests of our members in the legislative, judicial and regulatory arenas; to assure that our members are recognized financially and professionally for the value they provide; to be responsible stewards for our members by building an organization that works efficiently on their behalf."

## HORROR WRITERS ASSOCIATION

P.O. Box 50577, Palo Alto CA 94303. E-mail: hwa@horror.org. Website: www.horror.org. **Office Manager:** Nancy Etchemendy. Purpose of organization: To encourage public interest in horror and dark fantasy and to provide networking and career tools for members. Qualifications for membership: Complete membership rules online at www.horror.org/memrule.htm. At least one low-level sale is required to join as an affiliate. Nonwriting professional who can show income from a horror-related field may join as an associate (booksellers, editors, agents, librarians, etc.) To qualify for full active membership, you must be a published, professional writer of horror. Membership cost: $65 annually in North America; $75 annually elsewhere. Holds annual Stoker Awards Weekend and HWA Business Meeting. Publishes monthly newsletter focusing on market news, industry news, HWA business for members. Sponsors awards. We give the Bram Stoker Awards for superior achievement in horror annually. Awards include a handmade Stoker trophy designed by sculptor Stephen Kirk. Awards open to nonmembers.

## INTERNATIONAL READING ASSOCIATION

800 Barksdale Rd., P.O. Box 8139, Newark DE 19714-8139.(302)731-1600, ext. 293. Fax: (302)731-1057. E-mail: pubinfo@reading.org. Website: www.reading.org. **Public Information Associate:** Beth Cady. Purpose of organization: "Formed in 1956, the International Reading Association seeks to promote high levels of literacy for all by improving the quality of reading instruction through studying the reading process and teaching techniques; serving as a clearinghouse for the dissemination of reading research through conferences, journals, and other publications; and actively encouraging the lifetime reading habit. Its goals include professional development, advocacy, partnerships, research, and global literacy development." **Open to students.** Basic membership: $36. Sponsors annual convention. Publishes a newsletter called "Reading Today." Sponsors a number of awards and fellowships. Visit the IRA website for more information on membership, conventions and awards.

## THE INTERNATIONAL WOMEN'S WRITING GUILD

P.O. Box 810, Gracie Station, New York NY 10028. (212)737-7536. **Executive Director and Founder:** Hannelore Hahn. IWWG is "a network for the personal and professional empowerment of women through writing." Qualifications: open to any woman connected to the written word regardless of professional portfolio. Membership cost: $45 annually. "IWWG sponsors several annual conferences a year in all areas of the U.S. The major conference is held in June of each year at Skidmore College in Saratoga Springs, NY. It is a week-long conference attracting over 500 women internationally." Also publishes a 32-page newsletter, *Network*, 6 times/year; offers dental and vision insurance at group rates, referrals to literary agents.

## ☒ LEAGUE OF CANADIAN POETS

920 Younnge St., Suite 608, Toronto ON M4W 3C7 Canada. (416)504-1657. Fax: (416)504-0096. Website: www.poets.ca. **Acting Executive Director:** Joanna Poblocka. President: Mary Ellen Csamer. Inquiries to Program Manager: Joanna Poblocka. The L.C.P. is a national organization of published Canadian poets. Our constitutional objectives are to advance poetry in Canada and to promote the professional interests of the members. Qualifications for membership: full—publication of at least 1 book of poetry by a professional publisher; associate membership—an active interest in poetry, demonstrated by several magazine/periodical publication credits; student—an active interest in poetry, 12 sample poems required; supporting—any friend of poetry. Membership fees: full—$175/year, associate—$60, student—$20, supporting—$100. Holds an Annual General Meeting every spring; some events open to nonmembers. "We also organize reading programs in schools and public venues. We publish a newsletter which includes information on poetry/poetics in Canada and beyond. Also publish the books *Poetry Markets for Canadians*; *Who's Who in the League of Canadian Poets*; *Poets in the Classroom* (teaching guide), and online publications. The Gerald Lampert Memorial Award for the best first book of poetry published in Canada in the preceding year and The Pat Lowther Memorial Award for the best book of poetry by a Canadian woman published in the preceding year. Deadline for awards: November 1. Visit www.poets.ca for more details. Sponsors youth poetry competition. Deadline: December 1 of each year. Visit www.youngpoets .ca for details.

## LITERARY MANAGERS AND DRAMATURGS OF THE AMERICAS

P.O. Box 728, New York NY 10014. E-mail: lmda@lmda.org or lmdanyc@hotmail.com. Website: www.lmda.o rg. LMDA is a not-for-profit service organization for the professions of literary management and dramaturgy. Student Membership: $25/year. Open to students in dramaturgy, performing arts and literature programs, or related disciplines. Proof of student status required. Includes national conference, New Dramaturg activities, local symposia, job phone and select membership meetings. Active Membership: $60/year. Open to full-time and part-time professionals working in the fields of literary management and dramaturgy. All privileges and services including voting rights and eligibility for office. Associate Membership: $45/year. Open to all performing arts professionals and academics, as well as others interested in the field. Includes national conference, local symposia and select membership meetings. Institutional Membership: $135/year. Open to theaters, universities, and other organizations. Includes all privileges and services except voting rights and eligibility for office. Publishes a newsletter featuring articles on literary management, dramaturgy, LMDA program updates and other articles of interest.

## THE NATIONAL LEAGUE OF AMERICAN PEN WOMEN
1300 17th St. N.W., Washington DC 20036-1973. (202)785-1997. E-mail: info@americanpenwomen.org. Website: www.americanpenwomen.org. **President:** Dr. Bernice Strand Reid. Purpose of organization: to promote professional work in art, letters, and music since 1897. Qualifications for membership: An applicant must show "proof of sale" in each chosen category—art, letters, and music. Membership cost: $40 ($10 processing fee and $30 National dues); Annual fees—$30 plus Branch/State dues. Different levels of membership include: Active, Associate, International Affiliate, Members-at-Large, Honorary Members (in one or more of the following classifications: Art, Letters, and Music). Holds workshops/conferences. Publishes magazine 6 times/year titled *The Pen Woman*. Sponsors various contests in areas of Art, Letters, and Music. Awards made at Biennial Convention. Biannual scholarships awarded to non-Pen Women for mature women. Awards include cash prizes—up to $1,000. Specialized contests open to nonmembers.

## NATIONAL WRITERS ASSOCIATION
10940 S. Parker Rd., #508, Parker CO 80138. (303)841-0246. Fax: (303)841-2607. E-mail: ExecDirSandyWhelchel @nationalwriters.com. Website: www.nationalwriters.com. **Executive Director:** Sandy Whelchel. Purpose of organization: association for freelance writers. Qualifications for membership: associate membership—must be serious about writing; professional membership—must be published and paid writer (cite credentials). Membership cost: $65 associate; $85 professional; $35 student. Sponsors workshops/conferences: TV/screenwriting workshops, NWAF Annual Conferences, Literary Clearinghouse, editing and critiquing services, local chapters, National Writer's School. Open to non-members. Publishes industry news of interest to freelance writers; how-to articles; market information; member news and networking opportunities. Nonmember subscription: $20. Sponsors poetry contest; short story contest; article contest; novel contest. Awards cash for top 3 winners; books and/or certificates for other winners; honorable mention certificate places 5-10. Contests open to nonmembers.

## NATIONAL WRITERS UNION
113 University Place, 6th Floor, New York NY 10003. (212)254-0279. E-mail: nwu@nwu.org. Website: www.nwu.org. **Open to students.** Purpose of organization: Advocacy for freelance writers. Qualifications for membership: "Membership in the NWU is open to all qualified writers, and no one shall be barred or in any manner prejudiced within the Union on account of race, age, sex, sexual orientation, disability, national origin, religion or ideology. You are eligible for membership if you have published a book, a play, three articles, five poems, one short story or an equivalent amount of newsletter, publicity, technical, commercial, government or institutional copy. You are also eligible for membership if you have written an equal amount of unpublished material and you are actively writing and attempting to publish your work." Membership cost: annual writing income under $5,000—$95/year or $55/½ year; annual writing income $5,000-25,000—$155/year or $85/½ year; annual writing income $25,000-50,000—$210/year or $110/½ year; over $50,000—$260/year or $135/½ year. Holds workshops throughout the country. Offers national union newsletter quarterly, *American Writer*, issues related to freelance writing and to union organization for members. Offers contract and grievance advice.

## PEN AMERICAN CENTER
588 Broadway, Suite 303, New York NY 10012. (212)334-1660. Fax: (212)334-2181. E-mail: pen@pen.org. Website: www.pen.org. Purpose of organization: "To foster understanding among men and women of letters in all countries. International PEN is the only worldwide organization of writers and the chief voice of the literary community. Members of PEN work for freedom of expression wherever it has been endangered." Qualifications for membership: "The standard qualification for a writer to join PEN is that he or she must have published, in the United States, two or more books of a literary character, or one book generally acclaimed to be of exceptional distinction. Editors who have demonstrated commitment to excellence in their profession (generally construed as five years' service in book editing), translators who have published at least two book-length literary translations, and playwrights whose works have been professionally produced, are eligible for membership.' An application form is available upon request from PEN Headquarters in New York. Candidates

for membership should be nominated by 2 current members of PEN. Inquiries about membership should be directed to the PEN Membership Committee. Friends of PEN is also open to writers who may not yet meet the general PEN membership requirements. PEN sponsors public events in New York and elsewhere. They include tributes by contemporary writers to classic American writers, dialogues with visiting foreign writers, symposia that bring public attention to problems of censorship and that address current issues of writing in the United States, and readings that introduce beginning writers to the public. PEN's wide variety of literary programming reflects current literary interests and provides informal occasions for writers to meet each other and to welcome those with an interest in literature. Events are all open to the public. The Children's Book Authors' Committee sponsors annual public events focusing on the art of writing for children and young adults and on the diversity of literature for juvenile readers. The PEN/Phyllis Naylor Working Writer Fellowship was established in 2001 to assist a North American author of fiction for children or young adults (e-mail: awards@pen.org). Pamphlets and brochures all free upon request. Sponsors several competitions per year. Monetary awards range from $2,000-35,000.

### 🌐 PLAYMARKET

P.O. Box 9767, Te Aro Wellington New Zealand. (64)4 3828462. Fax: (64)4 3828461. E-mail: info@playmarket.org.nz. Website: www.playmarket.org.nz. **Director:** Anna Cameron. Script Development Manager: Mark Amery. Administrator: Katrina Chandra. Purpose of organization: funded by Creative New Zealand, Playmarket serves as New Zealand's script advisory service and playwrights' agency. Playmarket offers script assessment, development and agency services to help New Zealand playwrights secure professional production for their plays. Playmarket runs the NZ Young Playwrights Competition, The Aotearoa Playwrights Conference and the Adam Playreading Series and administers the annual Bruce Mason Playwrighting Award. The organization's magazine, *Playmarket News*, is published biannually. Inquiries e-mail: info@playmarket.org.nz.

### PUPPETEERS OF AMERICA, INC.

P.O. Box 330, West Liberty IA 52776. (888)568-6235. Fax: (440)843-7867. E-mail: pofajoin@puppeteers.org. Website: www.puppeteers.org. **Membership Officer:** Monica Leo. Purpose of organization: to promote the art of puppetry as a means of communications and as a performing art. Qualifications for membership: interest in the art form. Membership cost: single adult, $50; youth member, $30 (6-17 years of age); full-time college student, $30; family, $70; couple, $60. Membership includes a bimonthly newsletter (*Playboard*). Discounts for workshops/conferences, access to the Audio Visual Library & Consultants in many areas of Puppetry. *The Puppetry Journal*, a quarterly periodical, provides news about puppeteers, puppet theaters, exhibitions, touring companies, technical tips, new products, new books, films, television, and events sponsored by the Chartered Guilds in each of the 8 P of A regions. *The Puppetry Journal* is the only publication in the United States dedicated to puppetry in the United States. Subscription: $40 (libraries only). The Puppeteers of America sponsors an annual National Day of Puppetry the last Saturday in April.

### SCIENCE-FICTION AND FANTASY WRITERS OF AMERICA, INC.

P.O. Box 877, Chestertown MD 21620. E-mail: execdir@sfwa.org. Website: www.sfwa.org. **Executive Director:** Jane Jewell. Purpose of organization: to encourage public interest in science fiction literature and provide organization format for writers/editors/artists within the genre. Qualifications for membership: at least 1 professional sale or other professional involvement within the field. Membership cost: annual active dues—$50; affiliate—$35; one-time installation fee of $10; dues year begins July 1. Different levels of membership include: active—requires 3 professional short stories or 1 novel published; associate—requires 1 professional sale; or affiliate—which requires some other professional involvement such as artist, editor, librarian, bookseller, teacher, etc. Workshops/conferences: annual awards banquet, usually in April or May. Open to nonmembers. Publishes newsletter, *The Bulletin*. Nonmember subscription: $18/year in U.S. Sponsors SFWA Nebula™ Awards for best published science fiction in the categories of novel, novella, novelette and short story. Awards trophy.

### SOCIETY OF CHILDREN'S BOOK WRITERS AND ILLUSTRATORS

8271 Beverly Blvd., Los Angeles CA 90048. (323)782-1010. E-mail: info@scbwi.org. Website: www.scbwi.org. **President:** Stephen Mooser. Executive Director: Lin Oliver. Chairperson, Board of Advisors: Sue Alexander. Purpose of organization: to assist writers and illustrators working or interested in the field. Qualifications for membership: an interest in children's literature and illustration. Membership cost: $60/year. Plus one time $15 initiation fee. Different levels of membership include: full membership—published authors/illustrators; associate membership—unpublished writers/illustrators. Holds 100 events (workshops/conferences) worldwide each year. National Conference open to nonmembers. Publishes a newsletter focusing on writing and illustrating children's books. Sponsors grants for writers and illustrators who are members.

## SOCIETY OF ILLUSTRATORS

128 E. 63rd St., New York NY 10021-7303. (212)838-2560. Fax: (212)838-2561. E-mail: info@societyillustrators. org. Website: www.societyillustrators.org. **Contact:** Terrence Brown, director. "Purpose is to promote interest in the art of illustration for working professional illustrators and those in associated fields." Cost of membership: Initiation fee is $250. Annual dues for nonresident members (those living more than 125 air miles from SI's headquarters): $287. Dues for Resident Artist Members: $475 per year; Resident Associate Members: $552." Artist Members shall include those who make illustration their profession and earn at least 60% of their income from their illustration. Associate Members are those who earn their living in the arts or who have made a substantial contribution to the art of illustration. This includes art directors, art buyers, creative supervisors, instructors, publishers and like categories. The candidate must complete and sign the application form which requires a brief biography, a listing of schools attended, other training and a résumé of his or her professional career. Candidates for Artist membership, in addition to the above requirements, must submit examples of their work." Sponsors contest. Sponsors "The Annual of American Illustration," which awards gold and silver medals. Open to nonmembers. Deadline: October 1. Also sponsors "The Original Art: The Best of Children's Book Illustration." Deadline: mid-August. Call for details.

## SOCIETY OF MIDLAND AUTHORS

% SMA, P.O. 10419, Chicago IL 60610-0419. Website: www.midlandauthors.com. **Membership Secretary:** Thomas Frisbie. Purpose of organization: create closer association among writers of the Middle West; stimulate creative literary effort; maintain collection of members' works; encourage interest in reading and literature by cooperating with other educational and cultural agencies. Qualifications for membership: membership by invitation only. Must be author or co-author of a book demonstrating literary style and published by a recognized publisher and be identified through residence with Illinois, Indiana, Iowa, Kansas, Michigan, Minnesota, Missouri, Nebraska, North Dakota, Ohio, South Dakota or Wisconsin. **Open to students** (if authors). Membership cost: $35/year dues. Different levels of membership include: regular—published book authors; associate, nonvoting—not published as above but having some connection with literature, such as librarians, teachers, publishers and editors. Program meetings held 5 times a year, featuring authors, publishers, editors or the like individually or on panels. Usually second Tuesday of October, November, February, March and April. Also holds annual awards dinner in May. Publishes a newsletter focusing on news of members and general items of interest to writers. Sponsors contests. "Annual awards in six categories, given at annual dinner in May. Monetary awards for books published which premiered professionally in previous calendar year. Send SASE to contact person for details." Categories include adult fiction, adult nonfiction, juvenile fiction, juvenile nonfiction, poetry, biography. No picture books. Contest open to nonmembers. Deadline for contest: January 30.

## SOCIETY OF SOUTHWESTERN AUTHORS

P.O. Box 30355, Tucson AZ 85751-0355. Fax: (520)296-5562. E-mail: wporter202@aol.com. Website: www.azst arnet.com/nonprofit/ssa. **President:** Chris Stern. Purpose of organization: to promote fellowship among members of the writing profession, to recognize members' achievements, to stimulate further achievement, and to assist persons seeking to become professional writers. Qualifications for membership: proof of publication of a book, articles, TV screenplay, etc. Membership cost: $25 initiation plus $25/year dues. The Society of Southwestern Authors has annual 2-day Writers' Conference held the last weekend in January (check website for updated information). Publishes a bimonthly newsletter, *The Write Word*, about members' activities, achievements, and up-to-the-minute trends in publishing and marketing. Yearly writing contest open to all writers. Applications are available in September. Send SASE to the P.O. Box, Attn: Contest.

## SOUTHWEST WRITERS

3721 Morris NE, Suite A, Albuquerque NM 87111.(505)265-9485. Fax: (505)265-9483. E-mail: swriters@aol.c om. Website: www.southwestwriters.org. "Non-profit organization dedicated to helping members of all levels in their writing. Members enjoy perks such as newtworking with professional and aspiring writers; sustantial discounts on mini-conferences, workshops, and annual SWW writing contest; monthly newsletter; two writing programs per month; critique groups, critique service (also for nonmembers); discounts at bookstores and other businesses; and health and dental group insurance for New Mexico residents." Cost of membership: Individual, $60/year, $100/2 years; Two People, $50 each/year; Student, $40/year; Outside U.S., $65/year; Lifetime, $750. For more information, contact See webstie for information.

## TEXT AND ACADEMIC AUTHORS ASSOCIATION

P.O. Box 76477, St. Petersburg, FL 33734-6477. (727)563-0020 . Fax: (727)563-0020. E-mail: TEXT@tampabay.r r.com. Website: www.taaonline.net. **President:** Michael Sullivan. Purpose of organization: to address the professional concerns of text and academic authors, to protect the interests of creators of intellectual property at all levels, and support efforts to enforce copyright protection. Qualifications for membership: all authors and prospective authors are welcome. Membership cost: $30 first year; $75 per year following years. Workshops/conferences: June each year. Newsletter focuses on all areas of interest to text authors.

## VOLUNTEER LAWYERS FOR THE ARTS

1 E. 53rd St., 6th Floor, New York NY 10022-4201. (212)319-ARTS, ext. 1 (the Art Law Line). Fax: (212)752-6575. E-mail: askvla@vlany.org. Website: www.vlany.org. **Executive Director:** Elena M. Paul. Purpose of organization: Volunteer Lawyers for the Arts is dedicated to providing free arts-related legal assistance to low-income artists and not-for-profit arts organizations in all creative fields. Over 800 attorneys in the New York area donate their time through VLA to artists and arts organizations unable to afford legal counsel. There is no membership required for our services. Everyone is welcome to use VLA's Art Law Line, a legal hotline for any artist or arts organization needing quick answers to arts-related questions. VLA also provides clinics, seminars and publications designed to educate artists on legal issues which affect their careers. Membership is through donations and is not required to use our services. Members receive discounts on publications and seminars as well as other benefits. Some of the many publications we carry are *All You Need to Know About the Music Business*; *Business and Legal Forms for Fine Artists, Photographers & Authors & Self-Publishers*; *Contracts for the Film & TV Industry*, plus many more.

## WESTERN WRITERS OF AMERICA, INC.

1012 Fair St., Franklin TN 37064-2718. (615)791-1444. Fax: (615)791-1444. E-mail: candywwa@aol.com or tncrutch@aol.com. Website: www.westernwriters.org. **Secretary/Treasurer:** James A. Crutchfield. **Open to students.** Purpose of organization: to further all types of literature that pertains to the American West. Membership requirements: must be a *published* author of Western material. Membership cost: $75/year ($90 foreign). Different levels of membership include: Active and Associate—the two vary upon number of books published. Holds annual conference. The 2005 conference held in Spokane WA, 2006 in Cody WY, and 2007 in Springfield MO. Publishes bimonthly magazine focusing on western literature, market trends, bookreviews, news of members, etc. Nonmembers may subscribe for $30 ($50 foreign). Sponsors contests. Spur awards given annually for a variety of types of writing. Awards include plaque, certificate, publicity. Contest open to nonmembers.

## WOMEN WRITING THE WEST

8547 E. Arapahoe Rd., #J-541, Greenwood Village CO 80112.(303)773-8349. E-mail: WWWAdmin@lohseworks.com. Website: www.womenwritingthewest.org. **Contact:** Joyce Lohse, Administrator. Purpose of organization: "to gather and unite writers and other literature professionals fo the Women's West. The heart of this organization's interest is in the written record of women fo the American West." Qualifications for membership: Open to all interested persons worldwide. **Open to students.** Cost of membership: annual membership dues $50. Along with the annual dues there is an option to become a sustaining member for $100. Publisher dues are $50. "Sustaining members receive a WWW enamal logo pin, prominent listing in WWW publications, and the knowledge that they are assiting the organization. Note: WWW membership also allows the choice of participation in our marketing marvel, the annual *WWW Catalog of Author's Books*." Holds an annual conference the third weekend in October. Publishes newsletter. "The focus of the WWW newsletter is current WWW activities; feature market, research, and experience articles of interest pertaining to American West literature; and member news." Sponsors annual WILLA Literary Award. "The WILLA Award is given in several catagories for outstanding literature featuring women's stories set in the West." The winner of a WILLA Literary Award receives $100 and a plaque at the annual conference luncheon. Contest open to non-members.

## WRITERS GUILD OF ALBERTA

11759 Groat Rd., Edmonton AB T5M 3K6 Canada . (780)422-8174. Fax : (780)422-2663. E-mail: mail@writersguild.ab.ca. Website: www.writersguild.ab.ca. Purpose of organization: to provide meeting ground and collective voice for the writers in Alberta. Membership cost: $60/year; $30 for seniors/students. Holds workshops/conferences. Publishes a newsletter focusing on markets, competitions, contemporary issues related to the literary arts (writing, publishing, censorship, royalties etc.). Nonmembers may subscribe to newsletter. Subscription cost: $60/year. Sponsors annual literary awards program in 7 categories (novel, nonfiction, short fiction, children's literature, poetry, drama, best first book). Awards include $1,000, leather-bound book, promotion and publicity. Open to nonmembers.

## WRITERS OF KERN

P.O. Box 6694, Bakersfield CA 93386-6694. (661)399-0423. E-mail: Nanab5@bak.rr.com. Website: http://home.bak.rr.com/writersofkern/. **Membership:** Bertie Warren. Open to published writers and any person interested in writing. Dues: $45/year, $20 for students. Types of memberships: professional, writers with published work; associate—writers working toward publication, affiliate—beginners and students. Monthly meetings held on the third Saturday of every month. Bi- or tri-annual writers' workshops, with speakers who are authors, agents, etc., on topics pertaining to writing; critique groups for several fiction genres, poetry, children's, nonfiction, journalism and screenwriting which meet bimonthly. Members receive a monthly newsletter with marketing tips, conferences and contests; access to club library; discount to annual CWC conference.

## ◘ WRITERS' FEDERATION OF NEW BRUNSWICK

Box 37, Station A, 404 Queen St., Fredericton NB E3B 4Y2 Canada. (506)459-7228. E-mail: wfnb@nb.aibn.com. Website: www.umce.ca/wfnb. **Executive Director:** Mary Hutchman. Purpose of organization: "to promote New Brunswick writing and to help writers at all stages of their development." Qualifications for membership: interest in writing. Membership cost: $40, basic annual membership; $45, family membership; $50, institutional membership; $100, sustaining member; $250, patron; and $1,000, lifetime member. Holds workshops/conferences. Publishes a newsletter with articles concerning the craft of writing, member news, contests, markets, workshops and conference listings. Sponsors annual literary competition. Categories: fiction, poetry, children's literature—3 prizes per category of $150, $75, $50; Alfred Bailey Prize of $400 for poetry ms; The Richards Prize of $400 for short novel, collection of short stories or section of long novel; The Sheree Fitch Prize for writing by young people (14-18 years of age). Contest open to nonmembers (residents of Canada only).

# Conferences & Workshops

**W**riters and illustrators eager to expand their knowledge of the children's publishing industry should consider attending one of the many conferences and workshops held each year. Whether you're a novice or seasoned professional, conferences and workshops are great places to pick up information on a variety of topics and network with experts in the publishing industry, as well as with your peers.

Listings in this section provide details about what conference and workshop courses are offered, where and when they are held, and the costs. Some of the national writing and art organizations also offer regional workshops throughout the year. Write or call for information.

Writers can find listings of more than 1,600 conferences (searchable by type, location, and date) at The Writer's Digest/Shaw Guides Directory to Writers' Conferences, Seminars, and Workshops—www.writersdigest.com/conferences.

Members of the Society of Children's Book Writers and Illustrators can find information on conferences in national and local SCBWI newsletters. Nonmembers may attend SCBWI events as well. SCBWI conferences are listed in the beginning of this section under a separate subheading. For information on SCBWI's annual national conferences, contact them at (323)782-1010 or check their website for a complete calendar of national and regional events (www.scbwi.org).

**Information on conferences listed in the previous edition but not this edition of *Children's Writer's & Illustrator's Market* may be found in the General Index.**

## SCBWI CONFERENCES

### SCBWI; ANNUAL CONFERENCES ON WRITING AND ILLUSTRATING FOR CHILDREN

8271 Beverly Blvd., Los Angeles CA 90048. (323)782-1010. Fax: (323)782-1892. E-mail: scbwi@scbwi.org. Website: www.scbwi.org. **Conference Director:** Lin Oliver. Writer and illustrator workshops geared toward all levels. **Open to students.** Covers all aspects of children's book and magazine publishing—the novel, illustration techniques, marketing, etc. Annual conferences held in August in Los Angeles and in New York in February. Cost of conference (LA): approximately $390; includes all 4 days and one banquet meal. Write for more information or visit website.

### SCBWI; BOLOGNA DAY-BEFORE CONFERENCE

(33)1 42 73 33 75 (GMT + 1), (323)782-1892 (PST). E-mail: erzsideak@scbwi.org. Website: www.scbwi.org or www.kidbookprosworld.com. **Contact:** Erzsi Deàk, SCBWI International Advisor Chairperson and Day-Before Conference Organizer. Annual writer and illustrator conference for children's book professionals held in association with the largest international children's book rights fair in the world, the Bologna Children's Book Fair ( www.bookfair.bolognafiere.it). **Open to students.** Conference held annually in April, the day before the Bologna International Children's Book Fair. "A craft-based, hands-on, full day of talks and workshops and an introduction to the Bologna International Book Fair." A chance to meet editors, art directors and agents before the rights fair gets going. Registration limited to 100. Cost of conference: "We try to keep it under $100 US." Attendance fee covers presentations and workshops; lunch, closing cocktail party (to which many industry professionals are invited). Manuscript and illustration critiques available by reservation for additional fee (deadline for manuscripts to be received is January 31, 2006). Registration at www.scbwi.org Events page; PayPal payment accepted. Register early and reserve affordable rooms at local bed & breakfast establishments. 2005 topics and speakers included: "Why I Love this Book & Published It," with guest publishers Anne Schwartz (Schwartz & Wade Books/Random House U.S.); Barry Cunningham (The Chicken House U.K.); Deirdre McDermott (Walker Books Ltd U.K.); Isabelle Bézard (Bayard Editions France); Jennifer Wingertzahn (Clarion Books U.S.); Neal Porter (Neal Porter Books/Roaring Brook U.S.). Workshops: "Picture the Book: From Text to Dummy," with artist/author G. Brian Karas (*Atlantic*, and many other titles); "The Craft of Revision: Examining Motifs, Compression, Structure, & Character," with award-winning author Franny Billingsley (*The Folk Keeper*, *Well Wished*); and "Book Reviewing: Where Pictures & Words Intersect," with author/reviewer Leonard Marcus (*Dear Genius* and many other books, *Parenting* magazine).

### SCBWI—ALASKA

P.O. Box 84988, Fairbanks AK 99708-4988. (907)474-2138. E-mail: stihlerunits@mosquitonet.com. Website: www.scbwialaska.org. **Conference Organizer:** Cherie Stihler .

- SCBWI Alaska holds a conference every other year. Their next event will take place in 2006. Watch their website for details.

### SCBWI—ARIZONA

P.O. Box 26384, Scottsdale AZ 85255-0123. E-mail: rascbwiaz@aol.com. Website: www.scbwi-az.org. **Regional Advisor:** Michelle Parker-Rock. SCBWI Arizona will offer a variety of workshops, retreats, conferences, meetings and/or industry-related events throughout 2005. Open to members and nonmembers, published and non-published. Registration to major events is usually limited. Pre-registration always required. Visit website, write or e-mail for more information.

### SCBWI—CANADA; ANNUAL EVENT

E-mail: webinfo@SCBWIcanada.org; noreen@SCBWIcanada.org. Website: www.scbwicanada.org. **Regional Advisor:** Noreen Violetta. Writer and illustrator conference geared toward all levels. Offers speakers forums, book sale, portfolio displays, one-on-one critiques and a silent auction. Annual conference held in May. SCBWI Canada also holds Fall Retreats.

### SCBWI—CAROLINAS; ANNUAL FALL CONFERENCE

(704)894-0472. E-mail: eld513@bellsouth.net. **Regional Advisor:** Earl L. Davis. Conference will be held September 23-25, 2005 at the Sheraton Airport Hotel, Charlotte, NC. Speakers include Bruce Coville, Mark McVeigh, Stephanie Tolan, Lynne Polvino. Fee: $90 for SCBWI members, $100 for nonmembers by August 25; fees $100 and $110 respectively after August 25. Hotel has special room rates available for conference attendees. Critiques for writers available, illustration portfolio display. Conference open to adult students.

### SCBWI—EASTERN PENNSYLVANIA; FALL PHILLY CONFERENCE

Willford Country Club, Exton PA. (610)282-5460. E-mail: CathyGio@aol.com. **Conference Director:** Cathy

Giordiano. "Conference focuses on writing skills, the publishing market, and finding inspiration. Keynote speaker will be Bruce Coville, and a panel of editors will answer questions. Manuscript and Portfolio critiques with editors available for an additional fee. Lunch. Registration is limited to 150. Information will be posted on the website in July." Cost: $100. Registration includes buffet.

## SCBWI—FLORIDA REGIONAL CONFERENCE

(305)387-1658. E-mail: LindaBernfeld@hotmail.com. **Regional Advisors:** Linda Rodriguez Bernfeld and Sandy Smith Rubiera. Writer and illustrator workshops geared toward beginner, intermediate, advanced and professional levels. Subjects to be announced. Conference takes place in mid-January. Location to be announced. Mid-Year Writing Workshop: Features sessions led by editors and authors on writing and illustrating picture books, mid-grade books, and young adult books. The workshop is planned for June 11, 2005 at the Swan Hotel in Disney World. Write or e-mail for more information.

## SCBWI—HOUSTON; ANNUAL CONFERENCE

P.O. Box 19487, Houston TX 77024. Website: www.scbwi-houston.org. Annual conference featuring picture books will be held February 2006. For more information on all events, check website.

## SCBWI—IOWA CONFERENCES

E-mail: hecklit@aol.com. Website: www.schwi-iowa.org. **Regional Advisor:** Connie Heckert. Writer and illustrator workshops geared toward all levels. "Usually speakers include 1-4 nationally known experts in the children's literature field. Our annual conference is a major event over a weekend. Recent speakers include Candace Fleming, Cheryl Klein, Jeremy and Nicole Tugeau, Robert Sabuda, Michael Green, Stephen Mooser, and Carolyn Yoder. We also offer a one-day program, or a retreat geared to a specific genre, i.e., novel revision." Annual conferences. Cost of conferences: $60 and up for 1-day events; under $200 for a weekend conference. Individual critiques and portfolio reviews are an extra charge. See website for more information.

## SCBWI—LOS ANGELES; EVENTS

Pacific Palisades CA 90272. (310)573-7318. Website: www.scbwisocal.org. **Co-regional Advisors:** Claudia Harrington. (claudiascbwi@earthlink.net) and Edie Pagliasotti (edie_pagliasotti@paramount.com). SCBWI—Los Angeles hosts five major events each year: **Writer's Day** (spring)—a one-day conference featuring speakers, workshops, and a writing contest; **Critiquenic** (summer)—an informal critiquing session for writers and illustrators held after a picnic lunch; **Working Illustrators Retreat** (summer)—a 3-day, 2-night retreat featuring an editor, illustrators, and workshops on layout, design, portfolio presentation, and book dummies; **Illustrator's Day** (fall)—a 1-day conference featuring speakers, workshops, and portfolio review/display; and **Working Writer's Retreat** (winter)—a 3-day, 2-night retreat featuring an editor, speakers, and intensive critiquing. See calendar of events on website for details and dates.

## SCBWI—METRO NEW YORK; PROFESSIONAL SERIES

P.O. Box 646, New York NY 10116-0646. (212)545-3719. E-mail: scbwi_metrony@yahoo.com. Website: www.home.nyc.rr.com/scbwimetrony. **Regional Advisors:** Vicky Shiefman and Nancy Lewis. Writer and illustrator workshops geared toward all levels. **Open to students.** The Metro New York Professional Series meets the second Tuesday of each month, from October to June, 7-9 p.m., at Teachers and Writers Collaborative, 5 Union Square West (14th/15th Streets), 7th floor. See website for details and registration information. Cost of workshop: $12 for SCBWI members; $15 for nonmembers. "We feature an informal, almost intimate evening with coffee, cookies, and top editors, art directors, agents, publicity and marketing people, librarians, reviewers and more."

## SCBWI—MICHIGAN; CONFERENCES

1144 Buckingham Rd., Haslett MI 48840. Website: www.Kidsbooklink.org. **Co-Regional Advisors:** Ann Finkelstein and Paula Payton. One-day conference held in June and 3-day fall conference held in October. One day, $80 includes registration and lunch. Weekend, $270 includes registration, 6 meals and room. Speakers TBA. See website for details on all upcoming events.

## SCBWI—MIDATLANTIC; ANNUAL FALL CONFERENCE

Mid-Atlantic SCBWI; P.O. Box 3215; Reston, VA 20195-1215. E-mail: sydney.dunlap@adelphia.net; midatlanticscbwi@tidalwave.net. Website: www.scbwi-midatlantic.org. **Conference Chair:** Sydney Dunlap. **Regional Advisor:** Ellen Braaf. Conference takes place Saturday, October 28, 2006 in Arlington, VA from 8 a.m to 5 p.m. For updates and details visit website. Registration limited to 200. Conference fills quickly. Cost: $75 for SCBWI members; $90 for nonmembers. Includes continental breakfast.

## SCBWI—MISSOURI; CHILDREN'S WRITER'S CONFERENCE

St. Charles County Community College, P.O. Box 76975, 103 CEAC, St. Peters MO 63376-0975. (314)213-8000, ext. 4108. E-mail: suebe@brick.net. Website: www.geocities.com/scbwimo. **Regional Advisor:** Sue Bradford Edwards. Writer and illustrator conference geared toward all levels. **Open to students.** Speakers include editors, writers, and other professionals. Topics vary from year to year, but each conference offers sessions for both writers and illustrators as well as for newcomers and published writers. Previous topics included: "What Happens When Your Manuscript is Accepted" by Dawn Weinstock, editor; "Writing—Hobby or Vocation?" by Chris Kelleher; "Mother Time Gives Advice: Perspectives from a 25 Year Veteran" by Judith Mathews, editor; "Don't Be a Starving Writer" by Vicki Berger Erwin, author; and "Words & Pictures: History in the Making," by author-illustrator Cheryl Harness. Annual conference held in early November. For exact date, see SCBWI website: www.scbwi.org or the events page of the Missouri SCBWI website. Registration limited to 75-90. Cost of conference includes one-day workshop (8 a.m. to 5 p.m.) plus lunch. Write for more information.

## SCBWI—NEW JERSEY; ANNUAL SPRING CONFERENCE

E-mail: njscbwi@newjerseyscbwi.com. Website: www.newjerseyscbwi.com. **Regional Advisor:** Kathy Temean. This day-long conference brings in editors from top houses, an agent, art director and art rep to speak to small groups about timely topics. With various writer workshops running throughout the day, all writers will find workshops to fit their level of expertise. Illustrators can attend special sessions with an art director and art rep. Published authors attending the conference are invited to sign and sell their books in the afternoon. Illustrators have the opportunity to display their artwork during the day. Editors will do one-on-one ms critiques and portfolio critiques will be available for the illustrators who attend for an additional cost. Continental breakfast and lunch is included with the cost of admission. Conference is traditionally held during the beginning of June at Seton Hall, but the venue has been changed to Caldwell College, Caldwell, New Jersey in order to accommodate more members. E-mail for more information or see www.scbwi.org/events.htm.

## SCBWI—NORCA (SAN FRANCISCO/SOUTH); RETREAT AT ASILOMAR

Website: www.scbwinorca.org. **Regional Advisor:** Jim Averbeck. While we welcome "not-yet-published" writers and illustrators, lectures and workshops are geared toward professionals and those striving to become professional. Program topics cover aspects of writing or illustrating picture books to young adult novels. Past speakers include editors, art directors, Newbery Award-winning authors, and Caldecott Award-winning illustrators. Annual conference, generally held last weekend in February; Friday evening through Sunday lunch. Registration limited to 100. Most rooms shared with one other person. Additional·charge for single when available. Desks available in most rooms. All rooms have private baths. Conference center is set in wooded campus on Asilomar Beach in Pacific Grove, California. Approximate cost: $365 for SCBWI members, $500 for nonmembers; includes shared room, 6 meals, ice breaker party and all conference activities. Vegetarian meals available. One full scholarship is available to SCBWI members. Registration opens at the end of September and the conference sells out very quickly. A waiting list is formed. "Coming together for shared meals and activities builds a strong feeling of community among the speakers and conferees. For more information, including exact costs and dates, visit our website in September."

## Ⓝ SCBWI—NORTHERN OHIO; ANNUAL CONFERENCE

225 N. Willow Street, Kent OH 44240-2561.(330)678-2900. E-mail: jdaigneau@sbcglobal.net. Website: www.scb wiohio.org. **Regional Advisor:** Jean Daigneau. Writer and illustrator conference for all levels. **Open to students.** "This conference is the premier marketing/networking event of the year for Ohio SCBWI. The emphasis is on current market trends; what the market is publishing; what the market is seeking; getting manuscripts/portfolios market-ready; and staying alive in the market post-publication. Additional emphasis is on meeting/networking with peers." Annual event. Workshop held in September—2005 event held September 10-11 at the Cleveland Airport Sheraton Hotel. Registration limited to to 200. Conference costs will be posted on website with registration information. SCBWI members recieve a discount. Additional fess for later registration and critiques or portfolio reviews may apply. Cost includes an optional Friday evening Opening Banquet with keynote speaker from 6-10 p.m. and Saturday event from 8:30 am. to 5 p.m., including continental breakfast, full-day conference with breakout sessions, headliner presentations, lunch, and panel discussions. Conference schedule includes four headliners and a total of 16 breakout session. Also offered is an Illustrator Showcase open to all illustrators at no additional cost.

## Ⓝ SCBWI—NORTHERN OHIO; ANNUAL WRITERS' RETREAT

225 N. Willow Street, Kent OH 44240-2561.(303)678-2900. E-mail: jdaigneau@sbcglobal.net. Website: www.scb wiohio.org. **Regional Advisor:** Jean Daigneau. Writer retreat for advanced, professional levels. This Workshop focuses on specific aspects of writing (i.e. the 2005 Retreat focused on revision and had separate tracks for novels and picture books). Annual event. Workshop held April 2006 at Atwood Lake Resort, Delroy, Ohio.

Registration is limited; varies from year to year. See website for details. (For 2005, limit was 45.) Retreat costs posted on website with registration information. Costs include hotel, meals, workshops and most materials. Additional fee for extra/optional material may apply. Reqirements for registration may vary from year to year. See website for details. (For 2005, completed mss were required for both tracks, though only 15 pages were reviewed for the Novel track.)

## SCBWI—OREGON CONFERENCES

E-mail: robink@sparpungent.com. Website: www.sparpungent.com/scbwior. **Regional Advisor:** Robin Koontz. Writer and illustrator workshops and presentations geared toward all levels. "We invite editors, teachers, agents, attorneys, authors, illustrators, and others in the business of writing and illustrating for children. They present lectures, workshops, and on-site critiques on a first-registered basis." Critique group network fro local group meetings and regional retreats; see website for details. Two main events per year: Writers and Illustrators Retreat: held near portland Thursday-Sunday the 2nd week of October. Cost of retreat: $325 plus critique fee included double occupancy and all meals. Spring Conference: held in the Portland area—1-day event in May. Cost for conference: about $95 included continental breakfast and lunch. Registration limited to 55 for Retreat and 300 for Conference. SCBWI Oregon is a regional chapter for SCBWI; SCBWI members receive a discount for all events.

## SCBWI—POCONO MOUNTAINS RETREAT

(610)255-0514. (610)255-5715. E-mail: Lkiernan@tacsolutions.com. Website: www.scbwiepa.org. **Regional Advisor:** Laurie Krauss Kiernan. Held in the spring at Sterling Inn, Sterling PA. Faculty addresses writing, illustration, and publishing. Registration limited to 75. Cost of retreat: about $350; includes tuition, room and board. For information and registration form, visit website.

## SCBWI—ROCKY MOUNTAIN; EVENTS

E-mail: denise@rmcscbwi.org or chris@rmcscbwi.org. Website: www.rmcscbwi.org. **Co-Regional Advisors:** Denise Vega and Christine Liu Perkins. SCBWI Rocky Mountain chapter will offer these upcoming events in 2006/2006: Fall Workshop, Oct 8-9, 2005; Golden, CO; Spring Workshop 2006 (date TBA); Summer Retreat 2006 (date TBA); variety of mini-workshops. For more information check website.

## SCBWI—SAN DIEGO; CHAPTER MEETINGS & WORKSHOPS

San Diego—SCBWI, San Diego. CA E-mail: ra-sd@sandiego-scbwi.org. Website: www.sandiego-scbwi.org. **Regional Advisor:** Arlene Bartle. Writer and illustrator meetings and workshops geared toward all levels. Topics vary but emphasize writing and illustrating for children. Cost $7-140 (check website). Write or e-mail for more information. "The San Diego chapter holds meetings the second Saturday of each month from September-May at the University of San Diego's Olin Hall, room 125, from 2-4 p.m.; cost $7 (members), $9 (nonmembers)." 2005 meeting schedule: January 8, February 12, March 12, April 9, May 14, September 10, October 8, November 12, and December 10. May 14 is a conference with cost on the website; location is the Quality Resort in Mission Valley off highway 8. 2006 meetings will continue to be the second Saturday. 2006 Workshop will feature picture book authors/illustrators Andrea Zimmerman and David Clemasha; date to be announced on the website. Season tickets include all regular chapter meetings during the season and newsletter issues for one calendar year as well as discounts on workshops/conferences. If interested in taking a class, one may also sign up for Inside Children's books through University of San Diego for an extension class, 2 units credit. Class begins in September at 12:30 and includes the regular chapter meetings; ends in May. Fees are USD's fee plus season ticket. Class sessions include regular chapter meetings. See the website for conference/workshop dates, times and prices.

## SCBWI—SOUTHERN BREEZE; SPRINGMINGLE '05

P.O. Box 26282, Birmingham AL 35260. E-mail: JSKittinger@bellsouth.net. Website: www.southern-breeze.org. **Regional Advisors:** Jo Kittinger and Mary Ann Taylor. Writer and illustrator workshops geared toward intermediate, advanced and professional levels. Speakers typically include agents, editors, authors, art directors, illustrators. **Open to college students.** Annual conference held in one of the three states comprising the Southern Breeze region, this year Alabama. Usually held in March. Registration limited. Cost of conference: approximately $225; includes Friday dinner, Saturday lunch and Saturday banquet. Pre-registration is necessary. Send a SASE to Southern Breeze, P.O. Box 26282, Birmingham AL 35260 for more information or visit website: www.southern-breeze.org.

## SCBWI—SOUTHERN BREEZE; WRITING AND ILLUSTRATING FOR KIDS '05

P.O. Box 26282, Birmingham AL 35260. E-mail: jskittinger@bellsouth.net. Website: www.southern-breeze.org. **Regional Advisors:** Jo Kittinger and Mary Ann Taylor. Writer and illustrator workshops geared toward all levels. **Open to college students.** All sessions pertain specifically to the production and support of quality children's literature. This one-day conference offers 30 workshops on craft and the business of writing. Picture books, chapter books, novels covered. Entry and professional level topics addressed by published writers and illustrators, editors and agents. Annual conference. Fall conference is held October 15, 2005. All workshops are limited to 25 or fewer people. Pre-registration is necessary. Some workshops fill quickly. This is a metropolitan area with many museums, shopping, zoo, gardens in a short driving distance. Also universities and colleges. Cost of conference: $90 for members, $105 for nonmembers, $95 for students; program includes key note speaker, 4 workshops (selected from 30), lunch, and Friday night dessert party. Mss critiques portfolio reviews are available for an additional fee; mss must be sent early. Registration is by mail ahead of time. Manuscript and portfolio reviews must be pre-paid and scheduled. Send a SASE to: Southern Breeze, P.O. Box 26282, Birmingham AL 35260 or visit web page. "Fall conference is always held in Birmingham, Alabama. Room block at a hotel near conference site (usually a school) is by individual reservation and offers a conference rate. Keynote speakers to be announced."

### 🌐 SCBWI—TAIWAN; EVENTS
Fax: (886)2363-5358. E-mail: scbwi_taiwan@yahoo.com. Website: http://groups.yahoo.com/group/scbwi_tai wan. **Regional Advisor:** Kathleen Ahrens. Writer and illustrator workshops geared toward intermediate level. Open to students. Topics emphasized: "In 2005 we held a Weekend Workshop for Writing Success with Australian author Jen McVeity at Eslite Bookstore. We also regularly hold critiques for writers and for illustrators, and invite authors and illustrators to give talks. In 2006, we hope to invite a U.S. editor for a weekend workshop. See our webpage for more information."

### SCBWI—VENTURA/SANTA BARBARA; FALL CONFERENCE
Simi Valley CA 93094-1389. (805)581-1906. E-mail: alexisinca@aol.com. Website: www.scbwisocal-org/calend ar. **Regional Advisor:** Alexis O'Neill. Writers conference geared toward all levels. "We invite editors, authors and author/illustrators and agents. We have had speakers on the picture book, middle grade, YA, magazine and photo essay books. Fiction and nonfiction are covered." Conference held October 29, 2005. Scheduled at California Lutheran University in Thousand Oaks, California in cooperation with the School of Education. Cost of conference $75; includes all sessions and lunch. E-mail for more information.

### SCBWI—WISCONSIN; FALL RETREAT FOR WORKING WRITERS
15255 Turnberry Dr., Brookfield WI 53005. (262)783-4890. E-mail: aangel@aol.com. Website: www.scbwi-wi-com. **Co-Regional Advisor:** Ann Angel. Writer and illustrator conference geared toward all levels. All our sessions pertain to children's writing/illustration. Faculty addresses writing/illustrating/publishing. Annual conference held October in Racine, WI. Registration limited to 70. Bedrooms have desks/conference center has small rooms—can be used to draw/write. Program has free time scheduled in. Cost of conference: $375 for SBCWI member; $450 for non-members; includes program, meals, lodging, ms critique. Write or go to our website for more information: www.geocities.com/scbwiwi.

## OTHER CONFERENCES

Many conferences and workshops included here focus on children's writing or illustrating and related business issues. Others appeal to a broader base of writers or artists, but still provide information that can be useful in creating material for children. Illustrators may be interested in painting and drawing workshops, for example, while writers can learn about techniques and meet editors and agents at general writing conferences. For more information visit the websites listed or contact conference coordinator.

### AEC CONFERENCE ON SOUTHERN LITERATURE
(formerly Chattanooga Conference on Southern Literature), P.O. Box 4203, Chattanooga TN 37405-0203. (423)267-1218. Fax: (423)267-1018. E-mail: info@artsedcouncil.org. Website: www.artsedcouncil.org. **Executive Director:** Susan Robinson. **Open to students.** Conference is geared toward readers. No workshops are held. Biennial conference held in April. Cost of conference: $70, $15 for students. Visit website for more information. Featured panel discussions, readings and commentaries for adults and students by today's foremost Southern writers.

### AMERICAN CHRISTIAN WRITERS CONFERENCE
P.O. Box 110390, Nashville TN 37222-0390. 1(800)21-WRITE or (615)834-0450. Fax: (615)834-7736. E-mail: detroitwriters@aol.com. Website: www.ACWriters.com. **Director:** Reg Forder. Writer and illustrator work-

shops geared toward beginner, intermediate and advanced levels. Classes offered include: fiction, nonfiction, poetry, photography, music, etc. Workshops held in 3 dozen U.S. cities. Call or write for a complete schedule of conferences. 75 minutes. Maximum class size: 30 (approximate). Cost of conference: $99, 1-day session; $169, 2-day session (discount given if paid 30 days in advance) includes tuition only.

### ANNUAL SPRING POETRY FESTIVAL
City College, New York NY 10031. (212)650-6343. E-mail: barrywal23@aol.com. **Director, Poetry Outreach Center:** Barry Wallenstein. Writer workshops geared to all levels. **Open to students.** Annual poetry festival. Festival held May 1 6, 200 6. Registration limited to 325. Cost of workshops and festival: free. Write for more information.

### ⊕ ANNUAL WRITERS' CONFERENCE
Chinook, Southdown Road, Shawford near Winchester, Hampshire England S021 2BY. 44(0)1962 712307. E-mail: writerconf@aol.com. Website: www.gmp.co.uk/writers/conference. **Conference Director:** Mrs. Barbara Large MBE. Writers' conference geared toward beginner, intermediate, advanced and professional levels. **Open to students.** ''We offer mini courses, lectures, and week-long workshops given by professional children's authors and the opportunity to book one-to-one appointments with commissioning editors, literary agents and children's authors. Conference and week-long workshop held in June. Writing facilities available: Writing and revision facilities available throughout the conference. Cost of conference: 215 to include weekend accommodation and meals. Write for more information. Writers are encouraged to enter the Writing For Children competition which is open to delegates and non-delegates. Adjudications given on all submitted work. Prizes awarded at the Writers' Awards Reception, in June 2005. Accommodation/meals located on the campus of King Alfred's University College.

### AUTUMN AUTHORS' AFFAIR . . . A WRITER'S RENDEZVOUS
1507 Burnham Ave., Calumet City IL 60409. (708)862-9797. E-mail: exchbook@aol.com. Website: www.rendezvousreviews.com. **President:** Nancy McCann. Writer workshops geared toward beginner, intermediate, advanced levels. **Open to students.** Sessions include children/teen/young adult writing, mysteries, romantic suspense, romance, nonfiction, etc. Annual workshop. Workshops held in October. Cost of workshop: $75 for 1 day, $125 for weekend, includes meals, workshops, speeches, gifts. Call, write, or e-mail for more information.

### BUTLER UNIVERSITY CHILDREN'S LITERATURE CONFERENCE
199 North Madison Ave., Greenwood IN 46142. (317)882-1090. E-mail: kidsink@indy.net. Website: www.butler.edu/childlit/about.htm. **Contact:** Shirley Mullin. Writer and illustrator conference geared toward all levels. **Open to college students.** Annual conference held the last Saturday of the month of January each year featuring top writers in the field of children's literature. Includes sessions such as Nuts and Bolts for Beginning Writers. Registration limited to 350. Cost of conference: $85; includes meals, registration, 3 plenary addresses, 2 workshops, book signing, reception and conference bookstore. Write for more information. ''The conference is geared toward three groups: teachers, librarians and writers/illustrators.''

### CAPE COD WRITER'S CONFERENCE
Cape Cod Writer's Center, P.O. Box 408, Osterville MA 02655. (508)420-0200. Fax: (508)420-0212. E-mail: writers@capecodwriterscenter.org. Website: www.capecodwriterscenter.org. Courses and workshops geared toward beginner, intermediate and professional levels. Courses include: fiction, nonfiction, poetry, journalism, screen writing, and writing for the young reader. Evening programs include speakers, a master class, panels, poetry, and prose reading. Manuscript evaluations and personal conferences with faculty are available. The Young Writers' Workshop for student interested in prose and poetry is held concurrent with the conference for 12- to 16-year-olds. Annual conference held third week in August on Cape Cod; 43rd annual conference held August 21-26, 2005. Cost of conference: $70 to register; $100 for courses.

### CAT WRITERS ASSOCIATION ANNUAL WRITERS CONFERENCE
% President Fran Pennock Shaw, 1761 Wickersha, Lancaster PA 17603. (717)397-9531. E-mail: franshaw1@juno.com. Website: www.catwriters.org.

### CELEBRATION OF CHILDREN'S LITERATURE
Montgomery College, 51 Mannakee St., Rockville MD 20850. (240)683-2589. Fax: (240)683-1890. E-mail: theguild@childrensbookguild.org. Website: www.childrensbookguild.org. Writer and illustrator workshops offered in conjunction with Montgomery County Public Schools, Montgomery County Public Libraries, Children's Book Guild and other local organizations is geared toward all levels. **Open to students.** New workshops and activities will be offered providing literary development strategies, elementary school readiness activities for pre-school-

ers, "Babies & Books" (The Connection), hands on dictation narration and dramatic expression in pre-reading, pre-writing skill development. Annual workshop. Registration limited to 200. Art display facilities, continuing education classrooms and large auditorium. Cost of workshop: approximately $75; includes workshops, box lunch and coffee. Contact Montgomery College for more information.

## ▐ CENTAURI ARTS RETREAT

19 Harshaw Ave., Toronto ON MGS 1X9 Canada. (416)766-7124. Fax: (416)766-7655. E-mail: directors@centaur i.on.ca. Website: www.centauriarts.com. **Directors:** Julie or Craig Hartley. Writer and illustrator workshops geared toward beginner and intermediate levels. **Open to students.** Must be at least 18. Sessions include: Starting to Write; Writing for the Children's Market; Writing Nonfiction; Poetry Express; A Writer's Workshop; Writing Short Fiction; Watercolor I & II; A Painter's Workshop. Annual workshop. Four one-week residential retreats in July and August. Registration limited to 12 people per course. Writing/art facilities available: Fully equipped art studio, library, numerous work spaces, pleasant workshop rooms with views, computer lab. Cost of workshop: $650 (CDN/approx. $550 U.S.); includes food and accomodation for 1 week in beautiful rural retreat, 1-week writing or art course, elective classes and recreational activities. Write for more information. "Centauri Arts is a residential arts retreat which runs each summer at a lovely rural location one hour north of Toronto in Ontario. Writers and artists have a chance to meet others from around the world."

## CENTRAL OHIO WRITERS OF LITERATURE FOR CHILDREN, A Conference for Teachers, Parents, Writers & Illustrators

933 Hamlet St., Columbus OH 43201-3595. (614)291-8644. E-mail: cowriters@mail.com. Website: www.sjms. net/conf. **Director:** Hari Ruiz. Writer and illustrator conference geared toward beginner, intermediate and advanced levels. **Also open to full-time high school and college students.** Annual conference. See website for 2006 dates. Registration limited to 1860. Cost of conference: students and seniors $70; all others early-bird before January; regular before March $110 (approximately); late after March $120. $40 additional charge for ms or portfolio evaluations and workshops for writers and illustrators led by published authors and illustrators. $30 additional charge for "pitch sessions" with literary agent. "Event will be an all-day affair with two keynote speakers."

## CHILDREN'S AUTHORS' BOOTCAMP

P.O. Box 231, Allenspark CO 80510. (303)747-1014. E-mail: CABootcamp@aol.com. Website: www.WeMakeWr iters.com. **Contact:** Linda Arms White. Writer workshops geared toward beginner and intermediate levels. "Children Authors' Bootcamp provides two full, information-packed days on the fundamentals of writing fiction for children. The workshop covers developing strong, unique characters; well-constructed plots; believable dialogue; seamless description and pacing; point of view; editing your own work; marketing your manuscripts to publishers, and more. Each day also includes in-class writing exercises and small group activities." Workshop held 6-7 times/year at various locations throughout the United States. Bootcamps are generally held in March, April, June, September, October and November. Please check our website for upcoming dates and locations. Maximum size is 55; average workshop has 40-50 participants. Cost of workshop varies; see website for details. Cost includeds tuition for both Saturday and Sunday (9:00 a.m. to 4:30 p.m.); morning and afternoon snacks; lunch; handout packet.

## CHILDREN'S BOOK WORKSHOP WITH SARA LONDON AT CASTLE HILL

1 Depot Road, P.O. Box 756, Truro MA 02666-0756. (508)349-7511. Fax: (508)349-7513. E-mail: castlehilltruro@ aol.com. Website: www.castlehill.org. **Registrar:** Trish Newby. Writer workshops geared toward intermediate and advanced levels. **Open to students.** Annual workshop. Workshop held in July. Registration limited to 10-12. Writing/art facilities available: classroom space. Cost of workshop: $250; includes week long workshop and one-on-one conference with teacher. Write for more information.

## CHILDREN'S LITERATURE CONFERENCE

250 Hofstra University, U.C.C.E., Hempstead NY 11549. (516)463-5242. Fax: (516)463-4833. E-mail: uccelibarts @hofstra.edu. Website: www.hofstra.edu. **Contact:** Marion Flomenhaft, director, arts, culture and leisure. Writer and illustrator workshops geared toward all levels. Emphasizes: fiction, nonfiction, poetry, submission procedures, picture books. Workshops will be held in April. Length of each session: 1 hour. Cost of workshop: approximately $85; includes 2 workshops, reception, lunch, 2 general sessions, and panel discussion with guest speakers and critiquing of randomly selected first-ms pages submitted by registrants. Write for more information. Co-sponsored by Society of Children's Book Writers & Illustrators.

## CHRISTIAN WRITERS' CONFERENCE

P.O. Box 42429, Santa Barbara CA 93140-2429. (805)682-0316. E-mail: opalmac@bigplanet.com. **Coordinator:**

Opal Dailey. Writer conference geared toward beginner, intermediate and advanced levels. **Open to students.** We always have children writing instruction. Annual conference. Conference held October 1, 2004. Registration limited to 100. Cost of conference: approximately $65; includes breakfast, lunch, and refreshment breaks. Write for more information.

## THE COLLEGE OF NEW JERSEY WRITERS' CONFERENCE
English Dept., The College of New Jersey, Dept. of English, Hillwood Lakes CN4700, Trenton, New Jersey 08650-4700. (609)771-3254. Fax: (609)637-5112. E-mail: write@tcnj.edu. **Director:** Jean Hollander. Writer workshops geared toward all levels. Offers workshop in children's literature. Workshops held in April of every year. Length of each session: 2 hours. Cost of workshop: $40-70 (reduced rates for students); includes conference, workshop and ms critique. Write for more information.

## THE COLUMBUS WRITERS CONFERENCE
P.O. Box 20548, Columbus OH 43220-0176. (614)451-3075. Fax: (614)451-0174. E-mail: angelaPL28@aol.com. Website: www.creativevista.com. **Director:** Angela Palazzolo. Sessions geared toward all levels. "In addition to consultations with agents and editor, this two-day conference offers a wide variety of topics and has included writing in the following markets: children's, young adult, screenwriting, historical fiction, humor, suspense, science fiction/fantasy, travel, educational and greeting card. Other topics have included writing the novel, the short story, the nonfiction book; playwriting; finding and working with an agent; independent publishing; book reviewing; technical writing; and time management for writers. Specific sessions that have pertained to children: fiction, nonfiction, children's writing, children's markets, young adult and publishing children's poetry and stories. Annual conference. Conference held in August. Cost of conference is TBA. E-mail, call or write for more information; or visit website.

## CONFERENCE FOR WRITERS & ILLUSTRATORS OF CHILDREN'S BOOKS
51 Tamal Vista Blvd., Corte Madera CA 94925. (415)927-0960, ext. 229. Fax: (415)927-3069. E-mail: conferences@bookpassage.com. Website: www.bookpassage.com. **Conference Coordinator:** Marguerita Castanera. Writer and illustrator conference geared toward beginner and intermediate levels. Sessions cover such topics as the nuts and bolts of writing and illustrating, publisher's spotlight, market trends, developing characters/finding voice in your writing. Two-day conference held each June. Registration limited to 80. Includes 3 lunches and a closing reception.

## PETER DAVIDSON'S HOW TO WRITE A CHILDREN'S PICTURE BOOK SEMINAR
982 S. Emerald Hills Dr., Arnolds Park IA 51331-0497. E-mail: Peterdavidson@mchsi.com. **Seminar Presenter:** Peter Davidson. "This seminar is for anyone interested in writing and/or illustrating children's picture books. Beginners and experienced writers alike are welcome." **Open to students.** How to Write a Children's Picture Book is a one-day seminar devoted to principles and techniques of writing and illustrating children's picture books. Topics include Definition of a Picture Book, Picture Book Sizes, Developing an Idea, Plotting the Book, Writing the Book, Illustrating the Book, Formatting Your Manuscript, Copyrighting Your Work, Marketing Your Manuscript and Contract Terms. Seminars are presented year-round at community colleges. Even-numbered years, presents seminars in Minnesota, Iowa, Nebraska, Kansas, Colorado and Wyoming. Odd-numbered years, presents seminars in Illinois, Minnesota, Iowa, South Dakota, Missouri, Arkansas and Tennessee (write for a schedule). One day, 9 a.m.-4 p.m. Cost of workshop: varies from $40-59, depending on location; includes approximately 35 pages of handouts. Write for more information.

## THE DIY BOOK FESTIVAL
7095 Hollywood Blvd., Suite 864, Los Angeles CA 90028-0893. (323)665-8080. Fax: (323)660-1776. E-mail: diyconvention@aol.com. Website: www.diyconvention.com. **Managing Director:** Bruce Haring. Writer and illustrator workshops geared toward beginner and intermediate levels. **Open to students.** Festival focus on getting your book into print, book marketing and promotion. Annual workshop. Workshop held February-October, various cities. Cost of workshop: $50; includes admission to event, entry to prize competition, lunch for some events. Check out our website for current dates and locations: www.diyconvention.com.

## DUKE UNIVERSITY YOUTH PROGRAMS: CREATIVE WRITER'S WORKSHOP
Box 90702, Durham NC 27708. (919)684-6259. Fax: (919)681-8235. E-mail: youth@duke.edu. Website: www.learnmore.duke.edu/youth. **Contact:** Duke Youth Programs. Writer workshops geared toward intermediate to advanced levels. **Open to students.** The Creative Writer's Workshop provides an intensive creative writing experience for advanced high school age writers who want to improve their skills in a community of writers. "The interactive format gives participants the opportunity to share their work in small groups, one-on-one with instructors, and receive feedback in a supportive environment. The review and critique process helps writers

sharpen critical thinking skills and learn how to revise their work." Annual workshop. Every summer there is one 2-week residential session. Costs for 2005—$1,565 for this 2-week residential session. Visit website or call for more information.

## DUKE UNIVERSITY YOUTH PROGRAMS: YOUNG WRITER'S CAMP

P.O. Box 90702, Durham NC 27708. (919)684-2827. Fax: (919)681-8235. E-mail: youth@duke.edu. Website: www.learnmore.duke.edu/youth. **Contact:** Duke Youth Programs (919)684-6259. Writer workshops geared toward beginner and intermediate levels for middle and high school students. **Open to students** (grades 6-11). Summer Camp. The Young Writer's Camp offers courses to enhance participants skills in creative and expository writing. "Through a core curriculum of short fiction, poetry, journalism, and playwriting students choose two courses for study to develop creative and analytical processes of writing. Students work on assignments and projects in and out of class, such as newspaper features, short stories, character studies, and journals." Annual workshop. Every summer there are 3 2-week sessions with residential and day options. Costs for 2005—$1,565 for residential campers and $1,025 for extended/$775 for day campers. Visit website or call for more information.

## EAST OF EDEN WRITERS CONFERENCE

California Writers Club, 1125 Miguel Ave., Los Altos CA 94024. (650)691-9802. Fax: (650)390-0234. E-mail: eastofeden@southbaywriters.com. Website: www.southbaywriters.com. **Conference Director:** Beth Proudfoot. Writer workshops geared toward beginner, intermediate and advanced levels. **Open to students.** Bi-annual conference. 2004 event speakers includes Summer Laurie, editor, Tricycle Press and Ashley Grayson, literary agent, Ashley Grayson Literary Agency. Last held August 27-29, 2004, in Salinas, CA (at the National Steinbeck Center and the Salinas Community Center.) Registration limited to 400. Cost of conference: $225 (after May 1st—discount for CWC members and "Early Birds"); includes Friday night dinner and program; Saturday breakfast, lunch, and full day of workshops and panels; "Night Owl" sessions; Saturday dinner program and Sunday brunch at John Steinbeck's family home are available for a small additional fee. "This conference, run by the nonprofit California Writers Club, will include many top-notch seminars on the art and business of writing. We'll have panels where writers can meet literary agents and editors and an Ask-A-Pro program, where writers can sign up to speak individually with faculty members of their choice."

## EAST TEXAS CHRISTIAN WRITERS CONFERENCE

East Texas Baptist University, 1209 North Grove Street, Marshall TX 75670. (903)923-2269. Fax: (903)938-7798. E-mail: jhopkins@etbu.edu. **Humanities Secretary:** Donna Gribble. Writer workshops geared toward beginner, intermediate and advanced levels. **Open to students.** Children's literature, books, stories, plays, art, and general literature. Annual conference. Workshop held 1st Saturday in June each year. Cost of workshop: $50/individual; $40/student; includes 5 writing workshops, materials, luncheon. Write for more information.

## FESTIVAL OF CHILDREN'S LITERATURE

The Loft Literary Center, Suite 200, Open Book, 1011 Washington Avenue South, Minneapolis MN 55415. 612-379-8999. E-mail: loft@loft.org . Website: www.loft.org. Writer workshops geared toward all levels. Workshops have included: "Nuts and Bolts of Publishing Nonfiction for Children" (by 4 writers with multi-titles published); Annual conference held in the Spring; speaker s for 2005 includedSusan Kochan, Senior Editor, G. P. Putnam's Sons along with many more writers, editors, publishers, and illustrators of children's literature. Registration limited to 185 people; smaller groups for breakout sessions. Writing facilities available with a performance hall, classrooms and writers studios. Cost of conference: approximately $ 153 for Friday and Saturday; $142 for Loft members; includes admission to full and break-out sessions, Saturday lunch, discount on hotel room (3 blocks from conference site at Loft Literary Center). Write for more information.

## FESTIVAL OF FAITH AND WRITING

Department of English, Grand Rapids MI 49546. (616)526-6770. Fax: (616)526-8508. E-mail: ffw@calvin.edu. Website: www.calvin.edu/festival. E-mail all inquiries about attendance (for registration brochures, program information, etcetera). Geared toward all levels of readers and writers. **Open to students.** "The Festival of Faith and Writing has talks, panel discussions, and workshops by artists who compose, write, illustrate, and publish children's books and books for young adults. Each break-out session will have a session on children's books/young adult books. Please see website for list of authors and illustrators joining us for 2006." Conference held every other year. Registration limited to approximately 1,800 people. Cost of conference in 2004: $150/$75 for students (cost subject to change in 2006); includes all sessions, workshops, evening speakers. Write for more information. "This conference is geared towards a variety of writers. The Festival brings together writers and readers who wonder about the intersections of faith with words on a page, lyrics in a melody, or images on a screen. Novelists, publishers, musicians, academics, poets, playwrights, editors, screenwriters, agents, journalists, preachers, students, and readers of every sort sit down together for three days of conversation and celebration."

## FIRST COAST WRITERS' FESTIVAL

9911 Old Baymeadows Rd., Jacksonville FL 32256. (904)997-2669. Fax: (904)997-2746. E-mail: kclower@fccj.e du. Website: www.fccj.edu/wf. **Director, Media:** Kathleen Clower. Writer workshops geared to all levels. Illustrators workshops geared to beginner level. **Open to students.** " For our 2005 Festival, children's authors and illustrators will present workshops on writing and illustrating children's books. Several workshop will deal with publishing and marketing. Annual workshop held May of each year as The Sea Turtle Inn on the beach in Atlantic Beach, Florida; May19-22, 2005. Cost of workshop: 1-day festival (with lunch) $95 (early bird); 2-day festival (with lunch) $185 (early bird); Editors & Agents Day on Sunday $80 (early bird). "Children's writing/illustration is one of many offerings at the festival. Other presentations include freelancing, writing memoirs, poetry, humorous essay, nonfiction, working with an editor, getting published and screenwriting." Confirmed speakers to date include Gerald Hausman, Andrei Codrescu, William Least Heat-Moon, S.V. Date, Connie May Fowler, Lenore Hart, Leslie Schwartz, Larry Smith, Sophie Wadsworth, Steve Berry, Brian Jay Corrigan, Stella Suberman. More to be announced.

## FISHTRAP, INC.

400 Grant Street, P.O. Box 38, Enterprise OR 97828-0038. (541)426-3623. Fax: (541)426-3324. E-mail: rich@fisht rap. Website: www.fishtrap.org. **Director:** Rich Wandschneider. Writer workshops geared toward beginner, intermediate, advanced and professional levels. **Open to students.** Not specifically writing for children, although we have offered occasional workshops in the field. A series of eight writing workshops (enrollment 12/workshop) and a writers' gathering is held each July; a winter gathering concerning writing and issues of public concern held in February. Dates for the winter gathering are February 25-27, 2001 (2001 theme: "humor"); and for the summer gathering July 8-15, 2001 (2001 theme: "Legacy of Vietnam"). During the school year Fishtrap brings writers into local schools and offers occasional workshops for teachers and writers of children's and young adult books. Also brings in "Writers in Residence" (10 weeks). Cost of workshops: $100-240 for 1-4 days; includes workshop only. Food and lodging can be arranged. College credit is available. Please contact for more information.

## FLATHEAD RIVER WRITERS CONFERENCE

P.O. Box 7711, Kalispell MT 59937. E-mail: hows@centurytel.net. **Director:** Jake How. Writer workshops geared toward beginner, intermediate, advanced and professional levels. **Open to students.** Along with our presenters, we periodically feature a chidren's writer workshop. Annual conference held mid-October. Registration limited to 100. Cost of workshop: $150; includes all lectures and a choice of workshops plus breakfast and lunch. Write for more information.

## FLORIDA CHRISTIAN WRITERS CONFERENCE

2344 Armour Ct., Titusville FL 32780. (321)269-5831. Fax: (321)264-0037. E-mail: billiewilson@cfl.rr.com. Website: www.flwriters.org. **Conference Director:** Billie Wilson. Writer workshops geared toward all levels. **Open to students.** "We offer 56 one-hour workshops and 8 six-hour classes. Approximately 15 of these are for the children's genre." Annual workshop held March 3-6 2005. We have 30 publishers and publications represented by editors teaching workshops and reading mss from the conferees. The conference is limited to 200 people. Advanced or professional workshops are by invitation only via submitted application. Cost of workshop: $550; includes food, lodging, tuition and ms critiques and editor review of your ms plus personal appointments with editors. Write or e-mail for more information.

## GIG HARBOR WRITER'S CONFERENCE

P.O. Box 806, Gig Harbor WA 98335-0826. (253)265-1904. ( 253)265-1904. Fax: (253)265-8532. E-mail: Director @peninsulawritersassociation.org. Website: www.peninsulawritersassociation.org. **Director:** Kathleen O'Brien. Writer workshops geared toward beginner, intermediate, advanced and professional levels. **Open to students.** Annual workshop. Workshop held Spring. Registration limited to 150. Cost of workshop: $100, nonmember; $75 members; includes workshops, welcome reception, keynote speaker, and several presenters. Write for more information.

## GOTHAM WRITERS' WORKSHOP

New York NY 10023. (877)974-8377. (212)307-6325. E-mail: dana@write.org. Website: www.WritingClasses.c om. **Director, Student Affairs:** Dana Miller. Creative writing workshops taught by professional writers are geared toward beginner, intermediate and advanced levels. **Open to students.** "Workshops cover the fundamentals of plot, structure, voice, description, characterization, and dialogue appropriate to all forms of fiction and nonfiction for pre-schoolers through young adults. Students can work on picture books or begin middle-readers or young adult novels." Annual workshops held 4 times/year (10-week and 1-day workshops). Workshops held January, April, July, September/October. Registration limited to 14 students/in-person (NYC) class; 18

students/online class; 40 students for in-person (NYC) one-day workshops. Cost of workshop: $420 for 10-week workshops; $150 for 1-day workshops; 10-week NYC classes meet once a week for 3 hours; 10-week online classes include 10 week-long, asynchronous "meetings"; 1-day workshops are 7 hours and are held 8 times/year. E-mail for more information.

## GREAT LAKES WRITER'S WORKSHOP

Milwaukee WI 53234-3922. (414)382-6176. Fax: (414)382-6332. E-mail: nancy.krase@alverno.edu. Website: www.alverno.edu. **Program Assistant:** Nancy Krase. Writing workshops geared toward beginner and intermediate levels; subjects include publishing, short story writing, novel writing, poetry, writing techniques/focus in character development, techniques for overcoming writers block. Annual workshop. Workshop held 3rd or 4th weekend in June, Friday evening and all day Saturday. Average length of each session: 2 hours. Cost of workshop: $115/entire workshop; $99 if you register before June 1. See online brochure. Lunch is included in Saturday program with a featured author as keynote speaker. Write for more information or call.

## GREEN LAKE WRITERS CONFERENCE

Green Lake Conference Center, W2511 State Hwy 23, Green Lake WI 54941. (800)558-8898. Fax: (920)294-3848. E-mail: program@glcc.org. Website: www.glcc.org. **Program Coordinator:** Russann Hadding. Writer workshops geared toward beginner, intermediate, advanced and professional levels. **Open to students.** Participants under the age of 21 must be accompanied by an adult. Writing for Children, ms critique, publishing. Annual workshop. Workshop held mid-August. Writing facilities available: classrooms, library. Cost of workshop: $600/person; includes program fee and meals. Housing is double occupancy. Single rooms available at additional cost. Write for more information. Evening critique groups, editors on-hand for lecture and information. Per-page fee for additional ms critique.

## HANDSPRINGS: A CONFERENCE FOR CHILDREN'S WRITERS AND ILLUSTRATORS

P.O. Box 1084, Socorro NM. E-mail: scbwi_nm@blarg.net. Website: www.scbwi-nm.org. **Writers contact:** Chris Eboch, SCBWI-NM Regional Advisor. Conference level for writers: beginner, intermediate. Conference level for illustrators: beginner, intermediate. **Open to students.** "Each conference features three keynote speakers—editors, agents, and/or art directors. Writers and illustrators lead breakout sessions. 2004 workshop topics included: Business Basics, Children's Books in Rhyming Verse, Writing Easy Readers, The Art & Magic of Storytelling, Spectacular Sentences, Research for Writing and Illustrating, and Twelve Ways to Make Your Novel Stand Out." Annual event. Workshop held April 7-8, 2006. "Offers classroom-style workshops and large-group presentations." Cost: $80-110. Registration includes full day of speakers and breakout workshops, plus morning coffee and lunch; a Friday night cocktail party, panel discussion, and Illustrator's Display is an additional $10-20. For an additional fee, conference attendees can sign up for ms critiques with one of the editors or agents. Illustrators can schedule portfolio reviews with the art director or artist rep. Contact at address above for more information.

## HIGHLAND SUMMER CONFERENCE

Box 7014, Radford University, Radford VA 24142-7014. (540)831-5366. Fax: (540)831-5951. E-mail: jasbury@radford.edu. Website: www.radford.edu/~arsc. **Director:** Grace Toney Edwards. **Assistant to the Director:** Jo Ann Asbury. **Open to students.** Writer workshops geared toward beginner, intermediate and advanced levels. Emphasizes Appalachian literature, culture and heritage. Annual workshop. Workshop held first 2 weeks in June annually. Registration limited to 20. Writing facilities available: computer center. Cost of workshop: Regular tuition (housing/meals extra). Must be registered student or special status student. E-mail, fax or call for more information. Past visiting authors include: Wilma Dykeman, Sue Ellen Bridgers, George Ella Lyon, Lou Kassem.

## HIGHLIGHTS FOUNDATION WRITERS WORKSHOP AT BOYDS MILLS

Dept. CWF, 814 Court St., Honesdale PA 18431. (570)253-1192. Fax: (570)253-0179. E-mail: contact@highlightsfoundation.org. Website: www.highlightsfoundation.org. **Contac t:** Kent Brown, director. Writer workshops geared toward those interested in writing for children , intermediate and advanced levels. Classes offered include: Nonfiction Research, Word Play: Poetry for Children, Writing from the Heart, Heart of the Novel, Picturebook, Nature Writing for Kids, Illustration and more (see website for updated list). Spring/Fall workshops. Spring workshops held in March, April, May, June at home of the Founders, Boyds Mills, PA. Fall workshops held in September, October, and November. Workshops limited to 14. Cost of workshops range from $495 and up. Cost of workshop includes tuition, meals, conference supplies and housing. Call for availablility and pricing. Call for more information or visit the website.

## HIGHLIGHTS FOUNDATION WRITERS WORKSHOP AT CHAUTAUQUA

Dept. CWL, 814 Court St., Honesdale PA 18431. (570)253-1192. Fax: (570)253-0179. E-mail: contact@highlightsf oundation.org. Website: www.highlightsfoundation.org. **Contac t:** Kent Brown, director. Writer workshops geared toward those interested in writing for children; beginner, intermediate and advanced levels. Classes offered include: Children's Poetry, Book Promotion, Autobiographical Writing. Annual workshop held July 16-23, 2005 at Chautauqua Institution, Chautauqua, NY. Registration limited to 100/class. Cost of workshop: $2,100; $1,685 if registered by 2/15/05; includes tuition, meals, conference supplies. Cost does not include housing. Call for availability and pricing. Scholarships are available for first-time attendees. Call for more information or visit the website.

## HOFSTRA UNIVERSITY SUMMER WRITERS' CONFERENCE
250 Hofstra University, UCCE, Hempstead NY 11549. (516)463-5016. Fax: (516)463-4833. E-mail: uccelibarts@hofstra.edu. Website: www.hofstra.edu/Academics/conferences/writers/index_writers.cfm. Writer workshops geared toward all levels. Classes offered include fiction, nonfiction, poetry, children's literature, stage/screenwriting and other genres. Annual workshop. Workshops held for 2 weeks in July. Each workshop meets for 2½ hours daily for a total of 25 hours. Students can register for 2 workshops, schedule an individual conference with the writer/instructor and submit a short ms (less than 10 pages) for critique. Enrollees may register as noncredit students or credit students. Cost of workshop: noncredit students' enrollment fee is approximately $425; 2-credit student enrollment fee is approximately $1,100/workshop undergraduate and graduate (2 credits); $2,100 undergraduate and graduate (4-credits). On-campus accommodations for the sessions are available for approximately $350/person for the 2-week conference. Students may attend any of the ancillary activities, a private conference, special programs and social events.

## INSTITUTE FOR READERS THEATRE ANNUAL WORKSHOP
P.O. Box 17193, San Diego CA 92177. (619)276-1948. Fax: (858)576-7369. E-mail: wadams1@san.rr.com. Website: www.readerstheatre.net. **Director:** Dr. William Adams. Writer workshops geared toward beginner, intermediate and advanced levels. **Open to students.** Topics include oral interpretation; script writing (converting literary material into performable scripts); journal writing (for credit participants). Annual workshop held July 2005. Registration limited to 50. Cost of workshop: $1,795; includes 2 weeks room and breakfast Britannia Hotel, London, England airfare and university credit (optional) are extra. Write for more information.

## INTERNATIONAL CREATIVE WRITING CAMP
1930 23rd Ave., SE, Minot ND 58701-6081. (701)838-8472. Fax: (701)838-8472. E-mail: info@internationalmusiccamp.com. Website: www.internationalmusiccamp.com. **Camp Director:** Joseph T. Alme. Writer and illustrator workshops geared toward beginner, intermediate and advanced levels. **Open to students.** Sessions offered include those covering poems, plays, mystery stories, essays. Registration limited to 20. The summer camp location at the International Peace Garden on the Border between Manitoba and North Dakota is an ideal site for generating creative thinking. Excellent food, housing and recreation facilities are available. Cost of workshop: $275. Write for more information.

## INTERNATIONAL WOMEN'S WRITING GUILD "REMEMBER THE MAGIC" ANNUAL SUMMER CONFERENCE
P.O. Box 810, Gracie Station, New York NY 10028. (212)737-7536. **Executive Director:** Hannelore Hahn. Writer and illustrator workshops geared toward all levels. Offers 65 different workshops—some are for children's book writers and illustrators. Also sponsors 13 other events throughout the U.S. Annual workshops. "Remember the Magic" workshops held 2nd or 3rd week in June. Length of each session: 1 hour-15 minutes; sessions take place for an entire week. Registration limited to 500. Cost of workshop: $945/single, $810/double (includes complete program, room and board). Write for more information. "This workshop always takes place at Skidmore College in Saratoga Springs NY."

## IOWA SUMMER WRITING FESTIVAL
C215 Seashore Hall, Iowa City IA 52242. (319)335-4160. Fax: (319)335-4743. E-mail: iswfestival@uiowa.edu. Website: www.uiowa.edu/~iswfest. **Director:** Amy Margolis. Writer workshops geared toward beginner, intermediate and advanced levels. **Open to students.** "We offer writing workshops across the genres, including workshops for children's writers in picture books, structuring writing for children, the young adult novel, and nonfiction." Annual workshop. Workshop held June and July. Registration limited to 12/workshop. Workshops meet in university classrooms. Cost of workshop: $475-500/week-long session; $225/weekend; includes tuition. Housing is separate and varies by facility. Write or call for more information.

## KENTUCKY WRITER'S WORKSHOP
1050 State Park Road, Pineville KY 40977. (606)337-3066. Fax: (606)337-7250. E-mail: Dean.Henson@ky.gov. Website: http://parks.ky.gov/pinemtn2.htm. **Event Coordinator:** Dean M. Henson. Writer and illustrator work-

shops geared toward beginner and intermediate levels. **Open to students.** Annual workshop. Workshop held March 18-19, 2005. Writing facilities available: classroom setup. Cost of workshop: $175/single package; $245/ double; cost includes two nights accommodations, two evening buffet meals, and admission to all sessions. Write for more information.

## LAJOLLA WRITERS CONFERENCE

P.O. Box 178122, San Diego CA 92177. (858)467-1978. E-mail: jkuritz@san.rr.com. Website: www.lajollawriters conference.com. **Founder:** Antoinette Kuritz. Writer workshop geared toward beginner, intermediate and advanced levels. Illustrator workshops geared toward beginner and intermediate. **Open to students.** We offer sessions with children's book agents and editors; read and critique sessions with young adult authors, editors, agents and publishers, including Laura Rennert of the Andrea Brown Agency; IRA Award winner, John H. Ritter; Harcourt Children's Book Editor, Deborah Halverson. Annual workshop. Workshop held in October. Registration limited to 200. Cost of workshop: $305; early bird, $255; includes classes Friday-Sunday, lunch and dinner Saturday. Write for more information.

## LEAGUE OF UTAH WRITERS' ROUNDUP

P.O. Box 460562, Leeds UT 84746. (435)313-4459. Fax: (435)879-8190. E-mail: reelsweetjustwrite@juno.com. Website: www.luwrite.com. **Membership Chairman:** Dorothy Crofts. Writer workshops geared toward beginner, intermediate, advanced. **Open to students.** Annual workshop. Roundup usually held 3rd weekend of September. Registration limited to approximately 400. 2005 conference in St. George at the New Garden Inn Hilton, September 16-17. Cost of last year's workshop: $125 for members/$199 for nonmembers; includes 3 meals, all workshops, all general sessions, a syllabus of all handout materials and a conference packet. ''When requesting information, please provide an e-mail address and/or fax number.''

## LIGONIER VALLEY WRITERS CONFERENCE

P.O. Box B, Ligonier PA 15658-1602. (724)537-3341. Fax: (724)537-0482. E-mail: sarshi@wpa.net. **Contact:** Sally Shirey. Writer programs geared toward all levels. **Open to students.** Annual conference features fiction, nonfiction, poetry and other genres. Annual conference. Held in July. Cost of workshop: $200; includes full weekend, some meals, all social events. Write or call for more information and 2005 conference date.

## ◪ MARITIME WRITERS' WORKSHOP

UNB College of Extended Learning, P.O. Box 4400, Fredericton NB E3B 5A3 Canada. E-mail: k4jc@unb.ca. Website: unb.ca/extend/writers/. **Coordinator:** Rhona Sawlor. Week-long workshop on writing for children, general approach, dealing with submitted material, geared to all levels and held in July. Annual workshop. 3 hours/day. Group workshop plus individual conferences, public readings, etc. Registration limited to 10/class. Cost of workshop: $395 tuition; meals and accommodations extra. Room and board on campus is approximately $320 for meals and a single room for the week. 10-20 ms pages due before conference (deadline announced). Scholarships available.

## MAUI WRITERS CONFERENCE

P.O. Box 1118, Kihei HI 96753. (888)974-8373 or (808)879-0061. Fax: (808)879-6233. E-mail: writers@maui.net. Website: www.mauiwriters.com. **Director:** Shannon Tullius. Writer workshops geared toward beginner, intermediate, advanced. **Open to students.** ''We offer a small children's writing section covering picture books, middle grade and young adult. We invite one *New York Times* Bestselling Author and agents and editors, who give consultations.'' Annual workshop. Workshop held Labor Day weekend. Cost includes admittance to all conference sessions and classes only—no airfare, food or consultations.

## MID MISSISSIPPI RIVER WRITER'S CONFERENCE and Creative Writing Contest

John Wood Community College, Quincy IL 62305. (217)641-4903. Fax: (217)228-9483. **Contact:** Sherry Sparks. Speakers talk on a variety of topics including children's writing, poetry, fiction, songwriting. The college also sponsors a writing contest open to the entire area for poetry, fiction and nonfiction. In addition, the college sponsors writing workshops, readings, speakers, a humanities series, a photography show in spring, and an art competition in the fall.

## MIDWEST WRITERS WORKSHOP

Department of Journalism, Ball State University, Muncie IN 47306. (765)282-1055. Fax: (765)285-7997. Website: www.midwestwriters.org. **Director:** Earl L. Conn. Writer workshops geared toward intermediate level. Topics include most genres. Past workshop presenters include Joyce Carol Oates, James Alexander Thom, Bill Brashler and Richard Lederer. Workshop also includes ms evaluation and a writing contest. Annual workshop. Workshop will be held July 28-30, 2005. Registration tentatively limited to 125. Most meals included. Offers scholarships. Write for more information.

### MONTROSE CHRISTIAN WRITER'S CONFERENCE

Montrose PA 18801-1112. (570)278-1001. Fax: (570)278-3061. E-mail: mbc@montrosebible.org. Website: www .montrosebible.org. **Executive Director:** Jim Fahringer. **Secretary-Registrar:** Donna Kosik. **Open to adults and students.** Writer workshops geared toward beginner, intermediate and advanced levels. Annual workshop held in July. Cost of workshop: $130 tuition. Write for more information.

### MOONDANCE INTERNATIONAL FILM FESTIVAL

970 Ninth St., Boulder CO 80302. (303)545-0202. E-mail: moondanceff@aol.com (with MIFF or MOONDANCE in the subject line) Website: www.moondancefilmfestival.com. **Executive Director:** Elizabeth English. Film Festival Workshop Sessions include screenwriting, playwriting, short stories, filmmaking (feature, documentary, short, animation), TV and video filmmaking, writing for TV (MOW, sitcoms, drama), writing for animation, adaptation to screenplays (novels and short stories), how to get an agent, what agents want to see, and pitch panels. 2005 workshops and film festival held May 12-16, 2005. Cost of workshops, seminars, panels, pitch session: $50 each. Check website for more information and registration forms. The 2005 competition deadline for entries is April 1, 2005. ''The Moondance competition includes special categories for writers and filmmakers who create work for the children's market!'' Entry forms and guidelines are on the website.

### MOUNT HERMON CHRISTIAN WRITERS CONFERENCE

Mount Hermon Christian Conference Center, Mount Hermon CA 95041-0413. (831)335-4466. Fax: (831)335-9413. E-mail: rachelw@mhcamps.org. Website: www.mounthermon.org/writers. **Director of Adult Ministries:** David R. Talbott. Writer workshops geared toward all levels. **Open to students over 16 years.** Emphasizes religious writing for children via books, articles; Sunday school curriculum; marketing. 70 workshops offered include: Suitable Style for Children; Everything You Need to Know to Write and Market Your Children's Book; Take-Home Papers for Children. Workshops held annually over Palm Sunday weekend: April 7-11, 2006 and March 30-April 3, 2007. Length of each session: 5-day residential conferences held annually. Registration limited 45/class, but most are 20-30. Conference center with hotel-style accommodations. Cost of workshop: $660-990 variable; includes tuition, resource notebook, refreshment breaks, full room and board for 13 meals and 4 nights. Conference information posted annually on website by December 1. Write or e-mail for more information or call toll-free to 1-888-MH-CAMPS.

### THE NATIONAL WRITERS ASSOCIATION FOUNDATION CONFERENCE

P.O. Box 4187, Parker CO 80134. (303)841-0246. Website: www.nationalwriters.com. **Conference Coordinator:** Anita Whelchel. Writer workshops geared toward all levels. Classes offered include marketing, agenting, ''What's Hot in the Market.'' Annual workshop. The 2004 workshop was held in Denver, Colorado, June 12-14. Write for more information or check our website for 2005 conference dates.

### NORTH CAROLINA WRITERS' NETWORK FALL CONFERENCE

P.O. Box 954, Carrboro NC 27510-0954. (919)967-9540. Fax: (919)929-0535. E-mail: mail@ncwriters.org. Website: www.ncwriters.org. **Program Director:** Carol Henderson. Writing workshops geared toward beginner, intermediate, advanced and professional levels. **Open to students.** ''We offer workshops and critique sessions in a variety of genres: fiction, poetry, creative nonfiction, children's. Past young adult and children's writing faculty included: Louise Hawes, Jackie Ogburn, Clay Carmichael, Carol Boston Weatherford. Annual conference. The 2004 conference was held October 29-31 in Durham, NC. Cost of workshop: approximately $200/ NCWN members, $255/nonmembers; includes workshops, panel discussions, round table discussions, social activities and 2 meals. ''Cost does not include fee for critique sessions or accommodations.'' Write or e-mail for 2005 conference dates.

### OHIO KENTUCKY INDIANA CHILDREN'S LITERATURE CONFERENCE

% Greater Cincinnati Library Consortium (GCLC), Cincinnati OH 45206-2855. (513)751-4422. Fax: (513)751-0463. E-mail: gclc@gclc-lib.org. Website: www.gclc-lib.org. **Staff Development Coordinator:** Judy Malone. Writer and illustrator conference geared toward all levels. **Open to students.** Annual conference. Emphasizes multicultural literature for children and young adults. Conference held annually in November. Contact GCLC for more information. Registration limited to 250. Cost of conference: $50; includes registration/attendance at all workshop sessions, Tri-state Authors and Illustrators of Childrens Books Directory, continental breakfast, lunch, author/illustrator signings. E-mail or write for more information.

### OKLAHOMA WRITERS' FEDERATION, INC. ANNUAL CONFERENCE

P.O. Box 2654, Stillwater OK 74076-2654. (405)762-6238. Fax: (405)377-0992. E-mail: wileykat@cox.net. Website: www.owfi.org. **President:** Moira Wiley. Writer workshops geared toward all levels. Illustrator workshops geared toward beginner level. **Open to students.** "During 2003 event, Emily Mitchell, assistant editor with Charlesbridge Publishing, presented a session titled The Basics of Children's Book Contracts (Law Degree Not Required). Other noteworthy topics cover the basics of writing, publishing and marketing in any genre." Annual conference. Held first Friday and Saturday in May each year. Registration limited to 420. Writing facilities available: book room, autograph party, free information room. Cost of workshop: $100 before April 15, 2005; $125 after April 15, 2005; includes 2-day conference—all events including 2 banquets and one 10-minute appointment with an attending editor or agent of your choice (must be reserved in advance). "If writers would like to participate in the annual writing contest, they must become members of OWFI. You don't have to be a member to attend the conference." Write or e-mail for more information.

## OUTDOOR WRITERS ASSOCIATION OF AMERICA ANNUAL CONFERENCE

158 Lower Georges Valley Rd., Spring Mills PA 16875. (814)364-9557. Fax: (814)364-9558. E-mail: eking4owaa @cs.com. **Meeting Planner:** Eileen King. Writer workshops geared toward all levels. Annual 5-day conference. Craft Improvement seminars; newsmaker sessions. Workshop held in June. 2006 Conference to be held in Lake Charles, Louisiana. Cost of workshop: $325; includes attendance at all workshops and most meals. Attendees must have prior approval from Executive Director before attendance is permitted. Write for more information.

## OZARK CREATIVE WRITERS, INC. CONFERENCE

6817 Gingerbread Lane, Little Rock AR 72204. (501)565-8889. E-mail: ozarkcreativewriters@earthlink.net. Website: www.ozarkcreativewriters.org. **Counselor:** Peggy Vining. **Open to students.** Writer's workshops geared to all levels. "All forms of the creative process dealing with the literary arts. We sometimes include songwriting. We invite excellent speakers who are selling authors. We also promote writing by providing competitions in all genres." Always the second full weekend in October at Inn of the Ozarks in Eureka Springs AR (a resort town). Morning sessions are given to main attraction author. Six 1-hour satellite speakers during each of the 2 afternoons. Two banquets. "Approximately 200 attend the conference yearly. Many others enter the creative writing competition." Cost of registration/contest entry fee approximately $60-70. Includes entrance to all sessions, contest entry fees. "This does not include banquet meals or lodging. We block off 80 rooms prior to August 15 for the conference." Send #10 SASE for brochure by May 1st. "Reserve early."

## PACIFIC NORTHWEST CHILDREN'S BOOK CONFERENCE

(formerly Children's Book Conference), Portland State University Haystack Program, P.O. Box 1491, Portland OR 97207. (503)725-4186 or (800)547-8887, ext. 4186. Fax: (503)725-4840. E-mail: snydere@pdx.edu. Website: www.haystack.pdx.edu/children. **Contact:** Elizabeth Snyder, Haystack program coordinator. Focus on the craft of writing and illustrating for children while working with an outstanding faculty of acclaimed editors, authors, and illustrators. Daily afternoon faculty-led writing workshops. Acquire specific information on how to become a professional in the field of children's literature. Annual workshop for all levels. Conference held in July on the campus of Reed College, Portland, Oregon. Cost of conference: $590 noncredit; $860 for graduate credits; individual ms/portfolio reviews for an additional fee. Call more information. Linda Zuckerman, editor, coordinates, conference and collects knowledgeable and engaging presenters every year.

## PACIFIC NORTHWEST WRITER ASSN. SUMMER WRITER'S CONFERENCE

P.O. Box 2016, Edmonds WA 98020 (425)673-2665. E-mail: staff@pnwa.org. **Association Executive:** Dana Murphy-Love. Writer conference geared toward beginner, intermediate, advanced and professional levels. **Open to students.** Sample sessions: Constructing a Children's Book, The Art of Promoting Your Book, Breathing Life Into Your Characters, Writing a Home-run Book for Young Readers. Annual conference h eld July 6-9, 2006. Cost of conference: $350/members (limited scholarships available to members); $400/nonmember; includes all conference materials, continental breakfasts, refreshments, awards ceremony dessert reception, keynote dinners, appointments with editors/agents. "There are approximately 30 agents/editors that attend this conference. The Literary Contest Winners are announced as well. Conference is at the Hilton Seattle Airport, Seattle, WA."

## PERSPECTIVES IN CHILDREN'S LITERATURE CONFERENCE

School of Education, 226 Furcolo Hall, Amherst MA 01003-3035. (413)545-4325 or (413)545-1116. Fax: (413)545-2879. E-mail: childlit@educ.umass.edu. Website: www.umass.edu/childlit. **Coordinators of Conference:** Katelyn McLaughlin and Laura Ptaszynski. Writer and illustrator workshops geared to all levels. Presenters talk about what inspires them, how they bring their stories to life and what their visions are for the future. Conference held in April. For more information contact coordinators by phone, fax or e-mail."

## PUBLISHINGGAME.COM WORKSHOP

Newton MA 02459. (617)630-0945. E-mail: conference@PublishingGame.com. Website: PublishingGame.com.

**Coordinator:** Alyza Harris. Fern Reiss, author of the popular "Publishing Game" book series and CEO of Expertizing.com, will teach this one-day workshop. Writer workshops geared toward beginner, intermediate and advanced levels. **Open to students.** Sessions will include: Find A Literary Agent, Self-Publish Your Children's Book, Book Promotion For Children's Books. September—New York, NY; October—Boston, MA; November—TBD; December—Philadelphia, PA; January—Washington, DC; February—Boca Raton, FL; March—New York, NY; April—TBD; May—Washington, DC; June—Los Angeles, CA; July—San Francisco, CA; August—Seattle, WA. Registration limited to 18. Fills quickly! Cost of workshop: $195. Write for more information. Workshop now available as a 5-CD audio workshop.

### ROBERT QUACKENBUSH'S CHILDREN'S BOOK WRITING AND ILLUSTRATING WORKSHOP

460 E. 79th St., New York NY 10021-1443. Phone/fax: (212)861-2761. E-mail: rqstudios@aol.com. Website: www.rquackenbush.com. **Contact:** Robert Quackenbush. Writer and illustrator workshops geared toward all levels. **Open to students.** Four-day extensive workshop on writing and illustrating books for children, emphasizes picture books and chapter books from start to finish and provides instruction on how to create a ms and/or book dummy to submit to publishers. Also covered is writing fiction and nonfiction for middle grades and young adults, if that is the attendees' interest. Current trends in illustration are also covered. This July workshop is a full 4-day (9 a.m.-4 p.m) extensive course. Registration limited to 10/class. Writing and/or art facilities available; work on the premises; art supply store nearby. Cost of workshop: $650 for instruction. Cost of workshop includes instruction in preparation of a ms and/or book dummy ready to submit to publishers. Class limited to 10 members. Attendees are responsible for arranging their own hotel and meals, although suggestions are given on request for places to stay and eat. "This unique workshop, held annually since 1982, provides the opportunity to work with Robert Quackenbush, a prolific author and illustrator of children's books with more than 170 fiction and nonfiction books for young readers to his credit, including mysteries, biographies and song-books. The workshop attracts both professional and beginning writers and artists of different ages from all over the world." Recommended by Foder's *Great American Learning Vacations*.

### ⚟ SAGE HILL WRITING EXPERIENCE, Writing Children's & Young Adult Fiction Workshop

Box 1731, Saskatoon SK S7K 3S1 Canada . Phone/fax: (303)652-7395. E-mail: sage.hill@sasktel.net. Website: www.sagehillwriting.ca. **Executive Director:** Steven Ross Smith. Writer conference geared toward intermediate level. This program occurs every 2 or 3 years, but the Sage Hill Conference is annual. Conference held in July. Registration limited to 6 participants for this program, and to 37 for full program. Cost of conference approximately $795; includes instruction, meals, accommodation. Require ms samples prior to registration. Write or visit the website for more information and workshop dates.

### SAN DIEGO STATE UNIVERSITY WRITERS' CONFERENCE

The College of Extended Studies, San Diego CA 92182-1920. (619)594-2517. Fax: (619)594-8566. E-mail: extended.std@sdsu.edu. Website: www.ces.sdsu.edu. **Conference Facilitator:** Becky Ryan. Writer workshops geared toward beginner, intermediate and advanced levels. Emphasizes nonfiction, fiction, screenwriting, advanced novel writing; includes sessions specific to writing and illustrating for children. Workshops offered by children's editors, agents and writers. Workshops held near the end of January each year. Registration limited. Cost of workshop: approximately $300. Write for more information or see our home page at the above website.

### SAN FRANCISCO WRITERS CONFERENCE

1029 Jones St., San Francisco CA 94109. (415)673-0939. E-mail: sfwc@aol.com. Website: www.sanfranciscowritersconference.com. **Co-Founder:** Elizabeth Pomada. Writer workshops geared toward beginner, intermediate, advanced and professional levels. **Open to students.** Annual conference. Conference held President's Day weekend in mid-February. Registration limited to 700. Cost of workshop: $425-$495 depending on time of registration; includes continental breakfast and sit-down brunch. Write for more information. The 2005 preliminary program will be on the website by October 2004.

### ⚟ SASKATCHEWAN FESTIVAL OF WORDS AND WORKSHOPS

217 Main Street, Moose Jaw SK S6J 0W1 Canada. (306)691-0557. Fax: (306)693-2994. E-mail: word.festival@sasktel.net. Website: www.festivalofwords.com. **Manager of Operations:** Lori Dean. Writer workshops geared toward beginner, intermediate, advanced and professional levels. **Open to students.** Readings that include a wide spectrum of genres—fiction, creative non-fiction, poetry, songwriting, screenwriting, playwriting, children's writing, panels, interviews and performances. Annual workshop. Workshop held third weekend in July. Cost of workshop: $8/session—$125 for full festival pass. Write, e-mail, or visit website for more information.

### SOCIETY OF SOUTHWESTERN AUTHORS' WRANGLING WITH WRITING

P.O. Box 30355, Tucson AZ 85751-0355. (520)546-9382. Fax: (520)296-0409. E-mail: wporter202@aol.com;

barbara@clariticom.com. Website: www.azstarnet.com/nonprofit/ssa. **Conference Director:** Penny Porter. Writer workshops geared toward all genres. "Limited scholarships available." Sessions include Writing and Publishing the Young Adult Novel, What Agents Want to See in a Children's Book, Writing Books for Young Children. "We always have several children's book editors and agents interested in meeting with children's writers." Annual workshop held January 30-31, 2004. Registration limited to 500—usually 300-400 people attend. Hotel rooms have dataports for internet access. Tucson has many art galleries. Tentative cost: $250 nonmembers, $225 for SSA members; includes 3 meals and 2 continental breakfasts, all workshop sessions—individual appointments with agents and editors are extra. Hotel accommodations are not included. "Some editors and agents like to see mss prior to the conference; information about requirements is in the brochure. If you want a portfolio of artwork critiqued, please contact us directly, and we'll try to accommodate you." Write for more information. SSA has put on this conference for over 25 years now. "It's hands-on, it's friendly, and every year writers sell their manuscripts."

## SOUTH COAST WRITERS CONFERENCE

P.O. Box 590, 29392 Ellensburg Ave., Gold Beach OR 97444. (541)247-2741. E-mail: scwc@socc.edu. **Coordinator:** Janet Pretti. Writer workshops geared toward beginner, intermediate levels. **Open to students.** Include s fiction, nonfiction, nuts and bolts, poetry, feature writing, children's writing, publishing. Annual workshop. Workshop held Friday and Saturday of President's day weekend in February. Registration limited to 25-30 students/workshop. Cost of workshop: $50 before January 31, $60 after; includes Friday night author's reading and book signing, Saturday conference, choice of 4 workshop sessions, Saturday evening writers' circle (networking and critique). Write for more information. "We also have two six-hour workshops Friday for more intensive writing exercises. The cost is an additional $35."

## SOUTHWEST WRITERS CONFERENCES

3721 Morris NE, Suite A, Albuquerque NM 87111. (505)265-9485. Fax: (505)265-9483. E-mail: swriters@aol.c om. Website: www.southwestwriters.org. **Open to adults and students** Writer workshops geared toward all genres at all levels of writing. Various aspects of writing covered, including children's. Quarterly mini-conference and occasional workshops. Examples from mini-conferences: Beyond the Unknown conference: Steve Saffel of Del Rey and Liz Scheier of Penguin Groups lectured on science fiction/fantasy/horror and had one-on-one meetings with attendees for acquiring mss. Included other speakers, lunch, midnight reading event, and Old Town Ghost Tour. Cracking the Code: Secrets of Writing and Selling Compelling Nonfiction conference featured literary agents Michael Larsen, Elizabeth Pomoda, and Jeff Herman; Lee Gutkind, publisher; David Fryxell, editor; Lucinda Schroeder, criminologist/writer; and a panel of New Mexico publishers. Prices vary, but usually $99-$159. Also offers annual contest, two monthly programs, monthly newsletter, occasional workshops, critique service, and various discount perks. See website for information.

## SPLIT ROCK ARTS PROGRAM, University of Minnesota

360 Coffey Hall, 1420 Eckles Ave., St . Paul MN 55108-6084. (612)625-8100. Fax: (612)624-6210. E-mail: srap@c ce.umn.edu. Website: www.cce.umn.edu/splitrockarts/. Workshops including poetry, short stories, memoirs, novels, personal essays, young adult, and children's picture books are geared toward intermediate, advanced and professional levels. Workshops begin in July for 5 weeks. Optional college credits available. Registration limited to 16/workshop. Cost of workshop: $550 and up; scholarships available. Air-conditioned on-campus housing and food services available. Printed and online catalogs available in late February.

## STEAMBOAT SPRINGS WRITERS CONFERENCE

P.O. Box 774284, Steamboat Springs CO 80477. (970)879-8079. E-mail: sswriters@cs.com. Website: www.steam boatwriters.com. **Conference Director:** Harriet Freiberger. Writers' workshops geared toward intermediate levels. **Open to students.** Some years offer topics specific to children's writing. Annual conference since 1982. Workshops will be held in July. Registration limited to 35. Cost of workshop: $45; includes 4 seminars and luncheon. Write, e-mail or see website for more information.

## ▓ SUNSHINE COAST FESTIVAL OF THE WRITTEN ARTS

P.O. Box 2299, Sechelt BC V0N-3A0 Canada. (604)885-9631, 1-800-565-9631. Fax: (604)885-3967. E-mail: info@ writersfestival.ca. Website: www.writersfestival.ca. **Festival Producer:** Gail Bull. Writer and illustrator workshops geared toward professional level. **Open to Students.** Annual literary festival held every August. Pavilion seating 500/event. Festival pass $175; individual events $12. Fee schedule available upon request.

## ▓ SURREY INTERNATIONAL WRITER'S CONFERENCE

Guildford Continuing Education, 10707 146th St., Surrey BC U3R IT5 Canada (604)589-2221. Fax: (604)588-9286. E-mail: lkmason@telus.net. Website: www.siwc.ca. **Coordinator:** Lisa Mason. Writer and illustrator workshops geared toward beginners, intermediate and advanced levels. Topics include marketing, children's agents and editors. Annual Conference. Conference held in October. Cost of conference includes all events for 3 days and most meals. Check our website for more information.

### THE THIRD NEW-CUE WRITERS' CONFERENCE AND WORKSHOP IN HONOR OF RACHEL CARSON

The Spruce Point Inn, Boothbay Harbor ME. (845)398-4247. Fax: (845)398-4224. E-mail: info@new-cue.org. Website: www.new-cue.org. **President:** Barbara Ward Klein. Writer and illustrator workshops geared toward beginner, intermediate, advanced and professional levels. "Our conference emphasizes environmental and nature writing for juvenile fiction and non-fiction. Workshop held in June every 2 years on the even numbered year. Registration limited to 100 participants. Writing/art facilities available: Large meeting rooms for featured speakers, including Jean Craighead George. Smaller break-out rooms for concurrent sessions. Cost of workshop: $378/returning participants; $420/new-before 5/1/03. Includes all featured and keynote addresses, performance of one-woman play, *A Sense of Wonder*, concurrent sessions, workshops, guided outdoor activities and almost all meals. Submit writing sample, no longer than 3 pages. Write for more information. Additional information about featured speakers, The Spruce Point Inn, and the Boothbay Harbor Area is available on-line at www.new-cue.org.

### UMKC/WRITERS PLACE WRITERS WORKSHOPS

5300 Rockhill Rd., Kansas City MO 64110-2450. (816)235-2736. Fax : (816)235-5279. E-mail: seatons@umkc.e du. **Contact:** Kathi Wittfield. New Letters Writer's Conference and Mark Twain Writer' s Workshop geared toward intermediate, advanced and professional levels. Workshops open to students and community. Annual workshops. Workshops held in Summer. Cost of workshop varies. Write for more information.

### UNIVERSITY OF THE NATIONS SCHOOL OF WRITING AND WRITERS WORKSHOPS

YWAM Woodcrest, P.O. Box 1380, Lindale TX 75771-1380. (903)882-WOOD [9663]. Fax: (903)882-1161. E-mail: writingschooltx@yahoo.com. Website: www.ywamwoodcrest.com. **School Leader:** Carol Scott. Writer workshops geared toward beginner, intermediate, advanced levels. **Open to students.** Children's writing workshops include: Writing Children's Picture Books with Mona Gansberg Hodgson. Workshops held during various weeks between September and December. Cost for workshop: $20 registration fee (nonrefundable) plus $175 tuition per week (the 1st week) plus $175/week if staying on our campus. ($125 tuition each additional week.) $175 tuition/week covers lectures, critique groups, hands-on-training. Students may make own arrangements for lodging and meals. If you want college credit for the workshop or are taking the entire 12-week school of writing, you must have completed the YWAM's Discipleship Training School first. Write for more information. "Although we are associated with the Youth with A Mission missionary group, we welcome inquiries from all interested parties—not only missionaries."

### VANCOUVER INTERNATIONAL WRITERS FESTIVAL

1398 Cartwright St., Vancouver BC V6H 3R8 Canada. (604)681-6330. Fax: (604)681-8400. E-mail: viwf@writersf est.bc.ca. Website: www.writersfest.bc.ca. **Artistic Director:** Alma Lee. Annual literary festival. The Vancouver International Writers Festival strives to encourage an appreciation of literature and to promote literacy by providing a forum where writers and readers can interact. This is accomplished by the production of special events and an annual Festival which feature writers from a variety of countries whose work is compelling and diverse. The Festival attracts over 11,000 people and presents approximately 50 events in six venues during six days on Granville Island, located in the heart of Vancouver. The first 4 days of the festival are programmed for elementary and secondary school students and teachers. Held in late October (6-day festival). All writers who participate are invited by the A.D. The events are open to anyone who wishes to purchase tickets. Cost of events ranges from $10-25.

### THE VICTORIA SCHOOL OF WRITING

306-620 View St., Victoria BC V8W 1J6 Canada . (250)595-3000. E -mail: info@victoriaschoolofwriting.org. Website: www.victoriaschoolofwriting.org. **Director:** Jill Margo. Writer conference geared toward intermediate level. In the 2005 conference there will be 1 workshop that includes writing for children and young adults. Annual conference. Workshop third week of July. Registration limited to 12/workshop. Conference includes close mentoring from established writers. Cost of conference: $585 (Canadian); includes tuition and some meals. To attend, submit 3-10 pages of writing samples. Write for more information.

### VIRGINIA FESTIVAL OF THE BOOK

145 Ednam Dr., Charlottesville VA 22903. (434)924-6890. Fax: (434)296-4714. E-mail: vabook@virginia.edu. Website: www.vabook.org. **Program Director:** Nancy Damon. **Open to Students.** Readings, panel discussions,

presentations and workshops by author, and book-related professionals for children and adults. Most programs are free and open to the public. Held March 16-20, 2005 in Charlottesville. See website for more information.

## WESLEYAN WRITERS CONFERENCE

Wesleyan University, Middletown CT 06459. (860)685-3604. Fax: (860)685-2441. E-mail: agreene@wesleyan.e du. Website: www.wesleyan.edu/writers.**Director:** Anne Greene. Seminars, workshops, readings, ms advice; geared toward all levels. ''This conference is useful for writers interested in how to structure a story, poem or nonfiction piece. Although we don't always offer classes in writing for children, the advice about structuring a piece is useful for writers of any sort, no matter who their audience is.'' One of the nation's best-selling children's authors was a student here. Classes in the novel, short story, fiction techniques, poetry, journalism and literary nonfiction. Guest speakers and panels offer discussion of fiction, poetry, reviewing, editing and publishing. Individual ms consultations available. Conference held annually the third week in June. Length of each session: 5 days. ''Usually, there are 100 participants at the Conference.'' Classrooms, meals, lodging and word processing facilities available on campus. Cost of workshop: tuition—$565, room—$135, meals (required of all participants)—$210. ''Anyone may register; people who want financial aid must submit their work and be selected by scholarship judges.'' Call for a brochure or check website.

## WHIDBEY ISLAND WRITERS' CONFERENCE

P.O. Box 1289, Langley WA 98260. (360)331-6714. E-mail: writers@whidbey.com. Website: www.writeonwhid bey.org. **Writers contact:** Elizabeth Guss, conference director. ''Nurture your writing muse.'' Learn from a variety of award-winning children's book authors and very experienced literary agents. Topics inclue: ''Chang- ing Winds for Children's Books,'' "Dancing Backwards in High Heels: Writing Historical Fiction,'' and ''Well Kept Secrets of Children's Book Publishing.'' Workshop held in March 3-5, 2006. Registration limited to 275. Cost: $350. Registration includes workshops, fireside chats, high tea reception, various activities, and daily luncheons. The conference offers consultation appointments with editors and agents as well as opportunities for critiques from authors in many genres. A preconference retreat highlights children's writing. Registrants may reduce the cost of their conference by volunteering. See the website for more information. ''The uniquely personal weekend is specifically designed to be highly interactive.''

## WILLAMETTE WRITERS ANNUAL WRITERS CONFERENCE

9045 SW Barbur Blvd., Suite 5A, Portland OR 97219. (503)452-1592. Fax: (503)452-0372. E-mail: wilwrite@willi amettewriters.com. Website: www.willamettewriters.com. **Office Manager:** Bill Johnson. Writer workshops geared toward all levels. Emphasizes all areas of writing, including children's and young adult. Opportunities to meet one-on-one with leading literary agents and editors. Workshops held in August. Cost of conference: $285-350; includes membership.

## TENNESSEE WILLIAMS/NEW ORLEANS LITERARY FESTIVAL

938 Lafayette St., Suite 328, New Orleans LA 70113. (504)581-1144. Fax: (504)523-3680. E-mail: info@tennesseewill iams.net. Website: www.tennesseewilliams.net. **Executive Director:** Paul J. Willis. Writer workshops geared to- ward beginner, intermediate, advanced, and professional levels. **Open to students.** Annual workshop. Workshop held the third week in March. Master classes are limited in size to 100—all other panels offered have no cap. Cost of workshop: prices range from $15-35. Write for more information. ''We are a literary festival and may occasionally offer panels/classes on children's writing and/or illustration, but this is not done every year.''

## WINTER POETRY & PROSE GETAWAY IN CAPE MAY

18 N. Richards Ave., Ventnor NJ 08406. (609)823-5076. E-mail: info@wintergetaway.com. Website: wintergeta way.com. **Director:** Peter Murphy. Writer workshops geared toward all levels. **Open to students (18 years and over).** ''Writing for Children—You will learn to develop character, plot, setting, points of view. There will also be a discussion of genres in juvenile literature, of voice, of detail and of revision. Choose one of two sections: Picture books and younger readers or middle graders and teens.'' Annual workshop. Workshop held January 14-17, 2005. Registration limited to 8 writers in each workshop. Writing/art facilities available in hotel meeting and ballrooms. Cost of workshop: $475 double, $600 single, $300 commuter; double and single includes 3 nights at the Grand Hotel of Cape May with 3 breakfasts, lunches and snacks, most workshops and evening activities. Commuter rate includes workshop, snacks, evening activities and lunch on Saturday and Sunday. Write for more information. ''The Winter Poetry & Prose Getaway is well known for its challenging and support- ive atmosphere which encourages imaginative risk taking and promotes freedom and transformation in each participant's creative work.''

## WISCONSIN REGIONAL WRITER'S ASSOCIATION, INC.Spring and Fall Conferences

510 W. Sunset Ave., Appleton WI 54911-1139. (920)734-3724. E-mail: info@wrwa.net. Website: www.wrwa.n

et. **Contact:** Patricia Boverhuis, membership chair. Estab. 1948. Annual. Conferences held in May and September are dedictated to self-improvement through speakers, workshops and presentations. Topics and speakers vary with each event. Average attendance: 100-150. We honor all genres of writing. Spring conference is a one-day event that features speakers and awards for two contests (humor writing and feature article writing). Fall conference is a two-day event featuring the Jade Ring Banquet and awards for six genre categories. Cost of workshop: $40-75. Provides a list of area hotels or lodging options. "We negotiate special rates at each facility. A block of rooms is set aside for a specific time period." Award winners receive a certificate and a cash prize. First Place winners of the Jade Ring contest receive a jade ring. Must be a member to enter all contests. For brochure call, write, e-mail or visit our website.

## WRITE ON THE SOUND WRITERS CONFERENCE

700 Main St., Edmonds WA 98020-3032. (425)771-0228. Fax: (425)771-0253. E-mail: wots@ci.edmonds.wa.us. Website: www.ci.edmonds.wa.us/ArtsCommission/index.stm. **Cultural Resources Coordinator:** Frances Chapin. Writer workshops geared toward beginner, intermediate, advanced and professional levels with some sessions on writing for children. Annual conference held in Edmonds, on Puget Sound, on the first weekend in October with 2 full days of workshops. Registration limited to 200. Cost of workshop: approximately $99 early registration and $125 for late registration; includes two days of workshops plus one ticket to keynote lecture. Brochures are mailed in August. Attendees must pre-register. Write, e-mail or call for brochure. Writing contest and critiques for conference participants.

## ▧ WRITE! CANADA

(formerly God Uses Ink Conference), Box 487, Markham ON L3P 3R1 Canada. (905)471-1447. Fax: (905)471-6912. E-mail: info@thewordguild.com. Website: www.thewordguild.com. Estab. 1984. Annual conference for writers who are Christian. Hosted by The Word Guild, an association of Canadian writers and editors who are Christian. The Word Guild seeks to connect, develop, and promote its members. Keynote speaker, continuing classes, workshops, panels, editor appointments, reading times, critiques, and more. For all levels of writers from beginner to professional. Held at a retreat center in Guelph ON. June 16-18, 2005.

## WRITE-BY-THE-LAKE WRITER'S WORKSHOP & RETREAT

610 Langdon St., Room 621, Madison WI 53703. (608)262-3447. E-mail: cdesmet@dcs.wisc.edu. Website: www.dcs.wisc.edu/lsa/writing. **Coordinator :** Christine DeSmet. Writer workshops geared toward beginner and intermediate levels. **Open to students** (1-3 graduate credits available in English). "One week-long session is devoted to juvenile fiction. " Annual workshop. Workshop held the third week of June. Registration limited to 15. Writing facilities available: computer labs. Cost of workshop: $325 before May 23; $355 after May 23. Cost includes instruction, reception, and continental breakfast each day. Write for more information. "Brochure goes online every January for the following June."

## WRITE-TO-PUBLISH CONFERENCE

9731 N. Fox Glen Dr., #6F, Niles IL 60714-4222. (847)296-3964. Fax: (847)296-0754. E-mail: lin@writetopublish.com. Website: www.writetopublish.com. **Director:** Lin Johnson. Writer workshops geared toward all levels. **Open to students.** Conference is focused for the Christian market and includes classes on writing for children. Annual conference held in June. Cost of conference approximately: $400; includes conference and banquet. For information, call (847)299-4755 or e-mail brochure@writetopublish.com. Conference takes place at Wheaton College in the Chicago area.

## WRITERS' LEAGUE OF TEXAS WORKSHOP SERIES

1501 W. Fifth St., Suite E-2, Austin TX 78703. (512)499-8914. Fax: (512)499-0441. E-mail: wlt@writersleague.org. Website: www.writersleague.org. **Contact:** Helen Ginger. Writer workshops and conferences geared toward adults. Annual conferences. Classes are held during the week, and retreats/workshops are held throughout the year. Annual Teddy Children's Book Award of $1,000 presented each fall to book published from June 1 to May 1. Write for more information.

## WRITING FOR YOUNG READERS WORKSHOP

Brigham Young University, 348 Harman Bldg., Provo UT 84602-1532. (801)442-2568. Fax: (801)422-0745. E-mail: susan.overstreet@byu.edu. Website: wfyr.byu.edu.

# Contests, Awards & Grants

Publication is not the only way to get your work recognized. Contests and awards can also be great ways to gain recognition in the industry. Grants, offered by organizations like SCBWI, offer monetary recognition to writers, giving them more financial freedom as they work on projects.

When considering contests or applying for grants, be sure to study guidelines and requirements. Regard entry deadlines as gospel and follow the rules to the letter.

Note that some contests require nominations. For published authors and illustrators, competitions provide an excellent way to promote your work. Your publisher may not be aware of local competitions such as state-sponsored awards—if your book is eligible, have the appropriate person at your publishing company nominate or enter your work for consideration.

To select potential contests and grants, read through the listings that interest you, then send for more information about the types of written or illustrated material considered and other important details. A number of contests offer information through websites given in their listings.

If you are interested in knowing who has received certain awards in the past, check your local library or bookstores or consult *Children's Books: Awards & Honors*, compiled and edited by the Children's Book Council (www.cbcbooks.org). Many bookstores have special sections for books that are Caldecott and Newbery Medal winners. Visit the American Library Association website, www.ala.org, for information on the Caldecott, Newbery, Coretta Scott King and Printz Awards. Visit www.hbook.com for information on The Boston Globe-Horn Book Award. Visit www.scbwi.org/awards.htm for information on The Golden Kite Award.

For advice from a contest director, see the Insider Report with **Roxyanne Young**, creator of SmartWriters.com's Write It Now! competition, on page 364.

**Information on contests listed in the previous edition but not included in this edition of *Children's Writer's & Illustrator's Market* may be found in the General Index.**

## ACORN CONTESTS

Acorn, 1530 Seventh St., Rock Island IL 61201. (309)788-3980. **Submit entries to:** Betty Mowery, editor. Open to students. Annually. "Purpose of contest: to help young authors compete with others and to obtain discipline in preparing and submitting entries." Submissions must be unpublished. Submissions made by author. Rules/ entry forms are available for SASE. Entry fee: six 37¢ stamps. Awards subscription to Acorn. Judging by Acorn staff member. "Open to all young authors ages K-12th grade. Entries without SASE will not be returned and will not receive a reply. Entries without entry fee will not be judged."

## JANE ADDAMS CHILDREN'S BOOK AWARDS

Jane Addams Peace Association, Inc./Women's International League for Peace and Freedom, 777 United Nations Plaza, New York NY 10017. (212)682-8830. Fax: (212)286-8211. E-mail: japa@igc.org. Website: www.janeadda mspeace.org. **Contact:** Linda B. Belle. "Two copies of published books (in previous year only)." Annual award. Estab. 1953. Previously published submissions only. Submissions made by author, author's agent, a person or group, submitted by the publisher. Must be published January 1-December 31 of preceding year. Deadline for entries: January 1 each year. SASE for contest rules and entry forms but better to check website. Awards cash and certificate, $1,000 to winners (awards are for longer book, shorter book) and $500 each to Honor Book winners (split between author and illustrator, if necessary). Judging by national committee from various N.S. regions (all are members of W.I.L.P.F.).

## AIM, Magazine Short Story Contest

P.O. Box 1174, Maywood IL 60153-8174. (773)874-6184. **Contest Directors:** Ruth Apilado, Mark Boone. Annual contest. **Open to students.** Estab. 1983. Purpose of contest: "We solicit stories with lasting social significance proving that people from different racial/ethnic backgrounds are more alike than they are different." Unpublished submissions only. Deadline for entries: August 15. SASE for contest rules and entry forms. SASE for return of work. No entry fee. Awards $100. Judging by editors. Contest open to everyone. Winning entry published in fall issue of *AIM*. Subscription rate: $12/year. Single copy: $4.50.

## ⚡ ALCUIN CITATION AWARD

The Alcuin Society, P.O. Box 3216, Vancouver BC V6B 3X8 Canada. (604)732-5403. Fax: (604)985-1091. E-mail: leahgordon@shaw.ca. Website: www.alcuinsociety.com. Annual award. Estab. 1983. Purpose of contest: Alcuin Citations are awarded annually for excellence in Canadian book design. Previously published submissions only, "in the year prior to the Awards call for entries; i.e., 2005 awards went to books published in 2004." Submissions made by the publisher, author or designer. Deadline for entries: mid-March. Entry fee is $20/ book; include check and entry form with book. Awards certificate. Winning books are exhibited nationally. Judging by professionals and those experienced in the field of book design. Requirements for entrants: Winners are selected from books designed and published in Canada. Awards are presented annually at the Annual General Meeting of the Alcuin Society held in early June each year.

## AMERICAN ASSOCIATION OF UNIVERSITY WOMEN, NORTH CAROLINA DIVISION, AWARD IN JUVENILE LITERATURE

North Carolina Literary and Historical Association, 4610 Mail Service Center, Raleigh NC 27699-4610. (919)807-7290. Fax: (919)733-8807. E-mail: michael.hill@ncmail.net. **Award Coordinator:** Mr. Michael Hill. Annual award. Purpose of award: to recognize the year's best work of juvenile literature by a North Carolina resident. Book must be published during the year ending June 30. Submissions made by author, author's agent or publisher. Deadline for entries: July 15. SASE for contest rules. Awards a cup to the winner and winner's name inscribed on a plaque displayed within the North Carolina Office of Archives and History. Judging by Board of Award selected by sponsoring organization. Requirements for entrants: Author must have maintained either legal residence or actual physical residence, or a combination of both, in the state of North Carolina for three years immediately preceding the close of the contest period. Only published work (books) eligible.

## AMERICAS AWARD

CLASP Committee on Teaching and Outreach, %Center for Latin American and Caribbean Studies, Milwaukee WI 53201. (414)229-5986. Fax: (414)229-2879. E-mail: jkline@uwm.edu. Website: www.uwm.edu/Dept/CL ACS/outreach/americas.html. **Coordinator:** Julie Kline. Annual award. Estab. 1993. Purpose of contest: "Up to two awards are given each spring in recognition of U.S. published works (from the previous year) of fiction, poetry, folklore or selected nonfiction (from picture books to works for young adults) in English or Spanish which authentically and engagingly relate to Latin America, the Caribbean, or to Latinos in the United States. By combining both and linking the 'Americas,' the intent is to reach beyond geographic borders, as well as multicultural-international boundaries, focusing instead upon cultural heritages within the hemisphere."

Previously published submissions only. Submissions open to anyone with an interest in the theme of the award. Deadline for entries: January 15. SASE for contest rules and any committee changes. Awards $500 cash prize, plaque and a formal presentation at the Library of Congress, Washington DC. Judging by a review committee consisting of individuals in teaching, library work, outreach and children's literature specialists.

## AMHA MORGAN ART CONTEST

American Morgan Horse Association, Box 960, Shelburne VT 05482-0960. (802)985-4944. Fax: (802)985-8897. E-mail: info@morganhorse.com. Website: www.morganhorse.com. **Open to students.** Annual contest. The art contest consists of two categories: Morgan art (pencil sketches, oils, water colors, paintbrush), Morgan specialty pieces (sculptures, carvings). Unpublished submissions only. Deadline for entries: October 1. Contest rules and entry forms available for SASE. Entries not returned. Entry fee is $5 for children, $10 for adults. Awards $50 first prize in 2 divisions (for adults) and AMHA gift certificates to top 6 places (for children). Judging by *The Morgan Horse* magazine staff. "All work submitted becomes property of The American Morgan Horse Association. Selected works may be used for promotional purposes by the AMHA." Requirements for entrants: "We consider all work submitted." Works displayed at the annual convention and the AMHA headquarters; published in *AMHA News* and *Morgan Sales Network* and in color in the *Morgan Horse Magazine.* The contest divisions consist of Junior (to age 17), and Senior (18 and over). Each art piece must have its own application form and its own entry fee. Matting is optional.

## ARTS RECOGNITION AND TALENT SEARCH (ARTS)

National Foundation for Advancement in the Arts, 444 Brickell Ave., P-14, Miami FL 33131. (305)377-1140. Fax: (305)377-1149. E-mail: info@nfaa.org. Website: www.ARTSaward.org. **Contact:** Christopher D. Schram. Open to students/high school seniors or 17- and 18-year-olds. Annual award. Estab. 1981. "Created to recognize and reward outstanding accomplishment in dance, music, jazz, voice, theater, photography, film and video, visual arts and/or writing. Arts Recognition and Talent Search (ARTS) is an innovative national program of the National Foundation for Advancement in the Arts (NFAA). Established in 1981, ARTS touches the lives of gifted young people across the country, providing financial support, scholarships and goal-oriented artistic, educational and career opportunities. Each year, from a pool of more than 8,000 applicants, an average of 800 ARTS winners are chosen for NFAA support by panels of distinguished artists and educators. Deadline for entries: June 1 and October 1. Entry fee is $30/40. Fee waivers available based on need. Awards $100-10,000— unrestricted cash grants. Judging by a panel of authors and educators recognized in the field. Rights to submitted/winning material: NFAA/ARTS retains the right to duplicate work in an anthology or in Foundation literature unless otherwise specified by the artist. Requirements for entrants: Artists must be high school seniors or, if not enrolled in high school, must be 17 or 18 years old. Applicants must be U.S. citizens or residents, unless applying in jazz. Works will be published in an anthology distributed during ARTS Week, the final adjudication phase which takes place in Miami. NFAA will invite 2% of artists to participate in "ARTS Week 2005," in January in Miami-Dade County, Florida. ARTS Week is a once-in-a-lifetime experience consisting of performances, master classes, workshops, readings, exhibits, and enrichment activities with renowned artists and arts educators. All expenses are paid by NFAA, including airfare, hotel, meals and ground transportation.

## THE ASPCA HENRY BERGH CHILDREN'S BOOK AWARD

The American Society For the Prevention of Cruelty to Animals, 424 E. 92nd St., New York NY 10128-6804. (212)876-7700, ext. 4409. Fax: (212)860-3435. E-mail: education@aspca.org. Website: www.aspca.org/bookaw ard. **Award Manager:** Miriam Ramos, assistant director, National Education Programs. Competition open to authors, illustrators, and publishers. Annual award. Estab. 2000. Purpose of contest: To honor outstanding children's literature that fosters empathy and compassion for all living things. Awards presented to authors. Previously published submissions only. Submissions made by author or author's agent. Must be published between January 2006-December 2006. Deadline for entries: October 31, 2006. Awards foil seals, plaque, certificate. Judging by professionals in animal welfare and children's literature. Requirements for entrants: Open to children's literature about animals and/or the environment published in 2005. Includes fiction, nonfiction and poetry in 5 categories: Companion Animals, Ecology and Environment, Humane Heroes, Illustration, and Young Adult.

## ☑ ATLANTIC WRITING COMPETITION

Writer's Federation of Nova Scotia, 1113 Marginal Rd., Halifax NS B3H 4P7 Canada. (902)423-8116. Fax: (902)422-0881. E-mail: talk@writers.ns.ca. Website: www.writers.ns.ca/competitions.html. Annual contest. Purpose is to encourage emerging writers in Atlantic Canada to explore their talents by sending unpublished work to any of five categories: novel, short story, poetry, writing for children or magazine article. Unpublished submissions only. Only open to residents of Atlantic Canada who are unpublished in category they enter. Visit website for more information.

## BAKER'S PLAYS HIGH SCHOOL PLAYWRITING CONTEST

Baker's Plays, P.O. Box 6992222, Quincy MA 02269-9222. Fax: (617)745-9891. Website: www.bakersplays.com. **Contest Director:** Deirdre Shaw. **Open to any high school student.** Annual contest. Estab. 1990. Purpose of the contest: to encourage playwrights at the high school level and to insure the future of American theater. Unpublished submissions only. Postmark deadline: January 31. Notification: May. SASE for contest rules and entry forms. No entry fee. Awards $500 to the first place playwright with publication by Baker's Plays; $250 to the second place playwright with an honorable mention; and $100 to the third place playwright with an honorable mention in the series. Judged anonymously. Plays must be accompanied by the signature of a sponsoring high school drama or English teacher, and it is recommended that the play receive a production or a public reading prior to the submission. "Please include a SASE with priority postage." Teachers must not submit student's work. The work will be listed in the Baker's Plays Catalogue, which is distributed to 50,000 prospective producing organizations.

## BAY AREA BOOK REVIEWER'S ASSOCIATION, (BABRA)

% *Poetry Flash*, Berkeley CA 94710. (510)525-5476. Fax: (510)525-6752. E-mail: babra@poetryflash.org. Website: www.poetryflash.org. **Contact:** Joyce Jenkins. Annual award for outstanding book in children's literature, open to books published in the current calendar year by Northern California authors. Annual award. Estab. 1981. "BABRA presents annual awards to Bay Area (northern California) authors annually in fiction, nonfiction, poetry and children's literature. Purpose is to encourage writers and stimulate interest in books and reading." Previously published books only. Must be published the calendar year prior to spring awards ceremony. Submissions nominated by publishers; author or agent could also nominate published work. Deadline for entries: December. No entry forms. Send 3 copies of the book to attention: BABRA. No entry fee. Awards $100 honorarium and award certificate. Judging by voting members of the Bay Area Book Reviewer's Association. Books that reach the "finals" (usually 3-5 per category) displayed at annual award ceremonies (spring). Nominated books are displayed and sold at BABRA's annual awards ceremonies in the spring of each year; the winner is asked to read at the San Francisco Public Library's Main Branch.

## THE IRMA S. AND JAMES H. BLACK BOOK AWARD

Bank Street College of Education, New York NY 10025-1898. (212)875-4450. Fax: (212)875-4558. E-mail: lindag @bnkst.edu. Website: http://streetcat.bnkst.edu/html/isb.html. **Contact:** Linda Greengrass. Annual award. Estab. 1972. Purpose of award: "The award is given each spring for a book for young children, published in the previous year, for excellence of both text and illustrations." Entries must have been published during the previous calendar year (between January '05 and December '05 for 2006 award). Deadline for entries: mid-December. "Publishers submit books to us by sending them here to me at the Bank Street Library. Authors may ask their publishers to submit their books. Out of these, three to five books are chosen by a committee of older children and children's literature professionals. These books are then presented to children in selected second, third and fourth grade classes here and at a few other cooperating schools on the East Coast. These children are the final judges who pick the actual award winner. A scroll (one each for the author and illustrator, if they're different) with the recipient's name and a gold seal designed by Maurice Sendak are awarded in May."

## THE BOSTON GLOBE-HORN BOOK AWARDS

The Boston Globe & The Horn Book, Inc., The Horn Book, 56 Roland St., Suite 200, Boston MA 02129. (617)628-0225. Fax: (617)628-0882. E-mail: info@hbook.com. Website: www.hbook.com/bghbrules.shtml. Annual award. Estab. 1967. Purpose of award: "to reward literary excellence in children's and young adult books. Awards are for picture books, nonfiction, fiction and poetry. Up to two honor books may be chosen for each category." Books must be published between June 1, 2004 and May 31, 2005. Deadline for entries: May 2005. "Textboks, e-books, and audiobooks will not be considered, nor will mss. Books should be submitted by publishers, although the judges reserve the right to honor any eligible book. Award winners receive $500 and silver engraved bowl, honor book winners receive a silver engraved plate." Judging by 3 judges involved in children's book field. "*The Horn Book Magazine* publishes speeches given at awards ceremonies. The book must have been published in the U.S."

## ANN ARLYS BOWLER POETRY CONTEST

*Read* Magazine, Stamford CT 06912-0023. (203)705-3457. Fax: (203)705-1661. E-mail: jcohn@weeklyreader.c om. Website: www.weeklyreader.com/read.html. **Contest Director:** Jessica Cohn. **Open to students .** Annual contest. Estab. 1988. Purpose of the contest: to reward young-adult poets (grades 6-12). Unpublished submissions only. Submissions made by the author or nominated by a person or group of people. Entry form must include signature of teacher, parent or guardian, and student verifying originality. Maximum number of submissions per student: 3 poems. Deadline for entries: mid-January. SASE for contest rules and entry forms. No entry fee. Awards 6 winners $100 each, medal of honor and publication in *Read* . Semifinalists receive $50 each. Judging by *Read* and *Weekly Reader* editors and teachers. Requirements for entrants: the material must be original. Winning entries will be published in an issue of *Read* .

## ANN CONNOR BRIMER AWARD
Nova Scotia Library Association, P.O. Box 36036, Halifax NS B3J 3S9 Canada. (902)490-5875. Fax: (902)490-5893. **Award Director:** Heather MacKenzie. Annual award. Estab. 1991. Purpose of the contest: to recognize excellence in writing. Given to an author of a children's book who resides in Atlantic Canada. Previously published submissions only. Submissions made by the author's agent or nominated by a person or group of people. Must be published in previous year. Deadline for entries: October 15. SASE for contest rules and entry forms. No entry fee. Awards $1,000 and framed certificate. Judging by a selection committee. Requirements for entrants: Book must be intended for use up to age 15; in print and readily available; fiction or nonfiction except textbooks.

## BUCKEYE CHILDREN'S BOOK AWARD
Ada Kent % Ohio School for the Deaf, 500 Morse Rd., Columbus OH 43214. (614)728-1414. E-mail: agkent@columbus.rr.com. Website: www.bcbookaward.info. **President:** Ada G. Kent. Correspondence should be sent to Ada Kent at the above address. **Open to students.** Award offered every 2 years. Estab. 1981. Purpose of the award: "The Buckeye Children's Book Award Program was designed to encourage children to read literature critically, to promote teacher and librarian involvement in children's literature programs, and to commend authors of such literature, as well as to promote the use of libraries. Awards are presented in the following three categories: grades K-2, grades 3-5, grades 6-8 and grades 9-12 (Teen Buckeye)." Previously published submissions only. Deadline for entries: February 1. "The nominees are submitted by the students this date during the even year and the votes are submitted by this date during the odd year. This award is nominated and voted upon by children in Ohio. It is based upon criteria established in our bylaws. The winning authors are awarded a special plaque honoring them at a banquet given by one of the sponsoring organizations. The BCBA Board oversees the tallying of the votes and announces the winners in March of the voting year at www.bcbookaward.info and in a number of national journals. The book must have been written by an author, a citizen of the United States and originally copyrighted in the U.S. within the last three years preceding the nomination year. The award-winning books are displayed in a historical display housed at the Reinberger Children's Library at Kent State Library School."

## BYLINE MAGAZINE CONTESTS
P.O. Box 5240, Edmond OK 73083-5240. E-mail: mpreston@bylinemag.com. Website: www.bylinemag.com. **Contest Director:** Marcia Preston. Purpose of contest: *ByLine* runs 4 contests a month on many topics to encourage and motivate writers. Past topics include first chapter of a novel, children's fiction, children's poem, nonfiction for children, personal essay, general short stories, valentine or love poem, etc. Send SASE for contest flier with topic list and rules, or see website. Unpublished submissions only. Submissions made by the author. "We do not publish the contests' winning entries, just the names of the winners." SASE for contest rules. Entry fee is $3-4. Awards cash prizes for first, second and third place. Amounts vary. Judging by qualified writers or editors. List of winners will appear in magazine.

## BYLINE MAGAZINE STUDENT PAGE
P.O. Box 5240, Edmond OK 73083-5240. (405)348-5591. Website: www.bylinemag.com. **Contest Director:** Marcia Preston, publisher. **Open to students.** Estab. 1981. "We offer writing contests for students in grades 1-12 on a monthly basis, September through May, with cash prizes and publication of top entries." Previously unpublished submissions only. "This is not a market for illustration." Deadline for entries varies. "Entry fee usually $1." Awards cash and publication. Judging by qualified editors and writers. "We publish top entries in student contests. Winners' list published in magazine dated 2 months past deadline." Send SASE for details.

## RANDOLPH CALDECOTT MEDAL
Association for Library Service to Children, Division of the American Library Association, 50 E. Huron, Chicago IL 60611. (312)280-2163. E-mail: alsc@ala.org. Website: www.ala.org. **Executive Director:** Malore I. Brown. Annual award. Estab. 1938. Purpose of the award: to honor the artist of the most outstanding picture book for children published in the U.S. (Illustrator must be U.S. citizen or resident.) Must be published year preceding award. Deadline for entries: December 31. SASE for award rules. Entries not returned. No entry fee. "Medal given at ALA Annual Conference during the Newbery/Caldecott Banquet."

## CALIFORNIA YOUNG PLAYWRIGHTS CONTEST
Playwrights Project, 450 B St., Suite 1020, San Diego CA 92101. (619)239-8222. Fax: (619)239-8225. E-mail:

write@playwrightsproject.com. Website: www.playwrightsproject.com. **Director:** Deborah Salzer. **Open to Californians under age 19.** Annual contest. Estab. 1985. "Our organization and the contest is designed to nurture promising young writers. We hope to develop playwrights and audiences for live theater. We also teach playwriting." Submissions required to be unpublished and not produced professionally. Submissions made by the author. Deadline for entries: April 1. SASE for contest rules and entry form. No entry fee. Award is professional productions of 3-5 short plays each year, participation of the writers in the entire production process, with a royalty awarded. Judging by professionals in the theater community, a committee of 5-7; changes somewhat each year. Works performed in San Diego at the Cassius Carter Centre Stage of the Old Globe. Writers submitting scripts of 10 or more pages receive a detailed script evaluation letter upon request.

## CALLIOPE FICTION CONTEST

Writers' Specialized Interest Group (SIG) of American Mensa, Ltd., P.O. Box 466, Moraga CA 94556-0466. E-mail: cynthia@theriver.com. Website: www.us.mensa.org. **Fiction Editor:** Cynthia. **Open to students.** Annual contest. Estab. 1991. Purpose of contest: "To promote good writing and opportunities for getting published. To give our member/subscribers and others an entertaining and fun exercise in writing." Unpublished submissions only (all genres, no violence, profanity or extreme horror). Submissions made by author. Deadline for entries: changes annually but usually around September 15. Entry fee is $2 for nonsubscribers; subscribers get first entry fee. Awards small amount of cash (up to $75 for 1st place, to $10 for 3rd), certificates, full or mini-subscriptions to *Calliope* and various premiums and books, depending on donations. All winners are published in subsequent issues of *Calliope*. Judging by fiction editor, with concurrence of other editors, if needed. Requirements for entrants: winners must retain sufficient rights to have their stories published in the January/February issue, or their entries will be disqualified; one-time rights. Open to all writers. No special considerations—other than following the guidelines. Contest theme, due dates and sometimes entry fees change annually. Always send SASE for complete rules; available after April 15 each year. Sample copies with prior winners are available for $3 and large SAE with 3 first-class stamps.

## ◼ CANADA COUNCIL GOVERNOR GENERAL'S LITERARY AWARDS

350 Albert St., Ottawa ON K1P 5V8 Canada. (613)566-4410, ext. 5576. Fax: (613)566-4410. E-mail: joanne.laroc que-poirier@canadacouncil.ca. **Program Officer, Writing and Publishing Section:** Joanne Larocque-Poirier. Annual award. Estab. 1937. Purpose of award: given to the best English-language and the best French-language work in each of the seven categories of Fiction, Literary Nonfiction, Poetry, Drama, Children's Literature (text), Children's Literature (illustration) and Translation. Books must be first-edition trade books that have been written, translated or illustrated by Canadian citizens or permanent residents of Canada. In the case of Translation, the original work written in English or French, must also be a Canadian-authored title. English titles must be published between September 1, 2005 and September 30, 2006. Books must be submitted by publishers. Books must reach the Canada Council for the Arts no later than August 7, 2006. The deadlines are final; no bound proofs or books that miss the applicable deadlines will be given to the peer assessment committees. The awards ceremony is scheduled mid-November. Amount of award: $15,000 to winning authors; $1,000 to nonwinning finalists.

## CHILDREN'S WRITER WRITING CONTESTS

93 Long Ridge Rd., West Redding CT 06896-1124. (203)792-8600. Fax: (203)792-8406. Website: www.childrens writer.com. Contest offered twice per year by *Children's Writer*, the monthly newsletter of writing and publishing trends. Purpose of the award: To promote higher quality children's literature. "Each contest has its own theme. Any original unpublished piece, not accepted by any publisher at the time of submission, is eligible." Submissions made by the author. Deadline for entries: Last weekday in February and October. "We charge a $10 entry fee for nonsubscribers only, which is applicable against a subscription to *Children's Writer*' Awards: 1st place—$250 or $500, a certificate and publication in *Children's Writer*; 2nd place—$100 or $250, and certificate; 3rd-5th places—$50 or $100 and certificates. To obtain the rules and theme for the current contest go to the website and click on "Writing Contests," or send a SASE to *Children's Writer* at the above address. Put "Contest Request" in the lower left of your envelope. Judging by a panel of 4 selected from the staff of the Institute of Children's Literature. "We acquire First North American Serial Rights (to print the winner in *Children's Writer*), after which all rights revert to author." Open to any writer. Entries are judged on age targeting, originality, quality of writing and, for nonfiction, how well the information is conveyed and accuracy. "Submit clear photocopies only, not originals; submission will *not* be returned. Manuscripts should be typed double-spaced. No pieces containing violence or derogatory, racist or sexist language or situations will be accepted, at the sole discretion of the judges."

## CHILDREN'S WRITERS FICTION CONTEST

Stepping Stones, P.O. Box 601721, Miami Beach FL 33160. (305)944-6491. E-mail: verwil@alumni.pace.edu.

**Director:** V. Williams. Annual contest. Estab. 1993. Purpose of contest: to promote writing for children by giving children's writers an opportunity to submit work in competition. Unpublished submissions only. Submissions made by the author. Deadline for entries: July 31. SASE for contest rules and entry forms. Entry fee is $10. Awards cash prize, certificate; certificates for Honorable Mention. Judging by Williams, Walters & Associates. First rights to winning material acquired or purchased. Requirements for entrants: Work must be suitable for children and no longer than 1,500 words. Send SASE for list of winners. "Stories should have believable characters. Work submitted on colored paper, in book format, illustrated, or with photograph attached is not acceptable."

## COLORADO BOOK AWARDS
1490 Lafayette St., Suite 101, Denver CO 80218. (303)839-8320. Fax: (303)839-8319. Website: www.coloradocenterforthebook.org. **Interim Coordinator:** Sara Whelan. Annual award. Estab. 1993. Previously published submissions only. Submissions are made by the author, author's agent, nominated by a person or group of people. Requires Colorado residency by authors. Deadline for entries: January 15, 2004. SASE for contest rules and entry forms. Entry fee is $45. Awards $250 and plaque. Judging by a panel of literary agents, booksellers and librarians. "Please note, we *also* have periodic competitions for illustrators to design a poster and associated graphics for our other book programs. The date varies. Inquiries are welcomed."

## CRICKET LEAGUE
*Cricket* magazine, P.O. Box 300, 315 Fifth St., Peru IL 61354. (815)224-5803. Website: www.cricketmag.com. Address entries to: Cricket League. **Open to students** . Monthly contest. Estab. 1973. "The purpose of Cricket League contests is to encourage creativity and give young people an opportunity to express themselves in writing, drawing, painting or photography. There is a contest each month. Possible categories include story, poetry, or art. Each contest relates to a *specific theme* described on each *Cricket* issue's Cricket League page. Signature verifying originality, age and address of entrant and permission to publish required. Entries which do not relate to the current month's theme cannot be considered." Unpublished submissions only. Deadline for entries: the 25th of each month. Cricket League rules, contest theme, and submission deadline information can be found in the current issue of *Cricket* and via website. "We prefer that children who enter the contests subscribe to the magazine or that they read *Cricket* in their school or library." No entry fee. Awards certificate suitable for framing and children's books or art/writing supplies. Judging by *Cricket* editors. Obtains right to print prizewinning entries in magazine. Refer to contest rules in current *Cricket* issue. Winning entries are published on the Cricket League pages in the *Cricket* magazine 3 months subsequent to the issue in which the contest was announced. Current theme, rules, and prizewinning entries also posted on the website.

## DELACORTE DELL YEARLING CONTEST FOR A FIRST MIDDLE-GRADE NOVEL
Delacorte Press, Random House, Inc., 1745 Broadway, 9th Floor, New York NY 10019. Estab. 1992. Website: www.randomhouse/kids/games/dellyearling.html. Annual award. Purpose of the award: to encourage the writing of fiction for children ages 9-12, either contemporary or historical; to encourage unpublished writers in the field of middle grade fiction. Unpublished submissions only. No simultaneous submissions. Length: between 96-160 pages. Submissions made by author or author's agent. Entries should be postmarked between April 1 and June 30. SASE for award rules. No entry fee. Awards a $1,500 cash prize plus a hardcover and paperback book contract with a $7,500 advance against a royalties to be negotiated. Judging by Delacorte Press Books for Young Readers editorial staff. Open to U.S. and Canadian writers who have not previously published a novel for middle-grade readers (ages 9-12).

## DELACORTE PRESS PRIZE FOR A FIRST YOUNG ADULT NOVEL
Delacorte Press, Books for Young Readers Department, 1745 Broadway, 9th Floor, New York NY 10019. Website: www.randomhouse.com/kids/games/delacorte.html. Annual award. Estab. 1982. Purpose of award: to encourage the writing of contemporary young adult fiction (for readers ages 12-18). Previously unpublished submissions only. Manuscripts sent to Delacorte Press may not be submitted to other publishers while under consideration for the prize. "Entries must be submitted between October 1 and New Year's Day. The real deadline is a December 31 postmark. Early entries are appreciated." Length: between 100-224 pages. SASE for award rules. No entry fee. Awards a $1,500 cash prize and a $7,500 advance against royalties for world rights on a hardcover and paperback book contract. Works published in an upcoming Delacorte Press, an imprint of Random House, Inc., Books for Young Readers list. Judged by the editors of the Books for Young Readers Department of Delacorte Press. Requirements for entrants: The writer must be American or Canadian and must *not* have previously published a young adult novel but may have published anything else. Foreign-language mss and translations and mss submitted to a previous Delacorte Press are not eligible. Send SASE for new guidelines. Guidelines are also available on our website.

## DOROTHY CANFIELD FISHER CHILDREN'S BOOK AWARD

Vermont Department of Libraries, % Northeast Regional Library, St. Johnsbury VT 05819. (802)828-6954. Fax: (802)828-2199. E-mail: grace.greene@dol.state.vt.us. Website: www.dcfaward.org. **Chair:** Sally Margolis. Annual award. Estab. 1957. Purpose of the award: to encourage Vermont children to become enthusiastic and discriminating readers by providing them with books of good quality by living American authors published in the current year. Deadline for entries: December of year book was published. SASE for award rules and entry forms or e-mail. No entry fee. Awards a scroll presented to the winning author at an award ceremony. Judging is by the children grades 4-8. They vote for their favorite book. Requirements for entrants: "Titles must be original work, published in the United States, and be appropriate to children in grades 4 through 8. The book must be copyrighted in the current year. It must be written by an American author living in the U.S."

## FLORIDA STATE WRITING COMPETITION

Florida Freelance Writers Association, P.O. Box A, North Stratford NH 03590. (603)922-8338. Fax: (603)922-8339. E-mail: contest@writers-editors.com. Website: www.writers-editors.com. **Executive Director:** Dana K. Cassell. Annual contest. Estab. 1984. Categories include children's literature (length appropriate to age category). Entry fee is $5 (members), $10 (nonmembers) or $10-20 for entries longer than 3,000 words. Awards $100 first prize, $75 second prize, $50 third prize, certificates for honorable mentions. Judging by teachers, editors and published authors. Judging criteria: interest and readability within age group, writing style and mechanics, originality, salability. Deadline: March 15. For copy of official entry form, send #10 SASE or visit website. List of winners on website.

## DON FREEMAN MEMORIAL GRANT-IN-AID

Society of Children's Book Writers and Illustrators, 8271 Beverly Blvd., Los Angeles CA 90048. E-mail: scbwi@scbwi.org. Website: www.scbwi.org. Estab. 1974. Purpose of award: to "enable picture book artists to further their understanding, training and work in the picture book genre." Applications and prepared materials are available in October and must be postmarked between February 1 and March 1. Grant awarded and announced in August. SASE for award rules and entry forms. SASE for return of entries. No entry fee. Annually awards one grant of $1,500 and one runner-up grant of $500. "The grant-in-aid is available to both full and associate members of the SCBWI who, as artists, seriously intend to make picture books their chief contribution to the field of children's literature."

## ☪ AMELIA FRANCES HOWARD GIBBON AWARD FOR ILLUSTRATION

Canadian Library Association, 328 Frank St., Ottawa ON K2P 0X8 Canada. (613)232-9625. Website: www.cla.ca. **Contact:** Chairperson, Canadian Association of Children's Librarians. Annual award. Estab. 1971. Purpose of the award: "to honor excellence in the illustration of children's book(s) in Canada. To merit consideration the book must have been published in Canada and its illustrator must be a Canadian citizen or a permanent resident of Canada." Previously published submissions only; must be published between January 1 and December 31 of the previous year. Deadline for entries: December 31. SASE for award rules. Entries not returned. No entry fee. Judging by selection committee of members of Canadian Association of Children's Librarians. Requirements for entrants: illustrator must be Canadian or Canadian resident.

## GOLD MEDALLION BOOK AWARDS

Evangelical Christian Publishers Association, 4816 South Ash, Suite 101, Tempe AZ 85282. (480)966-3998. Fax: (480)966-1944. E-mail: mkuyper@ecpa.org. Website: www.ecpa.org. **President:** Mark W. Kuyper. Annual award. Estab. 1978. Categories include Preschool Children's Books, Elementary Children's Books, Youth Books. "All entries must be evangelical in nature and cannot be contrary to ECPA's Statement of Faith (stated in official rules)." Deadlines for entries: December 1. Guidelines available annually in October. SASE for award rules and entry form. "The work must be submitted by the publisher." Entry fee is $300/title for nonmembers. Awards a Gold Medallion plaque.

## GOLDEN KITE AWARDS

Society of Children's Book Writers and Illustrators, 8271 Beverly Blvd., Los Angeles CA 90048. (323)782-1010. E-mail: scbwi@scbwi.org. Website: www.scbwi.org. **Contact:** SCBWI Golden Kite Coordinator. Annual award. Estab. 1973. "The works chosen will be those that the judges feel exhibit excellence in writing, and in the case of the picture-illustrated books—in illustration, and genuinely appeal to the interests and concerns of children. For the fiction and nonfiction awards, original works and single-author collections of stories or poems of which at least half are new and never before published in book form are eligible—anthologies and translations are not. For the picture-illustration awards, the art or photographs must be original works (the texts—which may be fiction or nonfiction—may be original, public domain or previously published). Deadline for entries: December 15. SASE for award rules. No entry fee. Awards statuettes and plaques. The panel of judges will consist of professional authors, illustrators, editors or agents." Requirements for entrants: "must be a member of SCBWI and books must be published in that year." Winning books will be displayed at national conference in August. Books to be entered, as well as further inquiries, should be submitted to: The Society of Children's Book Writers and Illustrators, above address.

## N̄! THE MARILYN HALL AWARDS FOR YOUTH THEATRE
Beverly Hills Theatre Guild, P.O. Box 39729, Los Angeles CA 90039-0729. Website: www.beverlyhillstheatreguil d.org. **Contact:** Dick Dotterer. **Open to students.** Annual contest. Estab. 1998/99. Purpose of contest: "To encourage the creation and development of new plays for youth theatre." Unpublished submissions only. Authors must be U.S. citizens or legal residents and must sign entry form personally. Deadline for entries: between January 15 and last day of February each year (postmark accepted). Playwrights may submit up to two scripts. One nonprofessional production acceptable for eligibility. SASE for contest rules and entry forms. No entry fee. Awards: $500, 1st prize; $300, 2nd prize; $200, 3rd prize. Judging by theatre professionals cognizant of youth theatre and writing/producing.

## HIGHLIGHTS FOR CHILDREN FICTION CONTEST
803 Church St., Honesdale PA 18431-1895. (570)253-1080. Fax: (570)251-7847. Website: www.highlights.com. **Fiction Contest Editor:** Christine French Clark. Annual contest. Estab. 1980. Purpose of the contest: to stimulate interest in writing for children and reward and recognize excellence. Unpublished submissions only. Deadline for entries: February 28; entries accepted after January 1 only. SASE for contest rules and return of entries. No entry fee. Awards 3 prizes of $1,000 each in cash and a pewter bowl (or, at the winner's election, attendance at the Highlights Foundation Writers Workshop at Chautauqua). Judging by *Highlights* editors. Winning pieces are purchased for the cash prize of $1,000 and published in *Highlights*; other entries are considered for purchase. Requirements for entrants: open to any writer 16 years of age of older. Winners announced in June. Length up to 800 words. Stories for beginning readers should not exceed 500 words. Stories should be consistent with *Highlights* editorial requirements. No violence, crime or derogatory humor. Send SASE for guidelines and 2005 theme. See website for current theme and guidelines.

## INSIGHT WRITING CONTEST
*Insight Magazine*, 55 W. Oak Ridge Dr., Hagerstown MD 21740-7390. E-mail: insight@rhpa.org. Website: www.i nsightmagazine.org. **Open to students.** Annual contest. Unpublished submissions only. Submissions made by author. Deadline for entries: June. SASE for contest rules and entry forms. Awards first prizes, $100-250; second prizes, $75-200; third prizes, $50-150. Winning entries will be published in *Insight* . Contest includes three catagories: Student Short Story, General Short Story and Student Poetry. You must be age 22 or under to enter the student catagories. Entries must include cover sheet form available with SASE or on website.

## IRA CHILDREN'S BOOK AWARDS
International Reading Association, 800 Barksdale Rd., P.O. Box 8139, Newark DE 19714-8139. (302)731-1600. Fax: (302)731-1057. E-mail: exec@reading.org. Website: www.reading.org. Annual award. Awards are given for an author's first or second published book for fiction and nonfiction in three categories: primary (ages preschool-8), intermediate (ages 9-13), and young adult (ages 14-17). This award is intended for newly published authors who show unusual promise in the children's book field. Deadline for entries: November 1. Awards $500. For guidelines write or e-mail exec@reading.org.

## THE EZRA JACK KEATS NEW WRITER AND NEW ILLUSTRATOR AWARDS
Ezra Jack Keats Foundation/Administered by The Office of Children's Services, The New York Public Library, 455 Fifth Ave., New York NY 10016. (212)340-0906. Fax: (612)626-0377. E-mail: mtice@nypl.org. Website: www.ezra-jack-keats.org. **Program Coordinator:** Margaret Tice. Annual awards. Purpose of the awards: "The awards will be given to a promising new writer of picture books for children and a promising new illustrator of picture books for children. Selection criteria include books for children (ages 9 and under) that reflect the tradition of Ezra Jack Keats. These books portray: the universal qualities of childhood, strong and supportive family and adult relationships, the multicultural nature of our world." Submissions made by the publisher. Must be published in the preceding year. Deadline for entries: mid-December. SASE for contest rules and entry forms. No entry fee. Awards $1,000 coupled with Ezra Jack Keats Bronze Medal. Judging by a panel of experts. "The author or illustrator should have published no more than 3 children's books. Entries are judged on the outstanding features of the text, complemented by illustrations. Candidates need not be both author and illustrator. Entries should carry a 2004 copyright (for the 2005 award)." Winning books and authors to be presented at reception at The New York Public Library.

## EZRA JACK KEATS/KERLAN COLLECTION MEMORIAL FELLOWSHIP
University of Minnesota, 113 Elmer L. Andersen Library, Minneapolis MN 55455. (612)624-4576. Fax: (612)625-

5525. E-mail: clrc@tc.umn.edu. Website: special.lib.umn.edu/clrc/. Offered annually. Deadline for entries: May 1. Send request with SASE (6×9 or 9×12 envelope), including 60¢ postage. The Ezra Jack Keats/Kerlan Collection Memorial Fellowship from the Ezra Jack Keats Foundation will provide $1,500 to a "talented writer and/or illustrator of children's books who wishes to use the Kerlan Collection for the furtherance of his or her artistic development. Special consideration will be given to someone who would find it difficult to finance the visit to the Kerlan Collection." The fellowship winner will receive transportation and per diem. Judging by the Kerlan Award Committee—3 representatives from the University of Minnesota faculty, one from the Kerlan Friends, and one from the Minnesota Library Association.

## CORETTA SCOTT KING AWARD

Coretta Scott King Committee, Ethnic and Multicultural Information Exchange Round Table, American Library Association, 50 E. Huron St., Chicago IL 60611. (312)280-4294. Fax: (312)280-3256. E-mail: olos@ala.org. Website: www.ala.org/csk. "The Coretta Scott King Award is an annual award for books (1 for text and 1 for illustration) that convey the spirit of brotherhood espoused by M.L. King, Jr.—and also speak to the Black experience—for young people. There is an award jury of children's librarians that judges the books—reviewing over the year—and making a decision in January. A copy of an entry must be sent to each juror by December 1 of the juried year. Call or e-mail ALA Office for Literary Services for jury list. Awards breakfast held on Tuesday morning during A.L.A. Annual Conference. See schedule at website.

## LONGMEADOW JOURNAL LITERARY COMPETITION

% Rita and Robert Morton, 6750 N. Longmeadow, Lincolnwood IL 60712. (312)726-9789. Fax: (312)726-9772. **Contest Directors:** Rita and Robert Morton. Competition **open to students** (anyone age 10-19). Held annually and published every year. Estab. 1986. Purpose of contest: to encourage the young to write. Submissions are made by the author, nominated by a person or group of people, by teachers, librarians or parents. Deadline for entries: June 30. SASE. No entry fee. Awards first place, $175; second place, $100; and five prizes of $50. Judging by Rita Morton and Robert Morton. Works are published every year and are distributed to teachers and librarians and interested parties at no charge.

## LOUISE LOUIS/EMILY F. BOURNE STUDENT POETRY AWARD

Poetry Society of America, 15 Gramercy Park South, New York NY 10003-1705. (212)254-9628. Fax: (212)673-2352. E-mail: eve@poetrysociety.org. Website: www.poetrysociety.org. **Contact:** Program Director. **Open to students.** Annual award. Purpose of the award: award is for the best unpublished poem by a high or preparatory school student (grades 9-12) from the U.S. and its territories. Unpublished submissions only. Deadline for entries: Oct. 1 to Dec. 22. SASE for award rules and entry forms. Entries not returned. "High schools can send an unlimited number of submissions with one entry per individual student for a flat fee of $20. (High school students may send a single entry for $5.)" Award: $250. Judging by a professional poet. Requirements for entrants: Award open to all high school and preparatory students from the U.S. and its territories. School attended, as well as name and address, should be noted. PSA submission guidelines must be followed. These are printed in our fall calendar on our website and are readily available if those interested send us a SASE. Line limit: none. "The award-winning poem will be included in a sheaf of poems that will be part of the program at the award ceremony and sent to all PSA members."

## MAGAZINE MERIT AWARDS

Society of Children's Book Writers and Illustrators, 8271 Beverly Blvd., Los Angeles CA 90048. Fax: (323)782-1010. E-mail: scbwi@scbwi.org. Website: www.scbwi.org. **Award Coordinator:** Dorothy Leon. Annual award. Estab. 1988. Purpose of the award: "to recognize outstanding original magazine work for young people published during that year and having been written or illustrated by members of SCBWI." Previously published submissions only. Entries must be submitted between January 1 and December 15 of the year of publication. For rules and procedures see website. No entry fee. Must be a SCBWI member. Awards plaques and honor certificates for each of 4 categories (fiction, nonfiction, illustration, poetry). Judging by a magazine editor and two "full" SCBWI members. "All magazine work for young people by an SCBWI member—writer, artist or photographer—is eligible during the year of original publication. In the case of coauthored work, both authors must be SCBWI members. Members must submit their own work." Requirements for entrants: 4 copies each of the published work and proof of publication (may be contents page) showing the name of the magazine and the date of issue. The SCBWI is a professional organization of writers and illustrators and others interested in children's literature. Membership is open to the general public at large.

## MILKWEED PRIZE FOR CHILDREN'S LITERATURE

Milkweed Editions, 1011 Washington Ave. S., Suite 300, Minneapolis MN 55415-1246. (612)332-3192. Fax: (612)215-2550. E-mail: editor@milkweed.org. Website: www.milkweed.org. **Award Director:** H. Emerson

Blake, editor-in-chief. Annual award. Estab. 1993. Purpose of the award: to recognize an outstanding literary novel for readers ages 8-13 and encourage writers to turn their attention to readers in this age group. Unpublished submissions only "in book form." Please send SASE or visit website for award guidelines. The prize is awarded to the best work for children ages 8-13 that Milkweed agrees to publish in a calendar year by a writer not previously published by Milkweed. The Prize consists of a $5,000 advance against royalties agreed to at the time of acceptance. Submissions must follow our usual children's guidelines.

## MINNESOTA BOOK AWARDS

Minnesota Humanities Commission, 987 E. Ivy Ave., St. Paul MN 55106-2046. (651)774-0105. Fax: (651)774-0205. E-mail: mark@minnesotahumanities.org. Website: www.minnesotahumanities.org. **Award Director:** Jane Cunningham. Submit entries to: Martha Davis Beck, Minnesota Book Awards. Annual award. Estab. 1988. Purpose of contest: To recognize and honor achievement by members of Minnesota's book community. Previously published submissions only. Submissions made by author, publisher or author's agent. Fee for some categories. Work must hold 2004 copyright. Deadline for entries: late-December. Awards to winners and finalists, some cash. Judging by members of Minnesota's book community: booksellers, librarians, teachers and scholars, writers, reviewers and publishers. Requirements for entrants: Author must be a Minnesota author, editor or primary artistic creator. The Minnesota Book Awards includes 13 awards categories for children and young adult fiction and nonfiction titles and designs. For complete guidelines, visit website.

## MYTHOPOEIC FANTASY AWARD FOR CHILDREN'S LITERATURE

The Mythopoeic Society, P.O. Box 320486, San Francisco CA 94132-0486. E-mail: emfarrell@earthlink.net. Website: www.mythsoc.org. **Award Director:** Eleanor M. Farrell. Annual award. Estab. 1992 (previous to 1992, a single Mythopoeic Fantasy Award was given to either adult or children's books). Previously published submissions only. Submissions nominated. Must be published previous calendar year. Deadline for entries: February 28. Awards statuette. Judging by committee members of Mythopoeic Society. Requirements for entrants: books only; nominations are made by Mythopoeic Society members.

## NATIONAL CHILDREN'S THEATRE FESTIVAL

Actors' Playhouse at the Miracle Theatre, 280 Miracle Mile, Coral Gables FL 33134. (305)444-9293, ext. 615. Fax: (305)444-4181. E-mail: maulding@actorsplayhouse.org. Website: www.actorsplayhouse.org. **Director:** Earl Maulding. **Open to students.** Annual contest. Estab. 1994. Purpose of contest: to bring together the excitement of the theater arts and the magic of young audiences through the creation of new musical works and to create a venue for playwrights/composers to showcase their artistic products. Submissions must be unpublished. Submissions are made by author or author's agent. Deadline for entries: June 1. Visit website or send SASE for contest rules and entry forms. Entry fee is $10. Awards: first prize of $500, full production, and transportation to Festival weekend based on availability. Final judges are of national reputation. Past judges include Joseph Robinette, Moses Goldberg and Luis Santeiro.

## NATIONAL PEACE ESSAY CONTEST

United States Institute of Peace, 1200 17th St. NW, Washington DC 20036. (202)429-3854. Fax: (202)429-6063. E-mail: education@usip.org. Website: www.usip.org. **Open to students.** Annual contest. Estab. 1987. "The contest gives students the opportunity to do valuable research, writing and thinking on a topic of importance to international peace and conflict resolution. Teaching guides are available for teachers who allow the contest to be used as a classroom assignment." Deadline for entries is January 22, 2004. "Interested students, teachers and others may write or call to receive free contest kits. Please do not include SASE." Guidelines and rules on website. No entry fee. State Level Awards are $1,000 college scholarships. National winners are selected from among the 1st place state winners. National winners receive scholarships in the following amounts: first place $10,000; second $5,000; third $2,500. First place state winners invited to an expenses-paid awards program in Washington, DC in June. Judging is conducted by education professionals from across the country and by the Board of Directors of the United States Institute of Peace. "All submissions become property of the U.S. Institute of Peace to use at its discretion and without royalty or any limitation. Students grades 9-12 in the U.S., its territories and overseas schools may submit essays for review by completing the application process. U.S. citizenship required for students attending overseas schools. National winning essays will be published by the U.S. Institute of Peace."

## NATIONAL WRITERS ASSOCIATION NONFICTION CONTEST

10940 S. Parker Rd., #508, Parker CO 80134. (303)841-0246. **Executive Director:** Sandy Whelchel. Annual contest. Estab. 1971. Purpose of contest: "to encourage and recognize those who excel in nonfiction writing." Submissions made by author. Deadline for entries: December 31. SASE for contest rules and entry forms. Entry fee is $18. Awards 3 cash prizes; choice of books; Honorable Mention Certificate. "Two people read each entry;

third party picks three top winners from top five.'' Judging sheets sent if entry accompanied by SASE. Condensed version of 1st place published in *Authorship*

## NATIONAL WRITERS ASSOCIATION SHORT STORY CONTEST
10940 S. Parker Rd., #508, Parker CO 80134. (303)841-0246. **Executive Director:** Sandy Whelchel. Annual contest. Estab. 1971. Purpose of contest: ''To encourage writers in this creative form and to recognize those who excel in fiction writing.'' Submissions made by the author. Deadline for entries: July 1. SASE for contest rules and entry forms. Entry fee is $15. Awards 3 cash prizes, choice of books and certificates for Honorable Mentions. Judging by ''two people read each entry; third person picks top three winners.'' Judging sheet copies available for SASE.

## NEW ENGLAND BOOK AWARDS
New England Booksellers Association, 1700 Massachusetts Ave., Suite 332, Cambridge MA 02140. (617)576-3070. Fax: (617)576-3091. E-mail: neba@neba.org. Website: newenglandbooks.org. **Executive Director:** Rusty Drugan. Annual award. Estab. 1990. Purpose of award: ''to promote New England authors who have produced a body of work that stands as a significant contribution to New England's culture and is deserving of wider recognition.'' Previously published submissions only. Submissions made by New England booksellers; publishers. ''Award given to authors 'body of work' not a specific book.'' Entries must be still in print and available. SASE for contest rules and entry forms. No entry fee. Judging by NEBA membership. Requirements for entrants: Author/illustrator must live in New England. Submit written nominations only; actual books should not be sent. Member bookstores receive materials to display winners' books.

## NEW VOICES AWARD
Lee & Low Books, 95 Madison Ave., New York NY 10016. (212)779-4400. Fax: (212)532-6035. E-mail: general@leeandlow.com. Website: www.leeandlow.com/editorial/voices.html. **Editor-in-chief:** Louise May. **Open to students.** Annual award. Estab. 2000. Purpose of contest: Lee & Low Books is one of the few publishing companies owned by people of color. We have published over 50 first-time writers and illustrators. Titles include *In Daddy's Arms I Am Tall: African Americans Celebrating Fathers*, winner of the Coretta Scott King Illustrator Award; *Passage to Freedom: The Sugihara Story*, an American Library Association Notable Book; and *Crazy Horse's Vision*, a Bank Street College Children's Book of the Year. Submissions made by author. Deadline for entries: October 31. SASE for contest rules. No entry fee. Awards New Voices Award—$1,000 prize and standard publication contract (regardless of whether or not writer has an agent) along with an advance on royalties; New Voices Honor Award—$500 prize. Judging by Lee & Low editors. Restrictions of media for illustrators: The author must be a writer of color who is a resident of the U.S. and who has not previously published a children's picture book. For additional information, send SASE or visit Lee & Low's website, (leeandlow.com/editorial/voices3.html).

## JOHN NEWBERY MEDAL
Association for Library Service to Children, Division of the American Library Association, 50 E. Huron, Chicago IL 60611. E-mail: alsc@ala.org. Website: www.ala.org. **Executive Director, ALSC:** Malore Brown. Annual award. Estab. 1922. Purpose of award: to recognize the most distinguished contribution to American children's literature published in the U.S. Previously published submissions only; must be published prior to year award is given. Deadline for entries: December 31. SASE for award rules. Entries not returned. No entry fee. Medal awarded at Caldecott/Newbery banquet during ALA annual conference. Judging by Newbery Award Selection Committee.

## Ⓝ URSULA NORDSTROM FICTION CONTEST
HarperCollins Children's Books, 1350 Avenue of the Americas, New York NY 10019. (212)307-3628. Fax: (212)261-6668. Website: www.harperchildrens.com. **Director:** Alix Reid. Open to students and adults. Annually. Estab. 2004. Purpose of contest: ''to honor Ursula Nordstrom's committment to finding innovative new talent.'' Submissions must be unpublished. Submissions made by author or author's agent. Rules/entry forms are available for SASE.on website. Judging by a panel of editors. No rights to submitted material acquired. ''Only previously unpublished children's fiction is eligible.''

## NORTH AMERICAN INTERNATIONAL AUTO SHOW HIGH SCHOOL POSTER CONTEST
Detroit Auto Dealers Association, 1900 W. Big Beaver Rd., Troy MI 48084-3531. (248)643-0250. Fax: (248)283-5148. E-mail: sherp@dada.org. Website: www.naias.com. **Contact:** Sandy Herp. **Open to students.** Annual contest. Submissions made by the author and illustrator. Contact D.A.D.A. for contest rules and entry forms or retrieve rules from website. No entry fee. Awards in the High School Poster Contest are as follows: Chairman's Award and Designer's Best of Show (Digital and Traditional). A winner will be chosen in each category from

grades 9, 10, 11 and 12. Prizes: 1st place in 9, 10, 11, 12—$500; 2nd place—$250; 3rd place—$100. The winners of the Designer's Best of Show Digital and Traditional will each receive $500. The winner of the Chairman's Award will receive $1,000. Entries will be judged by an independent panel of recognized representatives of the art community. Entrants must be Michigan high school students enrolled in grades 9-12. Junior high students in 9th grade are also eligible. Winners will be announced during the North American International Auto Show in January and may be published in the *Auto Show Program* at the sole discretion of the D.A.D.A. "No shared work please."

## OHIOANA AWARD FOR CHILDREN'S LITERATURE: ALICE LOUISE WOOD MEMORIAL
Ohioana Library Association, 274 E. First Ave., Suite 300, Columbus OH 43201. (614)466-3831. Fax: (614)728-6974. E-mail: ohioana@sloma.state.oh.us. Website: www.ohioana.org. **Director:** Linda R. Hengst. Annual award. Estab. 1991. Purpose of award: "to recognize an Ohio author whose body of work has made, and continues to make a significant contribution to literature for children or young adults." Deadline for entries: December 31. SASE for award rules and entry forms. Award: $1,000. Requirements for entrants: "must have been born in Ohio, or lived in Ohio for a minimum of five years; established a distinguished publishing record of books for children and young people; body of work has made, and continues to make, a significant contribution to the literature for young people; through whose work as a writer, teacher, administrator, and community service, interest in children's literature has been encouraged and children have become involved with reading."

## OHIOANA BOOK AWARDS
Ohioana Library Association, 274 E. First Ave., Suite 300, Columbus OH 43201. (614)466-3831. Fax: (614)728-6974. E-mail: ohioana@sloma.state.oh.us. Website: www.OHIOANA.org. **Director:** Linda R. Hengst. Annual award. "The Ohioana Book Awards are given to books of outstanding literary quality. Purpose of contest: to provide recognition and encouragement to Ohio writers and to promote the work of Ohio writers. Up to six are given each year. Awards may be given in the following categories: fiction, nonfiction, children's/juvenile, poetry and books about Ohio or an Ohioan. Books must be received by the Ohioana Library during the calendar year prior to the year the award is given and must have a copyright date within the last two calendar years." Deadline for entries: December 31. SASE for award rules and entry forms. No entry fee. Winners receive citation and glass sculpture. "Any book that has been written or edited by a person born in Ohio or who has lived in Ohio for at least five years is eligible."

## OKLAHOMA BOOK AWARDS
Oklahoma Center for the Book, 200 NE 18th, Oklahoma City OK 73105. (405)521-2502. Fax: (405)525-7804. E-mail: gcarlile@oltn.odl.state.ok.us. Website: www.odl.state.ok.us/ocb. **Executive Director:** Glenda Carlile. Annual award. Estab. 1989. Purpose of award: "to honor Oklahoma writers and books about our state." Previously published submissions only. Submissions made by the author, author's agent, or entered by a person or group of people, including the publisher. Must be published during the calendar year preceding the award. Awards are presented to best books in fiction, nonfiction, children's, design and illustration, and poetry books about Oklahoma or books written by an author who was born, is living or has lived in Oklahoma. Deadline for entries: early January. SASE for award rules and entry forms. No entry fee. Awards a medal—no cash prize. Judging by a panel of 5 people for each category—a librarian, a working writer in the genre, booksellers, editors, etc. Requirements for entrants: author must be an Oklahoma native, resident, former resident or have written a book with Oklahoma theme. Winner will be announced at banquet in Oklahoma City. The Arrell Gibson Lifetime Achievement Award is also presented each year for a body of work.

## ONCE UPON A WORLD CHILDREN'S BOOK AWARD
Simon Wiesenthal Center's Museum of Tolerance Library and Archives, 1399 S. Roxbury Dr., Los Angeles CA 90035-4709. (310)772-7605. Fax: (310)553-4521. E-mail: bookaward@wiesenthal.net. Website: www.wiesenthal.com/library. **Award Director:** Adaire J. Klein. Submit 4 copies of each entry to: Adaire J. Klein, Director of Library and Archival Services. Annual award. Estab. 1996. Previously published submissions only. Submissions made by publishers, author or by author's agent. Must be published January-December of previous year. Deadline for entries: April 1. SASE for contest rules and entry forms. Awards $1,000. Judging by 3 independent judges familiar with children's literature. Award open to any writer with work in English language on subject of tolerance, diversity, human understanding, and social justice for children 6-10 years old. The next award will be presented on November 6, 2005. Book Seal available from the library.

## ORBIS PICTUS AWARD FOR OUTSTANDING NONFICTION FOR CHILDREN
The National Council of Teachers of English, 1111 W. Kenyon Rd., Urbana IL 61801-1096. (217)328-3870. Fax: (217)328-0977. E-mail: dzagorski@ncte.org. Website: www.ncte.org/elem/awards/orbispictus. **Chair, NCTE Committee on the Orbis Pictus Award for Outstanding Nonfiction for Children:** Sandijo Wilson, Husson

College, Bangor ME. Annual award. Estab. 1989. Purpose of award: To promote and recognize excellence in the writing of nonfiction for children. Previously published submissions only. Submissions made by author, author's agent, by a person or group of people. Must be published January 1-December 31 of contest year. Deadline for entries: November 30. Call for award information. No entry fee. Awards a plaque given at the NCTE Elementary Section Luncheon at the NCTE Annual Convention in November. Judging by a committee. ''The name Orbis Pictus commemorates the work of Johannes Amos Comenius, 'Orbis Pictus—The World in Pictures' (1657), considered to be the first book actually planned for children.''

## THE ORIGINAL ART

Society of Illustrators, 128 E. 63rd St., New York NY 10021-7303. (212)838-2560. Fax: (212)838-2561. E-mail: dir@societyillustrators.org. Website: www.societyillustrators.org. Annual contest. Estab. 1981. Purpose of contest: to celebrate the fine art of children's book illustration. Previously published submissions only. Deadline for entries: August 20. Request ''call for entries'' to receive contest rules and entry forms. Entry fee is $20/ book. Judging by seven professional artists and editors. Works will be displayed at the Society of Illustrators Museum of American Illustration in New York City October-November annually. Medals awarded; catalog published.

## HELEN KEATING OTT AWARD FOR OUTSTANDING CONTRIBUTION TO CHILDREN'S LITERATURE

Church and Synagogue Library Association, P.O. Box 19357, Portland OR 97280-0357. (503)244-6919. Fax: (503)977-3734. E-mail: csla@worldaccessnet.com. Website: www.worldaccessnet.com/ ~ csla. **Chair of Committee:** Barbara Graham. Annual award. Estab. 1980. ''This award is given to a person or organization that has made a significant contribution to promoting high moral and ethical values through children's literature.'' Deadline for entries: April 1. ''Recipient is honored in July during the conference.'' Awards certificate of recognition and a conference package consisting of all meals, day of awards banquet, two nights' housing and a complimentary 1 year membership. ''A nomination for an award may be made by anyone. It should include the name, address and telephone number of the nominee, plus the church or synagogue relationship where appropriate. Nominations of an organization should include the name of a contact person. A detailed description of the reasons for the nomination should be given, accompanied by documentary evidence of accomplishment. The person(s) making the nomination should give his/her name, address and telephone number and a brief explanation of his/her knowledge of the nominee's accomplishments. Elements of creativity and innovation will be given high priority by the judges.''

## PATERSON PRIZE FOR BOOKS FOR YOUNG PEOPLE

Poetry Center at Passaic County Community College, One College Blvd., Paterson NJ 07505-1179. (973)684-6555. Fax: (973)523-6085. E-mail: mgillan@pccc.edu. Website: www.pccc.edu/poetry. **Director:** Maria Mazziotti Gillan. Estab. 1996. Part of the Poetry Center's mission is ''to recognize excellence in books for young people.'' Published submissions only. Submissions made by author, author's agent or publisher. Must be published between January 1, 2004-December 31, 2004. Deadline for entries: March 15, 2005. SASE for contest rules and entry forms or visit website. Awards $500 for the author in either of 3 categories: PreK-Grade 3; Grades 4-6, Grades 7-12. Judging by a professional writer selected by the Poetry Center. Contest is open to any writer/illustrator.

## PEN/PHYLLIS NAYLOR WORKING WRITER FELLOWSHIP

PEN, 588 Broadway, New York NY 10012. (212)334-1660. Fax: (212)334-2181. E-mail: awards@pen.org. Website: www.pen.org. Submit entries to: awards coordinator. Must have published 2 books to be eligible. Annual contest. Estab. 2001. To support writers with a financial need and recognize work of high literary caliber. Unpublished submissions only. Submissions nominated. Deadline for entries: mid-January. Awards $5,000. Upon nomination by an editor or fellow writer, a panel of judges will select the winning book. Open to a writer of children's or young adult fiction in financial need, who has published at least two books, and no more than five during the past ten years. Please visit our website for full guidelines.

## PENNSYLVANIA YOUNG READERS' CHOICE AWARDS PROGRAM

Pennsylvania School Librarians Association, 148 S. Bethelehem Pike, Ambler PA 19002-5822. (215)643-5048. Fax: (215)646-7250. E-mail: bellavance@verizon.net. **Coordinator:** Jean B. Bellavance. Annual award. Estab. 1991. Submissions nominated by a person or group. Must be published within 5 years of the award for example, books published in 2001 to present are eligible for the 2005-2006 award. Deadline for entries: September 1. SASE for contest rules and entry forms. No entry fee. Framed certificate to winning authors. Judging by children of Pennsylvania (they vote). Requirements for entrants: currently living in North America. Reader's Choice Award is to promote reading of quality books by young people in the Commonwealth of Pennsylvania, to promote teacher and librarian involvement in children's literature, and to honor authors whose work has been recognized by the children of Pennsylvania. Three awards are given, one for each of the following grade level divisions: K-3, 3-6, 6-8.

## PLEASE TOUCH MUSEUM® BOOK AWARD

Please Touch Museum, 210 N. 21st St., Philadelphia PA 19103-1001. (215)963-0667. Fax: (215)963-0424. E-mail: kmiller@pleasetouchmuseum.org. Website: www.pleasetouchmuseum.org. **Contact:** Kathleen Miller. Annual award. Estab. 1985. Purpose of the award: "to recognize and encourage the publication of high-quality books for young children. The award is given to books that are imaginative, exceptionally illustrated and help foster a child's life-long love of reading. Each year we select one winner in two age categories—ages 3 and under and ages 4 to 7. These age categories reflect the age of the children Please Touch Museum serves. To be eligible for consideration, a book must: (1) Be distinguished in text, illustration, and ability to explore and clarify an idea for young children (ages 7 and under). (2) Be published within the last year by an American publisher. (3) Be by an American author and/or illustrator." SASE for award rules and entry forms. No entry fee. Publishing date deadlines apply. Judging by selected jury of children's literature experts, librarians and early childhood educators. Education store purchases books for selling at Book Award Ceremony and throughout the year. Autographing sessions may be held at Please Touch Museum, and at Philadelphia's Early Childhood Education Conference.

## PNWA LITERARY CONTEST

Pacific Northwest Writers Association, P.O. Box 2016, Edmonds WA 98020-9516. (425)673-2665. E-mail: staff@pnwa.org. Website: www.pnwa.org. **Contest/Award Director:** Dana Murphy-Love. **Open to students.** Annual contest. Purpose of contest: "Valuable tool for writers as contest submissions are critiqued (2 critiques)." Unpublished submissions only. Submissions made by author. Deadline for entries: February 21, 2006. SASE for contest rules and entry forms. Entry fee is $35/entry for members, $45/entry for nonmembers. Awards $600-1st; $300-2nd; $150-3rd. Awards in all 10 categories.

## POCKETS MAGAZINE FICTION CONTEST

*Pockets Magazine*, The Upper Room, P.O. Box 340004, Nashville TN 37203-0004. (615)340-7333. Fax: (615)340-7267. E-mail: pockets@upperroom.org. Website: www.pockets.org. **Contact:** Lynn W. Gilliam, senior editor. The purpose of the contest is to "find new freelance writers for the magazine." Annual competition for short stories. Award: $1,000 and publication in *Pockets* Competition receives 250-325 submissions. Judged by *Pockets* editors and 3 other editors of other Upper Room publications. Guidelines available on website or upon request and SASE. No entry fee. No entry form. Note on envelope and first sheet: Fiction Contest. Submissions must be postmarked between March 1 and August 15 of the current year. Former winners are not eligible. **Unpublished submissions only.** Word length: 1,000-1,600 words. Winner notified November 1. Submissions returned if accompanied by SASE.

## EDGAR ALLAN POE AWARD

Mystery Writers of America, Inc., 6th Floor, 17 E. 47th St., New York NY 10017. (212)888-8171. Fax: (212)888-8107. E-mail: mwa@mysterywriters.org. Website: www.mysterywriters.org. **Office Manager:** Margery Flax. Annual award. Estab. 1945. Purpose of the award: to honor authors of distinguished works in the mystery field. Previously published submissions only. Submissions made by the author, author's agent; "normally by the publisher." Work must be published/produced the year of the contest. Deadline for entries: November 30 "except for works only available in the month of December." SASE for award rules and entry forms. No entry fee. Awards ceramic bust of "Edgar" for winner; scrolls for all nominees. Judging by professional members of Mystery Writers of America (writers). Nominee press release sent after first Wednesday in February. Winner announced at the Edgar Banquet, held in late April/early May.

## MICHAEL L. PRINTZ AWARD

Young Adult Library Services Association, Division of the American Library Association, 50 E. Huron, Chicago IL 60611. Fax: (312)664-7459. E-mail: yalsa@ala.org. Website: www.ala.org. Annual award. The Michael L. Printz Award is an award for a book that exemplifies literary excellence in young adult literature. It is named for a Topeka, Kansas school librarian who was a long-time active member of the Young Adult Library Services Association. It will be selected annually by an award committee that can also name as many as 4 honor books. The award-winning book can be fiction, nonfiction, poetry or an anthology, and can be a work of joint authorship or editorship. The books must be published between January 1 and December 31 of the preceding year and be designated by its publisher as being either a young adult book or one published for the age range that YALSA defines as young adult, e.g. ages 12 through 18. The deadline for both committee and field nominations will be December 1.

### ⚑ PRIX ALVINE-BELISLE

Association pour l'avancement des sciences et des techniques de la documentation (ASTED) Inc., 3414 Avenue Du Parc, Bureau 202, Montreal QC H2X 2H5 Canada. (514)281-5012. Fax: (514)281-8219. E-mail: info@asted.org. **Award President:** Marie Helene Parent. Award open to children's book editors. Annual award. Estab. 1974. Purpose of contest: To recognize the best children's book published in French in Canada. Previously published submissions only. Submissions made by publishing house. Must be published the year before award. Deadline for entries: June 1. Awards $1,000. Judging by librarians jury.

### QUILL AND SCROLL INTERNATIONAL WRITING/PHOTO CONTEST

*Quill and Scroll*, School of Journalism and Mass Communication, University of Iowa, Iowa City IA 52242-1528. (319)335-3457. Fax: (319)335 -3989. E-mail: quill-scroll@uiowa.edu. Website: www.uiowa.edu/~quill-sc. **Contest Director:** Richard Johns. **Open to students.** Annual contest. Previously published submissions only. Submissions made by the author or school newspaper adviser. Must be published within the last year. Deadline for entries: February 5. SASE for contest rules and entry forms. Entry fee is $2/entry. Awards engraved plaque to junior high level sweepstakes winners. Judging by various judges. *Quill and Scroll* acquires the right to publish submitted material in the magazine if it is chosen as a winning entry. Requirements for entrants: must be students in grades 9-12 for high school division.

### 🌐 REDHOUSE CHILDREN'S BOOK AWARD

(formerly Children's Book Award), Federation of Children's Book Groups, 2 Bridge Wood View, Norsforth, Leeds LS18 5PE England 0113 258891. Fax: 0113 2588920. E-mail: marianneadey@aol.com. Website: www.redhousechildrensbookawards.co.uk. **Coordinator:** Marianne Adey. Purpose of the award: "The R.H.B.A. is an annual prize for the best children's book of the year judged by the children themselves." Categories: (I) books for younger children, (II) books for younger readers, (III) books for older readers. Estab. 1980. Works must be published in the United Kingdom. Deadline for entries: December 31. SASE for rules and entry forms. Entries not returned. Awards "a magnificent silver and oak trophy worth over $6,000 and a portfolio of children's work." Silver dishes to each category winner. Judging by children. Requirements for entrants: Work must be fiction and published in the UK during the current year (poetry is ineligible). Work will be published in current "Pick of the Year" publication.

### TOMAS RIVERA MEXICAN AMERICAN CHILDREN'S BOOK AWARD

Texas State University-San Marcos, EDU, 601 University Dr., San Marcos TX 78666-4613. (512)245-2357. Fax: (512)245-7911. E-mail: jb23@academia.swt.edu. **Award Director:** Dr. Jennifer Battle. Competition open to adults. Annual contest. Estab. 1995. Purpose of award: "To encourage authors, illustrators and publishers to produce books that authentically reflect the lives of Mexican American children and young adults in the United States." Unpublished mss not accepted. Submissions made by "any interested individual or publishing company." Must be published the year prior to the year of consideration. Deadline for entries: February 1 post publication year. Contact Dr. Jennifer Battle for nomination forms, or send copy of book. No entry fee. Awards $3,000 per book. Judging of nominations by a regional committee, national committee judges finalists. Annual ceremony honoring the book and author/illustrator is held during Hispanic Heritage Month at Texas State University-San Marcos.

### ⚑ SASKATCHEWAN BOOK AWARDS: CHILDREN'S LITERATURE

Saskatchewan Book Awards, 120-2505 11th Avenue, Regina SK S4P 0K6 Canada. (306)569-1585. Fax: (306)569-4187. E-mail: director@bookawards.sk.ca. Website: www.bookawards.sk.ca. **Award Director:** Glenda James. Open to Saskatchewan authors only. Annual award. Estab. 1995. Purpose of contest: to celebrate Saskatchewan books and authors and to promote their work. Previously published submissions only. Submissions made by author, author's agent or publisher by September 15. SASE for contest rules and entry forms. Entry fee is $20 (Canadian). Awards $2,000 (Canadian). Judging by two children's literature authors outside of Saskatchewan. Requirements for entrants: Must be Saskatchewan resident; book must have ISBN number; book must have been published within the last year. Award-winning book will appear on TV talk shows and be pictured on bookmarks distributed to libraries, schools and bookstores in Saskatchewan.

### SCBWI WORK-IN-PROGRESS GRANTS

Society of Children's Book Writers and Illustrators, 8271 Beverly Blvd., Los Angeles CA 90048. (323)782-1010. Fax: (323)782-1892. E-mail: scbwi@scbwi.org. Website: www.scbwi.org. Annual award. "The SCBWI Work-in-Progress Grants have been established to assist children's book writers in the completion of a specific project." Four categories: (1) General Work-in-Progress Grant. (2) Grant for a Contemporary Novel for Young People. (3) Nonfiction Research Grant. (4) Grant for a Work Whose Author Has Never Had a Book Published. Requests for applications may be made beginning October 1. Completed applications accepted February 1-April

1 of each year. SASE for applications for grants. In any year, an applicant may apply for any of the grants except the one awarded for a work whose author has never had a book published. (The recipient of this grant will be chosen from entries in all categories.) Five grants of $1,500 will be awarded annually. Runner-up grants of $500 (one in each category) will also be awarded. "The grants are available to both full and associate members of the SCBWI. They are not available for projects on which there are already contracts." Previous recipients not eligible to apply.

## SEVENTEEN FICTION CONTEST

1440 Broadway, 13th Floor, New York NY 10018. Fax: (212)204-3977. Website: www.seventeen.com. **Open to students.** Annual contest. Estab. 1945. Purpose of contest: To recognize and encourage talented, young writers. Unpublished submissions only. Deadline for entries: April 30. SASE for contest rules and entry forms; contest rules also published in December issue of *Seventeen*. Entries not returned. Submissions accepted by mail only. No entry fee. Awards cash prize and possible publication in *Seventeen*. Judging by "inhouse panel of editors, external readers." If 1st, 2nd or 3rd prize, acquires first North American rights for piece to be published. Requirements for entrants: "Our annual fiction contest is open to anyone between the ages of 13 and 21 who submit on or before April 30. Submit only original fiction that has not been published in any form other than in school publications. Stories should be between 1,500 and 3,000 words in length (6-12 pages). All manuscripts must be typed double-spaced on a single side of paper. Submit as many original stories as you like, but each story must include your full name, address, birth date, e-mail address, and signature in the top right-hand corner of the first page. Your signature on submission will constitute your acceptance of the contest rules."

## SHUBERT FENDRICH MEMORIAL PLAYWRITING CONTEST

Pioneer Drama Service, Inc., P.O. Box 4267, Englewood CO 80155-4267. Fax: (303)779-4315. E-mail: editors@pioneerdrama.com. Website: www.pioneerdrama.com. **Director:** Lori Conary. Annual contest. **Open to students.** Estab. 1990. Purpose of the contest: "To encourage the development of quality theatrical material for educational and family theater." Previously unpublished submissions only. Deadline for entries: March 1. SASE for contest rules and guidelines. No entry fee. Cover letter, SASE for return of ms, and proof of production or staged reading must accompany all submissions. Awards $1,000 royalty advance and publication. Upon receipt of signed contracts, plays will be published and made available in our next catalog. Judging by editors. All rights acquired with acceptance of contract for publication. Restrictions for entrants: Any writers currently published by Pioneer Drama Service are not eligible.

## SKIPPING STONES YOUTH HONOR AWARDS

*Skipping Stones*, P.O. Box 3939, Eugene OR 97403-0939. (541)342-4956. E-mail: editor@SkippingStones.org. Website: www.SkippingStones.org. **Open to students.** Annual awards. Purpose of contest: "to recognize youth, 7 to 17, for their contributions to multicultural awareness, nature and ecology, social issues, peace and nonviolence. Also to promote creativity, self-esteem and writing skills and to recognize important work being done by youth organizations." Submissions made by the author. Deadline for entries: June 20. SASE for contest rules. Entries must include certificate of originality by a parent and/or teacher and background information on the author written by the author. Entry fee is $3. Everyone who enters the contest receives the September-October issue featuring Youth Awards. Judging by *Skipping Stones*' staff. "Up to ten awards are given in three categories: (1) Compositions—(essays, poems, short stories, songs, travelogues, etc.) should be typed (double-spaced) or neatly handwritten. Fiction or nonfiction should be limited to 750 words; poems to 30 lines. Non-English writings are also welcome. (2) Artwork—(drawings, cartoons, paintings or photo essays with captions) should have the artist's name, age and address on the back of each page. Send the originals with SASE. Black & white photos are especially welcome. Limit: 8 pieces. (3) Youth Organizations—Tell us how your club or group works to: (a) preserve the nature and ecology in your area, (b) enhance the quality of life for low-income, minority or disabled or (c) improve racial or cultural harmony in your school or community. Use the same format as for compositions." The winners are published in the September-October issue of *Skipping Stones*, winner of Edpress, Name, and Parent's Choice Awards. Now in 16th year.

## KAY SNOW WRITERS' CONTEST

Williamette Writers, 9045 SW Barbur Blvd. #5A, Portland OR 97219-4027. (503)452-1592. Fax: (503)452-0372. E-mail: wilwrite@willamettewriters.com. Website: www.willamettewriters.com. **Contest Director:** Marlene Moore. Annual contest. **Open to students.** Purpose of contest: "to encourage beginning and established writers to continue the craft." Unpublished, original submissions only. Submissions made by the author. Deadline for entries: May 15. SASE for contest rules and entry forms. Entry fee is $10, Williamette Writers' members; $15, nonmembers; free for student writers grades 1-12. Awards cash prize of $300 per category (fiction, nonfiction, juvenile, poetry, script writing), $50 for students in three divisions: 1-5, 6-8, 9-12. "Judges are anonymous."

## SOCIETY OF MIDLAND AUTHORS AWARDS

Society of Midland Authors, P.O. Box 10419, Chicago IL 60610-0419. E-mail: writercc@aol.com. Website: www. midlandauthors.com. Annual award. Estab. 1915. Purpose of award: "to stimulate creative literary effort, one of the goals of the Society. There are six categories, including children's fiction and nonfiction, adult fiction and nonfiction, biography and poetry." Previously published submissions only. Submissions made by the author or publisher. Must be published during calendar year previous to deadline. Deadline for entries: February 1st. SASE for award rules and entry forms or check website. No entry fee. Awards plaque given at annual dinner, cash ($300). Judging by panel (reviewers, university faculty, writers, librarians) of 3 per category. Author must be currently residing in the Midlands, i.e., Illinois, Indiana, Iowa, Kansas, Michigan, Minnesota, Missouri, Nebraska, North Dakota, South Dakota, Ohio or Wisconsin.

## SOUTHWEST WRITERS ANNUAL CONTEST

SouthWest Writers, 3721 Morris NE, Suite A, Albuquerque NM 87111. (505)265-9485. Fax: (505)265-9483. E-mail: SWriters@aol.com. Website: www.southwestwriters.org. Submit entries to: Contest Chair. **Open to adults and students.** Annual contest. Estab. 1982. Purpose of contest: to encourage writers of all genres. Quarterly mim-conferences. Also offers critique groups (for $60/year, offers 2 monthly programs, monthly newsletter, annual writing contest, other workshops, various discount perks) and critique service (open to nonmembers). See website for more information or call or write.

## GEORGE G. STONE CENTER FOR CHILDREN'S BOOKS RECOGNITION OF MERIT AWARD

George G. Stone Center for Children's Books, Claremont Graduate University, 740 N. College Ave., Claremont CA 91711-6188. (909)607-3670. **Award Director:** Doty Hale. Annual award. Estab. 1965. Purpose of the award: to recognize an author or illustrator of a children's book or a body of work exhibiting the "power to please and expand the awareness of children and teachers as they have shared the book in their classrooms." Previously published submissions only. SASE for award rules and entry forms. Entries not returned. No entry fee. Awards a scroll. Judging by a committee of teachers, professors of children's literature and librarians. Requirements for entrants: Nominations are made by students, teachers, professors and librarians. Award made at annual Claremont Reading Conference in spring (March).

## THE JOAN G. SUGARMAN CHILDREN'S BOOK AWARD

Washington Independent Writers Legal and Educational Fund, Inc., P.O. Box 70437, Washington DC 20024-8437. (202)466-1344. E-mail: sugarman@Lefund.org. Website: www.Lefund.org/sugarman.html. **Award Director:** Rob Anderson. Submit entries to: Rob Anderson. Award offered annually. Estab. 1987. Previously published submissions only during the two-year time frame specified for each award. Submissions made by author. No entry fee. Awards $1,000 cash prize for book judged best overall. Three honorable mentions in the categories of early readers, middle readers, and young adult readers are also recognized. Judging by a committee drawn from selected fields of children's literature, such as library science, editing, teaching, and psychology. Books eligible for the award must be written by an author residing in Virginia, Maryland or the District of Columbia and be published works with the copyright of 2002 or 2003. The books must be geared for children 15 years or younger, be original and have universal appeal. Since the books are judged on the basis of their written content, picture books without text are not eligible.

## SUGARMAN FAMILY AWARD FOR JEWISH CHILDREN'S LITERATURE

Washington District of Columbia Jewish Community Center, 1529 16th St. N.W., Washington DC 20036. (202)518-9400. Fax: (202)518-9420. E-mail: jessikac@dcjcc.org. Website: www.dcjcc.org. **Award Director:** Jessika Cirkus. **Open to students.** Biannual award. Estab. 1994. Purpose of contest: to enrich all children's appreciation of Jewish culture and to inspire writers and illustrators for children. Newly published submissions only. Submissions are made by the author, made by the author's agent. Must be published January-December of year previous to award year. Deadline: May 2005. SASE for entry deadlines, award rules and entry forms. Entry fee is $25. Award at least $750. Judging by a panel of three judges—a librarian, a children's bookstore owner and a reviewer of books. Requirements for entrants: must live in the United States. Work displayed at the DC Jewish Community Center Library.

## SYDNEY TAYLOR MANUSCRIPT COMPETITION

Association of Jewish Libraries, 315 Maitland Ave., Teaneck NJ 07666. Fax: (201)862-0362. E-mail: rkglasser@aol.com. Website: www.jewishlibraries.org. **Coordinator:** Rachel Glasser. **Open to students.** Annual contest. Estab. 1985. Purpose of the contest: "This competition is for unpublished writers of fiction. Material should be for readers ages 8-11, with universal appeal that will serve to deepen the understanding of Judaism for all children, revealing positive aspects of Jewish life." Unpublished submissions only. Deadline for entries: December 30. Download rules and forms from website or send SASE for contest rules and entry forms must be enclosed.

No entry fee. Awards $1,000. Award winner will be notified in April, and the award will be presented at the convention in June. Judging by qualified judges from within the Association of Jewish Libraries. Requirements for entrants: must be an unpublished fiction writer; also, books must range from 64-200 pages in length. "AJL assumes no responsibility for publication, but hopes this cash incentive will serve to encourage new writers of children's stories with Jewish themes for all children."

## THE TORONTO BOOK AWARDS
City of Toronto, 100 Queen St. W, 10th Floor, West Tower, Toronto ON M5H 2N2 Canada. (416)392-8191. Fax: (416)392-1247. E-mail: bkurmey@toronto.ca. Submit entries to: Bev Kurmey, protocol officer. Annual award. Estab. 1974. Recognizes books of literary or artistic merit that are evocative of Toronto. Submissions made by author, author's agent or nominated by a person or group. Must be published the calendar year prior to the award year. Deadline for entries: last day of February annually. SASE for contest rules and entry forms. Awards $15,000 in prize money. Judging by committee.

## TORONTO MUNICIPAL CHAPTER IODE BOOK AWARD
Toronto Municipal IODE, 40 St. Clair Ave. E., Suite 205, Toronto ON M4T 1M9 Canada. (416)925-5078. Fax: (416)925-5127. E-mail: iodetoronto@bellnet.ca. **Contest Director:** Mary K. Anderson. Submit entries to: Theo Heras, Lillian Smith Library, 239 College St., Toronto. Annual contest. Estab. 1974. Previously published submissions only. Submissions made by author. Deadline for entries: November 1. No entry fee. Awards: $1,000. If the illustrator is different from the author, the prize money is divided. Judging by Book Award Committee comprised of members of Toronto Municipal Chapter IODE. Requirements for entrants: Authors and illustrators must be Canadian and live within the GTA.

## TREASURE STATE AWARD
Missoula Public Library, Missoula County Schools, Montana Library Assoc., 301 E. Main, Missoula MT 59802. (406)721-2005. Fax: (406)728-5900. E-mail: bammon@missoula.lib.mt.us. Website: www.missoula.lib.mt.us. **Award Directors:** Bette Ammon and Carole Monlux. Annual award. Estab. 1990. Purpose of the award: Children in grades K-3 read or listen to a ballot of 5 picture books and vote on their favorite. Previously published submissions only. Submissions made by author, nominated by a person or group of people—children, librarians, teachers. Must be published in previous 5 years to voting year. Deadline for entries: March 20. SASE for contest rules and entry forms. No entry fee. Awards a plaque or sculpture. Judging by popular vote by Montana children grades K-3.

## VEGETARIAN ESSAY CONTEST
The Vegetarian Resource Group, P.O. Box 1463, Baltimore MD 21203. (410)366-VEGE. Fax: (410)366-8804. E-mail: vrg@vrg.org. Website: www.vrg.org. Annual contest. **Open to students.** Estab. 1985. Purpose of contest: to promote vegetarianism in young people. Unpublished submissions only. Deadline for entries: May 1 of each year. SASE for contest rules and entry forms. No entry fee. Awards $50 savings bond. Judging by awards committee. Acquires right for The Vegetarian Resource Group to reprint essays. Requirements for entrants: age 18 and under. Winning works may be published in *Vegetarian Journal*, instructional materials for students. "Submit 2-3 page essay on any aspect of vegetarianism, which is the abstinence of meat, fish and fowl. Entrants can base paper on interviewing, research or personal opinion. Need not be vegetarian to enter."

## VFW VOICE OF DEMOCRACY
Veterans of Foreign Wars of the U.S., 406 W. 34th St., Kansas City MO 64111. (816)968-1117. Fax: (816)968-1149. Website: www.vfw.org. **Open to high school students.** Annual contest. Estab. 1960. Purpose of contest: to give high school students the opportunity to voice their opinions about their responsibility to our country and to convey those opinions via the broadcast media to all of America. Deadline for entries: November 1. No entry fee. Winners receive awards ranging from $1,000-25,000. Requirements for entrants: "Ninth-twelfth grade students in public, parochial, private and home schools are eligible to compete. Former first place state winners are not eligible to compete again. Contact your participating high school teacher, counselor, our website www.vfw.org or your local VFW Post to enter."

## VIRGINIA LIBRARY ASSOCIATION/JEFFERSON CUP
Virginia Library Association, P.O. Box 8277, Norfolk VA 23503-0277. E-mail: lhahne@coastalnet.com. Website: www.vla.org. **Executive Director:** Linda Hahne. **Open to students.** Award director changes year to year. Annual award. Estab. 1983. Purpose of award: "to encourage the writing of quality books for young people, to give recognition to authors who write in these disciplines, and to promote the reading of books that illustrate America's past." Previously published submissions only. Must be published in the year prior to selection. Deadline for entries: January 31. SASE for contest rules and entry forms. Judging by committee. "The book

must be about U.S. history or an American person, 1492 to present, or fiction that highlights the U.S. past; author must reside in the U.S." The book must be published especially for young people.

### VSA ARTS PLAYWRIGHT DISCOVERY AWARD

VSA arts, 1300 Connecticut Ave., NW, Suite 700, Washington DC 20036. (202)628-2800 or 1-800-933-8721. TTY: (202)737-0645. Fax: (202)737-0725. E-mail: info@vsarts.org. Website: www.vsarts.org. **Open to students.** Annual contest. Estab. 1984. "All scripts must explore an aspect of disability." Unpublished submissions only. Deadline for entries: April 15. Write to Performing Arts Coordinator for contest rules and entry forms. No entries returned. No entry fee. Judging by Artists Selection Committee. Entrants must be students, grades 6-12. "One-act script will be selected for production at The John F. Kennedy Center for the Performing Arts, Washington DC. The winning play(s) is presented each fall."

### WASHINGTON CHILDREN'S CHOICE PICTURE BOOK AWARD

Washington Library Media Association, P.O. Box 50194, Mukilteo WA 98275. E-mail: galantek@edmonds.wedn et.edu. **Award Director:** Kristin Galante. Submit nominations to: Kristin Galante, chairman; mail to Kristin Galante, WCCPBA, Lynndale Elementary School, 7200 191st SW, Lynnwood WA 98036. Annual award. Estab. 1982. Previously published submissions only. Submissions nominated by a person or group. Must be published within 2-3 years prior to year of award. Deadline for entries: March 1. SASE for contest rules and entry forms. Awards pewter plate, recognition. Judging by WCCPBA committee.

### WASHINGTON POST/CHILDREN'S BOOK GUILD AWARD FOR NONFICTION

E-mail: theguild@childrensbookguild.org. Website: www.childrensbookguild.org. **President:** Betsy Kraft, 2003-2004. Annual award. Estab. 1977. Purpose of award: "to honor an author or illustrator whose total work has contributed significantly to the quality of nonfiction for children." Award includes a cash prize and an engraved crystal paperweight. Judging by a jury of Children's Book Guild specialists, authors, illustrators and a *Washington Post* book critic. "One doesn't enter. One is selected. Our jury annually selects one author for the award."

### WE ARE WRITERS, TOO!

Creative With Words Publications, Carmel CA 93922. Fax: (831)655-8627. E-mail: cwwpub@usa.net. Website: members.tripod.com/CreativeWithWords. **Contest Director:** Brigitta Geltrich. **Open to students.** Twice a year (January, August). Estab. 1975. Purpose of award: to further creative writing in children. Unpublished submissions only. Can submit year round on any theme (theme list available upon request and SASE). Deadlines for entries: year round. SASE for contest rules and entry forms. SASE for return of entries "if not accepted." No entry fee. Awards publication in an anthology. Judging by selected guest editors and educators. Contest open to children only (up to and including 19 years old). Writer should request contest rules. SASE with all correspondence. Age of child and home address must be stated and ms must be verified of its authenticity. Each story or poem must have a title. Creative with Words Publications (CWW) publishes the top 100-120 mss submitted to the contest. CWW also publishes anthologies on various themes throughout the year to which young writers may submit.

### WESTERN HERITAGE AWARDS

National Cowboy & Western Heritage Museum, 1700 NE 63rd St., Oklahoma City OK 73111-7997. (405)478-2250. Fax: (405)478-4714. E-mail: editor@nationalcowboymuseum.org. Website: www.nationalcowboymuseu m.org. **Director of Public Relations:** Lynda Haller. Annual award. Estab. 1961. Purpose of award: The WHA are presented annually to encourage the accurate and artistic telling of great stories of the West through 13 categories of western literature, television, film and music; including fiction, nonfiction, children's books and poetry. Previously published submissions only; must be published the calendar year before the awards are presented. Deadline for literary entries: November 30. Deadline for film, music and television entries: December 31. Entries not returned. Entry fee is $45/entry. Awards a Wrangler bronze sculpture designed by famed western artist, John Free. Judging by a panel of judges selected each year with distinction in various fields of western art and heritage. Requirements for entrants: The material must pertain to the development or preservation of the West, either from a historical or contemporary viewpoint. Literary entries must have been published between December 1 and November 30 of calendar year. Film, music or television entries must have been released or aired between January 1 and December 31 of calendar year of entry. Works recognized during special awards ceremonies held annually at the museum. There is an autograph party preceding the awards. Awards ceremonies are sometimes broadcast.

### PAUL A. WITTY OUTSTANDING LITERATURE AWARD

International Reading Association, Special Interest Group, Reading for Gifted and Creative Learning, School of Education, P.O. Box 297900, Fort Worth TX 76129. (817)257-6938. Fax: (817)257-7480. E-mail: clock@tcu.edu.

**Award Director:** Dr. Cathy Collins Block. **Open to students** Annual award. Estab. 1979. Categories of entries: poetry/prose at elementary, junior high and senior high levels. Unpublished submissions only. Deadline for entries: February 1. SASE for award rules and entry forms. SASE for return of entries. No entry fee. Awards $25 and plaque, also certificates of merit. Judging by 2 committees for screening and awarding. Works will be published in International Reading Association publications. "The elementary students' entries must be legible and may not exceed 1,000 words. Secondary students' prose entries should be typed and may exceed 1,000 words if necessary. At both elementary and secondary levels, if poetry is entered, a set of five poems must be submitted. All entries and requests for applications must include a self-addressed, stamped envelope."

## PAUL A. WITTY SHORT STORY AWARD
International Reading Association, P.O. Box 8139, 800 Barksdale Rd., Newark DE 19714-8139. (302)731-1600. E-mail: exec@reading.org. Website: www.reading.org. "The entry must be an original short story appearing in a young children's periodical for the first time during 2005. The short story should serve as a literary standard that encourages young readers to read periodicals." Deadline for entries: The entry must have been published for the first time in the eligibility year; the short story must be submitted during the calendar year of publication. Anyone wishing to nominate a short story should send it to the designated Paul A. Witty Short Award Subcommittee Chair by December 1. Award is $1,000 and recognition at the annual IRA Convention.

## WOMEN IN THE ARTS ANNUAL CONTESTS
Women In The Arts, P.O. Box 2907, Decatur IL 62524-2907. (217)872-0811. **Open to students.** Vice President. **Open to students.** Annual contest. Estab. 1995. Purpose of contest: to encourage beginning writers, as well as published professionals, by offering a contest for well-written material in plays, fiction, essay and poetry. Submissions made by author. Deadline for entries: November 1 annually. SASE for contest rules and entry forms. Entry fee is $2/ms. Prize consists of $50—1st place; $35—2nd place; $15—3rd place. Send SASE for complete rules.

## ⓝ WRITE IT NOW!
SmartWriters.com, 10823 Worthing Ave., San Diego CA 92126-2665.(858)689-2665. E-mail: Editor@SmartWriters.com. Website: www.SmartWriters.com. **Editorial Director:** Roxyanne Young. Estab. 2994. Annual contest. "Our purposeis to encourage new writers and help get their manuscripts into the hands of people who can help further their careers." Unpublished submissions only. Submissions made by author. Deadline for entries: February 1. SASE for contest rules and entry froms; also see website. Entry fee is $10. Awards a cash prize, books about writing, and an editorial review of the winning mss. 2004's cash prize was $250. Judging by published writers and editors. Requirement for entrants: "This contest is open to all writers age 18 and older. There are 6 categories: Young Adult, Midgrade, Picture Book, Poetry, Non-Fiction, and Illustration." See website for more details.

## WRITER'S INT'L FORUM CONTESTS
Bristol Services Int'l., P.O. Box 1000, Carlsborg WA 98324-1000. Website: www.bristolservicesintl.com. Estab. 1997. Purpose of contest: to inspire excellence in the traditional short story format. "In fiction we like identifiable characters, strong storylines, and crisp, fresh endings. Open to all ages." SASE or see website to determine if a contest is currently open. Only send a ms if an open contest is listed at website. Read past winning mss online. Judging by Bristol Services Int'l staff.

## WRITING CONFERENCE WRITING CONTESTS
The Writing Conference, Inc., P.O. Box 664, Ottawa KS 66067. Phone/fax: (785)242-1995. E-mail: jbushman@writingconference.com. Website: www.writingconference.com. **Contest Director:** John H. Bushman. **Open to students.** Annual contest. Estab. 1988. Purpose of contest: to further writing by students with awards for narration, exposition and poetry at the elementary, middle school and high school levels. Unpublished submissions only. Submissions made by the author or teacher. Deadline for entries: January 8. SASE for contest rules and entry form or consult website. No entry fee. Awards plaque and publication of winning entry in *The Writers' Slate*, March issue. Judging by a panel of teachers. Requirements for entrants: must be enrolled in school—K-12th grade.

## ⓜ WRITING FOR CHILDREN COMPETITION
90 Richmond St. E, Suite 200, Toronto ON M5C 1P1 Canada . (416)703-8982, ext. 223. Fax : (416)504-9090. E-mail: projects@writersunion.ca. Website: www.writersunion.ca. **Open to students and Canadian citizens or landed immigrants who have not had a book published.** Annual contest. Estab. 1997. Purpose of contest: to discover, encourage and promote new writers of children's literature. Unpublished submissions only. Submissions made by author. Deadline for entries: April 24. Entry fee is $15. Awards $1,500 and submission of winner

# Roxyanne Young

*Contest helps open publishing
does for talented writers*

Roxyanne Young started SmartWriters.com in 2002 "as an informational website for children's writers, illustrators, and educators," she says. "My friend Kelly Milner Halls donated a lot of her old articles and I did a few interviews—Bruce Hale, creator of the Chet Gecko series, was my first." (See the Insider Report with Hale on page 132.)

Between them, Young and Halls started a small monthly Journal that has since grown in length and stature in the industry. SmartWriters.com now offers more than 200 pages of articles, interviews, market information, and other resources and has been named one of the 100 Best Web Sites for Writers by *Writer's Digest* magazine in 2003 and 2004. (The 2005 list was not out at press time, but SmartWriters.com was in the running again.) "We were the only children's website in the Genre listings in 2003. In 2004, we shared that with Jane Yolen's personal Web site. Pretty good company," says Young.

And Young's labor of love for the children's writing community continues to grow. In 2004, to add to the array of SmartWriters.com's offerings, she created a contest just for children's writers. "I started the Write It Now! Competition," says Young, "because I wanted to encourage newer writers to follow their dream and write their stories by acknowledging their talent and getting their work in front of people who can do something to help them start their careers." To that end, W.I.N. contest winners have their work reviewed by publishing professionals, and several contest winners have gotten book contracts as a direct result of Young's competition.

"So many of us get caught up in our everyday lives and we put off that dream because we've got to pick up the kids from school or finish this report for work or whatever," Young says. "All we need is the opportunity to make writing a priority, and that's what I wanted to help these writers do."

Here Young shares W.I.N. success stories and offers advice to writers entering contests. For more information on the Write It Now! Competition (including an impressive list of participating publishing pros), visit www.SmartWriters.com.

### You've got a great lineup of editors and art directors to review winning manuscripts. How were you so successful in gathering them?

Surprisingly, I just asked. I attend writing conferences all over the country, sometimes as a member of the faculty where I'm blessed to hang out with the editors and authors who are on the faculty, too. Others are just folks I've met or are friends of friends. Networking is key in this industry—sometimes it helps to know people who know people.

**How many entries did you receive for the first competition? Are some of your six categories more popular than others?**

Last year we received almost 900 entries. I was amazed and incredibly pleased. I think we had a big push because it was our first year and everyone was excited about a new competition for children's writers—there really aren't that many.

Of the six categories, Picture Books is by far the most popular category, both last year and this year. We're receiving four times the picture books as we get in all the other categories combined. Young Adult and Mid-Grade Fiction received about two hundred each, Non-Fiction received about fifty, and Illustration and Poetry receive the least number of entries with about twenty five each last year. The percentages are running about the same this year.

**As you process your entries have you noticed things multiple writers are doing wrong that you'd like to caution them against when they enter yours or any other contest?**

Well, I learned my lesson last year about issuing vague instructions. This year I put up a step-by-step checklist for entries and it's going much more smoothly. There are a few who have put their names on their manuscripts or artwork—a big no-no since we're doing this with completely blind judging, but that is the biggest transgression so far.

One has sent more than the 1,000 word maximum entry—he sent two full chapters, about twenty pages. While that might be okay for a regular unsolicited manuscript submission, it's not okay for this contest.

**Why is it a good idea for writers to enter contests? Have you entered them yourself in the past? How is W.I.N. different from other contests?**

I think entering a writing contest helps the writer make that public declaration: I am a Writer. When you're willing to put your manuscript up next to who knows how many others to be judged for professionalism and writing quality, you have to have a lot of faith in yourself and your work. I can tell from the manuscripts how hard people have worked on these entries and I begin reading each and every one totally in love with the idea, whatever that idea is.

If you win, it's a huge validation of your work—the subsequent recognition, prize money, and editorial review can all be a huge boost to your career. If you don't, that's okay, too. It's all part of honing your craft and getting out there in the professional circles, getting your work seen. For instance, last year there were several works that didn't make the final selections (I wasn't the final judge, so it wasn't my decision to make), but I liked them so much I shared them with an editor friend. I'll do the same this year if it happens again.

I have entered writing competitions in the past, yes. My mid-grade ghost story "Ghosts Under 12 Stay Free" placed third in the *Writer's Digest* Fiction Competition in 2003. How is W.I.N. different from other contests? I'm not really sure how to answer that. I know where we are coming from with our contest. We want to help new writers leapfrog out of the slush and into the hands of editors who can really do something to help their careers. We want to encourage new writers to write better, to create better books for young readers. Better books mean better readers—more readers—and that's good for all of us.

It's a mustard seed trying to be a mountain, this little dream of mine.

## How have you publicized your contest to writers?

The Children's Writers list (an online listserv through Yahoo! Groups) has been great. I've been an active member for years, so these people know me and know where I'm coming from when it comes to encouraging new writers. I've also partnered with Jon Bard and Laura Backes at www.write4kids.com who have sponsored prizes and posted the contest in their newsletter, as has Verla Kay (www.verlakay.com), another proponent of children's writers, and Writer's Digest Books has been kind enough to donate books for our prizes, so that helps get the word out, too.

## Some recent W.I.N.NERS have enjoyed publishing success. Please share the good news.

Well, Anne Bowen, who won first place in the picture book category for her *Harley Harrison, Tattle Tale*, sold it to Albert Whitman publishers. She said, "I do think it helped a great deal that I could say my manuscript took first place in the W.I.N. contest in my cover letter!"

Fiona Bayrock's *Bubble Homes and Fish Farts* came in third in our nonfiction category, and is now under contract at Charlesbridge, after a great review and editorial notes from Tanya Dean, the editor who gave her an editorial review as part of her prize, and Kelly Milner Halls, who judged the category.

Jennifer Roy came in second in our Mid-Grade category with a story about her grandmother, *Growing Up in the Lodz Ghetto*, which she later sold to Margery Cuyler (at Cavendish). "My win in the W.I.N Competition gave me the validation to submit my work to publishers," Jennifer wrote to me in an e-mail.

I think my favorite sale story is from Tammi Sauer, though, who had had her book, *Cowboy Camp*, with an editor for quite a long time—they had expressed interest in the book, but hadn't offered her a contract. When she placed second in the Picture Book category, she wrote him to let him know and was offered a contract two weeks later.

One of our other Mid-Grade winners has her novel with an editor, too, who loves it and wants to take it to acquisitions based on revisions the author is doing now. It's not final, so I can't talk about it in detail yet, but I'm extremely happy for this writer. This will be her first book sale.

Others have told me that their placing in the W.I.N. competition has led to art directors requesting their portfolios and editors requesting the full manuscripts of their entries. I'm really thrilled at the doors this seems to be opening up for people.

## Can you offer some general advice to writers preparing to enter contests?

Above all else, follow the directions for formatting your entry, and please, please, please make sure you're sending in the very best work you can. You're going up against professional-level competition, and your work will have to stand on its own.

Proofread your entry, and have someone else proof it, too, and double check your entry checklist before you put that envelope in the mail. I have received so many e-mails and follow-up letters with a corrected manuscript or a synopsis that was left out, etc. All the standard rules of manuscript submission apply. Be professional. Follow the guidelines. Don't make the work harder for the editor. (In this case, me.)

If you've sent your very best work and you know you followed all the guidelines of submission, sit back and relax for a day or two, then get busy on the next manuscript. Don't wait for this contest win to validate your dream. If you want to write for children, do it. Every day. And do it well. It's all in the name: Write It Now!

*—Alice Pope*

and finalists to 3 publishers of children's books. Judging by members of the Writers Union of Canada (all published writers with at least one book). Requirements for entrants: Open only to unpublished writers. Please do not send illustrations.

## ⚡ YOUNG ADULT CANADIAN BOOK AWARD

The Canadian Library Association, 328 Frank St., Ottawa ON K2P 0X8 Canada. (613)232-9625. Fax: (613)563-9895. Website: www.cla.ca. **Contact:** Committee Chair. Annual award. Estab. 1981. Purpose of award: "to recognize the author of an outstanding English-language Canadian book which appeals to young adults between the ages of 13 and 18 that was published the preceding calendar year. Information is available upon request. We approach publishers, also send news releases to various journals, i.e., *Quill & Quire.*" Entries are not returned. No entry fee. Awards a leather-bound book. Requirement for entrants: must be a work of fiction (novel or short stories), the title must be a Canadian publication in either hardcover or paperback, and the author must be a Canadian citizen or landed immigrant. Award given at the Canadian Library Association Conference.

## YOUNG READER'S CHOICE AWARD

3738 W. Central, Missoula MT 59804. (406)542-4055. Fax: (406)543-5358. E-mail: monlux@montana.com. Website: www.PNLA.org. **Award Director:** Carole Monlux, chair YRCA. "This award is not for unsolicited books—the short list for this award is nominated by students, teachers and librarians and it is only for students in the Pacific Northwest to vote on the winner." YRCA is intended to be a Book Award chosen by students—not adults. It is the oldest children's choice award in U.S. and Canada. Previously published submissions only (the titles are 3 years old when voted upon). Submissions nominated by a person or group in the Pacific Northwest. Deadline for entries: Febraury 1—Pacific Northwest nominations only. SASE for contest rules and entry forms. Awards medal made of Idaho silver, depicting eagle and salmon in northwest. Native American symbols. Judging by students in Pacific Northwest. "The Pacific Northwest Library Association's Young Reader's Choice Award is the oldest children's choice award in the U.S. and Canada. Only 4th- through 12th-graders in the Pacific Northwest are eligible to vote. PNLA strongly encourages people to nominate titles to be included in the ballot."

## THE YOUTH HONOR AWARD PROGRAM

Skipping Stones, P.O. Box 3939, Eugene OR 97403. (514)342-4956. E-mail: editor@skippingstones.org. Website: www.skippingstones.org. **Director of Public Relations:** Arun N. Toke. **Open to students.** Annual contest. Estab. 1994. Purpose of contest: "To recognize creative and artistic works by young people that promote multicultural and nature awareness." Unpublished submissions only. Submissions made by author. Deadline for entries: June. SASE for contest rules and entry forms. Entry fee is $3. "Ten winners will be published in our fall issue. Winners will also receive an Honor Award Certificate, a subscription to *Skipping Stones* and five nature and/or multicultural books." Requirements for entrants: Original writing (essays, interviews, poems, plays, short stories, etc.) and art (photos, paintings, cartoons, etc.) are accepted from youth ages 7 to 17. Non-English and bilingual writings are welcome. Also, you must include a certificate of originality signed by a parent or teacher. "Please include a cover letter telling about yourself and your submissions, your age, and contact information. Every student who enters will receive a copy of *Skipping Stones* featuring the five winning entries."

## THE ANNA ZORNIO MEMORIAL CHILDREN'S THEATRE PLAYWRITING AWARD

University of New Hampshire, Department of Theatre and Dance, Paul Creative Arts Center, 30 College Rd., Durham NH 03824-3538. (603)862-3038. Fax: (603)862-0298. E-mail: mike.wood@unh.edu. Website: www.unh.edu/theatre-dance. **Contact:** Michael Wood. Contest every 4 years; next contest is November 2008 for 2009-2010 season. Estab. 1979. Purpose of the award: "to honor the late Anna Zornio, an alumna of The University of New Hampshire, for dedication to and inspiration of playwriting for young people, K-12th grade. Open to playwrights who are residents of the U.S. and Canada. Plays or musicals should run about 45 minutes." Unpublished submissions only. Submissions made by the author. Deadline for entries: March 3, 2008. SASE for award rules and entry forms. No entry fee. Awards $1,000 plus guaranteed production. Judging by faculty committee. Acquires rights to campus production. Write for details.

# Helpful Books
# & Publications

The editors of *Children's Writer's & Illustrator's Market* suggest the following books and periodicals to keep you informed on writing and illustrating techniques, trends in the field, business issues, industry news and changes, and additional markets.

## BOOKS

**An Author's Guide to Children's Book Promotion**, by Susan Salzman Raab, 345 Millwood Rd., Chappaqua NY 10514. (914)241-2117. E-mail: info@raabassociates.com. Website: www.raabassociates.com/authors.htm.

**The Business of Writing for Children**, by Aaron Shepard, Shepard Publications. Website: www.aaronshep.com/kidwriter/Business.html. Available on www.amazon.com.

**Children's Writer Guide**, (annual), The Institute of Children's Literature, 93 Long Ridge Rd., West Redding CT 06896-0811. (800)443-6078. Website: www.writersbookstore.com.

**The Children's Writer's Reference**, by Berthe Amoss and Eric Suben, Writer's Digest Books, 4700 E. Galbraith Rd., Cincinnati OH 45236. (800)448-0915. Website: www.writersdigest.com.

**Children's Writer's Word Book**, by Alijandra Mogilner, Writer's Digest Books, 4700 E. Galbraith Rd., Cincinnati OH 45236. (800)448-0915. Website: www.writersdigest.com.

**The Complete Idiot's Guide® to Publishing Children's Books**, Second Edition, by Harold D. Underdown, Alpha Books, 201 W. 103rd St., Indianapolis IN 46290. Website: www.idiotsguides.com.

**Creating Characters Kids Will Love**, by Elaine Marie Alphin, Writer's Digest Books, 4700 E. Galbraith Rd., Cincinnati OH 45236. (800)448-0915. Website: www.writersdigest.com.

**Formatting & Submitting Your Manuscript**, Second Edition, by Cynthia Laufenberg and the editors of *Writer's Market*, Writer's Digest Books, 4700 E. Galbraith Rd., Cincinnati OH 45236. (800)448-0915. Website: www.writersdigest.com.

**Guide to Literary Agents**, edited by Kathryn S. Brogan, Writer's Digest Books, 4700 E. Glabraith Rd., Cincinnati OH 45236. (800)448-0915. Website: www.writersdigest.com.

**How to Write a Children's Book and Get It Published**, Third Edition, by Barbara Seuling, John Wiley & Sons, 111 River St., Hoboken NJ 07030. (201)748-6000. Website: www.wiley.com.

**Resources**

**How to Write and Illustrate Children's Books and Get Them Published**, edited by Treld Pelkey Bicknell and Felicity Trottman, Writer's Digest Books, 4700 E. Galbraith Rd., Cincinnati OH 45236. (800)448-0915. Website: www.writersdigest.com.

**How to Write Attention-Grabbing Query & Cover Letters**, by John Wood, Writer's Digest Books, 4700 E. Galbraith Rd., Cincinnati OH 45236. (800)448-0915. Website: www.writers digest.com.

**Ⓝ Illustrating Children's Books: Creating Pictures for Publication**, by Martin Salisbury, Barron's Educational Series, 250 Wireless Blvd., Hauppauge NY 11788. (800)645-3476. Website: www.barronseduc.com.

**It's a Bunny-Eat-Bunny World: A Writer's Guide to Surviving and Thriving in Today's Competitive Children's Book Market**, by Olga Litowinsky, Walker & Company, 104 Fifth Ave., New York NY 10011. (212)727-8300. Website: www.walkerbooks.com.

**Ⓝ Page After Page: discover the confidence & passion you need to start writing & keep writing (no matter what)**, by Heather Sellers, Writer's Digest Books, 4700 E. Galbraith Rd., Cincinnati OH 45236. (800)448-0915. Website: www.writersdigest.com.

**Picture Writing: A New Approach to Writing for Kids and Teens**, by Anastasia Suen, Writer's Digest Books, 4700 E. Galbraith Rd., Cincinnati OH 45236. (800)448-0915. Website: www.writersdigest.com.

**Story Sparkers: A Creativity Guide for Children's Writers**, by Marcia Thornton Jones and Debbie Dadey, Writer's Digest Books, 4700 E. Galbraith Rd., Cincinnati OH 45236. (800)448-0915. Website: www.writersdigest.com.

**A Teen's Guide to Getting Published**, by Danielle Dunn & Jessica Dunn, Prufrock Press, P.O. Box 8813, Waco TX 76714-8813. (800)998-2208.

**The Writer's Guide to Crafting Stories for Children**, by Nancy Lamb, Writer's Digest Books, 4700 E. Galbraith Rd., Cincinnati OH 45236. (800)448-0915. Website: www.writersdigest.com.

**Writing and Illustrating Children's Books for Publication: Two Perspectives**, Revised Edition, by Berthe Amoss and Eric Suben, Writer's Digest Books, 4700 E. Galbraith Rd., Cincinnati OH 45236. (800)448-0915. Website: www.writersdigest.com.

**Writing for Children & Teenagers**, Third Edition, by Lee Wyndham, revised by Arnold Madison, Writer's Digest Books, 4700 E. Galbraith Rd., Cincinnati OH 45236. (800)448-0915. Website: www.writersdigest.com.

**Writing for Young Adults**, by Sherry Garland, Writer's Digest Books, 4700 E. Galbraith Rd., Cincinnati OH 45236. (800)448-0915. Website: www.writersdigest.com.

**Writing With Pictures: How to Write and Illustrate Children's Books**, by Uri Shulevitz, Watson-Guptill Publications, 770 Broadway, New York NY 10003. (800)278-8477.

**You Can Write Children's Books**, by Tracey E. Dils, Writer's Digest Books, 4700 E. Galbraith Rd., Cincinnati OH 45236. (800)448-0915. Website: www.writersdigest.com.

**You Can Write Children's Books Workbook**, by Tracey E. Dils, Writer's Digest Books, 4700 E. Galbraith Rd., Cincinnati OH 45236. (800)448-0915. Website: www.writersdigest.com.

**The Young Writer's Guide to Getting Published**, by Kathy Henderson, Writer's Digest Books, 4700 E. Galbraith Rd., Cincinnati OH 45236. (800)448-0915. Website: www.writers digest.com.

## PUBLICATIONS

**Book Links: Connecting Books, Libraries and Classrooms,** editor Laura Tillotson, American Library Association, 50 E. Huron St., Chicago IL 60611. (800)545-2433. Website: www .ala.org/BookLinks. *Magazine published 6 times a year (September-July) for the purpose of connecting books, libraries and classrooms. Features articles on specific topics followed by bibliographies recommending books for further information. Subscription: $29.95/year.*

**Children's Book Insider,** editor Laura Backes, 901 Columbia Rd., Ft. Collins CO 80525-1838. (970)495-0056 or (800)807-1916. E-mail: mail@write4kids.com. Website: www.write4kid s.com. *Monthly newsletter covering markets, techniques and trends in children's publishing. Subscription: $29.95/year; electronic version $26.95/year.*

**Children's Writer,** editor Susan Tierney, The Institute of Children's Literature, 93 Long Ridge Rd., West Redding CT 06896-0811. (800)443-6078. Website: www.childrenswriter.com. *Monthly newsletter of writing and publishing trends in the children's field. Subscription: $24/year; special introductory rate: $15.*

**The Five Owls,** editor Dr. Mark West, 2000 Aldrich Ave. S., Minneapolis MN 55405. (612)890-0404. Website: www.fiveowls.com. *Bimonthly newsletter for readers personally and professionally involved in children's literature. Subscription: $35/year.*

**The Horn Book Magazine,** editor-in-chief Roger Sutton, The Horn Book Inc., 56 Roland St., Suite 200, Boston MA 02129. (800)325-1170. E-mail: info@hbook.com or cgross@hbook.c om. Website: www.hbook.com. *Bimonthly guide to the children's book world including views on the industry and reviews of the latest books. Subscription: $34.95/year.*

**The Lion and the Unicorn: A Critical Journal of Children's Literature,** editors Jack Zipes and Louisa Smith, The Johns Hopkins University Press, P.O. Box 19966, Baltimore MD 21211-0966. (800)548-1784 or (410)516-6987 (outside the U.S. and Canada). E-mail: jlorde r@jhu.edu. Website: www.press.jhu.edu/journals/lion_and_the_unicorn/. *Magazine published 3 times a year serving as a forum for discussion of children's literature featuring interviews with authors, editors and experts in the field. Subscription: $31/year.*

**Once Upon a Time,** editor Audrey Baird, 553 Winston Court, St. Paul MN 55118. (651)457-6223. E-mail: audreyouat@comcast.net. Website: www.onceuponatimemag.com. *Quarterly support magazine for children's writers and illustrators and those interested in children's literature. Subscription: $26/year.*

**Publishers Weekly,** editor-in-chief Sara Nelson, Reed Business Information, a division of Reed Elsevier Inc., 360 Park Ave. S., New York NY 10010. (800)278-2991. Website: www.p ublishersweekly.com. *Weekly trade publication covering all aspects of the publishing industry; includes coverage of the children's field and spring and fall issues devoted solely to children's books. Subscription: $199/year. Available on newsstands for $8/issue. (Special issues are higher in price.)*

**Society of Children's Book Writers and Illustrators Bulletin,** editors Stephen Mooser and Lin Oliver, SCBWI, 8271 Beverly Blvd., Los Angeles CA 90048. (323)782-1010. Website: www.scbwi.org/pubs.htm. *Bimonthly newsletter of SCBWI covering news of interest to members. Subscription with $60/year membership.*

# Useful Online Resources

The editors of *Children's Writer's & Illustrator's Market* suggest the following websites to keep you informed on writing and illustrating techniques, trends in the field, business issues, industry news and changes, and additional markets.

**Amazon.com:** www.amazon.com
Calling itself "A bookstore too big for the physical world," Amazon.com has more than 3 million books available on their website at discounted prices, plus a personal notification service of new releases, reader reviews, bestseller and suggested book information.

**America Writes for Kids:** http://usawrites4kids.drury.edu
Lists book authors by state along with interviews, profiles and writing tips.

**Artlex Art Dictionary:** www.artlex.com
Art dictionary with more than 3,200 terms

**Association for Library Service to Children:** www.ala.org
This site provides links to information about Newbery, Caldecott, Coretta Scott King and Michael L. Printz Awards as well as a host of other awards for notable children's books.

**Association of Illustrators:** www.theaoi.com
This U.K.-based organization has been working since 1973 to promote illustration, illustrators' rights and standards. The website has discussion boards, artists' directories, events, links to agents and much more.

**Authors and Illustrators for Children Webring:** http://t.webring.com/hub?ring=aicwebring
Here you'll find a list of link of sites of interest to children's writers and illustrators or created by them.

**The Authors Guild Online:** www.authorsguild.org
The website of The Authors Guild offers articles and columns dealing with contract issues, copyright, electronic rights and other legal issues of concern to writers.

**Barnes & Noble Online:** www.barnesandnoble.com
The world's largest bookstore chain's website contains 600,000 in-stock titles at discount prices as well as personalized recommendations, online events with authors and book forum access for members.

**The Book Report Network:** includes www.bookreporter.com; www.readinggroupguides. com; www.authorsontheweb.com; www.teenreads.com and www.kidsreads.com

All the sites feature giveaways, book reviews, author and editor interviews, and recommended reads. A great way to stay connected.

**Bookwire:** www.bookwire.com

A gateway to finding information about publishers, booksellers, libraries, authors, reviews and awards. Also offers frequently asked publishing questions and answers, a calendar of events, a mailing list and other helpful resources.

**Canadian Children's Book Centre:** www.bookcentre.ca

The site for the CCBC includes profiles of illustrators and authors, information on recent books, a calendar of upcoming events, information on CCBC publications, and tips from Canadian children's authors.

**Canadian Society of Children's Authors, Illustrators and Performers:** www.canscaip.org

This organization promotes all aspects of children's writing, illustration and performance.

**The Children's Book Council:** www.cbcbooks.org

This site includes a complete list of CBC members with addresses, names and descriptions of what each publishes, and links to publishers' websites. Also offers previews of upcoming titles from members; articles from *CBC Features*, the Council's newsletter; and their catalog.

**Children's Literature:** www.childrenslit.com

Offers book reviews, lists of conferences, searchable database, links to over 1,000 author/illustrator websites and much more.

**Children's Literature Web Guide:** www.ucalgary.ca/~dkbrown

This site includes stories, poetry, resource lists, lists of conferences, links to book reviews, lists of awards (international), and information on books from classic to contemporary.

**Children's Writing Supersite:** www.write4kids.com

This site (formerly Children's Writers Resource Center) includes highlights from the newsletter *Children's Book Insider*; definitions of publishing terms; answers to frequently asked questions; information on trends; information on small presses; a research center for Web information; and a catalog of material available from *CBI*.

**The Colossal Directory of Children's Publishers Online:** www.signaleader.com/childrens-writers

This site features links to websites of children's publishers and magazines and includes information on which publishers offer submission guidelines online.

**Database of Award-Winning Children's Literature:** www.dawcl.com

A compilation of over 4,000 records of award-winning books throughout the U.S., Canada, Australia, New Zealand and the U.K. You can search by age level, format, genre, setting, historical period, ethnicity or nationality of the protagonist, gender of protagonist, publication year, award name, or even by keyword. Begin here to compile your reading list of award-winners.

**The Drawing Board:** http://members.aol.com/thedrawing

This site for illustrators features articles, interviews, links and resources for illustrators from all fields.

**Editor & Publisher:** www.editorandpublisher.com

The Internet source for *Editor & Publisher*, this site provides up-to-date industry news, with other opportunities such as a research area and bookstore, a calendar of events and classifieds.

**Imaginary Lands:** www.imaginarylands.org
A fun site with links to websites about picture books, learning tools and children's literature.

**International Board on Books for Young People:** www.ibby.org
Founded in Switzerland in 1953, IBBY is a nonprofit that seeks to encourage the creation and distribution of quality children's literature. They cooperate with children's organizations and children's book institutions around the world.

**International Reading Association:** www.reading.org
This website includes articles; book lists; event, conference and convention information; and an online bookstore.

**National Association for the Education of Young Children:** www.naeyc.org.
This organization is comprised of over 100,000 early childhood educators and others interested in the development and education of young children. Their website makes a great introduction and research resource for authors and illustrators of picture books.

**National Writers Union:** www.nwu.org
The union for freelance writers in U.S. Markets. The NWU offers contract advice, greviance assistance, health and liability insurance and much more.

**Once Upon a Time:** www.onceuponatimemag.com
This companion site to *Once Upon A Time* magazine offers excerpts from recent articles, notes for prospective contributors, and information about *OUAT*'s 11 regular columnists.

**Picturebook:** www.picturebook.com
This site brought to you by *Picturebook* sourcebook offers tons of links for illustrators, portfolio searching, and news, and offers a listserv, bulletin board and chatroom.

**Planet Esmé: A Wonderful World of Children's Literature:** www.planetesme.com
This site run by author Esmé Raji Codell, offers extensive lists of children's book recommendations, including the latest titles of note for various age groups, a great list of links, and more. Be sure to click on "join the club" to receive Codell's delightful e-mail newsletter.

**Publishers' Catalogues Home Page:** www.lights.com/publisher/index.html
A mammoth link collection of more than 6,000 publishers around the world arranged geographically. This site is one of the most comprehensive directories of publishers on the Internet.

**The Purple Crayon:** www.underdown.org
Editor Harold Underdown's site includes articles on trends, business, and cover letters and queries as well as interviews with editors and answers to frequently asked questions. He also includes links to a number of other sites helpful to writers and excerpts from his book *The Complete Idiot's Guide to Publishing Children's Books*.

**Slantville:** www.slantville.com
An online artists community, this site includes a yellow pages for artists, frequently asked questions and a library offering information on a number of issues of interest to illustrators. This is a great site to visit to view artists' portfolios.

**Smartwriters.com:** www.smartwriters.com
Writer, novelist, photographer, graphic designer, and co-founder of 2-Tier Software, Inc., Roxyanne Young, runs this online magazine, which is absolutely stuffed with resources

for children's writers, teachers and young writers. It's also got contests, interviews, free books, advice and well—you just have to go there.

**Society of Children's Book Writers and Illustrators:** www.scbwi.org
This site includes information on awards and grants available to SCBWI members, a calendar of events listed by date and region, a list of publications available to members, and a site map for easy navigation. Follow the Regional Chapters link to find the SCBWI chapter in your area.

**The Society of Illustrators:** www.societyillustrators.org
Since 1901, this organization has been working to promote the interest of professional illustrators. Information on exhibitions, career advice, and many other links provided.

**U.K. Children's Books:** www.ukchildrensbooks.co.uk
Filled with links to author sites, illustrator sites, publishers, booksellers, and organizations—not to mention help with website design and other technicalities—visit this site no matter which side of the Atlantic you rest your head.

**United States Board on Books for Young People:** www.usbby.org
Serves as the U.S. national section of the International Board on Books for Young People.

**United States Postal Service:** www.usps.gov
Offers domestic and International postage rate calculator, stamp ordering, zip code look up, express mail tracking and more.

**Verla Kay's Website:** www.verlakay.com
Author Verla Kay's website features writer's tips, articles, a schedules of online workshops (with transcripts of past workshops), a good news board and helpful links.

**Writersdigest.com:** www.writersdigest.com
Brought to you by *Writer's Digest* magazine, this site features articles, resources, links, writing prompts, a bookstore, and more.

**Writersmarket.com:** www.writersmarket.com
This gateway to the *Writer's Market* online edition offers market news, FAQs, tips, featured markets and web resources, a free newsletter, and more.

**Writing-world.com:** www.writing-world.com/children
Site features reams of advice, links and offers a free bi-weekly newsletter.

# Glossary

**AAR.** Association of Authors' Representatives.

**ABA.** American Booksellers Association.

**ABC.** Association of Booksellers for Children.

**Advance.** A sum of money a publisher pays a writer or illustrator prior to the publication of a book. It is usually paid in installments, such as one half on signing the contract, one half on delivery of a complete and satisfactory manuscript. The advance is paid against the royalty money that will be earned by the book.

**ALA.** American Library Association.

**All rights.** The rights contracted to a publisher permitting the use of material anywhere and in any form, including movie and book club sales, without additional payment to the creator.

**Anthology.** A collection of selected writings by various authors or gatherings of works by one author.

**Anthropomorphization.** The act of attributing human form and personality to things not human (such as animals).

**ASAP.** As soon as possible.

**Assignment.** An editor or art director asks a writer, illustrator or photographer to produce a specific piece for an agreed-upon fee.

**B&W.** Black and white.

**Backlist.** A publisher's list of books not published during the current season but still in print.

**Biennially.** Occurring once every 2 years.

**Bimonthly.** Occurring once every 2 months.

**Biweekly.** Occurring once every 2 weeks.

**Book packager.** A company that draws all elements of a book together, from the initial concept to writing and marketing strategies, then sells the book package to a book publisher and/or movie producer. Also known as book producer or book developer.

**Book proposal.** Package submitted to a publisher for consideration usually consisting of a synopsis, outline and sample chapters. (See Before Your First Sale, page 8.)

**Business-size envelope.** Also known as a #10 envelope. The standard size used in sending business correspondence.

**Camera-ready.** Refers to art that is completely prepared for copy camera platemaking.

**Caption.** A description of the subject matter of an illustration or photograph; photo captions include persons' names where appropriate. Also called cutline.

**Clean-copy.** A manuscript free of errors and needing no editing; it is ready for typesetting.

**Clips.** Samples, usually from newspapers or magazines, of a writer's published work.

**Concept books.** Books that deal with ideas, concepts and large-scale problems, promoting an understanding of what's happening in a child's world. Most prevalent are alphabet and counting books, but also includes books dealing with specific concerns facing young people (such as divorce, birth of a sibling, friendship or moving).

**Contract.** A written agreement stating the rights to be purchased by an editor, art director or producer and the amount of payment the writer, illustrator or photographer will receive for that sale. (See Running Your Business, page 13.)

**Contributor's copies.** The magazine issues sent to an author, illustrator or photographer in which her work appears.

**Co-op publisher.** A publisher that shares production costs with an author, but, unlike subsidy publishers, handles all marketing and distribution. An author receives a high percentage of royalties until her initial investment is recouped, then standard royalties. (*Children's Writer's & Illustrator's Market* does not include co-op publishers.)

**Copy.** The actual written material of a manuscript.

**Copyediting.** Editing a manuscript for grammar usage, spelling, punctuation and general style.

**Copyright.** A means to legally protect an author's/illustrator's/photographer's work. This can be shown by writing ©, the creator's name, and year of work's creation. (See Running Your Business, page 13.)

**Cover letter.** A brief letter, accompanying a complete manuscript, especially useful if responding to an editor's request for a manuscript. May also accompany a book proposal. (See Before Your First Sale, page 8.)

**Cutline.** See caption.

**Division.** An unincorporated branch of a company.

**Dummy.** A loose mock-up of a book showing placement of text and artwork.

**Electronic submission.** A submission of material by modem or on computer disk.

**Final draft.** The last version of a polished manuscript ready for submission to an editor.

**First North American serial rights.** The right to publish material in a periodical for the first time, in the United States or Canada. (See Running Your Business, page 13.)

**F&Gs.** Folded and gathered sheets. An early, not-yet-bound copy of a picture book.

**Flat fee.** A one-time payment.

**Galleys.** The first typeset version of a manuscript that has not yet been divided into pages.

**Genre.** A formulaic type of fiction, such as horror, mystery, romance, science fiction or western.

**Glossy.** A photograph with a shiny surface as opposed to one with a non-shiny matte finish.

**Gouache.** Opaque watercolor with an appreciable film thickness and an actual paint layer.

**Halftone.** Reproduction of a continuous tone illustration with the image formed by dots produced by a camera lens screen.

**Hard copy.** The printed copy of a computer's output.

**Hardware.** All the mechanically-integrated components of a computer that are not software—circuit boards, transistors and the machines that are the actual computer.

**Hi-Lo.** High interest, low reading level.

**Home page.** The first page of a website.

**IBBY.** International Board on Books for Young People.

**Imprint.** Name applied to a publisher's specific line of books.

**Internet.** A worldwide network of computers that offers access to a wide variety of electronic resources.

**IRA.** International Reading Association.

**IRC.** International Reply Coupon. Sold at the post office to enclose with text or artwork sent to a recipient outside your own country to cover postage costs when replying or returning work.

**Keyline.** Identification of the positions of illustrations and copy for the printer.

**Layout.** Arrangement of illustrations, photographs, text and headlines for printed material.

**Line drawing.** Illustration done with pencil or ink using no wash or other shading.

**Mass market books.** Paperback books directed toward an extremely large audience sold in supermarkets, drugstores, airports, newsstands, online retailers, and bookstores.

**Mechanicals.** Paste-up or preparation of work for printing.

**Middle grade or mid-grade.** See middle reader.

**Middle reader.** The general classification of books written for readers approximately ages 9-11. Also called middle grade.

**Ms (mss).** Manuscript(s).

**Multiple submissions.** See simultaneous submissions.

**NCTE.** National Council of Teachers of English.

**One-time rights.** Permission to publish a story in periodical or book form one time only. (See Running Your Business, page 13.)

**Outline.** A summary of a book's contents; often in the form of chapter headings with a descriptive sentence or two under each heading to show the scope of the book.

**Package sale.** The sale of a manuscript and illustrations/photos as a ''package'' paid for with one check.

**Payment on acceptance.** The writer, artist or photographer is paid for her work at the time the editor or art director decides to buy it.

**Payment on publication.** The writer, artist or photographer is paid for her work when it is published.

**Picture book.** A type of book aimed at preschoolers to 8-year-olds that tells a story using a combination of text and artwork, or artwork only.

**Print.** An impression pulled from an original plate, stone, block, screen or negative; also a positive made from a photographic negative.

**Proofreading.** Reading text to correct typographical errors.

**Query.** A letter to an editor or agent designed to capture interest in an article or book you have written or propose to write. (See Before Your First Sale, page 8.)

**Reading fee.** Money charged by some agents and publishers to read a submitted manuscript. (*Children's Writer's & Illustrator's Market* does not include agencies that charge reading fees.)

**Reprint rights.** Permission to print an already published work whose first rights have been sold to another magazine or book publisher. (See Running Your Business, page 13.)

**Response time.** The average length of time it takes an editor or art director to accept or reject a query or submission and inform the creator of the decision.

**Rights.** The bundle of permissions offered to an editor or art director in exchange for printing a manuscript, artwork or photographs. (See Running Your Business, page 13.)

**Rough draft.** A manuscript that has not been checked for errors in grammar, punctuation, spelling or content.

**Roughs.** Preliminary sketches or drawings.

**Royalty.** An agreed percentage paid by a publisher to a writer, illustrator or photographer for each copy of her work sold.

**SAE.** Self-addressed envelope.

**SASE.** Self-addressed, stamped envelope.

**SCBWI.** The Society of Children's Book Writers and Illustrators. (See listing in Clubs & Organizations section.)

**Second serial rights.** Permission for the reprinting of a work in another periodical after its first publication in book or magazine form. (See Running Your Business, page 13.)

**Semiannual.** Occurring every 6 months or twice a year.

**Semimonthly.** Occurring twice a month.

**Semiweekly.** Occurring twice a week.

**Serial rights.** The rights given by an author to a publisher to print a piece in one or more periodicals. (See Running Your Business, page 13.)

**Simultaneous submissions.** Queries or proposals sent to several publishers at the same time. Also called multiple submissions. (See Before Your First Sale, page 8.)

**Slant.** The approach to a story or piece of artwork that will appeal to readers of a particular publication.

**Slush pile.** Editors' term for their collections of unsolicited manuscripts.

**Software.** Programs and related documentation for use with a computer.

**Solicited manuscript.** Material that an editor has asked for or agreed to consider before being sent by a writer.

**SPAR.** Society of Photographers and Artists Representatives.

**Speculation (spec).** Creating a piece with no assurance from an editor or art director that it will be purchased or any reimbursements for material or labor paid.

**Subsidiary rights.** All rights other than book publishing rights included in a book contract, such as paperback, book club and movie rights. (See Running Your Business, page 13.)

**Subsidy publisher.** A book publisher that charges the author for the cost of typesetting, printing and promoting a book. Also called a vanity publisher. (*Children's Writer's & Illustrator's Market* does not include subsidy publishers.)

**Synopsis.** A brief summary of a story or novel. Usually a page to a page and a half, single-spaced, if part of a book proposal.

**Tabloid.** Publication printed on an ordinary newspaper page turned sideways and folded in half.

**Tearsheet.** Page from a magazine or newspaper containing your printed art, story, article, poem or photo.

**Thumbnail.** A rough layout in miniature.

**Trade books.** Books sold in bookstores and through online retailers, aimed at a smaller audience than mass market books, and printed in smaller quantities by publishers.

**Transparencies.** Positive color slides; not color prints.

**Unsolicited manuscript.** Material sent without an editor's or art director's request.

**Vanity publisher.** See subsidy publisher.

**Work-for-hire.** An arrangement between a writer, illustrator or photographer and a company under which the company retains complete control of the work's copyright. (See Running Your Business, page 13.)

**YA.** See young adult.

**Young adult.** The general classification of books written for readers approximately ages 12-18. Often referred to as YA.

**Young reader.** The general classification of books written for readers approximately ages 5-8.

# Age-Level Index

This index lists book and magazine publishers by the age-groups for which they publish. Use it to locate appropriate markets for your work, then carefully read the listings and follow the guidelines of each publisher. Use this index in conjunction with the Subject Index to further narrow your list of markets. **Picture Books** and **Picture-Oriented Material** are for preschoolers to 8-year-olds; **Young Readers** are for 5- to 8-year-olds; **Middle Readers** are for 9- to 11-year-olds; and **Young Adults** are for ages 12 and up.

## BOOK PUBLISHERS

### Picture Books

## Young Readers

## Middle Readers

## Young Adult/Teen

## MAGAZINES

### Picture-Oriented Material

### Young Readers

### Middle Readers

## Young Adult/Teen

# Subject Index

This index lists book and magazine publishers by the fiction and nonfiction subject area in which they publish. Use it to locate appropriate markets for your work, then carefully read the listings and follow the guidelines of each publisher. Use this index in conjunction with Age-Level Index to further narrow your list of markets.

## BOOK PUBLISHERS: FICTION

### Adventure

## Animal

## Contemporary

## Fantasy

## Folktales

## Multicultural

## Nature/Environment

## Poetry

## Problem Novels

## BOOK PUBLISHERS: NONFICTION

### Activity Books

### Animal

## Arts/Crafts

Subject Index

## Hobbies

## How-to

## Nature/Environment

## Reference

# Writer's Digest

WRITE BETTER
GET PUBLISHED

## DISCOVER A WORLD OF WRITING SUCCESS!

Are you ready to be praised, published, and paid for your writing? It's time to invest in your future with *Writer's Digest!* Beginners and experienced writers alike have been relying on *Writer's Digest*, the world's leading magazine for writers, for more than 80 years — and it keeps getting better! Each issue is brimming with:

**Get 2 FREE ISSUES of *Writer's Digest!***

- Technique articles geared toward specific genres, including fiction, nonfiction, business writing and more

- Business information specifically for writers, such as organizational advice, tax tips, and setting fees

- Tips and tricks for rekindling your creative fire

- The latest and greatest markets for print, online and e-publishing

- And much more!

That's a lot to look forward to every month. Let *Writer's Digest* put you on the road to writing success!

## NO RISK!
### Send No Money Now!

☐ **Yes!** Please rush me my 2 FREE issues of *Writer's Digest* — the world's leading magazine for writers. If I like what I read, I'll get a full year's subscription (12 issues, including the 2 free issues) for only $19.96. That's 72% off the newsstand rate! If I'm not completely satisfied, I'll write "cancel" on your invoice, return it and owe nothing. The 2 FREE issues are mine to keep, no matter what!

Name _____

Address_____

City _____

State_____ZIP _____

E-mail _____

☐ You may contact me about my subscription via e-mail.
   (We won't use your address for any other purpose.)

Subscribers in Canada will be charged an additional US$10 (includes GST/HST) and invoiced. Outside the U.S. and Canada, add US$10 and remit payment in U.S. funds with this order. Annual newsstand rate: $71.88. Please allow 4-6 weeks for first-issue delivery.

## Writer's Digest

www.writersdigest.com

J5FCMK

# Get 2 FREE TRIAL ISSUES of

# Writer's Digest
**WRITE BETTER**
**GET PUBLISHED**

Packed with creative inspiration, advice, and tips to guide you on the road to success, *Writer's Digest* offers everything you need to take your writing to the next level! You'll discover how to:

- Create dynamic characters and page-turning plots
- Submit query letters that publishers won't be able to refuse
- Find the right agent or editor
- Make it out of the slush-pile and into the hands of publishers
- Write award-winning contest entries
- And more!

See for yourself — order your 2 FREE trial issues today!

## RUSH! 2 Free Issues!

## BUSINESS REPLY MAIL
FIRST-CLASS MAIL    PERMIT NO. 340    FLAGLER BEACH FL

*POSTAGE WILL BE PAID BY ADDRESSEE*

## Writer's Digest
PO BOX 421365
PALM COAST FL 32142-7104

**NO POSTAGE
NECESSARY
IF MAILED
IN THE
UNITED STATES**

## Self Help

## Social Issues

## MAGAZINES: FICTION

### Adventure

### Animal

### Contemporary

## Humor

## Multicultural

Subject Index

# MAGAZINES: NONFICTION

## Animal

## Arts/Crafts

Subject Index

**Travel**

# Photography Index

This index lists markets that buy photos from freelancers and is divided into book publishers, magazines, and greeting cards. It's important to carefully read the listings and follow the guidelines of each publisher to which you submit.

# General Index

Market listings that appeared in the 2005 edition of *Children's Writer's & Illustrator's Market* but do not appear in this edition are identified with a two-letter code explaining why the listing was omitted: **(NR)**—no response to our requests for updated information; **(OB)**—out of business; **(RR)**—removed by request; **(UC)**—unable to contact.

General Index